A Companion to German Cinema

A Companion to
German Cinema

Edited by

Terri Ginsberg
Andrea Mensch

⟨W⟩WILEY-BLACKWELL

A John Wiley & Sons, Ltd., Publication

This edition first published 2012
© 2012 Blackwell Publishing Ltd

Blackwell Publishing was acquired by John Wiley & Sons in February 2007. Blackwell's publishing program
has been merged with Wiley's global Scientific, Technical, and Medical business to form Wiley-Blackwell.

Registered Office
John Wiley & Sons Ltd, The Atrium, Southern Gate, Chichester, West Sussex, PO19 8SQ, UK

Editorial Offices
350 Main Street, Malden, MA 02148-5020, USA
9600 Garsington Road, Oxford, OX4 2DQ, UK
The Atrium, Southern Gate, Chichester, West Sussex, PO19 8SQ, UK

For details of our global editorial offices, for customer services, and for information about how to apply
for permission to reuse the copyright material in this book please see our website at www.wiley.com/
wiley-blackwell.

The right of Terri Ginsberg and Andrea Mensch to be identified as the authors of the editorial material in this
work has been asserted in accordance with the UK Copyright, Designs and Patents Act 1988.

Library of Congress Cataloging-in-Publication Data

A companion to German cinema / edited by Terri Ginsberg, Andrea Mensch. – 1st ed.
    p.   cm. – (Wiley-Blackwell companions to national cinema)
  Includes bibliographical references and index.
  ISBN 978-1-4051-9436-5 (hardback : alk. paper)   1. Motion pictures–Germany.   I. Ginsberg, Terri.
II. Mensch, Andrea.
  PN1993.5.G3C6455 2012
  791.430943–dc23
                                        2011041275

A catalogue record for this book is available from the British Library.

This book is published in the following electronic formats: ePDFs (ISBN 9781444345575); Wiley Online Library
(ISBN 9781444345605); ePub (ISBN 9781444345582); Mobi (ISBN 9781444345599)

Set in 11/13pt Dante by SPi Publisher Services, Pondicherry, India
Printed in Singapore by Ho Printing Singapore Pte Ltd

1   2012

Contents

Notes on Editors
and Contributors

Editors

Terri Ginsberg earned her PhD in Cinema Studies from New York University. She is coeditor (with Kirsten Moana Thompson) of *Perspectives on German Cinema* (G.K. Hall/Macmillan, 1996), author of *Holocaust Film: The Political Aesthetics of Ideology* (Cambridge Scholars, 2007), coeditor (with Chris Lippard) and contributor to *Historical Dictionary of Middle Eastern Cinema* (Scarecrow/Rowman & Littlefield, 2010), editor of a special issue of *International Journal of Contemporary Iraqi Studies* on film and media (2009), coeditor (with Dennis Broe) and contributor to a special issue of *Situations: Project of the Radical Imagination* on global cinema (CUNY, 2011), and coeditor (with Tareq Ismael) and contributor to a special issue of *Arab Studies Quarterly* on Middle East teaching (Pluto, 2011). She has taught film, media, and cultural studies at numerous institutions of higher learning, among them New York University, Rutgers University, Dartmouth College, Ithaca College, and Brooklyn College – including courses on German film and international cinemas. She is presently a director and programmer at the International Council for Middle East Studies in Washington, DC.

Andrea Mensch did her graduate work in English and German at the University of Cape Town, South Africa and doctoral work in English and Film Studies at Wayne State University. As well as being a senior lecturer in the English Department at North Carolina State University, she has taught film and literature courses in London and the NCSU Prague Institute. She was associate editor as well as book reviews editor for *Jouvert: A Journal of Post-colonial Studies*.

Contributors

Savaş Arslan is Associate Professor of Cinema and Television at Bahçeşehir University in Istanbul, Turkey. In addition to contributing articles on cinema, the arts, and culture to various journals, magazines, and edited volumes, he has published three books: *Cinema in Turkey: A New Critical History* (Oxford University Press, 2011), *Media, Culture and Identity in Europe* (coeditor; Bahçeşehir University Press), and *Melodrama* (in Turkish; L&M).

Dennis Broe's latest book, *Cold War Expressionism: Perverting the Politics of Perception / The American Style in a Global Perspective*, is forthcoming. His previous book, *Film Noir, American Workers and Postwar Hollywood*, was a Choice Outstanding Academic Book for 2009. His articles on film, politics, and culture have appeared in *Situations: Journal of the Radical Imagination*, *Cinema Journal*, *Framework*, *Social Justice*, and *Science and Society*. His work as a film critic and commentator has appeared in *Newsday*, *The Boston Phoenix*, and on Pacifica Radio in New York City. Dr Broe was the Graduate Coordinator in Media Arts at Long Island University.

David Clarke is Senior Lecturer in German at the University of Bath. His research interests include contemporary German film and literature, and the literature of East Germany. He is editor of *German Cinema since Unification* (Continuum, 2006) and coeditor of *The Politics of Place in Post-War Germany: Essays in Literary Criticism* (Edwin Mellen, 2009).

David Brandon Dennis is a doctoral candidate in modern European history at the Ohio State University. His primary research interests lie in examining formations of masculinity and sexuality in modern German history. He has been awarded fellowships for dissertation study in Germany through the Deutscher Akademischer Austauschdienst and the Fulbright Commission. Currently, he is completing a doctoral thesis on masculinity, labor, and the nation in the Wilhelmine merchant marine.

Gayatri Devi is an Assistant Professor of English at Lock Haven University of Pennsylvania where she teaches world literatures. She was co-chair of the Middle Eastern Caucus of the Society for Cinema and Media Studies and is a contributor to the *Historical Dictionary of Middle Eastern Cinema* (Scarecrow 2010). She writes frequently on South Asian and Middle Eastern literatures and films.

Anthony Enns is Assistant Professor of Contemporary Culture in the Department of English at Dalhousie University in Halifax, Nova Scotia. His books include *Screening Disability: Essays on Cinema and Disability* (2001), coedited with Christopher R. Smit, and *Sonic Mediations: Body, Sound, Technology* (2008), coedited with Carolyn Birdsall. His essays on film and media have appeared in such journals as *Screen*, *Journal of Popular Film and Television*, *Quarterly Review of Film and Video*, *Popular Culture Review*, *Studies in Popular Culture*, *The Senses and Society*, and *Culture, Theory and Critique*.

Tara Forrest is Senior Lecturer in Screen and Cultural Studies at the University of Technology, Sydney. She is the author of *The Politics of Imagination: Benjamin, Kracauer, Kluge* (2007), coeditor of *Christoph Schlingensief: Art without Borders* (2010), and editor of *Alexander Kluge: Raw Materials for the Imagination* (forthcoming, 2012).

Robert M. Gillett is Senior Lecturer in German at Queen Mary University of London, UK. His wide-ranging research interests cover German, Austrian, and comparative literature and culture from the nineteenth century to the present, with a special interest in the intersection of cultural studies and gender studies. He has made a particular study of the German author, ethnologist and filmmaker Hubert Fichte. His published interest in queer cinema goes back to 2003, with an article in *Moderna Språk* on "explaining queer through film," and he has recently coedited the book *Queer in Europe: Contemporary Case Studies* (Ashgate, 2011).

Frances Guerin teaches in Film Studies at the University of Kent, UK. She is the author of *A Culture of Light: Cinema and Technology in 1920s Germany* (University of Minnesota Press, 2005) and *Through Amateur Eyes: Film and Photography in Nazi Germany* (University of Minnesota Press, 2011) and coeditor of *The Image and the Witness: Trauma, Memory and Visual Culture* (Wallflower Press, 2007). Her articles have appeared in international journals, including *Cinema Journal, Screening the Past, Film and History,* and *Cinema e Cie.*

Jennifer Ruth Hosek took a PhD in Comparative Literature at Berkeley, then spent two years as a Stanford Fellow in the Humanities before accepting a position as an Assistant Professor of German at Queen's University, where she is crosslisted with Film and Media Studies. She has published on contemporary literature and film, critical theory and neuroscience, and on the women's movement. Her book entitled *Sun, Sex and Socialism: Cuba in the German Imaginary* (University of Toronto Press, forthcoming) was supported by the Berlin Abgeordnetenhaus, DAAD, Humboldt, Mellon, Berkeley, and Queen's. Jennifer's next project treats urban identity through filmic manifestations of Berlin and Havana and is funded by the Social Sciences and Humanities Research Council of Canada. She is also running an SSHRC-supported voiceover IP tandem learning project, WhirledPeas.ca. She has been on the Women in German steering committee and helps produce the WiG Bibliography.

Julia Knight is Professor of Moving Image at the University of Sunderland (UK), an Associate Director of the university's Centre for Research in Media and Cultural Studies, and coeditor of *Convergence: The International Journal of Research into New Media Technologies.* She is author of *Women and the New German Cinema* (Verso, 1992) and *New German Cinema: Images of a Generation* (Wallflower, 2004), but has more recently led a series of AHRC-funded research projects examining independent film and video distribution in the UK (see http://alt-fv-distribution.net).

Nadja Krämer received her PhD from Indiana University, focusing on the German colonial imagination and national identity through the construction of colonial space. Her research centers on issues of race and identity as well as minority and popular culture. She is interested in film studies, urban studies and the practice of place and works currently on *völkisch* concepts of urban planning in the early twentieth century. She is Assistant Professor of German at Minnesota State University, Mankato.

Priscilla Layne is an Assistant Professor in the Department of Germanic and Slavic Languages and Literatures at the University of North Carolina at Chapel Hill. She received her B.A. from the University of Chicago and her MA and PhD from the University of California at Berkeley. Her main interests are race, gender and rebellion in twentieth- and twenty-first-century German literature and culture. She has presented papers at Westfälische-Wilhelm-Universität in Münster, the German Studies Association, and the Society for Cinema and Media Studies. Her coedited volume, *Rebellion and Revolution: Defiance in German Language, History and Art*, was recently published by Cambridge Scholars.

Peter Limbrick is Associate Professor of Film and Digital Media at the University of California, Santa Cruz. He is the author of *Making Settler Cinemas: Film and Colonial Encounters in the United States, Australia, and New Zealand* (Palgrave, 2010) and his work has previously appeared in *Cinema Journal, Camera Obscura, Journal of Visual Culture*, and *Screening the Past*. His current research, teaching, and curation activities are focused on Arab film and video.

David James Prickett is an academic staff member of the English Philology section at Universität Potsdam's Center for Languages and Core Competencies (ZESSKO). He also teaches courses in German culture and language at the Europa-Universität Viadrina Frankfurt (Oder) and the Freie Universität Berlin (FUBiS). At the Humboldt-Universität zu Berlin, he is an associate member of the Center for Transdisciplinary Gender Studies (ZtG). He has published articles on topics including gender in the Early Modern Period (*Wahrnehmung und Herstellung von Geschlecht: Perceiving and Performing Gender*, 1999); literature, visual culture, and spatiality in Weimar Berlin (*Women in German Yearbook*, 2005; *Visual Culture in Twentieth-Century Germany: Text as Spectacle*, 2006; *Edinburgh German Yearbook*, 2007; *Leisure Studies*, 2011); and the image of women in post-Wall Germany (*Hat Strafrecht ein Geschlecht?*, 2010).

Claudia Pummer is currently completing her PhD in Film Studies at the University of Iowa on the work of Jean-Marie Straub and Danièle Huillet. In addition, she teaches courses in film studies at the University of Hawaii at Manoa.

Silke Arnold-de Simine studied at Munich, Karlsruhe, Oxford, and Mannheim, and was a DAAD-Lektorin at Sidney Sussex College, Cambridge. Since 2006 she has been a lecturer in German Studies at the Department of European Cultures, Birkbeck, University of London. Her research interests lie in nineteenth- and twentieth-century German literature and early film, gender studies, cultural memory, and museum studies. She is the author of *Leichen im Keller. Zu Fragen des Gender in Angstinszenierungen der Schauer- und Kriminalliteratur, 1790–1830* (St Ingbert, 2000) and editor of *Memory Traces: 1989 and the Question of German Cultural Identity* (Oxford, 2005). Currently she is working on a coauthored monograph on *Crossdressing in der deutschen Filmkomödie*.

Harald Steinwender, MA, DPhil, wrote a doctoral dissertation on the Italian director Sergio Leone with the publication title *Sergio Leone. Es war einmal in Europa* (Berlin, 2009). From 2007 to 2008 he was Lecturer for the Institute for Film Studies Mainz. He is currently working for the film department of the *Bayerischer Rundfunk* (Bavarian Broadcasting) in Munich.

Domenica Vilhotti, a graduate of North Carolina State University's Masters Program in American and British Literature, studied Holocaust cinema with Terri Ginsberg at the NCSU Film Studies Program in 2007. A former Teach for America teacher in eastern North Carolina, she presently teaches American Literature and Advanced Placement Literature at Mastery Charter School in West Philadelphia.

Vojin Saša Vukadinović, MA, studied modern history, German literature, and gender studies at the Universities of Freiburg and Basel before entering the doctoral program "Gender as Category of Knowledge" at Humboldt University, Berlin. He is currently a research assistant at the Center for Gender Studies at the University of Basel. His PhD project, tentatively entitled "Antifeminismus, Homophobie, Linksterrorismus: BRD 1970–1982," concerns the relationship between the antifeminist and homophobic reception of the RAF (Red Army Faction) in the first decade of its activities as well as the antifeminism and homophobia within the RAF itself. He has published on the history of antiracism, feminism, and leftist violence.

Sally Winkle received her PhD in German literature from the University of Wisconsin-Madison and is Professor of German and Director of Women's and Gender Studies at Eastern Washington University. She teaches German language, culture, film, and literature as well as women's and gender studies. She is the author of *Woman as Bourgeois Feminine Ideal* and coeditor of *The Nazi Germany Sourcebook*.

Alexander Zahlten, DPhil, is an Assistant Professor at Dongguk University, Seoul. From 2002 to 2009 he was a coorganizer of the Nippon Connection Film Festival in Frankfurt am Main. He is currently writing a book on media divergence issues with anime as a case study.

Acknowledgments

The editors thank the following persons and organizations for permission to reprint material that appears in this volume: Kamal Aljafari; Aelrun Goette; TAG/ TRAUM; and zero one film. We would also like to express gratitude to Dora Apel, Burkhard Engelmann, and Roy Grundmann for their intellectual assistance, and to Jayne Fargnoli, Margot Morse, Allison Kostka, Lisa Eaton, Felicity Marsh, Martin Noble, Annette Able, Jana Pollack, and Emily Howard at Wiley-Blackwell for their professional, editorial, logistical, and technical support and guidance. Appreciation also goes to Steven Edelstein, Alexander Eisenstein, Elaine Ginsberg, Joseph Gomez, Robin Mendelwager, and Heike Mensch for providing invaluable material and emotional sustenance throughout the course of this project.

Abbreviations

AIDS	Acquired Immune Deficiency Syndrome
ARD	Arbeitsgemeinschaft der öffentlich-rechtlichen Rundfunkanstalten der Bundesrepublik Deutschland/ Consortium of Public-law Broadcasting Institutions of the Federal Republic of Germany
BBC	British Broadcasting Corporation
BFI	British Film Institute
BMW	Bayrische Motorenwerke
BRD/FRG	Bundesrepublik Deutschland/Federal Republic of Germany
CCC	Central Cinema Company
CCTV	Closed-Circuit Television
CDU	Christlich Demokratische Union/Christian Democratic Union
CIA	Central Intelligence Agency
CNC	Centre national du cinéma/National Center for Cinema
DAAD	Deutscher Akademischer Austausch Dienst
DDR/GDR	Deutsche Demokratische Republik/German Democratic Republic
DEFA	Deutsche Film Aktiengesellschaft/German Film Corporation
Dffb	Deutsche Film und Fernsehakademie Berlin/German Film and Television Academy Berlin
EU	European Union
FDJ	Freie Deutsche Jugend/Free German Youth
FDP	Freie Demokratische Partei/Free Democratic Party
FIDMarseille	Festival International du documenataire de Marseille/ International Documentary Film Festival of Marseille
FLN	Front de Libération Nationale/National Liberation Front
FRG	Federal Republic of Germany

FSK   Freiwillige Selbstkontrolle der Filmwirtschaft/Organization
           for Voluntary Self-regulation (Film Classification Board of the
           German Film Industry)
GAYVN   Gay Video News
HFF   Hochschule für Film und Fernsehen/College for Film
           and Television
HIB   Homosexual Interest Community of (East) Berlin
HIV   human immunodeficiency virus
KHM   Kunsthochschule für Medien/Academy of Media Arts
MEDIA   Mesures d'encouragement pour le développement de l'industrie
           audiovisuelle/Measures for Encouraging Development of the
           Audiovisual Industry
MFA   Master of Fine Arts
MoMA   Museum of Modern Art
NATO   North Atlantic Treaty Organization
NRW   Nordrhein-Westfalen
OED   Oxford English Dictionary
ORF   Österreichischer Rundfunk/Austrian Broadcasting Corporation
PFLP   Popular Front for the Liberation of Palestine
RAF   Rote Armee Fraktion/Red Army Faction
RAI   Radiotelevisione Italiana
RTL   Radio Television Luxembourg
SDS   Sozialistischer Deutscher Studentenbund/Socialist German
           Student Union
SED   Sozialistische Einheitspartei Deutschlands/Socialist Unity Party of
           Germany
SPD   Sozialdemokratische Partei Deutschlands/Social Democratic Party
           of Germany
SPIO   Spitzenorganisation der Filmwirtschaft
SS   Schutzstaffel/Protection Squadron
SSHRC   Social Sciences and Humanities Research Council of Canada
Stasi   Ministerium für Staatssicherheit/Ministry for State Security
UAE   United Arab Emirates
UFA   Universum Film Aktiengesellschaft/Universum Film Corporation
UK   United Kingdom
UN   United Nations
UNRWA   United Nations Relief and Works Agency
US   United States
USSR   Union of Soviet Socialist Republics
WiG   Women in German
ZDF   Zweites Deutsches Fernsehen/Channel Two German Television
ZIJ   Zentralinstitut für Jugendforschung/Central Institute for Youth
           Research

Introduction

Terri Ginsberg and Andrea Mensch

If local war and global immiseration have now become the grossest manifestations of nation, race, gender, and class – note the continuing dismemberment of Bosnia/ Herzegovina and the sustained decimations of Haiti, Rwanda, and Iraq – then the polis of postnational disorderliness has already become the site of a violent and bloody graveyard. In view of this social fact, we conclude our introduction by stressing our belief that a public, political reengagement of these issues by the German cinema studies reader and the postmodern academy is eminently necessary at this time, the fiftieth anniversary of the end of World War II and the liberation of Auschwitz – July 1995 (Ginsberg and Thompson, 1996: 15)

By the time anyone is able to read the present volume, more than fifteen years will have passed since the above words were written as concluding remarks to an editorial collection on German cinema which stands as the authorial precursor to *A Companion to German Cinema*. Largely an arranged compilation of reprinted, canonical articles and essays, *Perspectives on German Cinema* (1996) served at once to consolidate what until that moment, with few exceptions (e.g. Kracauer, 1947; Elsaesser, 1989; Fehrenbach, 1995), had been a generally undertheorized mélange of journal articles and book chapters concerning one of history's most important and challenging national cinemas. German cinema studies, like the New German Cinema on which it had come centrally to focus and in which it was institutionally and politically invested, shared no consistent ideological orientation or discursive framework, while offering often conflicting and contradictory analyses of the aesthetic, philosophical, historiographic, and political-economic structures and implications of films made by persons self-identified as German, usually with the support of German public and, especially during earlier years, private industry funding, primarily in Germany but often for international more than local audiences.

Notwithstanding their discursive and ideological inconsistencies, these analyses had come veritably to define and delineate an academic-institutional field with certain disciplinary assumptions which *Perspectives on German Cinema* aimed to locate, grapple with, and problematize with respect to new and entrenched scholarly practices articulating variously and contradictorily to the "German." The volume assembled 43 articles – seven of them newly commissioned – along a contestational, or "differential," axis conceptualized in the tradition of ideology-critique and updated in postmodern context, calling for a "stereoscopic reader" who, as one reviewer (Knapp, 1997: 427) put it, "will be able to recognize the totality of meaning within the seemingly contradictory array" and in turn might be prompted to ask some anticipated difficult questions about the nascent field: What, after all, has "German cinema studies" come to mean for the US academy that is its institutional origin and platform? Who "speaks" this field, to whom, and for what purpose? Which perspectives are lent centrality within its disciplinary interpellation, which have been marginalized – and how? How might the contemporary film scholar theorize these implied enabling and constitutive conditions and their structuring absences? In effect, insofar as it was interested in "a more ideologically interventionist, socially critical configuration of scholarly inquiry" (Ginsberg and Thompson, 1996: 15), *Perspectives on German Cinema* pleaded that German cinema studies should not ignore or marginalize the social legacy of global conflagration – Imperialism, World War One, National Socialism, World War Two, the Holocaust, and the Cold War – for which German cultural scholarship more broadly speaking had long taken critical responsibility in a variety of useful, if limited ways.

Perspectives on German Cinema could only begin the daunting task of eliciting, much less answer such questions. As a scholarly compendium, moreover, it faced and symptomized ineluctable structural contradictions – the real and ideological limitations of academic centrism (e.g. Hake, 1998; cf. Fisher and Prager, 2010). Although its editors were criticized superficially by an H-Net review (Denham, 1998: para. 3) for apparently "not lik[ing] German film very much," their call, explicated succinctly by Gerhard Knapp in a prior review (1997: 426–427), was taken up within the field by serious scholarly endeavors (e.g. Reimann, 2003: 177) that have evidenced a determined pursuit of the volume's suggestion to register and reengage the "silent zone" (Ginsberg and Thompson, 1996: 15) of German cinema studies' disciplinary meanings and social import.

A good number of these key works are referenced, integrated, and critiqued by and within the contributions to *A Companion to German Cinema*, the aim of which is to rehearse while intellectually resituating the critical developments that have occurred in and around this field since the turn of the twenty-first century, a moment when German cinema studies, in its historically uneven relationship with German film production, began to experience a first post-Wall reinvigoration and institutional expansion beyond the US academy. Whereas the latter has seen a relative decrease in German studies generally,[1] the albeit belated establishment and acceptance of cinema studies as a legitimate area of academic inquiry within

German higher education (in addition to its longer presence in the vocational Hochschulen für Film und Fernsehen) has led to a growth of inquiry there, where scholarly publishing on German film has also noticeably increased.

A *Companion to German Cinema* also emerges at a moment in which the global conflagrations marking, but certainly not confined to, the German social legacy have not diminished, as Ginsberg and Thompson (1996: 15) had hoped they would when stressing a belief in the potential role scholarly inquiry could and should play in signaling "the formation of intellectual alliances along lines drawn toward ending (neo)fascism and (neo)nationalism, and toward ending prevailing assumptions that a radical theory of culture is no longer possible." Instead the world has seen – literally by means of new digital media as well as film and television – the totalities of nation, race, gender, and class manifest in many additional local wars and greater global immiseration than might previously have been imagined. Indeed, the decade preceding the present writing is marked by casualty and death far outstripping that which marred the years that produced the New German Cinema, its often avant-garde aesthetics and its critiques of US-led Western imperialism and neocolonialism. As the newly minted European Union has proceeded with much difficulty, and in the face of ongoing resistance, to consolidate economically in relation to these developments (see Habermas, 2010; Krugman, 2011), the neoliberal interests it represents as well as caters to and fosters, more often than not with the full backing of the United States, have redirected cultural and scholarly practices toward areas more fully concentrated on postcolonial regions. The ensuing sociocultural embrace of "otherness," to which Kira Kosnick (2007: 14) writing on Turkish-German media refers, quoting Ayşa Çağlar, as "ethnomarketing," has been a belated yet in many respects reductive and exploitative immersion by Europe, and the West generally, in renewed orientalisms and xenophobias disguised as benevolent multiculturalism.[2]

While German cinema studies throughout this period has by no means abandoned – infact it has increased critical attention to – *Vergangenheitsbewältigung* (mourning and coming to terms with the Nazi past),[3] the late 1990s and 2000s have seen a modest growth in the field's engagement with cultural studies areas such as feminism;[4] (homo)sexuality;[5] class politics, economic structures, and the former East Germany;[6] and race, (post)colonialism, globalization, and transnationalism.[7] These multi- and crosscultural foci have occasionally been addressed, if sometimes less directly and forcefully, in the context of more generic concerns, for instance reunification,[8] the ongoing legacy of West German film traditions and *Autoren*,[9] Weimar cinema,[10] and German cinematic/cultural relationships with Hollywood[11] and Austria.[12] Many of these investigations reflect a contemporary shift in German filmmaking away from international art-house and independent vehicles toward more sustained commercial-industrial, locally and regionally directed production. However, as several contributions to the present volume indicate, this turn to the local nonetheless articulates and implements larger structural shifts in the European film and media spheres to *transnational* schemes and collaborations.

Based upon the principle of subsidiarity "borrowed from the practices of Catholic Canon Law" (Norman Davies, quoted in Rivi, 2007: 28), these collaborations reenvision post-reunification Germany as a "heterogeneous, hybrid, and polycentric space" (Rivi, 2007, 6, 36) that stands ostensibly to overcome previous monolithic national configurations through the proliferation of popular regional markets.

In her analysis of contemporary European cinema's relationship to transnationalism, Luisa Rivi (2007) argues against such visions and practices, for instance those proffered by Tim Bergfelder (2005) writing on 1960s popular European co-productions. For her, these shifts toward localization have simply entailed further disenfranchising European culture's traditional "others." Recalling Thomas Elsaesser's (2005) concern that Germany's contemporary focus on (multi)culture, which was mandated by Article 151 of the revised Maastricht Treaty of 2001, is serving to position cultural production as a primarily commodificatory enterprise, Rivi (2007: 48, 56–57), following Foucault, sees the transnational turn not as a means of European "opening" but of its retrenchment. On her argument, dominant power structures and practices persist and proliferate by very way of their "decentralization and ubiquitous occupation" (p. 29); *because*, that is, they acknowledge otherness only to contain it (p. 48), they actually "safeguard … nationality at the core of supranationality" (p. 63) and therefore reinforce the very borders and exclusivisms which the so-called postnational, "deterritorialized" (Davidson, 1999) system purports to overcome.

The recent publication of several Germanophone books concerning animation, cinema technology, and digital media (DEFA-Stiftung, 2006; Kohlmann, 2007; Schenk, 2007; Brandlmeier, 2008) is conceivably related to this veritable postmodern systemics, even as philosophical interest continues in traditional German film aesthetics and avant-garde praxis and their legacy.[13] The increasingly transdisciplinary composition of German cinema studies, as evidenced by the bibliography to this Introduction and symptomatized by the departmental mergers referenced in note 1, likewise attests to this problematic structural turn. The transnational shift in post-*Wende* Germano-European film production has itself been enabled by sophisticated structural mechanisms of the new economic order. These include Mesures d'encouragement pour le développement de l'industrie audiovisuelle (Measures for Encouraging Development of the Audiovisual Industry) (MEDIA), which operates under the auspices of the European Commission of Cinematographic Co-Production and funds Europa Cinemas, an inter-European exhibition network promoting European films, the European Film Academy, an award-granting body modeled after the American Academy of Motion Picture Arts and Sciences, and Euromed Audiovisual, an uneven "partnership" between the European Union and ten "Mediterranean" countries/regions, including Turkey, the Palestinian Authority, Israel, and Algeria (Rivi, 2007: 60). This EU-based restructuring also includes Eurimages, a cinematic funding mechanism commonly decried for having fostered so-called "Europudding" films, well-intentioned popular-commercial fare that tends nevertheless to "replace national conflicts with a sweet but ultimately bland narrative than can only appeal to a least common denominator of culture" (Halle, 2008: 48; see also Wayne, 2002: 13–19; Galt, 2006: 103–105; Rivi, 2007: 64). Whereas these mechanisms have enabled a noticeable increase in the production of films addressing Germany's social and political-economic peripheries and their popular (re)locations within national borders (re)defined as "European" and endowed with "European values" (Kosnick, 2007: 13),[14] the imperative to turn a profit through mass appeal has frequently served to reproduce violently abstract cultural tropes and formal structures that encourage reactionary spectatorial positionings and ideological irredentism. In effect, the new Germano-European cinematic funding system is premised – as are some of Rivi's (2007: 9, 35) Jamesonian assumptions – upon the Euro-Western nation-state as the very foundation of culture, and thus upon measuring the success of multicultural integration on the degree to which immigrants assimilate and "become locals" within the so-called European value-system (Kosnick, 2007: 18; see also Milward, 2000). As Mike Wayne (2002: ix, 2–3) remarks in his political critique of new European cinema, these premises serve to confuse and conflate the systemic proliferation of local and regional media with the very differences such media presume to represent. As a result, what Guido Rings and Rikki Morgan-Tamosunas (2003: 15), writing on European film and identity, refer to as "other definitions of the 'postcolonial' developed by the periphery," for example the "subaltern oppositional practices" which Kosnick (2007: 19, 183) argues entail "actual minority participation and sharing of power," are implicitly excluded.

Although post-*Wende* German cinema studies has concerned itself more consistently with sociocultural "otherness," the revision of theoretical frameworks necessary to the genuine integration of intellectual differences entailed by such concerns has been less forthcoming (Rings and Morgan-Tamosunas, 2003: 15; see also Wayne, 2002: vii, 3–4; Galt, 2006: 3–7). As a partial antidote, Kosnick (2007: 6) proposes that German cultural scholarship link semiotic analysis, political and economic data-gathering, and historiographical investigation rather than continuing to separate them methodologically. The effect of this persisting nonintegration, echoing film production tendencies, is a plethora of lip-service paid to differences understood implicitly as capital surplus rather than, more constructively we believe, as genuinely transformative intellectual resources.

Perhaps most symptomatic of this problem is the array of above-referenced scholarly texts circulating on the state-run East German film studio, DEFA (Deutsche Film Aktiengesellschaft). According to Dennis Broe's contribution on East German Westerns, or *Indianerfilme*, which launches the present volume, and as David Brandon Dennis's ensuing paper on Heiner Carow's cinematic oeuvre stands to counter, contemporary DEFA scholarship has for all intents and purposes tended to throw out the socially emancipatory baby with the politically oppressive bathwater. As Meta Mazaj (2011) suggests in another context, Western European critics have continued to position Eastern European films as relatively transparent allegories of Communism and its legacy, thereby eliding through a process of metonymic projection the indigenous value of such films as well as the myriad forms of oppression and exploitation visible in and promoted by Western cinema that are critiqued variously, in often noteworthy fashion, by Eastern European cinema. While Broe questions Western scholarly resistance to the *Indianerfilme's* critiques of European colonialism and racism in the Americas, and as Dennis theorizes Carow's protoqueer cinema as a call for more genuinely democratic configurations of socialism, Julia Knight's contribution on immediate post-Wall documentaries regarding the effects of the *Wende* in Eastern Germany carries the tenor of such critiques into the post-reunification era, asking further, if implicitly, in relation to filmic examinations of nationalist identity formations on both sides of the former Berlin Wall, whether it is even possible any longer to answer such a call in light of the dire economic conditions faced by Eastern residents, their ongoing experiences of trauma, and the West's continued selective, veritably mythological viewing of their deteriorating situation.

For Anthony Enns, the answer to this implied question is a qualified "yes." Enns sees critical resistance to the failures and limitations of reunification inscribing the recent wave of German *Ostalgie* (postsocialist nostalgia) films. In contrast to widespread views deriding these films primarily as commercial compromises, Enns examines how they nonetheless illustrate the moral bankruptcy of a capitalist system that has been unable to address current economic and cultural challenges and a desire to reevaluate the state of a country still in flux fifteen years after the fall of the Berlin Wall. Similarly David Clarke's analysis of interstitial space within films of the post-*Wende* "Berlin School" demonstrates the extent to which these likewise popular, often internationally successful films undertake a critique of the post-reunification social and economic order by in some respects returning to the kind of political auteurism that characterized the New German Cinema and now is characterized by modes of territorial – and ideational – reappropriation. By the same token, but on the other hand, Jennifer Ruth Hosek's critique of post-*Wende* "Neue Heimat" (New Homeland) films, including but not limited to Berlin Films, locates and historicizes nostalgic "spaces of belonging" in this nascent genre in terms of their "-isms of propinquity," that is, their venerations of sameness which hearken to uncannily familiar nationalisms, racisms, sexisms, and classisms from within contemporary neoliberal conditions of crossborder capital flow and (de)regulation.

The prevalent, hotly contested issue of (post)national border-crossing is taken up in this context. While Hosek demonstrates the reinscription of neonationalist *Heimat* in popular German films of the post-*Wende* era, Gayatri Devi's appreciation of one such film, *Unveiled* (*Fremde Haut*, Angelina Maccarone, 2005), implicitly extends David Clarke's thesis to the register of critical spectatorship, in turn deconstructing and resituating *Heimat* as a matrix of radical social transformation in the era of neocolonialism. Likewise rethinking the cinematic articulation of national (un)homeliness is Claudia Pummer's critique of the canonized critical reception of the Alsatian avant-garde filmmaking team Straub–Huillet. Pummer retrieves and revisits the French auteurism that has begun to be mined by scholars in relation to Straub–Huillet's "German" cinematic oeuvre, in turn arguing for an anticolonialist as well as antinationalist allegoricality at its experimental core, and furthermore rejecting abstract formalist claims that these directors' biographical narratives and discursive-historical conditions are without significance for their materialist aesthetic concerns.

Not unpredictably, these investigations converge at the theoretical intersection of transnational cultural and economic conditions within post-reunification Germany and their implications for the country's public and intellectual spheres. How, in effect, they ask, to recall Rivi (2007: 1), does German totality "break down"? Implied, that is, by several of this volume's contributions is the radical potential of grounding the fetishistic mise-en-abyme of "otherness" promoted by European ethnomarketing in the situated coordinates of material history. Hence Peter Limbrick analyzes the experimental documentary work of Kamal Aljafari, whose cinematic critiques of national home extend from Germany to Iraq to Palestine/ Israel, at once symptomatizing and critically negotiating the Germano-European training and funding enabling and overdetermining such revisioning in the context of exilic diaspora. Similarly Savaş Arslan reunderstands the Turkish-German films of Fatih Akın as delineating a new, if evidently less oppositional post-reunification subjectivity located within, and to some extent against, predominant (trans)national formations because traceable historico-aesthetically to a really existing "other" home whose im/possible attainment stands to challenge the interests of the German self-same. For Priscilla Layne, such a critical redirection of the transnational marks a crucial missing link within Fassbinder scholarship. Layne argues that predominant privileging of the paradigmatic New German Cinema *Autor*'s reappropriation of Hollywood melodramas directed by exiled German filmmakers has served to neglect his appropriation of the popular genre's critique by the US Blaxploitation genre, as epitomized by Fassbinder's "least successful film," *Whity* (1970) – like the *Indianerfilme* a critical take on both Hollywood and revisionist Westerns and their nostalgic quests for racialized *Lebensraum*.

By contrastive extension, the relative dearth of sustained scholarly attention to historical German popular-commercial cinema is lent redress by Harald Steinwender and Alexander Zahlten's critical survey of the 1960s–1970s German sexploitation genre. Steinwender and Zahlten explore the contours of this underexamined genre, revealing its limited deconstruction of Germany's post-Marshall Plan, Cold War-era attempts to invigorate European national film cultures via intracontinental co-productions funded by television. Sexploitation's ironical destabilization of Euro-Western nation-statism marks the dialectical center of this ostensibly international and undeniably taboo-breaking endeavor, whereupon it serves as an instructive occasion for gauging the ideology-effects of popular-commercial cinematic innovation transnationally. On the other hand, the critically sidelined documentaries of Jochen Hick, made largely in and about gay male and transgender sex cultures in the post-AIDS United States and former Soviet bloc, break the ideological boundaries of their filmed subjects, even while arguably appearing structurally and stylistically rather conventional. According to Robert M. Gillett, these independent, internationally interested films at once historicize and problematize erotic and sexual exposure and the desire for it, its often simultaneous exploitation and suppression, while, recalling David Dennis on Heiner Carow's "third way," acknowledging the basic human need for sexual expression in its recognized manifold forms.

In this critical spirit, Nadja Krämer's critique of the post-Nazi era remasculization of German culture via the immensely popular and successful 1950s *Sissi* films exposes the ideological role these studio products played in advocating Cold War-era German rearmament. In turn Silke Arnold-de Simine supplies a crosscultural analysis of well-known German crossdressing films of the 1930s (Weimar period) and 1950s, and of their immensely popular and successful US remakes by European directors during the 1950s and 1980s. Both essays stand to recognize the contemporary tendency, marked by the post-Wall scholarly turn to popular-commercial German films, toward normalization, while proposing, apropos of Jennifer Hosek on *Neue Heimat* films, to critique it. The significance of feminism and queer theory for and within these endeavors cannot be overlooked, nor should their developing relationship to critical race and post-/anticolonial theories – which Krämer in turn exemplifies when highlighting the role played by enforced postwar family formations in facilitating German hegemony within the Western Germanophone bloc (in this instance Austria), and which Arnold-de Simine pursues when revealing the relative limits of cinematic gender-bending in comparative (inter)national contexts.

These issues are also of import to contemporary German cinema, whether commercial or art-house, where they have prompted public debates over key, ongoing German concerns about the Nazi period. Sally Winkle tests former New German Cinema *Autorin* Margarethe von Trotta's *Rosenstrasse* (2003) against critical claims that this film's portrayal of "Aryan" women's resistance to the Nazi-era arrests and deportations of their Jewish husbands instances a co-opted feminism in the service of apologetic right-revisionism. By contrast, Domenica Vilhotti discusses post-New German Cinema *Autor* Andres Veiel's post-Holocaust documentary, *Balagan* (1994), with respect to that film's provocative simulation of the "femininized" (see Vukadinović, Chapter 18, in this volume) abjection performed critically by Israeli/Palestinian avant-garde stage actors likewise engaged in reunderstanding the Holocaust for and in the present day. The abiding questions here of historical German violence and its cinematic inscriptions extend in turn to the post-Wall wave of RAF films, a veritable genre propagating revisionist views of the now-defunct Rote Armee Fraktion (Red Army Faction) and its controversial policy of *Linksterrorismus* ("leftist terrorism"). In his paper on the international box-office hit, *The Baader Meinhof Complex* (2008), Vojin Saša Vukadinović offers an immanent critique of mainstream/centrist criticisms of this phenomenon, especially its tenuous relationship to feminism and the popular mass base, thus contributing to current debates in the German public sphere, and across the political spectrum, over these issues and the function of moving-image culture in fostering critical thinking about political activism and social change.

Indeed the possibility that moving-image aesthetics and their modalities of (re)production are effective public intellectual occasions and vehicles for transformation in the transnational era comprises the problematics of Frances Guerin's appreciation of Harun Farocki's avant-garde documentary, *Videograms of a Revolution* (*Videogramme einer Revolution*, 1992), which supplies an aesthetic analysis of the televisual (mis)representation of the Romanian Revolution of 1989. The possibility that images are conceivable as nonlinguistic forms of communicative expression wielding objective power bespeaks rationales for their containment and censorship, as Terri Ginsberg discusses further within the context of critiquing a German academic feminist listserv debate over the "Jewish-German" film comedy, *Go for Zucker!* (*Alles auf Zucker!* 2004). Ginsberg's concern that objectivity not be misrecognized as ideology, and hence foreclosed, echoes an ironical comment by Michael Haneke, the internationally most renowned and celebrated of the post-*Wende Autoren*, who states in an interview that

> The demand for "objectivity" is quite strange in a medialized world in which the majority is concerned simply with reassuring and glossing over. Why *not* allow cinema to speak about the neglected areas of reality? Violence and emotional coldness are dominant characteristics of our neoliberal dog-eat-dog society – is it really one-sided to portray them in an exemplary way accordingly? We are living in a violent world. (Grabner, 2010: 19; our emphasis)

Via his contribution on the viscerally disturbing films of Eastern German filmmaker Aelrun Goette, whose oeuvre focuses a materialist feminist lens on violent mothers and their neglected children, David James Prickett fittingly reminds that cinema can – indeed must – intervene literally into a dysfunctional public sphere in order to prevent or ameliorate social injustice. This possibility may be what Tara Forrest likewise means to suggest as she extends Critical Theory to a reading of "utopianism" in Haneke's *71 Fragments of a Chronology of Chance* (*71 Fragmente einer Chronologie des Zufalls*, 1994); it is at least what we mean to suggest with the present anthological compilation.

In fact the socially transformative potential signified by the present volume's attention, by way of its 21 newly commissioned contributions, to marginalized, misunderstood, and neglected films, genres, directors, discourses, and theories marks what we believe is a necessary shift in the field away from overriding concerns with internal subjective states and spectator-effects toward reclaiming and (re)theorizing the objective orientation and significance of the larger moving-image apparatus and its filmic (and video and digital) occasionings. While by no means abandoning textual analysis, for instance – the majority of the contributions to this volume engage in this essential practice, through formalist and/or thematic methodologies – and while recognizing as well the nontextual determinants of any cinematic reading – all of the volume's contributions supply some form of contextual and/or structural historiography – *A Companion to German Cinema* aims to redirect the study of German cinema toward the question of its social-material *vanishing point*, a horizon-tal location through whose spectral scope the field may be repositioned to perform what Rivi (2007: 1) has called "Europe 'on the verge of a nervous breakdown,'" that is, to ramify a radically unsettled reenvisaging of that persistently contested geocultural place.

With this in mind, we have organized the contributions to this volume, with a nod to Michel Pêcheux (1982), into three barely marked, chronologically unordered "movements," each meant to signify a relative ideational moment in this proposed dialectics of objective vanishing: (1) destabilization; (2) dislocation; (3) disidentification. The reader will note in this respect that the contributions have not been selected in strict conformity with the disciplinary boundaries or protocols typically associated with the study of German cinema and culture; *A Companion to German Cinema* introduces several new scholars, some from fields traditionally not centered, conceptually or historically, upon the study of German cinema or visual culture. Whereas we do not necessarily agree with or condone all of their premises, approaches, or conclusions, we aim for each of these contributions to be judged, together and apart, on the basis of the potential it brings to exemplify and elaborate the delineated moments of German cinema's suggested reenvisaging and thus to transpose the theoretical vanishing point, structured by the volume, into its transformative reprise: a requiem for cinematic voices previously unheard and for cinematic images previously unseen, now at l(e)ast (re)emergent and projecting loudly and clearly from the vantage of their objective (un)timeliness – what Walter Benjamin might have called their *Jetztzeit*.

July 2011

Notes

1   An evident symptom of this decrease is the spate of German departmental and program closures and interdisciplinary mergers – or plans for such – across the United States in recent years. Affected institutions include Illinois Wesleyan University, Minnesota State University–Mankato, University of Iowa, University of Nevada–Reno, SUNY–Albany, and Virginia Commonwealth University – and numerous others.

2   Perhaps the public height of this sociocultural arrogance was reached in October 2010 by German Chancellor Angela Merkel of the conservative Christian Democratic Union, who, shortly following the release of a study by a German think-tank which revealed that more than 30% of Germans believe their country is "overrun by foreigners" (*Christian Science Monitor*, 2011), declared that multiculturalism in Germany "has utterly failed" (Weaver, 2010) – and blamed this purported failure on immigrants themselves for allegedly not having learned enough German to justify their sustained employment in the country. For another, by now notorious example of concomitant anti-immigrant discourse in the German public sphere, see Sarazzin, 2010. For a critical review of Sarazzin, see Ash, 2011.

3   E.g. Schulte-Sasse, 1996; Bonnell, 1998; Linville, 1998; Lungstrum, 1998; *New German Critique*, 1998; Thompson, 1999; Fox, 2000; Moeller, 2000; Reimer, 2000; Welch, 2000; Fox, 2001; Hake, 2001; Hoerschelmann, 2001; Romani, 2001; Shandley, 2001; Ascheid, 2003; Hake, 2002; Koepnick, 2002; Kansteiner, 2003; Moltke, 2003; Schoeps, 2003; Winkel, 2003a,b; Carter, 2004; Culbert, 2004; Lubich, 2004; Peukert, 2004; Dickie, 2005; Currid, 2006; Bendix, 2007; Gelbin, 2007; Horbrügger, 2007; *New German Critique*, 2007; Paver, 2007; Pelzer, 2007; Schmitz, 2007; Strobl, 2007; Fisher, 2008; Fuchs, 2008; Pages, Majer-O'Sickey, and Riehl, 2008; Prager, 2008.

4   E.g. Creech, 2008; Linville, 1998; Majer-O'Sickey and Zadow, 1998; Dassanowsky, 1999; Wager, 1999; Fox, 2000; McCarthy, 2000; Mennel and Onigiri, 2000; Müller, 2000; Wilke, 2000; McCormick, 2001, 2002; Specter, 2001; Mayne, 2004; Rupprecht, 2006; Stoicea, 2006; Pinkert, 2008.

5   E.g. Halle, 2000; Kuzniar, 2000; Davidson, 2002; Kaplan, 2002; Mitchell, 2004; Gelbin, 2007.

6   E.g. Müller-Bach, 1997; Allan and Sandford, 1999; Gemünden, 1999; Meurer, 2000; Fox, 2001; Feinstein, 2001; *New German Critique*, 2001; Naughton, 2002; Petrie, 2004; Pike, 2004; Steinmetz and Viehoff, 2004; Dittmar, 2005; Imre, 2005; Berghan, 2006; Stoicea, 2006; Dewald, 2007; Enns, 2007; Pinkert, 2008.

7   E.g. Davidson, 1999; Fenner, 2000; Koepnick, 2000; Betz, 2001; Oksiloff, 2001; Anderson, 2002; Jacobsen, 2003; Jones, 2003; *New German Critique*, 2004; Lieberfeld, 2005; Zwick, 2006; Benbow, 2007; Blumenrath *et al.*, 2007; Gerhardt, 2007; Halle, 2008; Kosnick, 2007; Bouchehri, 2008.

8   E.g. Costabile-Heming *et al.*, 2001; Majer-O'Sickey, 2002; *New German Critique*, 2002; Preece, 2003; Hantke, 2004; Lieberfeld, 2005; Clarke, 2006; Cormican, 2007; McAllister, 2007; *German Politics and Society*, 2007, 2008; *Screen*, 2007; Horn, 2008.

9   E.g. Cook and Gemünden, 1997; Lutze, 1998; Gunning, 2000; Jesinghausen, 2000; Lutze, 2000; Graf, 2002; Skidmore, 2002; Flinn, 2003; Halle and McCarthy, 2003; Praeger, 2003; Arnold-de Simine, 2004; Bergfelder, 2004; Birgel and Phillips, 2004; Robertson, 2004; Thomson, 2004; Hofer, 2005; Koestenbaum, 2005 / 2006; Silvestra, 2005; Langford, 2006; Moeller and Lelli, 2006; Davidson and Hake, 2007; Hosek, 2007; Praeger, 2007; Fujiwara, 2008; Hirsch, 2008; Horvath and Omasta, 2008; McIsaac, 2008; Rickels, 2008.

10 E.g. Levin, 1998; Robinson, 1998; Gleber, 1999; Steakley, 1999; Wager, 1999; Elsaesser, 2000; Calhoon, 2001; Ward, 2001; Aspetsberger, 2002; McCormick, 2002; Prawer, 2002; Kester, 2003; Knight, 2003; Mennel, 2003; Roper, 2003; Scheunemann, 2003; Winkler, 2003a; Pike, 2004; Roberts, 2004; Currid, 2006; Jelavich, 2006; Cowan, 2007; Ganeva, 2007; Ascárate, 2008; Ashkenazi, 2008; Hall, 2008; Richter, 2008; Roberts, 2008.

11 E.g. Dassanowsky and Steiner, 1997; Dimendberg, 1997; Dassanowsky, 2001; Latham, 2003; Petrie, 2004; Bahr, 2007; Gelbin, 2007; Haase, 2007; Fay, 2008.

12 E.g. Gemünden, 1998; *Maske under Kothern*, 2001; Dassanowsky, 2003, 2005; Krenn, 2007.

13 E.g. Wedel, 1999; Wege and Böger, 1999; Welsch, 1999; Koch, 2000; Strathausen, 2000; Szaloky, 2002; Halle and Steingröver, 2008; Elsaesser, 2004; Hansen, 2004; Nieberle, 2004; Claussen, 2005; Guerin, 2005; Vollmer, 2006; Bernhard, 2007; Ostermann, 2007; Schönfeld and Rasche, 2007; Stilwell and Powrie, 2007; Wheatley, 2009; Grundmann, 2010; Ornella and Knauss, 2010; Price and Rhodes, 2010; Speck, 2010.

14 Kosnick here avers, quoting Dominic Boyer, that such values are designated and promoted as "European" rather than "German" due to the perceived persisting need by Germany to shed its Nazi (violent racist) associations. For Kosnick, such "shedding" has become little more than disavowal in the context of multicultural ethnomarketing.

References

Aitken, I. (1998) Distraction and redemption: Kracauer, surrealism and phenomenology. *Screen*, 39 (2), 124–140.

Allan, S. and Sandford, J. (eds) (1999) *DEFA: East German Cinema, 1946–1992*, Berghahn Books, Oxford.

Alter, N.M. (1998) Ottinger's Benjamin: *Countdown*'s alternative take on unification. *Germanic Review*, 73 (1), 50–69.

Anderson, S.C. (2002) Outsiders, foreigners, and aliens in cinematic or literary narratives by Bohm, Dische, Dörrie, and Oren. *Germany Quarterly*, 75 (2), 144–159.

Arnold-de Simine, S. (2004) "Denn das Haus, was wir bewohnen, [...] ist ein Spukhaus": Fontanes *Effi Briest* under Fassbinders Verfilmung in der Tradition des *Female Gothic*. *Germanic Review*, 79 (2), 83–114.

Ascárate, R.J. (2008) Cinematic enlightenment: Franz Osten's *Die Leuchte Asiens* (1925). *Quarterly Review of Film and Video* 25 (5), 357–367.

Ascheid, A. (2003) *Hitler's Heroines: Stardom and Womanhood in Nazi Cinema*. Temple University Press, Philadelphia.

Ash, T.G. (2011) Germans, more or less. *New York Review of Books* 24 February, http://www.nybooks.com/articles/archives/2011/feb/24/germans-more-or-less/ (accessed February 26, 2011).

Ashkenazi, O. (2008) The incredible transformation of Dr. Bessel: alternative memories of the Great War films of the late 1920s. *Historical Journal of Film, Radio and Television*, 20 (1), 121–152.

Aspetsberger, F. (ed.) (2002) *Der Bergfilm 1920–1940*, Studien Verlag, Innsbruck.

Bahr, E. (2007) *Weimar on the Pacific: German Exile Culture in Los Angeles and the Crisis of Modernism*, University of California Press, Los Angeles, Berkeley.

Benbow, H.M. (2007) Ethnic drag in the films of Dorris Dörrie. *German Studies Review*, 30 (3), 517–536.

Bendix, J. (2007) Facing Hitler: German responses to *Downfall*. *German Politics and Society*, 25 (1), 70–89.

Bergfelder, T. (2004) Popular genres and cultural legitimation: Fassbinder's *Lola* and the legacy of the 1950s. *Screen*, 45 (1), 21–39.

Bergfelder, T. (2005) *International Adventures: German Popular Cinema and European Co-productions in the 1960s*, Berghahn, Oxford and New York.

Berghahn, D. (2004) Do the right think? Female allegories of nation in Aleksandr Askoldov's *Komissar* (USSR 1967/87) and Konrad Wolf's *Der Geteilte Himmel* (GDR, 1964). *Historical Journal of Film, Radio and Television*, 26 (4), 561–577.

Berghahn, D. (2007) Do the right thing? Female allegories of nation in Aleksandr Askoldov's *Komisar* (USSR 1967/87). *Historical Journal of Film, Radio and Television*, 26 (4), 561–577.

Bernhard, S. (2007) Cacography or communication? Cultural techniques in German media studies. *Grey Room*, 29, special issue on New German Media Theory, 26–47.

Betz, M. (2001) The name above the (sub)title: internationalism, coproduction, and polyglot European art cinema. *Camera Obscura*, 16 (1), special issue on Marginality and Alterity in New European Cinema, Part 2, 1–45.

Birgel, F.A. and Phillips, K. (eds) (2004) *Straight Through the Heart: Dorris Dörrie, German Filmmaker and Author*, Scarecrow Press, Lanham, MD.

Blumenrath. H., Bodenberg, J., Hillmann, R. and Wagner-Engelhaaf, M. (2007) *Transkulturalität: Türkisch-deutsche Konstellationen in Literature und Film*, Aschendorff Medien, Münster.

Bonnell, A.G. (1998) Melodrama for the Master Race: two films by Detlef Sierck (Douglas Sirk). *Film History*, 10 (2), 52–69.

Bouchehri, R. (2008) *Filmtitel im interkulterellen Transfer*, Frank and Timme, Berlin.

Brandlmeier, T. (2008) *Kameraautoren: Technik und Äesthetik*, Schüren, Marburg.

Calhoon, K.S. (ed.) (2001) *Peripheral Visions: The Hidden Stages of Weimar Cinema*, Wayne State University Press, Detroit, MI.

Carter, E. (2004) *Dietrich's Ghosts: The Sublime and the Beautiful in Third Reich Film*, BFI, London.

Christian Science Monitor (2010) Germany's Angela Merkel: Multiculturalism has "utterly failed." Global News Blog, October 17, http://www.csmonitor.com/World/Global-News/2010/1017/Germany-s-Angela-Merkel-Multiculturalism-has-utterly-failed (accessed February 26, 2011).

Clarke, D.C. (ed.) (2006) *German Cinema since Unification*, Continuum, London.

Claussen, D. (2005) Adorno and Fritz Lang. *Telos*, 130, 141–164.

Cook, R.F. and Gemünden, G. (1997) *The Cinema of Wim Wenders: Image, Narrative, and the Postmodern Condition*, Wayne State University Press, Detroit, MI.

Cormican, M. (2007) Goodbye Wenders: *Lola rennt* as German film manifesto. *German Studies Review*, 30 (1), 121–140.

Costabile-Heming, C.A., Halverson, R.J. and Foell, K.A. (eds) (2001) *Textual Responses to German Unification: Processing Historical and Social Change in Literature and Film*, Walter de Gruyter, Berlin, New York.

Cowan, M. (2007) The heart machine: "rhythm" and body in Weimar film and Fritz Lang's *Metropolis*. *Modernism/Modernity*, 14 (2), 225–248.

Creech, J. (2008) A few good men: gender, ideology, and narrative politics in *The Lives of Others* and *Good Bye, Lenin! Women in German Yearbook*, 24, 100–126.

Culbert, D. (ed.) (2004) *Historical Journal of Film, Radio and Television*, 24 (1), special issue on Nazi Newsreels in German-Occupied Europe, 1939–1945.

Currid, B. (2006) *A National Acoustics: Music and Mass Publicity in Weimar and Nazi Germany*, University of Minnesota Press, Minneapolis.

Dassanowsky, R.v. (1999) Male sites/female visions: four female Austrian film pioneers. *Modern Austrian Literature*, 32 (1), 126–140.

Dassanowsky, R.v. (2001) A mountain of a ship: locating the "Bergfilm" in James Cameron's *Titanic*. *Cinema Journal*, 40 (4), 18–35.

Dassanowsky, R.v. (2003) Going home again? Ruzowitzky's *Die Siebtelbauern* and the New Austrian *Heimatfilm*. *Germanic Review*, 78 (2), 133–147.

Dassanowsky, R.v. (2005) *Austrian Cinema: A History*, McFarland, Jefferson, NC.

Dassanowsky, R.v. and Steiner, G. (eds) (1997) *Filmkunst*, 154 (49), special issue on Austria's Hollywood/Hollywood's Austria.

Davidson, J.E. (1999) *Deterritorializing the New German Cinema*, University of Minnestora Press, Minneapolis.

Davidson, J.E. (2002) A story of faces and intimate spaces: form and history in Max Färberböck's *Aimée und Jaguar*. *Quarterly Review of Film and Video*, 19 (4), 323–341.

Davidson, J.E. and Hake, S. (eds) (2007) *Take Two: Fifties Cinema in Divided Germany*, Berghahn, New York, Oxford.

DEFA-Stiftung (eds) (2006) *Puppen im DEFA-Animationsfilm. Puppets in DEFA Animation Films*, DEFA-Stiftung, Berlin.

Denham, S. (1998) Review of T. Ginsberg and K.M. Thompson (eds), *Perspectives on German Cinema*. H-German, H-Net Reviews, October, http://www.h-net.org/reviews/showrev.php?id=2419 (accessed February 22, 2011).

Dewald, C. (2007) *Arbeiterkino: linke Filmkultur der Ersten Republik*, Filmarchiv Austria, Wien.

Dickie, G. (2005) The Triumph in *Triumph of the Will*. *British Journal of Aesthetics*, 45 (2), 151–156.

Dimendberg, E. (1997) From Berlin to Bunker Hill: urban space, late modernity, and film noir in Fritz Lang's and Joseph Losey's *M*. *Wide Angle*, 19 (4), 62–93.

Dittmar, C. (2005) Television and politics in the former East Germany (trans. B. Kraft). *Comparative Literature and Culture*, 7 (4), http://www.clcwebjournal.lib.purdue.edu (accessed October 4, 2008).

Elsaesser, T. (1989) *New German Cinema: A History*, Rutgers University Press, New Brunswick, NJ.

Elsaesser, T. (2000) *Weimar Cinema and After: Germany's Historical Imaginary*, Routledge, New York.

Elsaesser, T. (ed.) (2004) *Harun Farocki: Working on the Sightlines*, Amsterdam University Press, Amsterdam.

Elsaesser, T. (2005) *European Cinema: Face to Face with Hollywood*, Amsterdam University Press, Amsterdam.

Elsaesser, T. and Wedel, M. (eds) (1999) *The BFI Companion to German Cinema*, BFI, London.

Enns, A. (2007) The politics of *Ostalgie*: post-socialist nostalgia in recent German films. *Screen*, 48 (4), 475–491.

Fay, J. (2008) *Theaters of Occupation: Hollywood and the Reeducation of Postwar Germany*, University of Minnesota Press, Minneapolis.

Fehrenbach, H. (1995) *Cinema in Democratizing Germany: Reconstructing National Identity after Hitler*, University of North Carolina Press, Chapel Hill, London.

Feinstein, J. (2001) *The Triumph of the Ordinary: Depictions of Daily Life in the East German Cinema, 1949–1989*, University of North Carolina Press, Chapel Hill, London.

Fenner, A. (2000) Turkish cinema in the New Europe: visualizing ethnic conflict in Sinan Çetin's *Berlin in Berlin*. *Camera Obscura*, 15 (2), special issue on Marginality and Alterity in New European Cinemas, Part 1, 105–149.

Fisher, J. (2008) *Disciplining Germany: Youth, Reeducation, and Reconstruction after the Second World War*, Wayne State University Press, Detroit, MI.

Fisher, J. and Prager, B. (eds) (2010) *The Collapse of the Conventional: German Film and Its Politics at the Turn of the Twenty-First Century*, Wayne State University Press, Detroit, MI.

Flinn, C. (2003) *The New German Cinema: Music, History, and the Matter of Style*, University of California Press, Berkeley.

Fox, J. (2000) *Filming Women in the Third Reich*, Berg, Oxford.

Fox, T.C. (2001) *Stated Memory: East Germany and the Holocaust*, Camden House, London.

Fuchs, A. (2008) *Phantoms of War in Contemporary German Literature, Films and Discourse*, Palgrave, New York.

Fujiwara, C. (2008) *The World and Its Double: The Life and Work of Otto Preminger*, Faber & Faber, New York.

Galt, R. (2006) *The New European Cinema: Redrawing the Map*, Columbia University Press, New York.

Ganeva, M. (2007) Weimar film as fashion show. *German Studies Review*, 30 (2), 288–310.

Gelbin, C.S. (2007) Double visions: queer femininity and Holocaust film: from *Ostatni Etap* to *Aimée and Jaguar*. *Women in German Yearbook*, 23, 179–204.

Gemünden, G. (1998) Between Karl May and Karl Marx. *Film History*, 10 (3), 399–407.

Gemünden, G. (1999) *Framed Visions: Popular Culture, Americanization, and the Contemporary German and Austrian Imagination*, University of Michigan Press, Ann Arbor.

Gerhardt, C. (2007) Transnational Germany: Hito Steyerl's film *Die leere Mitte* and two hundred years of border crossings. *Women in German Yearbook*, 23, 205–233.

German Politics and Society (2007) 25 (4), special series on The *Denk ich an Deutschland* Films, Part 1.

German Politics and Society (2008) 26 (2), special series on The *Denk ich an Deutschland* Films, Part 2.

Ginsberg, T. and Thompson, K.M. (1996) *Perspectives on German Cinema*, G.K. Hall/Macmillan, New York and London.

Gleber, A. (1999) *The Art of Taking a Walk: Flanerie, Literature, and Film in Weimar Culture*, Princeton University Press, Princeton, NJ.

Grabner, F. (2010) "We live in a permanent state of war": an interview with Michael Haneke, in *Fascinatingly Disturbing: Interdisciplinary Perspectives on Michael Haneke's Cinema* (eds A.D. Ornella and S. Knauss), Wipf & Stock, Eugene, OR, pp. 13–33.

Graf, A. (2002) *The Cinema of Wim Wenders: The Celluloid Highway*, Wallflower Press, London.

Grundmann, R. (ed.) (2010) *A Companion to Michael Haneke*, John Wiley & Sons, Ltd, London.

Guerin, F. (2005) *A Culture of Light: Cinema and Technology in 1920s Germany*, University of Minnesota Press, Minneapolis.

Gunning, T. (2000) *The Films of Fritz Lang: Modernity, Crime and Desire*, BFI, London.

Haase, C. (2007) *When Heimat Meets Hollywood: German Filmmakers and America, 1985–2005*, Boydell & Brewer, Rochester, NY.

Habermas, J. (2010) Germany and the Euro-Crisis (trans. C. Cronin). *The Nation*, June 28, http://www.thenation.com/article/germany-and-euro-crisis (accessed February 26, 2011).

Hake, S. (1998) Review article. *Monatshefte*, 90 (1), 89–96.

Hake, S. (2001) *Popular Cinema of the Third Reich*, University of Texas Press, Austin.

Hake, S. (2002) *German National Cinema*, Routledge, New York.

Hales, B. (2007) Projection trauma: the femme fatale in Weimar and Hollywood film noir. *Women in German Yearbook*, 23, 224–243.

Hall, S.F. (2008) Moving images and the policing of political action in the early Weimar period. *German Studies Review*, 31 (2), 285–302.

Halle, R. (2000) "Happy ends" to crises of heterosexual desire: toward a social psychology of recent German comedies. *Camera Obscura*, 15 (2), special issue on Marginality and Alterity in New European Cinemas, Part 1, 1–39.

Halle, R. (2008) *German Film after Germany: Toward a Transnational Aesthetic*, University of Illinois Press, Urbana, Chicago.

Halle, R. and McCarthy, M. (eds) (2003) *Light Motives: German Popular Film in Perspective*, Wayne State University Press, Detroit, MI.

Halle, R. and Steingröver, R. (2008) *After the Avant-Garde: Contemporary German and Austrian Experimental Film*, Boydell and Brewer, Rochester, NY.

Hansen, M. (2004) Room-for-Play: Benjamin's gamble with cinema. *Canadian Journal of Film Studies*, 13 (1), 2–27.

Hantke, S. (2004) Horror film and the historical uncanny: the New Germany in Stefan Ruzowitsky's *Anatomie*. *College Literature*, 31 (2), 114–142.

Hirsch, F. (2008) *Otto Preminger: The Man Who Would Be King*, Random House, New York.

Hoerschelmann, O. (2001) "Memoria Dextera Est": Film and public memory in postwar Germany. *Cinema Journal*, 40 (2), 78–97.

Hofer, S. (2005) Das Ende der Generationseinheit von '68: Volker Schlöndorff's *Die Stille nach dem Schuß*. *Seminar*, 41 (2), 125–148.

Horbrügger, A. (2007) *Aufbruch zur Kontinuität – Kontinuität im Aufbruch: Geschlechterkonstruktionen im west – under ostdeutschen Nachkriegsfilm von 1945 bis 1952*, Schüren, Marburg.

Horn, E. (2008) Media of conspiracy: love and surveillance in Fritz Lang and Florian Henckel von Donnersmarck. *New German Critique*, 35 (1), 127–144.

Horwath, A. and Omasta, M. (2008) *Josef von Sternberg: The Case of Lena Smith*, Wallflower, London.

Hosek, J.R. (2007) Buena Vista Deutschland: Nation and Gender in Wenders, Gaulke and Eggert. *Downfall*. *German Politics and Society*, 25 (1), 46–69.

Imre, A. (2005) *East European Cinema*, Routledge, New York.

Jacobsen, J. (2003) Germans and Turks: cinematic encounters of the traveling kind. *Spectator*, 23 (2), 23–31.

Jelavich, P. (2006) *Berlin Alexanderplatz: Radio, Film, and the Death of Weimar Culture*, University of California Press, Los Angeles.

Jesinghausen, M. (2000) The sky over Berlin as transcendental space: Wenders, Döblin and the "angel of history," in *Spaces in European Cinema* (ed. M. Konstantarakos), Intellect, Exeter, Portland, OR.

Jones, S. (2003) Turkish-German cinema today: a case study of Fatih Akın's *Kurz und schmerzlos* (1998) and *Im Juli* (2000), in *European Cinema: Inside Out: Images of the Self and the Other in Postcolonial European Film* (eds G. Rings and R. Morgan-Tamosunas), Universitätsverlag Winter: Heidelberg, pp. 75–91.

Kansteiner, W. (2003) Entertaining catastrophe: the reinvention of the Holocaust in television of the Republic of Germany. *New German Critique*, 90, 135–162.

Kaplan, J.A. (2002) *Johanna d'Arc of Mongolia*: interview with Ulrike Ottinger. *Art Journal*, 61 (3), 7–21.

Kester, B. (2003) *Filmfront Weimar: Representations of the First World War in German Films from the Weimar Period (1919–1933)*, Amsterdam University Press, Amsterdam.

Knapp, G.P. (1997) Review of *Perspectives on German Cinema*. *Seminar*, 33 (4), 426–428.

Knight, J. (2003) *New German Cinema: The Images of a Generation*, Wallflower Press, London.

Koch, G. (2000) *Siegfried Kracauer: An Introduction* (trans. J. Gaines), Princeton University Press, Princeton, NJ.

Koepnick, L. (2000) Consuming the other: identity, alterity, and contemporary German cinema. *Camera Obscura*, 15 (2), special issue on Marginality and Alterity in New European Cinemas, Part 1, 41–73.

Koepnick, L. (2002) *German Cinema between Hitler and Hollywood*, University of California Press, Berkeley.

Koestenbaum, W. (2005–2006) *In the Funhouse*: five Fassbinder scenes. *Salmagundi*, 148–149, 58–70.

Köhler, I. (2006) *Der deutscshe Kinofilm: Perspektiven Visionen Erfolgschancen*, Vdm Verlag Dr. Müller, Saarbrücken.

Kohlmann, K. (2007) *Der computeranimierte Spielfilm. Forschungen zur Inszenierung und Klassifizierung des 3-D-Computer-Trickfilms*, Transcript Film, Bielefeld.

Kosnick, K. (2007) *Migrant Media: Turkish Broadcasting and Multicultural Politics in Berlin*, Indiana University Press, Bloomington, Indianapolis.

Kracauer, S. (1947) *From Caligari to Hitler: A Psychological History of the German Film*, Princeton University Press, Princeton, NJ.

Krenn, G. (2007) *"Ein sonderbar Ding": Essays und Materialien zum Stummfilm Der Rosenkavalier*, Filmarchiv Austria, Vienna.

Krugman, P. (2011) Can Europe be saved? *New York Times Magazine*, January 12, http://www.nytimes.com/2011/01/16/magazine/16Europe-t.html?ref=magazine (accessed February 26, 2011).

Kuzniar, A.A. (2000) *The Queer German Cinema*, Stanford University Press, Stanford, CA.

Langford, M. (2006) *Allegorical Images: Tableau, Time and Gesture in the Cinema of Werner Schroeter*, Intellect, Bristol, Chicago.

Latham, J. (2003) The Kaiser as best of Berlin: race and the animalizing of German-ness in early Hollywood's advertising imaginary. *West Virginia University Philological Papers*, 50, 16–30.

Levin, D.J. (1998) *Richard Wagner, Fritz Lang, and the Nibelungen: The Dramaturgy of Disavowal*, Princeton University Press, Princeton, NJ.

Lieberfeld, D. (2005) Globalization and terminal illness in *Goodbye, Lenin!* and *The Barbarian Invasion*. *Logos*, 4 (2), http://www.logosjournal.com/issue_4.2/lieberfeld.htm (accessed February 25, 2011).

Linville, S.E. (1998) *Feminism, Film, Fascism: Women's Auto/Biographical Film in Postwar Germany*, University of Texas Press, Austin.

Lubich, F.A. (2004) Rafael Seligmann's *Der Musterjude*: a master parody of German-Jewish *Führer* Phantasies. *German Studies Review*, 27 (2), 229–248.

Lungstrom, J. (1998) Foreskin fetishism: Jewish male difference in *Europa, Europa*. *Screen*, 39 (1), 124–140.

Lutze, P.C. (1998) *Alexander Kluge: The Last Modernist*, Wayne State University Press, Detroit, MI.

Lutze, P.C. (2000) Alexander Kluge's "cultural window" in private television. *New German Critique*, 80, 171–190.

McAllister, G.P. (2007) Romantic imagery in Tykwer's *Lola rennt*. *German Studies Review*, 30 (3), 517–536.

McCarthy, M. (2000) Teutonic water: effervescent otherness in Doris Dörrie's *Nobody Loves Me*. *Camera Obscura*, 15 (2), special issue on Marginality and Alterity in New European Cinemas, Part 1, 177–201.

McCarthy, M. (2004) Putting stones in place: Anne Duden and German acts of memory. *German Quarterly*, 77 (2), 210–229.

McCormick, R.W. (2001) Rape and war, gender and nation, victims and victimizers: Helke Sander's *Befreier und Befreite*. *Camera Obscura*, 16 (1), special issue on Marginality and Alterity in New European Cinema, Part 2, 99–141.

McCormick, R.W. (2002) *Gender and Sexuality in Weimar Modernity: Film, Literature, and "New Objectivity,"* Palgrave Macmillan, London.

McIsaac, P. (2008) Mapping German identities in Dorris Dörrie's *Bin ich schön?* *German Quarterly*, 77 (3), 340–362.

Majer-O'Sickey, I. (2002) Whatever Lola wants, Lola gets (or does she?): time and desire in Tom Tykwer's *Run Lola Run*. *Quarterly Review of Film and Video*, 19 (2), 123–131.

Majer-O'Sickey, I. and Zadow I.v. (1998) *Triangulated Visions: Women in Recent German Cinema*, SUNY Press, Albany.

Maske und Kothern (2001) 46 (1), special issue on Austrian Film of the Postwar Occupation.

Mayne, J. (2004) Marlene, dolls, and fetishism. *Signs*, 30 (1), 1257–1263.

Mazaj, M. (2011) Eastern European cinema on the margins. *Situations: Project of the Radical Imagination*, 4 (1), special issue on Global Cinema: Cinéma Engagé or Cinéma Commerciale?, 189–207.

Mennel, B. (2003) White law and the missing black body in Fritz Lang's *Fury* (1936). *Quarterly Review of Film and Video*, 20 (3), 203–223.

Mennel, B. and Onigiri, A. (2000) In a desert somewhere between Disney and Las Vegas: the fantasy of interracial harmony and American multiculturalism in Percy Adlon's *Bagdad Café*. *Camera Obscura*, 15 (2), special issue on Marginality and Alterity in New European Cinemas, Part 1, 151–175.

Meurer, H-J. (2000) *Cinema and National Identity in a Divided Germany 1979–1989: The Split Screen*, Edwin Mellen Press, Lewiston, NY, Queenston, ON, Lampeter, UK.

Milward, A.S. (2000) *The European Rescue of the Nation-State*, Routledge, London.

Mitchell, M. (2004) "Cabaret," America's Weimar, and mythologies of the gay subject. *American Music*, 22 (1), 145–157.

Moeller, F. (2000) *The Film Minister: Goebbels and the Cinema in the "Third Reich,"* Edition Axel Menges, Stuttgart, London.

Moeller, H. and Lelli, G. (2006) Heroes without compromise: an interview with Volker Schlöndorff. *Journal of Film and Video*, 58 (3), 43–53.

Moltke, J.v. (2003) Home again: revisiting the New German Cinema in Edgar Reitz's *Die Zweite Heimat* (1993). *Cinema Journal*, 42 (3), 114–143.

Müller, R. (ed.) (2000) *Discourse*, 22 (2), special issue on Valie Export.

Müller-Bach, I. (1997) Cinematic ethnology: Siegfried Kracauer's *The White Collar Masses*. *New Left Review*, 226, 41–56.

Naughton, L. (2002) *That Was the Wild East: Film Culture, Unification, and the "New" Germany*, University of Michigan Press, Ann Arbor.

New German Critique (1998) 74, special issue on Nazi Cinema.

New German Critique (2001) 82, special issue on East German Film.

New German Critique (2002) 87, special issue on Postwall Cinema.

New German Critique (2004) 92, special issue on Multicultural Germany: Art, Performance, and Media.

New German Critique (2007) 102, special issue on *Der Untergang?*: Nazis, Culture, and Cinema.

Nieberle, S. (2004) Das Grauen der Autorschaft: Angstnarrationen im Literarhistorischen Biopic. *Germanic Review*. 79 (2), 115–136.

Oksiloff, A. (2001) *Picturing the Primitive: Visual Culture, Ethnography, and Early German Cinema*, Palgrave Macmillan, London.

Ornella, A.D. and Knauss, S. (eds) (2010) *Fascinatingly Disturbing: Interdisciplinary Perspectives on Michael Haneke's Cinema*, Wipf & Stock, Eugene, OR.

Ostermann, E. (2007) *Die Filmerzählung: acht exemplarische Analysen*, Wilhelm Fink Verlag, Munich.

Pages, N.C., Majer-O'Sickey, I. and Riehl, M. (2008) *Riefenstahl Screened: An Anthology of New Criticism*, Continuum, London.

Paver, C. (2007) *Refractions of the Third Reich in German and Austrian Fiction and Film*, Oxford University Press, Oxford.

Pêcheux, M. (1982) *Language, Semantics, and Ideology* (trans. H.C. Nagpal), St Martin's Press, New York.

Pelzer, J. (2007) "The facts behind the guilt"? background and implicit intentions in *Downfall*. *Downfall*. *German Politics and Society*, 25 (1), 90–101.

Petrie, G. (2004) Bertolt Brecht and Béla Balász: paradoxes of exile. *Canadian Journal of Film Studies*, 13 (2), 2–21.

Peukert, B. (2004) The fascist choreography: Riefenstahl's tableaux. *Modernism/Modernity*, 11 (2), 279–297.

Pike, D.L. (2004) "Kaliko-Welt": the *Großstädte* of Lang's *Metropolis* and Brecht's *Dreigroschenoper*. *Modern Language Notes*, 119 (3), 474–505.

Pinkert, A. (2008) *Film and Memory in East Germany*, Indiana University Press, Bloomington.

Praeger, B. (2003) Werner Herzog's hearts of darkness: *Fitzcarraldo*, *Scream of Stone* and beyond. *Quarterly Review of Film and Video*, 20 (1), 23–35.

Praeger, B. (2007) *The Cinema of Werner Herzog: Aesthetic Ecstasy and Truth*, Wallflower, London.

Prager, B. (2008) Interpreting the visible traces of Theresienstadt. *Journal of Modern Jewish Studies*, 7 (2), 175–194.

Prawer, S.S. (2002) *The Blue Angel*, BFI, London.

Preece, J. (2003) Between identification and documentation, "autofiction" and "biopic": the lives of the RAF. *German Life and Letters*, 56 (4), 363–376.

Price, B. and Rhodes, J.D. (eds) (2010) *On Michael Haneke*, Wayne State University Press, Detroit.

Reimann, A. (2003) New German Cinema's boundaries opened: postmodern authorship and nationality in Monika Treut's films of the 1980s, in *Writing against Boundaries: Nationality, Ethnicity and Gender in the German-Speaking Context* (eds B. Kosta and H. Kraft), Rodopi, Amsterdam, New York, pp. 177–196.

Reimer, C. and Reimer C.J. (2008) *Historical Dictionary of German Cinema*, Scarecrow Press, Lanham, MD.

Reimer, R.C. (ed.) (2000) *Cultural History through a National Socialist Lens: Essays on the Cinema of the Third Reich*, Camden House, London.

Richter, S. (2008) The return of the queen of the night: Joseph von Sternberg's *Der Blaue Engel* and *Die Zauberflöte. German Life and Letters*, 61 (1), 171–185.

Rickels, L.A. (2008) *Ulrike Ottinger: The Autobiography of Art Cinema*, University of Minnesota Press, Minneapolis.

Rings, G. and Morgan-Tamosunas, R. (eds) (2003) *European Cinema: Inside Out: Images of the Self and the Other in Postcolonial European Film*, Universitätsverlag Winter: Heidelberg.

Rivi, L. (2007) *European Cinema after 1989: Cultural Identity and Transnational Production*, Palgrave Macmillan, Hampshire, UK, New York.

Roberts, I. (2008) *German Expressionist Cinema: The World of Light and Shadow*, Wallflower, London.

Roberts, J. (2004) Caligari revisited: circles, cycles, and counter-revolution in Robert Wiene's *Das Cabinet des Dr. Caligari. German Life and Letters*, 57 (2), 175–187.

Robertson, J.P. (2004) Teaching in your dreams: screen-play pedagogy and Margareth von Trotta's *The Second Awakening of Christa Klages. Canadian Journal of Film Studies*, 13 (2), 74–92.

Robinson, D. (1998) *Das Kabinett des Dr. Caligari*, BFI, London; Indiana University Press, Indianapolis.

Romani, C. (2001) *Tainted Goddesses: Female Film Stars of the Third Reich*, 2nd edn, Gremese International, Rome.

Roper, K. (2003) Fridericus films in Weimar society: Potsdamismus in a democracy. *German Studies Review*, 21 (3), 493–514.

Rupprecht, C. (2006) Post-war iconographies: wandering women in Brecht, Duras, Kluge. *South Central Review*, 23 (2), 36–57.

Sarazzin, T. (2010) *Deutschland schafft sich ab: Wie wir unser Land aufs Spiel setzen*, Deutsche Verlags-Anstalt, Munich.

Schenk, R. (2007) *Bilder einer gespaltenen Welt. 50 Jahre Dokumentar- und Animationsfilmfestival*, Bertz + Fischer Verlag, Berlin.

Scheunemann, D. (ed.) (2003) *Expressionist Film: New Perspectives*, Boydell and Brewer, Rochester, NY.

Schmitz, H. (ed.) (2007) *A Nation of Victims? Representations of German Wartime Suffering from 1945 to the Present*, Rodopi, Amsterdam, New York.

Schönfeld, C. and Rasche, H. (eds) (2007) *Processes of Transposition: German Literature and Film*, Rodopi, Amsterdam, New York.

Schoeps, K-H. (2003) *Literature and Film in the Third Reich*, rev. edn (trans. K.M. Dell'Orto), Boydell & Brewer, Rochester, NY.

Schulte-Sasse, L. (1996) *Entertaining the Third Reich*, Duke University Press, Durham, NC.

Screen (2002) 28 (2), special issue on The *Caché* Dossier.

Shandley, R.R. (2001) *Rubble-Films: German Cinema in the Shadows of the Third Reich*. Temple University Press, Philadelphia.

Siegert, B. (2007) Cacography or communication? Cultural techniques in German media studies. *Grey Room*, 29, special issue on New German Media Theory, 26–47.

Silvestra, M. (2005) Experience and memory in the films of Wim Wenders (trans. J. Sisneros), *SubStance*, 34 (1), 159–179.

Skidmore, J.M. (2002) Intellectualization and emotionalism in Margarethe von Trotta's *Die bleierne Zeit. German Studies Review*, 25 (3), 551–567.

Speck, O.C. (2010) *Funny Games: The Filmic Concepts of Michael Haneke*, Continuum, New York, London.

Specter, S. (2001) Was the Third Reich movie-made? Interdisciplinarity and the reframing of ideology. *American Historical Review,* 106 (2), 460–484.

Steakley, J.D. (1999) Cinema and censorship in the Weimar Republic. *Film History,* 11 (2), 181–202.

Steinmetz, R. and Viehoff, R. (eds) (2004) *Historical Journal of Film, Radio and Television,* 24 (3), special issue on East German Television History.

Stilwell, R.J. and Powrie, P. (eds) (2007) *Composing for the Screen in Germany and the USSR: Cultural Politics and Propaganda,* Indiana University Press, Bloomington.

Stoicea, G. (2006) Re-producing the class and gender divide: Fritz Lang's *Metropolis. Women in German Yearbook,* 22, 21–42.

Strathausen, C. (2000) The return of the gaze: stereoscopic vision in Jünger and Benjamin. *New German Critique,* 80, 125–148.

Strobl, G. (2007) "Zum Ruhme Englands": the "Vorgeschichte" of the Nazi film. *German Life and Letters,* 60 (2), 196–201.

Szaloky, M. (2002) Sounding images in silent film: visual acoustics in Murnau's "Sunrise." *Cinema Journal,* 41 (2), 109–131.

Thompson, B. (1999) The ministry of illusion: German cinema in the Goebbels era. *Stanford Humanities Review,* 5 (suppl.), 120–125.

Thomson, C.B. (2004) *Fassbinder: The Life and Work of a Provocative Genius,* Indiana University Press, Bloomington, Indianapolis.

Vollmer, U. (2006) Auf Leinwand begannt: Judith im (Miss-)Verständnis von Malerei und Film. *Biblical Interpretation,* 14 (2), 76–93.

Wager, J.B. (1999) *Dangerous Dames: Women and Representation in the Weimar Street Film and Film Noir,* Ohio University Press, Athens.

Ward, J. (2001) *Weimar Surfaces: Urban Visual Culture,* University of California Press, Berkeley.

Wayne, M. (2002) *The Politics of Contemporary European Cinema: Histories, Borders, Diasporas,* Intellect, Bristol, Portland, OR.

Weaver, M. (2010) Angela Merkel: German multiculturalism has "utterly failed": Chancellor's assertion that onus is on new arrivals to do more to integrate into German society stirs anti-immigrant debate. *Guardian,* October 17, http://www.guardian.co.uk/world/2010/oct/17/angela-merkel-german-multiculturalism-failed (accessed February 26, 2011).

Wedel, M. (1999) Messter's "silent" heirs: sync systems of the German music film 1914–1929. *Film History,* 11 (4), 464–466.

Wege, A. and Böger, A. (1999) Who decides what is "Haupstadtkultur," and what is not? *October,* 89, 127–138.

Welch, D. (2000) *Germany, Propaganda and Total War, 1914–1918,* Rutgers University Press, New Brunswick, NJ.

Welsch, T. (1999) Foreign exchange: German expressionism and its legacy. *Cinema Journal,* 38 (4), 98–102.

Wheatley, C. (2009) *Michael Haneke's Cinema: The Ethic of the Image,* Berghahn Books, London.

Wilke, S. (2000) The body politic of performance, literature, and film: mimesis and citation in Valie Export, Elfriede Jelinek, and Monika Treut. *Paragraph,* 22 (2), 228–247.

Winkel, R.vd. (2003a) The auxiliary cruiser: *Thor*'s death and transfiguration: a case study in Nazi newsreel propaganda in the Second World War. *Historical Journal of Film, Radio and Television,* 23 (3), 211–229.

Winkel, R.vd. (2003b). Nazi Germany's Fritz Hippler, 1909–2002. *Historical Journal of Film, Radio and Television*, 23 (2), 91–99.

Winkler, M.M. (2003a) Fritz Lang's mediaevalism: from *Die Nibelungen* to the American West. *Mosaic*, 36 (1), 135–146.

Winkler, M.M. (2003b) Nazi Germany's Fritz Hippler, 1909–2002. *Historical Journal of Film, Radio and Television*, 23 (2), 91–99.

Zwick, R. (2006) Mit "Esther" für Versöhnung Streiten: Zu Amos Gitais filmischer Aktualisierung der biblischen Erzählung. *Biblical Interpretation*, 14 (2), 54–75.

Further Reading

A more extensive bibliography on German cinema is available in Reimer and Reimer (2008).

First Movement: Destabilization

Whereas much contemporary writing on German cinema establishes an entry point into the subject at the moment of reunification, the first movement of this collection encourages inquiry into the cinematic treatment of the *Wende* by first presenting scholarly re-readings of GDR cinema. The movement ensues with analyses of post-reunification cinematic depictions of Eastern Germany in the context of the *Wende*, and follows with essays regarding depictions and portrayals of the West. In this way, the volume's first movement offers perspectives on post-reunification projections of the *Wende* that attend critically to the turn's uneven, destabilizing implications for German culture and national consolidation within the framework of the New Europe.

1

Have Dialectic, Will Travel

The GDR Indianerfilme *as Critique and Radical Imaginary*

Dennis Broe

It is almost impossible these days to conjure the GDR, the German Democratic Republic of 1948–1989, without the primary memory being that of surveillance, of an out-of-control police state, a drab, gray world of spies, counterspies and keeping tabs on your neighbor. Films such as the post-GDR *The Lives of Others* (2006), along with Western triumphalism, have effectively obliterated in the popular Western imagination any positive contribution of the GDR to its people and to present-day Germany as a whole. Rather than recalling exemplary social programs, a pronounced antifascism, and a vision of equality (cited as rationales for the existence of the GDR in Dorpalen, 1985), the best expression that memories of the former socialist republic are allowed is *"Ostalgie,"* a packaged, commodified "nostalgic" reduction of the principles of the GDR to a few of its artifacts. One of the most enduring brands of *Ostalgie* comprises books, merchandise, and festivals, particularly the annual event at Bad Segeberg, celebrating that campiest of East German relics, the *Indianerfilme*. Starring Yugoslavian hunk Gojko Mitic, these consisted of twelve films produced between 1965 and 1983, each from the perspective of different Native American tribes, detailing two centuries of their battles against the expansive power of the English Crown and the United States. The films were critically derided at the time, although they were popular successes, with crowds swarming to see them at huge, open-air summer festivals, and with their East European locations, directors, and casts standing as the Second World equivalent of the Hollywood global blockbuster. Three *Indianerfilme* have been released in the West over the past few years – *The Sons of Great Bear* (1965); *Chingachgook: The Great Snake* (1967); and *Apaches* (1973) – and have generally either been derided as protonationalist projections onto the Hollywood Western of a German colonial and racist past (Gemünden, 2001) or have been damned with faint praise as models

A Companion to German Cinema, First Edition. Edited by Terri Ginsberg and Andrea Mensch.
© 2012 Blackwell Publishing Ltd. Published 2012 by Blackwell Publishing Ltd.

of popular dissent, focusing around a yearning for national unity that the West and East could not permit (Dika, 2008).

This chapter will propose alternate readings of the *Indianerfilme*, preferring to see in their popular expression of Native American values and ways of life not a dangerous Socialist Utopia but the glimmerings of a shedding of dictatorship and the beginnings of a socialist democracy that were expressed at the time of the tearing down of the Berlin Wall and that were effectively demolished by the rapid unification and swallowing of East Germany whole by the capitalist West. On this reading, the *Indianerfilme*[1] will be seen as pointing the way toward the potential for social democracy in Eastern Europe, and the struggles they ostensibly project onto the Western as having been aimed first and foremost against the capitalist West and secondarily against the Russian colonizer to the East, thus giving the films much more currency in the present. This attempt at an alternative reading of these films, however, will begin by doing something that has apparently been considered outrageous by their extant interpreters: taking seriously their avowed intention to rewrite the Western from the perspective of the Native American, something that could only have been done in bits and pieces in Hollywood (as both Vera Dika and Gerd Gemünden point out), where the US foundational myth (and its rationale for future incursions) depends on a heroic story of freedom-loving "settlers" conquering "virgin" territory (Stam and Shohat, 1994).

This attempt to reposition the *Indianerfilme* takes Elsaesser and Wedel's dictum that any serious history of DEFA, or Deutsche Film Aktiengesellschaft (German Film Corporation), the East German film studio located on the grounds of the famed Weimar studio, UFA, or Universum Film Aktiengesellschaft, see that studio's production not as a complete exception in film and industry terms but as part of a continuum, in a dialogue with the West (and, I would add, with other countries to the East). To do otherwise is simply to accept a retrospective and teleological, Western triumphalist reading of GDR film history that always reduces cinematic and cultural expressions in the former Eastern bloc to "descriptions of a society longing for change" (from a West German telecast on the day of reunification, quoted in Elsaesser and Wedel, 2001: 5), and constitutes no break from the standard history that, in Walter Benjamin's terms, "is always written by the winners" (Elsaesser and Wedel, 2001: 7).[2] Hence this chapter will first position the *Indianerfilme* in relation to the Hollywood Western as a more complete form of that genre, one which appeared during the same period that the generic transformation of the Western, termed the Revisionist Western, was taking place in Hollywood as part of what was later referred to as Hollywood's New Wave, exemplified most seminally by Abraham Polonsky's *Tell Them Willie Boy Is Here* (1969), Arthur Penn's *Little Big Man* (1970), and Robert Altman's *Buffalo Bill and the Indians* (1976). Placed alongside Hollywood deconstruction of the Western, the *Indianerfilme*'s adoption of a Native American perspective can be understood in relation to the subset of those revisionist films which Steve Neale (1998) calls "Pro-Indian Westerns." Although they are not as sensitive as their Hollywood counterparts at rewriting the codes of Western action, they go much further in outlining the political economy of the West, in their emphasis, apropos of Native American cultural critic Ward Churchill's (2001) critique of the genre, on the various tribes and alternative histories of Native Americans, in their devaluation of the cowboy as a lumpen profiteer, and in their corresponding heightening of the power and strength of the Native American as guerilla and resistance fighter.

With respect to German film history of the period, the *Indianerfilme* will thus be seen as making a two-pronged contribution. The first is their rewriting of the West German Karl May, or "Isar," Westerns which preceded them, by offering a challenge to romantic notions that Indian nobility is affirmed only by conversion to Christianity, the religion and civilization of the West, and by critiquing Western political economy through the adoption of Brechtian and Eisensteinian distancing devices, which helped break through the veil that transformed the May Westerns from imperial primers during the Hitler years into elaborate adolescent (and capitalist) fantasies during the denazifying postwar period (Schneider, 1998). Their second contribution, of *Indianerfilm* and GDR cinema as a whole, was their consistent rewriting of popular West German genre films, for example *Fünf Patronenhülsen* (Five Cartridges, 1960), which, with its seldom explored setting during the Spanish Civil War (Bock, 1998), rewrote West German adaptations of the British, Edgar Wallace spy novels.

The most interesting way to see *Indianerfilme* as part of a German cinematic continuum would be to read them against the grain of their frequent interpretations as the degraded, popular East German statist flipside of the *Verbotsfilme*, 12 films made in the GDR during 1965 that were suppressed by the regime and that likely would have become the East German equivalent of New German Cinema, sometimes also referred to as the "Rabbit Films" (Elsaesser and Wedel, 2001: 7). One might instead see these films as aligned with the more avant-garde aspects of the New German Cinema, one of the New Wave movements in the West. In that case, the *Indianerfilme* might be considered that cinema's popular expression in the East, one that also drew from the European addition to the Revisionist Western, the "spaghetti Westerns" of Sergio Leone. Both the East and West German cinemas were highly concentrated on reworking genres that were popular during the fascist period by inserting reworked Hollywood strains – for example, Fassbinder's reinvention of the fascist and postfascist *Heimat* film, using tropes from the genre's Hollywood insertion by Douglas Sirk (Detlef Sierck) of those elements into the melodrama. In addition, both East and West elaborated respective versions of the Native American as source of resistance. Gemünden (2001: 36) notes that in the West the Native American was translated into a model of resistant *Stadtindianer* ("City Indians"), which for the New Left served as an attaché to the urban guerila. Although Gemünden discounts it, this is no less true for the (less industrially developed) East, where the Native Americans of the *Indianerfilme* were presented as a model for Third World peoples in their more rural struggles; guerila wars of independence that were still raging for most of the series' production period. Thus the *Indianerfilme* carry a double articulation; one, in their reexamination of the West as represented in Hollywood cinema, and two, in their proposing a new German imaginary in the process of rewriting the Western in light of its West German appropriation.

Finally, this chapter argues, via Gramsci, that, by referring to the *Indianerfilme* as the popular expression in the East of New German Cinema in the West, one is furthermore suggesting a cultural alliance of the precise sort that is forming – and which is much needed – in Germany today, where an attempt is ongoing to resuscitate the Left, grounded in *Die Linke* (The Left) party. That party, which now has the potential to join the government, is comprised of the former West German New Left faction – led until his recent illness by Oskar Lafontaine (a.k.a. "Red Oskar"), who is still the most prominent government representative of 1960s radicalism – as well as the remnants of the evolved social democratic element of the former GDR, led, also until recently, by Gregor Gysi, the former head of the reconstituted, hoped-for evolution of an Eastern democratic socialist and workers party. Thus the cultural-historical bloc formed by suggesting a continuum between the *Indianerfilme* and the New German Cinema, which marks a blending of a 1960s avant-garde, radical activist cinema with a more working-class-centered, popular cinema, is the imaginary currently being activated to counter the center- and hard-right's domination of a Germany which, after several years of experiencing a neoliberal destruction of its social welfare policies, is perhaps as "longing for change" as the West German media once declared East German citizens to be.

In arguing for an expanded place for the *Indianerfilme* in German consciousness, where they might become part of a radical imaginary that far surpasses *Ostalgie*, I want to refer to Dagmar Jaeger's interview with the Alfred Döblin prizewinner, Ingo Schulze, about his 1998 book, *Simple Stories*, a series of fictional accounts of East German characters who feel themselves, after the fall of the Wall, rapidly (dis)integrating into a commercialized West, perceived as being in the "midst of America" (Schulze, quoted in Jaeger, 2007: 145). Schulze expresses a certain strain of East German sentiment. He believed in 1989 that "we would build here a quite wonderful GDR" apropos of what at the time was termed the "Third Way" (Jaeger, 2007: 152). That possibility was quickly erased, he says, because the big power players surrounding the GDR, including the USSR, Britain, France, the United States, and West Germany (as he puts it: Gorbachev, Thatcher, Mitterand, Bush, and Kohl), would never allow it. After this *realpolitik* became clear, East Germans, Schulze reports, then went on about the reunification, until "one day people began to realize that major problems were emerging in everyday life that had not existed in the same form in East Germany" (Jaeger, 2007: 153). For him, many of these problems centered around the question of private property in a society that seeks at each moment of its everyday activity "to maximize profit" (he gives the example of a dentist about whose care he is never sure isn't primarily benefiting the dentist rather than the patient). What Easterners also found, he claims, is that in the new Germany there is no discussion of these fundamental principles: "This system is not willing to talk about certain things, meaning private property" (Jaeger, 2007: 153).

The West defines and defends itself as "natural," he says, which leads him to aver that "the GDR changes every year and becomes more important every year" (Jaeger, 2007: 148), and to declare, famously, "Only in the 1990s Did I Become East German." All of this points clearly to the contemporary relevance and importance of the *Indianerfilme* as a potential source of a radical imaginary, a site of remembering GDR culture that can point the way forward to a place where the fundamental values not only of neoliberalism but of capital as a whole may be questioned. The continued popularity of the *Indianerfilme* above and beyond *Ostalgie* may also be a sign of the ongoing need for questioning an ever more rapidly neoliberalizing Germany.[3]

This reading goes against the grain of much contemporary scholarship on the GDR, the role of DEFA, and its relationship to "building socialism." These studies range from characterizations of the GDR as, on the one hand, the bearer of an irrelevant legacy to, on the other hand, a seat of absolute and utter repression. Leonie Naughton's *That Was the Wild East* seems to find impractical the East German Left's deliberations at the time of the tearing down of the Berlin Wall over "what kind of society they wanted to build." She views this handwringing as putting the brakes on unification, a much desired phenomenon for the country as a whole, since East Germany was "a picture of indolence and decrepitude" (Naughton, 2002: xv) and "a technologically backward region" (Naughton, 2002: 5). Nevertheless, she admits that subsequent West German films about unification view the process positively while films that originate in the East are more negative (Naughton, 2002: 9).

In a more ideologically slanted appraisal, Joshua Feinstein argues, in *The Triumph of the Ordinary*, that the history of DEFA in the GDR begins and ends with the repression of what amounted to a whole year's production of films (the *Verbotsfilme*) at the Eleventh Plenum in 1965. This is a "TINA" study (following Thatcher's phrase that, with respect to Western capitalism, There Is No Alternative) that describes the GDR as a place of "stagnation and arrested development" where the "only factor that remained constant was massive political oppression" whose "significance lies only in its deficiency and aberrance" because it is not "a model Western democracy [which] embodies national progress" (Feinstein, 2002: 4). Given this view, then, it is not surprising that all film production culminates in the Eleventh Plenum suppression, with subsequent production consisting mainly of a reaction to the suppression and whose end result is a stagnation that lifts only when the films are finally shown in 1989. The "gap" from 1965 to 1989, in a monolithic characterization of the output of one of the primary production facilities of Eastern Europe, is seen as a "Rip Van Winkle sleep" (Feinstein, 2002: 4). One of the few more critical studies is Anke Pinkert's *Film and Memory in East Germany*, which argues that GDR films from 1945 to 1960 were involved, even if at times only marginally, in recounting, keeping alive, and mourning the "historical experience of war, death and mass murder" (Feinstein, 2002: 7), experience that was largely absent from the films in the West.

How the West Was Revised

The *Indianerfilme* can be viewed both as a lost branch of the Hollywood Revisionist Western, albeit one that adds significantly to the goals of that subgenre, and, within German cinema as a whole, as a kind of revisionist German Western. The films were a response to the Karl May films made from 1962 on by West Germans and shot on some of the same Yugoslav locations (using some of the same sets and extras). In that respect they followed the Hollywood model in which the Revisionist Westerns, also shot on the same locations as their 1950s predecessors, reworked the themes and contexts of the earlier films' dramatic actions. The shared sets and locations perhaps illustrated the degree to which Eastern Westerns were by no means an isolated phenomenon but instead stood in dialogic relation to their West German predecessors, especially in their critical reversal of the dramatic action played out against the same landscapes.[4]

While the Hollywood Western accounted for one quarter of all studio production up to 1960, the genre then began to fade, although by 1972, in what Jim Hoberman (1998: 90) calls the peak year of the Revisionist Western, the form still accounted for 12% of studio productions. But there were major differences. The Western, once the imperial genre par excellence, its films set mostly during the era of manifest destiny (1865–1885) when the United States was still expanding its domestic space through conquest (Churchill, 2001) and often concerned with the Indian Wars, could be seen as a backward projection onto the previous century of US postwar empire-building during the era when the United States, as the single most dominant world power, had declared the "Pax Americana." John Ford's independent production company, Argosy, which had investment ties to US intelligence (Saunders 2001: 286) and produced the trilogy comprised of *Fort Apache* (1948), *She Wore A Yellow Ribbon* (1949), and *Rio Grande* (1950), might stand for this moment most prominently.[5] But in light of a general questioning of US history, led by William Appleman Williams during the 1960s and brought on by reflection on the goals and means of empire *pace* Vietnam, the Western began to change. This was perhaps pioneered by Ford's own *Cheyenne Autumn* (1964) and marked by Sam Peckinpah's *The Wild Bunch* (1969), whose opening scene, an ambush, was famously discussed as duplicating the US combat experience in Vietnam, and *Little Big Man*, where the Indian Nations massacre similarly recalls military endeavors like Operation Phoenix, the aim of which was to attack and kill somewhat indiscriminately in a Vietnamese village in order to discourage peasants from aiding the Viet Cong. The period ends apocalyptically with the ultimate Revisionist Western, *Heaven's Gate* (1980), which, through the figure of the Scandinavian immigrant, questions the whole history of how and by whom the West was built.

Little Big Man, directed by New Wave stalwart Arthur Penn and starring *The Graduate*'s (1968) Dustin Hoffman as an unlikely John Wayne, was shot the year after Penn's validation of the mores of the counterculture, *Alice's Restaurant*. It projects a sixties movement and youth culture ethos onto the Western and uses this ethos to deconstruct many of the clichés of the genre. As such it stands as a kind of answer across the decades to Ford's assembling of those codes in *Stagecoach* (1939). However, Penn's sixties movement critique, while striking (witness the contrast at film's end of Old Lodgeskins' (Chief Dan George) playful death in tune with nature versus Custer's (evoking Nixon or Westmoreland) delusional ramblings as he makes his case for becoming the next president while leading his men to ruin), lacks grounding in the West's material aspects and, though it is one of the strongest onscreen depictions of Indian massacres, still deploys the old trope of positioning that massacre from the perspective of a (necessarily more detached?) white onlooker, thus still not registering full force the effects of a policy of genocide.

The *Indianerfilme*, Gemünden (2001: 35) claims, "did little to question established genre conventions," and while Dika (2008: 17) does acknowledge that *The Sons of Great Bear* "manipulates character, setting, and plot in a manner that sets itself apart as a notable addition to the history of the Western genre," she still claims that by offering blank parody or pastiche without the humor of, say, Penn's film, the *Indianerfilme* re- rather than de-mystify the Western, in a way that speaks not of the American West at all but only of East German experience at the time of the series' production. I would claim instead that the *Indianerfilme*, by centering on the political economy of the West, in a sense completed the project of the Hollywood Revisionist Western, adding elements that the US directors did not have in their repertoire, including discussions of class divisions in the West and of a more resistant, rather than merely victimized, image of Native Americans. In many ways the *Indianerfilme* strangely fulfilled what Ward Churchill (2001) would later call for: a thorough treatment of the various kinds of Native American experience. In the process of rewriting Western clichés, these films deepened the project of the Revisionist Western which, without a grounding in the materialist basis of the West, could only circumvent the ethos of the original Western with parodies which themselves failed to fully illuminate the problems inherent in the genre.

Das Kapital on the Plains

That there was a focus on a different way of viewing the West is apparent in the comments of DEFA Dramaturg (and what Hollywood studio had a dramaturg?) Dr Gunter Karl, who conceptualized the basis for the *Indianerfilme* and worked particularly on the second of the films, *Chingachgook*. Admitting that DEFA would retain some elements of the Western, including action orientation, landscapes, settings, and some character types, which conveyed "a certain romanticism," he explained that the studio would counter these generic tropes with "a different content. Most importantly, we had to assume a historic-materialist perspective of history, and make the focus on the historical truth the guiding theoretical principle" (quoted in Gemünden, 2001: 27). The films' star, Mitic, also displayed an alternative consciousness of Western history: "The white people invaded the land of the Indians and wanted to take away their habitat because they wanted to live there too … [they] wanted to build big ranches and have lots of land. When you consider *how the west was won* [the 1962 title of one of the last Hollywood Westerns to unremittingly celebrate colonization of the West, with a segment by John Ford], basically the whites ended up taking over the country" (Mitic, 2006).

Perhaps the most politically sophisticated of the films is *Chingachgook*, a rewriting of both the James Fenimore Cooper novel, *The Last of the Mohicans*, and of a number of its Hollywood adaptations, including a strong allusion to the Indian Wars in John Ford's *Drums Along the Mohawk* (1939) and, closer to home, a West German version, *Der letzte Mohikaner* [*The Last Tomahawk*], made two years earlier in 1965. The film opens, in a Brechtian flourish, with a Delaware war dance inside a lodge celebrating the rescue of a wounded chief; the music, choreography, and masks blend Brecht's Berliner Ensemble with the Native American research into a moment that is more alienating than cathartic. The audience, both immersed in and distanced from the story, and thus prepared to learn through Brecht's idea of combining entertainment with education through spectacle that was the epic theater, is then presented with a historical narrator who describes the political situation that will engender the drama. The voiceover describes the material basis of European invasion in the resources of the land, articulating the core of the *Indianerfilme* argument as to the purpose of the exploitation of, in this case New England and, later on in the series, the West. In 1740, the Indians have become both dependent on the economy of the invaders and in a constant state of war against each other (though of course this latter was also happening before the arrival of the whites) because of the presence of the trading post which created a situation of exploitation, aggression, and dependency. "Indians underestimate the value of hides" and subsequently "are overcharged for horses" and "pay inflated prices for metal goods," leading both to greater reliance on the trading post as a source of imported (horses) and manufactured (metal) goods and to competition for the goods where "tribal animosity is exploited." The imperial rivalry of the French and British, each choosing tribes to fight their battles by proxy, has also contributed to the Delaware becoming enemies of the Huron – a major conflict in the film. Part of the trading post's economy is the bounty paid for scalps, again a practice that existed before the Europeans arrived, but which now is brought into the exchange economy as a source of profit. The Delaware trade Huron scalps, the trapper and trader, Harry, has been forced to accept scalps since the price of furs has declined, and, when the British soldiers argue over whether to slaughter the Hurons, Harry makes the case for doing so by offering the British general and his soldiers equal parts profit in sharing the scalps: "You one-third, the soldiers one-third, me one-third" – here the profit motive explaining at the micro level the direct material basis for the Indian Wars. The British general, the main ideologist in the British camp, in answer to his junior officer's claim about the role of the British in helping fulfill the "hopes of a native for a better life," replies that "the crown wants power and riches." He sees the British mission as one of clearing the land so it can be looted of its resources; and, as part of that purpose, he recognizes that the European imperial powers, although at war, are colluding nonetheless to accomplish this task. "We pay the Delaware, the French pay the Hurons, and we watch them destroy themselves." Ordering the massacre of the Hurons on New York's Lake Ostego, he notes that the lake, where the Mohican Chingachgook is seen paddling peacefully, has "fantastic salmon."

The economic underpinning of the Indian Wars is also explored in *Sons of Great Bear* and *Apaches*. What underlies the fatal 1876 stabbing of Tokei ihto's father, the Great Bear, a Dakota chief in the Black Hills, by the cowboy "Red Fox" is the search for gold in those hills and the knowledge that the chief has a cache of the precious metal. Tokei ihto (Mitic) eventually uses that gold to purchase a resting place for his people, converting the metal back into the more enduring commodity of land for subsistence rather than circulating it for profit. In *Apaches*, the breaking by the Mexicans of a treaty with the Apaches, and their famous massacre at Santa Anita as a prelude to the Mexican-American War of the 1840s, is engineered by US advance army scouts, mostly cowboys interested in the Gila Valley area for its copper and silver. The US instigation of the massacre and the subsequent war against the Mexicans is viewed as a pretext for clearing the Indians from the grounds of the silver and copper mines and their more efficient exploitation by the Americans. Johnson, the cowboy scout, tells the Mexican commandant at Santa Anita, "You were content with copper, we want more." In all three films, the army is seen as the advance corps of capitalism, in league with trappers in the eighteenth, and cowboys in the nineteenth century to clear the Indians from the land in order to more fully exploit its resources. The cowboys and traders (Harry, Red Fox, Johnson) desire individual gain, whereas the army is a more rationalized, institutionalized instrument of long-term capitalist exploitation. This is not a view prevalent in Hollywood cinema.

If there are exploiters in the West, there are also the exploited. Of course, the main class division is the racialized one between Native Americans and Europeans, and while other conflicts are discussed and presented here in terms of class difference, in the American cinema if taken up at all, divisions were more likely to be projected as merely ethical disagreements. There is the division already pointed to in *Chingachgook* between the British commander and his second-in-command over the point of the mission; the younger, thinner officer argues for a civilizing mission; the older, more robust one for keeping paramount the idea of exploitation, of getting fat off the land.[6] There is a similar disagreement in *Sons of Great Bear*, again between the lieutenant and the commanding officer, over how to treat the Dakota. In *Apaches*, there is a division between the Mexican peasants who have been in Santa Anita working the mines, and the Mexican army which is supposed to be protecting them. The peasants are put in danger and attacked by the Apaches because of a massacre engineered by the Americans and aided by the Mexican soldiers. They are in a desperate situation but are not the helpless peasants of

The Magnificent Seven (1960) saved by the gunfighters. Instead the old peasant woman, Teresa, watches the soldiers deserting them and taking their horses to be slaughtered by the Apaches and says to the Mexican officer in charge, "You'd leave women and children?" The class antagonism reaches its peak when the Mexican commander, in his haste to get away, stabs Teresa's husband, Miguel, and Teresa responds by picking up a rifle and shooting the officer. Ulzana (Mitic) and the Apaches then spare the peasants but warn them "never to return to our land," in this way acknowledging a class similarity between the two groups but also maintaining their distinction while romanticizing neither.

Drums along the Danube

A key difference between the *Indianerfilme* and the classical Western (and to some extent the Revisionist Western) is the Native American mode of resistance. All three of the East German films depict the unity of the various tribes against the European threat, and this can clearly be read, as Dika does, as a cry for German unity against the capitalist world, on the one hand, and against the (Soviet) imperialist world hostile to any such unity, on the other hand. But within the context of the Western, it is also crucial in reminding us of the always grand imperial strategy of divide and conquer used against the Native Americans, as, for example, the Hurons are divided from the Delaware in *Chingachgook*. As for the Hollywood Western, even its most enlightened version, *Little Big Man*, still subscribes to the animosity between the Cheyenne and the Pawnee, without seeing both as divided by, and potentially allied against, the US army. The *Indianerfilme* also distinguishes itself by posing an alternative Native American view of the land, stressing the Indian as guerilla fighter, and by engaging an issue much debated in the Third (and former Second) World today: dependence and aid and how each pacifies populations.

In the classical Western, the Indian is simply transgressing on the land. Ford's *Stagecoach* moves from a shot of the stagecoach, as symbol of civilization, rolling peacefully over the plains accompanied by loping "folk" music to a shot of the barbarous Indian "other," all grunts and pockmarked aggression waiting to attack over menacing music, with no indication that the Native American's historical claim to the land might instead mark the stagecoach as the intrusive instrument. *Little Big Man* presents the attack on the stagecoach, opening in media res, without Ford's menacing preview, as humorous and chaotic, as simply parodic, which lightens the racist implications of Ford's image but does not directly address the imbalance. Even the Revisionist Western, when discussing the right to the land, usually claims that no one owns it, that the Native Americans worked the land but that they made no claim to it. The *Indianerfilme* counter this presentation. Here the land is owned by the Indians who do make a claim to it. In *Chingachgook*, the lead character, the Mohican, now without a tribe and, thus, any claim to land, says to the white trappers, "You steal our land and murder our people"; and of the lake and its surroundings, he says that this was "our land for a long time." This earliest event in the cycle, then, describes the original moment of capital accumulation as theft and asserts Indian ownership of the land. In the later periods of the West depicted in *Sons of Great Bear* and *Apaches*, the Indians, in both cases stripped of their now segmented land and forced to move to more barren land, must fight to retain their livelihood in land that can support them. The looser idea that the land is shared – the nomad idea that was bound up in the original European entitlement claims in lieu of Indian claims to its actual ownership – is not given credence in these films, which instead present an active struggle over this most valuable commodity.

While there is some trading in the *Indianerfilme* on the notion of the Native American as "Noble Savage," including a poignant theme in *Sons of Great Bear* concerning a Delaware scout for the army whose own tribe had long been wiped out and who in the end joins the Dakota, there is also much refutation of this image, since what makes the "savage" noble is his or her graceful endurance of defeat. The Indians in the *Indianerfilme* challenge their subjugation much more, and do so in a way that was linked to contemporary Third World struggles at the time. In *Sons of Great Bear*, made a year after John Ford's *Cheyenne Autumn*, the Dakota are, as in the Ford film, led across the plains to a barren reservation, but the focus here is on exploitation rather than, with Ford, on enduring pain, as a woman's baby is killed and the Indians are told to get packed and get out. This subjugation is countered, however, by Tokei ihto, who declares that he and his band want to live "as free men of the Prairie." He joins another tribe, the Sisika, gets outfitted with shirts, horses, guns, and, with this tribe, hides in the trees to attack the cavalry, fighting like a guerilla to take back the land he sees slipping away. The guerilla fighter moment was downplayed in the Revisionist Western as well, since it could be read as favoring Vietnamese independence. Even *Little Big Man*, with its intonations of My Lai and the systematic program to destroy villages in South Vietnam on the excuse that doing so would keep peasants from joining the independence struggle, as dramatized in a handheld, documentary-like scene of Indian Nations women and children being massacred, had to be careful about presenting the Indians as successfully fighting back.

The *Indianerfilme* also protest against the transformation of indigenous and colonized peoples from entirely subsistent to dependent. *Chingachgook* begins with a description of how this dependence was fostered in the eighteenth century, and *Apaches* picks up on its further development more than a century later. As that film opens, the Indians, apropos of a treaty they have signed, are going to Santa Anita for their annual handout of "relief flour" for baking. As an added bonus, one of them says, "Last year they gave me beefsteak." A central theme in *Apaches* is the awakening of the old man, Nana, who lives for the alcohol that is a part of the yearly feast, having gotten so drunk the year before that he "had to be tied to his horse to get home," and whose rationale is, "It wasn't my fault, they filled my glass." The Apaches are brutally murdered in the town (an actual event) when the white man breaks the treaty, and Ulzana, the chief who had refused to join the ceremony, sets fire to the "relief flour" and rescues Nana, who then transforms from being immobile to becoming Ulzana's second-in-command and an extraordinary fighter. This theme of being self-sufficient rather than beholden surely would have echoed with East Germans who saw themselves positioned between the East and West, but it would also resound with other subjugated colonial peoples; it became one of the main themes of Ousmane Sembene's *Guelwaar* (1993), a film about African dependence on the West for materials and for money to pay its international debt.

In *Fantasies of the Master Race*, Ward Churchill castigates the Hollywood Western not only for its racist portrayal of the Native American but for its limited historical grasp of the Native American, and its indifference to the multitude of tribes and ways of life. He notes that most of the films are set between 1865, the end of the US Civil War, and 1890, the final vanquishing of the Native American and conquest of the continent, with most projecting the Indian at that moment as an impediment to this conquest. By contrast, the twelve *Indianerfilme* cover a wide range of historical periods and tribes giving a much broader sense of the struggle between the Europeans and the Native American. Refusing to concentrate only on the period of the vanquishing, these films see that struggle as having taken place over two centuries, and thus they recount stories that more powerfully relate resistance.[7] Against Gemünden's claim that these films "ignore a wide spectrum of historical and regional difference" (2001: 28) is the fact that they include the following periods and tribes: the Delaware, Huron and Mohicans during the period of the 1740 Indian Wars (*Chingachgook*); Techumseh and the Shawnee in the early 1800s (*Tecumseh*, 1972); the Seminoles in Florida and their linkage to runaway slaves during the 1830s (*Oceola*, 1971); the Apaches and the onset of the Mexican-American War during the 1840s (*Apaches*); the Dakota in the Black Hills at the time of the gold rush (*Sons of Great Bear* and *Spur des Falken* (*The Trail of the Falcon*, 1968)); the Cheyenne and the Dakota in *Weiße Wölfe* (White Wolves, 1968); and the Cheyenne in 1864, again before the Civil War and in the aftermath of a massacre by the US army in *Blutsbrüder* (Blood Brothers, 1975). Finally, three *Indianerfilme* concern the later period of contending with life on reservations: *Ulzana* (1973), about the Mimbrano near Tucson who fight to keep businessmen from appropriating profits from the reservation; *Der Scout* (1982), about the Nez Peces facing extinction; and *Tödlicher Irrtum* (Fatal Error, 1969), set in 1896 Wyoming during the closing of the West, and about illegal oil drilling on Indian land. Even more wide-reaching is *Severino* (1978), which describes life among the Manzaneros of the Argentinean Andes.

Of course, this breadth is balanced by the imposition of a European consciousness on all these varied periods and tribes, but it does seem both spurious and a sort of postmodern posturing to claim, as Gemünden does, that these films failed to capture the so-called radical alterity of the Revisionist films. His example is Robert Aldrich's *Ulzana's Raid* (1972), where the Apache chief is a powerful force that is destructive and ultimately incomprehensible to Western eyes. That suggestion is plausible in the film, but the destructive force which eventually wreaks such havoc can also be read as continuous with Ford's *Stagecoach* Indian, since both are ultimately reduced to a menace which must be annihilated.

Doctor Mabuse, Der Cowboy

Any revival of an older form without a thorough questioning is likely to revive the racist and sexist stereotypes of that form. While it is true that the *Indianerfilme* did adopt many of the conventions of the Western and were guilty of resuscitating the residue of a colonial and imperial project, because of their orientation toward a materialist reading of the West, the films also altered and reversed many of those stereotypes. As Dika points out, centering the film around Native Americans reverses the polarity of the Civilization–Wilderness dichotomy, whereas in the classical Western, the Indian was merely a subset of the values of the wilderness. The orientation toward guerilla fighter, however, makes the Native American more than simply the backward-looking representative of a fading wilderness. Rather than being antimodern, the protagonists of the *Indianerfilme* struggle with finding a place in changing societies. In *Chingachgook*, Chingachgook and his white companion, Deerslayer, do return to the wilderness, but at that point the wilderness is still relatively untouched. By contrast, Tokei ihto in *Sons of Great Bear* uses gold, the basis of the white man's economy, to buy land for his people, and Ulzana in *Apaches* employs the tactics of guerilla warfare in his battle to retain control of Apache land. The meaning of landscape, so important in the Western, also changes along with this change in perspective. In Ford's films, the Western landscape connotes open spaces but often for conquest by the European settlers, his most popular image being the army patrol riding across the pristine desert with its beautiful, Death Valley mesas. Landscape in the *Indianerfilme* is often a battleground, as the Native American open space is reduced to the stones and rubble of the reservation of the forced relocation in *Sons of Great Bear*. It is a contested space rather than simply a blank space to be inscribed. To exemplify how perspective is reversed in these films, I will discuss three stereotypes which the *Indianerfilme* rewrite and explain how that rewriting revises notions of the West and the Western: the role of the cowboy; European as opposed to Native American "terrorism" in the West; and the place of alcohol.

Crucial to the conception of the *Indianerfilme* is the image of the cowboy as greedy, profiteering, petit bourgeois or lumpenproletariat scoundrel. The military was the imperial force of capital on the plains, but the cowboy was the advance dragoon. Obviously, this contrasts sharply with the noble image of the gunfighter, the ultimate individual who battled other lusty individuals and whose personal gain could also serve the community (*The Gunfighter*, 1950; *High Noon*, 1952; *Shane*, 1953). In *Chingachgook* the traders, frontiersmen, are the pre-image of the cowboy yet are revealed as reprehensible. The younger trader, Harry, defends taking women and children's scalps, and the older one, Tom, first seen as the loving father of Judith, the woman on his trading barge, is later revealed as the pirate murderer of her father and dies in front of her as she, after this revelation, stares at him, repulsed at his crime. In *Sons of Great Bear*, Red Fox, a sly reference to the Soviets (Giddins, 2006), murders Tokei ihto's father in the opening scene, when he refuses to turn over his gold in a saloon that is viewed as more funeral pyre than joyful watering hole. That same saloon is later the site of a Weimar-era, dirgelike Marlene Dietrich number that ends by characterizing the lumpen cowboys' lot as "Brandy and baccy, dragoons and damn it. What a shitty place." In a subsequent scene, Red Fox, who has appropriated Tokei ihto's white speckled horse, cannot master riding the horse and is thrown; Tokei ihto then jumps on the horse, and two bystanders erupt in laughter; the scene exposing the cowboy as incompetent in his supposed métier. *Apaches* opens with a fearsome band of horsemen galloping menacingly across the plains who then threaten the Indians they encounter. The band are American mercenaries led by the advance guard of the army, Johnson, who engineers the Santa Anita massacre and collects scalps for money as his personal booty. Here the cowboys are less the peaceful protectors of the plains than prototypes of Blackwater subcontractors in Iraq, showing up on the scene as adjuncts to the army who perform the dirty work the army might want to disavow – a pattern that predates the invasion of Iraq but predicts the subsequent privatizing or mercenarization of the imperial army.

Susan Faludi in *The Terror Dream* (2007) describes frontier literature and film as completely bound up in the image of the frightened white family, and particularly the white woman taken by the Indian. She also describes how almost none of the literature or cinematic accounts of these atrocities are based in fact: they are exaggerated and often contradict the experience of the white woman at whose expense the myth is constructed. The Revisionist Western was adept at countering the image of the lone pioneer family overwhelmed by Indians. In particular, *Soldier Blue* (1970) and *Little Big Man* are at great pains to present the more common occurrence (which we know to be true, since the Native American was close to disappearing at the close of the West): the massacre of Indian villages, often those guaranteed safety, as Indian land once deemed barren was found valuable. What the *Indianerfilme* add in their notable depiction of terrorism as practiced by the whites against Native Americans is both the methodical, systematic way this slaughter is accomplished and its "rational" motive as part of increased productivity and profit. In *Chingachgook*, an elaborate ritual with dancing, tomahawks, and arrows, practiced before the slaying of the Mohican Chingachgook by the Huron, is contrasted and broken up by the single-file, uniformed British military marching in unison over a hill and opening fire on the largely defenseless Huron, many of whom are simply slain on the spot. The image is of an efficient killing machine. Likewise in *Apaches*, rifles and cannon are deployed against the Indians, who have come only for their yearly subsistence. Johnson watches the slaughter and later keeps tabs on the number of scalps – his pay for this clearing of the Indian so the copper and silver mines can be exploited more effectively, while a shot of the slaughter's aftermath focuses on the deserted teepees as the few remaining stragglers limp home. When the Indians subsequently go on the offensive, there is a preindustrial, ludic reversal of a classical Western cliché, highlighting the prowess of the arrow over the gun. In *Stagecoach*, when the Indians attack, John Wayne seems to be firing the mythical single bullet of the Kennedy Assassination. Every time he fires, two Indians fall, as the bullet seems to hit them and their horses. Conversely in *Sons of Great Bear*, when Tokei ihto leads an attack on an army troop wagon train after the whites refuse the Dakota's offer to negotiate, his arrows match Wayne's bullets and often fell more than one soldier at the same time. A final deconstruction of the tropes around the massacre occurs in *Apaches*, when Johnson and his men are surrounded by Ulzana's raiding party, and one of the men sneaks off in the night to ask the cavalry for help. In the standard Western, such a desperate adventure is doomed, as the man frequently is waylaid by "savages." In *Apaches*, he breaks through and reaches the cavalry, pleading for rescue; however, the army commanders judge it more efficient to ensure the long-term objective of capturing the mines, so they proceed to attack the Mexicans in order to steal their territory, and thus no cavalry arrives for the rescue. The bugle blows in the camp, but only to summon the cavalry to a different, more important, imperial mission.

A final cliché the *Indianerfilme* shatter involves the communal feeling around alcohol. Ford never tired of presenting alcohol and inebriation as a character bond, most especially in *Fort Apache*, which is endlessly concerned with the "shenanigans" of three drunken sergeants (Hawks also relished such moments, e.g. the "hilarious" Eddy (Walter Brennan) in *To Have and Have Not* (1944), so debilitated he can no longer tolerate drinking water). Ford's lighthearted notions of drinking did a disservice to Irish culture, as it was often the Irish-American solider or sergeant who was portrayed as the imbiber, and served to disavow the colonizer's systematic deployment of alcohol to foster dependency and wreak damage on the Native American. The actor Mitic was himself blatantly antidrinking, aware of the damage it has wrought in Eastern European culture as well. His onscreen Indian persona, then, brought to each film a recognition of alcohol not as trivial and humorous but as an instrument of the colonizing project at a moment during the nineteenth century when Native American independence was being stripped, and that in hindsight served as a vivid precursor of the deployment of drugs to ameliorate tensions in twentieth-century urban communities. At the opening of *Sons of Great Bear*, Tokei ihto's father's drinking in the saloon results in his being stabbed by Red Fox for refusing to reveal the source of his gold. Later, at the fort, before a negotiation, alcohol is offered to Tokei ihto, who pointedly refuses. In *Apaches*, the old man Nana has embarrassed himself at the previous year's "relief flour" giveaway and again drinks as the massacre unfolds. He is rescued by Mitic's Ulzana, who refuses the drink and remains on his toes as a warrior. Later, Nana, having put down the drink, becomes Ulzana's trusted adjunct, at one point impersonating a Mexican peasant during a guerilla action meant to gain the Apaches entry to the soldier's camp. This anti-alcohol sentiment echoes that in the Algerian postindependence classic, *The Battle of Algiers* (1966), where the Front

Libération Nationale (National Liberation Front) enforces a clearing of the community's vices, seen as deliberate ways of promoting disorganization, in order to successfully challenge the French colonizers.

The Lives of Other(Genre)s

The *Indianerfilme* also intersect with two moments within West German cinema. They act both as a revisionist cinema vis-à-vis the West German commercial cinema, most prominently in terms of the 1960s Karl May Westerns and, to a lesser extent, the later sexploitative Edgar Wallace "thrillers," and as a popular correlative to New German Cinema, which expressed similar aspects of the youth rebellion, and whose lifecycle, mid-1960s to late 1970s, was roughly concurrent with the Eastern Westerns.

3:10 To Yugoslavia

The Western in German history is, in Benjamin's sense, a constellation that brings together various discursive fields, including historical projections of the colonial, capitalist-democratic, and fascist periods. The earliest German Westerns, shot near Munich during the 1920s were termed the "Isar Westerns" after the river that figured prominently in their landscapes (Schneider, 1998: 156). The so-called greatest moment of the West German film was marked by Cinemascope versions of the Karl May adaptations, beginning in 1962 with *Der Schatz im Silbersee* (*Treasure of Silver Lake*) and totaling 17 in all by 1968. The first film, an attempt to compete with Hollywood, was the most expensive West German film to date (3.5 million Deutschmarks), and achieved financial success throughout Europe (Schneider, 1998: 141). The films capitalized on the prior commercial success of May's adventure novels; May was the most frequently translated German-language author, whose Western novels concerning the relationship between a German settler, Old Shatterhand, and a Mescalero Apache, Winnetou, even outsold Louis L'Amour, the most popular English-language Western novelist (Schneider, 1998: 143). These films were so well-known to *Indianerfilme* audiences (and would have been known equally in the East and West), that the first Winnetou film begins with the narration, "Now we finally meet them face to face" (Schneider, 1998: 159). An American film critic (Allen Eyles, *Film and Filming*, 1965) praised one of the Winnetou Westerns for its "DeMille-like grandeur … the film revives the legendary West in its magnificent natural setting … There is respect too for traditional values" (quoted in Schneider, 1998: 146).

Formally, the Winnetou films, and particularly the trilogy *Winnetou I, II, II* (1963–1965), maintained their "respect for traditional values" in their use of the

Hollywood pattern of Western editing which consisted of the following: long-shot reserved for the settlers heroically trekking across the country stressing their communion with nature (going back to Ford's lyrical *Stagecoach* rolling across the plains); more frantic cutting of the battle scenes with the emphasis on the wagon trains under siege in the case of *Winnetou I* by the marauding Kiowas (for whom the shots are shorter and who are not individuated); and, elsewhere, a heavily analyzed standard crosscutting pattern usually from the perspective of the whites and particularly the blond German hero Shatterhand. The *Indianerfilme* employed the Soviet style of Eisensteinian montage (some of its directors having been trained in Moscow), which, when added to the preponderance of Brechtian distancing devices, created space for the Western to become a locus of reflection and a means for socialist political education rather than an affirmation of "traditional" (capitalist and colonial) values.

Sons of Great Bear's concluding sequence, Tokho ihto's battle with Red Fox, completely shuns continuity editing as practiced in the Hollywood Western, looking more in its editing pattern like the storming of the Winter Palace in Eisenstein's *October* (1927) than the gunfight in the hills at the conclusion of King Vidor's *Duel in the Sun* (1946). The final battle emphasizes Tokei ihto's cunning, as he fights barefisted against Red's gun, and Mitic's athleticism, as Tokei ihto is pulled by Red's horse and then pulls himself to the horse and leaps on. The cutting, however, distances the audience from an excessively emotional involvement in the battle, because many shots simply show Tokho ihto riding, and the antagonists are seldom in the same shot. This recalls the battleship gliding through the battalion during the final sequence of *Battleship Potemkin* (1925), where the ship is cut into its component parts and never seen in relation to the other ships in the fleet. *Sons of Great Bear* also frequently cuts without indicating that months or years may have passed in the narrative. The elongated time period of *Sons of Great Bear*, and of the *Indianerfilme* in general (the action of displacing the Dakota from their lands and of their attempt to reclaim a new space for themselves takes years) links these films more to the Melodrama than to the Western, which in Hollywood usually features a very condensed time period. In the melodrama, it is developmental aging within the family that is emphasized and time is elongated (Elsaesser, 1987), while, similarly, in the GDR Western, time is expanded to give the audience a better grasp of the historical situation, which in a materialist view is about, not personal, but historical transformation. In *Sons of Great Bear*, *Chingachgook*, and *Apaches*, the transformation is generally one of tribal land being lost, grabbed, and acquired – and the tribes' fighting back. The use of long-shots and extended takes in the first two films is reserved not for the settlers loping across the prairie, establishing their credentials as sedate civilizers, but rather for the Indian camps, which in this counter to Hollywood (and to Hollywood through the Winnetou films) are viewed lovingly as communal centers, places of harmony, which serve to validate an alternative view: that of a "civilization" in the process of being destroyed. *Apaches*, under the influence of the Leone Westerns, uses a more traditional extended long-take during its opening sequence to depict cowboys moving across the plains, but here they are presented as a destructive force of power and vengeance.

Chingachgook begins with a Brechtian flourish, a veritable catalogue of devices to highlight how the narrative is both story and teaching tool. The startling masks and dance of the Delaware are explained as their celebration of the wounded chief's rescue in a sequence that is part Native American re-creation and part early expressionist musical interlude. It is followed by offscreen narration recounting the socioeconomic moment of the tribe's entanglement in the British–French conflict and then Chingachgook himself acting out his version of the rescue in a way that emphasizes a Brechtian showing (*Darstellung*) with its emphasis within the spectacle on the gestural rather than on merely relating or telling. The combination of the editing and these extradiegetic devices, along with a deliberate editorial tendency to downplay the sensational element of Western violence by excluding it from the frame, make the West less a mythic place than a place of potential reflection – reflection about a colonial trajectory which continues in the present. In so doing, these Westerns counter the idea of myth, which generally works through emotional appeal to a past presumed to be understood as the same by all for all time. Instead, the materialist conception of the past is that it is a constantly evolving, specifically situated series of moments which must be understood rather than merely lauded for their place in leading to an equally unchallenged present.

The Winnetou Westerns were an attempt at a global transnational Western, or at least a trans-European one. They brought together a French actor, B-movie stalwart, aristocrat, and Indochine and Algerian War vet Pierre Brice (born Pierre-Louis Le Bris) as Winnetou, the Apache, and an American veteran of the *Tarzan* series, Lex Barker, as Old Shatterhand. They were shot in Yugoslavia and credited for creating the wave that led to the Sergio Leone Westerns, beginning with *A Fistful of Dollars* (1964), shot in Spain. The *Indianerfilme*, though, were equally transnational in their coordination of efforts from what at the time was called the Second World. Initially they were shot on the same Yugoslav locations as the Winnetou Westerns but soon expanded to locations in Romania, Bulgaria, Uzbekistan, and Slovakia, as well as boasting a Serbian lead actor, Mitic, and were often co-financed by other Eastern European countries; *Apaches*, for example, was co-produced by Buftea-Film in Bucharest and by Mosfilm in the USSR, and edited in the DEFA studios at Babelsberg. While the East and West German films both attempted to globalize the Western, the Winnetou films, evidenced by the lineage of their actors, simply localized the Hollywood Western, keeping intact its colonial and class pretensions, while the *Indianerfilme* attempted to employ the popularity of the genre while also questioning many of its basic assumptions, thus participating in a transnational, global dialogue rather than projecting globalization as Americanization.

The Karl May Winnetou adaptations also recall the colonialist and fascist associations that May's name conjures. May wrote these "naïve, boyhood version[s] of the classical Western" (Schneider, 1998: 146) with their tacit support for American manifest destiny from 1875 through 1910, at the same time also writing "adventure" novels about desert Arabs (*The Caravan of Death*, 1892, adapted into a film in 1920) and tales of Latin America Indians and peasants, all at the moment when the saturation of the domestic market at the height of German industrialization was compelling the country to expand its markets and catch up with the rest of Europe as a colonizer. Although the nominal hero is the Apache chief, Winnetou, the books and their West German film adaptations tend to celebrate the exploits, and more thoroughly focalize the narration through, the blond, resourceful German settler, Old Shatterhand. Winnetou may be noble, but his most noble moment in the novels occurs at his death, when he converts to Christianity. As one critic noted, "Winnetou ... combines the highest aspects of otherwise 'decadent' Indian cultures with the natural adoption of the romantic and Christian traits of Karl May's own vision of German civilization."[8] May also held to the most enduring principle of colonial rule, divide and conquer. From James Fenimore Cooper, he grafted onto his work not only the noble, if unequal, friendship of the Native American and the European, but also the division of the Indian tribes into morally just and unjust, or noble savage and just plain "savage." In keeping with this tradition, the Mescaleros in *Winnetou I* fulfill the noble function of the sadly defeated Indians who accept their defeat gracefully, while the Kiowas, pure evil and allied with the villainous whites, allow the usual colonial stereotyping to go on unimpeded. Against these "traditional values," the consistent message of the *Indianerfilme* was about warring tribes (the state of war being created or exacerbated by colonial rule) uniting to fight "settler" encroachment, and it is this resistance which makes them "noble."

The constellation of the Winnetou Westerns also encompasses fascism, not least because they were favorites of Hitler (in 1940, Klaus Mann's famously indicted May as "The Cowboy Mentor of the *Führer*"). During the fascist period, these tales of a solitary band of Indians facing all odds were reedited to align them more solidly with the "chauvinist 'healthy' German literary tradition of people's authors (*Volksschriftsteller*)" (Schneider, 1998: 143), and 300 000 copies were distributed to the German troops on the Russian front as examples of bravery during wartime. They also proved to the Führer, as outlined in Albert Speer's 1975 diary that, just as May had never visited the lands about which he was writing, so too, in waging war, "It was not necessary to know the desert in order to direct troops in the African theater of war ... it wasn't necessary to travel in order to know the world" (Speer, quoted in Liukkonen and Pesonen, 2008: para. 7). The *Winnetou* films simply ignore this context, while the New German Cinema, in particular Hans Jürgen Syberberg's collage film, *Karl May* (1974), highlights its repression. Gemünden justly points out that the *Indianerfilme*'s (and certainly, by implication, the *Winnetou* films') focus on the moment of genocide as a moment of resistance assuages German guilt for the genocide of the Jews. While this is undoubtedly a part of the films' appeal, it must also be pointed out that the East German Westerns evoke a historically resistant narrative that was also part of DEFA's avowed antifascist credo: the projection of the experience of partisans and freedom fighters against the Nazis in the countries in which these alternative stories of resistance were filmed. The films' publicity, for example, emphasized Mitic's lineage as the son of a Serbian partisan (Dika, 2008: 3), and Serbia was the Eastern region most active in resisting the fascists. Thus, in their symbolic layering, this Second World recounting of Indian resistance summons an anti-Nazi, antigenocidal past which did have an (albeit hidden) historical referent throughout the region and was not merely romantic projection or contemporary wish fulfillment.

The most prevalent ethos behind the West German Westerns, however, was not merely providing a diversionary world free of all actual conflict for the fulfillment of boyhood obsessions, as Tassilio Schneider maintains, but rather their distillation of the ruling and managerial ethos of the "economic miracle" that was taking place at the time of the films' conception, and the idea that this power always brought "progress." The films evidence a link to Weimar-era capitalism and depict 1960s West German society as led by a technologically resourceful class that, apropos of the contemporary German bourgeoisie's domination through economic force, entailed more than a hint of the will to power in an unsuccessfully denazified terrain. The bonding of Winnetou and Old Shatterhand in *Winnetou I* is not presented as an equal friendship but instead echoes the conclusion of Fritz Lang's Weimar classic, *Metropolis* (1927), where heart (the workers) and mind (the bosses) are urged to collaborate, though it is here justified as, the latter who control the former.[9] Winnetou is mostly passive, with Shatterhand, for example, freeing him at one point by figuring out the Kiowa camp's organizational structure, his superior intelligence enabling him to master Native customs to the extent that he knows the tribe better than the tribe knows itself. Shatterhand is an engineer who offers a technological solution to the problems centered around the battle of the Indians against the railroad. When the Kiowas attack his wagon train, he, a kind of thinking man's John Wayne, blows up the ammunition wagon to halt the attack. He later figures a way to dynamite the villainous railroad official and his gang out of their saloon. Finally, in a contest with Winnetou's father involving a boat race, while pursued by the entire tribe and against all odds, he deliberately capsizes his boat, thus abandoning his short-term protection, and, swimming to the chief's boat in order to overturn it, wins the contest by technologically outmaneuvering his opponent. (Is this a parable about the exporting genius of German industry in the Third World?!)

Shatterhand is also, pointedly, a defender of capitalist law, the sanctity of the contract. He believes, and the film validates the notion, that there is a legal solution to all disputes. The main dispute centers around the railroad breaking its compact and building on Apache land, but this dispute turns out to be not an inevitable clash of competing and unequal interests but merely a problem of one greedy local railroad official and his hired gunmen who want short-term profit by taking the Indian lands. Shatterhand and his cohorts defeat this illegal move and affirm the good intentions of the railroad owners, whose original pact preserved the native land, as well as a faith that building a railroad constitutes progress, or at least the best and only way forward. (Of course, their actions also reaffirm a capitalist ruling-class imperative for which long-term profit and stability, which would eventually involve systematically clearing Apache lands, should not be sacrificed for personal, short-term gain.) Clearly the *Indianerfilme*, with its focalization through the various tribes who witness the confiscation of the land which they inhabit by originary possession (*Chingachgook*), or watch treaties abrogated because the land has been found to contain valuable minerals (gold in *Sons of Great Bear*, copper and silver in *Apaches*) casts doubt on the rule of law as a guarantor of fairness. In *Winnetou I*, law is also backed up by force. The engineer acquires the nickname "Old Shatterhand" after he demonstrates the power of his fists in a barroom brawl, and his technical solutions to conflict frequently involve dynamite. Thus, beneath the technological know-how of capitalist economic power lies the threat of force should the fallacy of the law as equal guarantor of equality be exposed. In the contemporary context of only partial West German denazification, such power was also linked to a force with a history of exceeding all boundaries.

Beach Blanket Babelsberg: The *Indianerfilme*, the 1960s Youth Movement, and New German Cinema

If we continue to pursue Thomas Elsaesser and Michael Wedel's (2001: 11) dictum that GDR cinema in general was "less *sui generis* than generally assumed … in both its mainstream and art cinema idioms," we will find very tangible traces of the 1960s youth movement in the *Indianerfilme*, which, along with their relation to Hollywood and German popular genres, might also relate them to New German Cinema, in particular Fassbinder's project in the West. This view is contrary to the more commonplace notion in which the films are seen as counterparts to the *Verbotsfilme*, or Rabbit Films, the twelve films, virtually an entire year's production, that were banned and shelved by the GDR in 1965, the year of the first *Indianerfilme*, and that would likely have constituted the East German equivalent of the New German Cinema. Rather than letting this repression be the "moral, aesthetic, and historical vanishing point from which GDR cinema could be classified and judged" so that what is hidden is "authentic" and what is overt is necessarily suspect (Elsaesser and Wedel, 2001: 6), one might instead take up Elsaesser and Wedel's dictum and stress the links between the *Indianerfilme* and New German Cinema, both of which were engaged in rewriting popular West German cinema, questioning basic historical assumptions prevalent in (both) Germany(s), especially regarding the colonialist and fascist past, and using the mediating form of Hollywood genres to accomplish that questioning.

The youth movement was certainly a part of New German Cinema culture. It was also reflected in the *Indianerfilme*. Great change occurs in this respect between 1965's *Sons of Great Bear* and 1967's *Chingachgook*, the latter of which opens with Mitic, disallowed a female companion in the former film, now portrayed like a 1960s sex symbol, shirtless before a flower-decked Princess Wahtawah. Later, what Gary Giddins (2006) calls an Art Blakey jazz clarinet buttresses a scene in which

Chingachgook, along with his white companion, Deerslayer, a very hippyish-looking, thin blond student-type, and the trapper's daughter, Rebecca, who wears leather pants, all try on costumes from a treasure chest left by the trapper. A deliberate Haight-Ashbury feel to the sequence renders Deerslayer's and Rebecca's doomed romance closer to *The Graduate* than to *The Last of the Mohicans*.

Besides their cognizance of the 1960s youth movement, the projects of the East German popular and West German avant-garde films shared deep-structural similarities. Fassbinder's melodramas, for example, complexly negotiated a politically charged genre. Melodrama had been one of the primary Nazi genres and after the war became, along with the domestic *Heimat* ("Homeland") dramas, the dominant cinematic genre, constituting almost 30% of total genre output during the 1950s and 1960s (Schneider, 1998: 152). In terms of the continuity, for example, Veit Harlan, director of the infamous antisemitic *Jud Süß* (1940), after being cleared of Nazi sympathies by a judge who had previously ratified Hitler's purge of the Ukraine, went on to direct ten even more flamboyantly emotional *Heimat* films, mainly during the 1950s.[10] Fassbinder, however, in a Brechtian move, employed the melodrama but somewhat distanced himself from its German variant, instead adopting Sirk's Universal Melodramas as his overt source. Fassbinder deconstructed the genre by deploying its own techniques against itself, as exemplified by his critique of the still idealized Nazi past (*Lili Marleen*, 1981), his figuring of the colonial traces of the industrializing era (*Effi Briest*, 1974), and his dissatisfaction with both the drive to domination that accompanied the "economic miracle" (*The Marriage of Maria Braun*, 1979) and the psychical devastation commodification heaped upon German workers (*Mother Küsters Goes to Heaven*, 1975). The *Indianerfilme* was equally a corollary to the already antifascist thrust of GDR filmmaking; its first move being the funding of *Murderers Among Us* (1946), Germany's veritable *Open City* (1945), which examined the psychological effects of a fascism that had failed to dissolve at war's end. In its critique of the colonial and fascist associations of both the (West) German and the Hollywood Western, the *Indianerfilme*, like Fassbinder, also deployed a Hollywood form, yet distanced itself from it in order to make a point in the popular cinema arena, while Fassbinder made his on the art and festival circuits[11] (even as he also often expressed a desire to engage the popular, as evidenced by his persistent work on television).

One way the two forms are linked, as Elsaesser points out, is that the radicalized films which flowed from the 1960s youth movement in the West and the overt antifascist, anticolonial, and anticapitalist popular films of the East have both disappeared from the screen in today's Germany. The linking of these two cultural formations though suggests an alliance that is present and growing stronger today not in the cultural but in the political realm, and that is the alliance in *Die Linke* of the remnants of the 1960s youth movement in the West and of a reconstituted democratic socialist and workers party in the East.[12] Thus far the mainstream German Social Democratic Party (SPD), an ostensible workers party, has resisted bringing *Die Linke* into such an alliance and for that reason may have lost the 2005 election at a crucial moment when a Left coalition including *Die Linke*, the SPD, and the Green Party would likely have resulted in a Left parliamentary majority of forty seats (Anderson, 2009: 252). Instead, a largely do-nothing Christian Democratic Union (CDU)-SPD "grand coalition" of four years resulted in an ousting of the SPD from the government with the CDU joining forces with the overtly neoliberal Free Democratic Party (FDP). New Left alliances are starting to form nonetheless. In Berlin, the SPD mayor, Klaus Wowereit, has held power for seven years due to *Die Linke* support, and Germany is edging ever closer to challenging "the taboo" of its centrist parties forging alliances with the radical Left, the taboo having already been "broken in a Western *Land* (legislature) [election]" with this victorious coalition opening the possibility that "it could be replicated on the federal level" (Anderson, 2009: 253). If such alliances move into the mainstream, they will have been prefigured by the cultural Left's amalgamation of New German Cinema and popular GDR cinema. This was not an alliance that could have been discussed at the time it occurred because of the Cold War, but it is one that is fruitful to reconstruct as existing in essence in a crossborder formation that history, "written by the winners," has buried and not subsequently acknowledged; in that sense the Wall itself, once a physical enforcement, continues its existence as an enduring symbolic political and cultural blockade. (In which case, the relationship between the *Indianerfilme* and the Revisionist Western stresses a kind of global resistance and rethinking of embedded colonial and imperial concepts in both the former East and West and is important in continuing to dismantle this Wall.) If the cultural in the first instance prefigured the political, the political may yet prefigure a cultural renewal of a critical popular and avant-garde cinema that will take up a forward movement of Germany's workers and intellectuals in a way that continues to question its colonial and fascist past and posits a future free of the onerous and rapacious trappings of the capitalist present.

Notes

1 The sobriquet itself was not, as in the case of Leone's "spaghetti Westerns" or the term applied to the West German Karl May Films, "Kraut Westerns," an unflattering critical label imposed from outside the industry. *Indianerfilme* was the name DEFA assigned to the series (Bock, 1998), and, even in its contemporary US release, distributors have respected the intention of that name, terming the films, in highlighting their focalization through the Native American, "Westerns with a difference."

2 The quote is from Benjamin's 1939 essay, "Theses on the Philosophy of History" (Benjamin, 1968). The teleological reading is a trope of German film history much maligned in its application to Weimar Cinema by Siegfried Kracauer in *From Caligari to Hitler* (1947). For the primary critique, see Budd (1990), and for a formalist re-reading of the period, see Guerin (2005).

3   This moment, a general attack on what had been a strong German social welfare state, began with the SPD, the Labor Party, imposition of balancing the budget as an absolute priority. The reaction against the changes was negative but given the constraints of what amounts to a multiparty, two-party system, the country swung right and elected Angela Merkel but with an SPD, minority. In the 2009 election, though, Merkel won without the SPD, and with her new allies, the Free Democratic Party (FDP), an outright neoliberal group, she has continued the assault on workers rights and benefits.

4   The shared sets and locations also illustrate that the West is today as much a discursive field as a site of history and what matters is how and for what purpose the "authentic" sites are used, especially in this context, where the "authentic" locations themselves are chosen supposedly for their similarity to the original "authentic" sites, but even these are the sites of not the history of the West, but of the shooting, and history, of the Western.

5   For a treatment of how two other contemporary Westerns, *Red River* (1948) and *My Darling Clementine* (1946), accomplish this task, see Corkin (2000), and for a more extended treatment of the Western as empire building, see Corkin (2004). Corkin contends that both Westerns, though made when expansion was just beginning, are concerned with this expansion.

6   Zola makes a similar distinction between Florent, the thin prole revolutionary in the French Second Empire who has returned from Devil's Island and is hungry and thirsty for justice, and Beautiful Lisa, the robust self-satisfied shop owner who wants nothing to upset her prosperity in *Le Ventre de Paris* (The Belly of Paris).

7   What the *Indianerfilme* does not do, and what no Hollywood film has ever done, apropos Churchill (2001), is recount moments that occurred before the time of the European arrival which would even more validate Native American culture and traditions and more solidly establish the claim to the land.

8   The quote appears as part of a series of notes on an exhibition of Karl May's books at http://bancroft.berkeley.edu/Exhibits/nativeamericans/27.html (accessed May 22, 2011).

9   For a consideration of the antiworker aspect of *Metropolis* as clarified in the expanded 2010 version, see Atkinson (2010).

10 Information cited in the documentary *Harlan: In the Shadow of Jew Süss* (Felix Moeller, 2008).

11 Yet to be explored is the *Indianerfilme*'s links not only to the contemporary Revisionist Hollywood Westerns but also to what might be called "The Popular Front Western" which forms the basis of what Steve Neale (1998) discusses as "The Pro-Indian Western." (Blacklistee and Cultural Front stalwart Albert Maltz, for example, wrote the screenplay for *Broken Arrow*, 1950.) In this intertextual association, a feature such as Mitic's athleticism would place him as an actor in a relationship with actors like Burt Lancaster, also a non-Method actor from the Popular Front period who credited his acting ability to his early years as a circus performer (Buford, 2001). This establishes a further link between Mitic's Ulzana in *Apaches* and Lancaster's equally athletic *Apache* (1954), suggesting as well, in subjects for further research, a reexamination of Popular Front director Nicholas Ray's anti-McCarthy Western *Johnny Guitar* (1954).

12 Currently now giving way to a new generation led in the West by Klaus Ernst, a metal worker who will hopefully increase the party's working-class base, and in the East by a female linguist, Gesine Loetzsch, who has been adept at forming coalitions in her home district of Berlin.

References

Anderson, P. (2009) *The New Old World*. Verso, London.

Atkinson, M. (2010) The politics of a new metropolis. *In These Times*, November 25, http://www.inthesetimes.com/article/6649/the_politics_of_a_newi_metropolis_i/ (accessed January 28, 2011).

Benjamin, W. (1968) Theses on the philosophy of history, 1940, in *Illuminations* (ed. H. Arendt; trans. H. Zohn), Schocken, New York.

Bock, H-M. (1998) Excerpt from The DEFA story. Filmportal, *http://www.filmportal.de/df/54/ArtikelF97D9D32B474F7ADE03053D50B3733D7.html* (accessed January 28, 2011).

Budd, M. (1990) *Cabinet of Dr. Caligari: Texts, Contexts, Histories*, Rutgers University Press, New Brunswick, NJ.

Buford, K. (2001) *Burt Lancaster: An American Life*, Da Capo Press, Cambridge, MA.

Buscombe, E. and Pearson R.E. (eds) (1998) *Back in the Saddle Again: New Essays on the Western*, BFI, London.

Churchill, W. (2001) *Fantasies of the Master Race: Literature, Cinema and the Colonization of American Indians*, City Lights. San Francisco.

Corkin, S. (2000) Cowboys and free markets: post World-War II westerns and U.S. hegemony. *Cinema Journal*, 39 (3), 66–91.

Corkin, S. (2004) *Cowboys and Cold Warriors: The Western and U.S. History*, Temple University Press, Philadelphia.

Dika, V. (2008) An East German *Indianerfilm* – the bear in sheep's clothing. *Jump Cut*, 50, 1–17, http://www.ejumpcut.org/archive/jc50.2008/Dika-indianer/index.html (accessed January 28, 2011).

Dorpalen, A. (1985) *German History in Marxist Perspective: The East German Approach*, I.B. Tauris, London.

Elsaesser, T. (1987) Tales of sound and fury: observations on the family melodrama, in *Home Is Where the Heart Is: Studies in Melodrama and the Woman's Film* (ed. C. Gledhill), BFI, London, pp. 43–69.

Elsaesser, T. and Wedel, M. (2001) Defining DEFA's historical imaginary: the films of Konrad Wolf. *New German Critique*, 82, 3–24.

Giddins, G. (2006) When westerns made their way east. *New York Sun*, October 30, http://www.nysun.com/arts/when-westerns-made-their-way-east/42479/ (accessed January 28, 2011).

Faludi, S. (2007) *The Terror Dream: Fear and Fantasy in Post-9/11 America*, Metropolitan Books, New York.

Feinstein, J. (2002) *The Triumph of the Ordinary: Depictions of Daily Life in the East German Cinema 1949–89*, University of North Carolina Press, Chapel Hill.

Gemünden, G. (2001) Between Karl May and Karl Marx: the DEFA *Indianerfilme* 1965–1983. *New German Critique*, 82 (special issue on East German Film), 25–38.

Guerin, F. (2005) *A Culture of Light: Cinema and Technology in 1920s Germany*, University of Minnesota Press, Minneapolis.

Hoberman, J. (1998) How the west was lost, in *The Western Reader* (eds J. Kitses and G. Rickman), Limelight Editions, New York.

Jaeger, D. (2007) "Only in the 1990s did I become East German": a conversation with Ingo Schulze about *Remembering the GDR, Simple Stories*, and *33 Moments of Happiness*; with an introduction to his work. *New German Critique*, 101, 143–155.

Kracauer, S. (1947) *From Caligari to Hitler*, Princeton University Press, Princeton, NJ.

Liukkonen, P. and Pesonen, I. (2008) Karl May, http://www.kirjasto.sci.fi/karlmay.htm (accessed January 28, 2011).

Mann, K. (1940–1941) The cowboy mentor of the *Führer. The Living Age*, 359, 217–222.

Mitic, G. (2006) Interviews. *The Sons of Great Bear* (1965), *Chingachgook: The Great Snake* (1967) and *Apaches* (1973), DEFA Film Archive, University of Massachusetts, Amherst, MA.

Naughton, L. (2002) *That Was the Wild East: Film Culture, Unification, and the "New" Germany*, University of Michigan Press, Ann Arbor.

Neale, S. (1998) Vanishing Americans: racial and ethnic issues in the interpretation and context of post-war "pro-Indian" westerns, in *Back in the Saddle Again: New Essays on the Western* (eds E. Buscombe and R.E. Pearson), BFI, London, pp. 8–28.

Pinkert, A. (2008) *Film and Memory in East Germany*, Indiana University Press, Bloomington.

Saunders, F.S. (2001) *The Cultural Cold War: The CIA and the World of Arts and Letters*, New Press, New York.

Schneider, T. (1998) Finding a new *Heimat* in the wild west: Karl May and the German western of the 1960s, in *Back in the Saddle Again: New Essays on the Western* (eds E. Buscombe and R.E. Pearson), BFI, London, pp. 141–159.

Speer, A. (1976) *Spandau: The Secret Diaries* (trans. R. and C. Winston), Macmillan, New York, Toronto.

Stam, R. and Shohat, E. (1994) *Unthinking Eurocentrism: Multiculturalism and the Media*, Routledge, New York.

Zola, E. (1874) *Le Ventre de Paris*, 3rd edn, Charpentier & Cie., Paris.

Filmography

DEFA Westerns

Apaches [*Apachen*] (Gottfried Kolditz, East Germany, 1973).

Blutsbrüder [Blood Brothers] (W.W. Wallroth, East Germany, 1975).

Chingachgook: The Great Snake [*Chingachgook, die grosse Schlange*] (Richard Groschopp, East Germany, 1967).

Oceola (Konrad Petzold, East Germany, 1971).

Scout, Der [The Scout] (Konrad Petzold, East Germany, 1982).

Severino (Claus Dobberke, East Germany, 1978).

Sons of Great Bear, The [*Die Söhne der grossen Bärin*] (Josef Mach, East Germany, 1965).

Spur des Falken [The Falcon's Trail] (Gottfried Kolditz, East Germany, 1968).

Tecumseh (Hans Kratzert, East Germany, 1972).

Tödlicher Irrtum [Fatal Error] (Konrad Petzold, East Germany, 1969).

Ulzana (Gottfried Kolditz, East Germany, 1973).

Weiße Wölfe [White Wolves] (Konrad Petzold, East Germany, 1968).

General Filmography

Alice's Restaurant (Arthur Penn, USA, 1969).

Apache (Robert Aldrich, USA, 1954).

Battle of Algiers, The [*La battaglia di Algeri*] (Gillo Pontecorvo, Italy / Algeria, 1966).

Battleship Potemkin [*Bronenosets Potyomkin*] (Sergei Eisenstein, USSR, 1925).

Broken Arrow (Delmer Daves, USA, 1950).

Buffalo Bill and the Indians (Robert Altman, USA, 1976).

Caravan of Death [*Die Toteskarawane*] (Josef Stein, Germany, 1920).

Cheyenne Autumn (John Ford, USA, 1964).

Drums Along the Mohawk (John Ford, USA, 1939).

Duel in the Sun (King Vidor, USA, 1946).

Effi Briest [*Fontane - Effi Briest*] (R.W. Fassbinder, West Germany, 1974).

Fistful of Dollars, A [*Per un pugno di dollari*] (Sergio Leone, Italy / Spain / West Germany, 1964).

Fort Apache (John Ford, USA, 1948).

Fünf Patronenhülsen [Five Cartridges] (Frank Beyer, East Germany, 1960).

Graduate, The (Mike Nichols, USA, 1968).

Guelwaar (Ousmane Sembene, France / Germany / Senegal, 1992).

Gunfighter, The (Henry King, USA, 1950).

Harlan: In the Shadow of Jew Suess [*Harlan - Im Schatten von Jud Süss*] (Felix Moeller, Germany, 2008).

Heaven's Gate (Michael Cimino, USA, 1980).

High Noon (Fred Zinnemann, USA, 1952).

How the West Was Won (John Ford, USA, 1962).

Johnny Guitar (Nicholas Ray, USA, 1954).

Jud Süβ (Veit Harlan, Germany, 1940).

Karl May (Hans-Jürgen Syberberg, West Germany, 1974).

Last Tomahawk, The [*Der letze Mohikaner*] (Harald Reinl, Italy / Spain / West Germany, 1964).

Lili Marleen (R.W. Fassbinder, West Germany, 1981).

Little Big Man (Arthur Penn,USA, 1970).

Lives of Others, The [*Das Leben der Anderen*] (Florian Henckel von Donnersmarck, Germany, 2006).

Magnificent Seven, The (John Sturges, USA, 1960).

Marriage of Maria Braun, The [*Die Ehe der Maria Braun*] (R.W. Fassbinder, West Germany, 1979).

Metropolis (Fritz Lang, Germany, 1927).

Mother Küsters Goes to Heaven [*Mutter Küsters Fahrt zum Himmel*] (R.W. Fassbinder, West Germany, 1975).

Murderers Among Us [*Die Mörder sind unter uns*] (Wolfgang Staudte, East Germany, 1946).

My Darling Clementine (John Ford, USA, 1946).

October: Ten Days that Shook the World [*Oktyabr*] (Sergei Eisenstein, USSR, 1927).

Open City [*Roma, città aperta*] (Roberto Rossellini, Italy, 1945).

Red River (Howard Hawks, USA, 1948).

Rio Grande (John Ford, USA, 1950).

Shane (George Stevens, USA, 1953).

She Wore a Yellow Ribbon (John Ford, USA, 1949).

Soldier Blue (Ralph Nelson, USA, 1970).

Stagecoach (John Ford, USA, 1939).

Tell Them Willie Boy Is Here (Abraham Polonsky, USA, 1969).

To Have and Have Not (Howard Hawkes, USA, 1944).

Wild Bunch, The (Sam Peckinpah, USA, 1969).

Treasure of Silver Lake [*Schatz im Silbersee*] (Harald Reinl, West Germany / Italy / Yugoslavia, 1962).

Winnetou I [*Apache Gold*] (Harald Reinl, West Germany / Italy / Yugoslavia, 1963).

Winnetou II [*Last of the Renegades*] (Harald Reinl, West Germany / France / Italy / Yugoslavia, 1964).

Winnetou III [*The Desperado Trail*] (Harald Reinl, West Germany / Italy / Yugoslavia, 1965).

Ulzana's Raid (Robert Aldrich, USA, 1972).

2

Coming Out into Socialism
Heiner Carow's Third Way

David Brandon Dennis

Where should minorities, including gays and lesbians, be fully acknowledged and secure in their way of life, if not in socialism? (Heiner Carow qtd in Starke, 1994)

It is happenstance but nonetheless striking that Heiner Carow's *Coming Out* premiered on the same night that the Berlin Wall fell. This historical coincidence, along with the title's liberatory metaphor and Western connotations, helped to make the story of a young East Berlin teacher dealing with (homo)sexuality and self-acceptance into a hit among East German audiences and the recipient of a Silver Bear award at the 1990 Berlinale. As East Germany's first (and last) foray into queer cinema, Carow's film marked the high point of an increasingly public discussion of "homosexuality" that took place in East Germany during the late 1980s. The immediate causes of this discussion lay earlier in the decade, above all, in the formation of a grassroots lesbian and gay rights movement in the German Democratic Republic (GDR) that was searching for a third way between the "grey closet" of state socialism and the "rainbow ghetto" of the West (Thinius, 1994: 7–8).

Coming Out, one of the last feature films produced by the state-run Deutsche Film Aktiengesellschaft (DEFA), shared much in common with the grassroots lesbian and gay movement. Both film and movement were part of a reformist moment in East German history and were thus made possible by three overlapping historical developments. First, borrowing historian Dagmar Herzog's (2008) concept, both were products of and participants in East Germany's "sexual evolution." Second, both were made possible by German (state) socialism's overwhelmingly ambivalent and often contradictory stance toward same-sex sexuality. Finally, both were products of a loyal opposition: while maintaining a socialist framework, East German artists, intellectuals, and civil rights activists sought to make state socialism more adaptive to populist or grassroots pressures.

A Companion to German Cinema, First Edition. Edited by Terri Ginsberg and Andrea Mensch.
© 2012 Blackwell Publishing Ltd. Published 2012 by Blackwell Publishing Ltd.

Given this historical context, I read *Coming Out* as a reform-minded quest for a third way between social(ist) commitment and individual self-determination. Just like the demands of leading gay and lesbian activists, Carow's third way emerged in the fraught tensions between official and unofficial culture, between state and society, and between East and West.

Cinema marked not only the end of the GDR-specific struggle for lesbian and gay rights but also its beginning. If *Coming Out* provided the finale, then Rosa von Praunheim's *It Is Not the Homosexual Who Is Perverse, but the Society in Which He Lives* (*Nicht der Homosexuelle ist pervers, sondern die Situation in der er lebt*, 1971), a serious indictment of homophobia and antigay policy in West Germany, signaled the opening scene. In early 1973 von Praunheim's call for gay liberation premiered on West German television,[1] which had become an accessible and popular – albeit illegal – source of news and entertainment in the GDR. East German activists recall the 1973 premier as "the signal" to begin organizing (Soukup, 1990: 48; Silge, 1991: 89; Grau, 1995: 125). Given the close connection between film and lesbian and gay activism in East Germany, it makes sense to consider historiographical questions in light of film criticism and vice versa. With such an undertaking, however, it is important to keep in mind Barton Byg's (2002: 1) counsel against assessing DEFA films solely as evidence of GDR history. Using DEFA films as a historical source should therefore be less a matter "of positing them as 'mirrors' of some preexisting reality than of interpreting them as participants in what can be understood as a GDR-specific civic imaginary" (Feinstein, 2002: 11–12). In other words, by incorporating film-critical as well as historical interpretive tools, we can avoid one-sided readings of *Coming Out* and consider Carow's cinematic vision of sexual difference as both historical artifact and work of art.

Such an undertaking requires the recognition that cultural production in East Germany allowed for artistic license and responded to grassroots pressures within clearly identifiable state-imposed limitations. During the early 1990s this more nuanced understanding was overshadowed by the revival of totalitarian interpretations, which viewed East German society and culture as extensions of the official Socialist Unity Party of Germany's (SED) state (Jarausch, 1999: 52–55). Corey Ross and others have pointed out that the totalitarian approach takes the state's claim to total control as method, rather than object, of analysis (Ross, 2002: 34). Recognizing this problem, recent scholarship has produced more differentiated readings of GDR history, emphasizing for example "the limits of dictatorship" (Bessel and Jessen, 1996) or aspects of "care and coercion" in the "welfare dictatorship" (Jarausch, 1999). It is, of course, important to consider the structural blockages and ideological limits associated with the SED dictatorship.[2] Rather than accepting state claims to total control at face value, however, these should be the starting points for an analysis that goes beyond simple formulations of "state" and "society."

Following this methodological course, numerous recent studies have challenged totalitarian interpretations of East German culture in specific areas ranging from cabaret (Klötzer, 1999) and film (Feinstein, 2002) to working writers (Barck, 2003) and cultural functionaries (von Richthofen, 2009). This work suggests that understanding cultural production in the GDR requires not only recognition of its dictatorial aspects, but also exploration of the spaces that remained open for maneuvering within and around official structures of meaning. It provides a much needed corrective to the totalitarian narrative of GDR culture that informed the major historical syntheses of the 1990s (Schroeder, 1998: 579–583).

Our historical understanding of *Coming Out* is due for a reevaluation along similar lines. Denis Sweet's (Sweet 1997: 249; Sweet, 1998: 49) reading of the film locates it within a "conservative agenda" that aimed to "bolster" support for state socialism. Influenced by totalitarian models, this reading is predicated on an undifferentiated equation of the public sphere in the GDR with the organs of the state. East Germany's "official" public sphere certainly bore little resemblance to the classical Habermasian formulation of the term (although for other reasons neither did public spheres in twentieth-century Western democracies). Instead, Jürgen Habermas (1989: xviii) argued that a "variant type" of public existed in modern industrial dictatorships like the GDR, which he defined as a "plebiscitary-acclamatory form of regimented public sphere." In these "regimented" public spheres the regime "stages" public opinion in order to legitimate its power. The SED's "dictatorship of the proletariat" did, of course, aspire to regiment the East German public sphere. In doing so it used a range of powerful tools from censorship, control over associational life, and Stasi surveillance to staged rituals of public acclamation and the so-called "scissors in the head" – reflexive self-censorship mechanisms – of artists and journalists (Schroeder, 1998: 567). No doubt these tools produced formidable and, at times, insurmountable obstacles to artistic license and grassroots mobilization, but these should not be overestimated. For one thing, modern Western democracies have also used, to varying degrees, censorship and the staging of public opinion as tools of power (Lindenberger, 2006: 115–119). More importantly, in the East, "regimentation" was always an incomplete project. Socialist ideology's claim to esteem Enlightenment values along with the unpredictability of a complex bureaucratic state opened up historically shifting spaces for artists and other intellectuals to maneuver, as long as they demonstrated socialist commitment (Feinstein, 2002: 8). Neither the growth of a lesbian and gay rights movement in East Germany nor Heiner Carow's *Coming Out* can be fully explained without recognizing this delineated space for social and cultural movement.

A very different interpretation of *Coming Out* understands Carow's message essentially as "political dissidence." Katrin Sieg reads the film as "political criticism of socialist heteronormativity borrowed from GDR feminism, anchored in an anti-fascist minority discourse that takes the sting out of the dissident message" (Sieg, 2007: 288). Because it avoids the pitfalls of totalitarian interpretations, this reading is far more plausible than Sweet's. *Coming Out* is, indeed, suffused with explicit criticism of homophobia – the irrational fear of same-sex sexuality (Pharr, 1997) – and heterosexism – the structural privileging of heterosexual over other kinds of relationships (Herek, 1990) – in the GDR. Identifying these critiques as "political dissidence," however, requires further qualification, particularly in light of the extremely fraught historical debates over the meaning of dissent within the GDR.

Potentially, "dissidence" could refer to a wide range of activities from the smuggling and sabotage of the "Eisenberger Circle" to wearing blue jeans and long hair (Fulbrook, 1995: 151–170; Ross, 2002: 113–114).

Examining attitudes among East German cultural and intellectual figures during the 1970s and 1980s helps to identify where *Coming Out* lies on the spectrum of dissent. These decades witnessed the emergence of a renewed impulse which sought to reform state socialism from within rather than abandon it entirely. The strong inclination among East German intellectuals toward moderate dissent from within a socialist framework was unique within the Eastern Bloc because of the particular situation of divided Germany. The GDR's antifascist founding myth provided a potent ethical narrative, particularly for the generation that had come of age at the height of Nazi brutalities. For Heiner Carow, who was a teenager at the end of World War Two, antifascism provided a crucial element of personal history (Carow, 1983: 6–7). In addition, those who rejected the regime entirely could choose (with historically varying degrees of hardship) to "exit" East Germany for the automatic citizenship, guaranteed financial support, and cultural familiarity available to them in West Germany. Those who chose to remain behind and give "voice" to their concerns were more likely to identify with some version of socialist ideology and support the continued existence of the GDR as a separate state (Torpey, 1995: 8–9). Finally, a 1978 agreement between the Protestant Churches in the GDR and the state further bolstered the trend toward moderate political dissent, creating a semi-autonomous public sphere within the churches (Fulbrook, 1995: 109–125).

A far more helpful reading of *Coming Out* places its particular kind of dissent within this broad reformist impulse among East German cultural and intellectual figures. As will be argued below, Heiner Carow fit within this tradition as did most East German lesbian and gay rights activists. During the 1970s and the 1980s, reform-minded East Germans began to consider a host of possibilities – of "third ways" – that they believed would lead to a better, or more democratic, but still socialist GDR. Calls for a reimagined East German future reached a crescendo during the summer and fall of 1989, just as the production of *Coming Out* was wrapping up. The film is significant both historically and artistically because it captured the unique moment in East German history when "third ways" seemed desirable and possible, criticizing what was and imagining anew what life could be in the GDR. Still, Carow continued to privilege socialism as the ideological system through which "minorities, including gays and lesbians, [could] be fully acknowledged and secure in their way of life" (Thinius, 1994: 59).

"The Left and the Vice"

East Germans who were attracted to members of their own sex, like their Western cousins, had much cause for discontent. Over the course of GDR history they faced, among other problems, workplace and housing discrimination, social ostracism, forced "treatments," state surveillance, and police harassment. Even as conditions improved somewhat during the 1980s, they continued to encounter a state that treated them with a profound and contradictory ambivalence. Conflicting attitudes toward sexual minorities were part of a longstanding tradition on the German left. Although German leftists' responses to homosexuality were diverse and historically specific, they tended to fall into identifiable patterns. They shifted along an axis from outspoken support for homosexual rights to opportunistic use of homophobia as a political tool. When dealing with real or imagined enemies, German socialists rarely hesitated to associate them with homophobic stereotypes. Once in power, they reinscribed the heterosexism of bourgeois nationalist respectability within a production-centered project to construct socialism in the GDR.

A number of brief examples from the history of the German left illustrate these patterns. Before World War One, socialists construed homosexuality as a form of "bourgeois decadence" and mobilized homophobia for political gain even as they aided in early efforts to decriminalize sodomy. Marxist theorist Eduard Bernstein was one of the earliest voices to associate homosexuality with the bourgeois *Klassenfeind* ("class enemy"). In 1895 he covered the sensational Oscar Wilde trial in London for a leading German socialist journal. While decrying the British playwright's sentencing, Bernstein nevertheless held that the "cultural trend [*Geistesströmung*] [...] that [Wilde] represents and gives expression to cannot be eliminated with a penal code as long as it finds its nourishment in [bourgeois] social conditions" (Grumbach, 1995a: 23). Four years later, by contrast, Social Democratic Party leader August Bebel personally advocated the repeal of paragraph 175, Imperial Germany's antisodomy law, on the floor of the Reichstag. In doing so, Bebel and other socialists supported the efforts of Magnus Hirschfeld's Scientific Humanitarian Committee, the world's first homosexual rights organization, which was founded in Berlin in 1897. Countervailing Bebel's efforts, left-wing Wilhelmine newspapers used homophobic attacks to score political points in two high-profile German sex scandals – the Krupp Affair of 1902–1903 involving a prominent industrialist, and the Eulenburg Scandal within the conservative inner circle of Kaiser Wilhelm II.

After World War One, the German left continued its decriminalization efforts and almost succeeded in the late 1920s, even as it faced the emergence of right-wing radicalism. Again, German leftists instrumentalized homophobia to discredit their enemies. In the wake of revelations about Nazi SA chief Ernst Röhm's sexual preference for the men under his command, left-wing journalists and thinkers like Wilhelm Reich began crafting a powerful and lasting association between fascism and homosexuality (Reich, 1946: 165; Herzog, 2005: 12–13). They focused particular attention to Röhm's command of youthful storm troopers, characterizing him as a "seducer" of young men. In this spectacular fashion, German left-wing discourse linked homosexuality with fascism via the preexisting homophobic stereotype of the *Jugendverführer* ("seducer of youths"). Such homophobic sentiments hardened among German communists as the National Socialist regime drove them into exile during the mid-1930s (Zinn, 1995: 45–60). Many of them, including numerous future leaders and functionaries of the GDR, fled to the Soviet Union, where the relative sexual liberalization of the 1920s had already given way to Stalinist repression and the recriminalization of male homosexuality. There in 1934, Maxim Gorky, the key Soviet theorist of socialist realist art, cobbled together a series of homophobic images that had emerged from the contest between communists and Nazis, proclaiming,

> In the land where the proletariat governs courageously and efficiently, homosexuality, with its corrupting effect on the young, is considered a social crime punishable under the law. By contrast in [Germany], the "cultivated land" of the great philosophers, scholars, musicians, it is practiced freely and with impunity. There is already a sarcastic saying: "Destroy homosexuality and fascism will disappear." (Blasius and Phelan, 1997: 215)

By the mid-1930s, as evidence mounted of Nazi mass arrests and confinement of gay men, a few German exiles challenged the stereotype of the fascist homosexual. In a 1934 essay entitled "The Left and the Vice," Klaus Mann lamented the arrests and accused fellow antifascists of trying to "make scapegoats of homosexuals," suggesting that they had become "the Jews of the antifascists" (Zinn, 1995: 73). This view, however, remained on the margins of exile discourse.

The founders of the GDR were therefore heirs to a contradictory relationship between German socialism and homosexuality. On the one hand, humanist traditions on the German left spurred efforts toward cooperating with homosexual rights groups and advocating the decriminalization of homosexuality. In addition, a small minority of leftist exiles understood homosexuals as dual victims of Nazi brutality and antifascist prejudice. On the other hand, postwar German leftists possessed a repertoire of homophobic sentiments that associated homosexuality with bourgeois decadence, fascism, or *Jugendverführung*. They also inherited a tradition of using homophobia for political advantage. After World War Two, German communists were no longer political outsiders; as members of the SED, they became the rulers of a new, officially socialist East German state. The prevalence of former communist exiles in the state Party ensured a level of continuity in attitudes toward same-sex sexuality.

Sexual policies during the first two decades of SED rule freighted official ideologies of industrial production with older forms of heterosexism. Like Gorky, early SED leaders revived heterosexual respectability, an essential component of bourgeois nationalism (Mosse, 1985: 184–188), as a crucial basis for a productivist ethos that privileged labor as the ultimate human activity and the workplace as the main site of class struggle (Giddens, 1994: 175–182). Put another way, the SED appropriated a "quite oppressive brand of sexual conservatism" in support of its goals to make East Germans into "socialist personalities" (Herzog, 2008: 75). This new morality enlisted traditional gender roles, the reproductive family, and sexual respectability in the official project of building socialism. In her study of uranium miners in Thuringia and Saxony during the 1950s, Jennifer Evans (2005: 355–370) has shown how same-sex desire in the GDR, especially among men, threatened these categories. In particular, it destabilized the socialist masculine ideal, which glorified the sexually restrained, strong, and productive male worker. Furthermore, well into the 1970s East German sex advice literature, like its Western analogues, continued to incorporate psychological views of homosexuality as "perversion, pathology, or deviance" (Herzog, 2008: 76). It also repeated both nationalist and antifascist fears of youthful seduction. The centrality of working (male) youth to the future-oriented, productivist project of building state socialism meant that the antifascist exile image of homosexual men as *Jugendeverführer* took on even greater significance in the GDR.

Ironically, efforts to decriminalize sodomy accompanied the propagation of a sexually conservative morality in the GDR during its first two decades of existence. Reservations about the particularly invasive Nazi version of paragraph 175 led East German jurists to propose decriminalization in a 1952 draft proposal for the new legal code. Although this first attempt failed, a series of bureaucratic maneuvers quietly ended prosecutions in 1957.[3] When decriminalization arrived in East Germany in 1968, officials transformed the old paragraph 175 into a new age-of-consent law, which continued legal inequality for male and, for the first time in German history, female homosexuality.[4] These efforts, however, owed more to Bernstein's view that same-sex desire would disappear in a socialist society and, therefore, required no censure in criminal law, rather than to any officially sanctioned libratory impulse. During East Germany's first two decades, jurists understood homosexual love and desire as a "remnant of the bourgeois past" which they expected to gradually fade away in the GDR (Grau, 1995: 107).

During the late 1960s and 1970s the GDR was not immune to the calls for sexual liberation that swept through the West. But instead of Western-style sexual revolution, these decades witnessed an East German "sexual evolution." In light of the state's "apparent disorientation" concerning sexuality, progressive doctors, pedagogues, psychologists, and sexologists played a central role in steering the SED and East German national debate toward greater heterosexual freedom. This impulse resonated with ordinary East Germans, especially the young (Herzog, 2008). The privileged position of scientific discourse in Marxist-Leninist thought meant that social scientists and doctors were indispensible for the GDR's sexual evolution. Sexologist Siegfried Schnabel, author of East Germany's best-selling sex advice book, decoupled heterosexuality from reproduction, criticizing the "stupid procreation-ideology" of Christianity and Nazism and encouraging straight couples to revel in the "pleasure and delight" of sex (Herzog, 2005: 212–213). Heiner Carrow's 1973 run-away hit, *The Legend of Paul and Paula* (*Die Legende von Paul und Paula*), echoed Schnabel's contribution to the GDR's (hetero)sexual evolution. As will be discussed in a later section, this film was innovative for elevating fulfillment of sexual desire between its two straight protagonists over "respectable" socialist reproduction.

East Germany's sexual ethics evolved at a slower pace regarding lesbian and gay couples. As late as 1972, Schnabel, for example, still held to the old *Verführung* theory of homosexuality, although notably he claimed that "once homosexuality becomes firmly and untreatably rooted in the personality" it should not be a cause of concern since homosexuals could also develop partnerships based on "reciprocal loyalty, love, and respect" (Schenk, 2008: 47–48). During the 1980s, more positive attitudes toward same-sex desire increasingly became the norm within East German sexual science, ushering in a second phase of the "sexual evolution." When sociologists Kurt Starke and Walter Friedrich published their expansive 1984 study on sexual life in the GDR, they devoted an entire chapter to homosexuality, giving it a favorable reading as simply another variation among the broad range of human sexual behavior (Starke and Friedrich, 1984: 296–297). This development is all the more noteworthy considering Education Secretary Margot Honecker's hostility to Friedrich's Central Institute for Youth Research (ZIJ) in Leipzig, which from its inception in 1966 had become the closest thing to an institutional home for sexual science in the GDR. Scholars from the ZIJ circumnavigated Honecker's attempts to block their research by enlisting the help of other high-level functionaries, who allowed them to work with university students and workers' youth groups (Roberts, 2007: 131). It is precisely such contradictions within the state bureaucracy which suggest that the SED's position on (homo)sexuality was anything but clear. The state's lack of a clear position on same-sex sexuality, allowed openings not only for academic research but also grassroots pressure. In promoting greater tolerance, acceptance, and even equality for sexual minorities in East Germany, progressive sexual scientists had help from a nascent lesbian and gay rights movement.

Toward a Political *Lesbisch- und Schwulsein* in the GDR

Shortly after the *Wende* – the sweeping transformation of GDR politics and society during 1989–1990 – Kurt Starke published *Schwuler Osten* (Gay East), a comprehensive study of gay men in the GDR. The study's respondents answered questions during the months following German reunification in October 1990. They paint a bleak but generally improving picture of the lives of gay men under the East German regime. Interestingly, their views of the reform-focused *Wende* were far more positive than their opinions on reunification with the West. Almost two-fifths saw preunification reform as a positive development for gay men, while less than twenty percent viewed it negatively (with the remainder reporting no change). The numbers are almost exactly reversed concerning reunification, highlighting reservations among gay men about dismantling the GDR. The most frequent concerns they expressed about living as gay men in reunified Germany included the continued existence of paragraph 175 in the West, intolerance, discrimination, persecution, employment bans, violence, right-wing attacks, a loss of solidarity, commercialization of the gay subculture, and AIDS. Starke's study suggests that large numbers of gay East Germans welcomed changes within their native GDR but were skeptical of the West (Starke, 1994: 215–223). These popular sentiments reflect the attitudes of the East German lesbian and gay rights movement before and after November 1989. Well before the *Wende*, lesbian and gay activists were looking for a third way. The state apparatus responded to these efforts in fundamentally reactive and ambivalent ways.

Although most activists recall a 1982 church conference on the "Theological Aspects of Homosexuality" in Berlin as the founding moment of the East German lesbian and gay movement, there were a number of previous attempts to organize during the 1970s. Between 1974 and 1976 the Homosexual Interest Community of (East) Berlin (HIB), a small friendship circle, met in the Gründerzeit Museum of scene celebrity Charlotte von Mahlsdorf, held events, and petitioned authorities with their demands.[5] Intimidated by Stasi agents and with little to show for their efforts, the group's activities waned. In 1978 a lesbian group led by sociologist Ursula Silge tried to revive the Museum gatherings, only to be shut down by the authorities at the last minute (Silge, 1991: 89–92). Still, these efforts were noticed by higher-ranking bureaucrats in the administration, who finally issued an official statement against organizing independent lesbian and gay groups. The Ministries of the Interior, of Health, and of State Security in 1978 took the position that there was "no social need" for homosexual groups and advocated a policy whereby lesbians and gay men would be integrated into socialist society on an individual basis (Grau, 1995: 127).

The church–state agreement of 1978, however, created conditions that ultimately undermined the state's stalling tactics. Within three years, activists had organized "homosexual working groups" inside the semi-autonomous spaces of the Protestant Churches. Some of the groups that were uncomfortable in a religious setting began to seek institutional homes within state-based organizations such as *Kulturhäuser* (Cultural Houses) and the official youth groups of the *Freie Deutsche Jugend* (Free German Youth). By November 1989 there were over 20 church-based groups and half as many groups affiliated with state institutions. They existed in small towns like Aschersleben, but were concentrated mostly in the larger urban areas of Berlin, Leipzig, Dresden, Halle, and Magdeburg. The homosexual working groups cooperated through a loose coalition that met annually to share ideas and coordinate strategy and a "theoretical group" that met four times a year to formulate specific demands and political positions (Soukup, 1990: 47–57). Kurt Starke found that a little over 20% of his gay male respondents reported regular active work in the groups. This "hard core" of activists was subsumed within a much larger group, over two-thirds of respondents, who reported varying levels of participation in working group activities, which ranged from plays and dances to discussions and lectures (Starke, 1994: 187–194). The broad overview of the movement sketched here may suggest a level of uniformity that simply did not exist. Internal conflicts divided it along lines of gender, religious affiliation, and personality, among others (Silge, 1991: 99–106). Some, but not all, of these quarrels can be blamed on the Stasi. *Inoffizielle Mitarbeiter*, unofficial Stasi agents, infiltrated the movement in order to sow dissention, break up the groups, or steer them toward "state-friendly" positions (Grumbach and Grau, 1994).

It is relatively easy to show that East German state security infiltrated the lesbian and gay movement during the 1980s, but far harder to ascertain its motivations and goals. Journalist and theologian Eduard Stapel, co-founder of the first homosexual working group, has researched Stasi documents relating to the movement extensively (Stapel, 1999, 2008). He concluded that state security had no master plan regarding same-sex sexuality in East Germany. Nor was it acting on any particular set of orders from the SED leadership, for which homosexuality remained a "blind spot" until the end (Stapel, 2008: 100–102). These findings suggest that the state, or at least its security apparatus, was reactive rather than proactive regarding homosexuality. When confronted with independently organizing lesbians and gay men, Stasi agents and bureaucrats slipped reflexively into the homophobic and heterosexist patterns contained within German socialism's historic ambivalence and anchored in the postwar morality of the 1950s and 1960s. Furthermore, the gay rights movement was only one of many grassroots efforts – environmentalist, peace, feminist, and civil rights, among others – to attract particular interest from the Stasi. Ultimately the movement was politically suspect in the watchful eyes of state security not because of its lesbian and gay content per se, but rather because it infringed on the SED-state's essential claims to an absolute monopoly over political organization (Schenk, 2008: 54).

The East German medical and academic establishment reacted to the movement in a relatively positive manner compared with the Politburo's silence and the Stasi's politically motivated suspicion. The activities and petitions of lesbian and gay groups during the early 1980s eventually led municipal authorities in Berlin to commission an "Interdisciplinary Working Group on Homophilia" at Humboldt University. None of the grassroots gay and lesbian activists was invited to take part in this working group. However, a follow-up series of conferences sponsored by the Social-Hygienic Society of the GDR on the "Psycho-Social Aspects of Homosexuality" in Leipzig (1985) Karl-Marx-Stadt (1988) and Jena (1990) marked a new level of cooperation between activists and sexually progressive social scientists and medical doctors in the GDR (Silge, 1991: 96). In many cases the lines between the two groups blurred. Case in point, Günter Grau, a sexologist and consultant at the Marriage, Family, and Sexual Information Center in Berlin-Friedrichshain, participated in the conferences and went on to become one of the leading activists in the movement.

Grau, along with sociologist Ursula Silge, theologian Eduard Stapel, and other leading activist writers and organizers counted among those who chose to stay and "voice" their concerns in a socialist framework rather than "exit" to the West. As Silge (1991: 85) put it after the *Wende*,

> It's understandable that people could simply give up one day and leave, well, flee the GDR. But the opposite conviction that it was possible to change things was just as widespread. Homosexual women and men with their sympathizers were always

discussing in their groups how "faults and weaknesses" [of the socialist system] could be eliminated or, at least, reduced. (1991: 85)

Ultimately, these individuals constituted an interactive link between sympathetic practitioners within East Germany's medical and social scientific fields and grass-roots reform-minded sentiments like those Kurt Starke found in his study of gay East Germans.

Cooperation between the movement and progressive public health profession-als began to bear fruit by 1987. During the GDR's final two years a soft media buzz on the topic of homosexuality pierced the relative silence outside of academic, medical, and church environs. East Germans were informed that their fellow gay (male) citizens suffered from persecution and that "tolerance and acceptance" would be the order of the day. The first East German scientific monograph devoted to the subject of homosexuality appeared in 1987, going through two editions with over 100 000 copies (Werner, 1987). A second book regarding the work of the church groups and the ensuing church controversy appeared in 1989 (Grau, 1989). Over 200 articles about homosexuality appeared in newspapers, magazines, and journals. The subject of homosexuality was treated several times in GDR televi-sion programming including the program *Visite* (Visit) in 1987 and again in 1988 and the youth show *Hautnah* (Up Close) in 1989. The popular youth radio program *DT 64* broadcast a Q&A session with gay and lesbian youth. In association with the ZIJ in Leipzig, DEFA produced a "sex education" documentary, *Die andere Liebe* (The Other Love, 1989) featuring gay and lesbian youth. The release of *Coming Out* marked the peak of this groundswell of public discussion.

It might be tempting to read this support of "tolerance and acceptance for homosexuals" in the media and parts of the academic and medical establishments as evidence of a well-planned program of social engineering – a last-minute effort to "raise political capital" for the SED-state (Sweet, 1995: 351–364). But the histori-cal evidence simply does not support such a contention. State security had no over-arching goals in infiltrating the homosexual working groups apart from preserving the political monopoly of the SED. Berlin Party chief and Politburo member, Günter Schabowski, stated in an interview that the topic of homosexuality never came up in the East German Politburo (Starke, 1994: 95). Nor did the medical community speak with one voice on the issue. In late November 1989, Niels Sönnichsen, head of the AIDS Advisory Group in the GDR's Ministry of Health, warned in thinly veiled homophobic overtones that "the AIDS-infected and drug-addicted of the Western world" would soon throw themselves on East German youth (Soukup, 1990: 15). Furthermore, the relevant academic fields of Marxist-Leninist philosophy, ethics, and sociology ignored homosexuality and continued to be dominated by conservative views of the family and sexuality until the end of the regime (Schenk, 2008: 53).

Without instructions "from above," matters concerning homosexuality were often left to the discretion of local functionaries, who acted as capricious and unpredictable bureaucrats rather than executors of a coordinated strategy. Ursula Silge (1981: 86) recalls with frustration that whenever she tried to accomplish anything "the administrative apparatus turned into a black box that reacted in incalculable ways." In early 1986, for example, a cultural functionary allowed Silge's gay and lesbian Sonntags-Club (Sunday Club) to hold events at a Berlin youth facility. Almost a year later the Cultural Affairs Department of Berlin-Mitte found out what was going on and shut down the youth facility. "The state" spoke with many voices, not one. The quest for gay rights in the GDR unfolded within ideological and political limits imposed by a dictatorial state. But the political energy for greater acceptance of homosexuality within GDR society was generated primarily in the interactions among lower and midlevel functionaries, sexually progressive professionals, and the grassroots lesbian and gay rights movement.

"Cinema that Concerns Everyone"

As with East Germany's gay rights movement, *Coming Out* was not the product of a coordinated state initiative to integrate lesbian and gay East Germans (Sweet, 1997, 1998); instead, its production owes much to Heiner Carow's cinematic vision and personal engagement with cultural officials at DEFA and beyond. By the late-1970s Carow had developed a distinctive artistic vision for the future of East German cinema. He called for films that dealt with "everyday stories and people's emotions." Such films would make possible "a new way" for a "new generation" that was asking "new and different questions." Carow exhorted filmmakers,

> We must answer the questions that [young people] have with different answers than we were given, perhaps deeper answers about people themselves, how they think and how they feel, what they think about truth, about morality. And so we have to transform our artistic expressions and make new films with greater popular appeal. Our task will be to conquer the theaters again, so that we can make cinema into a form of stronger and greater revolutionary social debate. (1983: 7)

In short, he demanded an East German "cinema that concerns everyone" – a cinema that engages in a genuine class struggle by concerning itself with popular appeal.

Carow's new East German cinema was in many ways a subtle attack on the officially prescribed socialist realist approach to art that had dominated DEFA films since the early 1950s. It was also a defensive play against the growing popularity of Western imports on the East German big screen (Hake, 2008: 147–148). Socialist realist art valorized collective production and romanticized revolution through such elements as "positive" working heroes, optimism about the socialist future, class consciousness, and ideological conformity (Berghahn, 2005: 35). The strict interpretation of socialist realism favored by leading cultural functionaries in the SED viewed art as a didactic tool for educating the masses to become "socialist personalities." By the 1960s it had become clear that DEFA films made in the officially sanctioned socialist realist style, which paid little attention to grassroots and youthful concerns, had serious problems with popular appeal. In addition, the growth of television as a popular medium, which also meant competition from illegal West German TV, compounded DEFA's decline in popularity. An ensuing crisis of confidence among East German filmmakers spurred debates that focused on the issue of *Massenwirksamkeit* ("popular appeal").

Much of Carow's contribution to this debate unfolded on the pages of *Film und Fernsehen*. This journal catered specifically to East Germany's film specialists; it provided a venue in which they could express slightly more critical viewpoints than would be possible in major newspapers (Stott, 1999: 46–47). In the journal, Carow called for a "democratic attitude" among filmmakers, which would prevent them from "placing themselves above their audience" (Carow, 1983: 23). He also criticized the didacticism of typical DEFA films, in which "an outstanding workers' collective is shown on the screen along with a clearly expressed exhortation for the viewer to work better" (Carow, 1983: 92). This kind of cinema, he believed, would anger viewers who had far greater insight into the complexities of creating a socialist society than didactic films allowed. Instead, he advocated politically engaged films that were not only entertaining, but also exciting and controversial (Carow, 1983: 35). Carow's additional emphasis on the need to address concerns of a "new generation" signaled his sensitivity to the potential problems of an ossifying "gerontocracy" in the GDR – problems that would become painfully clear during the 1980s. His call to "conquer the theaters again" was therefore nothing less than a full-fledged attempt to save DEFA from obscurity by placing the individual viewer's emotions, needs, and questions at the center of socialist art.

During the 1970s Carow was at the forefront of an aesthetic shift in East German cinema that critics have associated with the representation of everyday life, or *Alltag*. Sigrun D. Leonhard (1989: 56–60) identifies an aesthetic movement toward a "new style of [everyday] realism." Similarly, Joshua Feinstein argues that the *Alltagsfilm* of the 1970s, which "emphasizes ahistorical existence, the diurnal," gradually replaced the *Gegenwartsfilm* (contemporary issue films) of the 1950s and 1960s, which contained "a strong sense of historical progression: the present as a mediating stage between the past and the future" (Feinstein, 2002: 6). Both scholars treat Carow's *The Legend of Paul and Paula* as a prototypical *Alltagsfilm*. The film places a premium on youth, love, personal fulfillment, and even such seemingly romantic elements as legend, dream, and fantasy. Its protagonist, Paul, a career-minded bureaucrat who is unhappy in his dull marriage, falls for his neighbor, Paula, an unpretentious grocery-store clerk and single mother. Despite their instantly passionate connection, Paul finds it difficult to give up the respectability of marriage and career for a single, working mother. When his hesitation almost costs him Paula's love, he forsakes social respectability and embarks on a comical and ultimately successful campaign to win her back. Tragically, Paula dies giving birth, but Paul takes comfort in their child as an enduring symbol of their love. *Paul und Paula* thus offers a critique of official socialist morality's conservative views of the family, sexuality, and reproduction. The film proved to contain a winning formula, conquering the theaters and becoming a cult classic and East Germany's most popular film along the way.

Carow's controversial films and reformist ideas brought him into subtle conflicts with the SED-state and the institutional hierarchy within DEFA. An earlier film of his, *The Russians Are Coming (Die Russen kommen,* 1968) – the story of young protagonist's emotional journey from Hitler Youth hero to Soviet prisoner and murder suspect – was shelved for 20 years because it departed from the fictitious yet official historical view that ordinary Germans had all welcomed the Soviet Army as liberators at the end of World War Two. Writing in 1979, Carow (1983:16) identified this film – and obliquely its censorship – as the moment in which he began to formulate an East German "cinema that concerns everyone." After the suppression of *The Russians Are Coming* and the success of *Paul and Paula*, Carow turned to a project based on Grimmelshausen's *Simplicissimus*, which he was forced to abandon after years of work because of opposition from DEFA functionaries. More ominously, he was among the filmmakers most watched by Stasi agents within DEFA (Geiss, 1997: 54). Despite such problems he remained a loyal SED party member. Like other reform-minded East German artists, he was a committed socialist who had no desire to overthrow the regime but resented state interference in the creative process. As with most active and ongoing participants in GDR cultural production he had learned the "rules of the game" – how to work with, through, and around the system to articulate his urgently felt personal and political concerns (von Richthofen, 2009: 17).

These skills were absolutely necessary in the late 1980s when Carow sought approval to film *Coming Out.* The film likely would not have been made, but for growing unrest within DEFA and Carow's determination to push it past the studio's institutional roadblocks. On the whole, scholars have interpreted the 1980s as a disheartening period of "resignation and disorientation" or "decline" among production teams at DEFA (Schittly, 2002: 241; Hake, 2008: 147). Rising Cold War tensions in the early years of the decade ushered in a return of heavy-handed policies toward film production. After the Ministry of Culture shelved Carow's *Simplicissimus* project in 1981, he was barred from working and did not make another film until conditions finally improved on the eve of DEFA's fortieth anniversary in 1986 (Schittly, 2002: 249; Hake, 2008: 151). By the late-1980s studio personnel had grown increasingly angry with this sort of repression, especially after leading cultural functionaries refused their calls for Soviet-style *glasnost* and *perestroika.* As tensions simmered within the studio, Carow approached DEFA director Hans Dieter Mäde about writing the script for *Coming Out.* Mäde refused to commission a film about homosexuality. Carow and Wolfram Witt wrote the screenplay anyway on their own initiative. Circumventing Mäde's opposition, they sent it directly to Kurt Hager, the SED's chief ideologue, along with letters of support from a psychiatrist, a sociologist, and a legal scholar. Hager approved the film (Poss and Warnecke, 2006: 453). This reliance on "enlightened" professionals to get around state-bureaucratic obstacles echoed the grassroots lesbian and gay movement's tactics. In the meanwhile, Mäde resigned in late 1988 over the turmoil at DEFA. His successors, whose sentiments were more favorable to artistic innovation than those of career functionaries like Mäde, were sympathetic to projects that challenged convention. Therefore, a confluence of Carow's rather plucky initiative, the support of progressive professionals, and the growing room for filmmakers to maneuver within DEFA's institutional structure during 1988–1989 ultimately made *Coming Out* possible.

Coming Out into Socialism

On screen *Coming Out* negotiates many of the same tensions that marked the East German lesbian and gay rights movement. But the resonance between film and movement extends only so far. One could argue that *Coming Out* fails precisely because it never once mentions the movement's existence. However, any scene featuring one of the GDR's grassroots civil rights movements would have had no chance to make it past DEFA's censors, even in the more tolerant atmosphere of 1989. In an interview for the film's official press release, Carow associated it with the "counter-movement against homophobia" in GDR society, likely a veiled reference to the homosexual working groups (Carow, 1989: 7). Whatever the case, both *Coming Out* and the movement shared a common vision of *Schwulsein* [being gay] in the GDR as a third way between political commitment to socialism and the individual self-determination. Carow was interested in a socialist humanism that did not give up on notions of "class struggle," but rather complicated them, equating class oppression with racial and sexual oppressions. In doing so he shared with the lesbian and gay movement at least four overlapping dynamics. These dynamics resulted from tensions between older and newer definitions of antifascism; between didacticism and *Massenwirksamkeit*; between the "welfare dictatorship" and *Eigen-Sinn* ("obstinacy," or an "individual sense of self"); and between Eastern "grey closets" and Western "colorful ghettoes."

At the beginning of the film, Philipp Klarmann (Matthias Freihof), an earnest and involved high school teacher, who is popular with his students and committed to socialism, seems poised for success at work. He literally runs into a fellow teacher, Tanja (Dagmar Manzel), in a school hallway and a romance quickly blossoms. They move into Tanja's apartment, although Philipp keeps his small efficiency with its breathtaking view of the East Berlin skyline. At first they are happy together, but Philipp's world begins to collapse after Tanja introduces him to her gay friend, Jakob, who turns out to have been Philipp's schoolboy crush. Try as he may, Philipp simply cannot return to normalcy. He wanders into an East Berlin gay bar where he meets Matthias (Dirk Kummer). Still masquerading as straight with Tanja, Philipp begins an affair with Matthias against the backdrop of the nightlights of Alexanderplatz. But when Tanja and Matthias find out about each other, Philipp loses them both. In the film's climactic scene, Philipp is finally forced to confront his sexuality by an old communist, Walter (Werner Dissel). With love life and professional reputation in shambles, Philipp has, nonetheless, come to accept himself.

Antifascism drives the first dynamic of Carow's third way, structuring Philipp's coming out process through symbols of the ghetto, Jewish resistance, racist violence, and the concentration camp. By dislocating present homophobia into the pre-GDR German fascist past, *Coming Out* revises the homophobic and heterosexist elements of historical antifascism into modern gay-friendliness. Philipp's path of self-realization leads through three scenes that are held together by a minority discourse embedded in Germany's Nazi past (Sieg, 2007: 288). In the first scene Philipp and Tanja attend an alternative concert in which antifascist resistance is emblematized by Yiddishkeit as performed in an unnamed Nazi ghetto, where Lutz, Philipp's student who is also gay, sings a "song from the ghetto." The camera pans between Philipp and Lutz, reinforcing their gay connection, as the soundtrack's Jewish folk melodies evoke the Holocaust and the resistance of the Jewish socialist Bund. The Bund, which had been active in Central and Eastern European Jewish cultures since the 1890s, played a significant role in organizing the Warsaw Ghetto Uprising in 1943. Jewish experience and resistance in Nazi ghettos stands in metaphorically for gay experience and resistance in the GDR.

The second scene takes place in a train car. Three neo-Nazi skinheads begin to threaten a fellow passenger, presumably an African guest-worker. Philipp, now acting the role of antifascist hero, takes the initiative of trying to prevent the assault. His students join in and together push the skinheads out of the train at the next stop. As a collective inspired by the heroic leadership of their teacher, the students win the battle against racism. At the train station, the camera lingers ambivalently on the station sign: "Marx-Engels Platz." Similar to the previous scene, the neo-Nazi attack stands in for the homophobic undercurrents in GDR society. And the station sign, viewed from within the mass-transit train car, clarifies that only a vibrant Marxism with a genuinely popular base holds the key to defeating racism and homophobia.

The final climactic encounter between Philipp and Walter solidifies this revamped, pro-gay antifascism. Following the loss of Matthias and Tanja, Philipp returns to the gay bar. Lonely, depressed, and terrified, he flits around the bar in an awkward frenzy until the host threatens to throw him out on the street. The more seasoned Walter intervenes, takes responsibility for the younger man, and begins to tell him about his experiences during the War. A former *Wehrmacht* soldier, Walter and his male lover had been discovered, deported to concentration camps, and forced to wear the pink triangle. Grateful to the comrades who saved him, Walter subsequently became a convinced communist after the war. But, finishing the story by quoting Marx, he highlights a glaring inconsistency: "We worked like crazy. We stopped mankind's exploitation by mankind, now it does not matter if the person you work with is a Jew or whatever. Except the gays. We forgot them somehow." In the process of invoking memories of the brutally homophobic policies of Nazism, *Coming Out* actually displaces the historically homophobic elements of antifascism. This scene is also the film's most politically pointed moment: Walter bluntly challenges the SED on its record regarding the emancipation of sexual minorities.

Carow's fundamental redefinition of the antifascist struggle as a struggle against residual bourgeois respectability within state-socialist ideology also evokes the generational conflict in the GDR's "gerontocracy" of the 1980s. *Coming Out* reverses the exile generation's stereotypes. In place of the homosexual fascist we now find Walter, the gay antifascist. In the confrontation scene between Walter and Philipp, *Coming Out* resolves the generational conflict by substituting alternative memories of antifascism that evoke Klaus Mann's 1930s critique of communist exiles. Walter instructs Philipp, representative of the next generation, that homosexuals were victims of fascism along with Jews. The confrontation scene also highlights the absurdity of the *Jugendverführer* stereotype. When Walter touches Philipp to try and calm him, Philipp calls him a "dirty old man." Only moments later, a tearful Philipp expresses fears to the older man about being an openly gay teacher.

The film's second dynamic operates in the tension between socialist realist didacticism and Carow's goals to make socialist films with popular appeal. Philipp faces a number of obstacles on his path out of the closet. Along the way various scenes show him confronted with the choice to remain closeted or to proceed with the process of coming out. Each is framed reflexively to convey a critical message about contemporary GDR society. In every instance, the particular character delivering the message dominates the mise-en-scène. The camera position sutures the perspective of a second character with that of the viewing audience. This formal construction reinforces the film's didactic function. Clearly social reform is its goal.

One such scene presents Philipp with his first opportunity to have sex with a man, Matthias. His own internalized heterosexism provides the obstacle here. This is the first real love scene of the film; those between Philipp and Tanja show little or no actual intimacy. Matthias sits on the bed waiting, but Philipp hesitates and finally tells Mattihias that he should leave, asking him, "Don't you want a family? To have kids some day?" The camera then cuts to Matthias, who now fills the screen. Matthias says, "No, I don't want any of that." The camera shift serves to align the point-of-view and, by extension, the perspectives of Philipp and the audience, whose civic imaginary is thusly contested by Matthias's rebuke. The message leaves little doubt as to its significance: socialist morality does not require, and should not entail, the valorization of heterosexual reproduction.

Philipp faces a second challenge when his distraught mother begs him to reconsider coming out. She blames his homosexuality for ruining her life. Wondering why he must justify himself to her or anyone, he asks her to accept his right to live as nature has apparently intended. As Philipp asks this question, his mother moves offscreen, and he comes to fill the screen. Again, the camera position merges his mother's point-of-view and, by extension her perspective with that of the contemporary audience. This scene teaches that being gay is "natural" and gay people deserve familial and social acceptance.

Tempering its didactic moments are the film's elements of *Massenwirksamkeit*. In a move that evokes *The Legend of Paul and Paula*, the quasi-romantic love story between Philipp and Matthias, situated in the margins of Philipp's collective labor experience, advances his coming out process. When a sympathetic colleague at school repeatedly tries to comfort him, he pushes her away, pretending everything is fine. Indeed, as the narrative progresses Philipp becomes increasingly estranged from his job. Onscreen his alienation from the working collective is embodied in the film's configuration of his relationships with two female characters: Tanja and the school director. Tanja, his colleague and fiancée, represents the ideological conflation of socialist production and heteronormative family life, while the school director stands for the exploitability of labor-power by state authority. The highly gendered nature of Philipp's alienation from the collective emphasizes the point that his capacity for true love and personal honesty exists primarily in his individual relationships with men. For Carow (1989: 6) this is a "film about love and honesty" with the message that "one can only develop [as a socialist personality] when one loves and is loved." Deploying an ostensibly insignificant but poignant love story, he simultaneously critiques the ideology of heteronormative reproduction and its aesthetic alignment with the strict socialist-realist glorification of labor and the workplace.

Coming Out's third dynamic involves a juxtaposition of aspects of the GDR's "welfare dictatorship" with individual *Eigen-Sinn*, to borrow key concepts from recent historical debates. Konrad Jarausch coined the term "welfare dictatorship" to capture the "central contradiction between socialism's emancipatory rhetoric and the corrupt practice of Stalinism within a single analytical category" (Jarausch, 1999: 60). For example, Matthias's medical treatment for attempted suicide, the subject of *Coming Out*'s opening scene, vividly depicts the elements of care and coercion that defined the GDR's welfare dictatorship: New Year's Eve fireworks light the night skies over East Berlin. A siren wails. An ambulance traverses the streets of East Berlin. The camera cuts to a team of nurses surrounding Matthias in an emergency room, focusing on his face as the nurses' hands roughly force a tube down his throat, all the while commanding him to "cooperate." They forcibly pump overdose pills, a potent metaphor for internalized homophobia, from his stomach. The camera cuts to Matthias sobbing alone in a hospital bed. When he confesses to the attending nurse that he had tried to kill himself because he is gay, she gently but firmly replies, "That's no reason to cry." In this context, the victimization of gay men appears as an apparent concern of the caring yet coercive state, embodied in the figure of the nurse.

Almost immediately after the suicide scene, the film proceeds explicitly to subvert the victimhood narrative that positions gay men as objects of the state's unyielding care. This is accomplished through a series of scenes which constitute Philipp's emerging sense of *Eigen-Sinn*, or "individual sense of self." Originally, Alf Lüdtke (1989) applied the term to Wilhelmine factory workers and the myriad small ways in which they distanced themselves not only vertically from capitalist labor discipline but also horizontally from their colleagues (see also von Richthofen, 2009: 10–12). The two bicycle-riding scenes that bracket Philipp's coming-out story emphasize his sense of difference and distance from other East Germans, even as they make clear his membership in that society. After the title shot, the film cuts to Philipp on his bicycle, self-propelled within busy traffic. However, this is no leisurely ride. He keeps pace with a line of cars along the wide Karl Marx Allee, riding uniformly in the direction of the traffic around him. But he is alone. He is the only bicyclist in a stream of cars, different and distant from – while among – the other drivers, a person driven alternatively to move both with and against the greater social whole. The film's final scene repeats this formal construction, only this time the camera angle gradually ascends as the final credits roll, tracking Philipp's film-length progress. This last bicycle scene, even more than the first, evokes a sense of Philipp's capacity to realize his personal difference within the framework of social(ist) commitment.

Philipp's *Eigen-Sinn* takes on political undertones when he is faced with an investigation after being outed at work. Four of his colleagues, including the school director, ominously arrive in the middle of class to observe his teaching. After looking each one of them in the eye, Philipp sits silently, staring out the window. The camera then zooms out the window, as if to suggest his desire to escape this moment of scrutiny and surveillance. The silence in the room is palpable. "Kollege Klarmann!" shouts the unnerved school director. Philipp remains obstinately mute for several seconds more before turning to face them. Here again, the camera position sutures the perspectives of the audience with that of the colleagues: Philipp stands, looks directly at the camera, and replies, "Yes." He knows why they are there and answers their accusation in the affirmative, but the critical pattern established by this formal construction belies any sense that he accedes to official ideology. At this point, heterosexist and homophobic policies have completely alienated him from the collective workplace he has loved and to which he had been committed – a deeply political charge in the GDR.

The fourth dynamic of Carow's film involves criticism of the Eastern "grey closet" paired with ambivalence toward a Western-style "colorful ghetto." The film's English-only title makes clear that Western discourses on lesbian and gay liberation form at least part of its cultural intertext. Additionally, capturing the "scene" in East Berlin's Prenzlauer Berg district was of major concern to Carow's production team, so they set *Coming Out* against a backdrop of actual gay bars and the "cruisy" Volkspark Friedrichshain. Many of the supporting actors were openly gay men and (a few) lesbians playing themselves, including a number who had appeared as themselves earlier that year in the DEFA documentary *Die andere Liebe*. Colorful and controversial scene personality Charlotte von Mahlsdorf[6] made a cameo appearance as a bartender, and Carow's openly gay assistant director, Dirk Kummer, played Matthias.

At first glance *Coming Out* portrays East Berlin's gay subculture as a warm, inviting space lit by bright colors and flashy characters, contrasting starkly with Philipp's closeted *Alltag*. On his first visit to a gay bar, he encounters flamboyant drag kings and queens, happily dancing couples, and plenty of men who show interest in him. The soundtrack behind this scene contains some of the film's liveliest music, interspersed with rock and English-language songs, evoking a Westernized atmosphere. The bright colors inside the gay bar contrast starkly with the grey or muted tones that shade other areas of Philipp's daily life and Western representations of East Germany. Most importantly, it is here that Philipp finds compassion, concern, and a chance at true love with Matthias.

But even in this scene Carow preempts any rose-colored image of ostensible Westernization, pairing brief shots of solitary men with distorted musical effects. In subsequent scenes this alternate, despairing image of the subculture moves to the forefront. After losing both Matthias and Tanja, Philipp is alone and scared. He goes cruising in the Volkspark hoping to find companionship. The gloomy park and dimly lit faces cast a colder, anonymous, and impersonal shadow on the subculture. Although the man he picks up in the park looks like Matthias, the sex they have is casual and emotionally unfulfilling. Deciding again to search for Matthias, Philipp goes back to the bar where the two met, only to learn from the otherwise cheerful host that "here everyone's alone." The last scene in the bar, which features Philipp's confrontation with Walter, also styles the flamboyant cheerfulness of the subculture as a farcical performance. The camera focuses on an exhausted drag queen, who, with a look of resignation, takes off her wig and earrings. *Coming Out* ultimately reveals Prenzlauer Berg's Western-style gay "ghetto" as an emotionally empty and unfulfilling space. This admittedly complex portrait of East Berlin's Western-style gay subculture subverts the antifascist minority discourse evoked earlier in the film, complicating the potent symbol of Lutz's "song from the ghetto."

The East German lesbian and gay movement negotiated similar dynamics in constructing *Schwulsein* as part of a reformed socialism. Activists redefined antifascism as gay-friendliness, framing their most comprehensive statement of demands, the Karl-Marx-Städter Platform of June 1989, with the memory of the pink triangle. The Platform called on the East German state to recognize and compensate the Nazis' lesbian and gay victims and to add homosexuals to the list of "victims of fascism" at public commemoration ceremonies (Soukup, 1990: 137–144).[7] The movement's organizers also struggled with questions of didacticism and *Massenwirksamkeit*. They wondered how to effectively "organize consensus across the entire social dimension" and worried that their movement, and other oppositional groups of the *Wende*, might turn out to be an "intellectual bubble" without real popular support (Soukup, 1990: 18–19). Likewise, the tension between the "welfare state" and *Eigen-Sinn* was difficult for lesbian and gay activists to resolve.

On one hand, they noted the "macabre advantages of Stalinist socialism" in making social change easier, given that people in positions of power were "enlightened" (Soukup, 1990: 18). On the other hand, many of them believed that their movement was not political enough and that only the "de-integration" of gay identity – a strategic separatism – would produce the political conditions necessary to demand social acceptance and equal rights (Soukup, 1990: 29).

Finally, lesbian and gay activists expressed skepticism toward a Western-style "ghetto," even as they tried to reform the GDR's "grey closet." Some defended the subculture as necessary for the creation of a gay political identity, averring that if a ghetto existed, society at large had "made" it (Soukup, 1990: 29). Still, the specter of "commercial ghettoization" in Western capitalist lesbian and gay life was a widespread concern (Soukup, 1990: 113). Western conditions, some warned, would end up with gay activists "retreating into themselves, staying at home, or in tranquil bars" (Soukup, 1990: 28). Discomfort with a Western-style subculture continued to resonate among former East German activists even after reunification. As Eduard Stapel (Starke, 1994: 106) observed in a 1994 interview, "At least we [gays and lesbians in the GDR] didn't build a ghetto ... where you get pumped full of loud music and anonymous and noncommittal sex." He insisted that "coming out doesn't happen through dancing ... neither personally nor socially."

During the year of the *Wende* and beyond, *Coming Out* became part of the broader conversation about *Lesben- und Schwulsein* in the GDR as activists sought to record their memories of the movement and scholars began to consider the significance of East German lesbian and gay life and politics. Almost invariably, activists cite the film as an important moment in the movement's history. Hubert Thinius (1995) dubbed the film *"Paul und Paul im Sozialismus,"* a reference to Carow's famous 1970s hit. A respondent in Kurt Starke's (1994: 146–147) study expressed the feelings of many gay East Germans, when he said "only through the film *Coming Out* – which up to now I've seen ten times – did I slowly gain self-confidence." In this way the film became an important component of the collective experience of a generation of gay East German men. On the other hand, the film's sparse portrayal of lesbians provoked a wave of criticism among female activists who linked it not only to the ongoing gender rifts within the movement but also to the longstanding invisibility of lesbians in German culture (Silge, 1991: 10–17).

Conclusion

The resonances between *Coming Out* and the grassroots network of East German "homosexual working groups" tell us much about a reformist moment in GDR history when East Germany's "sexual evolution" entered a lesbian and gay phase. It might be tempting to read the impulse in the GDR toward (homo)sexual liberalization as a state-driven effect of social engineering or Cold War positioning.

Historical evidence, however, suggests a far more complicated story that unfolded within officially prescribed limits but, in the end, became possible because of the regime's fundamental ambivalence toward homosexuality. Building on the hetero-sexual evolution of the 1960s and 1970s, the homosexual evolution of the 1980s involved the varied initiatives of sexually progressive doctors, social scientists, rights activists, and artists who worked to shift the official line toward greater sex-ual freedom. Heiner Carow, like East German lesbian and gay activists, remained part of a loyal opposition, equally committed to socialism and to reforming it from within. His vision of sexual freedom in the GDR captured the historical moment of the *Wende* when future possibilities seemed to multiply, at least for a short time. As Mary Fulbrook (1995: 16) reminds us, such reform-minded socialist dissent played a far more decisive – and unintentional – role in the demise of the GDR than did fundamental opponents of the regime. Perhaps, in this way, the premier of *Coming Out* on the same evening as the opening of the Berlin Wall should not seem so coincidental after all.

Notes

1   During the 1970s in particular, the West German government subsidized the artistic movement known as New German Cinema – of which von Praunheim's work was a part – with the goal of creating a state-legitimating "national cinema." Thomas Elsaesser (1989: 42–48) and John Davidson (1999: 8–12), among others, have pointed out the ways in which state subsidies had the paradoxical effect of allowing considera-ble airtime on West German television to forms of "self-expression" or "anti-imperialism" that were often quite radical. In this fashion, von Praunheim's work fits with other subsidized, but radical, critiques of West German society by such filmmak-ers as Rainer Werner Fassbinder and Helke Sander.

2   Cold War-era censorship was also part of the cinematic landscape of West Germany, although in forms different from those that existed in the East. Thomas Lindeberger's (2006) recent work provides an instructive comparative analysis of East and West German cinemas under Cold War conditions.

3   In dramatic contrast, officials in West Germany – under the auspices Family Minister Franz-Josef Wuermeling's sexually conservative and pronatalist *"Familienpolitik"* – renewed a virulent campaign to prosecute gay men during the 1950s and 1960s, result-ing in more than 100 000 cases with over 50 000 convictions between 1950 and 1965 (Sümke, 1989: 139–147; Moeller, 1994: 423–427).

4   West German officials decriminalized "mere" homosexual acts one year later in 1969. They rewrote paragraph 175 as a rather draconian and unequal age-of-consent law for male homosexuality.

5   In addition to the 1973 premiere of Rosa von Praunheim's *It Is Not the Homosexual Who Is Perverse* on West German television, there is evidence that contacts with West German gay rights activists at the 1973 World Festival of Youth and Students in East Berlin helped inspire the formation of the HIB (Grau, 1995: 125).

6   Charlotte von Mahlsdorf (Lothar Berfelde) and her published autobiography (von Mahlsdorf, 1995) have been the subject of considerable celebration and controversy since the 1990s. Among other things, she has been accused of being an informal Stasi agent during the mid-1970s. Her life has been the subject of a film, *I Am My Own Woman* (1992), by Rosa von Praunheim, as well as a Tony Award-winning play, *I Am My Own Wife* (2003), by American playwright Doug Wright.

7   Lesbian and gay activists in the GDR also invoked the symbolism of the concentration camp to reformulate a politically useful antifascism. In early 1984 a lesbian group from East Berlin repeatedly sought to place a commemorative wreath at the Ravensbrück concentration camp memorial to honor the lesbians murdered there by the Nazi regime. This highly symbolic action staged the quest for lesbian rights as an antifascist undertaking, in line with official ideology. Each time the activists returned, however, the wreath was missing and their group name had been erased from the guestbook. The strategy worked nonetheless – their actions led, in large part, to the creation of the "Interdisciplinary Working Group on Homophilia" at Humboldt University (Kenawi, 2008: 58–62).

References

Allan, S. and Sandford, J. (eds) (1999) *DEFA: East German Cinema, 1946–1992*, Berghahn, New York.

Amendt, G. (ed.) (1989) *Natürlich anders: zur Homosexualitätsdiskussion in der DDR*, Pahl-Rugenstein, Cologne.

Barck, S. (2003) "Ankunft im Real-Sozialismus" Anno 1970. Anmerkungen zu sozialen Irritationen und kulturellen Diffusionen am Beispiel der Bewegung Schreibender Arbeiter. *Potsdamer Bulletin*, 28/29, 60–72.

Berghahn, D. (2005) *Hollywood Behind the Wall: The Cinema of East Germany*, Manchester University Press, Manchester and New York.

Bessel, R. and Jessen, R. (eds) (1996) *Die Grenzen der Diktatur: Staat und Gesellschaft in der DDR*, Vandenhoeck & Ruprecht, Göttingen.

Blasius, M. and Phelan, S. (1997) *We Are Everywhere: A Historical Sourcebook of Gay and Lesbian Politics*, Routledge, New York.

Byg, B. (2002) Introduction: reassessing DEFA today. *AICGS Humanities Program Series*, 12, 1–23.

Carow, H. (1983) *Filmkunst, die alle angeht-Ausgewähltes-70er Jahre. Eine Dokumentation*, Aus Theorie und Praxis des Films, no. 3. Betriebsakademie des VEB DEFA Studio für Spielfilme, [East] Berlin.

Carow, H. (1989) Interview mit dem Regisseur. *Progress. Pressebulletin. Kino DDR* (November suppl.), 6–9.

Davidson, J. (1999) *Deterritorializing the New German Cinema*, University of Minnesota Press, Minneapolis and London.

Elsaesser, T. (1989) *New German Cinema: A History*, Rutgers University Press, New Brunswick, NJ.

Evans, J.V. (2005) The moral state: men, mining, and masculinity in the early GDR. *German History*, 23 (3), 355–370.

Feinstein, J. (2002) *The Triumph of the Ordinary: Depictions of Daily Life in the East German Cinema 1949–1989*, University of North Carolina Press, Chapel Hill.

Fulbrook, M. (1995) *Anatomy of a Dictatorship: Inside the GDR 1949–1989*, Oxford University Press, Oxford.

Geiss, A. (1997) *Repression und Freiheit. DEFA-Regisseure zwischen Fremd- und Selbstbestimmung*, Brandenburgische Landeszentrale für politische Bildung, Potsdam.

Giddens, A. (1994) *Beyond Left and Right: The Future of Radical Politics*, Blackwell, Cambridge.

Grau, G. (ed.) (1989) *Und diese Liebe auch. Theologische und sexualwissenschaftliche Einsichten zur Homosexualität*, Evangelische Verlagsanstalt, Berlin.

Grau, G. (1995) Sozialistische Moral und Homosexualität: Die Politik der SED und das Homosexuellenstrafrecht 1945 bis 1989 – ein Rückblick, in *Die Linke und das Laster: Schwule Emanzipation und linke Vorurteile* (ed. D. Grumbach), Männerschwarm, Hamburg, pp. 85–141.

Grumbach, D. (1995a) Die Linke und das Laster: Arbeiterbewegung und Homosexualität zwischen 1870 und 1933, in *Die Linke und das Laster: Schwule Emanzipation und linke Vorurteile* (ed. D. Grumbach), Männerschwarm, Hamburg, pp. 17–37.

Grumbach, D. (ed.) (1995b) *Die Linke und das Laster: Schwule Emanzipation und linke Vorurteile*, Männerschwarm, Hamburg.

Grumbach, D. and Grau, G. (1994) Die Stasi und die Schwulen. *Magnus*, 6 (2), 10–17.

Habermas, J. (1989) *The Structural Transformation of the Public Sphere: An Inquiry into a Category of Bourgeois Society* (trans. T. Burger and F. Lawrence), MIT Press, Cambridge, MA.

Hake, S. (2008) *German National Cinema*, 2nd edn. Routledge, London and New York.

Herek, G.M. (1990) The context of anti-gay violence: notes on cultural and psychological heterosexism. *Journal of Interpersonal Violence*, 5, 316–333.

Herzog, D. (2005) *Sex after Fascism: Memory and Morality in Twentieth-Century Germany*, Princeton University Press, Princeton, NJ, Oxford.

Herzog, D. (2008) East Germany's sexual evolution, in *Socialist Modern: East German Everyday Culture and Politics* (eds K. Pence and P. Betts), University of Michigan Press, Ann Arbor, pp. 71–95.

Jarausch, K.H. (1999) Care and coercion: the GDR as welfare dictatorship, in *Dictatorship as Experience: Towards a Socio-Cultural History of the GDR* (ed. K.H. Jarausch, trans. E. Duffy), Berghahn, New York, pp. 47–72.

Joppke, C. (1995) *East German Dissidents and the Revolution of 1989: Social Movement in a Leninist Regime*, New York University Press, New York.

Kenawi, S. (2008) Die Ersten werden die Letzten sein. Thesen zur Lesbenbewegung in der DDR. *Lesben und Schwule in der DDR. Tagungsdokumentation*, Heinrich-Böll-Stiftung Sachsen-Anhalt and LSVD Sachsen-Anhalt, Halle, Magdeburg, pp. 57–66.

Klötzer, S. (1999) "Volldampf Voraus?": Satire in der DDR. "Eulenspiegel" und "Kabarett am Obelisk" in den siebziger und achziger Jahren, In *Herrschaft und Eigen-Sinn in der Diktatur. Studien zur Gesellschaftsgeschichte der DDR* (ed. T. Lindenberger), Bohläu, Cologne, pp. 267–313.

Lemke, J. (1989) *Ganz normal anders. Auskünfte schwuler Männer*, Aufbau-Verlag, Berlin.

Leonhard, S.D. (1989) Testing the borders: East German film between individualism and social commitment, in *Post New Wave Cinema in the Soviet Union and Eastern Europe* (ed. D.J. Goulding), Indiana University Press, Bloomington, pp. 51–100.

Lindenberger, T. (1999) *Herrschaft und Eigen-Sinn in der Diktatur. Studien zur Gesellschaftsgeschichte der DDR*, Zeithistorische Studien, no. 12. Böhlau, Cologne.

Lindenberger, T. (2006) Looking West: the Cold War and the making of two German cinemas, in *Mass Media, Culture, and Society in Twentieth-Century Germany* (eds K.C. Führer and C. Ross), Palgrave Macmillan, New York, pp. 113–128.

Lüdtke, A. (1989) *Alltagsgeschichte. Zur Rekonstruktion historischer Erfahrungen und Lebensweisen*, Campus, Frankfurt, New York.

Mahlsdorf, C.v. (1995) *I Am My Own Wife: The True Story of Charlotte von Mahlsdorf* (trans. J. Hollander), Cleis, San Francisco.

Moeller, R.G. (1994) The homosexual man is a "man," the homosexual woman is a "woman": sex, society, and the law in postwar West Germany. *Journal of the History of Sexuality*, 4 (3), 395–429.

Mosse, G. (1985) *Nationalism and Sexuality: Respectability and Abnormal Sexuality in Modern Europe*, Howard Fertig, New York.

Pence, K. and Betts, P. (eds) (2008) *Socialist Modern: East German Everyday Culture and Politics*, University of Michigan Press, Ann Arbor.

Pharr, S. (1997) *Homophobia: A Weapon of Sexism*, Chardon, Berkeley.

Poss, I. and Warnecke, P. (eds) (2006) *Spur der Filme. Zeitungen über die DEFA*, Christoph Links, Berlin.

Reich, W. (1946) *The Mass Psychology of Fascism*, 1933 (trans. T.P. Wolfe), Orgone Institute Press, New York.

Richthofen, E.v. (2009) *Bringing Culture to the Masses: Control, Compromise, and Participation in the GDR*, Berghahn, New York, Oxford.

Roberts, B.M. (2007) Heikle Fagen. DDR-Sexualpädagogik und der DEFA-Aufklärungsfilm, in *Die Imaginierte Nation. Identität, Körper und Geschlect in DEFA-Filmen* (ed. B. Mathes), DEFA-Stiftung, Berlin, pp. 110–144.

Ross, C. (2002) *The East German Dictatorship: Problems and Perspectives in the Interpretation of the GDR*, Arnold, London.

Schenk, C. (2008) Die Partei(en) in der DDR. Ihre Politik und ihre Ideologie(n) im Blick auf lesbische Lebenswelten, in *Lesben und Schwule in der DDR. Tagungsdokumentation*. Heinrich-Böll-Stiftung Sachsen-Anhalt and LSVD Sachsen-Anhalt, Halle, Magdeburg, pp. 35–56.

Schenk, R. (ed.) (1994) *Das zweite Leben der Filmstadt Babelsberg DEFA-Spielfilme 1946–1992*, Henschel Verlag, Berlin.

Schittly, D. (2002) *Zwischen Regie und Regime. Die Filmpolitik der SED im Spiegel der DEFA-Produktionen*, Christoph Links, Berlin.

Schroeder, K. (1998) *Der SED-Staat. Partei, Staat und Gesellschaft 1949–1990*, Carl Hanser, Munich, Vienna.

Sieg, K. (2007) Homosexualität und Dissidenz. Zur Freiheit der Liebe in *Coming Out* von Heiner Carow, in *Die Imaginierte Nation. Identität, Körper und Geschlect in DEFA-Filmen* (ed. B. Mathes), DEFA-Stiftung, Berlin, pp. 284–311.

Silge, U. (1991) *Un-sichtbare Frauen: Lesben und ihre Emanzipation in der DDR*, Christoph Links Verlag, Berlin.

Soukup, J.J. (ed.) (1990) *Die DDR. Die Schwulen. Der Aufbruch: Versuch einer Bestandsaufnahme*, Schriftenreihe des Waldschlößchens, Göttingen.

Stapel, E. (1999) *Warme Brüder gegen Kalte Krieger. Die DDR-Schwulenbewegung im Visier des Ministeriums für Staatssicherheit*, Landesbeauftragte für die Unterlagen des Staatssicherheitsdienstes der ehemaligen DDR Sachsen-Anhalt, Magdeburg.

Stapel, E. (2008) Warme Brüder gegen Kalte Krieger. Die DDR-Schwulenbewegung im Visier des Ministeriums für Staatssicherheit. In: *Lesben und Schwule in der DDR*.

Tagungsdokumentation, Heinrich-Böll-Stiftung Sachsen-Anhalt and LSVD Sachsen-Anhalt, Halle, Magdeburg, pp. 99–108.

Starke, K. (1994) *Schwuler Osten: Homosexuelle Männer in der DDR*, Christoph Links Verlag, Berlin.

Starke, K. and Friedrich, W. (1984) *Liebe und Sexualität bis 30*, Deutscher Verlag der Wissenschaften, (East) Berlin.

Stott, R. (1999) "Letting the Genie out of the Bottle": DEFA Film-makers and *Film und Fernsehen*, in *DEFA: East German Cinema, 1946–1992* (eds S. Allen and J. Sandford), Berghahn, New York, pp. 42–57.

Stümke, H-G. (1989) *Homosexuelle in Deutschland. Eine politische Geschichte*, Beck, Munich.

Sweet, D.M. (1995) The Church, the Stasi, and socialist integration: three stages of lesbian and gay emancipation in the former German Democratic Republic. *Journal of Homosexuality*, 29 (4), 351–367.

Sweet, D.M. (1997) Bodies for Germany, bodies for socialism: the German Democratic Republic devises a gay (male) body, in *Gender and Germanness: Cultural Productions of Nation* (eds P. Herminghouse and M. Mueller), Berghahn, Providence, RI, pp. 248–262.

Sweet, D.M. (1998) Die DEFA und ihre "Anderen": Heiner Carow's "Coming Out" als Coming Out den "Anderen." *Film und Fernsehen*, 1, 42–47.

Thinius, B. (1994) *Aufbruch aus dem grauen Versteck. Ankunft im bunten Ghetto? Randglossen zu Erfahrungen schwuler Männer aus der DDR und Deutschland Ost*, Bundesverband Homosexualität, Berlin.

Thinius, B. (1995) Paul und Paul im Sozialismus. *Mitteilungen aus der kulturwissenschaftlichen Forschung*, 36, 143–169.

Torpey, J.C. (1995) *Intellectuals, Socialism and Dissent: The East German Opposition and Its Legacy*, Contradictions in Modernity, no. 4. University of Minnesota Press, Minneapolis.

Werner, R. (1987) *Homosexualität. Herausforderung an Wissen und Toleranz*, VEB Verlag Volk und Gesundheit, Berlin.

Zinn, A. (1995) "Die Bewegung der Homosexuellen:" Die soziale Konstruktion des homosexuellen Nationalsozialisten im antifaschistischen Exil, in *Die Linke und das Laster: Schwule Emanzipation und linke Vorurteile* (ed. D. Grumbach), Männerschwarm, Hamburg, pp. 38–84.

Further Reading

During the past two decades East German history has been the subject of vigorous and, at times, heated public debate. Corey Ross's (2002) thorough historiographical survey sketches and evaluates the major scholarly debates concerning the GDR. For a shorter introduction to historiography that concerns the debate about the nature of the SED-regime in particular see Konrad Jarausch (1999). One major drawback to these broad surveys is their relative lack of attention to cultural history. For those interested in GDR culture, a good place to start would be the fine collection of articles edited by Katherine Pence and Paul Betts (2008) or, for film history in particular, Joshua Feinstein's (2002) compelling monograph. Other essential historical surveys of DEFA include the Filmmuseum Potsdam's classic historical overview edited by Ralf Schenk (1994) and Darmar Schittly's

(2002) helpful monograph on DEFA film policy. Recent work has also written DEFA history in transnationally (Lindenberger, 2006) or chronologically (Hake, 2008) comparative frameworks. Scholarship on sexuality in the GDR, particularly on same-sex sexuality, is still in its infancy. Jennifer Evans's (2005) piece on masculinity, morality, and miners in the GDR, and Dagmar Herzog's (2008) article on East Germany's "sexual evolution" provide a welcome introduction to the literature that exists so far. The history of the lesbian and gay movement in the GDR has been written almost entirely by "insiders." Major works in this category include Ursula Silge (1991), Bert Thinius (1994), Günter Grau (1995), and Eduard Stapel (1999). Published documents pertaining to the movement may be found in these histories and also in Amendt (1989), Starke (1994), and especially in Soukup (1990). Aside from *The Legend of Paul and Paula* (1973), Heiner Carow's life and work have remained relatively unexplored. Additional scholarly film criticism of *Coming Out* can be found in Denis Sweet (1997, 1998) and Katrin Sieg (2007). Carow's (1983) collection of interviews remains one of the best published sources for his views on socialist cinema.

Filmography

Coming Out (Heiner Carow, East Germany, 1989).

I Am My Own Woman [*Ich bin meine eigene Frau*] (Rosa von Praunheim, West Germany, 1992).

Legend of Paul and Paula, The [*Die Legende von Paul und Paula*] (Heiner Carow, East Germany, 1973).

It Is Not the Homosexual Who Is Perverse, but the Society in Which He Lives [*Nicht der Homosexuelle ist pervers, sondern die Situation in der er lebt*] (Rosa von Praunheim, West Germany, 1971).

Other Love, The [*Die andere Liebe*] (Helmut Kissling and Axel Otten, East Germany, 1989).

Russians Are Coming, The [*Die Russen kommen*] (Heiner Carow, East Germany, 1968 (1988)).

3

German Identity, Myth, and Documentary Film

Julia Knight

In 1991 the Goethe-Institute toured a package of films made during the year or so following the opening of the Berlin Wall. It included five documentaries which form the focus of this chapter: *November Days* (Marcel Ophus, 1990), *In the Splendour of Happiness* (Johann Feindt and Helga Reidemeister, 1990), *Locked Up Time* (Sibylle Schönemann, 1990), *Last Year in Germany* (Lars Barthel *et al.*, 1990) and *Last Year – Titanic* (Andreas Voigt, 1991). All five films undertook an exploration of East Germany in light of the recent opening of its border with West Germany. They are informed either by the realization that what was happening during 1989–1990 was history in the making, as it were, and should therefore be documented as it happened and/or by the desire to examine what had happened in order to establish causes and responsibility. All the filmmakers are German (East, West or expatriate), but come from a range of different backgrounds. Although there are points of similarity between some of these films, they differ in terms of style, approach, choice of interviewees, emphasis and conditions of production.

In his introduction to the touring package which included these films Ulrich Gregor (1991) observed that: "One must recognize [them] as having the quality of historical documents [...] There is hardly a precedent for the German cinema being so close to reality." This chapter argues that the films are indeed historical documents – not because they were "so close to reality," but because they articulate a very particular and historically specific German identity. However, paradoxically, they did so at a moment when time and again commentators both in and outside Germany suggested that, given the dramatic and rapid changes sweeping across the country, Germans had *no* clear sense of national identity. This view was exemplified for instance in the very title of Alan Watson's 1992 book and accompanying Channel 4 documentary series: *The Germans – Who Are They Now?*

A Companion to German Cinema, First Edition. Edited by Terri Ginsberg and Andrea Mensch.
© 2012 Blackwell Publishing Ltd. Published 2012 by Blackwell Publishing Ltd.

When the East German government opened the Berlin Wall on November 9, 1989, it allowed German Democratic Republic (GDR) citizens to come and go at will for the first time in the 28 years of the Wall's existence. Given the momentous nature of this occasion it was greeted at the time almost universally as cause for celebration. Once the celebrations were over, however, a realization that no one knew anything for certain quickly replaced the initial elation. As a Swiss journalist working in West Germany observed: "No-one can foresee what relations will prevail here in two, five or ten years' time. No one knew ten, five or even two weeks ago that the Federal Republic would look the way it looks now" (Weck, 1989: 3). Such uncertainty, compounded by the subsequent collapse of the Sozialistische Einheitspartei Deutschlands (SED) regime, invited speculation about the future of the two Germanies. While economic and political concerns tended to predominate initially, the possibility of redrawing national boundaries inevitably raised questions about national identity and generated an extensive public debate about what it meant to be German.

Although – as will be discussed below – commentators advanced a range of ideas in response to that question, the debate is more remarkable for the way in which it highlighted the fundamental *instability* of national identity. As Etienne Balibar (1991: 94) has observed, identity may be individual but is always formed within the wider sociohistorical context. The possibility of a specifically *national* identity is a relatively recent phenomenon, made possible in Europe – as Balibar, Benedict Anderson (1991), Ernest Gellner (1983) and others have demonstrated – with the emergence of the nation-state and spread of nationalism in the eighteenth century which changed the previously dominant ways of thinking. However, since nation-states – their political regimes, the makeup of their populations, together with their languages and territorial boundaries – do not remain static for all time, any sense of national identity will necessarily also change over time. Just as importantly – and perhaps more so – at any one time, any nation-state invariably encompasses different social and ethnic groups,[1] and as Balibar (1991) explains that difference and diversity has to be "relativized" if "a people" are to develop a unified sense of national belonging.

Thus national identity is not an essence and has instead to be constructed. Given the historically changing and diverse nature of lived experience, academic work on national, European and cultural identity has argued that such identity is, as Colin McArthur (1984: 55) has expressed it, "a *process* rather than an *essence*, a process which has constantly to be reworked and restated." As Hans Joachim Meurer (2000: 52–55) has demonstrated in the context of his discussion of cinema and national identity in a divided Germany, theorists have employed a range of approaches – including psychological, sociological, and philosophical – to examine the precise nature of that process. Although it is evident that many things can contribute to the process – including, for instance, "the political struggle for power" (Meurer, 2000: 52) – this chapter will draw on the approach exemplified by McArthur, which suggests that, with the invention of cinema and television, audiovisual culture now also plays a crucial role in it. Hence it is unsurprising that the five documentaries listed above can be viewed as articulating German identity. However, the fact that they can be viewed in this way conflicts with the contemporaneous public debate, which suggested that Germans *lacked* a clear sense of national identity. The chapter starts therefore by exploring this apparent paradox. To do so, in contrast to Meurer's (2000: 55–59) tracing of the process of German identity formation over time and in relation to changing historical conditions, this chapter looks at the process in operation at a particular point in time in relation to a particular historical context. It does so by employing the concept of myth and then, building on that discussion, goes on to undertake a textual analysis of each film to demonstrate the way in which each can be viewed as articulating German identity.

The Question of German Identity

According to Philippe Lacoue-Labarthe and Jean-Luc Nancy (1990: 26), for the Germans there has in fact always been "a problem of identity." However, in the period immediately following the opening of the Berlin Wall that problem and the issue of what constituted German identity became the subject of a particularly extensive public debate. In 1991 Andreas Huyssen (1991: 142), for instance, asserted that "postwar Germans East or West have no emphatic sense of national identity, nor are they likely to develop it soon," and in one form or another, this view was widely expressed by commentators both in and outside Germany. It stemmed in part from a belief that the political and economic reality of forty years of a divided Germany had in turn impeded the development of "a truly national identity" (Bohrer, 1991: 80). According to Jürgen Habermas (1991: 86), for instance, coping in the West with the realities of the postwar situation led to the Federal Republic's economic achievements becoming a substitute for a sense of national identity, while the East German dramatist Heiner Müller asserted that for East Germans the experience of living under two dictatorships lasting over fifty years resulted in "the neurosis of an entire generation" (Bohrer, 1990: 184). Taking a wider view, Karl Heinz Bohrer (1991: 79–80) maintained that not only division, but the loss of former territories in 1945 and a deep-seated desire to forget the "shameful" Nazi past, produced a general loss of memory in both German states which precipitated a collective identity crisis. For others, however – such as the filmmaker Marcel Ophuls (e.g. Jeffries, 2004) – the memory of the Holocaust in itself meant that "an easy, unbroken sense of national identity will never again be granted to the Germans" (Zimmer, 1990: 68).

As Huyssen seemed to imply and others explicitly argued, the suddenness and speed with which the events of 1989–1990 unfolded made it seem unlikely that the Germans would be able to resolve their national "identity crisis" in the near future. A poll taken in East Berlin in July 1990 reported that less than half of East Germans felt themselves to be "German" and concluded that it would take them at least a decade "to find a new identity in a new Germany" (Evans, 1991: 20). For some even this was optimistic, suggesting it would take at least a generation for East and West Germans to "melt" together (Unger, 1991: 72–73). And still others suggested that the haste with which unity was being pursued would produce its opposite: long-term practical and psychological chaos (Leicht, 1990; Grass, 1991).

This is not to suggest, as already noted above, that national identity is something which can be "granted" or simply "found." Nor is it to suggest that these commentators, intellectuals, and analysts all shared the same political views; Bohrer (1990, 1991), for instance, argued that unification would "remedy" rather than compound the identity crisis. Rather it is to highlight the fact that when the subject of national identity was discussed – in whatever manner – there appeared to be no clear idea of what was meant by the term "German." It very quickly became apparent that it meant different things to different people, and commentators frequently felt the need to qualify the term, as Huyssen did: "postwar Germans *East or West*" (my emphasis).

According to Duncan Petrie (1992: 1), however, it is precisely at times of upheaval, transition, and uncertainty that "the search for identity and belonging becomes increasingly pertinent." And implicit in the various observations about the Germans' lack of any clear sense of national identity is precisely the assumption that there *should* be that sense of identity. The notion that national identity is something that can be lost and subsequently found suggests that it is a preexisting entity. Yet, as already observed, this is not the case. It is more accurate to conceptualize national (as well as cultural) identity as a *process*, constantly performed in the present – indeed it is possible to argue that it never actually *becomes*, but is always on the point of *just* becoming (McArthur, 1984; Bhabha, 1990; Petrie, 1992). Drawing on the work of "Third World" and postcolonial theorists Homi Bhabha and Frantz Fanon, John Caughie (1992) utilized this idea of "identity as a process" to shed light on the concern with European identity that emerged at the beginning of the 1990s – precisely in the wake of the collapse of East Germany and other Soviet-supported regimes, along with the push toward greater economic and political integration with the West. He asserts,

> The *"just"* refers to the liminality of a national culture, to its place on the threshold of enunciation, its shape sensed but never grasped in a single gesture, an identity which always seems about to be but never is, never achieves the stability which can be looked back on. (1992: 36)

Any sense of national identity is therefore illusory – it is only the *aspiration* to stability – and conceals a lived reality of "instability." Consequently, as Caughie goes on to argue,

> In order to represent itself as national culture instability has to misrecognize itself as stable, collective and representative; but that necessary misrecognition, the political

and intellectual will towards identity and unity, is always destabilized by the recognition and the experience of difference and diversity.

This ongoing cycle of misrecognition–destabilization–misrecognition is the historical process that produces a sense of national identity. (1992: 36)

If this is the case, it is possible to suggest that the events of 1989–1990 made Germans extremely conscious of the lived reality of instability and the social experience of difference and diversity. Any aspiration to stability could not at the time misrecognize instability sufficiently enough to produce the illusion of a stable, collective and representative national identity – hence producing the perception that Germans had no clear sense of what it means to be "German." But this does not mean that they lacked *any* sense of German identity. The process – "the search for identity and belonging" – nonetheless continued. Indeed, apropos of Petrie's argument, the collapse of the SED, the ensuing uncertainty about Germany's future, and the subsequent disappointments of unification served to fuel a search for identity and belonging.

If we accept the above analysis, the public debate surrounding the 1989–1990 events can be viewed as part of the process by which national identity is (re)constructed. But, unable to allow the misrecognition of instability needed to produce an illusory *unified* identity, those events instead led ironically to a foregrounding of post-Wall social reality, which in turn highlighted *a number* of often conflicting ideas about what it means to be "German."

As the possibility of unification became a concrete reality, several commentators, for instance, referenced the Nazi past and the political problems bequeathed by Bismarck to suggest that German unity "must always from the outset be politically poisonous" (Bohrer, 1991: 77; see also: Miller, 1990; Watson, 1992). Such a past, combined with the dramatic growth in unemployment that rapid monetary union was likely to precipitate, and the East Germans' lack of experience of participating in a political democracy, aroused fears that unification would permit the reemergence of German fascism (Grass, 1991; Hirsch, 1990). Moreover, for the Jewish community the Holocaust meant that the Germans had lost any right to exist as a unified nation-state. While commentators differed on the cause of the Wall – some argued it was World War Two, others the Cold War, while Watson (1992: 39–40) argued it could even be traced back to World War One – the division of Germany into two states was seen as their punishment for the Nazi atrocities and acceptance of it a sign of their penitence. Thus the Wall had become a highly potent symbol, and its dismantling almost unthinkable (Gilman, 1991).

At the same time there was also a broad perception that unification was the "logical" or "natural" course for the future. For some, the only reason for a separate East German state had been socialism – with its collapse there was no need for two capitalist German states (Heym, 1989). Others argued that a shared culture draws and binds the German people together, making it possible to speak of a German "cultural nation" which would always transcend any political boundaries that attempted to divide them. Günter de Bruyn, for instance, declared,

I had relatives, friends and readers in both parts of Germany; my life-long interest in German history and literature constantly showed me the artificiality of the border line drawn in 1945, and whenever I was able to make comparisons on journeys, I found the correctness of the concept verified by inspection: the mutual similarities of the two states thought to be so different were always popping up from under the surface. (1991: 60)

However, some observers drew upon history to assert that a German *national* identity was anything but "natural." Although a historical precedent existed for a single unified German nation-state, it spanned only a matter of decades (Walser, 1988; Bruyn, 1991). For the greater part of German history, there have been a number of German states and, if anything, the Germans have always been divided by marked regional identities. Bruyn (1991: 64), for instance, argued that the historical evidence clearly indicated unification was not a wise choice. Although federalism has in fact not been without its own perceived problems, he asserted that "the happiest times were not characterized by nation-state centralism ... but rather by a highly developed federalism."

Furthermore, 40 years of division and the experience of very different political regimes had produced undeniable differences. For instance, despite the initial rush to embrace "westernization," a high percentage of East Germans still wanted the two East German television channels (DDR 1 and 2) to continue. When it was decided to merge the two channels, the East German broadcaster was surprised at the number of complaints they received from the East Germans (Nowell-Smith and Wollen, 1991: 50). While a number of intellectuals and political activists also argued the possibility of resisting Western capitalism and pursuing a so-called "third path" of democratic socialism, time and again the idea of "difference" was articulated in the romantic notion of the former GDR as a blissful idyll, safely removed and protected from the noise, pace and pressures of the modern industrialized West. Although Eastern Europe was usually associated with a lack of political freedom, Martin Ahrends (1991: 42) argued that living in the East offered another kind of freedom: "To wait, to dream, to be allowed to daydream time away. That is, that was, the freedom of the East." For West German visitors it represented "a romantic Germany, long since lost in the West" (Bohrer, 1991: 75) and was frequently noted for the "human warmth and belonging that supposedly obtain there" (Bruyn, 1991: 63). It is as if there was a desire to preserve the former GDR as a separate state *precisely because* it represented a completely different way of life.[2]

In complete contrast, however, according to Frank Unger (1991) there was a prevalent perception of East Germans as second-class citizens in relation to their West German counterparts. He does not identify the basis of such a perception, but in the immediate wake of unification he observed: "My impressions, distilled from countless conversations with East Germans ... is this: that no matter how much life has changed for them, no matter how much harder and more insecure it will be, they enjoy being elevated to the status of 'real Germans'" (Unger, 1991: 72). In this connection, it is impossible to ignore the fact that a significant element of Germany's social experience was (and still is) its substantial "immigrant" population, resulting from the recruitment of *Gastarbeiter* from countries such as Turkey, Morocco, Greece, and Italy during the 1950s and 1960s. Many of these workers put down permanent roots in West Germany, raising families there, but have frequently been subject to racist attacks because of their perceived "outsider" status marked largely by racial and religious difference. Thus Unger went on to suggest that, for many East Germans, becoming "real Germans" was also akin to becoming "white Germans" – instead, that is, of remaining "mere" workers, subjugated like the *Gastarbeiter* had been, in the newly reunified State. Günter Grass (1991), Habermas (1991) and others have in fact argued that, rather than the two former Germanies unifying, West Germany simply annexed or colonized East Germany. Their assertion has some validity, since the West German Basic Law, under article 146, allowed for the founding of an entirely new German state, but the five East German *Länder* instead simply acceded to the Federal Republic via article 23.[3]

At the same time, parallels were also drawn between the GDR and Nazi Germany. Both were politically repressive regimes and prompted similar questions: "What had been the moral duty of the individual in a dictatorship? Did silence equal support?" (Brockmann, 1991: 27). Reflecting on the imprisonment of Erich Honecker and former Minister for State Security Erich Mielke, Daniela Dahn (1991: 58) also noted another similarity: "To bring to trial an entire leadership elite – the only previous example of that was in Nuremberg."

Although not an exhaustive exploration of what it has meant to be "German," the above is nevertheless a representative selection of the ideas that dominated public debate around the 1989–1990 events. Unsurprisingly, some of these ideas were hotly contested. Bohrer, for instance, reexamined Bismarck's Reich in an attempt to disprove the contention that German unity would necessarily be "politically poisonous" (1991: 76–77), while others asserted that the GDR's corruption, mismanagement and temporary imprisonment of political dissidents bore no comparison to the acute racism, systematic genocide, and military aggression of Nazism (Dahn, 1991; Christy, 1993) or aspects of its persistence in either of the ostensibly "denazified" Germanies. It is obviously necessary not to simply accept the ideas at face value – they are a range of viewpoints, reflections, and arguments offered from a range of perspectives – but it is equally necessary to address their existence. As is evident, they are not discrete, but form a series of intermeshing and competing ideas, which can be most productively discussed as a series of contemporaneous myths.

National Identity as Mythic Narrative

In studying nonliterate tribal societies, anthropologists have noted that the stories those communities designate as myths are taken very seriously and often considered "true" in some way. The narrative details may be obviously fictitious to the outsider, but "realism" is not the issue – rather it is the fact that any story termed "myth" is perceived to be dealing in some way with something that is relevant and important to the community or society that has produced it.[4] After spending years studying the Trobriand Islanders, for instance, Bronislaw Malinowski (1974: 101) maintained that myth "expresses, enhances, and codifies belief; it safeguards and enforces morality; it vouches for the efficiency of ritual and contains practical rules for the guidance of man" and as such "is not an idle tale, but a hard-worked active force." Heavily influenced by structural linguistics and based on his studies of various Amer-Indian tribes, Claude Lévi-Strauss (1972, 1978) asserted that myth functions either to overcome a contradiction that exists within the society that produces it, or to reconcile members of that society to it. Although formulations differ – in fact there is little agreement on the *precise* nature and function of myth – the work of such anthropologists has been borrowed by other disciplines and applied to the study of cultural products and practices in modern technological and pluralist societies (e.g. Barthes, 1973; Jung, 1978; McConnell, 1979; Schatz, 1981; Hobsbawm and Ranger, 1983; Fiske, 1990; Lacoue-Labarthe and Nancy, 1990; Hill, 1993). Indeed, historians (Samuel and Thompson, 1990) and others, such as Roland Barthes (1973), have suggested that it's not just stories that can perform the function of myth – whether via oral storytelling, novels, or cinema and television fictions – but a whole range of practices, including rituals, ceremonial occasions, social customs, family and social relationships, oral history, social movements and religion, as well as images, fantasies, fears, emotions, and psychological attitudes. This work is in some cases concerned with how societies have developed, but it is also centrally concerned with examining the *existence* of myth in those societies at any given time and the role it plays. Although specific perspectives and applications vary, broadly speaking, in this context, "myth" has been defined as any means by which a society in some way makes sense of, organizes, understands, or comes to terms with itself: it is effectively a society talking to itself about itself (O'Sullivan *et al.*, 1994: 192). While societies may evolve and change, myth will always play a crucial role in articulating and shaping that society's self-identity, and therefore the concept is certainly appropriate to any discussion of *national* identity.

The concept of myth also embodies the idea of a historical process that is so central to the work of Bhabha, Fanon, Caughie, and others on national identity. Myths circulate through repetition, through being continually "retold" – this is precisely how they fulfill their role. Any myth will only be retold for as long as it is relevant to the society that produces it: its relevance perpetuates it. Thus no myth is eternal, fixed for all time, but is instead historically specific and exists in a dynamic relationship to the society which produces it. Consequently myths will change, disappear, and resurface as that society's needs or values change over time.[5] Any single myth will only exist *as myth* while it is in active circulation. Or as Lévi-Strauss (1972: 229) expressed it, "myth grows spiral-wise until the intellectual impulse which has produced it is exhausted." So, myth, like national identity, is a historical process, being performed repeatedly through time. Rather than "myth" being merely appropriate to a discussion of national identity, this suggests that the articulation of national identity can be viewed as a form of mythic narrative.

Finally, the concept of myth also permits a consideration of the *series* of intermeshing and competing ideas of German identity discussed above. As John Fiske (1990: 90) has observed: "no myths are universal in a culture. There are dominant myths, but there are also counter-myths." To use Lévi-Strauss's terminology, a number of "intellectual impulses" addressing a particular concern or issue will coexist at any one time. It's possible to argue, for instance, that in contemporary culture, there are a number of myths in circulation concerning the benefits or otherwise of digital technology. This means that, by viewing national identity as a form of mythic narrative, we can acknowledge that there will always be a series of identities which exist in dynamic relationships to one another and to the society that produces them. Any sense of a single, representative identity would stem from the dominance of one particular myth.

Thus, the series of intermeshing and competing ideas about what it has meant to be "German" can be conceptualized as a series of contemporaneous myths. Although in terms of lived experience, Germany's *Gastarbeiter* population provides a complicating factor, broadly speaking, the myths that have dominated the public debate around the events of 1989–1990 articulate a range of ideas around the fundamental question of German unity versus East–West difference which had been brought to the fore by the possibility of redrawing national boundaries. Either *all* Germans share a common bond or belong together in some way – be that through their alleged predisposition toward authoritarian rule, a purportedly shared cultural heritage or economic logic – or important differences exist – whether expressed in terms of differing regional identities, differing social status, via the "demonization" of the GDR or by its idealization as a "protected" idyll.

The exuberant nature of the celebrations surrounding the opening of the Wall, the East Germans swapping of their chant of "We are the people" for "We are one people" (Maron, 1991), the speed with which then-Chancellor Helmut Kohl put forward his ten-point plan for reunification, and the haste with which unification was implemented all helped perpetuate a myth of German unity. However, the myth of East–West difference was also well represented in the public sphere, and is in fact privileged in the five documentaries noted above. Although documentary filmmaking is popularly thought of as a form of *factual* program-making, the following discussion of those films will not be directly concerned with establishing the accuracy, veracity or authenticity of the viewpoints expressed in and by the documentaries. By undertaking a textual analysis of each film – analyzing the materials used and their arrangement within the work – the intention is rather to demonstrate that a process of "narrative shaping" has occurred which not only articulates the idea of general difference and diversity among Germans as opposed to German unity, but also privileges – albeit in different ways – a specific myth of East–West difference which implicitly favors Western ideological perspectives on German nationhood through a generalized "othering" of the GDR.

East–West Difference in Documentary Film

November Days – Voices and Choices

Commissioned by the BBC in conjunction with a West German producer, *November Days – Voices and Choices* was directed by Marcel Ophuls. Ophuls is well-known, both as the son of Jewish film director Max Ophuls, who fled Nazi Germany for France in 1933, and as a documentary filmmaker who has addressed recent German history in a number of films, with *Hotel Terminus* (1985–1988), about Klaus Barbie, winning him the Academy Award for Best Documentary Feature in 1988. Like many of his films, *November Days* is a collection of interviews interspersed with archival footage, and has Ophuls frequently appearing onscreen as the interviewer. The interviews are with a number of East German public figures – including Egon Krenz (former Communist Party General Secretary and a former Head of Security Police), Günter Schabowski (former Communist Party leader), the playwright Heiner Müller, the writer Stefan Hermlin, the former Stasi general Markus Wolf, and Barbara Brecht-Schall (daughter of Marxist playwright Bertolt Brecht) – party officials and East German citizens. In the months following the fall of the Berlin Wall but prior to unification, Ophuls asks his interviewees about the ways in which the politicians had handled the demonstrations and mounting unrest in East Germany in October–November 1989, their feelings about Erich Honecker and the former SED regime, about the Wall, antisemitism and freedom. The interviews are filmed in a variety of settings, but invariably include shots of Ophuls asking questions and reacting to his interviewees' answers.

The opening section of the film includes a compilation of television news footage shot on the evening of November 9, 1989 showing the reactions of people as they witness the opening of the Wall. The general atmosphere is joyous and celebratory, and those persons questioned by reporters repeatedly refer to the event as both "wonderful" and "beautiful." This is intercut with newsreel footage of celebrations at the end of World War Two showing women hugging sailors and troops. Such juxtaposing seems to suggest that, just as the end of the war returned men to their loved ones, so the opening of the Wall brought families back together, implying a parallel between Nazism and SED rule – an unavoidable one given that both historical moments marked the end of politically repressive regimes in Germany. Thus the film begins with an apparent representation of the Wall as something which had denied people their freedom, and its opening as something greeted overwhelmingly as cause for joy. This way of viewing the events is made more explicit at the end of the opening section with the inclusion of press announcements by British politicians Margaret Thatcher (Conservative) and Neil Kinnock (Labor) giving their responses to the event. Kinnock expresses interest only in the future plans of the GDR politicians, while Thatcher describes her reactions to watching the news coverage: "You see the joy on people's faces and you see what freedom means to them. It makes you realize that you can't stifle or suppress people's desire for liberty." When Ophuls asks Krenz which politician judged the historical moment most accurately, he asserts it was Thatcher.

However, Ophuls's filmmaking style has frequently been noted for its ironic juxtaposing of material to create a montage which exposes contradictions and fosters a critique of popularly held notions.[6] Even in the opening section discussed above, Ophuls includes interview footage which starts to undermine Krenz's endorsement of Thatcher's view and the perception that the opening of the Wall reunited people. An East German couple, for instance, explains how it in fact made them feel "scared" and "insecure," while in another case it split up a marriage because the husband moved to the West while the wife chose to remain in the East. Thus the film quickly starts to "destabilize" any sense of a unified German identity around the fall of the Wall, and to acknowledge the reality of lived experience and the diversity of social perspectives regarding it.

As the film develops, this technique is repeatedly employed – particularly highlighting the differing or contradictory viewpoints of the interviewees – to cast the former SED regime in an unfavorable light. For instance, Ophuls talks to party official Herr Ludwig, who made a speech at a political rally the weekend following the opening of the Wall. Ludwig claims he was "told" to make the speech and that Krenz helped him write it, while Krenz asserts that he may have "advised" but had no time to write other people's speeches. On another occasion, Stefan Hermlin describes Honecker as a "good, warm human being," while a woman on the street asks: "Has [Honecker] cared about the sick these last 40 years? He didn't consider anybody." This also creates some very humorous moments by appearing to "expose" the shaky foundations of the SED regime: those who were supposed to be united in the socialist struggle seem unable to agree on anything! On occasion, the film also suggests that an interviewee is lying, as when Ophuls asks Barbara Brecht-Schall if she was personally acquainted with Honecker. She maintains she met him only twice to request help for the Brecht Archive. After her assertion is contradicted by Heiner Müller, who suggests her work with the Berlin Ensemble would have brought her into close contact with the ex-leader, we are shown archival footage of her seated next to Honecker in the East Berlin theater.

In this context the archival footage functions as a form of critical commentary, with the material guiding us toward a particular conclusion. In this instance, it purports to reveal the "truth," but on other occasions extraneous material is included primarily for humorous effect, and it is precisely the humor which undermines any possible veracity of the interviewees' comments. For instance, the retired Stasi General Markus Wolf attempts to distance himself from repressive measures taken against political dissidents, maintaining he was only involved in intelligence and did not cause a single death. Wolf refers to himself as naive and says, "that may make you laugh," at which point a montage of people laughing is inserted. The montage contains a clip from Ernst Lubitsch's film, *To Be Or Not To Be* (USA, 1942), followed by shots of Schabowski and Krenz. Given that the

Lubitsch film revolves around the idea of impersonation, and the fact that one might reasonably expect two senior GDR politicians to have known the extent of Wolf's activities, the montage is not only humorous but highly pointed.

This critical perspective is frequently reinforced by Ophuls's interviewing style. For example, after showing footage of Communist Party member Herr Golle attending an SED rally, Ophuls asks Golle: "Were you ordered to attend the demonstration that evening?" The nature of the question seems to presuppose that the SED regime was totalitarian. On several occasions, Ophuls also makes explicit the parallel implied in the opening section between Nazism and the SED regime. For instance, when party member Thomas Montag describes how the state security police would arrest political dissidents during the night, Ophuls inquires, "As in the Third Reich?" And during the Markus Wolf interview, Ophuls says Wolf's assertion reminds him of Klaus Barbie's defense in Lyon. Thus, while the film challenges popular assumptions about what the opening of the Wall has meant for the average East German citizen-worker, its textual strategies also construct a generally unfavorable, rather one-dimensional representation of the former GDR, effectively repositioning it as the "enemy" of the West.

Indeed the film tends to link the notion of "freedom" with Western political concepts while downplaying the economic constraints they entail – and which the GDR, at least ideally, tried to rectify. This is implicit in the opening section, with its representation of the Wall as something which denied East Germans freedom of movement, alongside its concomitant questioning of the overwhelmingly joyous response to its opening. As one East German citizen explicitly states: "A bird can fly where wings will take him. But not us!" But the connection is also made through Ophuls's presence in the film. As a Jew who fled Nazi Germany, his opposition to fascism is in a sense public knowledge, and he has continued to live and work in the West. Although Ophuls states in the film that he favors social democratic forms of government, after interviewing Markus Wolf, he observes,

> Listening to you, I think … Marcel, how lucky *you* are! Because in the 20s and 30s our fathers shared the same views. In the Weimar Republic, who wasn't on the Left? Who wasn't communist? And I think: weren't you lucky that the film director Max Ophuls and his family fled to the West and not to the East.

While Ophuls's recognized political position suggests that one should not accept such an observation at face value, his own "image" does contrast with the "images" of his interview subjects, setting up a tension between East and West which at once denigrates the former for its denial of personal freedoms, and praises the latter for its albeit limited endorsement of them. At the same time, however, the film's use of ironic juxtapositions – widely recognized as Ophuls's auteur signature – constantly calls this very judgment into question. Since we regularly see Ophuls onscreen and hear his voice on the soundtrack throughout *November Days*, this dual tension informs much of the film. Indeed, given his public profile, his directing, and his interviewing credits, the film is most easily "read" as Ophuls's personal critique of GDR socialism, combined with an autocritique of Western presuppositions about it.

This dual tension is made more explicit toward the end of the film, during an interview with Bärbel Bohley, the so-called Mother of the Revolution. Talking three months before unification, she is saddened that the GDR was not given a chance to stand on its own, and expresses fears about how East Germans will suffer amid the rush to monetary and political union. Bohley's demeanor suggests that, for some, the collapse of the GDR was experienced as a deeply felt loss, a turn to focusing on monetary gain over what an earlier interviewee terms the "national soul," but Ophuls juxtaposes his own seemingly contrary view. When she asks him how he feels about the events, he asserts: "I can't get over the fact that the Wall has gone. That's so positive, I can't understand the other anxieties, including yours." On the one hand, Ophuls's comment reinforces the prior linking of the West to the notion of personal freedom. Yet Bohley's interview is intercut ironically with clips of Liza Minnelli and Joel Grey singing "Money Makes the World Go Around" from Bob Fosse's film *Cabaret* (1972), along with shots of East German citizens frantically swapping East German Marks for Deutschmarks on the day of monetary union, which also suggests Ophuls's awareness of reunification's foreseeable problems. As if to underline this dual tension, the film ends with an East German woman asserting the pleasure she gets from "the feeling of being free," of being able to "speak your mind over a beer," as she expresses her genuine fears about the future.

November Days highlights the push toward German unity while offering a critique of that, and in so doing, it destabilizes the historically disastrous German "will to unity." However, it is also clearly critical of the former SED regime, and by drawing certain parallels between it and the Third Reich, it implicitly favors the Western notion of "freedom," thus privileging a myth of East–West difference that is largely consonant with Western ideological perspectives.

In the Splendour of Happiness

In contrast to *November Days*, which can be read as an *auteur* film, *In the Splendour of Happiness* was made by a group of East and West German filmmakers. Shot during February–March 1990, the film is loosely based around a journey through East Germany in an attempt to find out "what's it like now?" Although the film includes several interviews, there is also an emphasis on the "landscape" of East Germany – via an "observational" camera style – that contrasts starkly with Ophuls's film. Indeed, *Splendour* is subtitled "Observations in Berlin (East and West), Potsdam, Leipzig, Wasungen/Thuringia, Passau." The interviews are usually fairly informal, with people often carrying on working as they talk. The film mixes a range of interviewing styles – discussed below – is filmed in both black/white and color, and on occasion intercuts old GDR newsreel footage of parades, children exercising, and the like. Overall, the film appears less deliberately structured than *November Days* and more of a haphazard collage of impressions of and reactions to recent events.

On the one hand, this collage includes footage of rousing political speeches, celebratory rallies and festive parades. Often the source of this footage is not identified, which invites us to read it as signifying that Germans generally – wherever they are – are indeed "in the splendour of happiness." It is often accompanied by a soundtrack of lively, upbeat music, and the impression is that many, East and West, welcome the prospect of unification. At one rally, for instance, an East German politician observes, to much applause, that "we're bringing in sixteen million people who are bursting with hope." At a similar event, an elderly West German declares to the filmmakers: "We prefer a thousand East Germans to one foreigner or immigrant. They are our brothers and sisters. They're part of us … We belong together as we once were." And later, we also see footage of Helmut Kohl addressing the crowd, replete with German flags, in a public square. He asserts, again to much applause: "The symbol of a united German society should never again be the comrade's clenched fist, but the outstretched hand of a partner." Thus, in the context of raising the specter of racism toward Germany's immigrant population, the film clearly evidences a German "will to unity," and indeed ends on a shot of a demolished border watchtower with a voiceover saying, "To close our rally, let's sing together the national anthem," followed by clapping, cheering, and whistling.

On the other hand, the film also includes a number of interviews mainly with ordinary East German citizen-workers, such as a schoolteacher, a car mechanic, factory workers, a policeman, people on the street, and (a notable exception) a former Stasi psychologist. Some talk at length, reflecting primarily upon their lives under socialism, and in the process demonstrate that the opening of the Wall precipitated much more than simply the possibility of German unity. Most of them express both disillusionment with the SED regime and a deep sense of loss or bewilderment at the GDR's demise, and several admit – as do some of Ophuls's interviewees – awkwardly their naiveté or shame at having colluded with the former regime's oppressive policies.

However, as noted above, these interviews are conducted via a range of interviewing techniques. At times, the filmmakers allow their interviewees to talk more or less directly into the camera with no interruption, as is the case with the schoolteacher, Cornelia Reum. As the camera is static and she is reflecting about her own collusion and naiveté, the scene becomes almost painfully voyeuristic. On other occasions, when they are filming on the street, we hear the filmmakers' voices over the soundtrack as they ask questions from behind the camera in order to precipitate some response from an assembled crowd. When, for instance, they visit a former Stasi prison, they talk to a policeman who used to patrol outside, asking if he was aware of what went on inside. His denial triggers a spontaneous discussion between him and gathering onlookers, who express hostile disbelief at his professed ignorance, prompting one man to draw a parallel with similar denials made at the end of World War Two. On yet another occasion, when filmmaker Tamara Trampe is interviewing the Stasi psychologist, J. Girke, she makes herself as much the focus of the interview as Girke. The film includes nearly ten minutes of Girke, filmed via a series of static camera shots, as he attempts – prompted by questions from an offscreen Trampe – to explain and justify his involvement with the Stasi. Occasional black-and-white photographic stills of Trampe are intercut, and gradually her questioning becomes quite insistent. Eventually the camera pans to include her in-shot with Girke, and she takes over the interview by explaining *her* feelings to Girke and the difficulty she has had in trying to understand how he could have used fear to fight for the same socialist ideals as she. This is followed by a sequence in which Trampe herself, filmed against a stark white backdrop, talks directly into the camera – almost in the manner of a video diary – about her opposition to oppressive SED policies and her decision to keep quiet about them for fear of reprisal. This mix of interview techniques suggests that the film is attempting both to "observe" *and* consciously articulate a particular viewpoint, but in the process it unleashes an unexpected anger from members of the public and Trampe, for which the film – with its remit to explore "What's it like now?" – is unable to account.

This unexpected element not only affords the film a somewhat incoherent feel, but also tends to foreground the filmmakers themselves, in that we are made very aware of their presence. Much as Ophuls in *November Days* is positioned in ironical tension to his interviewees, the *Splendour* filmmakers are also frequently at odds with theirs. This is evident in the Trampe-Girke interview, but is also apparent in their street interviews. The spontaneity with which the hostility of the crowd takes over the discussion with the policeman at the Stasi prison, completely usurping the filmmakers' role as interviewers, suggests the filmmakers do not anticipate – and may not fully appreciate – the extent of the underlying anger that their questioning can bring to the surface. This is more explicit in another street interview, where their questions appear to display a degree of naiveté and provoke indignant responses. An elderly East German man begins by voicing his support for the CDU – the Christian Democratic Union, West Germany's conservative party[7] – by saying "We're all for the CDU." This prompts the filmmakers to ask: "So you didn't all agree with the fascists? … And the Stalinists?" He replies vehemently,

> "Never! […] No way […] I'm on an invalid pension. Only a few marks. They screwed us for forty years. Those red bums. Why weren't they locked up? They were in fine health. Now suddenly they're too sick to be jailed! They should be killed."

Immediately following this, a young man declares he would happily shoot ex-Stasi officers. From off screen, one filmmaker comments that this is not a very Christian attitude for a declared CDU supporter. An older woman retorts that if the film-maker had experienced what they had, she would give the man more credence. Although *Splendour*'s directors have adopted a more observational style of filmmaking than Ophuls – frequently letting the camera roll and filming what happens – their presence and act of filming nevertheless directly precipitate many of these interactions. In the process, the interviews they conduct suggest that the opening of the Wall precipitated a range of responses – much more than simply an overarching or one-dimensional notion of German unity.

Indeed, although most of the interviewees' comments throughout the film are directed at the former GDR, they contrast so sharply with the celebratory tone of the political speeches, rallies, and other festive occasions that they tend to undermine the unification rhetoric. This makes the title of the film – taken from the German national anthem – ironic. Unlike *November Days*, however, *Splendour*'s selection and juxtaposing of material does not function as a humorous "exposé" of such rhetoric. There is no single authorial presence, no use of Hollywood film clips, and no rapid montage to suggest a sharply directed critique. Instead, the observational style of *In the Splendour of Happiness* seems to invite and encourage extended reflection. Yet, like *November Days*, the textual strategies it employs do suggest the existence of markedly different ways of seeing and understanding the 1989–1990 events.

In *Splendour*, however, the contrast between perspectives is so marked that it tends to rupture the film's coherence – something which is compounded by the mixed interviewing techniques. As a consequence, the function of inserting old GDR newsreels is not immediately apparent. On the one hand, taken individually, the newsreel clips give an impression of the country's former socialist aspirations, especially since the film *begins* with one of these clips. As the GDR citizens subsequently express their disillusionment and senses of loss, the inserted clips afford a glimpse of the "better future" – one of social equality for their children, for instance – toward which many East Germans had always felt themselves to be working. On the other hand, the clips act as reminders that, due to corruption and mismanagement combined with Western pressure, that future failed to materialize. Given *Splendour*'s observational style, the multiple meanings that can be attributed to the inserted GDR newsreel clips invite further speculation about the rhetoric of unification – as evidenced by the contemporary footage of political speeches, rallies, and parades – implying it may prove as hollow as SED sloganeering.

Overall, precisely because of its fragmentary nature, *In the Splendour of Happiness* powerfully conveys a sense of the problems that emerged in the wake of the Wall opening. Insofar as it was filmed almost entirely in East Germany, and includes footage of conservative politician Kohl offering the "outstretched hand of a partner," however, the film also suggests – incorrectly – that such problems were the sole provenance of the former GDR, and hence articulates the myth of East–West difference from a perspective that favors Western hegemony.

Last Year – Titanic

This DEFA[8] production was directed by Andreas Voigt, co-written with the film's cinematographer, Sebastian Richter, and shot over an extended period – December 1989 to December 1990 – in Leipzig. As with *In the Splendour*, *Last Year – Titanic* combines a series of fairly informal interviews with an "observational" rather than reflexive filmmaking style. According to Voigt, the people who appear in the film were both "chance encounters and longer-standing friendships," and he describes the film as concerned with "everyday events ... with people's hopes, dreams, failures, successes, battles, injuries, resignation and new hopes."[9]

Although both Voigt and Richter are East German, they are not from Leipzig, and as the film's opening and conclusion clearly indicate, they are visitors to that city. The film begins with a tracking shot along the railway line into the Leipzig train station, and ends with the same shot in reverse. These opening and closing shots are in color, while the rest of the film is in black and white, which gives the impression that this filmic visit to Leipzig is a journey into an entirely different world.

Once in this "other" world, the film conveys a sense of celebration. After "arriving" at the station we see shots at night of people dressed as clowns, crowds swarming across a public square, parades, people singing and dancing in the streets, accompanied by a soundtrack of chanting, whistling and honking car horns. These sorts of scenes recur intermittently throughout the film; and whereas the concluding scene returns to color, its initial shots are of a firework display. Although television news footage is included which announces the East Germans' first opportunity to vote in a parliamentary election, the rest of the film is constructed in a way that suggests the celebrations have more to do with simply gaining access to the West and what it supposedly has to offer in consumerist terms than with the serious implications of prospective political-economic unification. For instance, at one point we are shown the words "Heute kommt die Deutsche Mark" ("The Deutschmark arrives today") rolling across a huge dot-matrix display on the roof of an office block, while later an East German policeman proudly tells the filmmakers how the Tübingen police department has presented him and his colleagues with an Audi car.[10]

Most of *Last Year*'s interviews – all conducted by an offscreen interviewer – reinforce a common Western assumption that East Germans are more interested in the prospects of Western-style economic consumption than anything else, by implying the *Wende*-era GDR is, as the title suggests, a sinking ship. Only one interviewee, a journalist, actually reflects on her past involvement with the SED regime, but in the problematic respect of her having cooperated for a time with the Stasi. Several interviewees, however, express feelings of insecurity about their futures in postunification Leipzig. A group of female factory workers fears for their jobs, while a younger woman has armed herself with a gun as protection against the violence of neofascist groups – which increased in number and size following the withdrawal of Soviet support under Gorbachev (in the name of *glasnost* ("openness" to the West) and *perestroika* (neoliberal "restructuring")), and would yet again after reunification. But the vast majority announce plans to leave for West Germany, mainly due to lack of opportunity and insufficient means in the privatized GDR. We see a barmaid arranging her farewell party, and a man explaining his departure as resulting from a belief that there is no longer any future for him in the East, but also a factory worker who had twice attempted an escape to the West during the 1960s talking about his imminent plans at last to depart at will.

The image of a sinking ship is compounded by recurring shots of people packing up their belongings, and of derelict buildings, half-demolished houses, and empty streets. Shots of empty factories toward the end of the film also contrast poignantly with the hustle and bustle of the opening sequence. Not only are the interviewees deserting a sinking ship, their very departure would seem to be hastening its demise.

At the same time, some of the interviewees seem reluctant to talk, because there seems little to say. The filmmakers must therefore repeatedly ask questions – any questions ("what are your children's names?") – to prompt the interviewees to speak. As with *In the Splendour*, not only does this strategy make us aware of the filmmakers' presence and limitations, it also precipitates the unexpected. While filming in a bar, the camera lingers on a group of black African musicians (possibly immigrants or *Gastarbeiter*), then pans to some white Germans. The latter start complaining that the filmmakers seem interested in filming only the "foreigners," asserting in classic racist, anti-immigrant fashion that they, the East Germans, are getting walked on all over again.

Paradoxically, these interviewee–filmmaker dynamics reinforce the filmmakers' overt positioning as visitors, outsiders. Even though they are East German, the filmmakers do not seem to share or understand the Leipzigers' experiences. The fact that they never appear in front of the camera seems entirely appropriate, precisely because they do not come from or belong in Leipzig. Thus, when they "leave" at the end of the film, we are left with the impression that they – and we as viewers – have only passed through this "other" world as tourists. Yet Leipzigers' experiences of unemployment and insecurity – as evidenced in both *November Days* and *In the Splendour* – are comparable to thousands of East Germans in the wake of reunification, whereupon Leipzig may be viewed as a microcosm. Therefore, when the film returns to color upon the filmmakers' departure, it gives the impression that they, too, are fleeing a sinking ship. Since the interviewees – and by implication the filmmakers – are positioned as fleeing to the West, this conclusion very vividly underscores the Western myth of East–West difference.

Locked Up Time

The director of *Locked Up Time*, Sibylle Schönemann, is also East German and worked for the DEFA Studios until she left the GDR in 1985. In the film, made entirely in black and white, the director undertakes a journey back to her homeland to investigate the circumstances which precipitated her departure. As the film unfolds, we learn through interviews and her voiceover that Schönemann and her husband had lived with their children in Potsdam. She explains that they both regularly submitted production applications to DEFA for films about "real" people, films that would present a recognizable "reality." She doesn't explain beyond this, but the implication is that she and her husband wanted to make films about the lived experiences of GDR citizens which would, as a result, in some way criticize the SED regime. She reports that all of their applications were rejected, so they decided to apply for exit permits, at which point they were put under police surveillance. Eventually, in 1984, they were arrested, and Schönemann was imprisoned in Thuringia. The West German authorities obtained her release a year later – exactly how is not made clear – whereupon she emigrated to the FRG and was finally reunited there with her family who had also been granted exit permits.

Schönemann's declared aim is to try to make sense of what happened to her in the former GDR. She does this by seeking out the people who played a role in her arrest and imprisonment, such as the man who interrogated her after her arrest, and the prosecutor at her trial. In contrast to Ophuls, whose often confrontational form of interviewing means his interviewees frequently respond to him defensively about their implied past actions, Schönemann appears at times less interested in making people account for their actions or in apportioning blame. In these instances, her manner of questioning suggests that she is more concerned with trying to understand the process, and with finding someone who can explain *why* these things happened to her. An implied feminine discourse invoked by numerous references to motherhood and family also pervades this more tempered approach.

When Schönemann meets with the people involved in her case, she frequently starts by asking them if they remember her. The Educator at the Thuringia prison remembers her, since she was the only film director detained there, and recalls that Schönemann is a mother of two. Later, Schönemann visits the former General Manager of the DEFA Studios, Herr Mäde, who not only recognizes her but greets her warmly. Once she starts asking questions about her arrest and imprisonment, however, almost without exception these people become reticent and vague. The Educator suddenly "cannot possibly remember every detail" about an individual case, while Mäde is first too busy and then too ill to give even an informal interview.

Schönemann also finds that most of those involved in her arrest and imprisonment have readily adapted to the post-Wall situation, having completely detached themselves from their former roles. When she visits her interrogator, he claims not to reproach himself for his past actions and declares simply that "it's all over now anyway." Similarly, while disliked by his rural neighbors, an ex-Stasi officer who liaised with Mäde has settled comfortably into a new life as a forester and sees no problem in having colluded with the denunciation and persecution that led to Schönemann's imprisonment. He insists that one either accepted the "system" and worked accordingly, or challenged it and bore the consequences, but maintains that there were no half measures. It is as though Schönemann's interviewees are not so much unwilling to talk about the SED past as they are indifferent to its recollection.

A few of those interviewed do give *some* indication of the systemic conditions which led to her imprisonment. For instance, a woman at DEFA admits having signed a report containing lies about Schönemann, because she was told to do so by Mäde. The prosecutor at Schönemann's trial explains he could not have acquitted her, because her statements were deemed threatening to the State, and he did not have the courage to challenge it. On the whole, however, Schönemann's investigation actually reveals very little of the purportedly desired concrete evidence she is seeking; apropos of its feminine tenor, *Locked Up Time* is less an exploratory analysis than a gentle assessment of the past. But from this standpoint, the film does clearly suggest that Schönemann's story is not unique. While visiting the prisons in which she was held and the courtroom in which she was tried, she reenacts or reconstructs her arrest and incarceration. Part of this process involves meeting up again with Birgit, a former cellmate. Schönemann recalls having assumed that Birgit had been convicted of murder, only to discover that she had also been subject to persecution and arrest after submitting an application to emigrate, that her husband was likewise imprisoned, and that they, too, have children. Indeed, the conclusion of *Locked Up Time* reveals that the women's experiences were shared by at least 35 000 political prisoners, most of whom were released in the years leading up to or following reunification.

Because, in the context of Schönemann's interview technique, none of her interview subjects is willing or able to explain these actions, the film tends to interpret them as arbitrary and senseless rather than as systemic. By the same token, the fact that virtually all of those interviewed are shown trying – and generally able – to distance themselves from the past indicates that a significant degree of willful collusion was in fact necessary to realize such actions. As one reviewer asserts: "Ironically, by focusing solely on one woman's story, *Locked Up Time* seems to have captured the East German national psyche where more ambitious projects have failed."[11] The reviewer does not indicate which "more ambitious projects" are being referenced, but Schönemann's film focuses on an individual's experience and thus differs markedly from – and can be viewed as less ambitious than – the other four documentaries discussed in this chapter (and other films made at the time) which tried to capture "history" in the making or explore the wider GDR experience. For Schönemann, accordingly, the system at fault is not really a "system" but a psychological disposition toward a particular form of national unity. Although she, Birgit, and 35 000 other political prisoners may have wished to emigrate not because they favored Western capitalism but precisely because they were committed socialists, then, the film offers an idealist understanding of East–West difference, which frames their eventual departures in rather unrealistic terms – in contrast to Schönemann's stated intentions as a filmmaker, and in line with Western ideological proclivities which would have indeed raised the ire of SED bureaucrats – as a matter of fundamentally distinct national identities.

Last Year in Germany

A British-German co-production, this film was shot between November 1989 and December 1990 by four Germans, two from the East and two from the West. As with *In the Splendour*, *Last Year* is loosely structured as a journey through Germany, this time, as a voiceover explains, with the filmmakers accompanying people "who are close to us – friends, acquaintances, relations." Rather than *Splendour*'s collage of impressions and reactions to recent events, *Last Year in Germany* plots how its interviewees alter their perceptions of such events over the course of one year.

The film begins with a series of criticisms leveled at the GDR by its former citizens. These range from accusations of social conservatism, bureaucratic mismanagement, and sloppy work practices, to complaints about feelings of entrapment, lack of personal freedom, and having little to show for 40 years of struggling for socialism. The complaints are followed by clips from the news coverage of the opening of the Wall, complete with a soundtrack of rousing music, cheering, whistling, and honking car horns. Thus in a manner not dissimilar to *November Days*, *Last Year in Germany* begins by representing the opening of the Wall as at least achieving freedom from the worst excesses of the SED regime.

Through an ensuing series of interviews, the film explores the fundamental question this "freedom" raises for East Germans. As one interviewee comments: "The decision 'to leave or not to leave' is the hardest I've ever made. You go mad churning it over for weeks." Another continues: "It's peculiar to the GDR since we all identify with the problem. Everyone has to decide 'to go or not to go.'" Of those who do decide to leave, the film follows two in particular – Ina, a potter, who is separating from her husband, and Tina, a barmaid. A third woman, Suzanne, would like to leave like her friend Teresa, who left in October 1989 and now lives in the West, but her husband wants to stay. In addition to Suzanne's husband Stefan, their elderly next door neighbor and a psychologist are among those who want to stay.

Throughout the film, a female voiceover marks the passage of time and notes the changing national "landscape" through the course of the year. When the filmmakers reach their second port of call, the voiceover announces: "Karl Marx Stadt in February 1990. Three months later the town will be called Chemnitz again." As they move on: "The people of Dresden are staging their first uncensored carnival, and the West German politicians their first election campaign in the GDR." And later, as the camera pans across a former border zone, she expresses how difficult it is for her to imagine that, only a few months ago, one could get shot for entering the area.

Set against this changing "landscape" and the passage of time are the observations of people who appear in the film. As late as May 1990, some of them are still strident in their criticisms of the former East German state. One woman asserts: "I'm glad those so-called Communists are gone. They are the GDR. The GDR isn't socialism, it's a state run by lousy bigwigs." But, with one or two exceptions on which the film focuses only briefly, disillusionment and disappointment with reunification gradually set in. During the year of filming, Suzanne visits Teresa in Aalen, Swabia, to find her changed and unfriendly, and life in the West uncomfortably hectic. Tina moves to West Berlin but finds difficulty in coping with the contradiction between "all the free choice of where you work" and her actual inability to find work; while Ina's attempt to open a business in the West fails, and she decides to return to the East.

Those who stay in the East are shown faring little better, as they find their way of life gradually eroded by the free market economy. By summer, a young man is complaining that life under the SED regime may have been restrictive, but once the Wall was opened, his mother lost her job, and his friend's father deserted his family for the West. Stefan informs the viewer that the cost of construction materials has risen threefold, and complains that governmental decisions are now made in Bonn. By autumn 1990, Suzanne has lost her waitressing job, virtually without notice, because without state-subsidized childcare in the post-reunification era's privatizing system of diminished social services, she can no longer work evenings. And an artist friend of Ina finds herself with nothing left to show for her many years of effort, her studio having collapsed after losing contracts due to monetary union.

With the gift of hindsight, *Last Year*'s voiceover also repeatedly warns the viewer that the situation will probably worsen. For instance, at a point signaled as March 1990, she observes that, while several months earlier, GDR citizens were shouting "We are the People" and sweeping away the SED regime, one year later they will have demonstrated again – against Kohl, against reunification, and for preservation of their jobs. At times, the voiceover assumes the position of a unitary enunciating subject, articulating "we" or "us." Thus, whereas another artist friend of Ina is shown (albeit briefly) asserting that things happen to be improving for him, and although Tina does eventually find a job and acclimates to life in West Berlin, the voiceover frames a generally pessimistic future vision for East Germans. This vision is underscored by the filmmakers' declared close relationships with many of the interviewees, as signaled clearly in the voiceover at the beginning of the film and reiterated upon arrival at Karl-Marx-Stadt: "This is where Beate [one of the filmmakers] grew up. Ina lives near Beate's parents' house." By these assertions of acquaintance or friendship with the interviewees, the film positions its ability to know, understand and assess the situation, like Schönemann, on somewhat abstract, personal-psychological grounds.

As a result, *Last Year*'s suggestion is superficial: that, because of their socialist upbringing or proclivities, most East Germans are ill-equipped, even unable, to adapt to the post-Wall situation, which has both rendered the "freedom" of the West accessible to them and unleashed its harsh realities upon them. Whereas any such inability is undoubtedly due in large part to the economic restrictions of monetary union, and also to the dizzying pace of historical change it has entailed, the film would locate its roots in East German "identity." Stefan talks about "feeling" like a GDR citizen and thinking of that country as his *Heimat*, a term which can only inadequately be translated as "homeland." Thomas Elsaesser (1988: 1) has explained that "*Heimat* is an intensely emotional concept, a feeling before it assumes precise meaning, evocative of loss but also of hope: for a return to imagined or real origins." Understood in this context, Stefan's use of the term highlights a deeply ingrained, perhaps utopic sense of East Germanness. In a similar vein, both his elderly neighbor and Tina explain that living in the GDR has come to shape their self-identities. The psychologist explains,

> GDR citizens have certain attitudes, we've grown up with them. We sense the difference when we go West, or talk to people from the FRG. We feel, and I speak not only

for myself but for others, we have something specifically East German, but at the same time it's not identification with the State.

Yet *Heimat* is known most famously as a term commonly associated with German national identity above and beyond the East–West divide, especially in the name of "Aryan" racial unity. By including Stefan's use of the term, *Last Year* positions the East–West divide in a manner which echoes Schönemann's film, despite certain aesthetic differences, in that it proffers an idealist conception of German nationalism. In this instance, East German disidentification with the SED regime is easily interpreted, falsely and out of context, as an anti-Statist sentiment favorable to the Western putsch to deregulate and privatize government – which, in the real context of German history, has paved the road to fascism.

The "Othering" of East Germany

In conducting these textual analyses, my aim – as explained above – has not been to establish the accuracy of the subject documentaries, but rather to highlight the process of "narrative shaping" which they conduct. Although the films may include evidence of celebration at the prospect of Germany unity – and thus incorporate a myth of German unity – they all nevertheless privilege a positioned myth of East–West difference. Each film in some way articulates ideas of difference and diversity among Germans – be that of opinion, psyche, reaction to the post-Wall situation, or ability to cope with it – but these ideas crystallize and are structured around a likewise mythical differentiation. While its precise nature varies from film to film, this myth of difference is always articulated in a way that positions East Germany as West Germany's "other." This is evident in *November Days'* implicit representation of the GDR as the enemy of the "free" West, in *Splendour's* positioning of East Germany as "the problem" vis-à-vis FRG offers of partnership, and in *Last Year – Titanic's* microcosmic representation of Leipzig as an "other" world. In *Locked Up Time*, it is apparent as a psychological tendency toward conformism and authoritarian ethics, and in *Last Year in Germany*, it is projected onto a naive conception of the GDR as a safe haven protected from the "real" (Western capitalist) world.

This positioning of East Germany as "other" is reinforced through an embedding of the filmmakers' gaze in their respective texts. Each film draws attention to the relationship between its director(s) and the interview subjects – whether by including the filmmaker(s) onscreen, presenting the narrative as a personal story, or interviewing and filming which precipitates the unexpected. On one level, these techniques promote awareness of the act itself of filming, of the fact that the filmmakers have traveled through East Germany specifically to "look," in one way or another, at what is happening there since the fall of the Wall. Although most of the filmmakers aver their entitlement in this respect – they know the interviewees personally, they are returning to their home country and have a special relationship to it – their largely idealist constructions of East–West difference belie an underlying voyeurism and tendentious viewer manipulation. This voyeurism – the act of privileged, ostensibly unobserved "looking" – becomes explicit in some of the films by the use of long, static "observational" shots of certain interviewees.

The opening of the Wall and the prospect of unification, however, affected *West* Germany as well as East Germany. McKenzie Wark has argued that

> One thinks of Europe in 1989 as the opening night at the theater where the curtain goes up and the audience comes face to face with another audience. Each thinks the other is the spectacle, themselves the real audience. One has to be outside the theatre altogether to see it as a double game. (1990: 35)

Yet this "double game" is never evident in these films, it is mainly East Germany which comes under scrutiny – the "West" is largely absent. The primacy of "looking" at the East, combined with a demonstrably inadequate understanding of the East German interviewees creates an impression that the former GDR has been put under a *Western* microscope – irrespective of the filmmakers' national origins. Despite its apparent absence, the "West" in fact becomes the films' *structuring* absence, the unstated defining term against which the GDR is measured, finally, and by which it is repeatedly (mis)represented as infinitely more damaging psychologically and worthy of forgetting, rejecting, and fleeing than the "free," "democratic" West.

Given that this narrative shaping occurs in a *documentary* format – a format that within mainstream audio-visual culture purports to offer a "window on the world" – the films also imply that their particular positioning of East Germany is simply the way things were. Thus the film *form* functions to conceal the fact that it is only one way of viewing the former GDR. In doing so, the films themselves exemplify the cultural process that Roland Barthes (1973) termed myth – a process he identified at work in French culture whereby cultural artefacts and practices function to naturalize history, making that which has come about through a specific set of historical circumstances appear to be simply "there."

Notes

1   Balibar (1991) has also argued – as has Immanuel Wallerstein (1991) – that "ethnicity" itself is equally a construct.
2   More recently of course there has also been the rise of *Ostalgie*, the nostalgia for certain aspects of life in the former GDR. This is evident, for instance, in films like Leander Haußmann's *Sonnenallee* (Sun Alley) (Germany, 1999), Hannes Stöhr's *Berlin Is in Germany* (2001) and Wolfgang Becker's *Good Bye, Lenin!* (2003). See e.g. Blum (2000); Jozwiak and Mermann (2006); Leeder (2009).

3   It is worth noting, however, that Micha Brumlik (1991: 108) argued at the time that with the predominance of conservative voters in both Germanies, "nothing indicates that the result of a new constitutional debate would result in anything as emancipatory or universalist as what we now have in the Basic Law."

4   This is particularly evident in myths of origin. According to Bronislaw Malinowski (1974: 111), for instance, the Trobriand Islanders believed that: "The world [...] was originally peopled from underground. Humanity had there led an existence similar in all respects to the present life on earth [...] They emerged, establishing by this very act certain rights in land and citizenship."

5   This is also akin to Walter Benjamin's view of literature. According to Terry Eagleton (1982: vii), Benjamin "dismissed the view that all literary works were equally 'readable' at all times. For Benjamin, a work may fall into obscurity for centuries, only to be suddenly reactivated as the history to which it belongs flashes into a freshly relevant relationship to our own epoch."

6   This has been particularly noted in discussions of his *The Sorrow and the Pity* (1969), which exposed French collaboration with the occupying Germans during World War Two.

7   The CDU is Germany's center-right political party. Founded in 1949, it advocates conservative values and laissez-faire economic policies alongside an extensive welfare system, now undergoing gradual privatization and reduction. The CDU has enjoyed varying levels of support but was the dominant party during the 1950s, at the height of the Cold War, and experienced a resurgence of popularity when the Berlin Wall fell.

8   DEFA stands for Deutsche Film Aktiengesellschaft. Founded in 1946, in the Soviet zone of occupied Germany, it became the state-owned East German film production company. Based in Potsdam, it had a prolific output of films and continued to operate until its dissolution in 1992, shortly after reunification. For a history of the DEFA studios, see Allan and Sandford (1999); Claus (2002).

9   From an uncredited translation of the film notes accompanying the screening of the film at the Berlin Film Festival in 1991.

10 West German engineering had a reputation for extremely high quality and hence the country's cars were usually among the more expensive on the market.

11 Quoted in the 35th London Film Festival program, November 6–21, 1991: 56.

References

Allan, S. and Sandford, J. (eds) (1999) *DEFA: East German Cinema, 1946–1992*, Berghahn, New York, Oxford.

Ahrends, M. (1991) The great waiting, or the freedom of the East: an obituary for life in Sleeping Beauty's castle. *New German Critique*, 52, 41–49.

Anderson, B. (1991) *Imagined Communities: Reflections on the Origin and Spread of Nationalism*, rev. edn, Verso, New York and London.

Balibar, E. (1991) The nation form: history and ideology, in *Race, Nation, Class: Ambiguous Identities* (eds E. Balibar and I. Wallerstein), Verso, New York and London.

Barthes, R. (1973) *Mythologies* (trans. A. Lavers), Paladin Grafton, London.

Bhabha, H. (ed.) (1990) *Nation and Narration*, Routledge, London.

Blum, M. (2000) Remaking the East German past: "ostalgie," identity, and material culture. *Journal of Popular Culture*, 34 (3), 229–253.

Bohrer, K.H. (1990) Und die Erinnerung der beiden Halbnationen? *Merkmur*, 493, 183–188.

Bohrer, K.H. (1991) Why we are not a nation – and why we should become one. *New German Critique*, 52, 72–83.

Brockmann, S. (1991) Introduction: the reunification debate. *New German Critique*, 52, 3–30.

Brumlik, M. (1991) Basic aspects of an imaginary debate. *New German Critique*, 52, 102–108.

Bruyn, G.d. (1991) On the German cultural nation. *New German Critique*, 52, 60–66.

Caughie, J. (1992) Becoming European – art cinema, irony and identity, in *Screening Europe* (ed. D. Petrie), BFI, London, pp. 32–44.

Christy, D. (1993) Storyteller to the Stasi. *Guardian*, February 4, http://www.lexisnexis.com:80/uk/legal/results/docview/docview.do?start=7&sort=BOOLEAN&format=GNBFULL&risb=21_T11189496799 (accessed February 8, 2011).

Claus, H. (2002) DEFA – state, studio, style, identity, in *The German Cinema Book* (eds T. Bergfelder, E. Carter, and D. Göktürk), BFI, London, pp. 139–147.

Dahn, D. (1991) Conformists like me. *New German Critique*, 52, 50–59.

Eagleton, T. (1982) *The Rape of Clarissa*, Basil Blackwell, London.

Elsaesser, T. (1988) The Heimat-film, in *Deutscher Heimatfilm* progamme notes, Goethe-Institute, London.

Evans, R. (1991) Germany's morning after. *Marxism Today*, June, 20–23.

Fiske, J. (1990) *Introduction to Communication Studies*, 2nd edn, Routledge, London.

Gellner, E. (1983) *Nations and Nationalism*, Blackwell, Oxford.

Gilman, S.L. (1991) German reunification and the Jews. *New German Critique*, 52, 173–191.

Grass, G. (1991) What am I talking for? *New German Critique*, 52, 66–72.

Gregor, U. (1991) Foreword. *Filmfestival: 1989/1990 Post-Wall Germany*, Goethe-Institut, Munich.

Habermas, J. (1991) Yet again: German identity – a unified nation of angry DM-Burghers? *New German Critique*, 52, 84–101.

Heym, S. (1989) Es ging immer unmoralisch zu in dieser Parte. *Süddeutsche Zeitung*, November 25–26, 12.

Hill, G. (1993) *Illuminating Shadows – The Mythic Power of Film*, Shambhala, Boston.

Hirsch, H. (1990) Der Neubeginn als Selbstaufgabe? *Die Zeit*, March 16, 3.

Hobsbawm, E. and Ranger, T. (eds) (1983) *The Invention of Tradition*, Cambridge University Press, Cambridge.

Huyssen, A. (1991) After the Wall: the failure of German intellectuals. *New German Critique*, 52, 109–143.

Jeffries, S. (2004) Patriotism is a lie: Stuart Jeffries talks to Marcel Ophuls, the director who shattered postwar myths about France and the Nazis. *Guardian*, May 24, http://www.guardian.co.uk/film/2004/may/24/1 (accessed October 27, 2010).

Jozwiak, J.F. and Mermann, E. (2006) "The wall in our minds?" Colonization, integration, and nostalgia. *Journal of Popular Culture*, 39 (5), 780–795.

Jung, C.G. (ed.) (1978) *Man and His Symbols*, Pan Books, London.

Lacoue-Labarthe, P. and Nancy, J-L. (1990) The Nazi myth (trans. Brian Holmes). *Critical Inquiry*, 16, 291–312.

Leeder, K. (ed.) (2009) From Stasiland to ostalgie: the GDR twenty years after. *Oxford German Studies*, 38 (3) special issue.

Leicht, R. (1990) Der nächste Schritt zur Einheit. *Die Zeit*, March 16, 1.

Levi-Strauss, C. (1972) *Structural Anthropology*, Penguin, Harmondsworth.

Levi-Strauss, C. (1978) *Structural Anthropology Two*, Penguin, Harmondsworth.

McArthur, C. (1984) National identities, in *National Fictions* (ed. G. Hurd), BFI, London.

McConnell, F. (1979) *Storytelling and Mythmaking: Images from Film and Literature*, Oxford University Press, Oxford.

Malinowski, B. (1974) *Magic, Science and Religion*, Condor, London.

Maron, M. (1991) Writers and the people. *New German Critique*, 52, 36–41.

Meurer, H.J. (2000) *Cinema and National Identity in a Divided Germany 1979–1989: The Split Screen*, Edwin Mellen Press, New York, Lampeter.

Miller, A. (1990) Anschluss, angst and a great enigma. *Guardian*, May 29, http://www.lexisnexis.com:80/uk/legal/search/newssubmitForm.do (accessed February 8, 2011).

Nowell-Smith, G. and Wollen, T. (1991) (eds.) *After the Wall*, BFI, London.

O'Sullivan, T., Hartley, J., Sanders, D., Montgomery, M. and Fiske, J. (1994) *Key Concepts in Communication and Cultural Studies*, 2nd edn, Routledge, London.

Petrie, D. (ed.) (1992) *Screening Europe: Image and Identity in Contemporary European Cinema*, BFI, London.

Samuel, R. and Thompson, P. (eds) (1990) *The Myths We Live By (History Workshop)*, Routledge, New York, London.

Schatz, T. (1981) *Hollywood Genres*, Random House, New York.

Unger, F. (1991) Speaking of unity, in *After the Wall* (eds G. Nowell-Smith and T. Wollen), BFI, London, pp. 69–76.

Wallerstein, I. (1991) The construction of peoplehood: racism, nationalism, ethnicity, in *Race, Nation, Class: Ambiguous Identities* (eds E. Balibar and I. Wallerstein), Verso, London, New York.

Walser, M. (1988) Über Deutschland reden. *Die Zeit*, November 4, 65–67.

Wark, M. (1990) Europe's masked ball: East meets West at the Wall. *New Formations*, 12, 33–42.

Watson, A. (1992) *The Germans – Who Are They Now?* Thames Methuen, London (the accompanying Channel 4 series was broadcast in January and February 1992).

Weck, R.d. (1989) Im besten Sinne deutsch. *Die Zeit*, November 24, 3.

Zimmer, D.E. (1990) Den Völkern Gespött oder Furcht: die Deutschen und das Nationgefühl. *Die Zeit*, April 6, 68.

Further Reading

This chapter draws on a diverse range of sources – from film studies, German studies, anthropology and communication studies, as well as contemporaneous news and journal coverage – in order to provide both an overview of the public discussion that accompanied the opening of the Berlin Wall and a conceptual framework within which to analyze the documentary films discussed. Hence it is difficult to isolate a small number of key texts for follow-up reading. However, as a starting point I would recommend the following:

For an accessible cross-section of the debates surrounding the 1989–1990 events in Germany, see *New German Critique*, 52 (Winter 1991). This was a special issue on German Unification and most of the articles appeared originally in German language sources between November 1989 and June 1990. For a sense of the wider media landscape in Europe at the time and its role in the 1989–1990 events, see Geoffrey Nowell-Smith and Tana Wollen (eds), *After the Wall* (1991). This is a collection of papers presented by broadcasters, analysts and commentators at a conference entitled "How Do You See Germany?" and organized by the British Film Institute a year after the Berlin Wall came down. For a broader discussion of national and European identity in relation to film, see Duncan Petrie (ed.), *Screening Europe: Image and Identity in Contemporary European Cinema* (1992). This is the published proceedings of another British Film Institute conference held in June 1991 addressing the theme of European identity and its expression through film in a Europe no longer divided by the Iron Curtain.

Filmography

Berlin Is in Germany (Hannes Stöhr, Germany, 2001).

Cabaret (Bob Fosse, USA, 1972).

Good Bye, Lenin! (Wolfgang Becker, Germany, 2003).

In the Splendour of Happiness [*Im Glanze dieses Glückes*] (Johann Feindt and Helga Reidemeister, with contributions from Jeanine Meerapfel, Dieter Schumann and Tamara Trampe, West Germany, 1990).

Last Year in Germany [*Letztes Jahr in Deutschland*] (Lars Barthel, Dagmar Benke, Beate Schönfeldt and Jürgen Seidler, East Germany / West Germany, 1990).

Last Year – Titanic [*Letztes Jahr Titanic*] (Andreas Voigt, East Germany / West Germany, 1991).

Locked Up Time [*Verriegelte Zeit*] (Sibylle Schönemann, East Germany / West Germany, 1990).

November Days – Voices and Choices [*Novembertage – Stimmen und Wege*] (Marcel Ophuls, UK/ West Germany, 1990).

Sonnennallee [Sun Alley] (Leander Haußmann, Germany, 1999).

To Be Or Not To Be (Ernst Lubitsch, USA, 1942).

4

Post-Reunification Cinema
Horror, Nostalgia, Redemption

Anthony Enns

This chapter will examine how the social impact of German reunification has been depicted in contemporary German cinema, and it will particularly focus on three narrative modes that are frequently employed in cinematic depictions of German reunification: horror, nostalgia, and redemption. Many of the earliest films that address the impact of German reunification employ horror or thriller narratives to represent the perceived threat that reunification posed to the former German Democratic Republic (GDR) and its citizens. By representing this threat in the most explicit terms imaginable, these narratives were quite effective at addressing public concerns surrounding the loss of East German identity and the impact of Western capitalism. These early narratives were followed by more ambiguous films that expressed a certain degree of nostalgia for the former GDR. While these nostalgic films do not necessarily condemn reunification, they do express a profound sense of loss and they offer an implicit critique of post-reunification Germany by pointing to some of the more positive aspects of the former GDR, which have since vanished. The third and most common narrative is overtly celebratory, as it portrays the fall of the Berlin Wall and the reunification of Germany as a moment of salvation and redemption. These films function as confessional narratives that allow East German characters to atone for past sins and to embrace an ostensibly more optimistic vision of the nation's future. This third mode has been the most prevalent in recent years, yet this chapter will show that there are still many other competing narratives concerning German reunification. This proliferation of competing narratives is to some extent contingent upon and reflects ongoing historical and social developments in Germany, and it is therefore unlikely that any single narrative mode will ever be capable of capturing and conveying the wide range of attitudes and opinions concerning the impact of reunification on German society.

A Companion to German Cinema, First Edition. Edited by Terri Ginsberg and Andrea Mensch.
© 2012 Blackwell Publishing Ltd. Published 2012 by Blackwell Publishing Ltd.

Horror

One of the first and most widely discussed films about German reunification is Christoph Schlingensief's *Das deutsche Kettensägenmassaker* (The German Chainsaw Massacre, 1990). As the title already indicates, *Das deutsche Kettensägenmassaker* was a take-off on Tobe Hooper's genre-defining splatter film *The Texas Chainsaw Massacre* (1974), yet the subtitle of the film, "Die erste Stunde der Wiedervereinigung" (The First Hour of Reunification), also emphasized the significance of the film's immediate social context. The film was shot only fourteen days after the fall of the Berlin Wall, and it even received a special prize for the Best Film on German Reunification at the Hofer Filmtage (Germany's second largest film festival after the Berlin Film Festival). The importance of this context is also emphasized by the opening shots of the film, which consist of actual documentary footage of the reunification festivities in Berlin on October 3, 1990. As Anthony Coulson points out, Schlingensief's splatter film signifies an attack on the process of image-making that this documentary footage represents:

> Schlingensief … targets his onslaught, in drastic hyperbole, on the image-making itself, on the screen drama of national celebration. For him the depravity of these images, and of the society that apparently believes in them, consists in camouflaging the unsavory realities of unification, realities which, with few inhibitions, his satire then proceeds to expose. (1995: 218)

The purpose of Schlingensief's film, in other words, is to offer an alternative to such "shiny images of jubilation" (Coulson, 1995: 221) by exposing the darker and more sinister aspects of reunification.

This documentary footage is followed by a title card that reads as follows: "Since the borders opened on November 9, 1989, hundreds of thousands of GDR citizens left their old home. Many of them live to this day unacknowledged among us. Four percent never arrived." The premise of Schlingensief's film is that this missing "four percent" have fallen victim to a family of cannibals who operate a West German meat-packing facility located near the border of the former GDR. As Kris Thomas-Vander Lugt points out, within the context of this massive population migration the term "arrived" takes on a double meaning:

> The idea of "not arriving" in West Germany plays both literally and figuratively. As the narrative unfolds, we discover that these four percent were in all likelihood literally ground into wurst and devoured by a West German family of butchers. But the phrase also plays on another meaning of "never arrived" – there were some East Germans who did manage to make it to the West with their bodies in one piece, but never "arrived" in a metaphorical sense, that is, they failed to adapt to capitalism and fell through the cracks of the system. (2007: 172)

In other words, the film employs a familiar horror film genre – the "splatter" film – to describe the problem of assimilation and integration following German reunification. Many of the East Germans in the film fail to escape the marauding West German cannibals, just as many East Germans were unable to make a life for themselves in the newly unified Germany. The literal dismemberment of East Germans in the film thus illustrates how the former GDR was figuratively torn apart by the former Federal Republic of Germany (FRG). As Coulson points out, the contrast between the documentary style of the opening and the obviously surreal imagery of the splatter narrative also reflects the film's political critique:

> In making the "splatter movie" – the epitome of mindless, "state-of-the-art" media savagery – the metaphor of German political fratricide, in projecting the time and place of this national embrace onto the screen-space of the video nasty, factualized, as it were, by the "documentary" pose of the prologue, Schlingensief fuses political and media critique into one, suggesting that another, and more subtle, form of violence, other than the whining chain-saws of the unifiers, is also at work. His satire reveals in the pictures of togetherness another kind of daily massacre: the liquidation of realities on the television screen. *Das deutsche Kettensägenmassaker* parodies a media-made world that is already grotesquely distorted; it offers a caricature of images and words that themselves can batter and brutalize our political consciousness. (1995: 221)

The film thus employs the splatter genre not only to criticize the social impact of German reunification, but also to attack the distorted representations of reunification in the mainstream media. While the film does not claim to depict reality, in other words, its horrific imagery serves to deconstruct the very sense of social reality engendered by the allegedly "true" images shown on television news programs.

The connection between capitalism and cruelty is made explicit at several key moments in the film when the desire for personal gain drives the characters to betray and murder one another. Upon hearing the news of the fall of the Berlin Wall, for example, the film's protagonist Clara (Karina Fallenstein) immediately stabs her husband and drives across the border to join her West German boyfriend Artur (Artur Albrecht). She meets her boyfriend at a barren industrial site (filmed near Duisburg in the western province of North Rhine-Westphalia), and he attempts to force her to have sex with him despite the fact that she rejects his advances. From the very beginning of the film, therefore, viewers are invited into a world where demand and consumption are valued above basic human rights. The horrors of capitalism are most vividly illustrated by the family of West German cannibals, who kill East Germans and grind their bodies into sausages. The family's meatpacking factory clearly demonstrates how the economic impera-tives of a capitalist economy treat humans as nothing more than commodities. At one point, for example, the family encounters an East German couple driving along and immediately run them off the road while shouting "Welcome!" and asking "How much do you weigh?" When the East German woman gets out of the car, one of the cannibals holds a knife to her throat and yells, "This here's the free market, got it?" The notion that capitalism negates the value of human life is further emphasized by the cannibals' repeated refrain: "In a time when everything is possible, it is unimportant whether something is good or bad." The "free market" economy is fundamentally unethical, in other words, because it reduces all human behavior to acts of exploitation and consumption. The film also presents this cycle of exploitation and consumption as virtually limitless, as human bodies literally become raw material for the mass production of consumer products.

More importantly, the film emphasizes the idea that the logic of capitalism has overwhelmed any sense of collective identity or national solidarity. As the aforementioned East German woman is killed by a chainsaw-wielding cannibal, for example, she screams: "But we are one people!" This comment not only reveals how capitalism reduces all human relationships to those of predator and prey, but it also shows how belief in a collective identity can make people more vulnerable to economic exploitation. This sense of futility is also conveyed through Clara's story. Clara is initially held captive in the basement of the meatpacking facility, but after escaping she attempts to look for Artur. When they are reunited it turns out that he, too, has been infected by the family's cannibalistic mania, which illustrates yet another aspect of Western capitalism: its vampiric character. Clara flees from him as well, and at the end of the film she manages to jump onto the back of a passing pickup truck. She believes she has been rescued until she looks into the window of the cab and discovers that the driver is none other than Artur. The ending thus clearly suggests that true escape is impossible, as German reunification can only result in the dismembering of the GDR and its assimilation into the FRG. This idea is further emphasized in the film's closing image, a burning Trabi (the iconic East German automobile), which once again emphasizes the ominous notion of a reunification that may only result in the destruction of the former GDR.

Schlingensief's film was shocking not only because of its gratuitous use of gore and fake blood but also because it openly rejected the more moderate approach to German reunification that was commonly employed in public discourse at the time. As Lugt points out,

> Schlingensief departs from "politically correct" avenues of social critique, most especially from discourses of tolerance that arose in the postwar and post-reunification context. Instead, Schlingensief recognizes conflict and confrontation as being at the center of contemporary debates and works from within the logic of violence to explode it from the inside out. (2007: 166)

The violent content of the film's narrative is thus essential to its underlying message, as Schlingensief was attempting to expose a conflict that was not being addressed in contemporary debates concerning the impact of reunification.

Randall Halle (2003: 296) also identifies Schlingensief's film as part of a wave of German horror films that appeared shortly after reunification, to which he refers as "unification horror." According to Halle, these films used the familiar tropes of the genre to address the social turmoil associated with reunification, and they thus represent a form of "cheap therapy … to make bearable the lack of cohesion of the social body outside the film fantasy."

Carsten Fiebeler's *Die Datsche* (Home Truths, 2002) employs a similar narrative mode to address the impact of reunification on former East Germans. The film takes place in the former GDR in 1996, at a time when many of the fears expressed in the "unification horror" films had indeed come true. The protagonists, Elke and Arnold (Catherine H. Flemming and Michael Kind), are a childless couple with marital problems. In an effort to resolve their difficulties, Arnold has agreed to sell their weekend home, although he is clearly proud of the house and does not want to lose it. The house is filled with GDR furniture and memorabilia, and Arnold's attachment to the house appears to be symbolic of his pride in his former country. Further evidence of his inability to "just let go" is provided by the GDR jacket he wears throughout the film. Elke, on the other hand, seems to despise the house and its contents, which also reflects her dislike for both her husband and the former GDR. The house thus becomes a symbol of the marriage and the nation, both of which Elke desires to escape. Elke's sense of confinement is also conveyed by locating practically the entire film in the same cramped room. The limited use of sets was largely due to the fact that the film was based on Ulv Jakobsen's stage play *Keine Bewegung*, yet by adhering to the play's original setting and stage directions Fiebeler's adaptation effectively conveys the claustrophobic impression that this vacation home has become a prison.

Real estate developer Martin Stein (Alexander Hörbe) has agreed to purchase the house, which he is planning to turn into a thoroughfare to an "Erlebnisbad" resort. Stein thus becomes an embodiment of capitalism itself, which threatens to exploit the country's remaining resources and erase all traces of its socialist history. As the couple spend their last night in the house, they are assaulted by two burglars (Uwe Kockisch and Nils Nellessen), who ransack their home and then leave. Like the real estate developer's desire to buy the property and demolish the house, the burglars' assault similarly represents an attempt to pillage the former GDR, taking whatever is left of value and discarding the rest. The film thus conflates criminals and capitalists, who are only interested in exploiting other people and maximizing their own profits, and in this way the film allegorically represents the theft of East German culture following German reunification. After the burglars have gone, Elke decides to destroy whatever is left in order to claim a larger insurance settle-ment. Like the capitalists and criminals, in other words, Elke too is only interested in maximizing profit, even though it hurts Arnold to see her destroy their home – a place that he still cherishes due to the many positive memories he associates with it. The tensions between the married couple are thus closely related to their conflicting notions of value; while Elke sees the home and its contents as worthless relics of the past that should either be sold or discarded, Arnold still recognizes the value in the home, even if that value is purely sentimental.

The burglars return soon afterwards, as one of them is injured and they need a place to stay for the night. Although they take the couple hostage, Elke gradually begins to sympathize with them. The criminals not only represent a more potent form of masculinity which her husband evidently lacks, but they also share her desire to escape. Like the criminals, Elke also yearns for what they call the "wild life" – not necessarily in the sense of a hedonistic life of crime, which is how the criminals use this term, but rather in the sense of personal freedom and liberation from social restrictions, which is clearly what this term implies. Arnold is the only character who truly wishes for everything to remain the same; he desires nothing more than to hold onto whatever is left of the past, even though it is already gone. Elke's shift in allegiance from her husband to the criminals becomes increasingly obvious when Stein appears the following morning. One of the criminals, posing as Elke's husband, sells the house for a much larger sum than Arnold originally agreed upon, and Elke appears to be genuinely in love with him, as she yearns to run away with the criminals when they make their final escape. When she is left behind and finds herself alone with her husband once again, she ultimately decides to kill him and flee on her own. It thus appears that Elke has been infected by the same capitalist logic that informs the behavior of the criminals and the businessman. Rather than remaining trapped in the past and in her marriage, she chooses instead to cut her ties to her former life and become a liberated outlaw. In this way, German reunification can be seen as the motivating force behind a wide variety of criminal acts, from real estate swindles and theft to insurance scams and finally murder.

German reviews of the film stressed its concern with the psychological problems faced by East Germans as well as its more universal themes, such as the frustrated longings and disappointments that accompany middle age. Rolf-Ruediger Hamacher (2003: 35), for example, described the film as "a macabre and excessive mixture of thriller and psychodrama that illuminates the East German mentality, which turns out to be all-German, at least when it comes to garden idylls and secret longings" (my translation).[1] Such a focus on the universality of the narrative, however, obscures the most essential feature of the plot: every act of cruelty depicted in *Die Datsche* is the direct result of German reunification and its impact on the former GDR, which has effectively become a wasteland of selfish exploitation and barbaric cruelty.

Nostalgia

The first film to depict life in the former GDR in a more positive and nostalgic way was *Sonnenallee* (Sun Alley, 1999). Based on Thomas Brussig's novel *Am kürzeren Ende der Sonnenallee* (At the Shorter End of Sonnenallee, 1999), and directed by

Leander Haußmann, *Sonnenallee* is set in the 1970s on the east side of Sonnenallee, a street that lay directly on the border between East and West Berlin. The film tells the story of 17-year-old Micha (Alexander Scheer), a teenager with two driving obsessions: a passion for rock 'n' roll and a crush on a young woman named Miriam. Both of these interests entail considerable challenges. The music he loves is banned in the GDR, forcing Micha and his friends to discover creative ways of purchasing illegal records by the Beatles, Rolling Stones, T. Rex, etc. Miriam remains similarly out of reach, and her relationship with a glamorous, wealthy youth from West Berlin is a painful reminder to Micha that he is out of her league. Haußmann purposefully constructs this film as a universal tale of adolescent growing pains, not unlike George Lucas's *American Graffiti* (1973), and in the end Micha eventually overcomes his teenage angst and wins over Miriam once she snubs her West German boyfriend. Micha's neighbors, who include Stasi informers, black marketeers, party administrators, young pioneers, and rebellious youth, are also able to overcome their personal and political differences. In the closing scene of the film the entire neighborhood is miraculously unified through the power of rock 'n' roll, as they dance together in the street, their movements perfectly choreographed to Dynamo 5's hit song "The Letter."

Rather than providing an accurate depiction of life in the GDR, this light-hearted story represents a pointed attempt to characterize the former GDR in a "sunnier" fashion. In other words, the film does not depict the way the GDR really was, but rather the way it has been transformed through the narrator's own nostalgic memories of youth. The film was also closely linked to the phenomenon of *Ostalgie* – a term that combines the German words for "nostalgia" and "East." This concept was used to refer to a growing appreciation for GDR culture commonly held by former East Germans, many of whom had fond memories of growing up in the GDR.[2] As Immanuel Kant (1798: xxxii) points out, however, nostalgia does not represent a desire to return to the place where a person spent his childhood, but rather it represents the desire to recapture childhood itself. This sensibility is clearly emphasized in *Sonnenallee* by the voiceover at film's end, presented by the now presumably middle-aged Micha, who characterizes this long-ago time as the best of his life because "I was young and in love." The comment thus serves as a framing device for reminding the audience that Micha's story has been told from the perspective of the present, whereupon the film's levity is clearly licensed by the presumed fact that, because the political system it describes no longer exists, it is also no longer in need of critique. This is certainly a risky strategy, and it would indeed be easy to accuse the film of promoting a kind of historical amnesia, of failing to make the audience more politically aware by ignoring the harsh realities of life in the GDR. For example, Haußmann's humorous approach deflects the seriousness of Micha's mother's attempts to abandon her family and escape to the West – a serious issue faced by many East Germans. The problem of smuggling is similarly treated in a comical manner by depicting the regime's control as completely innocuous and ineffectual. For example, Micha's "eccentric" uncle from West Berlin (who is coded as gay in a rather obvious, stereotypical fashion) regularly smuggles Western products across the border, such as panty-hose and underwear, yet he appears to be engaged in such illegal activity simply for the thrill of getting away with it. And when Micha's forbidden recording of Wonderland's song "Moscow" is confiscated, it merely serves to highlight the incompetence of the police, who mistake the song for an authentic Soviet release. The quirky neighborhood guard (Detlev Buck) endures a constant, comical dance of being promoted and demoted in rank from "Herr Meister" to "Herr Obermeister," thus mocking the title-obsessed and overly hierarchical bureaucracy of the GDR. All of these examples clearly illustrate the director's own assertion that the private moments of people's lives are far more important than the political realities they experience.[3]

Several reviewers criticized the film for precisely this reason, arguing that *Sonnenallee* presents life behind the Berlin Wall as a virtual "petting zoo" and that the young protagonists are not in touch with the realities of everyday life in the GDR (Einax, 1999: 19), yet other critics argued that the very notion of representing life in the GDR as "normal" was in itself a political statement. As Elke de Wit (2000: para. 5) points out, *Sonnenallee* "pleads for recognition from West Germans that life for young East Germans was just as valid." Haußmann's personal background would seem to support this argument: since he was born in 1959 in the eastern city of Quedlinburg, it is easy to read the film as Haußmann's attempt to assert the validity of his own experiences growing up in the former GDR – and indeed the experiences of his entire generation. There is certainly some truth to the argument that even the mere depiction of everyday life in the GDR serves a political purpose, as such depictions are indeed quite rare and many East Germans increasingly feel that their experiences are being erased from Germany's collective cultural memory. Yet such arguments often ignore or simply overlook more obvious political readings of the film. There is a marked satirical tone in *Sonnenallee* that exposes and criticizes Western stereotypes of East Germans and of the former GDR as a whole. Haußmann is particularly drawn to the cut-off section of Sonnenallee in which the central characters live, for instance, because it lay directly on the border between East and West Berlin, and Westerners could observe the eastern section of Sonnenallee from observation platforms that were set up on the western side. This neighborhood was thus constantly under the microscope of Western surveillance, and there are several moments in the film during which Western tour groups come to gaze upon the street's supposedly unfortunate inhabitants. Prompted by jeers from West German adolescents, Micha and his friends at one point angrily play to their stereotypes of East Germans by threatening the onlookers with violent words and gestures. Micha and his friends also exaggerate the presumed clichés held by Western visitors when they run after a tour bus with pleading, outstretched arms. One of the naive Western tourists exclaims: "Look at those boys. They're just like those people we saw in Africa." "It's so sad," responds another. This satirical representation of Westerners clearly illustrates the film's desire to provide a more positive depiction of life in the former GDR. By portraying Westerners as both gullible and hopelessly out of touch, the film invites viewers to witness life in the former GDR from an explicitly East German perspective, and instead of invoking sympathy or pity this perspective is designed to convey a genuine sense of collective identity and solidarity. The film thus rejects the cultural stereotypes associated with the GDR and celebrates certain aspects of life in the GDR that might even seem preferable to the FRG.

This strategy suggests that the film's nostalgia might represent something more complex and potentially more political than Micha's simple recollections of youth. Throughout the film Micha describes the GDR as a thriving environment where employment rates were high and everyone could afford housing and food. In the closing shot of the film, the camera tracks down the empty street and crosses the former border between East and West Berlin, which is now gone. By shifting from color to black-and-white and eliminating all signs of life, this shot clearly suggests that the sun has finally set on Sonnenallee, and the uncertain future that lies ahead will be nothing more than a bleak and lonely night. Here the reference to reunification does not carry a promise of a better tomorrow; rather, the film's retrospective look at life in the GDR is informed by the subsequent failure of reunification to have met the nation's hopes and expectations. This failure points to a deeper, contemporaneous void in the present: life on Sonnenallee is far bleaker today than it was prior to reunification. As Susanne Rost (2003: 24) points out, unemployment and crime have only increased in this part of the city since the fall of the Berlin Wall.

Leander Haußmann's next film, *Herr Lehmann* (Berlin Blues, 2003), tells a similar story of a young man who is more focused on the trials and tribulations of love than the political events taking shape around him. This film, however, is set just prior to the fall of the Berlin Wall, and the action takes place in the former West Berlin neighborhood of Kreuzberg, a bohemian district that was geographically isolated from other parts of West Berlin as it was surrounded by eastern sections of the city. Illuminating the culture of all-night watering holes patronized by customers and bar-owners alike, the story is told through the eyes of Herr Lehmann (Christian Ulmen), a 29-year-old bartender whose circle of eclectic characters includes his best friend Karl (Detlev Buck), a cafe manager and struggling sculptor, and Lehmann's love interest Kathrin (Katja Danowski), a cranky and outspoken cook at Karl's cafe. Throughout the film Lehmann struggles to endure the emotional turbulence of his relationships with these two characters. His love for Kathrin, which incorporates his fantasies of her as his bride and the mother of his children, is not reciprocated, and his enduring hopes for a union with her come to a crashing halt when he finally discovers her kissing another man. Karl's delicate hold on reality eventually gives way to a nervous breakdown, perhaps in response to his upcoming sculpture exhibition, and Lehmann is forced to deliver his friend to a psychiatric ward. After these disturbing events, which take place on Lehmann's thirtieth birthday, he dulls his pain with beer at a Kreuzberg bar. Yet that final evening turns out to be momentous for a completely different reason, as it occasions the fall of the Berlin Wall. Just as Haußmann privileges the private over the political in *Sonnenallee*, therefore, the events surrounding the fall of the Berlin Wall are overshadowed by Lehmann's personal crises.

Critics immediately recognized these two films as companion pieces because of their mutual nostalgia for pre-reunification Berlin; some critics even employed the term *Westalgie* to describe *Herr Lehmann*'s nostalgia for the former FRG (e.g. Bartels, 2003: 15; Heine, 2003). As with *Sonnenallee*, the film's emphasis on the private moments of Lehmann's life also seems to diminish the seriousness of the film's historical context by obscuring any reference to the ongoing events leading up to the fall of the Berlin Wall. The only exception is Lehmann's attempt to bring money to a relative who lives in East Berlin, which is confiscated by border guards after a prolonged interrogation. The political weight of the situation is undercut, however, by the guards' frivolous obsession with the minutia of customs declaration terminology. The historical import of the film's final scene, in which Lehmann learns of the fall of the Berlin Wall, is also dramatically undercut, as the characters fail to acknowledge the magnitude of the event. After ordering a beer, for example, an anonymous woman mentions almost in passing that the Wall is open. Herr Lehmann appears unsurprised as the bartender turns on a tiny television set. The camera then focuses on the television, which broadcasts actual footage of a man driving his family across the border in a Trabi. Herr Lehmann turns to his drunken friend Sylvio and tells him to wake up: "The Wall is open." Sylvio, in a stupor, suggests they go and see what's going on, to which Herr Lehmann responds: "First, let's drink up." This scene provides perhaps the most salient instance of a pivotal moment in German history being treated merely as an apolitical, almost inconsequential backdrop to Lehmann's personal life.

However, there is still something potentially subversive about this nostalgic and idealistic look at life in 1980s Kreuzberg. In the previous scene, for example, the characters' repeated refrain that "now they will all come over" seems to offer an implicit critique of West German attitudes and prejudices, which still remain prevalent in Germany today, such as the ongoing allegations that the western provinces or *Bundesländer* have been forced to bear an unreasonable economic burden following reunification. Rather than privileging the personal over the political, which suggests that the film's appeal primarily lies in its discussion of universal themes like friendship or unrequited love, the film actually seems to illustrate the degree to which the political is always already embedded in the personal, and how the political turmoil taking place in Berlin in the 1980s repeatedly parallels Lehmann's own first-hand experiences. His sadness over the loss of Kathrin and Karl ultimately leaves him adrift at the end of the film, for example, a consequence that parallels the loss of the unique character of Kreuzberg itself. Like *Sonnenallee*, *Herr Lehmann* also portrays a community of innocence and vitality that has since been lost or corrupted. And in contrast to most depictions of the fall of the Berlin Wall, the film represents that event as a lamentable and uncertain moment: the world of Lehmann's past is gone, and rather than being the hopeful start of a promising new era, the Wall's dismantlement seems merely to signal the end of a happy one. As in *Sonnenallee*, therefore, German reunification does not carry with it the promise of a better tomorrow. Instead, its depiction is already informed by the subsequent failure of reunification to meet people's hopes and expectations, a failure that points to a deeper void in the present.

The notion that many Germans were disillusioned following reunification is also explored in Wolfgang Becker's *Goodbye, Lenin!* (2003), which employs a Rip van Winkle device to emphasize the sudden and overwhelming changes that took place in Germany after the fall of the Berlin Wall. The film begins just prior to this moment, as a loyal GDR citizen named Christiane Kerne (Katrin Sass) witnesses her son Alex (Daniel Brühl) being beaten by East German police during a demonstration. This traumatic event causes her to fall into a coma, and when she wakes up eight months later, the doctor informs her son that the slightest shock may kill her. Knowing that his mother would be shocked to discover that the GDR has collapsed, Alex attempts to prevent his mother from learning the truth, and he resurrects the family's old GDR furniture in order to transform his mother's bedroom back into the way it was prior to reunification. As most of the food products manufactured in the GDR are no longer available, Alex also searches for old containers, which he then fills with newly imported foods. This search provides some of the most humorous moments in the film – moments that may be lost on foreign audiences – as the most mundane aspects of daily life in the GDR suddenly take on tremendous significance. In this way, it could be argued that *Goodbye, Lenin!* reflects and even contributes to the current fascination for GDR culture, as it reminds spectators about common products such as "Mocca Fix" coffee and "Spreewaldgurken" pickles. Because the fall of the Berlin Wall also resulted in an enormous shift in fashion, as Easterners quickly discarded their old-fashioned clothes in favor of new Western imports, Alex must search for old clothing for his family to wear. This becomes a source of humor as well, as the family members end up wearing clothes from the former GDR that they themselves now find appallingly unfashionable. Alex's sister Ariane (Maria Simon) expresses disbelief that she ever wore such clothing, even though her current clothes would not have been available in the GDR less than a year earlier. The film thus repeatedly illustrates the differences between East and West as a confrontation between the former GDR and Germany's post-reunification present as seen through the lens of mass culture, and Alex becomes a kind of archeologist sifting through the detritus of a vanished culture and transforming his family home into a time capsule or living museum.

In order to create the illusion that the GDR is still functioning as normal, Alex hires local children to wear young pioneer uniforms and sing traditional songs for his mother, who used to conduct a young pioneer choir. Because the current television news would be too shocking for his mother, Alex also produces his own fake news broadcasts with the help of his friend Denis (Florian Lukas). When an advertisement for Coca-Cola goes up on a building wall directly visible from his mother's window, Alex even accommodates this potentially shocking change by faking a news report that claims Coca-Cola was actually invented in the GDR. Alex's broadcasts thus allow him to reinvent the country's history, and as the narrative progresses this reinvention increasingly diverges from reality. For example, once Christiane unexpectedly leaves the confines of her controlled environment and takes a walk outside, she witnesses a large number of Westerners living in her neighborhood, whereupon Alex creates another news story, claiming that Erich Honecker has agreed to take in West German refugees disillusioned with capitalism. Through this conscious play of simulation and representation, Alex's idealized depiction of life in the former GDR gradually becomes completely removed from actual, lived reality, and Alex himself realizes that he is not recreating the GDR as it was, but rather as he would like it to have been. By editing the history of the GDR, in other words, Alex is effectively editing his own country's cultural memory, and the sanitized version of the GDR that finally emerges on his television screen represents a pure product of his own nostalgia. At the end of the film, he even reedits the footage of the fall of the Berlin Wall such that the collapse of the GDR represents the ultimate achievement of socialism rather than its last great failure.

By refusing to address the more serious and disturbing aspects of the GDR, however, Becker's film has been frequently criticized for its apparently apolitical stance. Anna Funder (2003a: para. 9) argues, for example, that the film obscures the fact that the GDR was a totalitarian regime employing the most sinister methods of surveillance to control and manipulate its citizens: "If a similar film were made about the end of the De Klerk regime in South Africa, it would be strange not to mention apartheid at all." Becker justifies this oversight by focusing on the universal appeal of the film rather than its specific social and political context, claiming that the film can be "totally separated from this specific past" (quoted in Iordanova, 2003: 28). Becker also rejects the idea that this film has anything to do with *Ostalgie*, because it is equally as popular in the former FRG as in the former GDR. Katrin Sass, a veteran of the East German DEFA film studio, also claims that "'it is not a film about the fall of the Wall ... It's about a mother and a son, a family. It's a story the audience should be able to relate to with or without the historical background'" (Iordanova, 2003: 28). This interpretation has also been reinforced in the international press, whose reviewers often seem to be both unfamiliar with the film's historical background and oblivious to the *Ostalgie* phenomenon in general. In his review of *Goodbye, Lenin!* for example, Roger Ebert (2004: paras 6, 7) writes,

Goodbye, Lenin! ... never quite addresses the self-deception which causes Christiane to support the communist regime in the first place. Many people backed it through fear, ambition or prudence, but did anyone actually love it and believe in it? ... Imagine a film named *Goodbye, Hitler!* in which a loving son tries to protect his cherished mother from news of the fall of the Third Reich. (2004: paras 6, 7)

Ebert's inability to understand that there were indeed many aspects of life in the GDR that its citizens loved and believed in reveals a profound lack of attention to the film's specific cultural context, yet he ultimately rescues the film from its allegedly misguided politics by stressing instead its exploration of universal themes concerning parent–child relationships: "The underlying poignancy in this comedy is perhaps psychological more than political: How many of us lie to our parents, pretending a world still exists that they believe in but we have long since moved away from?" (Ebert, 2004: para. 8).

It is certainly understandable that the filmmakers would want to distance this film from the more gimmicky overtones of *Ostalgie*. The characterization of the film as the product of pure nostalgia could easily reduce it to nothing more than an empty stereotype of East German culture or leave it open to criticism for being politically irresponsible. By representing young pioneers, Stasi informers, and bureaucrats as harmlessly comical and largely ineffectual members of a now defunct state apparatus, the film clearly runs the risk of transforming the former GDR into a safe commodity. The reading of the film as a simple family melo-drama with universal appeal thus allows filmmakers and critics to dehistoricize, decontextualize and depoliticize the film, yet this strategy fails to address more complicated questions about the political function of nostalgia itself. For example, Alex's recreation of the GDR does not simply represent a conservative restoration of the past, but rather it also represents an idealized version of that past. In other words, Alex is also explicitly reassessing the country's guiding principles and questioning what the GDR could have been had it had the opportunity to be critiqued and improved. *Goodbye, Lenin!* thus clearly illustrates how nostalgia also functions as a form of political engagement, as it expresses the utopian desire to imagine new social possibilities.

This can be most clearly seen in Alex's fake news reports, which explicitly acknowledge the ways in which the former GDR has been transformed into a media construction. While the news effectively illustrates national identity as a composite of media representations, it simultaneously exposes the malleability of such representations, and the end result is a self-consciously nostalgic version of GDR history that is not actually true but nevertheless speaks to the problems and issues faced by East Germans after reunification. These news reports also provide a perfect example of what Svetlana Boym refers to as "countermemory," a phenomenon that emerged in Eastern Europe prior to the collapse of the Soviet Union. Boym (2001: 61) describes countermemory as "a prototype of a public sphere that already had emerged under the Communist regime," in which an "alternative vision of the past, present and future ... was communicated through half words, jokes and doublespeak." This process involved "finding blemishes in the official narrative of history" as well as deconstructing the dominant political rhetoric. Countermemory is "not merely a collection of alternative facts and texts but also an alternative way of reading by using ambiguity, irony, doublespeak, private intonation that challenged the official bureaucratic and political discourse"

(Boym, 2001: 62). Countermemory thus recognizes that history itself consists of nothing more than representations, and it provides people with a humorous and lighthearted way of deconstructing official versions of national identity while simultaneously constructing alternative versions that are more closely connected to their own lived experiences. When Alex realizes that he is constructing an alternative version of GDR history that more closely matches his own personal sense of national identity, as well as that of his immediate community, his lighthearted and well-intentioned prank similarly becomes a countermemory that retains a far greater political significance. By restaging the circumstances surrounding the fall of the Berlin Wall, for example, Alex's final news broadcast clearly illustrates a desire to resurrect useful aspects of socialism that have since been buried under the weight of history.

The most recent film to represent the history of the former GDR in a positive light is Carsten Fiebeler's *Kleinruppin forever* (2004), which tells the story of two twins who grew up on opposite sides of the country. The film takes place in 1985 when Tim, who lives in the Western city of Bremen, is an affluent tennis star on the verge of going pro and his twin brother Ronnie, who lives in the fictitious Eastern city of Kleinruppin, is a poor factory worker dreaming in vain of one day studying architecture (both characters are played by Tobias Schenke). The two brothers finally meet when Tim's high school goes on a field trip to the GDR, and Ronnie's curiosity for the West leads him to forcefully assume Tim's identity and return in his place.[4] The rest of the film chronicles Tim's attempts to return home and his eventual realization that his new life in the East is more complete and meaningful than the empty life he led in the West. While Tim remains critical of the GDR's political and economic systems, the film describes this gradual conversion as the valuing of personal relationships over political allegiances; as with earlier nostalgia films, therefore, the personal is valued over the political. While many of the negative aspects of life in the GDR are represented in this film, such as the Stasi agents who constantly spy on Tim and his family or the blatant corruption he witnesses at work, the film focuses more on the positive bonds Tim develops with his new community. Tim's father in the West, for example, is a cold, self-serving and insensitive businessman, who mocks Tim's tennis ambitions and urges him instead to join the family firm, yet Ronnie's father Erwin (Michael Gwisdek) is a kind, warmhearted man, who quickly becomes the caring father Tim never had. Tim's girlfriends conform to the same model. While his girlfriend in the West is depicted as wealthy, superficial and unemotional, his new Eastern girlfriend Jana (Anna Brüggemann) eventually teaches him the true meaning of love. These personal bonds also have political connotations, however, as they illustrate the ways in which interpersonal relationships in the West were created through materialism and the acquisition of capital, while those in the East were strengthened through mutual struggle and interdependence. The importance of personal bonds that override professional and financial security is also the basis for Tim's ultimate decision to reject his tennis scholarship and remain in the GDR.

Like Haußmann, Fiebeler also grew up in the former GDR. Unlike his first film, *Die Datsche*, which was a far more brutal depiction of the hardships suffered by East Germans after the fall of the Berlin Wall, *Kleinruppin forever* was clearly designed to inspire viewers to wish that they too could live in the GDR. The fact that Fiebeler's second film is far more lighthearted has encouraged reviewers like Jan Brachmann (2004: 30) to conclude that "now, according to Fiebeler, the time for licking wounds has passed, and he strives instead to claim the right to view the East in a positive way" (my translation).[5] Brachmann also points out, however, that the story is told from a Western perspective, which suggests that East German filmmakers are increasingly being deprived of their own voice: "When a young director can only view the country in which he was born and raised in a partially loving way by adopting a Western perspective, it is a sign of … self-expropriation" (Brachmann, 2004: 30; my translation).[6] This argument certainly has merit, and the nostalgia in this film is tempered to some degree by the fact that it focuses primarily on Tim rather than Ronnie, yet Fiebeler ultimately subverts this Western perspective by repeatedly switching back and forth between the East and the West, thus providing a detailed analysis of the many differences between these two cultures. While the GDR functions as an object of critical scrutiny at the beginning of the film, for example, the same can also be said of the FRG, as its negative aspects are similarly exaggerated and contrasted with the GDR's socialist alternative. This is particularly evident when Tim manages to escape from the GDR and return to his previous home. The presence of his twin brother Ronnie, who has since happily assimilated into Tim's former life, serves as a virtual mirror that allows Tim to see more clearly what he once was. The extremely gaudy and extravagant lifestyles of the West Germans – the clothes, the swimming pools and the overabundance of fruity cocktails – now appear as strange and foreign to him as the GDR did when he first arrived. Perhaps the most radical aspect of the film is that this shift in perspective is so subtle and convincing: while Tim's character ostensibly represents an initial point of identification for Western viewers, these same viewers are gradually led to identify with an Eastern perspective, and by the end of the film they are even asked to view themselves as Easterners view them.

Like many other nostalgic films, therefore, *Kleinruppin forever* illustrates a direct confrontation between two competing ways of life, and it employs nostalgia as a critical tool for evaluating contemporary German society and identifying potentially positive aspects of life in the former GDR that seem to have disappeared since reunification. It seems that this strategy was designed to speak directly to a particular historical moment, as the release of this film coincided with the fifteenth anniversary of the fall of the Berlin Wall, an event that generated considerable public debate in Germany concerning the impact of German reunification. This debate allowed many former East Germans to express their dissatisfaction with the Western model that had been imposed upon them, which was seen as the solution for all of the GDR's problems but which has only increased the economic disparity between the East and the West. By allowing Eastern voices to be heard and explicitly criticizing the effects of reunification, films like *Kleinruppin forever* clearly employ nostalgia as both a form of mourning for what has been lost and a means for effecting positive political change.

Redemption

Although Brussig's best-selling novel *Helden wie wir* (*Heroes Like Us*, 1995) was published four years before *Am kürzeren Ende der Sonnenallee*, it was not adapted until 1999. Sebastian Peterson's film version, which debuted on the tenth anniversary of the fall of the Berlin Wall on November 9, 1999, was clearly designed to capitalize on the recent success of *Sonnenallee*, yet the tone of the two novels could not be more different. *Helden wie wir* tells the story of a young man growing up in the GDR who becomes a model citizen by joining the young pioneers, spying on his neighbors and eventually joining the Stasi. Like *Am kürzeren Ende der Sonnenallee*, this novel similarly employs absurdist humor, yet its criticism of the state is much more overt. The surge of nationalism at the end of the novel, for example, is quickly replaced by anxieties concerning the impending threat of Western capitalism, as the main character suspects that the disintegration of one oppressive political regime will simply allow another one to take its place. As Brad Prager points out,

> While some of the novel may at first appear to describe a romantic revolutionary fantasy of political and sexual liberation, Brussig depicts how the turn away from the GDR inevitably brought about a turn towards yet another set of equally confining ideological strictures … [I]ts discourses of political and sexual emancipation are accompanied by a critical reflection on the impossibility of such emancipation for the subjects of either Germany. (2004: 983)

The novel was not nostalgic, therefore, but instead highly critical of the negative aspects of both the GDR and German reunification. In Peterson's film, however, an effort was made to incorporate elements of both nostalgia and redemption into the narrative, and the result is an odd mixture of two narratives modes that often seem incompatible.

The film's protagonist, Klaus Uhltzscht (Daniel Borgwardt), was born on August 20, 1968, the day that Soviet tanks entered Czechoslovakia, bringing an end to the Prague Spring. Klaus also claims to have single-handedly caused the fall of the Berlin Wall by exposing himself to border guards and allowing the crowds to break through. His autobiography thus parallels the story of socialism's decline and fall. This is emphasized early in the film when a parallel is drawn between his upbringing by his parents and his education by the state. This parallel is made even more apparent when Klaus discovers that his father is actually employed in the Ministerium für Staatssicherheit (Ministry for State Security). It is also established early in the film that Klaus has developed an inferiority complex as a result of both his parents and the state, whose numerous prohibitions have stunted his psychosexual development. Both the film and the novel thus depict the experience of living in the GDR as an Oedipal drama, in which the character's struggles with the repressive state apparatus represented by the Stasi parallel his struggles with the ideological state apparatus represented by home and family. Klaus's struggle to resolve his psychological and sexual issues similarly parallels the struggle of East Germans to resolve their political issues, as the film concludes by simultaneously depicting both the growth of Klaus's penis (a symbol of his psychosexual develop- ment) and the fall of the Berlin Wall. Klaus's emotional and sexual maturity is thus deeply connected to and perhaps even dependent on the collapse of the GDR. The object of Klaus's affections is Yvonne Anders (Xenia Snagowski), the daughter of a dissident who clearly rejects the propagandistic curriculum disseminated by the state's educational institutions. Instead of seeing Western Europe as the enemy, Yvonne fantasizes about Holland. In this way, Klaus's own sexual desire is closely linked to the West, and, insofar as he joins Yvonne in Holland at the end of the film, it becomes clear that the resolution of his personal-political Oedipus complex can only be accomplished by rejecting the GDR and escaping from Eastern Europe. The film as such presents the history of the GDR as the history of an immature country, its policy of containment having effectively stunted the mental, spiritual, and even sexual development of its inhabitants. The fall of the Berlin Wall is hence understood as a moment of both political and personal liberation. In direct contrast to *Sonnenallee*, in other words, there is nothing negative for *Helden wie wir* about German reunification. Rather, reunification becomes a moment of salvation and redemption – the ultimate defeat of an oppressive totalitarian regime.

This underlying message is partially undercut, however, by certain formal devices that add an element of absurdist comedy to the film's otherwise serious political critique. While the film obviously demonizes the Stasi and their methods of control and surveillance, the scenes depicting them are extremely humorous, which serves to deflate any genuine threat or danger usually associated with them. One technique used to add humor to these scenes is the use of rear-screen projection to introduce a level of parody and irony to the film. While Klaus is being trained by the Stasi, several officers are shown sitting in a parked car spying on people walking down the street. During these scenes actual documentary footage of GDR street scenes is projected in the background. However, unlike Schlingensief's *Das deutsche Kettensägenmassaker*, where the fictional footage is designed to counterbalance the overly celebratory documentary footage, Peterson's pastiche of documentary and fictional images serves to highlight the constructed nature of the film and make the Stasi officers appear ridiculous and ineffectual, which potentially obscures the very real impact of their social surveillance practices. Peterson employs a similar technique during the interior scenes in Karl's apartment, where the exterior view from the living-room window always looks out onto animated footage of buildings being erected in fast motion.

As with the use of rear-screen projection in the previous scene, this animated sequence repeatedly reminds the viewer that Klaus's apartment is merely a set that has been constructed in a film studio. The animation also reflects a common theme in East German socialist propaganda: the unrealized promise of economic growth and development. Much like the comical devices in *Sonnenallee*, not least the closing scene in which the entire neighborhood dances together in the street, these cinematic techniques serve to undercut the seriousness of the film's political critique and make the oppressive nature of the GDR's state apparatus seem ineffectual and simply absurd. While Peterson clearly employed these techniques in order to capitalize on the success of *Ostalgie* films like *Sonnenallee*, the film's critique of the former GDR is absolutely fundamental to the underlying narrative. Rather than depicting the GDR in a nostalgic way by emphasizing its positive aspects and addressing the failures of reunification, *Helden wie wir* clearly represents the fall of the Berlin Wall as a moment of redemption that effectively rescued East Germans from an oppressive totalitarian regime.

A similar ambiguity informs the two versions of Hannes Stöhr's debut, *Berlin Is in Germany* (1998 and 2001). The 2001 feature-length film was based on a short film of the same title, which was released in 1998. However, the feature-length version illustrates a shift between two different ways of depicting the impact of reunification: the horror mode and the redemption mode. Both films narrate the story of a former GDR citizen who has been released from prison after the fall of the Berlin Wall. In the original short film, the protagonist is suddenly thrust into a strange new world that he seems barely to recognize. His old East German currency is now worthless and can only be used for building paper airplanes. His clothes are also outmoded, and he finds it impossible to conform to contemporary fashion. He also discovers that his wife is working as a travel agent and has a foreign boyfriend, which emphasizes the fact that the border between East and West is now open and as a result Berlin has dramatically changed. In the end, it gradually becomes clear that he simply does not belong in this strange new world. One of the most effective devices used to convey this sense of alienation is the almost complete absence of dialogue. The main character has effectively lost his voice, which further emphasizes his estrangement from his former country that is also his former home. Stöhr's short film thus represents reunification as a shocking and traumatic experience of loss for the citizens of the former GDR, from which the main character may never recover.

The feature film released three years later departs significantly from the bleak pessimism of the short film. The protagonist of the feature film is Martin Schulz (Jörg Schüttauf), who is released from prison 11 years after the fall of the Berlin Wall. At the end of the film, it is revealed that his crime was actually an accident, thus transforming his imprisonment into an explicit indictment of the flaws of the GDR's legal system. His prison sentence also seems to function as a metaphor for the GDR itself, as the fall of the Berlin Wall effectively liberated the inhabitants of the former GDR from their own unjust confinement. But the film's main focus is on Berlin and the radical changes that occurred there over the course of the previous decade. Not only have massive construction projects changed the city's outer face, but even the streets have been reorganized and renamed. The elimination of places like "Stalinallee" and "Leninplatz" provide obvious examples of the ways in which the history of the city has been rewritten to eliminate any trace of its socialist past. The disorienting effect of these geographical changes is emphasized when Martin applies for a taxi license and realizes he can no longer navigate his own hometown. Martin is thus forced to study the layout of the new Berlin, but due to his criminal record he is ultimately let go before he even has a chance to take his final examination. The film thus builds on the prison metaphor of the GDR by suggesting that former East Germans are often treated like convicted felons, as they are seen as second-class citizens and are often unable to find work in a free market economy where their training and education are considered substandard or simply irrelevant. The changes that have taken place in Germany also parallel changes in Martin's family, as his wife now has a new boyfriend from West Germany and his son Rokko no longer recognizes him. Although these problems are ultimately resolved by the end of the film, viewers are left to ponder its more disturbing social and political implications. The film's English title, for example, comes from one of Rokko's homework assignments, which illustrates a shift in curriculum from Russian to English as the primary foreign language taught in the German public school system. This change is disorienting for Martin, as it crystallizes the new generation gap between parents and children and emphasizes the feeling that he is a foreigner in his own country.

This general sense of being a foreigner in one's own country forms the thematic basis of both the short film and the feature film. The key difference between these two films, however, is that in the short film the changes to Berlin are the direct cause of the main character's suffering, while in the feature film it is the character's resistance to change that appears to prevent him from moving forward. By introducing a back-story that establishes that Martin was labeled a criminal by the Stasi because he originally wanted to flee the GDR, his allegiance to his former country is far more tenuous than in the short film. His continued efforts to escape the past and resolve the trauma of his former life in the GDR thus prevent him from assimilating into the newly reunified Germany. His inability to let go of the past becomes particularly apparent when he is arrested by the police for the second time. He immediately falls into old patterns by assuming that his interrogator was trained by the Stasi, despite the fact that he is actually from Bremen. Martin thus continues to struggle with a system that exists only in his mind. As the film concludes with his release from custody, its final scenes mirror the opening scenes in which he is released from prison. Unlike those scenes, however, the ending implies that Martin will eventually manage to start over again. With the help of his wife and a sympathetic social worker, his transition will eventually be successful, and his dream of reuniting with his family will parallel the nation's collective hopes for reunification.

One of the most successful of the cinematic redemption narratives is Florian Henckel von Donnersmarck's *Das Leben der Anderen* (*The Lives of Others*, 2006). The film takes place in 1984 and depicts the Stasi's surveillance of a fictional playwright named Georg Dreyman (Sebastian Koch). Dreyman is not a dissident, but rather Cultural Minister Bruno Hempf (Thomas Thieme) is in love with Dreyman's girlfriend, actress Christa-Maria Sieland (Martina Gedeck), and is looking for an excuse to place Dreyman in prison. The Stasi agent assigned to observe Dreyman (Ulrich Mühe) eventually discovers Hempf's true motives, and he then attempts to intervene on their behalf in order to free them from Hempf's influence. Despite his efforts, or perhaps inadvertently because of them, Dreyman becomes increasingly critical of the state and Sieland is arrested and forced to inform on her boyfriend. The Stasi agent struggles to protect Dreyman by concealing some potentially incriminating evidence, yet Sieland is so overwhelmed with guilt that she eventually commits suicide. At the end of the film, Hempf encounters Dreyman at the theater and notes that Dreyman has not been able to write since the fall of the Berlin Wall. He concludes that the GDR was not such a bad place after all: "What is there to write about in this new Germany? Nothing to believe in, nothing to rebel against. Life was good in our little republic. Many realize that only now." In other words, the suffering endured by artists and intellectuals at the hands of the Stasi also served as a source of positive inspiration by giving them a cause to fight for and an opponent to fight against.

Donnersmarck's parents were both from the GDR, and he has stated in interviews that when he visited the GDR as a child he could sense the fear they had as subjects of the state. By allowing the major villain of the film to be the only character who voices any nostalgia for the former GDR, and by making it clear that the reasons for his nostalgia are absolutely unconscionable, Donnersmarck was clearly providing a counternarrative to the nostalgic depictions of the former GDR presented in films like *Sonnenallee* and *Goodbye, Lenin!* Reviews of the film frequently acknowledge this subtext. Reinhard Mohr (2007: para. 4) claims, for example, that "*Das Leben der Anderen* is the first German motion picture to seriously tackle the GDR without expressing nostalgia for Trabis or Spreewaldgurken" (my translation),[7] and Holger Lodahl (2007: para. 5) similarly claims that "after the GDR has been all dressed up and nostalgically represented in successful film comedies, *Das Leben der Anderen* finally shows the other side of the GDR. This film begins to fill the historical gap left behind by *Goodbye, Lenin!* and *Sonnenallee*" (my translation).[8] Tobias Vetter (2006: para. 9) nicely sums up this viewpoint by describing the film as "an efficient antidote to the *Ostalgie* overdose" (my translation).[9] Such reviews would seem to indicate that *Das Leben der Anderen* represents more than simply another version of GDR history; rather, the film seems to signal a more widespread cultural backlash against the Ostalgie phenomenon.

The only negative reviews of the film suggest that its critique of the GDR was simply not severe enough. By presenting a Stasi agent as a sympathetic figure who becomes disillusioned after recognizing that his government is corrupt,

Donnersmarck's film apparently runs the risk of being interpreted as an overly naive depiction of life in the former GDR. Slavoj Žižek (2007: para. 2) argues, for example, that the film soft-pedals the oppressive nature of the former GDR because "the horror that was inscribed into the very structure of the East German system is relegated to a mere personal whim [of the minister of culture]." Anna Funder similarly argues that the film is unrealistic because it would have been impossible for a Stasi operative to have hidden information from his superiors:

> No Stasi man ever tried to save his victims, because it was impossible … [T]otalitarian systems rely on thoroughgoing internal surveillance (terror) and division of tasks. The film doesn't accurately portray the way totalitarian systems work, because it needs to leave room for its hero to act humanely (something such systems are designed to prevent). (2007: para. 4)

In response to Donnersmarck's claim that "*The Lives of Others* is a human drama about the ability of human beings to do the right thing, no matter how far they have gone down the wrong path" (quoted in Funder, 2007: para. 14), Funder replies: "What is more likely to save us from going down the wrong path is recognising how human beings can be trained and forced into faceless systems of oppression, in which conscience is extinguished" (2007: para. 14). What these critics do not question, however, is the fundamental premise of the film: that the GDR was a corrupt regime that was responsible for the suffering of its citizens, and that the fall of the Berlin Wall represented the liberation and salvation of these people by the FRG. By arguing that the film was not harsh enough, in other words, these critics are clearly calling for filmic representations that would criticize the former GDR even more emphatically. As Žižek concludes: "We are still waiting for a film that would provide a complete description of the GDR terror" (Funder, 2007: para. 12).

Conclusion

The tremendous success of *Das Leben der Anderen* shows how the redemption narrative seems to have become the "official" narrative of German reunification. The notion that the GDR represents nothing more than a totalitarian regime and that reunification represents the liberation of an oppressed people is certainly a compelling story, and it is supported by many horrific accounts of the treatment of former GDR citizens by the Stasi. Many of these atrocities are catalogued in Funder's 2003 book *Stasiland: Stories from Behind the Berlin Wall*. Like many writers, Funder sees the GDR's techniques of state control as informing every aspect of East German culture. Consider, for example, Funder's (2003b: 275) description of a typical GDR apartment: "What surprises me about living here is that, no matter how much is taken out, this linoleum palace continues to contain all the necessities for life, at the same time as it refuses to admit a single thing, either accidentally or arranged, of beauty or joy. In this, I think, it is much like East Germany itself." Because East German culture appears to lack any trace of "beauty" or "joy," Funder is at a loss to explain the recent outpouring of nostalgia for these objects, and she can only conclude that this nostalgia "takes the place of a sense of belonging." Like many writers, therefore, Funder is clearly dismissive of *Ostalgie*, and she describes the fall of the GDR as a narrative of liberation and salvation. As I have attempted to show in this chapter, however, there are many other ways of telling this story, and none of them are necessarily truer than the others. While few East Germans would want to go back to the way things were prior to November 9, 1989, many still feel that their country was taken away from them and they were simply forced to accept Western capitalism rather than having the opportunity to reform their political system in potentially more positive ways. The impact of German reunification thus remains a highly contested issue, and it is unlikely that any single narrative mode will ever be able to capture the many conflicting viewpoints of former East and West Germans.

A very different version of this chapter's argument appeared in *Screen* (2007) 48 (4), 475–491, under the title "The politics of *Ostalgie*: post-socialist nostalgia in recent German film."

Notes

1 "… eine makaber überhöhte Mischung aus Thriller und Psychodrama, das nebenbei auch ostdeutsche Befindlichkeiten beleuchtet, die sich aber durchaus als gesamtdeutsche entpuppen – zumindest was Schrebergartenidylle und geheime Sehnsüchte anbelangt."
2 For a more detailed discussion of the concept of *Ostalgie* in relation to contemporary German cinema, see Enns (2007).
3 This comment is taken from an interview with the director featured on the DVD release of *Herr Lehmann*.
4 A similar premise was employed in the ZDF television series *Schulz und Schulz* (1989).
5 "Jetzt, meint Fiebeler, sei die Zeit des Wundenleckens vorbei, und er strengt sich an, den Osten gut finden zu dürfen."
6 "Wenn aber ein junger Regisseur auf das Land, in dem er geboren wurde und aufgewachsen ist, nur mit einem Westblick halbwegs liebevoll schauen kann, ist das ein Zeichen von … Selbstenteignung."
7 "… 'Das Leben der Anderen' [ist] der erste deutsche Spielfilm, der sich durchgehend ernsthaft, ohne Trabi-Nostalgie, Spreewaldgurken-Romantik …"
8 "Nachdem die DDR mit erfolgreichen Komödien im Kino geschönt und (n)ostalgisch dargestellt wurde, zeichnet *Das Leben der Anderen* endlich die anderer Seite der DDR. Dieser Film beginnt die filmhistorische Lücke zu schließen, die nach *Good Bye, Lenin!* *Sonnenallee* …"
9 "Ein effizienteres Gegenmittel gegen die Ostalgie-Überdosis …"

References

Bartels, G. (2003) Wie die Westlagie das Laufen lernt. *Die tageszeitung*, September 4, 15.

Boym, S. (2001) *The Future of Nostalgia*, Basic Books, New York.

Brachmann, J. (2004) Buddelt euch ein! *Berliner Zeitung*, September 9, 30.

Coulson, A. (1995) New land and forgotten spaces: the portrayal of another Germany in post-reunification film, in *The New Germany: Literature and Society after Unification* (eds O. Durrani, C, Good and K. Hilliard), Sheffield Academic Press, Sheffield, pp. 213–230.

De Wit, E. (2000) The sunnier side of East Germany. *Central European Review*, 2 (9), http://www.ce-review.org/00/9/kinoeye9_dewit.html (accessed February 22, 2011).

Ebert, R. (2004) Review of *Goodbye, Lenin! Chicago Sun-Times*, March 26, http://rogerebert.suntimes.com/apps/pbcs.dll/article?AID=/20040326/REVIEWS/403260304/1023 (accessed February 22, 2011).

Einax, R. (1999) Aufguss. *Frame*, 25 (5), 19.

Enns, A. (2007) The politics of *Ostalgie*: post-socialist nostalgia in recent German film. *Screen*, 48 (4), 475–491.

Funder, A. (2003a) Review of *Goodbye, Lenin! Prospect* 89, http://www.prospectmagazine.co.uk/2003/08/5680-berlinerbrief/ (accessed February 22, 2011).

Funder, A. (2003b) *Stasiland: Stories from Behind the Berlin Wall*, Granta, London.

Funder, A. (2007) Tyranny of terror. *The Guardian*, May 5, http://books.guardian.co.uk/review/story/0,,2072454,00.html (accessed February 22, 2011).

Halle, R. (2003) Unification horror: queer desire and uncanny visions, in *Light Motives: German Popular Film in Perspective* (eds R. Halle and M. McCarthy), Wayne State University Press, Detroit, pp. 281–303.

Hamacher, R-R. (2003) Die Datsche. *Film-dienst*, 56 (2), 35.

Heine, M. (2003) Es war nicht alles schlecht. *Die Welt*, July 1, http://www.welt.de/data/2003/07/01/126863.html (accessed February 22, 2011).

Iordanova, D. (2003) East of Eden. *Sight and Sound*, 148, 27–28.

Kant, I. (1798) *Anthropologie in pragmatischer Hinsicht*, Nicolovius, Königsberg.

Lodahl, H. (2006) *Das Leben der Anderen*: Das nächste große Ding? *kino-zeit* http://www.kino-zeit.de/filme/artikel/4463_das-leben-der-anderen.html (accessed February 22, 2011).

Lugt, K. (2007) Better living through splatter: Christoph Schlingensief's unsightly bodies and the politics of gore, in *Caligari's Heirs: The German Cinema of Fear after 1945* (ed. S. Hantke), Scarecrow Press, Lanham.

Mohr, R. (2006) Stasi ohne Spreewaldgurke. *Spiegel Online*, March 15, http://www.spiegel.de/kultur/kino/0,1518,406092,00.html (accessed May 23, 2011).

Prager, B. (2004) The erection of the Berlin Wall: Thomas Brussig's *Helden wie wir* and the End of East Germany. *Modern Language Review*, 99 (4), 983–998.

Rost, S. (2003) Straße ohne Sonne. *Berliner Zeitung*, April 30, 24.

Vetter, T. (2006) Das Leben der Anderen. *Filmrezension*, March 21, http://www.filmrezension.de/+frame.shtml?/filme/das_leben_der_anderen.shtml (accessed February 22, 2011).

Žižek, S. (2007) The dreams of others. *In These Times*, May 18, http://www.inthesetimes.com/article/3183/the_dreams_of_others (accessed February 22, 2011).

Filmography

Berlin Is in Germany (Hannes Stöhr, Germany, 2001).

Das deutsche Kettensägenmassaker [The German Chainsaw Massacre] (Christoph Schlingensief, Germany, 1990).

Die Datsche [Home Truths] (Carsten Fiebeler, Germany, 2002).

Goodbye, Lenin! (Wolfgang Becker, Germany, 2003).

Helden wie wir [Heroes like Us] (Sebastian Peterson, Germany, 1999).

Herr Lehmann [Berlin Blues] (Leander Haußmann, Germany, 2003).

Kleinruppin forever (Carsten Fiebeler, Germany, 2004).

Leben der Anderen, The [*The Lives of Others*] (Florian Henckel von Donnersmarck, Germany, 2006).

Sonnenallee [Sun Alley] (Leander Haußmann, Germany, 1999).

5

"Capitalism Has No More Natural Enemies"
The Berlin School

David Clarke

The Berlin School in Context of the German Film Industry

Debates among academics, film critics, industry insiders and makers of cultural policy about the state and future of the German cinema industry are characterized today by a competition between different models of economic and cultural viability in a global marketplace dominated by the United States. Following the demise of the New German Cinema movement of the 1970s and 1980s, these debates in the 1990s and in the new millennium centered on the tension between promotion of commercial cinema and other forms of cinema considered aesthetically innovative as well as politically or socially critical. For a wave of filmmakers who debuted in the early 1990s, Hollywood genre cinema offered a clear model, for example in the wave of romantic comedies that briefly enjoyed commercial success in the first half of the decade, such as Katja von Garnier's *Making Up!* (*Abgeschminkt!* 1993), Sönke Wortmann's *Maybe, Maybe Not* (*Der bewegte Mann*, 1994) or Rainer Kaufmann's *Talk of the Town* (*Stadtgespräch*, 1995). These films in particular drew the criticism of leading film scholar Eric Rentschler (2000) and the veteran critic Georg Seeßlen (Seeßlen and Jung, 1997) for their apparently apolitical stance. These critics implicitly expressed the fear that the dominance of a German genre cinema reaching large audiences would exclude the development of more challenging films. This view of the mutual exclusivity of commercial and "art" cinema in the national film culture has doubtless been fed by the myth of the New German Cinema's supposed overcoming of commercial genres in the 1970s; a myth that, as Tim Bergfelder (2005: 1–2) points out, tends to ignore that it was Hollywood and not the films of Fassbinder, Wenders, and others that really killed off these homegrown entertainments. In the discussions surrounding the group of filmmakers I will discuss in this

A Companion to German Cinema, First Edition. Edited by Terri Ginsberg and Andrea Mensch.
© 2012 Blackwell Publishing Ltd. Published 2012 by Blackwell Publishing Ltd.

chapter, the so-called Berlin School that emerged around the turn of the millennium, this kind of argumentation is reversed, but follows essentially the same logic. Here it is the supporters of commercial cinema who worry over the emergence of a style of filmmaking that might undermine the recent box-office successes of mainstream German productions. Well-known German director Oskar Roehler,[1] for example, sees the films of the Berlin School as "brittle and severe."

> Nothing actually happens in these films. They are always slow, always depressing, nothing is ever really said in them – and that is what is called the "Berlin School"; they are always well thought of and have an audience of between five and ten thousand. (Suchsland, 2004)

The terms in which Roehler distances himself from the Berlin School are revealing in relation to his own implicit claim to accessibility and commercial viability, despite his own auteurist sensibility; but his comments chime in with much press coverage of this movement that typically accuses the films of the being too slow and lacking clear narrative impetus, making them indigestible to a mainstream audience (e.g. Ströbele, 2006). This concern is also present in the critique formulated by established German director Dominik Graf,[2] who used the occasion of his appointment to an honorary chair at the International Film School in Cologne in May 2006 to express his concerns about the alleged formalism of what he describes as "the German new wave" (Graf, 2006: 64). Graf's argument is that this lack of narrative action is related to the personalities of the directors themselves, who, Graf rather patronizingly suggests, have yet to emerge from their "student situation" and engage with the real world. Their academic training has allegedly left them with excellent filmmaking skills, but little experience of reality, so that they "carry form before them like a shield against real life" (Graf, 2006: 64).

Veteran German producer Günter Rohrbach attacked the Berlin School less directly in an article for news magazine *Der Spiegel* in early 2007, where he criticized the work of German film critics, who, to simplify Rohrbach's argument only very slightly, were advising German filmgoers to see the wrong films. Rather than encouraging them to see good quality, high-budget films such as Tom Tykwer's blockbuster *Perfume* (2006), critics were supporting low-budget productions with small audiences, such as work by Valeska Griesbach[3] and Christoph Hochhäusler[4] (two key directors of the Berlin School) and making themselves the servants of a clique rather than of the mass public (Rohrbach, 2007). Rohrbach's article caused considerable debate, but the most perceptive assessment of his position was formulated by Georg Seeßlen (2007), who pointed to the almost hysterical reaction of defenders of the mainstream, who perceive the existence of anything outside of the film culture they support as a "moral insult," "as if it was a matter of alternatives – as if the evil realists and ascetics wanted to take away all our fun films, from James Bond to Florian von Donnersmark's [*The Lives of Others*], and use the art house to spoil our [...] weekly feelgood movie." As Seeßlen goes on to point out, this unease about the Berlin School in particular is often formulated in terms of the perceived danger of a return to the low-budget, niche film that is seen as a threat to the viability of the German film industry. However, the very fact that these are low-budget productions means that they can survive on lower returns. As both Susanne Gupta (2005) and Marco Abel (2010) also observe, the number of viewers, particularly when the films are screened on television, is more than enough to make these inexpensive films viable: this is not an anticommercial production model, even if these films are not as widely known in Germany as mainstream commercial productions (Abel, 2008).

In this light, the sensitivity of the defenders of the popular against the supposedly off-putting aesthetic of what has become known as the Berlin School arguably speaks of a deeper unease that these films not only challenge the aesthetics and ideology of mainstream productions, but also the social order they ultimately affirm. In this sense, the Berlin School, as Abel (2011) has been the first to recognize, should be read as a "counter-cinema."

Defining the Berlin School

Commentators on the Berlin School have generally identified a sizeable list of potential adherents, divided into a slightly older generation and a younger band of followers. As Abel points out, critic Rüdiger Suchsland (Abel, 2008) was the first to attempt a general definition of what this new cinematic movement might be. In a 2005 essay, Suchsland points out that significant figures in what he sees as the older generation of the School, Christian Petzold, Angela Schanelec and Thomas Arslan, were all trained at the German Film and Television Academy in Berlin in the late 1980s to mid 1990s and have since produced feature films that have secured limited cinema releases but achieved their most significant audiences through the "Little Television Play" ("Kleines Fernsehspiel") broadcasts on Germany's second public television channel, ZDF. Debuting only a few years later, Suchsland (2005) points a diverse group of directors, many of whom trained in Munich but who are now largely based in Berlin, whose films have much in common with the work of these earlier three. The names mentioned in this context, and later by other commentators, include Henner Winckler, Benjamin Heisenberg, Ulrich Köhler, Christoph Hochhäusler, Valeska Griesbach and Maria Speth (cf. Knörer, 2007).

Suchsland (2005) describes the films of the Berlin School as "coolly observed" and "sober," with a strong concern for reality. The central characters in these films, he observes, tend to be represented wandering through a world which is "normal, yet strangely unfamiliar"; they struggle with family problems and intergenerational conflict, and are often at odds with society, yet the films themselves do not offer any utopian alternative. In tune with Suchsland, Abel (2010), who has produced the most significant academic analyses of the films of the Berlin School to date, describes their shared "aesthetics of reduction": the films in question tend, he points out, to be characterized by "long takes, long shots, clinically precise framing, [and] a certain deliberateness of pace." Abel stresses the aesthetic points of contact between the various filmmakers, but other commentators have, like Suchsland, identified thematic concerns that might help to define the School, even if this definition is sometimes accompanied by skepticism regarding the existence of a clearly defined group. For example, Baute *et al.* (2006) also identify a concern with the family and the private sphere as a key theme, as does Hanns-Georg Rodek (2006), while Michael Sicinski (2009: 6) defines the "pseudomovement" of the Berlin School in terms of a concern with "late modernist themes of transnationalism, alienation, and spatial dislocation."

As will be clear from the above, while there is a widely held perception among critics that the work of some contemporary directors does allow us to identify certain aspects in common in terms of aesthetics and thematics, the definition and significance of the Berlin School is likely to remain open to debate and, within certain contexts, highly controversial. This is unsurprising when we compare this School to other filmmaking "movements," for example to the "New German Cinema" of the 1970s, whose definition is always the product of a combination of factors, not least the desire of critics and academics to identify an object of study and the desire of filmmakers themselves to market their products under a convenient banner (Rohnke, 2006).

The aim of the rest of this chapter will not be to offer a watertight definition of what the Berlin School might be or to merely synthesize the views detailed above. Rather, I will argue that it is more productive to see in the films of certain contemporary filmmakers a reaction to a particular set of historical circumstances, a reaction that has comparable but not identical consequences in terms of themes, narrative structure, and filmic form. In the space available, it is impossible to cover all of the films potentially belonging to the Berlin School, but I hope to provide a starting point for further analysis by discussing the work of three key directors, addressing two films by each.

The Social Context

The films of the New German Cinema were strongly identified with the generation of 1968, that is to say the first generation born after World War Two, whose cultural and political vanguard went on to challenge the values of the postwar Federal Republic and its political and economic system: for example, like the student movement, films of the New German Cinema critiqued consumerist capitalism, the alleged authoritarianism of the postwar Federal Republic, patriarchy and West Germany's failure to adequately address the legacy of National Socialism.

By the late 1990s, this generation, in the shape of the Schröder government, had reached the end of its "march through the institutions," to use student revolutionary Rudi Dutschke's famous phrase,[5] and was regarded by many, especially by disgruntled conservatives, as representing the new political and cultural hegemony in the country, a position it had achieved to a large extent by giving up many of its more radical positions or allowing them to be co-opted by the mainstream. The young directors of the early 1990s who rejected the supposedly somber and worthy model of the New German Cinema in favor of lightness and entertainment value were, it could be argued, simultaneously rejecting the albeit varied aesthetic strategies of the filmmakers of the 1968 generation while falling into line with that same generation's increasing acceptance of the capitalist status quo. As Paul Cooke and Chris Homewood (2011: 3) have put it, this was a cinema for a postideological "fun society."

The society into which young Germans enter today is nevertheless beset by uncertainties. High unemployment, the de-industrialization and depopulation of Eastern Germany (a favored setting for Berlin School films), the increasing insecurity of life for many low-skilled workers in service industries, and the rolling back of the German welfare system are all experiences reflected in films of the Berlin School. Despite recent strong electoral showings for *Die Linke* ("The Left"), a political party comprising postcommunists from Eastern and Western Germany, the main political parties, both Christian Democrats and Social Democrats, have tended to subscribe to the notion of the inevitability of these social conditions in a globalized capitalism where utopian projects no longer seem viable.

The representations of German society to be found in the films of the Berlin School are a response to these social conditions, and it will be the task of this chapter to establish the nature of that response. The films often show young people attempting but failing to establish a satisfying sense of identity and purpose under these conditions, but equally portray adults struggling to find meaning in an apparently monotonous and unfulfilling day-to-day existence characterized by alienation and ennui. Although some of the filmmakers discussed here (such as Angela Schanelec, Ulrich Köhler, or Christoph Hochhäusler) focus on middle-class figures rather than those on the margins of society (who are a feature of films by, for example, Maria Speth, Christian Petzold, or Henner Winckler), their apparent material security belies a rootlessness and alienation from their surroundings. This is often expressed in a restless and directionless wandering (Suchsland, 2005; Abel, 2008) through a mise-en-scène characterized by a blankness and anonymity associated with capitalist modernity. Cooke and Homewood (2011: 7) argue that such narratives and the "slow-paced, evacuated frames" employed can either be seen as a critique or as perhaps only the "straightforward declaration" of "the emptiness of everyday life after the 'end of history,'"[6] whereas Abel's (2010) analyses have tended to view these films very much in terms of a critique of such emptiness and as an attempt to offer an aesthetic alternative to it. While I share in the following Abel's insight that these films tend to stress the spatiotemporal aspect of their characters' existence, I will suggest that these films both allow us access to different constructions of the spatial and, at the same time, undertake to reveal spaces beyond the domination of the social order.

Theorizing the Spatial in the Films of the Berlin School

Henri Lefebvre (1991: 165–167) makes an important distinction between "conceived" and "lived" space. The former is space as organized by scientists, planners, architects, technocrats, the interests of capital and those of government; it is also what Lefebvre sees as "dominated space," and I will tend to use this term for the sake of clarity in what follows. Like Michel Foucault, Lefebvre regards such space as being subordinated to the requirements of power, while at the same time pointing out that such dominated space tends to simultaneously make opaque the social relations it expresses (Soja, 1989: 61). Dominated space, just as we will find it in the films of the Berlin School, is "sterilized, emptied out" (Lefebvre, 1991: 165). "Lived" space, however, is the space that subjects inhabit, try to make meaning in and "appropriate" to their needs. This space can be subjective in the extreme: imagination and fantasy, perhaps even psychosis create this space that does not need to be coherent or consistent as much as it needs to be satisfying to the subject (Lefebvre, 1991: 41). The "highest form" of the appropriation of space is, according to Lefebvre, the work of art (1991: 165).

The films of what has become known as the Berlin School tend to show us space from all of these three perspectives. First of all, they tend to focus on the effects of the contemporary social and economic order as it shapes physical spaces and imposes different forms of control and discipline on its subjects. Second, the protagonists attempt to project their own desires and needs on their physical surroundings, often through fantasy or imagination. At times these projections are incoherent, but in all cases the physical environment proves ultimately resistant to them. Third, we find in these films an aesthetic appropriation of space by the camera itself, an appropriation relatively independent of the desires and projects of the protagonists.

As noted, the films of the Berlin School are characterized, broadly speaking, by the predominance of long-shots, of a static or relatively immobile camera, slow editing, and a frequent use of long-shots or extreme long-shots. This style, rather than participating directly in the protagonists' struggle to appropriate space, or encouraging viewer identification with this struggle, serves to create an alternative representation of space, an aesthetic "appropriation" (Lefebvre) of space in its own right, but one inherent in the film itself as a work of art rather than one lived by the characters. A typical example of such an aesthetic appropriation of space can be found, for example, in Thomas Arslan's *Vacation* (*Ferien*, 2007), a tale of fraught family relationships set in and around a country house in the Uckermarck region of Eastern Germany. Although this film is almost entirely private in its subject matter, in that it does not seek to demonstrate the workings of power in spatial terms in the way that other Berlin School films do, it is notable for the insertion of a number of static shots of the landscape and nature around the house at the center of the story. These shots are neither identifiably shown from the point of view of any of the characters, nor do they work in the same fashion as conventional establishing shots. Whereas the rest of the film is focused tightly on the interactions of the film's characters, we occasionally see, for example, a shot of a field of tall grass or a blue sky with clouds passing through it. Sometimes these apparently unmotivated shots of the natural world are retrospectively attributed to the point of view of the characters, as when we see an extended close-up of an ants' nest followed by a long-shot of the two grandchildren of the house's owners observing the ants. Despite this attribution, the shot of the ants initially gains autonomy from the narrative, like the later shots of clouds and landscape, so that the viewer has the impression that this is a view of the filmic world existing alongside, rather than coinciding with, the perspectives of the characters, who are in any case too wrapped up in their own problems to pay much attention to their surroundings.

It is tempting to read this stylistic device, which finds parallels elsewhere in the Berlin School films, as producing an effect of distanciation for the viewer. We are deliberately placed in the position of detached observers, party to a perspective on the world that the characters in the film do not share, and we are therefore perhaps less likely to enter into an emotional identification with them. This coolness or distance might be compared to that produced in the films of directors of the New German Cinema, for example with Rainer Werner Fassbinder or Wim Wenders, whose use of framing, long-shots and a camera that assumes a point of view relatively independent from the action seeks to create a sense of critical distance. However this distanciation in Fassbinder and Wenders is amplified by other Brechtian alienation effects (*Verfremdungseffekte*), for example nonnaturalistic acting, dialogue and characterization, whereas in the films of the Berlin School these elements remain resolutely naturalistic, including in many cases the use of nonprofessional actors, which frequently leads to a reception of these films in terms of a realist aesthetic.

In order to reach some preliminary conclusions about the consequences of this aesthetic strategy I will focus briefly on one film, Angela Schanelec's *Marseille* (2004). This film fits in with the theme of restlessness and rootlessness already mentioned: it focuses on a young woman, Sophie, who seems unable to feel at home in her native Berlin and searches for a space that she can appropriate on her own terms. This film provides a particular useful example of theme of spatial appropriation in that Sophie's relationship to her surroundings is mediated by art. She is a photographer who wanders around the streets of Marseille, through its shopping centers, and in its commercial and industrial areas, creating images that she then pins to the wall of her flat around a map of the city. This map, the result of an administrative and economic process of domination in Lefebvre's terms, is set against her own imaginative appropriation of the urban space. However, this environment proves to be resistant to that appropriation in a number of ways.

The locations employed by Schanelec tend in themselves to express such resistance. They are often blank, emptied of human figures, or spaces of transit like bridges, escalators, roads, or crossroads. Despite some use of steadicam, what predominates is a static camera that often shows Sophie in a long-shot, sometimes reduced to a tiny figure in the urban landscape, or receding into that landscape, as in one scene where she leaves a bus and walks away from it down the street while the camera remains inside the vehicle. These spaces can be described, with French anthropologist Marc Augé, as "nonplaces," that is to say locations that express the conditions of an advanced capitalist modernity, favoring the anonymous movement of individuals through often highly administered and commercialized zones that resist attempts to linger and connect with others. Augé (1995: 79) lists the car park, the supermarket and the shopping mall among such typical "nonplaces" of advanced modernity, and these are also among the sites of Sophie's wandering. Furthermore, even if Sophie believes that she is appropriating space freely on her own terms, there are numerous reminders of the fragility of such a project. In one telling scene, Sophie is reprimanded twice by a security guard for attempting to take a photograph inside an anonymous-looking shopping mall, suggesting that, although she attempts to appropriate such spaces artistically on her own terms, the strictures imposed by the power defining them cannot simply be pushed aside. Sophie's autonomy is also challenged at the end of the film when her clothes and bag are stolen by an escaping robber. This bizarre crime leads to her being questioned in a police station wearing a prison-issue yellow dress. Here the questioning is just as intrusive and traumatic as the robbery that proceeded it; an impression heightened by our not having been shown the robbery, whereas the camera is present during the interrogation. Here Sophie's freedom to appropriate space is curtailed by the needs of one of the state's disciplinary agencies as it goes about the business of maintaining order and security.

The end of Schanelec's film, after Sophie leaves the police station, consists of a sequence of extreme long-shots of the empty Marseille beach at sunset, in the last of which we are just about able to pick out Sophie in her yellow clothing. This ending finds parallels in a number of the films I will discuss below, where we see the disappearance of the protagonists into the environment, either swallowed up by it or moving away from the camera until they disappear. In all of these cases, there is a suggestion of the futility of their attempts to master the world around them, yet perhaps also a hint at the contingency of the human ordering of space in general, including that control of space that Lefebvre attributes to the dominant social order. Here space is no longer anthropocentric, resisting attempts to impose meaning. From this perspective, one might interpret this aesthetic strategy as fundamentally pessimistic. By presenting space as exceeding the ability of the protagonists to appropriate it in any meaningful way, by consistently presenting them as overwhelmed by it, the films call into question the capacity of these figures to escape their essentially stagnant existences. What is left for the viewer, particularly here in the case of Schanelec's film, is an undoubtedly beautiful final image that offers access to the reality of a physical world independent both of the spatial domination of power and of the struggles and fantasies of the protagonists. It is perhaps in this sense that we can understand Hochhäusler's claim that the films of the Berlin School represent an "intrusion [*Einbruch*] of reality" (quoted in Rohnke, 2006). This intrusion of the real does not offer liberation for the protagonist of the film, nor does it function like one of Siegfried Kracauer's "flashes of reality" (Aitken, 2006: 180), that allow the viewer to intuit a totality beyond the fragmentation and alienation of modernity; but it does hint at something that exists outside the social order, even if that "outside" can for now be captured only by the camera.

This strategy, I would argue, is symptomatic of the fundamental ambiguity of these films in relation to contemporary capitalism, whose inescapable spatial order functions here as a metaphor for its apparently unchallengeable hegemony in the post-Cold War period. While the films I will discuss in this chapter point toward a beyond of the capitalist social order, they demonstrate that its subjects are ill-equipped to resist and overcome the circumstances which oppress them, circumstances which are, again, experienced in spatial terms. Indeed, such an overcoming can only be gestured toward on an aesthetic level through the directors' use of the camera.

Christian Petzold's *The State I Am In* (*Die innere Sicherheit*, 2000) and *Ghosts* (*Gespenster*, 2005)

Christian Petzold is the most prolific and (in relative terms) commercially successful director associated with the Berlin School, gaining widest recognition for his film of 2000 *The State I Am In* (*Die innere Sicherheit*). This film directly addresses the intergenerational conflict between the generation of 1968 and those who came after by portraying the relationship between a couple of Red Army Faction (RAF) members as they return to Germany with their daughter after many years on the run. Although the film can be read as criticizing the parents for their inherent selfishness in subjecting their daughter to this precarious life and for imposing their ideology upon her, it also paints a bleak picture of the Germany created by those who came to an arrangement with the capitalist system after the political upheavals of the 1960s and 1970s. While the parents' former radical friends now have comfortable existences, the film critiques the inherent social inequity and materialism of the Federal Republic of the late 1990s, where the lives of the young are characterized by boredom, apoliticism and a striving after the material (Palfreyman, 2006: 21–22). Jeanne, the daughter of the terrorist couple, and her co-generationalists appear to lack the wherewithal and the impetus to change a society that is presented as fundamentally alienating. Instead, fantasy and aspiration to the pleasures of a consumer society appear to be their only means of personal expression. In the case of Heinrich, the young "McJobber" Jeanne falls in love with, such fantasizing includes the appropriation of space: when he first meets Jeanne, he encourages her to imagine the luxury villa he claims he grew up in and tells her invented tales of his globe-trotting lifestyle. Heinrich has few opportunities to escape his limited world: in fact, he can only fantasize about what it would be like to be one of the economically powerful and mobile members of his society.

The attitude of Jeanne's parents to the spaces they inhabit as they cross the hostile terrain of the Federal Republic at first appears laughably paranoid. Here again we see characters largely in "nonplaces," such as anonymous motels, motorway laybys, service stations, road junctions, and so on. Yet in this case, Jeanne's parents recognize such spaces as only superficially open to the free movement of individuals. Instead, they understand that such spaces as always potentially subject to the surveillance and control of authority. Sometimes their fear is misplaced, as when Jeanne's father believes they are about to be arrested because a traffic light has been slow to change. However, their view of the relationship between power and space is not entirely without foundation, as the final sequence, when police cars apparently appear from nowhere to run the family off a deserted road, amply demonstrates. Equally, when the family witness a group of illegal immigrants being rounded up by police by a motorway, it becomes clear that, even without a focus on the threat of ultraleft terrorism, the state remains keen to control those spaces where people may try to slip between the cracks of power.

The denouement of the film, when Jeanne is in one sense freed from the life her parents have imposed upon her, is ambiguous: she has been liberated by the representatives of a social order that, to judge by the lives of the other young people she encounters, does not offer an especially attractive alternative to the underground existence of her family. Here it would be quite wrong to suggest, as Stefanie Hofer (2009: 188) has, that Petzold is somehow affirming the suggested reintegration of Jeanne into the social order of the Federal Republic. It is characteristic of Petzold's films in general that his protagonists' attempts at escape either fail or lead to their further entrapment in the order that oppresses them, his film *Yella* (2007) being a good case in point; yet the analysis of such processes in his films by no means amounts to an affirmation, much less a celebration of them.

The theme of escape and its failure is also important for Petzold's film *Ghosts*, that tells two parallel stories: the first is about Nina, a teenage offender being rehabilitated in Berlin; the second is about a French woman, Françoise. Françoise has returned to Berlin with her husband in search of her daughter, who was kidnapped many years before outside a supermarket in the city and who, we only learn at the very end of the film, was in fact murdered by her abductor. After a chance meeting, Françoise becomes convinced that Nina is really her daughter Marie, and there is in fact some evidence for this, given that Nina and Marie share a distinctive scar on their left ankles and a heartshaped birthmark on the back of their necks. Despite this amazing coincidence, Françoise knows that Marie is dead and that Nina therefore cannot be her daughter. Nevertheless, her mental illness drives her to continually seek out young women with whom to play out the fantasy of discovering Marie alive.

In this narrative, Nina is primarily represented in terms of her situation in dominated space. She is integrated into the penal system, collecting rubbish in Berlin's Tiergarten under the supervision of a state-employed overseer and living in a home for juvenile delinquents. She escapes from this situation, under threat of arrest, when she meets Toni, a young homeless woman with whom she runs away and begins to shoplift to survive. Nina and Toni are sexually attracted to each other, but it becomes clear that Toni is far more streetwise and prepared to use sex as a means of manipulating those around her. Despite Toni's rebelliousness, she clearly sees in Nina, at least initially, the possibility of finding a temporary refuge, and later in the film she will abandon Nina in order to seek just such a refuge with a married man.

The urban space that Toni moves through, accompanied by Nina, is dominated by interests over which she has little or no influence: she is powerless in economic terms and has to play cat and mouse with security guards and CCTV cameras in order to survive. The backdrop to Toni and Nina's wanderings in the city is that of the "Neue Mitte," the regenerated old center of the city around the Potsdamer Platz, now a landscape of high-tech buildings and shopping malls that continually repels them and forces them to keep moving.

Françoise moves in the same spaces as the two young women, but has a very different relationship to her surroundings. She is staying in a luxurious hotel in "Mitte" with her husband and cruises the area in their BMW cabriolet. She is characterized by her freedom of movement, clearly linked to her economic status, but this freedom also gives her mental illness scope to make of the city a fantasy space, out of which her murdered daughter will reappear unharmed. It is in this fantasy appropriation of the urban environment that Nina's needs and Françoise's needs momentarily coincide. Nina accepts that she must be Françoise's daughter (although we have no clear indication that her own parentage is uncertain) and sits happily with Françoise eating breakfast in the foyer of the hotel. Here she is finally admitted into the spaces reserved for the use of the wealthy, until Françoise's husband leads his wife away, much to Nina's distress.

What Petzold's film emphasizes here is that Nina's inability to appropriate the dominated space of the "Neue Mitte" is the counterpart to Françoise's merely illusory appropriation of that space. That illusion is, true enough, a product of psychosis, but it is also an illusion supported by her economic status, that gives her the freedom to act out her fantasies. The space of the "Neue Mitte," however, is not as amenable to her appropriation as it seems. Whereas Nina is faced with the hard fact of this space's resistance, Françoise can allow herself the delusion that this is not the case for her. This contrast is neatly demonstrated in the two brief sequences in the film that make use of images treated so as to appear like those of a monochrome CCTV camera. The first shows Nina and Toni leaving a branch of H&M in the shopping center at Potsdamer Platz. Although the camera fails to spot the stolen goods they carry, its gaze clearly signifies attempted control and surveillance in the interests of the capitalist consumer economy. The second sequence of this kind is the only flashback in the film, and shows Françoise's daughter being snatched from outside a supermarket in Berlin, which she also visits during the course of the film. This reference to the presence of CCTV cameras highlights the disjuncture between the primary function of the video surveillance in terms of protecting economic interests against criminal or disruptive behavior and the frequently stated justification of such surveillance in terms of making the public at large safer: the space Françoise inhabits is not organized around her interests, nor in such a way that will protect her from violence and danger. She is ultimately as exposed in and alienated from that space as is Nina.

The resistance of the space of the "Neue Mitte" to Nina's attempts at appropriation is clearly expressed in the film's mise-en-scène. Nina is constantly on the move in urban spaces that are empty and featureless, shown walking at speed along deserted streets flanked by blank façades. Even the green spaces of the city offer no respite or refuge, since they too are empty and inhospitable. In a similar fashion to the denouement of Schanelec's *Marseille*, *Ghosts* ends with Nina's virtual disappearance. Returning to a park to find the wallet she and Toni earlier stole from Françoise, Nina discovers in it a series of computer-generated photographs showing Françoise's child as she would appear if she had lived; the last bearing an uncanny resemblance to Nina. Unmoved, Nina screws up the paper and throws it into a trash can before retreating from the camera, which initially follows her before stopping to let her slowly recede into the landscape. The mise-en-scène is particularly important here, in that Nina's disappearing form is finally less important in the image than the trees swaying in the breeze in the foreground. Similar shots of Berlin's green spaces have already appeared at various points throughout the film and, as with the beach in *Marseille*, offer an image of the world as "intrusion of reality," an image that escapes the concerns of the disappearing and defeated female protagonist.

Both of the films discussed in detail here, along with *Yella*, form a loose trilogy of what Petzold has describe as "ghost films," and it is indeed characteristic of the *The State I Am In*, *Ghosts*, and *Yella* that the spaces the characters move through seem to resist their presence: that movement is not characterized by a high degree of interaction with others and the protagonists barely leave their mark on the locations they pass through. Indeed they seem to almost exist in a parallel reality, as if they were already dead. In fact, in *Yella*, the protagonist already is dead, whereas Nina in *Ghosts* is confused with a murdered girl.

However, this ghostliness need not only be understood on this narrative level. Jacques Derrida (1994) has analyzed Marx's critique of capitalism precisely in terms of the theme of "spectrality," describing the specter as "what one imagines, what one thinks, what one sees and what one projects – on an imaginary screen on which there is nothing to see" (Derrida, 1994: 100–101). For Derrida, Marx conceives of capitalism as a form of society in which all relations, both social and economic, are reduced to such specters or fantasy projections, whereas Marxist critique seeks to dissipate such phantoms by attempting to access the real (Derrida, 1994: 170). Although Petzold's films and others of the Berlin School do not adopt an explicitly Marxist standpoint, we can see in them a similar contrast between the fantasy projections of their protagonists and the real that the films seek to reveal in shots such as those described above. Although they do not propose means for the protagonists to overcome their immersion in spectral social relations, they do point to a beyond of these relations and therefore implicitly resist them.

Ulrich Köhler's *Bungalow* (2003) and *Windows on Monday* (*Montag kommen die Fenster*, 2006)

Ulrich Köhler's debut feature *Bungalow* has been called the quintessential Berlin School film (Abel, 2008). His protagonist is of a similar age to Jeanne and Nina in Petzold's films, and as in the case of Jeanne, the film dramatizes the tension between the rebellious generation of the 1960s and their children within one family. The film's protagonist, the 19-year-old conscript Paul, is a late child of parents whose older son is already in his midthirties. Although we never see these parents, the action takes place largely in their house, itself a metaphor for the apparently stable and comfortable social order that their generation has built in the Federal Republic. The director himself makes these links between the microcosm of his fictional family and contemporary Germany explicit in an interview for the left-wing weekly newspaper *Junge Welt*:

> He [Paul] probably comes from the pretty much ideal family, but he rejects this world and signs up. His parents probably vote for the Schröder government. In these circles there is a consensus that the children will refuse to serve in the army, but that … the parents will vote for parties that use the military as an instrument of foreign policy. […] I have a similar background, I also vote for these parties, so I'm part of this contradiction. Sometimes I miss the things that people from less liberal backgrounds have to overcome. This comfortable embrace sometimes really got to me. (Hesler, 2003)

It is worth noting in this quotation that Köhler, who identifies himself in the same interview with Paul's older brother Max, has chosen to project his own ambivalent feelings toward the parental generation onto a younger character. In a variation on the search for freedom in contemporary Germany, Köhler presents us with a youthful protagonist whose conflict with society does not stem from disadvantage, as for example in the case of Nina in *Ghosts*, but who experiences all of the benefits of a society that still fails to provide him with a sense of meaning and purpose. The irony highlighted by Köhler is that, in such an apparently perfect world, the only means of escape (Paul's unconventional decision to do military service rather than the social work favored by most middle-class young men) actually involves his deeper integration into the institutions of this society.

Paul's desire for escape is expressed in spatial terms. After an opening sequence where he allows himself to be left behind by his platoon at a motorway service station before making his way back to his parents' bungalow, the remaining action takes place largely in spaces of transit: on roads, in supermarket car parks, at motels and roadside service stations, at road junctions and roundabouts. Paul spends a good deal of the latter part of the film on the road, on foot, driving, or on his skateboard, escaping from the military police who appear from time to time to try to arrest him, yet there seems little prospect that this movement will allow him to appropriate space for himself according to his needs. He is repeatedly expelled from the bungalow, a building that represents a potential retreat and refuge from the inhospitably blank dominated space outside: Köhler carefully chooses feature-less exterior locations that are eerily empty and muted. However, the space of the bungalow is also resistant to appropriation by Paul: it is comfortable and middle-class, it is spacious and modern, the parents who provided it for him are described as tolerant, even perhaps too tolerant, according to Paul's increasingly frustrated older brother. Yet, in order to escape from this environment, Paul fantasizes about traveling to exotic locations, such as Africa, and the lure of an imagined space that is radically other is perhaps also the root of his attraction to his brother's Danish girlfriend, Lene, who is not only a foreigner, but also an actress rehearsing for a part as an alien in a film to be made in Munich.

In this film, the absent and therefore distant parental generation is presented as having built the Germany through which the younger generation moves: we discover that Paul's father is an architect, and in a half-hearted act of rebellion Paul draws a line through a design for a bungalow, not unlike the one the family inhabits, that he finds in his father's study, thereby rejecting the world that his father has helped to shape. Despite his stance of rejection, Paul's many abortive attempts to leave the bungalow for good are hindered by his clear inability to for-mulate any alternative to the life that this environment represents. As the director says of his antihero,

> because he never really breaks away: *Bungalow* is for me a failed road movie. The protagonist has many reasons to leave, but he can't do it. Paul has no goal. Nothing he can get excited about, nothing he can oppose to the world he rejects. Perhaps that is why he can't find the strength to leave. (Köhler, 2003: 6)

Paul's world seems to offer no possibility of formulating alternatives to an established order that threatens to sink into eventlessness. Here Köhler implicitly reflects on those neoliberal diagnoses of a new posthistorical world order in the wake of the fall of state socialism, where the promise of radical change is sidelined in favor of a capitalist status quo described by Patrick Brantlinger (1998: 68) as a "New World Order of eternal peace, plenty and boredom." At the same time, older means of rebellion are presented as exhausted and futile. Early in the film, Paul, Max and Lene hear an explosion and watch a plume of smoke rise from the center of the town as they stand on the roof of the bungalow. A number of the characters assume that this must have been an ultraleft terrorist attack, despite the fact that the RAF laid down its weapons in 1998. Later, however, it becomes clear that this was an accident caused by a faulty gas cylinder, supporting Max's claim that "capitalism has no more natural enemies."

In a similar fashion to Nina in *Ghosts* or Sophie in *Marseille*, Paul finally disappears at the end of the film. After seducing Lene, he calls the military police himself and walks from the motel where he has slept with her to be arrested. The camera views the whole scene in a high-angle static long-shot, as if from one of the windows of the motel. As Paul is about to be arrested, a truck pulls in front of the military vehicle and pulls away only when the police are ready to leave with Paul. However, as we cannot see him enter the military jeep, this scene gives the uncanny impression that Paul has simply vanished into thin air. As is often the case with the photography in this film, and in keeping with the style of realism typical of the Berlin School, the camera remains static as the jeep vacates the space, capturing a fragment of the real that transcends Paul's own projects and the domination of a state apparatus that finally reincorporates him, much as it reincorporated Jeanne in *The State I Am In*.

Köhler's second feature, *Windows on Monday*, also ascribes a symbolic importance to houses. Here there are two: first, the parental home of the female protagonist Nina and her brother Christoph, where they retreat when their adult relationships become too much for them, but that has apparently been abandoned by the parents themselves; second, the house that Nina, a doctor, is renovating with her husband Frieder. During her holiday, when Nina is supposed to help Frieder, she decides to leave him, spending a good deal of the first half of the film wandering around the woods around her parents' house, where she discovers a new hotel and leisure complex. Here Nina stays the night, observing the revels of a group of corporate customers, who are being entertained by former tennis star David Ionesco. Nina has a brief sexual encounter with Ionesco, but eventually returns and moves toward a (nevertheless inconclusive) reconciliation with Frieder.

Nina's wanderings seem to express a desire to return to adolescence or to a time before commitment to adult relationships and careers: she goes back to her parents' house, spends time with her brother, sleeps in a child's bunk bed and borrows her brother's clothes, giving her a tomboyish appearance. Her adventures at the hotel, where she seems to move with a ghostlike freedom, as if invisible, are an encounter with a world designed to facilitate fantasies and satisfy desires, as demonstrated by the general debauch of the customers there. With Ionesco, she is able to slip into a new identity, to play at being someone else, in a way that the appropriation of space represented by the renovation of the house with Frieder seems not to permit: on the contrary, this project is experienced as oppressive.

Again, as in *Bungalow*, the world of the everyday is portrayed here as largely eventless and directionless. The characters spend a good deal of time asleep: the opening sequence provides a key metaphor in this respect, showing Nina's daughter visiting her at work, where the child sees rows of beds with comatose patients: "Are they dead?" she asks, to which Frieder replies, "No, they're only sleeping." The implication here is that life for affluent citizens of contemporary Germany is a kind of death-like sleep, where nothing really happens, and where directionless lives can only be escaped through rare moments of fantasy. Once again, this desire for escape is expressed in spatial terms, in Nina's almost sleepwalk wandering.

Christoph Hochhäusler's *This Very Moment* (*Milchwald*, 2003) and *I Am Guilty* (*Falscher Bekenner*, 2005)

Like a number of the films discussed so far, Christoph Hochhäulser's first two features draw on intergenerational conflict in order to express dissatisfaction with the affluent world of Germany's middle class. In *This Very Moment*, the director retells the story of Hansel and Gretel in a contemporary context. The parents in the story are the biological father of a girl and her younger brother, and, in keeping with the fairytale, a reluctant stepmother. The family occupies a newly built house on an expensive-looking private development in Eastern Germany. The interior of the building – that like the house in *Windows on Monday* is still being decorated – is white, blank and cool. It is very much presented as the realm of the parents: in fact, because the children are abandoned by their stepmother at the beginning of the film during a shopping trip over the Polish border, they are never actually shown in the house itself. The borderland where the characters move is depicted as largely empty and featureless, so that the newly built house is reminiscent of a settler's homestead in a newly colonized land. Equally, the Polish side of the border is also shown to be a largely vacant space, characterized by empty roads and deserted service stations, reminiscent of the spaces of transit so characteristic of *Bungalow* and *Ghosts*, for example.

The hostility of the children toward their stepmother seems to be chiefly the product of the daughter Lea's jealousy, reversing the situation described in Grimms' fairytale. As the children move on foot through the Polish countryside, however, a distinct shift takes place in the relationship between the adults of the film and the children. Soon after being abandoned, the children are given a ride by the Polish sanitation engineer, Kubak, who attempts to sell them back to their parents for a substantial reward; yet the parents' quest to recover the children becomes less and less determined as the narrative progresses. The parents' relationship grows closer without the children: in one pivotal sequence, the stepmother faints outside a Polish service station restaurant after having caught a glimpse of her stepson being cleaned up ready for the handover by Kubak in the very same building. Rather than telling her husband what she has seen, she makes love to him in a motel room at the service station, and the search simply seems to peter out. The denouement that follows soon after this episode equally shows a rejection of the world of adults by the children. Whereas, until this point, the children have been seeking to return home, the final shot of the film shows them walking away from the camera down a straight road toward the horizon, over which they eventually disappear. In the empty spaces shown in the film, the adults struggle to express their interests and fulfill their desires; yet the children's disappearance implicitly acknowledges that their interests cannot and will not be acknowledged in the society their parents accept. Once again, in the film's final static shot, we are left with the image of a reality resistant to the projections of desire that many of the characters engage in.

Similar processes of fantastic projection are also at work in Hochhäusler's second feature, *I Am Guilty*, that tells the story of Armin. Like Paul in *Bungalow* he is the late child of a family whose parents can be identified with the generation of 1968. His father, played by veteran actor Manfred Zapatka (b. 1942), clearly lives comfortably from a material point of view, and is determined that his son should take up a white-collar profession (working as a travel agent is one option), whereas Armin's real aptitude and one talent is to work with car engines. In one telling scene, Armin's father calls him away from advising a neighbor on his car, obviously keen to dissuade Armin from indulging this interest as somehow inappropriate for the son of such a family.

Armin's response to this situation is to retreat into a world of fantasy, claiming responsibility for an accident whose aftermath he witnesses and a series of crimes reported in the local paper. This is one form of Armin's general attempt to reempower himself through imaginative projections, an attempt that takes roads as its preferred location. For example, we also see Armin's fantasies of engaging in group sex with a gang of leather-clad bikers in a roadside public toilet. Eventually, Armin even imagines one of these bikers having sex with him in his father's house, thus reclaiming for himself a sense of control of this parental space.

The use of the road as a fantasy space is revealing here. As I have shown, the road and movement are often features of Berlin School films, but here they most explicitly provide a metaphor for the protagonist's attempt to appropriate a space for himself within an oppressive social order. The road system, and the motorways that feature here in particular, are after all the expression of a complex modern planning apparatus designed to impose a mathematical organization on space according to principles of rationality, efficiency, and safety (Zeller, 2007: 181–223). The road system is therefore a prime example of "conceived" and "dominated space" in Lefebvre's terms. At the same time, this system produces "nonplaces" like the intersections and roadside rest-stops that Armin moves through and that serve as a screen onto which he projects his fantasies of escape. When he is eventually arrested by the police for his sabotage claims, he smiles as he is driven away to be questioned. This ending is ambiguous, but we can perhaps see his satisfaction in terms of having escaped his father's plans for his respectable middle-class career, of somehow having finally become the transgressive outlaw he imagined himself to be. However, as we have seen with other figures from Berlin School films, liberation is accompanied by a further subjection to the dominant social order, here manifested in its police force.

At the same time as Armin's subversion of the dominated space represented by the motorway fails to achieve the hoped-for liberation, the images of the roadway and traffic featured in the film are not infrequently reminiscent of those images of empty "nonplaces" already discussed. Before Armin enters the frame, for example in the very opening of the scene of the film, but also at other points, the viewer is presented with static framings of this space that allow Armin's projections yet ultimately remain unchanged by them. Nevertheless, these often aestheticized images transcend the function of the motorway within the social and economic order that it otherwise represents.

Conclusion

While it has not been the aim of this chapter to establish a rigid definition of the Berlin School, the films discussed allow us to identify a number of key themes and aesthetic strategies, establishing points of contact between a number of directors. Further work would doubtless allow us to establish parallels with the films of directors such as Thomas Arslan (mentioned only briefly here), Maria Speth, Maren Ade, Henner Winckler, and others. Clearly, these films mount an aesthetic challenge to the mainstream of German film, rejecting the models of popular cinema defended by the likes of Rohrbach and Graf, but they also seek to problematize the very foundations of such a mainstream by questioning the value of a life lived though fantasy projections, those spectral relationships to the world identified by Derrida and often promoted by the cinematic mainstream. At the same time, however, it is clear that the protagonists of these films do not establish successful strategies for escaping the domination of the forces that oppress them, and remain trapped in their own failing attempts to imaginatively appropriate the spaces they inhabit. In this sense, the inescapable spatial order that contains these characters becomes a metaphor for the apparently unchallenged dominance of the capitalist social order in contemporary Germany, an order which apparently has no more effective "enemies." The challenge mounted here by the eye of camera, which at least allows the viewer glimpses of a real that stubbornly refuses domination, expresses a desire for the overcoming of the status quo without actually furnishing the protagonists of these films with the strategies to achieve it.

Notes

1 Roehler's best-known films are *No Place to Go* (*Die Unberührbare*, 2000), *Agnes and his Brothers* (*Agnes und seine Brüder*, 2004), and his adaptation of Michel Houellebecq's novel *Atomised* (*Elementarteilchen*, 2006).
2 Graf is a prolific director, who is especially known for crime films made for cinema and television. Recent work includes *The Rock* (*Der Felsen*, 2002) and *The Red Cockatoo* (*Der rote Kakadu*, 2005).
3 Griesbach has made two features, *My Star* (*Mein Stern*, 2001) and *Longing* (*Sehnsucht*, 2006).
4 Hochhäusler's work will be discussed in detail below.
5 Rudi Dutscke (1940–1979) was a key figure in the student movement in West Berlin in the 1960s.
6 The notion of the "end of history" was popularized in the early 1990s by the American philosopher Francis Fukuyama, who argued in his book *The End of History and the Last Man* (1992) that the fall of communism pointed to an inevitable development of all societies toward an economically liberal, democratic model, marking the end point of human history.

References

Abel, M. (2008) Intensifying life: the cinema of the "Berlin School." *Cineaste* 33 (4), http://www.cineaste.com/articles/the-berlin-school.htm (accessed October 9, 2010).

Abel, M. (2010) Imagining Germany: the (political) cinema of Christian Petzold, in *The Collapse of the Conventional: German Cinema and its Politics at the Turn of the Twenty-First Century* (eds B. Prager and J. Fischer), Wayne State University Press, Detroit, pp. 258–284.

Abel, M. (2011) "A sharpening of our regard": realism, affect, and the redistribution of the sensible in Valeska Griesbach's *Longing*, in *Beyond the Cinema of Consensus? New Directions in German Cinema since 2000* (eds P. Cooke and C. Homewood), I.B. Tauris, London, pp. 200–218.

Augé, M. (1995) *Non-Places: Introduction to an Anthropology of Supermodernity* (trans. J. Howe), Verso, London.

Aitken, I. (2006) *Realist Film Theory and Cinema: The Nineteenth-Century Lukácsian and Intuitionist Realist Traditions*, Manchester University Press, Manchester.

Baute, M., Knörer, E., Pantenburg, V., Pethke, S. and Rothöhler, S. (2006) "Berliner Schule" – Eine Collage. *Kolik.Film*. Sonderheft, 6, http://www.kolikfilm.at/sonderheft.php?edition=20066&content=texte&text=1 (accessed October 9, 2010).

Bergfelder, T. (2005) *International Adventures: German Popular Cinema and European Co-Productions in the 1960s*, Berg, Oxford.

Brantlinger, P. (1998) Apocalypse 2001; Or, what happens after posthistory? *Cultural Critique*, 38, 59–83.

Cooke, P. and Homewood, C. (2011) Beyond the cinema of consensus? New directions in German cinema since 2000, in *Beyond the Cinema of Consensus?* (eds P. Cooke and C. Homewood), I.B. Tauris, London, pp. 1–19.

Derrida, J. (1994) *Spectres of Marx: The State of the Debt, the Work of Mourning, and the New International*, Routledge, London, New York.

Fukuyama, F. (1992) *The End of History and the Last Man*, Free Press, New York.

Graf, D. (2006) Unerlebte Filme. *Filmschnitt*, 43 (3), 62–65.

Gupta, S. (2005) Berliner Schule: Nouvelle Vague allemande. *fluter.de*, http://film.fluter.de/de/122/film/4219/ (accessed October 9, 2010).

Hesler, J. (2003) *Bungalow* in deutschen Kinos: Phlegma statt Weltverbesserungsgestus? J.H. sprach mit dem Regisseur Ulrich Köhler. *Junge Welt*, February 6, http://www.jungewelt.de/2003/02-06/017.php (accessed October 9, 2010).

Hochhäusler, C. (2006) Kino muss gefährlich sein, in *Revolver: Kino muss gefährlich sein* (ed. M. Seibert), Verlag der Autoren, Frankfurt a.M., p. 47.

Hofer, S. (2009) "…Von der Unmöglichkeit der Gegenwart": Gechlecht, Generation, und Nation in Petzolds *Die innere Sicherheit* und Sanders-Brahms' *Deutschland, bleiche Mutter. German Life and Letters* 62, 2, 174–189.

Knörer, E. (2007) Longshots: Luminous Days. Notes on a New German Cinema. *Vertigo* 43, 5, http://www.vertigomagazine.co.uk/showarticle.php?sel=andsiz=1andid=772 (accessed 9 October 2010).

Köhler, U. (2003) Interview mit Ulrich Köhler, in *Bungalow: Ein Film von Ulrich Köhler*, Basis-Filmverleih, Berlin, pp. 4–7.

Lefebvre, H. (1991) *The Production of Space* (trans. D. Nicholson), Blackwell, Oxford.

Palfreyman, R. (2006) The fourth generation: legacies of violence as quest for identity in post-unification terrorism films, in *German Cinema since Unification* (ed. D. Clarke), Continuum, London, 11–42.

Rentschler, E. (2000) From New German Cinema to the post-Wall cinema of consensus, in *Cinema and Nation* (eds M. Hjort and S. Mackenzie), Routledge, London, pp. 26–77.

Rodek, H-G. (2006) Reality ping-pong. *Sign and Sight*, http://www.signandsight.com/features/1074.html (accessed October 9, 2010).

Rohnke, C. (2006) Die Schule, die keine ist – Reflektionen über die "Berliner Schule." *Goethe Institut*, http://www.goethe.de/kue/flm/fmg/de1932607.htm (accessed October 9, 2010).

Rohrbach, G.v. (2007) Das Schmollen der Autisten: Hat die deutsche Filmkritik ausgedient? *Der Spiegel*, 4, January 22, 156–157.

Seeßlen, G. and Jung, F. (1997) Das Kino der Autoren ist tot: Glauben wir an ein neues? Eine Polemik zum deutschen Film. *epd Film*, 9, 18–21.

Seeßlen, G. (2007) Die Anti-Erzählmaschine: Ein Gegenwartskino in der Zeit des audiovisuellen Oligopols oder der Versuch, die "Berliner Schule" zu verstehen. *Freitag*, September 14, http://www.freitag.de/kultur/0737-stilfrage (accessed October 9, 2010).

Sicinski, M. (2009) Once the wall has tumbled: Christian Petzold's *Jerichow, Cinema Scope*, 38, 6–9, http://www.cinema-scope.com/cs38/feat_sicinski_jerichow.html (accessed October 9, 2010).

Soja, E.W. (1989) *Postmodern Geographies: The Reassertion of Space in Critical Social Theory*, Verso, London.

Ströbele, C. (2006) Muss das sein? *Die Zeit*, 4, n.p.

Suchsland, R. (2004) "Man macht sich was vor, und das ist auch gut so…": Oskar Roehler unplugged. *Artechock*, October 24, http://www.artechock.de/film/text/interview/r/roehler_2004.htm (accessed October 9, 2010).

Suchsland, R. (2005) Langsames Leben, schöne Tage kino: Annäherungen an die "Berliner Schule." *Film-Dienst*, 13, http://film-dienst.kim-info.de/artikel.php?nr=151062&dest=frei&pos=artikel (accessed October 9, 2010).

Zeller, T. (2007) *Driving Germany: The Landscape of the German Autobahn, 1930–1970*, Berghahn, Oxford.

Filmography

Agnes and His Brothers [*Agnes und seine Brüder*] (Oskar Roehler, Germany, 2006).

Atomised [*Elementarteilchen*] (Oskar Roehler, Germany, 2006).

Bungalow (Ulrich Köhler, Germany, 2003).

Ghosts [*Gespenster*] (Christian Petzold, Germany, 2005).

I Am Guilty [*Falscher Bekenner*] (Christoph Hochhäusler, Germany, 2005).

Lives of Others, The [*Das Leben der Anderen*] (Florian Henckel von Donnersmarck, Germany, 2006).

Longing [*Sehnsucht*] (Valeska Griesbach, Germany, 2006).

Making Up! [*Abgeschminkt!*] (Katja von Garnier, Germany, 1993).

Marseille (Angela Schanelec, Germany, 2004).

Maybe, Maybe Not [*Der bewegte Mann*] (Sönke Wortmann, Germany, 1994).

My Star [*Mein Stern*] (Valeska Griesbach, Germany, 2006).

No Place to Go [*Die Unberührbare*] (Oskar Roehler, Germany, 2000).

Perfume: The Story of a Murderer [*Das Parfum: Die Geschichte eines Mörders*] (Tom Tykwer, Germany/France/Spain/USA).

Talk of the Town [*Stadtgespräch*] (Sönke Wortmann, Germany, 1994).

Red Cockatoo, The [*Der rote Kakadu*] (Dominik Graf, Germany, 2005).

Rock, The [*Der Felsen*] (Dominik Graf, Germany, 2002).

State I Am In, The [*Die innere Sicherheit*] (Christian Petzold, Germany, 2000).

This Very Moment [*Milchwald*] (Christoph Hochhäusler, Germany, 2003).

Vacation [*Ferien*] (Thomas Arslan, Germany, 2007).

Windows on Monday [*Montag kommen die Fenster*] (Ulrich Köhler, Germany, 2006).

Yella (Christian Petzold, Germany, 2007).

6

Projecting *Heimat*
On the Regional and the Urban in Recent Cinema

Jennifer Ruth Hosek

For Ed

Although cinema continues to shape imagined communities (Anderson, 1991), national cinema may be anachronistic and is certainly elusive today. Randall Halle (2008) has used film from Germany as a case study to explain ways in which global forces shape even the most independent, low-budget productions. How are we then to read the return to the local in so many post-1990 features by German directors, particularly the dissimilar local spaces of New *Heimat* films and Berliner Schule (Berlin School) films set in the new capital? This chapter explores their poetic and narrative specificities diachronically, through critical archaeologies of *Heimat* ("Homeland") in the West German film tradition, and synchronically, in relation to post-1990 discourses around national community. It exposes what I shall call "-isms of propinquity" that are widespread in New *Heimat* and intermittent in Berlin films, notwithstanding the heterodoxies of urban *Heimat* in the latter.

A brief word on definitions is in order. The examples considered here are commonly understood as belonging to genres that, especially in the latter case, are contested. While films and their filmmakers can gain attention and attendance by being classified as part of a burgeoning genre, this same categorization can also constrict. Fatih Akın and Thomas Arslan are examples of filmmakers who continue to negotiate these pros and cons successfully by producing work and presenting themselves in ways that build upon and break stereotypes of Turkish-German filmmaking. Akın's *Solino* (2002), for instance, treats the (im)migrant experience in Germany through Italian, not Turkish workers. *The Edge of Heaven* (*Auf der anderen Seite*, 2007) cites canonical German literature. Arslan has moved from a trilogy about urban Turkish-Germans to featuring white Germans and mainstream

A Companion to German Cinema, First Edition. Edited by Terri Ginsberg and Andrea Mensch.
© 2012 Blackwell Publishing Ltd. Published 2012 by Blackwell Publishing Ltd.

German concerns such as West–East unification in *Vacation (Ferien,* 2007). Arslan's productions are classified with the Berliner Schule for the most usual reasons: aesthetic style and his training and work at the German Film and Television Academy in Berlin (*dffb*).While it is not necessary for this contribution on *Heimat* in German film from about 1990 to 2010 to engage directly in definitional wrangling, this analysis does in fact participate insofar as it will demonstrate some surprising commonalities between categories. My selection of films aims not to be exhaustive, but rather representative enough to convince.

Troubles with *Heimat*

Heimat is being reclaimed in public debate in unified Germany. Roughly translatable as Homeland, this affective notion was spurned by intellectuals and artists in both postwar Republics due to its mobilizations by fascists. In the mainstream intellectual landscape, a "normalized" Germany is now perceived as desirable to further policy agendas of Germany, Europe, and the global North. Accordingly, this European state should again bear arms abroad and cut domestic spending, and its populace should abandon principled commitments, conditioned over forty years, to left-leaning socioeconomic models. Normalization debates have turned on two related questions: What is German? – the Leading Culture (*Leitkultur*) dispute – and What are its foundations? – what will shore up the new imagined community following the age of constitutional patriotism and the German Mark (Taberner and Cooke, 2006).

New *Heimat* films respond with regionally specific belonging narratives that unfold in rural homogeneity. Although some New *Heimat* films overtly deride constrictions of such spaces, fundamentally they shore up a normative organization in which time is cyclical and place and belonging eternal and familiar. These contemporary renditions of Homeland venerate sameness and tradition in seemingly benign ways reminiscent of the West German *Heimat* films of the 1940s and 1950s. The recent turn to the regional has coincided with a discreet turn from overtly transnational cinema. By transnational cinema here I mean: films by Germans with a migrant background and those that depict identities as in excess of the national; New German Cinema, whose critical *Heimat* genres sought to unsettle nationalism and to further internationalist affinities; and DEFA film, whose German *Heimat* bears internationalist and transnational valences (Hosek, 2010; Boa and Palfreyman, 2000).[1]

New *Heimat* movies focus overtly on the local; yet, this circumscribed attention is a transnational phenomenon and this local is best understood as glocal. New *Heimat* film participates in a contemporary wave of European, even worldwide, regionalist filmmaking whose particularisms are shaped by and are responses to globalization. In a study whose results also speak to other regionalist filmmaking, Maria Irchenhauser (2009) has shown in detail how the filmic homelands in

New *Heimat* films express and shape social disorientation exacerbated by post-1990 globalization.[2] New *Heimat* films feature particular communities, geographies, and themes using particular aesthetics. Such circumscription responds to and expresses variegated trepidation around the movement of capital and its cultures across borders, brought and followed by people including privileged cosmopolitans and undocumented (im)migrant workers. New *Heimat* films concern themselves with the concomitant difficulties of im/mobility for those populations who are the primary subjects and protagonists of their films – white, Christian, middle-class, heterosexual, rural Germans.

"-isms of Propinquity"

In his anthology, *Giving Ground: The Politics of Propinquity*, Michael Sorkin (1999: 4) defines propinquity as neighborliness. Propinquity is also proximity, understood as familial, natural, or physical. From the Latin *propinquitas* ("nearness"), it is understood to further interpersonal attraction. Sorkin's anthological arrangement maps a dialectics of physical and psychological propinquities, regarding which he argues that "It is no tautology to suggest that the only training for living together is living together. Racial tolerance is never concretized in the absence of the other, which is why anti-Semitism, and racism of all forms, thrives where there are no Jews, no racial others, in sight" (Sorkin, 1999: 7). Sorkin's notion of propinquity highlights how lived spatiality and affective familiarity perpetuate homogeneity in community and thwart heterogeneity in it.

"-Isms of propinquity" expands the analytic lens to include all bigotries and particularly their flipside, preferential proximity. My use of the term propinquity is meant to highlight how, rather than simply expressing active -isms, filmic representations of homogeneous spaces and communities articulate a more or less conscious preference for similarity. Propinquity's Janus-face is a passive "racism without racists" (Bonilla-Silva, 2006), sexism without sexists, classism without classists, and so on. Or, as Zygmunt Bauman (1993: 13) writes, "Rejection of strangers ... verbalizes itself in terms of incompatibility ... of cultures, or of the self-defence of a form of life bequeathed by tradition." This logic resonates increasingly in what is sometimes termed Fortress Europe. It is found in attempts to crystalize and promulgate a German Leading Culture. German nationalisms and New Right formations have developed alongside and perhaps in some ways vis-à-vis a protean multicultural *Heimat* that Boa and Palfreyman (2000) see exemplified in the works of Turkish-German authors in the 1990s.

I argue that certain *Heimat* narratives, notably in New *Heimat* films but also latently in works of the Berliner Schule, resist and contain notions of heterodox, constitutionally supported multicultural nationalism such as those anticipated by Boa and Palfreyman. Examples I discuss from the New *Heimat* genre are Marcus H. Rosenmüller's oeuvre, *Wer früher stirbt ist länger tot* (He who dies sooner is dead longer, 2006), *Beste Zeit* (Best Time, 2007), and *Beste Gegend* (Best Place, 2008), and even *Räuber Kneißl* (The Robber Kneißl, 2008); as well as Hans Steinbichler's *Hierankl* (2003) and *Winter Journey* (*Winterreise*, 2006). A variant on these -isms of propinquity based in a logic of inversion flows through Christoph Hochhäusler's *This Very Moment* (*Milchwald*, 2003), Ulrich Köhler's *Windows on Monday* (*Am Montag kommen die Fenster*, 2006), Ann-Kristin Reyels's *Hunting Dogs* (*Jagdhunde*, 2007), Thomas Arslan's *Vacation*, and Maren Ade's *Everyone Else* (*Alle Anderen*, 2007) – all Berliner Schule films set in insular and largely unattractive provincial spaces, in which urban transplants, now positioned as "migrants," have no real place. Angela Schanelec's *Ich bin den Sommer über in Berlin geblieben* (I stayed in Berlin over the summer, 1993), *Passing Summer* (*Mein langsames Leben*, 2001), and *Afternoon* (*Nachmittag*, 2006–2007), and Christian Petzold's *Ghosts* (*Gespenster*, 2005) – all Berliner Schule films set in Berlin, are strikingly different from one another and from New *Heimat* films in both their plots and poetic structures. Yet each employs regionally specific *Heimats* legible to preferred insider audiences. Their similarity lies, that is, in the respective regional monocultures they depict and address through -isms of propinquity that undercut heterogeneity, notwithstanding its implied endorsement in notions of urban *Heimat*.

Heimat Film

-isms of propinquity share in a tradition of othering common in the first wave of *Heimat* films. One of the most popular *Heimat* features, attracting 19 million viewers, was Hans Depp's *Green Is the Heath* (*Grün ist die Heide*, 1951) (Naughton, 2002: 133). Reasons commonly supplied for its popularity are mainstream West German desires for Germanocentric, escapist entertainment in lives marked by war, thoughtful and didactic Rubble Films (*Trümmerfilme*), and US Hollywood fantasies. Government funding furthered and met these apparent interests; *Green Is the Heath* was the first movie financed by the Ministry of the Interior and also in this way can be seen as quintessentially *Heimat*.

The film tells of the patrician Lüderson and his daughter Helga, who have found a second home on the West German Lüneburger heath. They are expellees (*Vertriebene*), Germans who were forced to relocate from Eastern European regions that under the Nazi occupation were part of the Reich to what became East and West Germany. Lüderson's homesickness for his former lands in what now is Poland fuels his uncontrollable addiction to poaching in Lüneburg's public forest. To save him from punishment, Helga convinces him to move to the city. Prior to departure, father and daughter attend the village festival, spectacularly depicted with a variegated panorama of German regional flags, white Germans in regional dress (*Tracht*), and traditional German music and dance. Inspired by his melancholy and acculturation problems, Lüderson's impassioned speech at the

Stammtisch-like beer trestles set up outdoors is the didactic core of the film: "Don't be too hard on the people who have fled to you. Whoever has not been compelled to leave his home cannot know what it means to be without one."[3]

Lüderson's concerns speak to the situation in 1951, as many expellees were experiencing political, religious, class, and/or cultural conflict vis-à-vis the locals. The didactics of the film thus aim, as Johannes von Moltke (2005) points out, to encourage integration of German regional differences, which the panning shots of regional dress and flags metonymize. Von Moltke's work is path-breaking in that it does not read *Heimat* films as primarily reactionary, which most scholarly commentary to date has done. Instead, it seeks to place these movies into the discursive arc of post/ modernity by highlighting what it reads as significant ambivalences. In Von Moltke's analysis, *Green Is the Heath* values both change and tradition, for instance when a motorcar rescues a blue-blood Prussian equestrian, or female protagonists wear modern attire. I suggest, instead, that the embrace of such change in the narrative is less about appreciating modernity than about appreciating modern commodities made available by the economic upswing in West Germany from about 1948. On a more fundamental level, the film validates sameness and stasis.

This message becomes clear as the story develops. A parallel plot has been the arrival of a traveling circus whose grand opening in spatial and temporal proximity to the village festival suggests mutual benefit. For von Moltke (2005: 85), this circus is a surplus visual adornment typical of the genre. "Such non-narrative digressions [range] from contemplations of nature to moments of pure performance [such as those in the circus ring]." As attractions the performers are welcome, as actual neighbors they are strangers. Georg Simmel (1950: 402) calls the stranger "a social position defined by ... a combination of nearness and farness [whose] position in [a] group is determined, essentially, by the fact that he imports qualities into it, which do not and cannot stem from the group itself."[4] The exotically presented, exotically talented performers of spectacle are others against which intra-German differences pale; these outsiders cause the real trouble in *Heimat*. While German foresters expertly manage the German *Wald* and nature-loving former landowners struggle to engage harmoniously with it, a circus hand poaches the local wildlife to use as lion fodder. Discovered, this egregious misappropriation camouflages and relativizes Lüderson's actions. As the foreign shysters leave for their preferred destination, America, German–German amalgamation succeeds libidinally through the pairing of two female expellees with two male natives.

Melodramatic conventions – musical and visual spectacle, romance and beautiful people, comedy, and Happy Endings – tempt viewers to understand *Heimat* films as innocuous. Close analysis of *Green Is the Heath* exemplifies the inadequacy of such preferred readings. Comparison of Hans Behrendt's proto-*Heimat* feature *Green Is the Heath* (1932) and Depp's film is equally illuminating. In the former, Lüderson's poaching is censured; he dies dishonourably at film's end. In the latter, it is symbolically vindicated by his expellee status; he is neither castigated nor rehabilitated, but integrated. The earlier version maintains distinctions between

German wrongdoers, in this case marked along class lines. The later version amalgamates all German difference into a nationally inflected, regional community imagined as homogeneous; homeland troubles are solved by the departure of irritating foreigners. As so often in the narrative arc of *Heimat* films, problems develop and are solved in spaces of pastoral tranquility. Their cause is the strange or the stranger; their solution is the expulsion of this other.

New *Heimat* Film

New *Heimat* filmmakers and films stand overtly in the *Heimat* film tradition. In the credits, Rosenmüller expresses indebtedness to Luggi Waldleitner, the founder of Roxy Kino, *Wer früher stirbt ist länger tot*'s production company. An established commercial producer, Waldleitner importantly represents 1950s and 1960s traditional cinema (*Papas Kino*), although (or perhaps because) he convinced Rainer Werner Fassbinder to direct *Lili Marleen* (1981). Hans Steinbichler sees *Hierankl* as a Homeland film that critiques failed 1960s and 1970s progressive and radical movements (Storz *et al.*, 2005). These films reference the *Heimat* genre thematically, narratively, and aesthetically.

The smash hit *Wer früher stirbt* shores up a traditional, homogeneous and secure diegetic "perfect world" (*heile Welt*), even as certain filmic elements ostensibly unsettle it. The 11-year-old Sebastian becomes obsessed with guilt over his mother's death. He lives with his innkeeper father, Lorenz, and older brother, Franz, in an idyllic Bavarian town in an idyllic Bavarian valley. Interestingly, Rosenmüller emphasized the difficulties he experienced locating a traditional German inn (*Gasthaus*) to use as the Schneider family's "Kandlerwirt" (Von Poser, 2006). The very scarcity of such formerly ubiquitous locales seemingly made an exemplary centerpiece indispensible. A diegetic unity, the larger filmic space is an amalgamation of bits of lower Bavarian villages and valleys. While such filmic stitching is not uncommon, here it is overdetermined by the play between generic mythologies of unity and geographical unities that have ceased to exist. Filmic time is equally anachronistic. Although the tale is set explicitly in 2006, the modern trappings of daily village life harken to the late 1980s and early 1990s. The world of the village is that of West German life before unification brought threatening spectres of a larger Germany. While small towns may characteristically be thought of as out-moded in terms of consumer trends, the 1980s styles worn by Sebastian and the other children who are still growing and require new clothes regularly serve to maintain the narrative within a figuratively innocent, preunification period. The fact that the female protagonists dress in somewhat more up-to-date fashion underscores the temporal messaging; adult female characters clothed in fashions from the prior decade would likely awaken viewer recognition of the ruse. *Wer früher stirbt*'s costume designer, Steffi Bruhn, also points out that the women are always clad in skirts to express traditional gender dynamics (Von Poser, 2006). This anachronism suggests an innocence involving more than just Sebastian, which is why innocence itself is multiply conjured. Mid-2000s debates around the dangers of a larger German nation recalled the Nazi past and interrogated the status of German guilt (e.g. Moses, 2007; Hosek, 2007). Certainly the young Sebastian is innocent. Not only do several characters state that he is innocent under the law, his "sins" are typical childhood pranks, and only his simple-minded brother considers Sebastian's birth, which entailed their mother's death, Sebastian's "crime." Guilt is rendered similarly benign through humorous critiques of the medieval Catholicism influential in the village. Moreover, the film is marketed as a comedy, which works to preempt substantive readings of these aspects. It is within mid-2000s debates that this dogged production of blamelessness makes sense as a complement to the leitmotivs of culpability, death, and violence.

Wer früher stirbt's plot is driven precisely by misplaced guilt and killing. The film thus seems unlike the early *Heimat* films, which avoid questions of wartime responsibility and violence. Whereas those productions employ ideologically unburdened locales, the space of *Wer früher stirbt* is one in which war guilt is putatively at its most benign: southern West Germany well after 1945 but prior to 1989. Although Bavarian *Heimat* was famously employed by the Nazis, *Wer früher stirbt*'s filmic pastoral suggests a Homeland reclaimed from such influence. The idyllic location is an expanse for innocent fascination with guilt, killing, and death. It enables an allegorical working through of the past (*Vergangenheitsbewältigung*) that evokes only ultimately to render benign. As I will demonstrate in examples below, death and killing are presented here as normative and regenerative, and the ensuing guilt as literally out of place.

In his analysis of the significance of World War Two within postunification Germany, Michael Geyer points to the "stigma of violence" – the mark of those who killed defenseless others – and corresponding, unexpressed feelings of guilt. While it would indeed be out of place to map the killings in *Wer früher stirbt* directly onto the systematic exterminations under German Fascism, it is illuminating to read the film as speaking to those social structures of violence and culpability. Geyer (1997: 49) argues that the psychic legacy of the Nazi death cult coupled with both apathy and panic toward mass death foreclosed public debate. "Once this discussion took hold in the 1970s, the paralysis of emotions was eased, leading in the eighties to a veritable German cult of remembering. That is the secret of the strange double success of the television series *Holocaust* on the one hand, and *Heimat* on the other."

In *Wer früher stirbt*, remembering is a recollection of death and (mis)recognition of guilt that leads to a presumption of innocence and an orderly positioning of death and killing in the *Heimat*. When Sebastian accidently runs over Franz's caged rabbits with a truck, the teenager ties his little brother to a post in the barn, strikes and burns him, shows him the date on their mother's *In Memoriam* card, and forces him to apologize for the killings to avoid the flames of purgatory

(*Fegefeuer*). During these acts of torture, Franz slowly rises and removes a Zippo lighter from his tight jeans in a threatening gesture that evokes violent male fantasies of war (Theweleit, 1987). Zippos bear a well-known connection not only to both world wars but to the Vietnam conflict, notably the torching of village thatches by US soldiers. While the West German government supported US military actions in Vietnam, many Germans criticized its tactics. The allusion here unsettles the postwar narrative of the singularity of German guilt by expanding it beyond national borders. As I detail below, *Wer früher stirbt*'s complementary dominant logic condenses negative forces of culpability into the US peacenik, rock-and-roll counterculture embodied in the DJ character, Alfred. Symbolic excision of this ostensibly foreign element enables a rebirth of traditional *Heimat*. In this Homeland, not only are death and killing part and parcel of life, but the 1970s and 1980s political dissent engendered by the German guilt question is either washed away or transformed into lifestyles that foreground bourgeois self-actualization.

In *Over Her Dead Body*, Elisabeth Bronfen (1992) argues that certain representations of death enable viewers to reinforce myths of personal immortality while simultaneously confronting them with the reality of imminent death. Likewise, the death confronted through Sebastian is at first final, then escapable, then a perpetual cycle of mortality and immortality bound within a naturalized ethos. Killing – of animals, of the mother – is organized according to this ethos.[5]

Bronfen's work, which explains the gendering of death as a form of patriarchal othering, can also help explain the connection between woman and death that is central to *Wer früher stirbt*. Because in Western culture at least, women are positioned as sites of alterity, the representation of women's death becomes a site of its misrecognition in the interests of male subjectivity. "Death is localized away from the (man's) self onto a dead woman" (Bronfen, 1992: xi). In *Wer früher stirbt*, Sebastian first understands his alleged killing of his mother as monstrous. This notion engenders his projection of her as monstrous, first as a vengeful undead seeking to draw him violently into her grave and eternal damnation, later as a beautiful water spirit seeking to draw him gently to an earthly death and everlasting paradise.

Culpability shapes these interrelated mother fantasies. During his nightmare, Sebastian is ridden with guilt for supposedly having caused his mother's death. By the time of the second, barbiturate-induced, hallucination, Sebastian has apparently freed himself from guilt in two ways. First, he has performed the "good work" of finding his father a new love – his teacher, Frau Dorstreiter – with his deceased mother's imagined consent. Second, rather than following her perceived directive to kill Frau Dorstreiter's husband, the rock-and-roll DJ, Alfred, Sebastian has saved the eccentric character from self-imposed strangulation. This moment of rebellion against the older generation, as expressed in his refusal to carry out his mother's putative directive, marks Sebastian's fullest disavowal of the guilt she also represents.

The material absence of the woman provokes guilt in multiple ways. In these fantasies, the boy's monstrously reappearing, absent–present mother embodies the guilt of the past, enticing her beloved into death and canceling out his future. Guilt as well as death is displaced onto this female "other," especially guilt that might entail – and be entailed by – violence. Moreover, an absent mother is a culpable mother. If Franz blames Sebastian for her death, the narrative blames her absenteeism for Sebastian's cheeky attitude and mischievous behavior. According to the male town elders, the widower Lorenz is overwhelmed raising their two boys alone. Told overtly on the individual level, this story is also about the stigma of violence and its attendant guilt at the social level.

The normalized future that Sebastian engineers is one in which killing and death are as integral to the cycle of life as are traditional gender roles and cultural heritage. By the same token, Frau Dorstreiter is already married to her counterculture DJ; it would seem anathema to tradition to break up a marriage. The film legitimates this plot turn in four ways. First, as described above, the reinstatement of conventional structures occurs largely through the postunification generation's – Sebastian's – earnest and naive efforts to right his alleged wrongs. Second, the female protagonist is symbolically virginal. Her marriage to Alfred is barren; never "Veronika" and always the formal second-person "*Sie*," she is proper; her white dress and a baptismal plunge of the pair prepare the innocence of their morning kiss; the close-up on her snow-white, modest brassiere as Lorenz hangs laundry metonymizes her move into the Schneider home as a domestic act. Third, the relationship between Veronika and Lorenz is instigated by Alfred himself, who during his New Age radio show inadvertently redirects libidinal energy to flow between them. Finally, because the foreign influence associated with Alfred is also associated with tragic death, the community benefits from its excision in the form of the DJ's symbolic exile.

Just as the Zippo lighter recalls American-style killing, in *Wer früher stirbt*, US counterculture is linked to disruptive death – by 1960s and 1970s rock-and-roll music and its heroes who died young, by the guitar of Sebastian's dead mother, by Alfred's attempted suicide. This wide-ranging connection between outside influence and death is intimated from the film's opening: as US-style rock-and-roll music[6] sweeps from Alfred's mountaintop radio station into the valley, the camera sweeps like a fighter jet toward its targets. A beer truck driver's excitement over the rock-and-roll song broadcast by this counterculture guru DJ sets off the film's opening chain of accidents, in which Sebastian is nearly run over and he in turn runs over and kills the rabbits.

Alfred is the primarily embodiment of troublesome foreignness. His fetishization of US counterculture and music is accompanied by uncanny powers that also have foreign valence. Although depicted humorously as is characteristic for the film, they are nevertheless often destructive. In one sequence at the Dorstreiter residence, Alfred sports a John Lennon-style T-shirt with a "Home" logo, literally translating *Heimat* into English. His tendency to contaminate the native with the foreign in such ways is underscored here by the film's only moment of magical realism: during the ensuing, heated telephone conversation between the male competitors for Veronika, some of Alfred's spaghetti dinner ends up in Lorenz's fresh slaughter all the way at the Kandlerwirt. Thus, on an allegorical level, the DJ's visual relegation to the mountaintop, away from the village in which Lorenz, Frau Dorstreiter, Franz, and Sebastian end up recreating a nuclear family, simultaneously expels tragic death. Extended into the German cultural imaginary, this denouement overcomes the stigma of violence and culture of guilt through the institution of a new homogeneous *Heimat*.

Rosenmüller's other films reveal similar logics. *Beste Zeit* and *Beste Gegend* also present *Heimat* as a beautiful space in which time and life are cyclical and community members ever-present. In these films, the "foreign" is a disruptive element initially appearing as unquenchable *Wanderlust* for abroad. *Heimat* is rectified by transforming this disturbance into exotic tourism, with its concomitant assurance of return. These first two parts of a cinematic trilogy are female coming-of-age films set in the Bavarian village of Tandern. In *Beste Zeit*, Kati desires to see the world by participating in a student exchange at a US university, but finally decides to remain in her village with her family and friends. In the sequel, Kati and her best friend Jo's pact to travel the world together after sitting for their A-level exams (*Abitur*) ends in a car breakdown at Europe's Brenner bridge and news of Jo's grandfather's collapse, which brings them back home before they get more than a short distance past the border but after they have had to spend much of their money on the repair. Miscommunications throughout lead each young woman to lose faith in the other's capacity to uphold the pact on its romanticized terms of "tailwind and freedom" (*Fahrtwind und Freiheit*). Apparently believing that Kati will finally choose to stay in Tandern with Lugge, her long-time flame and now suddenly potential relationship, rather than resume their road trip, Jo purchases an airline ticket to Johannesburg. The film's denouement consists in part of frontal takes, shot slightly from above and framing Kati beside Jo's own boyfriend, Toni, as both hang out the windows of a car that their responsible, mutual friend, Rocky, drives briskly down a familiar country road. The mutual exuberance of the close-knit group furthers a joyous chorus; these takes are interspersed with interior shots of the airplane, in which Jo softly continues the refrain, half surrounded by thirty-something, tall, and very dark African men. This juxtaposition suggests at once that freedom lies at home and that the other is so foreign that it is only worth a visit; any appropriate engagement will remain only an unfulfilling flirt with the exotic.

In *Räuber Kneißl*, a Robin Hood tale based on the Bavarian folk hero, Mathias Kneißl (1875–1902), history repeats itself with different players. Following the diegetic Kneißl's beheading, the neighborhood policeman is pelted by youngsters in a scene hearkening to the opening scene with the Kneißl brothers and the police. This figurative repetition resolves an important interpretative ambivalence around Mathias, for the plot, music, and camerawork construct him as the primary identificatory locus, while his actions and positioning other him in his own community. When the next generation takes up weapons, Kneißl becomes legible as individual embodiment of a particular and recurring role in this socopolitically stratified society, that of socially minded rebel. The film's temporal structure gains significance in an extradiegetic, geographical return: the main intersection of the town in *Räuber Kneißl* strongly resembles the village intersection in *Wer früher stirbt*. No doubt rationalized logistically, this spatial repetition underscores the cyclical logic in Rosenmüller's *Heimat* oeuvre.

Steinbichler's *Hierankl* and *Winter Journey* likewise turn on tropes of contagion by outside influences. In a manner reminiscent of *Beste Gegend*, *Winter Journey* concretizes the other as Black Africa. A largely unsympathetic – egocentric, racist, megalomaniacal – German protagonist faces impending financial ruin exacerbated by competition from transnational corporations. These Northern winners of global capitalism are everywhere and nowhere, and it is unclear how a regionally bound German could beat them. Neither is such a course of action intimated, for the aging, emasculated, and psychologically unstable Franz Brenninger is bewitched by their Southern twin, an other embodied, finally, by a mafia mogul, Michael Uyi, head of a racketeering scheme originating in Nairobi. Franz's struggle within a veritable urban heart of darkness, and his eventual triumph over Uyi, sublates his own, imminent downfall, and he decides to take his own life. It is in this limited triumph that German Homeland is preserved: Franz's wife will obtain a desired surgical procedure to regain her sight, and his grown children will continue their bourgeois lives. His suicide is redeemed indirectly through the words of a tribal wise man, spoken in voiceover by Franz's translator; African characters are disallowed subjectivity. The white characters best their African others while colonial histories are obscured. The 1886 Anglo-German treaty partitioned East Africa: future Kenya in the British sphere, future Tanzania in the neighboring German sphere. Franz's weak English and his visit to Kenya highlight only a British past, as does Jo's choice of Johannesburg in *Beste Gegend*. Such particular representations of Africa speak both to selective othering and further evidence that New *Heimat* sensibilities are reactions to globalization.[7]

By contrast, *Hierankl* incorporates anti-*Heimat* elements while validating the traditional *Heimat*, which it suggests is endangered. The solitary alpine farmhouse to which family members and close friends return for the birthday celebration of the patriarch, Lukas, is opulent and beautiful – but dark. Its surrounding, craggy hills are lushly forested but threatening. The musical soundtrack is uplifting but penetrating. Internecine quarreling escalates as secrets are aired and rivalries emerge. In generically reflexive scenes, Lukas's son, Paul, derides the penchant of *Heimat* films for positive affective relationships and Happy Endings. Lukas suggests that change is necessary and normal when he worries to Paul about Paul's seeming desire to maintain the status quo. And the film is framed by modern social questions raised by Lene, his twenty-something daughter now living in Berlin, in an interior voiceover monologue: "Are you having sex? Do you have family? Are you on the move?" *"Hast du Sex? Hast du Familie? Bist du in Bewegung?"* Yet *Hierankl's* main problematic, an Electral tragedy, is of foreign, not indigenous provenance. Lene takes her parents' friend,

Götz, as her lover to spite her mother, Rosemarie. An Oedipus of sorts as well, this Electra does not know that Götz is actually her father via her married mother. The eventual revelation destroys what remains of the family harmony.

More significant, however, is that the crisis is predicated upon 1960s countercultural values, to which both Lukas and Götz adhered in their youth. Dinner conversation reveals Lukas's changed opinions about ultraleftism, for instance when he refers to the late Red Army Faction member, Ulrike Meinhof, as a Hitlerite-turned-Stalinist. What remains for him are John Lennon images; his current penchant is for canonical German culture, especially Goethe. His marriage is based on similarly conservative values. Lukas was attracted to Rosemarie's beauty and elegance; the Munich aristocrat was drawn to him for his earthy roots. Their now-strained relationship recalls a pervasive mythology of ideal union between ruled and ruler found in many German film narratives, from the paradigmatic *Heimat* films of the blockbuster *Sissi* series to the recent telefilm, *Die Flucht* (The Flight), in which a beautiful and resourceful blonde, blue-eyed Junker aristocrat is portrayed saving her needy and grateful servants from the Soviet army. Götz does not articulate his current political views at length, but he was or is heavily engaged in international politics that have influenced his personal life as well. He worked at the US embassy, where his US beloved was murdered, presumably for political reasons by German ultraleftists, and he never married.[8] His rakish, urban intellectual demeanor, his sexually permissive comportment, and his comment to Lene that he feels like a foreigner at Hierankl, underscores how foreign and left-leaning influences continue to contaminate him in ways that seemingly also make him disposed to Lene's advances.

These New *Heimat* films share aesthetic tendencies. Each showcases natural settings as beautiful, lush, vast, inviting, and unspoiled. Scenes open, close, or are interspersed with panoramic shots of landscapes from bird's-eye views. Characters stroll through and explore them; they also bicycle and sometimes drive through them. They play, dance, lounge, swim, and make love in them. Although small in comparison with the shots framing them, such actions emphasize freedom: the characters know these familiar territories. Colors tend toward warm palettes; the sun is often angled to project friendly, golden rays across the expanses. Houses, roads, and other markers of human life also fit the domesticated, *heimisch* environments, as they are likewise attractive; even the run-down Kneißl farmhouse sports a green mossy waterwheel and cozy, clean rooms.

Rural *Heimat* in the Berliner Schule

Films with hamlet motifs by Berliner Schule filmmakers picture nature less invitingly. *This Very Moment* includes verdant fields and thick woods and one particularly arresting take features a white stork strutting across a bright grassy track leading into a moist, lush forest. Yet in contrast to New *Heimat* films, such images serve primarily to advance the plot rather than stoke visual pleasure, in this case by metonymizing a Hansel and Gretel leitmotiv with its stepmother trope. The Polish landscape near the German border in which the two abandoned children wander is uncomfortable and foreboding, whether in the form of messily pollinating fields full of buzzing insects, rainy, dark woods, or dilapidated socialist-era housing developments. *Windows on Monday* features a slushy, gray, early winter, a nondescript suburb, a heavily logged forest, and a charmless hotel complex. *Vacation* is set primarily in a Brandenburg dacha to which Western Germans have retired. The nearby beach and motocross track are unspectacular. While certain images suggest a lazy summery lushness, frequent long-takes evoke an ennui that turns the hideaway into a metaphorical prison.

In these films, long-time rural dwellers are intolerant toward the more recent arrivals. Many of the main protagonists come from or want to live in Berlin. In *Vacation*, each expresses desire for the city as presumed antidote to the rural. Notwithstanding their initial preference to leave the metropolis, the newcomers increasingly perceive the physical surroundings as enervating and they do not associate with the locals. *Vacation*'s matriarch, Anna, laments that visitors came by to visit only in the first years after her relocation to Brandenburg. By this, she evidently means people from the city. One of her current visitors, Paul, speaks with only one stranger, who turns out also to be from Berlin. The reason for this continued rift between long-time and new inhabitant is given by Anna's husband, Robert, who explains to his son, Max, that the local village youth do not accept Robert, because "we are the immigrants [*Zugezogene*]." This conversation takes place in Max's room, which features an old wooden folding table carved with the words West Berlin, evidently brought from their previous residence. The scene redeploys neoliberal logics to blame Easterners for Western–Eastern divisions and ignore power differentials between Westerner urbanites who moved into the Eastern countryside and those Easterners who continued living there. In *Hunting Dogs*, the Western Berliner Henrik's village Christmas party remains unattended. His teenage son Lars's forays into the surrounding wood are infused with injury and death. A thwarted Happy Ending drives home the message. After finally gaining some acceptance from Reschke, his friend Jana's father, Lars drowns in the frozen lake near the site where his dog had previously been attacked. A highly stylized scene of the forest night shot in the blue tone of Romantic hope underscores the message through an inverse of the pathetic fallacy: this Berlin family has no place in Brandenburg, which for them remains a dangerous site of isolation and alienation.

While these contemporary German films are in many ways very different, they each transport similar logics of *Heimat* and -isms of propinquity. If Brandenburg natives are intolerant and rural areas uninviting, a disassociated Berlin is legitimated as *Heimat*. It is notable that the suffering others in these films are generally not the non-German (im)migrant workers who have indeed fared so badly in these provincial regions. Instead, it is the protagonists with their class, racial, religious, and sexual privileges who are positioned as society's victims. Having opted for outward mobility, they are cosmopolitan ruralists, temporary residents by choice. These characters mirror the tendency of actual peripatetic cosmopolitans to neglect local concerns in order to attend to more private issues (Kofman, 2007). In these films, their practices are justified by the elision of power disparities and by persistent representation of native bigotry toward new inhabitants.

While nominally set outside of Germany, *Everyone Else* plays within a myopically German surround and milieu. Two thirty-somethings, Gitti and Chris, are spending their summer holiday at Chris's family vacation home in Sardinia. Their interactions consist of microrelationship problems and deriding the(ir fellow) bourgeoisie. When they meet Chris's German friends, a successful and more traditional couple, their relationship begins to suffer from insecurity-driven comparisons. Most of the action takes place in the couples' homes. Largely absent is Sardinia, except as supermarket. The extradomestic, figuratively non-German surroundings are here demoted to mere framing devices. Tourism domesticates and minimizes the potentially exotic, as the protagonists bring their cultural accoutrements and community with them. Meanwhile the German characters' mini identity crises engendered by imperfect role-play and overblown mimetic desires enliven what some viewers might recognize as an economy of homogeneity. Insignificant interactions and individual differences gain exaggerated importance, which works to monopolize the attention of characters and viewers alike and to foreclose recognition of these narcissistic practices as expressions of -isms of propinquity.

So far we have seen that Berliner Schule films set outside the capital city depict unwelcoming *Heimats* to which new inhabitants from urban areas do not belong. Their protagonists' social and economic privileges are elided, while the rural natives are held responsible for intolerance toward these newcomers or are simply absent. What of Berliner Schule films set in Berlin? Is an urban *Heimat* articulated, and what messages does it bear? Here I suggest that -isms of propinquity course through many of these Berlin films, and that these -isms are worth recognizing because of the ways in which the resultant filmic messages form and express the growing conservatism in today's Germany, Europe, and global North.

This is not the first time that Berliner Schule films have been criticized for their political quiescence, which their directors have been quick to refute or defend (e.g. Köhler, 2007). While few of these counter-Hollywood movies do well at the box office, they have a particular following among a certain demographic – thirty- to forty-something, university level, white, often West Germany-raised, Protestant or agnostic city dwellers, often Berliners by choice (*Wahlberliner*) who inhabit the more central neighborhoods such as Kreuzberg, Schöneberg, and Prenzlauer Berg. What do these audiences see? *Everyone Else* strong film festival showing suggests that Gitti and Chris's experiences and overt navel-gazing resonates with these German cinephiles, many of whom are in analogous subject positions. Schanelec's *Ich bin den Sommer über in Berlin geblieben Passing Summer*, and *Afternoon* focus likewise on the concerns of a similar Berlin milieu, expressing and shoring up propinquities that allow no space for concerns of other city inhabitants. Of *Passing Summer*, Schanelec writes: "The film is the attempt to examine life from outside, to win distance, not to intervene, but to watch. I wanted to find a smooth transition from life to film and back. Two young women in a café, at the beginning, I have seen a thousand times, in some café or other on some summer day or other. […] I asked myself what happens when one tries to hold onto nothing but normality."[9]

Yet what is "normality"? The normality represented in *Passing Summer*'s opening scene is that of a mythological Prenzlauer Berg milieu, whose presentation of self in everyday life performs carefully managed difference and obfuscates backstories of similarity (Sussebach, 2007). Homogeneity of ethnicity, gender, creed, political stripe, beauty, sexual orientation, participation in the "creative class" is visually apparent, by its presence as well as absence. The thirty-something main protagonist Valerie muses to her close friend about her plans for the summer – perhaps she will work, perhaps she will take up piano again. Later, the young writer chats about the heat inside sunny Berlin apartments in the summer. In a trendy restaurant over dinner, she then monologues about the compulsion of yearly vacations away from the city. Valerie's concerns, particularly her decision to stay in Berlin for the summer, has experiential and cognitive meaning for the primary intended audience. In characteristic Schalenec style, these utterances are not presented forcefully; the other characters do not engage with Valerie's commentary, the camera does not focus on her, there is no musical underscoring. For these narrative elements to resonate, viewers must be able to bring their own understandings and experiences of a particular Berlin; they must share a certain experiential propinquities.

Notable is a tendency away from class analysis and toward elision of class difference, in part through the relative absence of blue-collar protagonists, salaried labour, time pressures, and markers of financial need and benefit. (Petzold's films are an important exception.) In *Ich bin den Sommer über*, the main protagonist states lightly that she lives "from her friends." In *Passing Summer*, Valerie cannot afford a large apartment, but there seems no correlation between her perhaps unremunerated occupation and her eatery visits and fashionable looks. In *Nachmittag*, none of the characters is marked by class difference, whether in dress, mannerism, or personality. Indeed, here a Great Gatsby trope emerges: the most tragic characters are those with the most money. Such logic flatters Berlin viewers whose class status is only somewhat correlated to their current wages or salaries and yet who do not desire to self-identify with the leisure class. These Berlin films mirror idealized versions of their primary audience and foster ideological misrecognition. They offer topics of interest to these insiders in aesthetic codes legible to them. (Re)experienced and (re)articulated on film and in daily life, particular lifestyle practices gain in complexity among these communities of propinquity. The performed urban *Heimat* appears richly filled with difference, which obscures the monoculturalism in this social environment of the new Berlin Republic.

Here I am suggesting that, just as the plotlines of many Berliner Schule films have milieu-specific legibility, so too do many of their aesthetic patterns speak the insider language of certain privileged and homogeneous imagined communities. Marco Abel elucidates this insider logic in his essay on Petzold's *Ghosts*:

> In Petzold's hand, this in-between world around Potsdamer Platz is nearly unrecognizable. Unless one actually knows the area rather well, the viewer is not invited to recognize the mise-en-scène as anything specific – as anything that is represented and that, as such, is supposed to be decodable. Completely refusing to provide establishing shots that would specifically demarcate the cinematic location as an empirically real location – and thus allow viewers to enjoy the comforts of recognition ("ah, it's Berlin") [...] what he really does is find new images for a space whose images have turned into clichés. (2010: 270)

In effect, those who know Berlin as urban *Heimat* recognize the sites, increase their understandings of the narrative, and further their community belonging. The wealthy Frenchwoman Françoise's electronic spying on the young, underprivileged Nina in the changing room of the Arcaden shopping mall on Potsdamer Platz resonates much more strongly both in terms of plot coherence and commentary on surveillance when one knows the debates about this central square. Crosscutting between the automobile transit of the French couple around the Victory Column (*Siegessäule*) and Nina and her new acquaintance Toni's simultaneous breakfast in the outdoor café at this transit hub foreshadows their later meeting. The acting tryouts take place at the hypercommodified *Mediaspree*; for knowledgeable viewers, the scopophilia of the casting director can also be read as a critique of recent urban development. Indeed, I contend, echoing Abel, that such insider understandings further the affective relationship of the viewers to the narrative, to the film, to the cinematic city, and to the experiential relationship with this urban *Heimat*.

Locations are even more important in Schalenec's films because their sparse emplotment creates spaces in which these sites can communicate loudly. The opening described above resonates among a particular Berlin society for whom the café's sleek interior points to a particular type of clientele. The housing preference of the character in *Ich bin den Sommer über* is legible for those who live this Berlin's unique urban tapestry. Her desire for a new apartment and grudging acceptance of one in a classic turn-of-the-century Berlin building (*Gründerzeit Altbau*) complete with bare, polished wooden floors sets her slightly at odds with her cohort, for whom the latter is the gold standard. The isolation of the characters in *Nachmittag* gains a political touch for viewers who see that these protagonists living in an Eastern German villa are Western Germans for whom Berlin has remained the expensive Western district of Charlottenburg.

Of the centrality of nonlinguistic elements in contemporary German film, Jaimey Fisher and Brad Prager (2010: 15) write, "Certainly, the language(s) of a film are central [because they] serve as a gesture of recognition from the filmmakers toward their addressees, their presumed audiences." I suggest that the tendency toward the interpolation of certain demographics risks an urban *Heimat* that incorporates -isms of propinquity. Indeed, interpretation of such cinema can further the same. Consider Abel's (2010: 273–274) reading of *Ghosts'* red-filtered scene in which Nina and Tina dance: "This visually most intense moment of the film [...] corresponds to Nina's refusal to join what others consider normalcy. Instead, the normalcy she desires is the one that she imagines." Abel deftly connects aesthetics to subjectivity here, yet, Nina does not refuse normalcy; she cannot obtain it. Tina and Françoise reject her and she wanders off into the in-between space of the park. To suggest that this is her choice is not only to misread multiple cinematic cues, but to risk legitimating the -isms of propinquity that would contend that the other does not want to assimilate, that in the words of Chancellor Merkel, "multiculturalism has failed in Germany" (FLO/DPA, 2010).

In a recent podium discussion, Christian Petzold pointed to the ways in which the city does not afford the same *Heimat* as that found in the New *Heimat* films. In an era of new -isms, longstanding rivalries between German states such as Bavaria and Berlin may be coming again to the fore (Saldern, 2008). These rivalries are also expressed in arts funding, which in turn shapes the resultant filmic productions (Hosek, 2010; Bomnüter and Scheller, 2009). New Regionalism is increasingly shaping Europe (Schaser, 2007) and some see it as a means of combating nationalism (Veggeland, 2000). This contribution seeks to add to this debate about spaces of belonging with its cautionary notes on -isms of propinquity.

Notes

1   For a recent exploration of definitions of transnationalism, see Ginsberg and Lippard (2010: 395–400).
2   Jennifer Kapczynski (2010) has recently made a similar argument about contemporary film in general.
3   "Macht es den Menschen, die zu euch geflüchtet sind nicht schwer. Wer nicht von der Heimat weg musste, der kann es nicht ermessen, was es bedeutet, heimatlos zu sein."
4   "Er ist innerhalb eines bestimmten räumlichen Umkreises – oder eines, dessen Grenzbestimmtheit der räumlichen analog ist – fixiert, aber seine Position in diesem ist dadurch wesentlich bestimmt, dass er nicht von vornherein in ihn gehört, dass er Qualitäten, die aus ihm nicht stammen und stammen können, in ihn hineinträgt." (Simmel, 1908: 509–512).
5   An earlier iteration of this section entitled, "Generation Guilt? Normalization, Heimat and *Wer früher stirbt ist länger tot* benefitted from presentation at the Modern Languages Association Conference in the Women in German panel, "Changing Notions of Belonging in German Literature and Culture," organized by Friederike Eigler, Jens

Kugele, and Andrea Reimann (San Francisco, December 2008). I would particularly like to thank Andrea for her many insightful suggestions.

6   Gerd Baumann composed the music and has a cameo role as the fictional John Ferdinand Woodstock, Alfred's rock-and-roll idol who also died young. Their English lyrics mark the songs as foreign and further the connection between foreign influence and death. Pragmatically, it may have been expedient to use original music by a Munich native; rights to popular songs can be expensive and the film was also largely financed by the state of Bavaria. Symbolically speaking, the English lyrics further -isms of propinquity on the narrative level, while the German songs further them on the production level by keeping the film itself uncontaminated by foreign composition.

7   See also Irchenhauser (2005).

8   The reader may notice a recurring leitmotiv involving critique of US involvement in Germany. A sustained pursuit of this topic, however, would hyperextend this article.

9   "Der Film ist der Versuch, das Leben von außen zu betrachten, Distanz zu gewinnen, nicht einzugreifen, sondern zuzusehen. Ich wollte einen fließenden Übergang finden vom Leben zum Film und wieder zurück. Die zwei jungen Frauen im Cafe, zum Beginn, hab' ich tausendfach gesehen, in irgendwelchen Cafés an irgendwelchen Sommertagen. Jede Situation gibt es tausendfach, die Familie, die am Flughafen ankommt, die ältere Frau, die allein im Zug sitzt, die erwachsenen Kinder vor dem Krankenhaus, in dem der Vater stirbt. Es ist normal. Ich hab' mich gefragt, was passiert, wenn man versucht, sich an nichts als an die Normalität zu halten ..." http://www.peripherfilm.de/meinlangsamesleben/inhalt.htm (accessed May 24, 2011).

References

Abel, M. (2010) Imaging Germany: The (political) cinema of Christian Petzold, in *The Collapse of the Conventional: German Cinema and its Politics at the Turn of the Twenty-First Century* (eds J. Fisher and B. Prager), Wayne State University Press, Detroit, pp. 258–284.

Anderson, B. (1991) *Imagined Communities: Reflections on the Origin and Spread of Nationalism*, Verso, London.

Bauman, Z. (1993) *Postmodern Ethics*, Blackwell, Oxford.

Boa, E. and Palfreyman, R. (2000) *Heimat – A German Dream: Regional Loyalties and National Identity in German Culture 1890–1990*, Oxford University Press, Oxford.

Bomnüter, U. and Scheller, P. (2009) *Filmfinanzierung. Strategien im Ländervergleich: Deutschland, Frankreich und Großbritannien*, Nomos, Baden-Baden.

Bonilla-Silva, E. (2006) *Racism without Racists: Color-Blind Racism and the Persistence of Racial Inequality in the United States*, Rowman & Littlefield, New York.

Bronfen, E. (1992) *Over Her Dead Body: Death, Femininity and the Aesthetic.* Manchester UP, Manchester.

Fisher, J. and Prager, B. (2010) Introduction, in *The Collapse of the Conventional: German Cinema and its Politics at the Turn of the Twenty-First Century* (eds J. Fisher and B. Prager), Wayne State University Press, Detroit, pp. 1–38.

FLO/DPA (2010) Merkels Multikulti-Absage sorgt für weltweites Aufsehen. *Spiegel Online*, October 19, http://www.spiegel.de/politik/deutschland/0,1518,723993,00.html (accessed February 12, 2011).

Geyer, M. (1997) The place of the Second World War in German memory and history. *New German Critique*, 71, 5–40.

Ginsberg, T. and Lippard, C. (2010) *Historical Dictionary of Middle Eastern Cinema*, Scarecrow Press, Lanham, MD.

Halle, R. (2008) *German Film after Germany: Toward a Transnational Aesthetic,* University of Illinois Press, Urbana-Champaign.

Hosek, J.R. (2007) Buena Vista Deutschland: gendering Germany in Wenders, Gaulke and Eggert. *German Politics and Society*, 25, 46–69.

Hosek, J.R. (2010) Materialities of urban film space: interpolating a European capital. *German Studies Association*, Oakland, CA.

Irchenhauser, M. (2005) Narzisstische Blicke auf Afrika. Der "dunkle Kontinent" als Spiegel im deutschsprachigen Roman und Film. MA thesis. Queen's University.

Irchenhauser, M. (2009) Heimat im Spannungsfeld Globalisierung: Studien zu zeitgenoessischen Heimatfilmen und Heimattexten. Ph.D. dissertation. Queen's University.

Kapczynski, J. (2010) Imitation of life: the aesthetics of Agfacolor in recent historical cinema, in *The Collapse of the Conventional: German Cinema and its Politics at the Turn of the Twenty-First Century* (eds J. Fisher and B. Prager), Wayne State University Press, Detroit, pp. 39–62.

Kofman, E. (2007) Figures of the cosmopolitan, in *Cosmopolitanism and Europe* (ed. C. Rumford), Liverpool University Press, Liverpool, pp. 239–256.

Köhler, U. (2007) Warum ich keine "politischen" Filme mache. *New filmkritik*, April 23, http://newfilmkritik.de/archiv/2007-04/warum-ich-keine-"politischen"-filme-mache/ (accessed September 3, 2010).

Moltke, J.V. (2005) *No Place Like Home: Locations of Heimat in German Cinema*, University of California Press, Berkeley.

Moses, A.D. (2007) *German Intellectuals and the Nazi Past,* Cambridge University Press, Cambridge.

Naughton, L. (2002) *That Was the Wild East: Film Culture, Unification, and the "New" Germany*, University of Michigan Press, Ann Arbor.

Poser, F.v. (dir.) (2006) *Hinter den Kulissen (Bonus Interview on Wer früher stirbt ist länger tot DVD)*, Roxy Film.

Saldern, A. (2008) Citizenship in twentieth-century German history: changes and challenges of a concept, in *Citizenship and National Identity in Twentieth-Century German History* (eds G. Eley and J. Palmowski), Stanford University Press, Stanford, CA, pp. 198–213.

Schanelec, A. (n.d.) Die Regisseurin über ihren Film, http://www.peripherfilm.de/meinlangsamesleben/inhalt.htm (accessed October 10, 2010).

Schaser, A. (2007) The challenge of gender: national historiography, nationalism, and national identities, in *Gendering Modern German History: Rewriting Historiography* (eds N.K. Hagemann and J.H. Quataert), Berghahn Books, USA, pp. 39–62.

Simmel, G. (1908) Exkurs über den Fremden Soziologie. *Untersuchungen über die Formen der Vergesellschaftung*, pp. 509–12, http://socio.ch/sim/unt9f.htm (accessed February 5, 2011).

Simmel, G. (1950) The Stranger, in *The Sociology of Georg Simmel* (ed. K. Wolff), Free Press, New York, pp. 402–408.

Sorkin, M. (1999) Introduction: traffic in democracy, in *Giving Ground: The Politics of Propinquity* (eds J. Copjec and M. Sorkin), Verso, London, pp. 1–15.

Storz, F., Jauker, N. and Steinbichler, H. (directors) (2005) *Interview on Hierankl DVD.*

Sussebach, H. (2007) Bionade – Biedermeier: Der Berliner Stadtteil Prenzlauer Berg ist das Experimentierfeld des neuen Deutschlands. Doch wer nicht ins Raster passt, hat es schwer im Biotop der Schönen und Kreativen. *Die Zeit Online*, 46, 44.

Taberner, S. and Cooke, P. (eds) (2006) *German Culture, Politics, and Literature into the Twenty-First Century: Beyond Normalization,* Camden House, Rochester, NY.

Theweleit, K. (1987) *Male Fantasies,* University of Minnesota Press, Minneapolis.

Veggeland, N. (2000) Neo-regionalism: planning for devolution, democracy and development. Research Report no. 52. Lillehammer College, Lillehammer, Norway, http://domino2.hil.no/web/forskning.nsf/0/4073e9553a7113b5c1256c7e0034ad29/$FILE/Forskningsrapport%20522000.pdf (accessed November 2, 2008).

Filmography

Afternoon [Nachmittag] (Angela Schanelec, Germany, 2006–2007).

Beste Gegend [Best Time] (M.H. Rosenmüller, Germany, 2008).

Beste Zeit [Best Place] (M.H. Rosenmüller, Germany, 2007).

Edge of Heaven, The [Auf der anderen Seite] (Fatih Akın, Germany / Turkey / Italy, 2007).

Everyone Else [Alle Anderen] (Maren Ade, Germany, 2007).

Ghosts [Gespenster] (Christian Petzold, Germany, 2005).

Green Is the Heath [Grün ist die Heide] (Hans Behrent, Germany, 1932).

Green Is the Heath [Grün ist die Heide] (Hans Depp, West Germany, 1951).

Hierankl (Hans Steinbichler, Germany, 2003).

Ich bin den Sommer über in Berlin geblieben [I stayed in Berlin over the Summer] (Angela Schanelec, Germany, 1993).

Hunting Dogs [Jagdhunde] (A-K. Reyel, Germany, 2007).

Lili Marleen (R.W. Fassbinder, West Germany, 1981).

Passing Summer [Mein langsames Leben] (Angela Schanelec, Germany, 2001).

Räuber Kneißl (M.H. Rosenmüller, Germany, 2008).

Solino (Fatih Akın, Germany, 2002).

This Very Moment [Milchwald] (Christoph Hochhäusler, Germany, 2003).

Vacation [Ferien] (Thomas Arslan, Germany, 2007).

Wer früher stirbt ist länger tot [He who dies sooner is dead longer] (M.H. Rosenmüller, Germany, 2006).

Windows on Monday [Am Montag kommen die Fenster] (Ulrich Köhler, Germany, 2006).

Winter Journey [Winterreise] (Hans Steinbichler, Germany, 2006).

7

No Happily Ever After
Disembodying Gender, Destabilizing Nation in Angelina Maccarone's Unveiled

Gayatri Devi

1

In one of the earliest expository scenes in Angelina Maccarone's *Fremde Haut* (Stranger's Skin or *Unveiled*, its English title), Fariba Tabrizi tells fellow Iranian asylum-seeker in Germany Siamak Mustafai that she has no hopes of ever being granted political asylum in Germany. Both Fariba and Siamak are temporarily held in the transit shelter at an unspecified German airport, "in orbit," so to speak. "I didn't tell them the truth … I didn't flee the country for political reasons … The real reason is I was with a woman," Fariba tells Siamak. "Tell them that now," Siamak encourages a distraught and teary Fariba, both of them hiding inside the holding center's unisex stark bathroom. "I did," Fariba tells Siamak, "but they are sending me back anyway. Now they don't believe anything I say."

To many Western viewers, the distinction Fariba draws between her "truth" and her "lie" appears naive; isn't the personal the political? Isn't sexual orientation a political provision for us? In some sense, it is impossible for us living in the West to conceptualize personal freedom if that freedom does not also include free expressions of the fullest potential of our gender identity, including our sexual orientation. Early women's movements and feminism in particular were collective social movements to claim a discursive space and representational rights, visibility in its fullest sense, for women as autonomous entities with equal rights to men, the traditional Other which valorizes women's private and public identities in most societies. It is in this sense that Fariba's comment that "she didn't flee for political reasons" astounds, because persecuting an individual based on that person's erotic and sexual preferences is a political decision endorsed and supported by the State (see Tait, 2005; and "Iran Country Report," pp. 104–105). Siamak, we later find

A Companion to German Cinema, First Edition. Edited by Terri Ginsberg and Andrea Mensch.

out, fits Fariba's understanding of a "political" refugee; he is in Germany seeking asylum as a member of a dissident student group in Iran. Yet, very clearly, Fariba does not claim the same status for herself. In some ways, *Unveiled* presents Fariba's emerging awareness of herself as a lesbian, the lesbian as a gender identity, and gender identity as a political category. And yet, the problem with identity categories is that categories by definition are built of certain essentialist properties, features, actions, and ends that can reify the very concepts the categories attempt to question: for instance, the connection between biology and gender, gender and sexual orientation, etc. Though gender identity based on biological and sexual differences between men and women and feminism's various attempts to posit an essentialist and categorical quality to this difference while also attempting to unravel this difference are both useful historical moments in the ongoing discourse on identity politics in the West, the fundamental question remains: is gender a process of consolidation or is it a process of divestment and dissolution – or is it something else that may defy "identity"? *Unveiled* occupies a space in this ongoing discourse where we see a double erasure of women within patriarchy – woman as woman and woman as lesbian – an erasure equally applicable to both the Iranian Fariba and her German lover, Anna.

Fariba's German lover Anna's predicament is particularly telling in the light of Maccarone's critique of the liberal posturing about sexual identity in the West, particularly in Germany, which has one of the most sexually liberated societies as indexed by the positive representations of onscreen homosexuality, at least since the Third Reich, if not the Weimar Republic itself (see Dyer, 1990: 6–8). Anna, the straight woman, becomes the emblem of Germany's heterosexual norms, which come to life with bristling violence when Anna becomes a woman's object of desire. Maccarone's film successfully pushes us to question how best to establish our presence, our subjectivities, our desires – ultimately our identities – within contexts that constrain their very expressions. Anna's affair with Fariba/Siamak in its Siamak stage (long before Siamak is revealed to be the woman Fariba) also is offensive to her German friends because of Siamak's Iranian and specifically Muslim ethos. Anna's friends in the sauerkraut factory tauntingly address Siamak as "Hey Ayatollah," without an ounce of irony or self-consciousness at their reduplication of the very dogmas about the inferiorities of different races, genders, religions, and ethnicities they seek to mock through such an address. Indeed, from Fariba/Siamak's subjective position, life in Germany as an Iranian is as unsatisfying as life in Iran as a lesbian. Both preclude aspects of Fariba's identity. Fariba/Siamak is constantly under threat of being deported back to Germany; as a refugee immigrant awaiting "paperwork," Fariba/Siamak's options are acutely limited. In fact, the switch in the English title is an interesting glimpse into the nondiegetic forces acting on the cinema-text; the English title, *Unveiled*, makes implicit what is suppressed in the German title, *Fremde Haut* – "Stranger's Skin": the stranger is also a political category, a racial category, the word "veil" evoking the Muslim ethos as the estranged ethos of the film's diegetic world, which comes back with the vengeance of the return of the repressed. Paradoxically, the film attempts to contain all of these identities – lesbian, Iranian, Muslim – Fariba wants to be all – using the presence of one to stabilize/de-stabilize the other. Fariba/Siamak's life as a crossdressing and closeted lesbian in Iran at the conclusion of the film is an analogue to Fariba/Siamak's life as a crossdressing Muslim refugee in Germany. With so much of one's self constantly hidden, so much veiled, as much of one's self is also revealed and unveiled; with so much of one's identity constantly surveyed and attacked, is it possible to have any sort of agency as a human being? More importantly, are we to read in Fariba's (forced) return to Iran and her decision to enter Iran as a "man" (Siamak) a capitulation and ultimately an instance of gender performance? Or are we to read in this act Maccarone's challenge to Western epistemes of subjectivity, selfhood, agency, freedom, autonomy, etc. – what are usually offered as cardinal values of the West? Given the Western world's stated interest in institutionalizing these Enlightenment values on the rest of the world, particularly what are considered in Western media and discourse to be rogue regimes in the Middle East, through war, if necessary, this chapter examines *Unveiled* from the perspective of an abject (see Meijer and Prins, 1998: 281–282) female body's challenge to Western ideas of autonomy, freedom, agency, and self-hood as national values. It is only by learning to see the world through the barbed wire of a holding shelter that the West can begin to understand its connections to the rest of the world. In *Unveiled* a Muslim, Iranian lesbian looks at Germany and to the possibility of an authentic life that is as prohibited there as it is in Iran.

2

Though *Unveiled* does not make any explicit references to the Jewish holocaust, barring a highly coded and tendentious reference to "submarines" in an iconic scene which I shall discuss later, or to the persecution of homosexuals under the Nazi regime, several well-known mainstream and independent German films treat these two holocausts as, in a sense, sharing a common history of violence. Several noteworthy films centered around both the subjective experience of homosexuality, as well as its persecution in open society, had become thematic material for German films almost from the first days of film itself. We can even say that German cinema in the 1920s used the medium for "outing" purposes. Films such as *Different from the Others* (1919) or the romantic melodrama *Michael* (1924) had homosexual characters as their protagonists, gifted, talented, and high-born artists whose calm acceptance of their sexual orientation is at odds with the numerous vicissitudes of fortune that persecute them. While these films featured homosexual characters, they were romances modeled after existing heterosexual romances. The intrusion of class and gender differences into this homosexual romantic matrix gave rise to movies such as *Pandora's Box* (1929) and *Diary of a Lost Girl* (1929), movies which, while not exclusively oriented thematically around homosexuality, nevertheless portray an urban German society that is repressively patriarchal, mercenary, and exploitative of women in general and of the poor and the normatively different. At once portrayed as "fallen," diabolical, and eventually "punished" for her crimes, but also victimized, lost and angry, Lulu in *Pandora's Box*, or Thymian and Erika in *Diary of a Lost Girl*, who are stock victims of an oppressive male world, nevertheless hint at a new form of storytelling that privileges the voice and experiences of social outsiders. The most notable film from this era that encapsulates this new aesthetic of privileging a repressed voice is justifiably Leontine Sagan's 1931 film *Mädchen in Uniform*, which tells the story of a pure and righteous romance between a young schoolgirl, Manuela, and her ideal teacher, Fraulein von Bernburg, in an all-female boarding school. The film ends melodramatically and on an upbeat note with the tyrannical headmistress of the school – a proxy for patriarchy who had demanded the expulsion of both Manuela and Bernburg – chastised by Bernburg for her wrongheaded tyranny. The film with its all-female cast boldly include a sensual kiss between the young girl and the older woman and became a cult hit in Germany and Europe, although it faced competition from director Josef von Sternberg's *The Blue Angel* (1930). *The Blue Angel* tells the story of a serious and virtuous man, Dr Rath, brought down by his infatuation for the wild and promiscuous cabaret dancer, Lola Lola, the role that launched Marlene Dietrich's screen career. The cabaret is the antithesis of the classroom, and both movies appear to critique the strict moral codes of the Prussian school system, although in Sternberg's movie, the system wins, whereas in Sagan's movie, we are left with a more ambiguous ending. Both movies subversively show the powerlessness and subjugation of women inside German society, whether it is the vilified female energy of a Lola Lola in a cabaret or the anguished and suicidal shame of a young Manuela in *Mädchen in Uniform*. Feminist critic B. Ruby Rich, in her well-known essay on *Mädchen in Uniform*, identifies the movie as a "coming-out" of lesbian films and sees Fraulein Bernburg as a woman coming to terms with her bonafide lesbian identity (Rich, 1981: para. 48); at the same time, it is interesting to note that Manuela, the film's protagonist, belongs to the category of passive, suffering, and victimized lesbian characters who resort to suicide, unsuccessfully it is true, in the absence of social acceptance of their sexual identity.

In the aftermath of World War Two, lesbian love-themed films in Germany recast the historical violence of the Jewish holocaust into plotlines of interracial romance where the Nazi regime is made to contain both German society's xenophobia as well as homophobia and thus provide the collective "Other" against which both Jewishness and lesbianism must define themselves. Not an easy task, and as evidenced by films dealing with this topic, lesbianism is often erased when Jewishness is reclaimed. Many of the narratological and ideological problems underlying this genre may be seen, for instance, in critical responses to a paradigmatic postwar German lesbian film such as *Aimée and Jaguar* (1999), with "its focus on the everyday dimension of the Holocaust, the titillation promised by a lesbian romance, and its appeal as a tragic love story" (Sieg, 2002: 304). *Aimée and Jaguar* recounts the love affair between a German mother of four, Lilly "Aimée" Wust, and the Jewish "submarine" – Jews who went into hiding after the 1942 "Final Solution" which resulted in the forced deportation of Jews into the death camps – Felice "Jaguar" Schragenheim during the height of World War Two; Schragenheim's arrest, deportation, and death in 1945; Wust's unsuccessful search for Schragenheim and her attempts to forge an anti-Nazi, antifascist activist consciousness and to work on behalf of oppressed Jews. It is important to note that while male homosexuality was criminalized in Germany, lesbianism was not. It is also significant, then, that lesbianism has been co-opted inside other resistance discourses, particularly that of the Jewish holocaust, as in *Aimée and Jaguar*, women's rights, and with a movie such as *Unveiled*, perhaps the refugee crisis and immigration, but with a crucial and refreshing difference. In abeyance, lesbian identity is "shown" onscreen as the matrix of bodies / identities that cannot be shown and are not accorded political visibility and power. When multiple valences tug at the control centers of the discourse of identity politics in Holocaust cinema, the co-opting of lesbianism, however, has largely meant denying its historical fullness and complexity by reducing it to an identity and in turn collapsing it into other modalities of social protest such as reclaimed racial and ethnic identities or gender equality. *Unveiled* deliberately rejects investing lesbian identity as a historical and political position that serves other activist causes in order to give it a far more profound political signature: lesbian identity, and its proverbial "desire that dare not speak its name," as a historical and political signifier for countless bodies that are denied historical and political materialization. In effect, *Unveiled* retrieves "lesbianism" from its prevailing metonymic usage and resituates it metaphorically, along lines evocative of its more radical allegorical theorizations. I will briefly focus on one specific critical response to *Aimée and Jaguar* in order to exemplify the ultimately dangerous political consequences of the discourse of identity politics negotiating the mined terrains of gender and racial "allegiances," in order to clarify the radical questions about identity politics raised by *Unveiled*.

In her interesting and in many ways paradigmatic reading of *Aimée and Jaguar*, Katrin Sieg (2002: 305) argues that the efforts of the film and Erika Fischer's book on which the film is based "to secure Jewish identity against German appropriations leads her to conscript lesbian sexuality into an ethnic logic of identity by organizing both around collective loyalty. As a result, however, both sexuality and ethnicity attain a degree of impermeability that mitigates against the conceptualization of change or the articulation of antifascist alliances across communities. When change becomes associated with injustice and appropriation, social transformation becomes increasingly difficult to conceptualize outside of a logic of betrayal." Despite the reservations listed above, Sieg's reading of the book and the movie does ultimately find both texts to be wanna-be and partially realized instances of "social transformation" through lesbian love. For instance, Sieg states that the movie adaptation dramatizes "romance in which lesbian desire is flatly at odds with Jewish survival and reserves heroism only for the woman who renounces that desire," and that one way in which to restore the elided social history of the lesbian is to "restore the sexual dimension of the story as socially and politically meaningful" and that "stresses the potential of transformation over the preoccupation with preserving and betraying integrity" (Sieg, 2002: 305–306). But *Unveiled* raises the question of whether it is possible or even desirable ultimately to long for fixed identities – lesbianism being understood as one such vested identity – given the multiple levels of abjection with which essentialized constituencies of nation, race, gender, and class are burdened, by definition. *Unveiled* is a modest but firm effort to answer this question in the negative. Fariba seeks to assert her lesbian identity by fleeing Iran for Germany, where she has to pass as a man in order to function in society. With German citizenship turning into a xenophobic nightmare, Fariba returns to Iran as a woman turning into a man, in transit. The German title of the film, *Fremde Haut*, or "stranger's skin," is also a synonym for "crossdressing." Such performativity of gender in *Unveiled* is best read not as an act of political submission, but as a deliberate act of resistance against being silenced, though Sieg in her reading of *Aimée and Jaguar* condemns "performativity" as a weak alternative to the pitfalls of "essentialism." Sieg sees the many instances of gender subversion in Färberböck's movie – the crossdressing, the drag, the sartorial aspects of the butch–femme gendered role-play between Wust and Schragenheim – as ultimately and always already "homophobic" in the manner of mainstream Hollywood homosexual-themed films; quoting Teresa de Lauretis's *The Practice of Love* (1994), Sieg asserts that "women's putative inability to tell the difference between wanting another woman and wanting to be her indicates a failure on the part of Hollywood cinema (but also some feminist theory) to imagine and represent lesbian desire *as sexual*" (Sieg, 2002: 312). Sieg's reading of *Aimée and Jaguar* is a fascinating attempt to arrive at a full investiture of gender and racial essentialism, the very essentialism that she seeks to critique and appears to deplore. It makes for interesting intellectual gymnastics, but we do find "lesbian desire" and "lesbian sexuality" conflated with a racial essentialism which in Sieg's reading of the movie and the book takes form as an albeit limited solidarity with oppressed Jews. *Unveiled* distinctly runs counter to such ideological co-opting in its resistance to "servicing" another cause, such as nation, race, class, or even gender itself. After all, Fariba returns to Iran in the skin of a "wanted," dead, antigovernment activist. In Fariba's solidarity with persecuted Iranian youths, lesbianism once again gains an active, disidentificatory ground as a modality of effective, organized, and collective resistance.

3

While homoerotic content has been a mainstay, at least in a spiritual form in Iranian literature, in the poetry of the mystic Sufis and the visual arts, and indeed both homoerotic sentiment as well as homoerotic practice in the Islamic Middle East as discussed extensively by Samar Habib in *Islamic Texts on Female Homosexuality 800–1500 AD* (2009) and *Female Homosexuality in the Middle East: Histories and Representations* (2007), the practice of homosexuality in postrevolutionary Iran is a criminal offense punishable by execution. In a distressing adaptation of the three-strikes model, homosexual acts up to three times are punished by lashings, a pardon issued upon recanting, but a fourth offense results in execution. Most recently, Iran's position on homosexual rights achieved a certain notoriety in Western media when Iran's president was quoted (or misquoted) as having stated: "In Iran, we don't have homosexuals like in your country … In Iran we don't have this phenomenon" ("President misquoted", 2007: para. 2). Similarly, while mainstream and art-house Iranian cinema are deafeningly silent about homosexual themes, Iranian-born, New York-based filmmaker Tanaz Eshaghian's wrenching documentary, *Be Like Others* (2008), tells the story of gays and lesbians in Iran who are advised/coerced into undergoing sex change operation rather than practice their natural sexual orientation in their biological bodies, Eshaghian observed that this was

> a very public phenomenon … These sex changes are legal and are endorsed by the leading clerics. It's embraced. I asked for a press permit before I went. After a month, I was given the OK. Officially, I was allowed to do what I needed to do. It's not like I was doing a film on nuclear strategy – they don't see it as an openly political issue. (2008: section 5)

Eshaghian's observation that Iranians do not seem to perceive this coercion as "political" echoes Fariba's comment to Siamak that she is not a "political" refugee. Parvez Sharma's documentary, *A Jihad for Love* (2007), likewise narrates the experiences of gay and lesbian Iranians, among others, who opt to live their sexual orientations rather than undergo punishment or a sex-change operation in Iran (Morrow, 2008: paras 6–7).

Although gender roles are firmly ensconced in Iranian films, woman-centered themes and stories are seriously addressed in Iranian films by Iran's sophisticated film industry and its artful directors, but homosexuality as a theme has yet to find enduring articulation through the medium of cinema in Iran. Intimations of homoeroticism, however, appear as the return of the repressed, most often in films with crossdressing as theme or mise-en-scène. For instance, crossdressing is treated comedically in Davood Mir-Bagheri's *Adam Barfi* (Snowman, 1995), where an Iranian man desperately seeking a visa to immigrate to the United States dresses up as a woman in the hopes of marrying an American man. Abbas, the hero, wins his masculinity and returns to his Iranian citizenship when he marries an Iranian woman in the film's black comedic resolution. Likewise, in Majid Majidi's *Baran* (2001), Lateef falls in love with Rahmat/Baran, an Afghani girl crossdressing as a boy to secure employment.

Crossdressing has a long history within films; while early crossdressing characters provided cheap comic relief, especially male-to-female crossdressers, they also started to embody a certain sinister quality, particularly in film noir; crossdressing as a dangerous killer in female clothing with petticoats and frills intensified the psychopathology of the killer; not only was he a criminal, but a deviant as well.[1] Here we must make a distinction between filmic representation of characters who consider "drag" as their gender identity, as opposed to a biological man or woman who is forced by the diegetic context to wear the opposite gender's clothes.[2] Often such characters crossdressed to gain access to the social universe of the opposite gender that would otherwise be closed to them due to any number of social, cultural, and political reasons: crossdressing as part of "passing" and social acceptance into a different world. Women traditionally crossdressed to gain entrance into the military or to go where no woman had gone before; depending on the social milieu, various social spheres were closed off to women: the bar, the football field, the army, the adventure. Men usually crossdressed to gain entrance into women's spheres of work or play; *Mrs. Doubtfire* wants his family back, while *Tootsie* wants work. In racial contexts, crossdressing across racial ethos afforded "blacks" to pass as "whites," as in Nella Larsen's acclaimed novel, *Passing* (1929), and Jews to pass as non-Jews, as discussed extensively by Sieg.

Fariba does not fall into the category of either drag or intentional crossdressing; Fariba's original intent in coming to Germany is to seek asylum from being persecuted as a lesbian; she hopes to live in Germany as a lesbian. It is only when her application is denied after being exposed for her "lie" that she is a "political" refugee that she decides to pass as a man. *Unveiled* thus belongs to a lesbian feature film genre where the lesbian character accepts her lesbian identity; she does not wish that she were different. She does not wish that she were straight. She wants to live as a lesbian, and if it is not possible in one place, she will seek out another society that allows her to express her sexuality and identity like anyone else. But in its reluctance to afford a satisfactory resolution to the love affair between the two women, *Unveiled* posits such a desire for a mutually reciprocal and socially blessed love as, in line with Fariba's ostensible lie, politically loaded. In other words, "romantic love" and its sexual expression are re-revealed not as solutions to xenophobia or homophobia, as envisioned by Sieg's reading of *Aimée and Jaguar*, for instance; instead they are shown to be part of the structural problematics of traditional social institutions.

Is the alternative suggested by a fused lesbian love a corrective to the tyranny of patriarchy and heteronormativity? There is considerable debate in contemporary lesbian studies on the "lesbian continuum" first proposed by Adrienne Rich in her then controversial essay, "Compulsory Heterosexuality and Lesbian Existence" (1990), which posits a "woman-identified" "lesbian continuum" united against heteronormative patriarchy, that being Rich's true subject in her essay. Gender theorist Teresa de Lauretis (1994: 190–192), among others, has read Rich's "lesbian continuum" as a form of oversimplified woman-to-woman bonding, which does not take into account what de Lauretis terms in her neo-Freudian framework the sexual dimension of lesbian subjectivity. *Unveiled* would fall somewhere in between these two theories, if only because it sees gender and sexuality neither as ends in themselves nor as abstract objectives but as real concepts marked by social alienation and political struggle in a violent and exploitative world, concepts that mediate – and are mediated by – experience, both sexual and social, and that may be engaged critically through acts of material and ideological solidarity. For a movie that deals at least partly with lesbian desire, *Unveiled* is remarkably economical, even reticent in portraying this desire, the reticence less a statement about the measure of diegetic or nondiegetic sexuality than an unwillingness to hand over lesbianism to interpersonal romance. We are left with the clear lingering conclusion that love is not enough to enable its sustained sexual expression and offer meaningful redress to its very real abjection.

Maccarone uses just one snapshot to portray lesbian life in Iran. Fariba looks at a photo of herself with Shirin, her lover, before burning it: two women, fully covered in black chador, heads covered in scarves, eyes hidden in dark glasses, sit facing each other, their bodies leaning toward each other, their mouths smiling at each other. We don't see their faces. The photo has content, but it is contentless at the same time. Nothing distinguishes it as a "coming-out" photo or a "coming-out" scene, other than the emotional quotient suggested by its tendentious destruction by Fariba – she burns it – even far away from Iran. There are two proper "coming-out" scenes in *Unveiled*; together, they complicate the social trans-formative power of romantic love with its happy ending for the lesbian couple, of narratologically fused lesbian desire as a confident expression and experience of such love. *Unveiled* underscores the insufficiency of the former and refuses to elaborate on the latter, perhaps owing to the film's fundamental refusal to submit "lesbian desire" for suspect commodity consumption onscreen. Female desire whether exchanged between men and women, or women and women has the power to commodify this desire for its very abjection; *Unveiled* appears to be aware of this representational constraint. One is the outing of Anna, the hetero-sexual woman, and the second one is the imminent outing of Fariba/Siamak as a crossdresser by a prostitute. In the scene where Fariba and Anna make love, their lovemaking is shown through Anna's eyes; she unbinds Fariba's breasts in horror, and when they touch one another, they are touching politicized bodies; the sheer act of a woman sensuously touching another woman embodies the social threat posed by women who intentionally desire other women, both in Germany and in Iran. In an ordinary morning punctuated with eating breakfast after a night together, Anna's and Fariba's lives spiral out of control as they are discovered by Anna's male friends, both homophobic and xenophobic. The unveiling of Anna's sexual desire in this scene is in stark contrast to the sexual silence, indeed the complete absence of visual eroticism in the snapshot of Fariba with her Iranian lover, Shirin. It is also an ironic counterpoint to Fariba's "outing" at a brothel by a prostitute who refuses to "service" her on account of her gender, and who agrees to be silent only because she has already been paid. The lingering vertical depth of this scene, with its real-time waiting for a male–female sexual union to be over – Fariba and the prostitute have to make sure that the macho buddies waiting outside the sordid love booth are convinced that they are indeed having sex – lays bare the terrible and terrifying sexual economy inside which women labor in patriarchy. *Unveiled* decisively stages romantic, erotic lesbian love as just not enough for social transformation, thus placing into question the very notion of that love's vested experience. Love and sexual desire are shown as insufficient holdings for historical identities in sociopolitical crisis.

Maccarone does not merely make Fariba adopt a male identity; she has her step into a dead man's shoes. This is a significant equation between two ways of being: a living closeted/persecuted woman in Iran is equal to a dead Iranian man in Germany. The ethical center of *Unveiled*, what makes the movie a powerful critique of Western epistemological assumptions about identity as an endowed category and selfhood as an evident category, is beautifully achieved by Maccarone in this unthinkable equation she draws between a dead Iranian refugee who committed suicide inside a transit shelter, whose body is buried without evidence in an unnamed German countryside, who has no record as it were, with that of a persecuted Iranian woman who steps into this nonexistent space, a signifier for what is contentless, but whose voice we continue to hear through real letters that Fariba writes Siamak's parents in his voice assuming his identity. This transubstantiation of essences between Siamak and Fariba is of a painfully tender kind. Siamak, the dissident student, arrives in Germany from Iran after the state police take away his brother who assumes his identity when they come to arrest Siamak. Siamak knows intuitively that his incarcerated brother will die in prison. Siamak merely delays his own suicide in Germany until he learns that his brother was killed in prison. In one scene, we do see Siamak trying to escape from the bus taking the asylum-seekers from the holding center to the airport offices; it is his first suicide attempt because he knows that he will be contained or shot inside the fenced acres of the airport. Thus Fariba's assumption of Siamak's identity is an act of profound political resistance, an instance of solidarity with the hundreds of nameless and unknown youths killed for their criticism of the Iranian state. Maccarone's injunction, articulated in an interview about the film, against settling for the comfort zone of "constricted polarities" or binary thinking is particularly applicable to the ethical and political abiding by Iran, by Muslims, and lesbians that Fariba/Siamak represents; in its unwillingness to acquiesce to the monolithic options offered by an "Iran" or a "Germany," "man" or "woman," "homosexual" or "heterosexual" (particularly in Ann's case: Anna falls in love with Fariba/Siamak, not with Fariba or with Siamak), Maccarone takes the prescriptive imperative to reductive comparison and abides by the vast humanity that the "nation" discards, whether in Iran or in Germany.[3] In fact, the entire mise-en-scène at the airport holding center is a metonymic displacement of that other prison with its abject bodies that we will not see or hear about. The holding center with its cell-like rooms, its crowded bunkbeds, women, children, and men packed like sardines, the undistinguished number of Muslim men offering their prayers to God on dirty floor mats before they are deported back to the countries they came from or released into Germany, the little boy who draws a picture of going to America – by manipulating the mise-en-scène Maccarone invests scene after scene with the depths of two incarcerations, one in Iranian prison cells and the other in the German holding shelters, both filled with people awaiting their freedom. In these scenes we see the tragic relation between the countries these men and women have left behind in their exile to foreign lands in search of a better life, and their betrayal by the West a second time around.

Maccarone gives us brief but pointed glimpses into the fragile existence of those in the liminal state between asylum-seeker, refugee, immigrant, and citizen. Fariba / Siamak's roommate spends every minute of his spare time watching videos of his home. Fariba narrates the amenities Germany offers to its immigrants in her letters to Siamak's parents while saving whatever money she can to buy a German passport on the black market. A qualified translator who is fluent in German and English, Fariba ends up working illegally at a sauerkraut factory and later at a car rental service as a janitor. In many ways, Fariba's existence is a poignant extrapolation of what Siamak's (and by extension any immigrant's) own life would have been in Germany. Once again, Maccarone suggests the constrained and constricted world of immigrants largely through a carefully crafted mise-en-scène: Siamak's cramped living quarters are far removed from the open countryside seemingly there for the taking by any free individual. This feeling of cramped space, of being against a wall with nowhere to turn is Maccarone's preferred style in portraying Siamak's life as an illegal immigrant in Germany. The hunted and haunted nature of an illegal immigrant's day-to-day survival is memorably caught in the scene at the sauerkraut factory, where the local police drop in unannounced to check for illegal employees. Fariba and her friend are literally forced to hide inside a giant sauerkraut mixer with mountains of white shredded cabbage hiding them from the police. The camera looks down on them hidden inside the mixer, vulnerable, barely escaping exposure.

Maccarone's manipulation of the setting adds unexpected depth to the unspoken and perhaps unspeakable emotional content of the film in its earlier parts where Fariba's identity is known only to us and not to any of the other characters. The first real meeting and conversation between Fariba and Anna in the cabbage field adjacent to the airport wonderfully captures Maccarone's technique of making the scene tell a story. Through a simple long-shot carefully composed, Maccarone evokes a scene of pastoral calm and peace, giving just the minimal suggestion of powerlessness to its human characters. We see Fariba and Anna foregrounded against the sprawling cabbage patch, beyond which is open land and an open sky into which an airplane takes off. Fariba looks up and Anna starts a conversation about being homesick. Fariba is clearly more educated and more urbane than Anna. They speak about Teheran, a big city where Fariba is from, and the rural town of Esslingen, where the two are now, which Anna wishes to leave. "I tried to leave once, "Anna says, "but it didn't work out." In this scene, Anna and Fariba are mostly facing each other and also partly facing us, their heads close together, their bodies directed into each other, much like the photograph of Fariba and her lover taken in Iran, focused on the work of prying the cabbages from the bushes. The emotional energy of this scene is that of work as well as confession and camarade-rie. It is that of a private space inside a much bigger public space. There is nowhere for the women to go other than from the patch to the truck and back and forth, but it is a wonderfully rested scene with everything in its place: the land, the farm, the sky, and the two characters talking and walking. Unbeknownst to Fariba, Anna had been dared to secure a date with the "new Iranian guy" by her friend, Bina; Bina will give Anna a bike for her son if she goes out on a date with Siamak. Anna uses this moment to tell Fariba/Siamak that she would like to take him out to see the countryside of Fildern if he likes. Fariba/Siamak whispers "Yes." The fact that Anna considers Fariba/Siamak one of the boys is evident when she leans close and asks Fariba/Siamak, "But why are you whispering?" The scene ensconces an ambiguous gender perspective when Fariba replies, "Because I am happy." Again, in keeping with the film's drive to deconstruct and redirect essentialized positions, we hear in this barely audible admission something unsettling, unpredictable and unstabilizing; it is not the sort of response Anna is used to hearing from her regular male suitors. We see in Anna's surprised but accepting smile that she is aware that she is in the presence of a different experience.

For a movie that is largely shot in cramped indoor quarters or barbed-wired outdoors, this scene and the following one with Anna and Fariba/Siamak riding in Anna's scooter through the Fildern countryside are notable not merely for the visual contrast they bring, but also for the confluence of themes they spark; in particular, Anna's sense of being at odds with her environment, her struggles as a young, attractive, single mother in a small town, the good-natured horseplay of her male friends that hides a violent possessiveness, and her growing desire for something different in her life. In Anna's "night-out" with her friends we see small-town life: bowling alley and beer while her mother watches Anna's young son. And yet, Maccarone is exact in showing us the West's instinctive feelings of superiority over the countries it demonizes and caricatures as inferior. Anna's friends taunt Fariba/Siamak with a number of racially derogatory remarks; they refer to him as being from Tajikistan (Iran? Tajikistan? What is the difference?), they constantly address him as "Ayatollah," they dare him to drink beer instead of "rice brandy" and taunt him to sing or dance for them, to do an "expressive dance." Both men and women taunt Fariba/Siamak: it is Bina who mockingly acts out "the expressive dance" in a primitive gesture of sashaying belly dancers. Maccarone shows these men and women as individuals essentially blind to the implications of their own existence. Fariba/Siamak, precisely because of her outsider/outcast status, is capable to put the type of pressure on the social strata that will cause it to crack and reveal the weakness of its structure. When her friend, Bina, tells Anna that with Siamak, she will have no future, Anna replies, "Future? What about now? I want something different in my life."

The movie makes explicit its preoccupation with women's struggles for self-definition and autonomy through Anna's character. But unlike the gritty female heroines of Margarethe von Trotta, in particular, Christina Klages from *The Second Awakening of Christa Klages* (1978), or either of the two sisters from *Marianne and Juliane* (1981), Anna is essentially powerless to make a better life for herself and her son, primarily because of her class and concomitant economic status. Anna's agency for personal or social reform is severely limited, and in this sense she is a Western foil for Fariba. In fact, there is little difference between Fariba's Iranian lover, Shirin, who asks Fariba never to contact her again, and Anna, who stands powerless as Fariba is taken away by the authorities during the film's painful climax. As an employee in Bina's father's factory, Anna, like Fariba/Siamak, does not have any political voice or power, and it is in this sense that Anna's solidarity with Fariba/Siamak figures into the movie's critique of Western power but is ultimately a weak, imploded resistance. The notion of self-identity and autonomy that enters heavily into Western claims of philosophical, political, economic, and social superiority over other cultures rides on the back of an oppressed working class, particularly working-class women. Anna signifies one such powerless entity and is ultimately entrapped in a situation far more insidious than the one into which Fariba/Siamak enters upon her deportation from Germany and forced return to Iran.

If it is her nationality and sexual orientation that make Fariba powerless, then it is her gender and class origins that make Anna an equally abject body. Just as love and sexual desire cannot promise Fariba the freedom that she craves, Anna is also imprisoned within her gender and class by her inability to form an effective resistance against patriarchy. Contrasting while in some ways complementing von Trotta's films, which posit at least the possibility of a collective struggle against the gender confines of patriarchy, Maccarone's critical focus is on the socially implied moral equivalence between Fariba's and Anna's transformative needs, a false symmetricality that transcends collective recognition. Whereas any organized, collective, and antipatriarchal resistance must also necessarily involve protecting other differences, such as that of homosexuality, Anna is not part of a collective; in fact, *Unveiled* is distinctly postfeminist in its insistent challenge to mainstream feminism's real or perceived inability to reach women such as Anna or Fariba. We see Anna always in the company of her friends, bourgeois families, we might note, where conversations revolve around such banalities as a pregnant woman's "glow." Maccarone shows us the length, breadth, and depth of Anna's social interactions during her son's birthday party; her portrayal of Anna the struggling single parent is both gentle in its ideological critique as well as uncompromising in its challenge to the banalities of Anna's existence. Nowhere is this thwarted solidarity between women, between Anna and Fariba, more evident than in the scene at the birthday party where Fariba nervously digs through Anna's bathroom supplies in search of tampons. Anna's young son interrupts her search by asking her what she is doing with his mother's tampons. They are submarines, Fariba tells the little boy. Little torpedos. They fill the bathroom sink up with water and play, watching the tampons float in water. Lily Wust had eagerly co-opted her Jewish "submarine" lover's identity in *Aimée and Jaguar*; Wust ostensibly solidifies her loyalty to oppressed Jews by individually helping three additional Jewish women. In *Unveiled*, such a model of German solidarity with the oppressed and the persecuted is swiftly undone through the tampon scene. The German woman is revealed sans-community, reduced to her biological sex. She is in no position to organize or initiate the defense of anyone she loves. Fariba/Siamak, through shifting the boundaries of her identities, poses a far greater subversive challenge to the hegemonic power of an established order in Germany or Iran than Anna can ever hope to achieve in Esslingen. Anna's options are few; very likely, she has no avenues other than to go back to the sauerkraut factory as one of its superexploited, unempowered workers.

The "coming-out" scenes discussed earlier also helps us connect Maccarone's thematic and ideological positioning of the status of women inside patriarchy. Fariba/Siamak experiences first-hand the social subordination of women during the second half of the boy's "night out," when they take Fariba/Siamak to a bar in the entertainment district of Stuttgart where Uwe pays for a prostitute to "service" Fariba/Siamak. It is an ironic scene: the prostitute immediately discovers that Siamak is a woman and refuses to have sex with her, while Fariba/Siamak begs the woman to stay the whole time in the cubicle in order to protect her gender cover. This is a classic set-up: man pays money to watch man and woman having sex. Maccarone nullifies the exploitative potential of this pornographic arrangement by making evident its ideological message: the sexual commodification of the woman's body is for male, not female, pleasure. The prostitute's rejection of Fariba underscores the power of this sexual ideology. It is also in stark contrast to the later scene where Fariba and Anna make love for the first and last time, where a straight woman falls in love with a lesbian of her own choice. While the prostitute's encounter with Fariba follows the frustrated expectation of conventional roles played by both genders, Fariba and Anna represent a fluid give and take of these gender norms, of desire for an "other," which in Anna's admittedly Eurocentric case becomes, in a circuitous manner, a love of her own Self.

Several narrative features distinguish Fariba's and Anna's courtship and consummation of love, most important of which is the explicit "female bonding" that the two characters undergo, most of the time under watchful male and heteronormative eyes. There is no love at first sight for Fariba and Anna; their relationship develops over a period of time and interaction in which they learn about each other – certainly what Anna might want from a lover, we are led to believe. How women (make) love outside the dictates of a patriarchal order becomes the tender focus in the scene where the men and women go riding in the car during their night out. Anna and Fariba hold hands in the back seat of the car where Anna starts to examine Fariba's hands. Lesbian desire and love come together in this beautiful scene, Anna "seeing" in Fariba's hands the key to her identity, an echo back to their earlier conversation about the "Hand of Fatima" pendant with its "seeing eye" worn by Fariba; it protects the wearer from the Evil Eye. However, *Unveiled* provides no metaphysical solutions to social problems; perhaps this is its reluctance to valorize "love" as an emotion with socially redemptive and transformative potential. Riding with the boys, stopped by a cop, Fariba and Anna are shown equally powerless to claim an autonomous space for themselves either as women or as lovers.

On the one hand, *Unveiled* portrays lesbian desire as a whole and complete woman-ness that is divested of any claims to socially arbitrated feminine norms. Thus it is significant that Anna, a straight woman, chooses the object of her desire – another woman. The lesbian, by her very choice, may be held suspect by societies with arbitrary enumeration of binary sexuality and any form that curves away from this dual division of sex assignation as deviant definitions of gender behavior – this is often the reason behind the forced sex-change operations in Iran; if you desire a woman, you must want to be a man; if you desire a man, you must want to be a woman. Maccarone presents Anna's coming-out scene with Fariba as situationally constructed as well as an authentic need from within herself – something Fariba already possesses. Through Fariba, Anna embodies the lesbian position as one that consciously has no need to answer to a male position: both Fariba and Anna potentially embody a subjectivity that need not define itself against a gendered or sexualized Other. Anna's lesbianism is represented as organically evolved, a personally meaningful choice, which points toward desire as a force directed toward the similarities of and within differences; not the Other, much less another, but the Same and ultimately the Self misrecognized as We. Such a choice, whose expression is represented as foreclosed to Fariba due to socopolitical constraints, is given representational content in the character of Anna. It is possible to see that what Anna loses by way of direct political action to intervene on behalf of Fariba and to stop her deportation is consolidated through one existential act of personal meaning that shapes the film's ideological stance on sexual orientation.

However, Maccarone is careful to cast this sexual desire and ultimately erotic love as politically suspect; by juxtaposing Anna's powerlessness as a woman, even the lesbian desire she experiences as a genuine transformation on a personal level is refused a social function. For instance, we do not know at all whether Anna will lead a lesbian lifestyle after Fariba leaves. We do not see her discussing her sexuality with anyone. We are shown her helplessness as the authorities take Fariba away, much as Shirin must have done in Iran. This is where the reflexive identification between Anna and Fariba is directed, against their shared helplessness against patriarchal institutions. Anna does not want to become Fariba or vice versa; we might have to call their deep awareness of each other even as they are denied a future together an honest and possible approximation to solidarity. Anna's "identification" with Fariba is mirrored in Fariba's return to Iran as Siamak, another existential act that represents the film's radical solidarity with the anonymous dead young men – and women – that are victims of state violence.

It might be tempting to read in Anna's love for Fariba and Fariba's metonymic stepping-in in the shoes of Siamak/dead young men in Iran the kind of essentialist appropriation of gender and resistance politics, a process of assimilation that threatens our awareness of necessary differences that so often provide the cautionary caveat especially for those of us interested in the nexus between activism and epistemological work. *Unveiled* avoids this homogenization of the resistance collective – both in the sexual domain and in the political domain – by deconstructing, in the sexual domain, the fixity of binary gender as an ethical act for Anna. Likewise, Maccarone confers on Fariba/Siamak the power of a repressed memory, a powerful signifier that every refugee is a citizen exiled by his/her own country. The film itself uses the conventions of the modern, Western lesbian romance – the courtship and successful consummation leading to a successful integration with the mainstream society – only to sacrifice such a resolution toward a more theoretically open-ended question as to the ethical status of such legitimized desires.

For instance, as audience, we do not "identify" with either woman or wish for their thwarted love affair to be made whole again, for that would be an exercise in fantasy. In the film's broken resolution, we see Maccarone's challenge to feminist activism in our times; how can we as women build a collective struggle against oppressive actions of communities and nations appealing to either our similarities or differences? In Anna's and Fariba's case, mere love is not enough, because race complicates that love. Political asylum complicates that love. Rise of radical fundamentalism complicates that love. Anna is no Wust and Fariba is no Schragenheim and Anna can neither "save" Fariba nor redeem herself inside the changed permutations of what constitutes personal identity in our times. There is no racialized collective – much as there is the Jewish community in *Aimée and Jaguar* – to which Anna pledges her devotion and commitment. *Unveiled* makes no historical apology from the West toward the East, but it does something far more politically radical. In Fariba's case, what does it mean to say that you live your life as a free lesbian when the very freedom you experience is predicated on a borrowed identity? To an extent equally applicable to Fariba and Anna, more to Fariba in a nationalist context and Anna inside a capitalist exploitative context, *Unveiled* asks what it means to be a nation when your very identity as a nation depends on the exclusion and execution of your own citizens? In its deliberate rejection of the romance paradigm, *Unveiled* interrogates the giant Western epistemes of attainable selfhoods for individuals as well as nations. In the film's uncertain final act – is Fariba/Siamak walking into another suicide or is it a chance at living? – we are forced to acknowledge categorically and once and for all that real social transformation is more than momentary subversion of hegemonic power structures through crossdressing or ethical, transformative love. Ultimately, the challenge *Unveiled* offers to the viewer in the twenty-first century is to formulate the theoretical connections between gender, race, class, and nationalism when these constituents are shown to be neither "essences" nor "performances," and how best to forge epistemological as well as activist alliances across these constituencies as traditional binaries such as

East–West, man–woman, straight–gay, etcetera prove insufficient to resolve if not to ascertain the nature of the problems facing our current historical moment.

Notes

1   I am thinking specifically of Alfred Hitchcock's *Murder* (1930) and *Psycho* (1960).
2   Drag as an identity character may be seen, for instance, in *The Rocky Horror Picture Show* (1975), *Hairspray* (1988), *The Crying Game* (1992), *To Wong Foo Thanks for Everything, Julie Newmar* (1995), and *The Bird Cage* (1996).
3   "I think one of the main problems is our thinking within constricted concepts like polarities. There is good or evil, the 'free world' or suppression. I believe the world, the human, is more complex than that. The simple solutions that are suggested by polarities are dangerous. Thinking like 'we are good, they are evil' has existed for a long time and justified a lot of horrible things people do to each other. I wanted to show that on either side there are humans. If the 'bad guys' are human too they do have a bigger responsibility for their decisions" (Swartz, 2005: para. 7).

References

De Lauretis, T. (1994) *The Practice of Love: Lesbian Sexuality and Perverse Desire*. Indiana University Press, Bloomington.

Dyer, R. (1990) Less and more than women and men: lesbian and gay cinema in Weimar Germany. *New German Critique*, 51, 5–60.

Habib, S. (2007) *Female Homosexuality in the Middle East: Histories and Representations*, Routledge, London.

Habib, S. (2009) *Islamic Texts on Female Homosexuality 800–1500 A.D.*, Teneo Press, New York.

Hays, M. (2008) Iran's gay plan. *CBC News*, August 26, http://www.cbc.ca/arts/film/story/2008/08/26/f-homosexuality-iran-sex-change.html (accessed January 1, 2011).

Iran Country Report (2002) *UNHCR/ACCORD: 7th European Country of Origin Information Seminar Berlin, 11–12 June 2001 –Final report*, http://www.ecoi.net/file_upload/mv100_cois2001-irn.pdf (accessed January 1, 2011).

Meijer, I.C. and Prins, B. (1998) How bodies come to matter: an interview with Judith Butler. *Signs*, 23 (2), 275–286.

Morrow, M. (2008) Forbidden love: a brave documentary reveals the lives of gay and lesbian Muslims. *CBC News*, July 16, http://www.cbc.ca/arts/film/story/2008/07/16/f-jihad-for-love.html (accessed January 1, 2011).

President misquoted over gays in Iran: aide (2007) *Reuters*, October 10, http://www.reuters.com/article/idUSBLA05294620071010 (accessed January 1, 2011).

Rich, A. (1980) Compulsory heterosexuality and lesbian existence. *Signs*, 5 (4), 631–660.

Rich, B.R. (1981) *Maedchen in Uniform*: from repressive tolerance to erotic liberation. *Jump Cut*, 24–25, http://www.ejumpcut.org/archive/onlinessays/JC2425folder/MaedchenUniform.html (accessed January 1, 2011).

Sieg, K. (2002) Sexual desire and social transformation in "Aimee and Jaguar." *Signs*, 28 (1), 303–331.

Swartz, S. (2005) Interview with "Unveiled" director Angelina Maccarone. *Afterellen*, November 17, http://www.afterellen.com/Movies/2005/11/unveiled.html (accessed January 1, 2011).

Tait, R. (2005) A fatwa for freedom. *Guardian*, July 27, http://www.guardian.co.uk/world/2005/jul/27/gayrights.iran (accessed January 1, 2011).

Filmography

Adam Barfi [Snowman] (Davood Mir-Bagheri, Iran, 1995).

Aimée and Jaguar (Max Färberböck, Germany, 1999).

Baran (Majid Majidi, Iran, 2001).

Be Like Others (Tanaz Eshaghian, Canada/Iran/UK/USA, 2008).

Blue Angel, The [*Der Blaue Engel*] (Josef von Sternberg, Germany, 1930).

Birdage, The (Mike Nichols, USA, 1996).

Crying Game, The (Neil Jordan, UK/Japan, 1992).

Diary of a Lost Girl [*Das Tagebuch einer Verlorenen*] (G.W. Pabst, Germany, 1929).

Different from the Others [*Anders als die Andern*] (Richard Oswald, Germany, 1919).

Hairspray (John Waters, USA, 1988).

Jihad for Love, A (Parvez Sharma, USA/UK/France/Germany/Australia, 2007).

Mädchen in Uniform (Leontine Sagan, Germany, 1931).

Marianne and Juliane [*Die Bleierne Zeit*] (Margarethe von Trotta, West Germany, 1981).

Michael (Carl Theodor Dreyer, Germany, 1924).

Mrs. Doubtfire (Chris Columbus, USA, 1993).

Murder (Alfred Hitchcock, USA, 1930).

Pandora's Box [*Die Büchse der Pandora*] (G.W. Pabst, Germany, 1929).

Psycho (Alfred Hitchcock, USA, 1960).

Rocky Horror Picture Show, The (Jim Sharman, USA, 1975).

Second Awakening of Christa Klages, The [*Das zweite Erwachsen der Christa Klages*] (Margarethe von Trotta, West Germany, 1978).

To Wong Foo Thanks for Everything, Julie Newmar (Beeban Kidron, USA, 1995).

Tootsie (Sydney Pollack, USA, 1982).

Unveiled [*Fremde Haut*] (Angelina Maccarone, Germany, 2005).

Second Movement: Dislocation

Marked by transnationally inflected historiography for which borders and their transgression are of central concern, contemporary German film scholarship has often repositioned the nation-state within the limits of such border-crossings as persistently necessary to German – and by extension, European – sociocultural vitality. By contrast, the present volume's second movement offers a series of chapters which challenge that tendency by analyzing films and film movements that stand either to critique or to symptomatize it. They do so from (im)migrant/ diasporic, feminist and queer, and critical class perspectives regarding avant-garde/ experimental and alternative/independent works or films and genres that instance the exploitation and co-optation of marginalized ethnoracial, religious, and sex-gender positions internationally. The second movement thereby offers a critical dislocation of prevailing theoretical support and advocacy for transnational capital mobility in the Germano-European cinematic sphere and beyond. It points to the often violent displacement of globally subjugated and indigenous populations which is the preeminent result of such mobility.

8

Views across the Rhine

Border Poetics in Straub–Huillet's Machorka-Muff (1962) and Lothringen! (1994)

Claudia Pummer

1. Border Crossings

Danièle Huillet and Jean-Marie Straub met in Paris in November 1954. In the same month, the first severe clashes between Algerian Front de Libération Nationale (FLN) troops and the French colonial army broke out in Algeria; the Algerian War had begun. Four years later, a 25-year-old Jean-Marie Straub fled across the French–German border to escape the draft into the war. Huillet joined him shortly after and by the end of 1959, the couple had found a new residence in Munich.

Two years later, in the fall of 1962, Straub–Huillet completed their first film, the German-language production *Machorka-Muff*. An adaptation of postwar novelist Heinrich Böll's short story, *Bonn Diary* (*Hauptstadt Journal*, 1958), the film dealt with one of the most controversial current political matters at the time: the Federal Republic's rearmament and military restoration after World War Two. Also the three other German-language films the couple made in the following ten years of their Munich residence (1958–1968) were heavily infused with German culture and subject matter; their second Böll adaptation, *Not Reconciled* (*Nicht Versöhnt*, 1964–1965), was one of the first films made in the Federal Republic that addressed explicitly the country's difficulties to deal with its National Socialist and military past; their first feature-length film, *The Chronicle of Anna Magdalena Bach* (*Die Chronik der Anna Magdalena Bach*, 1967), was about the life and work of a German cultural icon: the Baroque composer Johann Sebastian Bach; and *The Bridegroom, the Comedienne, and the Pimp* (*Der Bräutigam, Die Komödiantin, und der Zuhälter*, 1968), Straub's collaboration with the young Rainer Werner Fassbinder, dealt with contemporary class conflicts in postwar West German society.

A Companion to German Cinema, First Edition. Edited by Terri Ginsberg and Andrea Mensch.
© 2012 Blackwell Publishing Ltd. Published 2012 by Blackwell Publishing Ltd.

Filmed on location in Bonn and Munich, the making of *Machorka-Muff* coincided, in addition, with the emergence of the Young German Film (whose official outbreak had been declared a few months earlier in the Oberhausen Manifesto). Although they were not signatories of the manifesto, the film is often considered "an early milestone of the Young German Cinema (Byg, 1995: 35)." In his attempt "to demonstrate the significance of Straub–Huillet's work as a cinematic confrontation of German history and culture," Barton Byg inevitably undermines the transnational characteristics in Straub–Huillet's work. And, he is not alone. Even though Straub–Huillet are less present in more recent surveys on postwar German cinema (following the general disciplinary shift away from modernist and new German filmmaking practices toward previously neglected phenomena, like popular cinema, reception studies, or culturally specific genre films), the couple was for a long time primarily known and discussed for their contributions to New German Film culture of the 1960s and 1970s, especially within Anglo-American scholarship (Turim, 1984, 1986; Byg, 1995; Magisos, 1996; Rentschler, 1996).

This German orientation appears even greater in light of Straub–Huillet's conspicuous absence in national or modernist surveys on either French or Italian postwar cinema, despite of the fact that the two filmmakers lived and worked primarily in Italy since 1968. And until Huillet's passing in 2006, they filmed most of their work on locations in Italy, including a substantial and growing number of French- and Italian-language films.

In this chapter, I address Straub–Huillet's contributions to German cinema from a transnational angle. I draw attention first to the influence that French New Wave film culture and criticism had on Straub–Huillet's work, especially during the early years. I do not argue for historicizing their work as an intrinsic part of French New Wave Cinema; I propose to understand it rather as deriving from the position of *the border*, thus belonging neither fully to one nor the other national film culture. Straub–Huillet's involuntary border-crossing in late 1958 placed the two filmmakers squarely in-between two national film cultures: while producing their first films in the geographical, cultural, linguistic, and partially institutional context of the Young German Film, their artistic approach remained indebted to a critical and aesthetic model that was central to the formative years of French New Wave Cinema. Following a brief overview of Straub–Huillet's affiliations and occupations during their Parisian residence (1954–1958), I read their debut film, *Machorka-Muff*, in terms of a *border poetics*, a reading practice in which the border emerges as a central figure that works across temporal, formal, textual, linguistic, and cultural limits (e.g. Michaelsen and Johnson, 1997; Schimanski, 2006; Schimanski and Wolfe, 2007). Thus, breaching a number of different planes and categories, I treat the border as a zone rather than a line, "in which case the border becomes not only the division between two territories or places, but also a territory or place in itself (with its own borders)" (Schimanski, 2006: 49).

For instance, in reference to François Truffaut's seminal article "A Certain Tendency of the French Cinema" (1954), I argue in the first part of this chapter, that

Machorka-Muff is deeply informed by an ethical position that structures the relationship between filmmaker and subject matter. Bearing itself structural similarities to a borderline position, this ethical imperative was central to a theory of New Wave filmmaking, while it differed radically from notions of authorship developed by Young German filmmakers a few years later. This is part of the reason why critics and viewers in West Germany reacted at first rather negatively to *Machorka-Muff*.

In the second part of this chapter, I am showing how figurations of borderlines inform Straub–Huillet's films also on a textual, discursive, and formal basis in *Machorka-Muff* and in one of the couple's later works, the French–German co-production *Lothringen!* (*Lorraine!* 1994). Developed in response to specific personal and biographical experiences (which were themselves triggered by geopolitical border politics and conflicts), both films are inscribed by discernible traces of border formations that appear on multiple levels: first, in reference to extratextual discourses that reference geopolitical events as well as the filmmakers' biographies external to the film texts; second, in the form of intertextual and intermedial relations (operating between texts or between text and profilmic location); and, third, as part of formal figurations of borderlines that are directly inscribed into the filmic mise-en-scène.

The choice of these two films is not coincidental. Straub–Huillet made *Lothringen!* only a few years after the Berlin Wall had come down in 1989, followed by German unification in 1990 and the founding of the European Union in 1993. Bracketing the beginning of these events, *Machorka-Muff* had been filmed one year after the Berlin Wall was erected in 1961. Marking the beginning and end of Cold War politics as they had been mapped onto a German topography, the two films are structured around multiple border zones that unfold a genealogy of West European, in particular French–German, territorial conflicts. While dealing, for instance, at the outset with the nationally specific topic of 1950s West German defense politics, *Machorka-Muff* also bears traces of the French colonial conflict that took place around that time in Algeria. In addition, the film opens its view onto Straub's birthplace in the Alsace-Lorraine region, a place he experienced as a child under Nazi occupation. This same place provides the main setting in *Lothringen!* and connects it to a broader history of French–German border conflicts from the Franco-Prussian War of 1870–1871 to the post-Wall landscape of Germany in the early 1990s.

One of the border's most distinct features (and effective measures) is its ability to institute conflicting meanings. With its "polysemic nature," the border means different things to different people (Balibar, 2002: 81). It welcomes and invites some to cross, while (violently) prohibiting others to do the same. For instance, in the winter of 1958, the military draft forced Straub to cross the border into neighboring West Germany, a territory that was itself heavily divided by interior borderlines.

In the following months, Straub (who was frequently accompanied by Huillet) traveled freely across those interior borderlines while conducting research of archival material and scouting for original locations for the couple's long-term Bach film project. The Bach project and, more precisely, the biographical parameters established by the historical figure Johann Sebastian Bach, compelled, in a sense, the couple's border-crossing into German territory and determined their journey across German–German borderlines. Outside of France, Straub's involuntary exile turned into an expedition of two filmmakers on the trail of Bach. Since it followed Bach's map, and not the territorial reconfigurations of a divided German landscape, *Chronicle* became a German–German "co-production," at least in terms of filming on original locations in both East and West Germany. Unlike most East Germans (and Eastern Europeans) at the time, the French émigré filmmakers had a certain mobility in exile, which allowed them to cross inner German–German state lines. This kind of mobility stands in contrast to the conditions Straub had been running from in France. Threatened by the draft, he (and many other young French men) had only three options which all substantially limited their mobility and implied various forms of expulsion beyond either social, national, or imperial borderlines: to go to war meant, first, to participate in a colonial border conflict; second, to refuse the draft meant either to be sent to prison, a place of social and civil deportation within the country's inner borders, or it meant, third, emigration and exile.

To conclude thus far, Straub–Huillet's border-crossing in the late 1950s is informed by a number of contradictory meanings and movements, involving passages across exterior and interior boundaries, some of them restrictive and others transgressive.

Another variation of the border's polysemic function lies in the possibility that a person can experience the "same" border in more than one way. Something like this happened in regard to Straub's own biographical experiences with the French–German border. Born in 1933 in Metz, in the border region of Alsace-Lorraine, he spent parts of his childhood under Nazi occupation. His later ostensible engagement with German-language arts and culture appears especially interesting in this regard. In 1958, Germany must have presented, in this respect, both a certain familiarity and a difficult choice. Moreover, in Straub's first experience it was the border that moved, crossing and violating an entire region and its people. But in the late 1950s, the "same" borderline had changed its meaning: this time Straub was the active crosser (rather than the other way around) while the border functioned as a barrier that protected him from being sent across the sea, where he would himself have become part of an occupying army involved in the redrawing of France's colonial map.

2. Border Criticism

Straub–Huillet's professional collaboration had already begun during the couple's Parisian residence, a period that coincided precisely with the formative years of the French New Wave. The "film that brought Straub and Huillet together" (Byg, 1995: 51) was based on an idea that existed at least since 1954 (Roud, 1972; Heberle and Funke Stern, 1982). Already engaged in the idea of making a biographical film about Bach, Straub asked Huillet if she would help him write the screenplay for the film. Even though the film was not realized until more than a decade later, the Bach film is largely considered Straub–Huillet's first project.

Whereas our knowledge about the couple's early Parisian residence is mostly anecdotal, we can infer that the two were part of a vital young French film culture. Critics often claim that Straub worked as an assistant for the, at the time, already established filmmakers Jean Renoir, Abel Gance, and Robert Bresson, yet the only credit he actually received during that time was for a low-budget short film called *Fool's Mate* (*Le Coup du Berger*, 1956), retrospectively considered one of the first films of French New Wave Cinema (Douchet, 1998; Neupert, 2002; Marie, 2003). Directed by Jacques Rivette, the film was written and produced by Claude Chabrol and made in collaboration with the young *Cahiers du cinéma* critics: Jacques Doniol-Valcroze, Jean-Luc Godard, and François Truffaut. Jean-Marie Straub was second unit and assistant director.

Straub already knew some members of the *Cahiers* group before he came to Paris in 1954. He had managed the local student film club in his hometown of Metz, and *Cahiers* critics like Bazin or Truffaut showed up frequently to give introductions to, or lectures on, the films (Bronnen and Brocher, 1973). Straub once claimed that he was at first only interested in becoming a film critic and considered directing only under Huillet's influence. In comparison with Straub, we know even less about Huillet's professional activities during the Parisian years. But it is safe to say that Huillet was from the beginning determined to become a filmmaker and, more precisely, that she wanted to specialize in ethnographic documentary filmmaking (Gregor, 1976).

A rare visual trace depicting Straub's New Wave affiliations during the mid-1950s exists in the form of a photograph depicting a young François Truffaut and a young Jean-Marie Straub walking side-by-side on an urban sidewalk in November 1954 (coincidentally, also the month in which Huillet met Straub and in which the Algerian War broke out). This photograph appeared, first, in an interview that Michel Delahaye conducted for *Cahiers* in July 1966 (right after the French release of *Not Reconciled*). However, the article contains no explicit references to the photograph's origins or Straub's Parisian past, nor to his expatriation. The article situates Straub's career, instead, solely in the context of contemporary German cinema. In 1999, the photograph reappeared, printed on glossy paper and blown-up in scale, as part of a bulky volume on the French New Wave (Douchet, 1998: 47). At this point, the photograph marks Straub–Huillet's retrospective integration into the canon of French New Wave Cinema. The pair Truffaut and Straub form a rather odd couple. Most critics would define Truffaut, in terms of style, practice, and politics, rather in opposition to Straub, who is instead usually associated with Jean-Luc Godard or Jacques Rivette. Yet, as I will show in the following, Straub–Huillet share with Truffaut a basic formative tendency in their treatment and adaptation of original authors and texts.

The French New Wave historian Michel Marie (2003) has suggested that in spite of their apparent differences in style and personality, many filmmakers associated with the French New Wave were "tied to a collection of critical concepts held by a fairly coherent group. [Their] tastes and ideas found a material form in a large number of articles, public debates, and interventions in the press ... throughout the 1950s." Marie stresses the importance of Alexandre Astruc's article "The Birth of a New Avant-garde: La Caméra-Stylo" (1948) and Truffaut's "A Certain Tendency of the French Cinema" (1954) as key texts in the formation of the French New Wave's critical agenda. Often reduced to the polemical rant of a rebellious youngster, Truffaut's article is much more considerate, complex, and analytical than critics usually admit. Combining Astruc's definition of film authorship as a form of cinematic *écriture* with Bazin's theory of ontological realism, Truffaut is specifically concerned with the nature of the relationship between filmmaker and filmic subject. Focusing explicitly on the artistic practice of adaptation – a practice also fundamental to Straub–Huillet's work – Truffaut presents the auteur as a counterfigure to the *metteur-en-scène*, the screenwriter or director who works in what Truffaut polemically refers to as the "Tradition of Quality." Unlike the auteur, the *metteur-en-scène* holds all authority over his characters, the scenery, and ultimately the meaning expressed in the work. Following in the tradition of the nineteenth-century novel, the *metteur-en-scène* produces "literary" films that present a hermetically sealed-off world, that is, a world whose outer limits cannot be breached. This is a world without borders (in the most totalizing sense of the expression).

> The school which aspires to realism destroys it at the moment of finally grabbing it, so careful is the school to lock these beings in a closed world, barricaded by formulas, plays on words, maxims, instead of letting us see them for ourselves, with our own eyes. The artist cannot always dominate his work. He must be, sometimes, God and, sometimes, his creature. (Truffaut, 1954: 232)

The auteur, in contrast to the godlike attitude of the *metteur-en-scène*, makes room for another view, a new perspective; he "lets us see with our own eyes." Two faculties function to restrain the auteur from exercising too much control over the subject matter; one is the voice provided by the original text; the other is an intervention of the real exercised through the cinematic apparatus's ability to record its encounter with the profilmic world. Ignoring these two faculties, thus forging a filmic representation in accordance with the director's singular worldview, leads ultimately, according to Truffaut, to the distortion and exploitation of the original characters.

> In the films of "psychological realism" there are nothing but vile beings, but so inordinate is the authors' desire to be superior to their characters that those who, perchance, are not infamous are, at best, infinitely grotesque. (Truffaut, 1954: 233)

Truffaut condemns, in addition, the technique of inventing new (so-called "equivalent" scenes or dialogues) in order to compensate for scenes in the original literary text that are considered "unfilmable" (Truffaut, 1954: 226). The invention of new scenes is nothing but "a decoy," since its actual purpose is to give screenwriters and directors the possibility of imposing their own political convictions (and moral judgments) onto the adapted text (Truffaut, 1954: 233). In doing so, screenwriters and directors show nothing but contempt, not only towards the original author and the characters, but also for their public that is given "its habitual dose of smut, nonconformity and facile audacity" (Truffaut, 1954: 230). Truffaut does not only raise formal concerns and should therefore not be brushed off as either conservative or apolitical. He does not criticize the leftist, "antibourgeois," "antimilitarist," or "anticlerical" attitude of French screenwriters and directors because he necessarily disagrees with their politics, but because he deems the way in which these political objections enter the film text as hypocritical, if not reactionary (Truffaut, 1954: 234). He shares this attitude, as we will see shortly, with the declared Marxists Huillet and Straub.

Maureen Turim (1984: 336) once defined the couple's "liaison with Paris film circles [as] a major factor in the presentation of their films to a broader public. Their work, however," she concludes, "is still primarily seen at international film festivals and on the German cultural television channel" (Turim, 1984: 336). Yet when *Machorka-Muff* came out in 1963, West German critics and viewers reacted to the film with resentment and harsh criticism. Failing, in particular, to condemn the title character, the redeemed ex-Nazi officer Erich von Machorka-Muff, the film was criticized for its political conformism. "No agitation, no satire, no bitterness, no cynicism. Instead: Colonel von Machorka-Muff shaves. He orders drinks … he ties his tie …" a critic tried to describe that which infuriated German audiences (Färber, 1966: 36). In effect, the film was excluded from the Oberhausen film festival and struggled to find a distributor. Straub–Huillet's second short film *Not Reconciled* solicited similar reactions. Even the leftist journal *Filmkritik*, which would eventually become one of Straub–Huillet's strongest voices of support, attacked both films at first:

> "The greatest German film since Murnau and Lang" (Michel Delahaye)? Certainly not. The mistakes are frustrating, especially in terms of directing – or failing to direct – the actors. Badly recited is not necessarily well alienated, as Straub, who credits Brecht, […] seems to believe. (Patalas, 1965: 474)

As the quote insinuates, the reactions left of the Rhine were quite different. In fact, both *Machorka-Muff* and *Not Reconciled* became instant successes with French film critics, especially those associated with *Cahiers*, where Jacques Rivette called *Machorka-Muff* "the first (small) film d'auteur produced in postwar Germany" (Rivette, 1963: 36). But *Cahiers*' rival publication *Positif* also reacted favorably to the two Böll adaptations:

The seriousness and the courage of such a film did only incite hostility among the majority of German critics who, in a well-known fashion criticized the form [...] in order to avoid judging the central issues instead. In this light, it is remarkable how Straub sets out to treat taboo subjects in such an innovative manner within the mediocre world of German cinema. (Ciment, 1965–1966: 61)

Whereas old alliances certainly helped to promote Straub–Huillet's cause in France, they cannot fully explain the specific resentment the films received in the Federal Republic. As the quote from *Positif* rather suggests, the roots for this kind of criticism corresponded to more general and frequent notions of cultural criticism that were based on fundamentally different ideas of addressing political issues in writing and artworks. Moreover, the way in which Straub–Huillet treated their characters as well as subject matter, and the way in which they addressed the film audience, differed considerably from the way in which Young German filmmakers like Alexander Kluge, Werner Herzog, or Volker Schlöndorff approached their material.

We may think in this regard of the recurring disputes between Straub and Kluge that erupted precisely along these lines (Kluge, 1976; Straub, 1977). B. Ruby Rich's analysis of Kluge's filmmaking practice and mode of address is at this point especially illuminating:

[Kluge's] narrator holds a position of omniscience as a deus ex machina privy to information unavailable to the film's characters and inaccessible with the film text. In this guise, the narrator quickly becomes the favored replacement for the viewer in search of identification. The narrator, in his display of wit and wisdom, wins the respect of the viewer over the course of the film. The viewer, in turn, repays this narrative generosity with downright chumminess, uniting in a spirit of smug superiority with the narrator over and against the character(s). (1998: 239)

Rich's words echo the words that Truffaut employs in order to criticize the patronizing stance that the *metteur-en-scène* occupies vis-à-vis his characters and the audience in an attempt to get his political message across. Furthermore, Kluge's technique is not so much a personal form of expression as a staple of authorial address within Young German filmmaking. Young German filmmakers, Thomas Elsaesser has pointed out, treated "their protagonists as case studies, while exposing them to ridicule or patronising sentiment" (Elsaesser, 1989: 73).

On these grounds Straub identifies not Kluge but John Ford as "one of the most Brechtian of all film-makers" (Engel, 1970: 21). In Ford's films, he says, the viewer is allowed to notice for a moment, "for a fraction of a second," that something is false. In other words, Ford presents ideological conflicts and contradictions beneath rather than on the surface of the text (similar to our everyday experiences of social and political structures). Straub explained, that after seeing Ford's *The Searchers* (1956),

I understood better the attitude of the settlers in Algeria – I had really tried hard to understand them when I was in Paris during the Algerian war; when I saw the film by John Ford, the one that shows the settler and the Indian-hunter with a certain initial respect because he understands him. (Engel, 1970: 21–22)

Treating the characters with a certain initial respect, even those that one disagrees with, is then – as the reference to Ford emphasizes – not a practice exclusive to the figure of the auteur or to 1950s French New Wave criticism. The concept evokes, instead, an ethical mandate that is able to traverse temporal as well as cultural boundaries. In this light, it is not surprising, that Straub–Huillet found similar attitudes toward filmmaking even in Munich, at the margins of the Young German Film. After *Not Reconciled* had received recognition and awards at a few international film festivals, the overall critical climate toward Straub–Huillet's films began to shift markedly, especially among West German film critics writing for *Filmkritik*. Thus, only one year after his slanting critique (see above), editor-in-chief Enno Patalas (1966b) organized a fundraising campaign after the Bach film had been denied funding by the *Kuratorium Neuer Deutscher Film* (the Federal Republic's official film subsidy board). Alexander Kluge and Volker Schlöndorff, the internationally most renowned Young German filmmakers at the time, cosigned the appeal.

Yet Straub–Huillet's alliances lay elsewhere: in the opening credits to *Chronicle* they thanked their old colleagues and continuous supporters: Rivette, Godard, Delahaye, and, in addition, the German filmmaker Peter Nestler. Like Straub–Huillet, Nestler was part of the so-called "New Munich Group" (Patalas, 1966a), an informal circle of local documentary and short-film directors (that included also Klaus Lemke, Eckhart Schmidt, Rudolf Thome, and Max Zihlmann). None of them managed to enter the canon of the Young German Film in the way in which Kluge, Herzog, and even Straub–Huillet did. Yet during the early 1960s, some members of the group received significant critical attention at short-film and documentary film festivals, especially among West German and French critics. Also Straub considered them important. "What's missing in contemporary German cinema is humility," he explained in this regard to Michel Delahaye.

I'm thinking of the humility of a Jean Rouch. At heart, my characters are similarly free as his, because they speak like his characters. It is this kind of humility that gives importance to the films of Nestler and of three others who are currently making something. (1966: 56)

Straub argues, here, for a genealogical trace that links him and Huillet to Rouch and Nestler, a lineage we can extend further to Ford or Truffaut. For what Straub describes here as "Rouchian humility" is very close to the concept that Truffaut defines as auteurism, and it works similar to the respectful treatment he admires in Ford. The common principle described here is the willingness to inhabit a position in which the filmmaker's relationship to the world or to others is generally defined as a nonposition, as the refusal to occupy a preconceived, stable territory. "That which counts is tone, or emphasis, nuance, as one will call it," Rivette (1961: n.p.) writes in a similar vein,

> that is to say, the point of view of a man, the auteur, badly needed, and the attitude that this man takes in relation to that which he films, and therefore in relation to the world and to everything: that which can be expressed by a choice in situations, in the construction of the storyline, in the dialogue, in the play of actors, or in the pure and simple technique [...].

The auteur's position points, in fact, to a "nonposition," another borderline figure. This is not a conformist stance, but a standpoint that must continuously be renegotiated. Like borderlines that shift their meaning in the course of time and in regard to different human or material conditions, a filmmaker's relationship to the world is not only bound to change continuously, but is also inscribed with more than one meaning.

3.   Border Poetics

As filmmakers, Straub–Huillet emerged from various conditions of biographical, historical, and geopolitical border-crossings. On these grounds, figurations of borderlines dissect and conjoin their film texts on multiple levels: between texts (as intermedial and intertextual boundaries), outside of the text (as discursive historical or biographical references), and within the text (as formal inscriptions of borderlines).

The Border between Texts

Whereas "Böll's story met with objections from the Right; [*Machorka-Muff*] was very badly received by the Left" (Roud, 1972: 30). This is even more surprising as "the film seems to follow the story word for word." In consideration of the original author, Heinrich Böll, Straub–Huillet not only refrain from inventing new scenes or plot events (another example of their agreement with Truffaut's directives), but also keep the original literary text intact by using all elements written in direct speech as part of the dialogue. They treat Böll's short story, in other words, like an original screenplay. In doing so, Straub–Huillet insist on maintaining the boundaries between literary original and filmic adaptation. On one side, the original text does not disappear, is not assimilated into the film, but rather remains discernible, its outer borders clearly visible as part of the film's overall structure. On the other side, the literary text changes its materiality, because only as screenplay does it continue to exist as written word material. But in the film, Böll's writing is presented as part of a spoken dialogue and physiological performance that comes to light in the cinematographic inscription of audible and visual material. This means that also on the level of the film text, we encounter the contradictory and polysemic nature of the border. As a filmic adaptation, the original text crosses a borderline when changing from one material form of expression to another. But as a quotation in the film text, the original text remains intact and is prevented from traversing any textual boundaries. In effect, *Machorka-Muff* renders not only the adapted text visible but also the process of adaptation. The reason why Böll's text maintains its "original" features within the larger structure of the film results not only from the literal quotations, but also from the specific technique of reciting Böll's text. The performers, many of them nonprofessional actors, speak each word and perform each gesture without any recognizable emotional attachment, without any "psychological" interpretation. In doing so, they present Böll's text *as* text. Nothing is there but the bare word. In doing so, Straub–Huillet take Truffaut's suggestions on adaptation to a whole new level, giving it, so to speak, a decisively "Brechtian" twist without compromising, on the other hand, the call for a unique ontological relationship between cinema and world.

Due to cinema's material specificity, this relationship is nonetheless as crucial as the film's relationship to the original artwork. Present in the film, besides the bare words, are the filmmakers', the actors', and the technological apparatus's encounter with a place. As in most of Straub–Huillet's films, the location is always doubly inscribed: as a setting or stage (for the histrionic performance or recital of the text) and as original location (marked by a quotidian reality). The borderline between these two realms is, once again, polysemic; it remains imperceptible, on the one hand, since it is impossible to define where one realm begins and the other ends, but on the other hand, it is present, since neither the histrionic nor the quotidian become sublimated or resolved within one image. Quite the contrary, each one of them remains clearly present and discernible.

In *Machorka-Muff* it is the Federal Republic's capital city of Bonn, which functions at once as narrative location (the stage for the formal recital of Böll's text) and as a space of quotidian reality. As in Böll's text, the city obtains, in addition, a figurative meaning: Bonn is synonymous with West German politics after World War Two, especially the Cold War and European politics established during the Adenauer era. But aside from this metonymic meaning, the film captures the city of Bonn as part of a material encounter between camera and actual place. Filmed on original locations, the Bonn depicted in *Machorka-Muff* emerges in a direct relationship between camera lens and the real. In numerous scenes, Bonn in the fall of 1962 intervenes, loses the histrionic narrative out of its sight, and becomes the protagonist of the film. The borderline evoked at this point derives from an intermedial encounter between narrative setting and the quotidian reality of the location. The image depicts Bonn both in its figurative meaning (the setting for the postwar politics under Adenauer) and in terms of a filmic encounter with everyday street life and people.

Insistence on a representation of quotidian reality beyond any figurative connotation is reflected also in Straub–Huillet's refusal to use additional sound recordings that had been made in Munich instead of in Bonn. Even though the endeavor was much more costly, the couple chose instead to return to "Bonn to record the tramways," since "the sound on a corner of Bonn is not all the same as on a corner in Munich" (Engel, 1970: 17). The border that emerges at this point in between the histrionic and the quotidian reminds one of Jean Rouch's ethnographic rituals and performances, a reference that also seems justified considering Huillet's early career focus on ethnographic documentaries.

The techniques of direct quotation and an insistence on filming on original locations remained central to Straub–Huillet's filmmaking practice throughout their career. Thus, when Straub–Huillet adapted Maurice Barrès' novella *Colette Baudoche: The Story of a Young Girl From Metz* (*Colette Baudoche: Histoire d'une Jeune Fille de Metz*, 1908) they employed a similar process of adaptation as they had done in *Machorka-Muff*. Yet *Lothringen!* pushes the border between intertextual and intermedial relations one step further by including, in addition, the vicissitude of linguistic specificity and translation. Barrès' story is about the courtship between the young Collette and the German Professor Asmus during the German annexation of the region, following the Franco-Prussian War of 1870–1871. Like *Machorka-Muff* the film is largely filmed on original locations, in this case in Metz and its surrounding countryside.

A co-production between the regional German television network *Saarländischer Rundfunk* and the independent French producer Pierre Grise, the 20-minute short film was made with a small French production crew and cast. Based on a French-language text and shot mainly on locations in France, one would assume that the film could easily be labeled a French film. However, *Lothringen!* is, strictly speaking, not one but two films, since Straub–Huillet officially released a French-language and a German-language version of the film. This practice of creating different linguistic versions of the same film (in contrast to dubbing one film into different languages) revives somewhat the so-called multiple-language films that were made in Europe during the 1930s (see Vincendeau, 1988). Even though two versions exist, the images remain largely the same. It is only the voiceover narrative that is significantly altered: in the French version it is divided between a female voice ("Colette's grandmother" spoken by Dominque Dosdat) and a male voice (the narrator spoken by André Warynski). Yet in the German-language version, the entire text is spoken by Jean-Marie Straub. Thus, the native French-speaker Straub reads with a French accent the German translation of a text originally written in French. By speaking the entire voiceover narrative, Straub assumes, furthermore, the roles of two different characters in the novella: that of Colette's grandmother and that of the narrator. We could read this as an act of taking control over the narrative, speaking, so to say, for one of the female characters and erasing the distinction between the grandmother's direct mode of address and the more impersonal tone of the narrator (who, however, addresses the reader directly in the novella).

I am proposing, however, that Straub appears instead as a reader: a reader who reads Barrès' text in translation which means, in this case, as someone who insists on *reading his native language with an accent and in a foreign tongue*. Straub does so, because he reads the novella in reference to his own biography. Born in 1933 in Metz, he spent most of his childhood under Nazi occupation. Straub once recalled the violence he experienced in terms of being forced to learn and to speak the language of the occupier (Gregor, 1976). At this point, we are no longer simply moving between texts but stepping markedly overboard and outside the immediate textual system involved in the filmic adaptation process. Deriving from biographical experiences and historical events, as we will see next, these extratextual references figure in the film texts as discursive borderlines.

The Border outside the Text

A continuous strategy that runs throughout Straub–Huillet's entire oeuvre is to expose the lineage and shared characteristics among distinct historical, geopolitical, or cultural phenomena. This process often demands the introduction of another, a foreign perspective into the filmic representation. By reading a German translation of Barrès'novella, that is, in a language that was once forced upon him, Straub performs a type of border-crossing that opens the text to discursive events that remain outside, as they are never explicitly acknowledged within the text.

While Straub–Huillet largely refrain from making changes to the original text quotations, the changes they do make often involve the omission of specific parts of an original text. This leads to the following effect: the two filmmakers incorporate their own point of view through the specific material they select. *Lothringen!* includes a particular passage from Barrès' text in which the male narrator describes in detail how French school children are forced to learn German. The fictional quotation echoes the biographical recollection of Straub's childhood mentioned above. *Lothringen!* – the title itself exclaims the violence of linguistic coercion and translation.

In contrast to Straub, Huillet had no prior German language skills, but only began to learn the language through the couple's work on the Bach film, mainly with the help of the baroque scripts of Bach's cantatas (Heberle and Funke Stern, 1982). As a result she learned to speak at first a rather strange and antiquated German. The accented and foreign tongue is, in this case, twice removed, because Huillet engages with a foreign language by crossing both intermedial and temporal borderlines. The language she acquires is not only that of another country, but also a written German from another era. These temporal and intermedial transgressions also occur in *Lothringen!* for instance, when Straub assumes the voice of the old Alsatian woman. He transgresses historical, textual, linguistic, and, not to forget, gender lines. And yet, all of these boundaries remain, at the same time, intact, since the character of the old woman only exists in the novel and since the biographical references to him or Huillet remain outside of the text. By quoting, in addition, passages dealing with the enforced exile of Alsace's indigenous population in the aftermath of 1871, *Lothringen!* furthermore evokes Straub's (and Huillet's) enforced exile in 1958.

This brings us back to the earlier film, *Machorka-Muff*. Straub–Huillet's first meeting in November 1954 not only coincided with the outbreak of the Algerian War but also happened right after the signing of the so-called Paris Agreements, which guaranteed (under conditions) the German Federal Republic's sovereign status while integrating it simultaneously into the Western military alliance. This agreement paved, in addition, the way of the reconstitution of the West German army in 1955. Straub recalls:

> The reason I wanted to make [*Machorka-Muff*] was precisely my first strong political feelings, as I was still a student in Strasbourg … That was my first bout of political rage – exactly this story of the European defense community … the fact that Germany had been rearmed – the story of a rape. That is to say – the only country in Europe which, after a certain Napoleon, the first gangster in the series, had the chance to be free. This chance was destroyed. I know … that in Hamburg people threw stones at the first uniforms … people didn't want them, they had had enough of it. (Engel, 1970: 17)

In this quotation, Straub refuses markedly to understand the Federal Republic's rearmament after World War Two as a topic of national (or historical) specificity. Instead, he sees the politics of rearmament as part of a much broader tradition by backdating it to the beginnings of modern European imperialism under Napoleon. West Germany's rearmament continues this legacy not only because it subscribes to a similar spirit of military power, but also because it occurs under the explicit condition of the country's Western integration. From Straub's perspective, German rearmament is simply a means to larger ends, which supports mainly the North/Western alliance in the conflict of the Cold War. The alleged sovereignty (or freedom) is, therefore, nothing but a decoy in the service of widening Western European economic, territorial, and political interests in the world. Written in direct response to these politics, Böll's short story stresses similar notions of historical continuity: "A democracy in which we have the majority of Parliament on our side is a great deal better than a dictatorship," remarks one of the characters involved in military restoration.

But *Machorka-Muff* not only points to the historical continuity in postwar West German state politics, but also views a nationally specific debate from an outside position. A scene in *Machorka-Muff* opens with the principal character, Erich von Machorka-Muff, sitting on the outside patio of a café. He is reading the newspaper. Directly quoting from the Böll text, his offscreen voice-over commentary states: "In honor of the occasion I permitted myself an aperitif, looked through some news-papers, and tried to imagine what Schnomm – if he were still alive – would have said had he read these newspapers." During his final words, the images change and a two-minute-long sequence consisting of cinematographic depictions of 18 different newspaper clippings begins. All of the articles stem from West German newspapers, published in the 1950s, and cover debates about the country's military restoration. However, under closer examination the selection appears to be more specific than that: all articles (or advertisements) are specifically about the issue of military enlistment: "Those who enlist voluntarily, remain in control of their own time and their own free decisions!" reads the first line of an advertisement in favor of the draft. This specific theme does not appear in Böll's original story *Bonn Diary*, where the newspaper articles are only described with the words "a few editorials on defense policy" (Böll, 1958: 58).

Throughout the sequence, the camera emphasizes the draft as its central theme by tracking and panning across some of the pages, highlighting, for instance, the quotation of a 19-year-old young man, who is quoted in support of a "humane" military service: "With good conscience we gladly want to fulfill this duty for our country and our people." Quite clearly, the selection and montage of these articles does not simply have the function of cinematically illustrating Böll's original text, nor does it provide us with an "objective" documentation of a nationally publi-cized debate about the Federal Republic's military rearmament. The overt focus on one specific part of this debate – military conscription – presents rather an issue that played a principal role in Straub and Huillet's own biography, an issue that was directly responsible for the couple's border-crossing and exile. In his *Bonn Diary*, Böll does not even bring up the issue of military conscription. This does not mean, however, that Straub–Huillet merely use Böll's story in order to get their personal political agenda across. In fact, Straub–Huillet's personal take never overpowers the film text. The theme of the draft is never explicitly pointed to and only deci-pherable when watching the scene many times. During a regular screening situation, the movement of the camera and the framing of the articles produce a rather fragmentary, if not disorienting, impression, which is reinforced through the atonal musical score that accompanies the sequence on the audible level. In other words, the sequence contains undeniably a viewpoint specific to Straub–Huillet's own experience; yet this viewpoint gains neither superiority over the nar-rative, nor does it become the film's main political lesson. If at all, it has a place at the margins of the overall story, which exhibits why Straub–Huillet were drawn to Böll's story in the first place. It renders visible in what way these two young French filmmakers were able to add something else to Böll's satire about the Federal Republic. In this sense, the newspaper sequence inscribes a discursive borderline into the film text, since it invokes an incident (and a place) that is not explicitly addressed. Thus, in addition to the intertextual encounter between Böll's text and the newspaper articles, Straub–Huillet's cinematographic montage invokes an event that remains outside of the text, an event pointing across national bounda-ries. However, paradoxically, the view that refers to something that never enters the text can only be produced in connection to the film's intertextual and formal workings (as the montage sequence of the newspaper articles exemplifies). We turn, last, to the way in which the border inscribes this view as part of a point-of-view structure into the filmic mise-en-scène.

The Border within the Text

Machorka-Muff contains a shot that inscribes a slow panoramic view across the Rhine. The camera is located on the right riverbank, and in a semicircular pan to the left, the camera scans the landscapes on the other side, stretching out into the West in the background. After a 180-degree turn, Erich von Machorka-Muff appears suddenly screen-left, looking onto the river, and the shot is retroactively revealed as his point of view. This shot renders more than merely the fictional character's perspective. Pointing into the direction of the French–German border region and France behind it, the view invokes also the two French filmmakers' point of view toward their native country.

A second shot in the film repeats this cinematographic gesture of a view onto the Rhine in the direction of the French–German border. This time the 180-degree pan scans the river's left bank from a position located in the mountains, near Bonn. The specific setting is the outside terrace of the Petersberg Hotel. Taken from Böll's novel, this location has a significant historical connotation: from 1945 until West Germany regained conditional sovereignty and military power in 1955, the Petersberg Hotel was the seat of the Allied high commissioner. Beginning in 1955 it became the official guesthouse of the German Federal Republic. Böll chooses this specific setting to connote a figurative meaning: Erich von Machorka-Muff and his bride Inn (a descendent of an old, aristocratic line) celebrate their marriage here. The new union between two old German traditions, the military and the aristocracy, is thus staged at a location that is overtly inscribed by the most recent changes in postwar German state politics.

Aside from this figurative meaning, the view from the Petersberg Hotel allows Straub–Huillet, in addition, to point the camera's gaze, once again, across the Rhine in the direction of the French–German border and toward their native country. Panning across and alongside the river, the cinematographic movement literally underlines the Rhine's bordering function in this image. As a so-called natural line of geographic demarcation, the river figures as a supplement for the actual border between the two countries. On an aesthetic level, the figure inscribes a horizontal line into the image and dissects it in two halves: a foreground, where the action takes place, where both character and camera perform their looks and gestures; and a space that lies behind or beyond the left river bank, the quotidian landscape that stretches out into the background of the image. In so doing, the image itself produces a specific layering of historical and geopolitical connotations: the reinstitution of West Germany as a military power, played out in the foreground, is staged in view of the French–German borderland.

Almost all shots in *Lothringen!* contain similar figurations of natural borderlines as part of their mise-en-scène. However, there are differences. Like many Straub–Huillet films that were made in the later period of their career, *Lothringen!* has a much stronger documentary vibe than *Machorka-Muff.* Moreover, almost all quotations from Barrès' novella are spoken as disembodied offscreen voice-over monologues. The only visual representation of a fictional character from the novella is the character of Collette, who appears, however, in only two shots (dressed in historical costume, but placed into the contemporary twentieth-century landscape). In the first shot, Collete is positioned directly in front of a metal railing. Her back is turned to the camera and she gazes out onto a lake. In the second shot, she is seated on an old stone wall, located on a hill, the city of Metz stretching out in the far background behind her. Both shots echo the inscription of borderlines in *Machorka-Muff* in their function of dissecting the image into two halves. The foreground is marked as the realm in which the histrionic performance takes place, a space occupied by the fictional and the camera; the background displays the quotidian setting of the rural and urban landscapes. Once again, the line is clearly discernible, yet it is impossible to state clearly where one realm ends and the other begins.

The rest of the film is composed of similar shots, yet without the fictional character present in the scene. In each image, a horizontal or diagonal line runs across the mise-en-scène (e.g. a fence, train tracks, a wall in ruins, a country road, or a line of trees). The bordering function is highlighted by the camera's panning or tracking movement alongside these structures. Positioned in the foreground of the images, the camera observes the space behind the borderline from a distance yet never physically approaches or enters it. In other words, neither the actor nor the camera ever cross beyond and violate the iconographic marker of the border.

Continuing the evocation of historical layers and references that had already impacted the formal composition in *Machorka-Muff,* *Lothringen!* embeds Barrès' original narrative into a contemporary landscape of the post-Wall era. The film opens on an exterior location that does not, however, belong to the narrative setting established in the novella: it depicts instead the city of Koblenz, a place located at the so-called German Corner, the juncture of the rivers Rhine and Moselle (that also divide the regions of Alsace and Lorraine). The camera performs a 360-degree pan that gives us the view from the position of the place. We see the memorial statue of Emperor Wilhelm I, which had been destroyed in World War Two yet was newly erected in honor of the German unification. The statue refers directly to the legacy of German imperialism – one of them the annexation of Alsace-Lorraine in 1871 – as well as to an implied continuity of these politics in a reunited Germany. A 360-degree pan captures a circular arrangement of 16 flags representing the 16 German federal states (including the five new ones), placed below the statue. This representation of a reunited Germany (that still remains divided by a set of political, regional, and administrative interior state-lines) arises against the backdrop of a view onto Germany's outer borders, figured by the riverbanks of the Rhine and Moselle in the image. Not coincidentally, the camera (and "we" with it) are positioned at the border, the place where the two rivers, both figurations of borderlines, meet. From here we are given a contemporary view of border traffic: in the background, a camping site stretches out on the left bank of the Rhine, while a steady number of sight-seeing boats and cargo ships pass up and down the two riverbeds. On "our" side (where camera and microphone are located), we see and hear tourists, visiting the memorial site.

Within this image of a reunited Germany, the border lies embedded in a seemingly peaceful site of recreational, leisure, and business transactions. After lingering a few minutes at this site, Straub–Huillet dissolve the image to that which lies underneath historically and geopolitically. The image cuts to a historical map of the region around Metz, acoustically accompanied by a string rendition of the German national anthem and gunfire explosions. This transition epitomizes how border zones unfold and function within the narrative, formal, and discursive structure of Straub–Huillet's films: from *Machorka-Muff* to *Lothringen!*. Informed by aporetic or polysemic characteristics, these border zones insist on understanding each specific territorial or military conflict in relation to similar events, ideas, or practices. A history, however, that is less about seamless progressions or continuities than about common principles, actions, and their effects. In other words: a genealogy, to borrow a concept developed by Michel Foucault (1971); a genealogy that records "the singularities of events outside of any monotonous finality" and that "isolates the different scenes where they engaged in different roles" (Foucault, 1971: 76). A genealogy, to be more precise, that unfolds in a series of temporal, physical, or other border-crossings. Such a genealogy can be populated by "a series of gangsters" (to paraphrase Straub), who each played a part in shaping the history of French–German border politics in the past two hundred years. But it can also refer to the appearance of a critical concept of a filmmaking practice shared among diverse filmmakers like Ford, Rouch, Truffaut, or the members of the New Munich group.

For better or worse, Straub–Huillet's films urge us to recognize these shared principles and common characteristics that structure politics, culture, and aesthetics. "You can be a citizen or you can be stateless, but it is difficult to imagine *being* a border," Etienne Balibar (2002: 88) cites the psychoanalyst André Green. "But isn't this precisely what, all around us, many individuals, groups and territories must indeed try to imagine?" he asks further. Instead of rooting for a borderless world, imagining "being" a border means, strictly speaking, to refuse being "*neither this nor that*" (Balibar, 2002: 89). By directing our view continuously and consistently toward such a position, Straub–Huillet's films refuse to dwell in trans-national harmony. Instead of imagining a borderless world, they insist, for instance, on including an émigré perspective into a familiar landscape or on speaking one's native language with a foreign tongue.

References

Astruc, A. (1948) The birth of a new avant-garde: La Caméra-Stylo, 1968, in *The New Wave: Critical Landmarks* (ed. P.J. Graham), Doubleday, Garden City, NY, pp. 17–23.

Balibar, E. (2002) *Politics and the Other Scene*, Verso, London.

Barrès, M. (1908/2010) *Colette Baudoche: The Story of a Young Girl of Metz* (trans. F.W. Huard), Nabu Press, Charleston SC.

Böll, H. (1958) Bonn diary, 2006 (trans. L. Vennewitz), in *Heinrich Böll: Stories, Political Writings, and Autobiographical Works* (ed. M. Black), Continuum, New York, pp. 54–62.

Bronnen, B. and Brocher C. (1973) *Die Filmemacher: Der Neue Deutsche Film nach Oberhausen*, Bertelsmann, Munich.

Byg, B. (1995) *Landscapes of Resistance: The German Films of Danièle Huillet and Jean-Marie Straub*, University of California Press, Berkeley.

Ciment, M. (1965–1966) Suite Bergamasque. *Positif*, 72, 61.

Delahaye, M. (1966) Entretien avec Jean-Marie Straub. *Cahiers du Cinéma*, 180, 52–57.

Douchet, J. (1998) *The French New Wave*, D.A.P., New York.

Elsaesser, T. (1989) *New German Cinema: A History*. Rutgers University Press, New Brunswick, NJ.

Engel, A. (1970) Andi Engel talks to Jean-Marie Straub. *Cinemantics*, 1, 20–24.

Färber, H. (1966) Machorka-Muff. *Filmkritik*, 10, 36.

Foucault, M. (1971) Nietzsche, genealogy, history, 1984, in *The Foucault Reader* (in P. Rabinow), Pantheon Books, New York, pp. 76–100.

Gregor, U. (ed.) (1976) *Herzog, Kluge, Straub*, C. Hanser, Munich.

Heberle, H. and Funke Stern, M. (1982) Das Feuer im Innern des Berges (interview with D. Huillet). *Frauen und Film*, 32, 4–12.

Kluge, A. (1976) Straub. *Filmkritik*, 240, 576–577, 586–589.

Magisos, M. (1996) *Not Reconciled*: the destruction of narrative pleasure, in *Perspectives on German Cinema* (eds T. Ginsberg and K. Thompson), G.K. Hall/Macmillan, New York and London, pp. 497–507.

Marie, M. (2003) *The French New Wave: An Artistic School*. Blackwell Publishing, Malden, MA.

Michaelsen, S. and Johnson, D. (eds) (1997) *Border Theory: the Limits of Cultural Politics*. University of Minnesota Press, Minneapolis.

Neupert, R. (2002) *A History of the French New Wave Cinema*, University of Wisconsin Press, Madison.

Patalas, E. (1965) Nicht Versöhnt. *Filmkritik*, 9, 474.

Patalas, E. (1966a) Ansichten einer Gruppe. *Filmkritik*, 10, 247–249.

Patalas, E. (1966b) In eigener Sache. *Filmkritik*, 10, 601–602.

Rentschler, E. (1996) The use and abuse of memory: New German film and discourse of Bitburg, in *Perspectives on German Cinema* (eds T. Ginsberg and K. Thompson), G.K. Hall/Macmillan, New York, London, pp. 163–183.

Rich, B.R. (1998) She says, he says: the power of the narrator in modernist film politics, in *Chick Flicks: Theories and Memories of the Feminist Film Movement*, Duke University Press, Durham, NC, pp. 238–253.

Rivette, J. (1961) On abjection, http://www.dvdbeaver.com/rivette/OK/abjection.html (accessed February 12, 2011).

Rivette, J. (1963) Machorka-Muff. *Cahiers du Cinéma*, 145, 36.

Roud, R. (1972) *Jean-Marie Straub*, Viking Press, New York.

Schimanski, J. (2006) Crossing and reading: notes towards a theory and a method. *Nordlit*, 19, 41–63.

Schimanski J. and Wolfe, S. (eds) (2007) *Border Poetics De-limited*, Wehrhahn, Hannover.

Straub, Jean-Marie (1977) Zum Kluge. *Filmkritik*, 241, inside front cover.

Truffaut, F. (1954/1976) A certain tendency of the French cinema, in *Movies and Methods: An Anthology* (ed. B. Nichols), University of California Press, Berkeley, pp. 224–237.

Turim, M. (1984) Oblique angles on film as ideological intervention, in *New German Filmmakers: From Oberhausen through the 1970s* (ed. K. Phillips), Frederick Ungar, New York, pp. 335–358.

Turim, M. (1986) Textuality and theatricality in Brecht and Straub/Huillet: *History Lessons* (1972), in *German Film and Literature: Adaptations and Transformations* (ed. E. Rentschler), Methuen, New York, pp. 231–245.

Vincendeau, G. (1988) Hollywood Babel: the multiple language version. *Screen*, 20 (2), 24–39.

Further Reading

Armes, R. (1976) Jean-Marie Straub: strict counterpoint, in *The Ambiguous Image*, Secker & Warburg, London, pp. 208–215.

Aumont, J. (2006) The invention of place: Danièle Huillet and Jean-Marie Straub's *Moses and Aaron*, in *Landscape and Film* (ed. M. Lefebvre), Routledge, New York, pp. 1–18.

Böser, U. (2004) *The Art of Seeing, the Art of Listening: The Politics of Representation in the Work of Jean-Marie Straub and Danièle Huillet*, Lang, Frankfurt a.M.

Brady, M. (2008) Brecht in Brechtian cinema, in *Verwisch die Spuren! Bertolt Brecht's Work and Legacy: A Reassessment* (eds R. Gillett and G. Weiss-Sussex), Rodopi, Amsterdam, pp. 295–308.

Deleuze, G. (1985) *Cinema 2: The Time Image*, 2003 (trans. H. Tomlinson and R. Galeta), University of Minnesota Press, Minneapolis.

Deleuze, G. (1998) Having an idea in cinema (on the cinema of Straub–Huillet), in *Deleuze and Guattari: New Mappings in Politics, Philosophy, and Culture* (eds E. Kaufman and K.J. Heller), University of Minnesota Press, Minneapolis, pp. 14–19.

Fairfax, D. (2009) Jean-Marie Straub and Danièle Huillet. *Senses of Cinema*, 52, http://www.sensesofcinema.com/2009/52/jean-marie-straub-and-daniele-huillet/ (accessed February 12, 2011).

Shafto, S. (2010) On Straub–Huillet's Une Visite au Louvre. *Senses of Cinema*, 53, http://www.sensesofcinema.com/2009/feature-articles/on-Straub–Huillets-une-visite-au-louvre-1/ (accessed February 12, 2011).

Walsh, M. (1981). *The Brechtian Aspect of Radical Cinema* (ed. K.M. Griffiths), BFI Publishing, London.

Filmography

Bridegroom, the Comedienne, and the Pimp, The [*Der Bräutigam, Die Komödiantin und der Zuhälter*] (Jean-Marie Straub, West Germany, 1968).

Chronicle of Anna Magdalena Bach, The [*Die Chronik der Anna Magdalena Bach*] (Jean-Marie Straub/Danièle Huillet, West Germany/Italy, 1967).

Fool's Mate [*Le Coup du Berger*] (Jacques Rivette, France, 1956).

Lothingen! [*Lorraine!*] (Jean-Marie Straub/Danièle Huillet, France/Germany, 1994).

Machorka-Muff (Jean-Marie Straub/Danièle Huillet, West Germany, 1962).

Not Reconciled, Or Only Violence Helps Where Violence Rules [*Nicht Versöhnt, Oder Es Hilft Nur Gewalt Wo Gewalt Herrscht*] (Jean-Marie Straub, West Germany, 1964–1965).

Searchers, The (John Ford, US, 1956).

9

Contested Spaces

Kamal Aljafari's Transnational Palestinian Films[1]

Peter Limbrick

In an online interview to accompany a festival screening of his film *Port of Memory* (2009), Palestinian filmmaker Kamal Aljafari begins by quoting the German philosopher, Theodor Adorno (2005: 87): "Adorno said, 'for a man who no longer has a homeland, writing becomes a place to live.'" Reconfiguring that reflection, Aljafari then continues, "For a Palestinian, cinema is a homeland" (Aljafari, 2010). The filmmaker's citation of Adorno in the course of his interview might profitably be read alongside an epigraph that appears near the beginning of Aljafari's second film, *The Roof* (2006). After a brief introductory sequence, we encounter a title on a black background, a quotation from an essay on Palestine by Palestinian writer Anton Shammas (2002: 111): "And you know perfectly well that we don't ever leave home – we simply drag it behind us wherever we go, walls, roof and all." Placing these two quotations together, we might say that the second – from Shammas – articulates the conditions under which the first – via Adorno – becomes meaningful for the filmmaker-as-author. That is, if home as place is experienced under erasure for Palestinians who must perforce carry its memory and burdens wherever they go (even within historic Palestine) then under such conditions cinema is one of the few sites in which one can articulate that absent or impossible home; as a transnational Palestinian filmmaker, Aljafari himself does so under material conditions that are highly mobile.

This chapter will consider the films that Kamal Aljafari has made from a German production base and will argue that the politics and aesthetics of his documentary-fiction practice are generated from a transnational frame in which neither Germany nor Palestine/Israel are fixed, unproblematic sites from which to locate or explain his work. I begin from the starting point that German cinema itself has become thoroughly transnational in its production, distribution, and reception as well as in its film narratives, as others have argued (Davidson, 1999; Schindler and Koepnick,

A Companion to German Cinema, First Edition. Edited by Terri Ginsberg and Andrea Mensch.
© 2012 Blackwell Publishing Ltd. Published 2012 by Blackwell Publishing Ltd.

2007; Halle, 2008). Some critical accounts of this transnationality stress the advent of a "cinema of border crossings" best exemplified by the films of Turkish-German filmmakers who critically interrogate concepts of German national identity and global migration (Hake, 2008: 216–221; Halle, 2008, 129–168). But Aljafari's work demands that we also build an account of media practices whose locations and narrative focus are situated beyond the borders or spaces of Germany and Europe. In *The New European Cinema: Redrawing the Map* (2006), Rosalind Galt develops a nuanced study of the relationship between aesthetics and politics in recent European films. Galt ends by devoting attention not just to European films that move outside Europe, but even to films like Tsai Ming-Liang's *The Hole* (1998) that inhabit a space of transnational production (Taiwanese/French, commissioned within a global art film series of auteur films) while creating an aesthetic at once locally specific and charged with transnational references (in the case of Tsai's film, through its musical scenes and travel narrative, in particular). Galt concludes that "both industrially and aesthetically, [*The Hole*] makes us question the ways that disparate places engage with their national, regional, and global histories" (Galt, 2006: 236). Just as Tsai's careful and aesthetically "spectacular" film resonates with the politics and history of Taiwan even as it is formed out of a transnational film culture, so too are Aljafari's films embedded within Palestinian history and politics while simultaneously existing within a transnational field of cinematic production in which Germany has provided, thus far, a physical and financial base for his work. Like Tsai (a filmmaker whom Aljafari particularly reveres), Aljafari's two latter films are completely embedded in Palestinian locations and politics while remaining transnational in their finance, their personnel, and even in their aesthetic which, I will show, deploys the kind of aesthetic beauty and "spectacle" that Galt identifies in some European transnational cinemas. Yet, as I will demonstrate throughout this chapter, whatever his films' indebtedness to a European cinematic frame, his work studiously refuses Euro*centrism* in that it avoids an orientalizing gaze from the position of a Europe looking out to "its others." Like the work of Elia Suleiman (another Palestinian filmmaker raised in Israel and based in Europe), Aljafari's films utilize their European art cinema affiliations to expose and subvert Western discourses on Arabs and Arab locations especially as those collude with Zionist narratives of Israel as a model of a liberal democracy.

In many respects, then, Aljafari is typical of the "interstitial" filmmakers discussed by Hamid Naficy in his influential account *An Accented Cinema* (2001). Rather than assume easy definitions of national agency or, in contrast, complete alterity to the concept of nation, Naficy exposes the way in which many migrant or exilic filmmakers (whose status is definitional of the term "accented" film-maker) inhabit an interstitial mode of belonging with respect to the state: "It would be inaccurate," he states, "to characterize accented filmmakers as marginal, as scholars are prone to do, for they do not live and work on the peripheries of society or the media or film industries. They are situated inside and work in the interstices of both" (2001: 46). Indeed, Naficy argues elsewhere that interstitial filmmakers "are simultaneously local and global, and they resonate against the prevailing cinematic production practices, at the same time as they benefit from them" (Naficy, 2001: 4). For this reason, Naficy continually stresses complexity and multivocality: funding sources are diverse and often transnationally organized (funding from TV stations, state grants, private money and so on) and production conditions are always "convoluted," with a mixture of languages, labor roles and conditions, etc. Tellingly, Palestinian-Belgian filmmaker Michel Khleifi is one of Naficy's case studies for the interstitial mode: a Palestinian born within Israel, Khleifi attended film school in Belgium and retained it as his base. He raised money for his *Wedding in Galilee* (1987) from a mixture of public and private capital in Belgium, France, Britain, and Germany including TV companies Zweites Deutsches Fernsehen or ZDF (Germany) and Canal Plus (France) (Naficy, 2001: 58–60; Al-Qattan, 2006: 113). Typical, then, of an interstitial mode of production, filmmakers like Khleifi and Aljafari negotiate multiple politics of location and belonging to make films that inevitably stand in ambivalent relation to questions of national production and nationhood, be it Israeli, Palestinian, Belgian, or French.

As Naficy argues elsewhere (2001: 60–62), the position of interstitial filmmakers is not confined to the cracks within state and private capital: filmmakers like Aljafari are also produced within the worlds of festival programming, academic research and publishing, and university teaching, all of which can establish the artisanal filmmaker-subject as a kind of global commodity while simultaneously offering visibility and agency.[2] Since the publication of Naficy's study, the sources of potential finance for interstitial filmmakers have expanded. In this regard, the production circumstances of Aljafari's most recent work, *Port of Memory*, are indicative of the shift occurring in many aspects of Arab arts and culture as the financial center of gravity for artists based in the Middle East and in diaspora shifts from Europe to the Gulf states of Qatar and the United Arab Emirates (UAE). Such shifts, while acting to diversify sources of funding for such transnational productions, nonetheless maintain fundamental aspects of the interstitial and highly mobile modes of practice for transnational Palestinian artists, many of whom cannot freely travel in and out of Israel and the West Bank nor the adjacent Arab states.

From Jerusalem to Köln to *Visit Iraq*

Aljafari grew up in the town of Ramle, Israel (originally Al-Ramla before Israel's establishment in 1948) and lived there and in Jaffa through his school years. Attending university in Jerusalem, Aljafari began to immerse himself in cinema by frequenting the Jerusalem Cinematheque. It was at this time that he also began to apply for postgraduate education outside of Israel, influenced, he recounts, by a desire both to study cinema and to "free myself from the status I had as a Palestinian in Israel" by moving outside the country (Aljafari, 2009). Prompted in part by a friend's move to Germany, Aljafari applied and was accepted to the Kunsthochschule für Medien (Academy of Media Arts, or KHM) in Köln, where he was awarded a Heinrich Böll Stiftung student scholarship in 2000 and went on to complete a three-year MFA degree, concentrating in cinema. There he produced a final-year thesis project, *Visit Iraq* (2003), and retained Köln as his base to make *The Roof* (2006) and *Port of Memory* (2009), as well as an installation project called *Album* (2008), created for the "Home Works" arts forum in Beirut.

Visit Iraq is a film about an empty space – the abandoned office of Iraqi Airways in Geneva, Switzerland. Aljafari first visited the city shortly after the first Gulf War, where he photographed the street-front office vacated by the airline, which had been subject to a Western embargo at that time. Returning to the site during his time at the KHM, Aljafari decided to organize a film around its exploration and was encouraged by one of his KHM advisors. This particular work, then, emerged directly from his position within the German art academy and was further facilitated by that specific educational environment: Aljafari's advisor, for example, introduced him to the work of British filmmaker Patrick Keiller, whose film *London* (1994) made a strong impression on Aljafari for its highly aestheticized exploration of urban space through static, carefully composed shots of the eponymous city, accompanied by an ironic voiceover by an unnamed narrator who recalls encounters with a mysterious character named Robinson. Keiller's essay film asks complex questions about the political and social aspects of urban space in London but does so in a highly self-conscious style, creating a fictional frame around its documentation of the city by fragment. To make *Visit Iraq*, Aljafari shot for approximately two weeks in Geneva, constructing multiple perspectives on the empty Iraqi Airways office from a variety of angles: from across the street, with the camera's object of study refracted through the windows of other shops; at unusual angles from the sidewalk, distorting our perspective of the exterior; from a position pressed against the windows of the office, focusing on the broken furniture and discarded appliances littering the floor (Figure 9.1).[3]

Interwoven with the beauty of *Visit Iraq*'s shots of space is a series of interviews with passers-by who discuss what they know or imagine about the office. Here Aljafari introduces a dry humor into the film in a method quite similar to Keiller's: the interviews create a composite narrative of the space that veers from the plausible to the outlandish. Aljafari's "characters" tell stories of bomb scares, mysterious staff movements, and even an elaborate tale of political espionage involving the CIA, Swiss secret service, and Yasir Arafat, that may or may not have anything to do with the empty office. The film's final credit sequence is bookended by two shots of one of the interviewees who offers an acapella impersonation of a cavalry drum and brass band and then, after the credits finish, creates his own, one-man sound rendition of a cavalry-vs.-Indian charge. While the film proffers nothing definitive about the space it investigates, the viewer is left with a subtle and uneasy sense that this Arab-identified space has been the subject of a kind of

Figure 9.1 Exploring an empty space, in *Visit Iraq* (dir. Kamal Aljafari, prod. Kunsthochschule für Medien).

everyday surveillance from the city's European inhabitants, most of whom now have little more than conjecture to offer about its history.

While *Visit Iraq* was specifically enabled by the KHM and took place under its institutional umbrella, Aljafari by his own account felt remarkably independent during its making, considering himself to have been unconstrained by any kind of institutional, funding-oriented, or nationally-inflected limitations (Aljafari, 2009). His next project, *The Roof*, however, was the first in which he was required to arrange funding outside of the art school environment. While this process marked his entry into the world of independent production beyond the sponsorship of the academy, it also constituted a rude awakening for Aljafari, who had imagined himself to have secured creative independence along with financial backing. Instead, it soon became clear that the film's major funder "owned" Aljafari's artistic choices in ways he had not envisaged. The film was partially financed by Filmstiftung Nordrhein-Westfalen (a state film fund) and the Kunststiftung NRW (an arts organization also from Nordrhein-Westfalen), but the bulk of the film's finance came from the state-owned German television channel ZDF, still one of the largest funders of German independent film. Aljafari's proposed film was to screen in ZDF's "new directors" slot, one which had facilitated many first features, both German and non-German (Jim Jarmusch's *Stranger than Paradise* (1984), for example).

Shooting for *The Roof* proceeded without incident but, during the editing process, a conflict arose between Aljafari and the film's German producers. Speaking with hindsight, Aljafari has admitted he was naive to have imagined that ZDF would not wish for a strong degree of creative control; however, at the time, his disavowal of the company's role led to a dramatic sequence of events in which, after objecting to what ZDF was requiring, he "stole" his footage back from the network's editing suite, finished his own cut of the film, and screened it at FIDMarseille in 2006 (winning an award for sound design), all unbeknownst to the film's producers. Seeing the film advertised there, the ZDF belatedly realized Aljafari had completed his film without their assent and sued him. The circumstances that led to this rupture are undoubtedly symptomatic of the contradiction Naficy (2001: 93) identifies between the artisanal nature of many "accented" films and the simultaneous reality of their dependence on capital. However, the problem of the disagreement, when placed in the context of a discussion of the film's style, reveals more than simply the creative constraints experienced by artisanal, European-based, interstitial filmmakers. It speaks profoundly to the politics that underpin Aljafari's careful, precise film – those of being Palestinian within Israel – and the way in which such politics may be rendered or made visible within Europe. I will return to the controversy of production after considering more closely the question of the film's style and discourse.

The *Roof* and the Politics of Home

The Roof is a film that can certainly be considered a documentary, although, taking Bill Nichols' (2001: 99–138) well-worn taxonomy as a guide, one could question the film's adherence to more common documentary aesthetics by noting its refusal of the expository mode (except for a brief minute of voiceover explanation near the beginning), its reliance only partially on observation (it also places the filmmaker interactively in the frame, in dialogue with its subjects), and its inclusion of elaborately scripted and quite discursively performative moments that utilize nonnaturalistic sound and camera placements. More specifically, I would argue, its form is essayistic in ways that Michael Renov (2004: 109) has outlined: it relies upon a multifaceted approach to past events that "regards history and subjectivity as mutually defining categories" and that constructs a self that is articulated within a broad and complex social sphere. Such an essayistic approach is also, as one might expect, argumentative, although not in a way that lends itself to obvious polemic. By the end of *The Roof*, one has gained an impression of the marginalized nature of this particular family and its near-mute filmmaker subject as he appears at various moments in the film, but such an understanding is not born of arguments articulated by the documentary characters themselves, nor does the film lay out an extensive historical explanation of the events that have led to this situation. At certain moments, the film does offer scenes in which characters speak of the everyday realities of Palestinian life in Israel. In one such scene, Aljafari's sister describes to him her job working for an Israeli judge in Jerusalem and the response she gets when speaking Arabic on the street: uncomprehending stares, "as if they do not know that there are Arabs who live here." In a later scene, a wiry young man speaks directly to the camera (his interviewer is offscreen and unheard) and complains that, with an influx of Russian Jewish immigrants pushing the Arab population from Ramle, Palestinians have become "the tail" of the country. Beyond these brief scenes, however, the film essays its arguments as much through a rhetoric of visual style as through verbal argumentation or spoken narration.

Within this essayistic mode, which eschews exposition for a more complex imbrication of the subjective and historical, the film develops a sustained, almost fetishistic attention to inanimate material objects – the texture of a flat concrete wall, the ruins of a former neighborhood – and to the presentation of found sounds, ranging from the roar of the Jaffa coastline to the chirping of caged birds and the mechanical sounds that accompany work on the ever-enlarging separation wall between Israel and the occupied West Bank (which annexes large swathes of the latter). *The Roof* constructs Aljafari's family members as mostly mute characters. In successive scenes we observe his parents, siblings, and extended family in Jaffa engaged in a variety of mundane activities – eating, sleeping, working. But the central conceit of the film, the thing that gives it its title and helps organize its cinematic style beyond the usual genres of documentary, is the unfinished second storey over Aljafari's family home. Through its obsessive interest in this space, the film develops a style that, while not incompatible with the aims of a social history of Palestinians in Israel, relies more on a spatial discourse that deemphasizes active human subjects and does not rely upon their testimony or visible actions for its impact. Where it engages Palestinians – Aljafari himself, his family, and others they encounter – it places them as bodies within a spatial environment that is structured by a logic of "erasure and reinscription,"[4] an environment which they do not appear to actively control. Such processes of erasure and overwriting, common to settler colonial environments more generally, are particularly resonant in the case of Israel/Palestine because of the relatively short and accelerated history of spatial transformation since the end of British Mandate Palestine.[5] In constructing a spatial history of Ramle and its surrounding areas and placing a set of subjects (his family) within that history, Aljafari's film unsettles a dominant mode of media representation in which the state of Israel is depicted as homogeneously Jewish and Palestinians are visible only in relation to the Occupied Territories of Gaza and the West Bank – engaged in conflicts and violent encounters with soldiers and Jewish settlers – rather than also as second-class citizens of Israel itself. Aljafari's refusal of this kind of dichotomous logic created a crisis for his German funders, whose liberal intentions regarding the prospect of a Palestinian documentary were nonetheless mired in such a discourse of conflict. Moreover, the film questions the "settled state" of Israeli spatial control, insofar as the Jewish state renders invisible and invalid Palestinian claims to a prior and ongoing spatial practice within the terrain now claimed by/as Israel proper. In drawing attention to the colonial politics that have affected all of Palestine, including that part of it which is now Israel, the film essays a deeply complex set of historical events and relationships in the present by showing the sedimented histories of the past as they are found in architectural structures and in uses of space. The family house in Ramle with its half-built roof, never quite "centered" in the frame of Aljafari's film, stands askew and unfinished as a metaphor for the broken histories and "roofless" state of Israel, with its dispossessed Palestinian inhabitants and its genuinely *un*settled Jewish majority.

The house in which we find Aljafari's family was never really theirs to begin with, we learn. A few minutes into the film, as we move to a static, foreshortened, straight-on shot of the Jaffa waterfront, with abandoned fishing boats, a sea wall, and crashing waves, we hear the following words in voiceover narration, spoken in Arabic and subtitled in English as follows:

> Everything began in 1948. In May. My grandparents were on a boat on their way to Beirut after their city of Jaffa had been bombed. Over those few days the waves got too big, so they were forced to return … But when they got back, Palestine was already gone. Their homes were gone as well. The people who remained were forced to live in one neighborhood and they were given the houses of other Palestinians … In 1948 the owners of this house were still building the second floor. Today the house is still the same: My parents live on the first floor and the past lives above them.

While the voiceover proceeds, the camera begins tracking slowly across an empty space of gravel and broken rubble in an abandoned part of Ramle, coming to rest in a static long-shot of the tower of *Al-Masjid al-Abyad* (Ramle's "White Mosque") which appears behind the ruins of a cemetery. We cut from there to two static shots of semideserted Ramle streets, before cutting again to a slow and carefully controlled tracking shot along a concrete wall, a shot held close enough that we can study in detail the texture of the wall which is yet without context as to its placement or function. Cutting from there to a daylight interior shot, the film presents three single beds with three figures napping, and a succession of close-ups: toiletries, family photos, a barred window, a caged bird.[6] A man watches television in another room; his daughter prepares food; the young man, who we by now assume is the filmmaker, watches television too; all are silent. The somewhat discontinuous montage of shots continues as we see the family, now numbering six, seated around a table, eating, but barely talking.

The overwhelming impression in this sequence of exterior and interior shots is of staging and of carefully calculated performance rather than straightforward observation: Aljafari's family seems to be performing a perhaps exaggerated version of itself or, equally plausibly, a script of the filmmaker. The carefully structured views of the exterior streetscape and the slow tracking along the wall, accompanied by nondiegetic music, suggest not the seemingly objective look of an observational film, but that of a carefully framed composition invested in conveying a precise aesthetic impression from the material of the everyday. As we shall see, Aljafari's most recent film, *Port of Memory*, takes the already blurred lines

There isn't another house like this in Jaffa.

Figure 9.2 Urban "renovation," in *The Roof* (dir. and prod. Kamal Aljafari).

between documentary and staged fiction that one sees in certain sequences of *The Roof* and extends them into the more ambiguous terrain of history and memory. Further, by returning to some of the recognizable subjects of the earlier film (his uncle, aunt, and grandmother) but treating them even more insistently as characters within an ever-more vulnerable and colonized space (Jaffa), *Port of Memory* prompts one to interpret *The Roof* as a narrative primarily about home and its built, lived, buried, and broken properties.

In addressing a spatial politics of home, Aljafari and director of photography Diego Martínez Vignatti, shooting on digital video, offer many shots of flat surfaces and the layers that comprise them, excavating the built environment around Ramle and Jaffa as if an archaeological site. Their camera does so with precisely orchestrated tracking shots or with long static takes that resemble tableaux vivants – one can see movement in the frame, but that movement is minimal and barely disturbs the surface of what seems like a photographic still image. Several examples of this are found in the film's first few minutes, as the film sets up its montage of Ramle scenes, exterior and interior to the family home. But the focus on built environments and the ways in which they are configured by various colonial practices of appropriation, demolition, or control is a continual issue through the film, resulting in several important scenes. Several of these involve sequences that function like "tours": in one, we are led by Aljafari's uncle, Salim, from his house through his neighborhood. As he walks, followed by a handheld camera, we come upon a house whose entire front wall has been reduced to rubble, leaving its interior bizarrely unscathed and open to the elements (Figure 9.2).

In successive shots through the crumbled masonry and up into its rooms, the building appears like a half-destroyed doll's house, with beds and furniture and wall hangings still in place amid the ruins in front. One of the owners speaks directly to the camera and to those assembled about how the house had been one of the most ornate and beautiful in Jaffa, and that she will insist it be rebuilt exactly as it was (the "room" in which she stands will appear in a key scene in *Port of Memory*). Some of the men present, with whom Salim converses, suggest that an Israeli bulldozer "made a mistake" and hit the foundations of the house, triggering a collapse of the wall. Yet the film here suggests that the official explanation of a "mistake" appears unlikely and even disingenuous; Salim's interlocutors talk about the deliberate "renovation" of the neighborhood by Israeli developers and how that will result in a future neighborhood exclusively for Israeli Jews despite the ongoing presence of Palestinians there even after 1948. This sequence is followed by a silent panning of the camera across the environment immediately adjoining the half-destroyed house, showing us piles of dirt, open lots scraped clean of the buildings that once stood there, and signs of new construction all around. The shot ends on the same stretch of seashore that we have seen previously, with its abandoned, rusted fishing boats, as the sound of waves comes up in the mix and we cut to Aljafari's grandmother describing again the events of their attempted flight in 1948, including the loss of family members to unrest in Lebanon or bombs in Jaffa as the city fell to the new Israeli forces.[7]

In this carefully controlled transition from the exteriority of the neighbor's house to the interiority of the uncle and grandmother's Jaffa home, the film constructs an historical and political narrative that insists on linking the events of the 1948 War with the dispossession of Palestinian families in Jaffa and Ramle today.[8] Rather than through images of overt conflict, *The Roof* makes its argument about the loss of home through a focus on the often mundane physical properties of spatial transformation and its causes and effects. In this way the film shares much in common with the many recent interventions into Israeli and Palestinian history that focus on architecture, geography, and mapping. Among these many interventions, many of them scholarly or popular written works, are other films too: as Ella Shohat (2010: 278) has reiterated with respect to films about Palestine/Israel, film work can be "fundamentally historiographical" and one should read such "photographic and cinematic documents as a vital part of the archive and the reassessment of history." As well as Aljafari's work, one could point to films like Amos Gitai's *House* (1980), which exposes the multiple histories of a house in Jerusalem whose original Palestinian owner lost it to Israel in 1948, after which time it was acquired by the government and rented first to Jewish Algerian immigrants before being sold to an Israeli professor; or the more recent *In Working Progress* (2006), which follows Palestinian construction workers as they build Israeli settlement colonies in the occupied West Bank.

Writers and scholars have attempted to make sense of what these visual artists have shown so succinctly, focusing attention on the ways that architecture and the demarcation of space are organized within Zionist colonial logics.[9] Similarly, in *Sacred Landscapes*, Meron Benvenisti details the process of literal remapping that

Zionist organizations instigated during the British Mandate, the pace of which accelerated as part of official policy post-1948 (Benvenisti, 2000: 12–14). As Benvenvisti shows, the process of remapping had two related aspects: it found Hebrew equivalents or replacements for Arabic names, resulting in a "Hebraization of the landscape" (Benvenisti, 2000: 37), and it reflected the new "facts on the ground" in the wake of 1948: entire Palestinian villages had been razed and no longer existed. Thus the existing maps of Mandatory Palestine, already the result of British imperial practices, enabled a further transformation of terrain such that an extensive Hebrew symbolic system could be constituted over the remains of an Arabic symbolic landscape.[10] As Benvenisti explains, this was not limited to the renaming of certain villages, rivers, or sites with biblical Hebrew names – a process that the mapmakers saw as a "national duty" of "redemption" (Benvenisti, 2000: 30–31) – but also extended to creating Hebrew names even where there were no historical precedents for them, transforming Arabic names into similar-sounding Hebrew words or immortalizing modern immigrant Jewish figures with Hebrew placenames (even when those figures had non-Hebrew names themselves) (Benvenisti, 2000: 35–36). *The Roof* succinctly demonstrates the results of this process in an early sequence around the family home, when a succession of close-ups reveals the names of surrounding streets: the English names on the signs are Dr. Koch Street, Dr. Salk Street, Dr. Sigmund Freud Street, but these are inscribed first in their Hebrew versions. While Arabic appears too, the Arabic name is simply a transliteration of the English and Hebrew.

The film continues its focus on the reinscription of space and the elision of Palestinian spaces of home in a sequence set in the viewing tower of a Tel Aviv skyscraper. The filmmaker appears in frame and walks across the empty floor toward a circular wall of windows that offers a full panorama of the Jaffa-Tel Aviv area. As he gets closer, the sound of his shoes squeaking on the polished floor gives way to a close-up of Aljafari wearing headphones, and we hear the sound of the audio tour to which he is listening. A polished American-accented voice begins: "We're now facing the center of the city that some refer to as the cultural center of Israel – Tel Aviv." Classical music begins and continues through the voice-off; after a description of the immediate vicinity, the audio tour turns toward Jaffa:

> To the left of the Shalom Tower, toward the horizon, you can see Jaffa's small fishing harbor and its ancient city. During the settlement period, Jaffa was a Canaanite city. It was then conquered by the Hezmonians and became a Hebrew city. Since then, Jaffa fell into the hands of the Egyptians, Philistines, Cisyrrians, Babylonians, Persians and the people of Sour and Sidon. It was destroyed and then rebuilt by the Greeks, Romans, Byzantines, Arabs, Crusaders and Mamluks. It was destroyed again by Napoleon's army and again rebuilt by the Turks. Then came the British conquest and finally the Israelis. What a history!

The linguistic slippage around the issue of Palestinian habitation is significant: quickly establishing the Hebrew credentials of the city, the narration makes scant reference to any Palestinian habitation of the town (allowing only for "Arabs" and "Philistines" and relegating their residency to pre-Crusader periods). As Mark LeVine (2005: 28) argues, such a narrative typifies official Israeli tendencies to stress the period of Jaffa's history from biblical times to the Crusaders while "ignoring the Ottoman period because of the assumption that Palestine experienced stagnation and even decline during this time." Thus, Jaffa was "rebuilt again by the Turks," according to this narration, but the ellipses between the mentions of "Napoleon's army" (which invaded in 1799), "the Turks" (Ottomans, who occupied it earlier, in 1517, and then again from 1807), the "British conquest" (1917), and "the Israelis" (1948) render invisible and nonexistent the local Palestinian population, who in fact experienced all of these moments – French and Ottoman rule, British colonialism, and Israeli conquest.[11]

Aljafari places this eliding narration next to a scene that further exposes and undermines the marginalized position of Palestinians within Israeli discourses of subjectivity and home. Again, the scene relies on a certain performativity and calculated irony rather than on straightforward documentary denotation. A carefully arranged shot shows a cup of coffee or tea next to which an outstretched hand enters the frame to first show and then set down on the table an array of sugar sachets emblazoned with the faces of twentieth-century Zionist leaders. Over this shot we hear the song, "I Believe," sung in English by the El Avram Group (1995), and in the next shot its refrain, "I exist, I exist, tell the world that I am well/I believe, I believe, I'm the son of Israel," begins as we see Aljafari slumped in a chair, motionless, in a hotel lobby. The dissonance between the upbeat song and the maudlin look of the film's authorial subject continues to emphasize the air of passivity and lack of agency that seems to have attached to him throughout. In a drole learning-to-drive sequence, the filmmaker-character is first interrogated by his Israeli instructor's long list of health and law enforcement questions and then, after first stalling and then making halting progress through the gear changes, is directed into the unpaved streets that lead to the Arab neighborhood of Ramle, where he is warned that the car may be damaged by potholes and unsigned railway crossings. Through the entire sequence, he remains silent, as he does in many earlier scenes within the family home or at his father's tire shop. In his silence and apparent inability to transcend physically the limitations of his environment, his character is thoroughly reminiscent of the character of "E.S." in Elia Suleiman's three features, *Chronicle of a Disappearance* (1996), *Divine Intervention* (2002), and *The Time that Remains* (2009), where Suleiman plays a Keatonesque character who resembles the director but is not reducible to him. Aljafari never creates for himself a character by name, but, with the exception of the already-mentioned brief voiceover, the film more often than not positions him as an icon within a diegesis rather than as an authorial subject commenting on the film or explaining things for a viewer.

In two significant sequences in *The Roof* in which we do see the filmmaker speak, what is said reinforces the literal and metaphorical sense of incarceration and imprisonment that the film establishes. In the film's opening sequence, for example, Aljafari recounts to his sister the condition of his imprisonment during the first Intifada (for a reason that the film does not disclose), and the description of prison conditions includes a reference to a friend, Nabieh, whom Aljafari later telephones. In that scene, shot at night as Aljafari speaks to Nabieh, who is in Lebanon, via mobile phone, a dominant chord in the conversation is Aljafari's inability to meet him: as a citizen of Israel with an Israeli passport, Aljafari will not be admitted to most Arab countries. Here, then, the film builds a chain of images that are suggestive of incarceration, as the successive shots of blank walls and surfaces are juxtaposed with personal narratives of a literal imprisonment that also suggest a larger shared sense of entrapment, one in which Palestinian citizens of Israel feel imprisoned by a state that stands in as the locus of "home."

Moreover, the discussion of the weather and the sound of the sea in Beirut creates a strong sense of spatial proximity despite the supposedly impermeable borders to which the men refer. Aljafari and Nabieh discuss whether or not it's raining in their respective locations, and when Aljafari asks Nabieh to hold the phone out so that he, Aljafari, can hear the Beirut waves, the soundtrack brings up in the mix the diegetic sound of waves on the beach in Jaffa, which becomes a sound bridge as the film cuts back to that location and a new scene. What figures first as a neat and humorous transition – the wave sounds are louder and carry more fidelity than one would expect from a telephonic transmission – has in effect produced a more meaningful connection, not only bridging the seemingly impossible distance between the two men, who are in fact just a few hundred kilometers apart, but also evincing the historical maritime axis by which the port towns of Jaffa and Beirut were connected in earlier periods. This very axis is what Aljafari's family tried to access in 1948; its inaccessibility in that time is redoubled in the telephone call, as Aljafari and Nabieh expose the various impediments to travel between Ramle and Beirut, Israel and Lebanon, at this actual historical moment. The waves that connect Beirut to Jaffa, the rain that is falling in Beirut but not yet on Ramle, evoke a Levantine space whose recent political borders, the products of many European colonialisms – British, French, Israeli – belie a far longer history of proximity and interaction between the numerous peoples of the region.[12] Thus the film evokes a longer historical sense of home in Palestine, one that is not, as official Zionist narratives would have it, exclusively Jewish or biblical.[13] *The Roof* exposes the pressures on and disavowals of this more inclusive home by an exceptionalist Israeli state whose attempts to write history in an exclusivist and questionable discourse of Jewish ethnonationhood are rendered quietly obvious and absurd by the film.

I have suggested, then, that Aljafari's film, with its interest in home and built spaces, deploys a carefully stylized cinematic discourse to render visible the logics of Israeli urban planning, historiography, and spatial conquest and their dehumanizing effect on Palestinians in "the interior." That is, *The Roof* demonstrates that the "1948 Palestinians" are effectively invisible to the state except to the extent to which they occupy a marginalized position within Zionist discourse, one in which they are made to signify a pathological premodernity and backwardness before the coming-into-being of the modern Israeli state. Shohat (2010: 106) reminds us that Golda Meir also famously constructed Mizrahim, or Oriental Jews, in such a fashion, considering them to have arrived unevolved from another time: "Shall we be able to elevate these immigrants to a suitable level of civilization?" she asked. As Shohat shows, the "Arabness" both of Mizrahi Jews and Palestinian Arabs is constructed within a racialized discourse, while the differential position of Israel's various populations results in a complexity that is belied by simplistic constructions of "Arab vs. Jew" or "Arab vs. Israeli" (*Port of Memory* will embody this recognition even more overtly). Thus *The Roof* seems to offer in its slow-moving images and near-mute characters a fragmented nonidentity as a direct result of a colonial state logic, and the film – in its concentration on rubble, walled surfaces, incompletely buildings, and spatial divisions – cinematically constructs a fractured and ruinous home space whose many-layered past is contrasted with the eerily smooth surface of the separation wall which dominates the film's final scenes. I have written elsewhere that this cinematic style creates an effect that is uncanny and even queer in its discursive effects: the gendered masculine authority of the filmmaker is undermined rather than recovered, and the Palestinian family is rendered such that it appears pathological within heteronormative Zionist ideology (Limbrick, 2011). Rather than contest such signs of lack with a compensatory filmic mechanism of explicit nationalism, however, the film uses the marginality of its characters as a means to unsettle and expose the discursive logics of Zionism, revealing its structuring logics of racism and spatial hierarchization.[14] Moreover, the film also rejects the familiar documentary iconography of Palestine. Aljafari's characters (and, as we have seen, they appear to us more as characters than as documentary subjects in privileged relation to the real) do not appear in the positions or settings in which many non-Arab audiences are used to seeing Palestinians appear: in contrast to mass media representations, they are not traversing checkpoints within the West Bank or crossing into Israel, they are not in visible conflict with Israeli soldiers, they are not protesting or waving flags or being shot at; in other words, they do not conform to the limited and partial imaginary created in and for the West as the result of decades of occupation, resistance, and conflict. It was precisely this absence that perturbed the ZDF representatives who shared the editing suite with Aljafari in his first attempts to cut his film.

The production liaison, relates Aljafari (2009), would take copious notes during his viewing of the rushes, scribbling in a notebook as Aljafari's images appeared on screen. At first the ZDF representative did not impose judgment or demands; eventually, however, he became more vocal. He could not understand why Aljafari's family members "looked more Italian" than they did Palestinian, why they "talked so softly," and why nothing seemed to happen in his film. What was required, he argued, was a voiceover to explain things better to an audience, and more conflict between the characters and their setting. Certainly we can attribute such comments in part to the contradictory conditions of production already noted in the artisanal mode of film practice; the avowedly noncommercial filmmaker with his personal vision placed in direct conflict with the capitalist mode of production that he depends upon, in the personage of a producer whose desired choices rest on a presumed threshold of audience comprehension and accessibility. One must at the same time, however, recognize the overdetermined cultural logic of such a scenario: a transnational and interstitial filmmaker, whose work creates a critical engagement with notions of home by essaying the internal displacement of his subjects, is here pulled back into his European production context – one that financially enables his work but that refuses to "see" its critical vision of Palestinian life inside Israel. The German producer's inability to countenance Aljafari's images reveals a kind of nativism that cannot see "1948 Palestinians" because it recognizes Palestinians solely as a people geographically external to a bounded and bordered Jewish state with which they are in combat. Such a misrecognition of the realities of Palestinian life across all of Palestine/Israel, not only Gaza and the West Bank, reorientalizes Palestinians and fails to comprehend the specificity of spatial destruction and reinscription that *The Roof* presents.[15] Further, and more disturbingly, the funders' call for more visible conflict and expression of an oppositional Palestinian-ness evinces a desire wrongly to transform questions that the film demonstrates are political – having to do with colonial policies and spatial control – into a singular and dichotomized issue of ethnic or religious identities in conflict. The desire for a more simplistic and obfuscatory discourse on Palestine/Israel is, of course, neither generalizable across all German settings, nor is it only found in Germany; my point is rather that it represents a logic that is both Eurocentric and ultimately coextensive with ideological conceptions of a homogeneous Jewish nation locked in inevitable and timeless conflict with non-Jewish antagonists. As a logic, it depends upon a constructed binarism between Western/European/ modern settings and non-Western/Arab/primitive ones and is thus antithetical to Aljafari's films in which the discourse on home is irresolveably produced across axes of difference, through multilayered histories, and across borders. Against the reductive tendencies embraced by his German producers, Aljafari's cinema is neither programmatic nor driven by simplistic or literal-minded expositions; rather, it is attentive to the small details that render "Palestine" an unrealized or yet-untenable concept within the current incarnation of a settler state.

Port of Memory and the Spatial Politics of Jaffa

In Aljafari's most recent work, *Port of Memory*, the politics of home within the "unsettled" settler state are presented even more keenly as producing a kind of slow-burning psychological damage. While the sense of suspended animation created in *The Roof*'s domestic settings is continued in the latter film, here an even more disquieting air of collective trauma prevails, manifest in disturbing images of Jaffa residents who have seemingly gone mad. Like Aljafari's two previous films, *Port of Memory* is evocative of a very particular locality and space – the neighborhood of Ajami in Jaffa – but it is also a film that, beyond the intense localness of its representation, demonstrates even more compellingly the relativity of Aljafari's German production base and the increasingly decentered and transnational scope of his practice. The film again received funding from Filmstiftung Nordrhein-Westfalen and postproduction was carried out in Munich, but this time financial support for the film came from a diverse list of parties that included the Sundance Institute (from which he received script development funds), the Arab Fund for Arts and Culture (based in Jordan), Fonds Sud Cinéma (France), the Ministère des Affaires Etrangères et Européennes (France), Ministère de la Culture et de la Communication CNC (France), and the Middle East International Film Festival (since renamed the Abu Dhabi film festival), whose funds reserved the right to premier the film at their festival. Certainly all European-based filmmakers are now familiar with a degree of transnational funding but, as Randall Halle (2010: 306) explains, many European funds are also now explicitly addressed to filmmakers in and from the Mediterranean and North Africa. Aljafari's project stands between these different strands of transnational production, since he has worked from a European base and is thus eligible for local sources such as German television, but he also inhabits the role of a Palestinian filmmaker on a transnational stage, which places him within the orbit of funds external to Europe or earmarked for Arab or Middle Eastern filmmakers. These sources of capital extend as far as the United States, and not only via festivals like Sundance: Aljafari completed the subtitling of *Port of Memory* while a Radcliffe Fellow at Harvard University.

Thus, the financing of *Port of Memory* is indicative of two major cultural and political trends that contextualize the transnational coordinates of his practice over these three films. One is the increased interest in Middle Eastern cultural production on the part of US funds, as evidenced by Sundance's support. In part as a consequence of the post-9/11 political environment (in which government and nongovernment organizations have been more actively engaged in projects of "cultural bridge-building"), some US arts and cultural organizations are increasingly engaged in sponsoring Arab or Middle Eastern projects, both those that originate from within the United States itself and those that take shape internationally. As examples of this trend one might point to the success of an organization like ArteEast, which, as a nonprofit, has been able to secure US philanthropic funds for the curation of important, well-publicized programs of Arab films and art at venues like Lincoln Center and the Museum of Modern Art and has toured them at universities, schools, and museums. The magazine *Bidoun*, based in New York but with founding editors and writers based in Dubai, Beirut, and other key transnational Arab cities, has become part of the international cadre of art/culture magazines. At the same time (and often in conjunction with US organizations and institutions), the past decade has seen new projects of massive capital investment in arts and education infrastructure within the Gulf states of Qatar and the UAE. Major new museums have opened or are under construction in Dubai, Doha, and Abu Dhabi; film festivals in Dubai, Abu Dhabi, and Sharjah have recruited famous international directors and curators and continue to create new funds for filmmakers. In Qatar, the Doha Tribeca Film Festival was launched in 2009 as a joint venture between the Doha Film Institute and the Tribeca Film Institute (based in New York City), and the Doha Film Institute is positioning itself as a financing source for film production as well as promoting an educational program of workshops, creative labs, and short film competitions. Such initiatives, financed jointly by the oil wealth of Emirati and Qatari governments and the cultural and financial capital of US institutions, are not only transforming the coordinates of local production in the region in their attempts to create a culture industry in the Gulf, but are also simultaneously challenging the earlier primacy of established European sources like Fonds Sud or Arte television. Thus we might position Aljafari's film, like the work now in production by many other Arab filmmakers, within the shifting coordinates of arts funding that is increasingly located in the Gulf states and is articulated to new centers of global finance.[16]

Port of Memory extends some of the preoccupations that Aljfari has developed as a filmmaker in both *Visit Iraq* and *The Roof*. However, it essays even further the dislocated politics of home that the prior films addressed. It does so, first, by loosening a relationship to the real through an even more hybridized form of documentary fiction. As in *The Roof*, members of Aljafari's family play key roles. Shot partly in their actual house, the film centers around the home of Aljafari's uncle, aunt, and grandmother which is threatened with acquisition by the Israeli state. As the film begins, Salim pays a visit to his attorney, who remains offscreen and casually reports that he has lost the deed of title to Salim's home. Through the course of the film, we return to the same living room and to conversations conducted between Salim and his sister, Fatmeh (Aljafari's aunt) about the immediacy of the eviction threats to which they, and the Palestinian families around them, are subjected. The film develops this sense of attenuated life by alternating scenes of the domestic rituals of a middle-aged woman and her mother, whose home we have in fact seen in *The Roof*; it is the house damaged by a bulldozer, now repaired. The film also stresses the extreme psychological toll experienced by Palestinians within this environment by returning to other characters whose actions are disturbing or inexplicable. One such figure (whom we have already seen in the lawyer's office, too) is placed in a kind of sparsely furnished working-men's club, where he and two older men pass their time wordlessly, watching television, staring vacantly across the room, and tending a charcoal grill, respectively. In the first scene in which we are introduced to this character, he uses tongs to pick up a glowing coal which he proceeds to hold just centimeters from his neck as it undoubtedly begins to burn his skin. The television in the club displays a broken and repetitive excerpt from the Chuck Norris film, *The Delta Force* (1986), whose production, as I will show later, violently affected Jaffa's

urban fabric; in effect, the older man watches the televised reoccupation of his neighborhood from within its very ruins. Another character who is central to the film's mood, yet who remains unnamed and without dialog, is a young man on a scooter who, upon his first appearance in the film, rips his helmet from his head, throws it to the ground, and begins screaming uncontrollably without provocation. And, at significant moments in the film, we see a close-up shot of the hands of Aljafari's aunt, who washes at the sink in a slow and beautifully choreographed ritual that nonetheless has the appearance of an obsessive-compulsive behavior. By the end of the film's remarkably simple narrative, Salim dreams that his lawyer locates the missing title, but visits his office one more time, only to find it vacant, its occupant disappeared without explanation.

The film thus stages this simply sketched story within a larger, nonnarrative discourse that reflects the actual logic of dispossession currently taking place in the Jaffa area. As does *The Roof*, *Port of Memory* exhibits a documentary attention to built environments, especially those under demolition and construction: we see signs of new housing developments for Israelis and a public park at the water's edge, and examine the scars of neglected or damaged buildings that are being torn down or renovated by Israelis in search of "authentic" and "historical" environs with which to construct a "New-Old Jaffa" next to modern Tel Aviv (LeVine, 2005: 226–248). However, this documentary material becomes a scaffold for a series of vignettes that further test the borders between documentary and fiction and combine to render Jaffa a densely conflicted and multilayered space. Signaling the ongoing way in which everyday relations between residents are constructed within a dynamic of urban renewal and dispossession, Aljafari constructs a scene in which a young Israeli woman comes to the door of Salim and Fatmeh's home to ask politely but insistently, in Hebrew, if it is for sale or if she can at least enter and look around. This scene, isolated in the film (we never see the visitor again) is nonetheless contextualized by other shots in which we see posters lamenting the loss of Palestinians in the neighborhood ("we miss you," says their text in Arabic), flyers encouraging residents to call if a home is for sale or rent, and leaflets that document evictions of Palestinian families, all of them signs from the actual lived reality of Jaffa. In a decision that was again the source of some dissent between Aljafari and one of his producers (this time French), the subtitling of this sequence for European and US release prints did not signal the linguistic shifts from Arabic to Hebrew and back. While his producer insisted upon a need for clarity in light of her audience, Aljafari maintained that leaving the languages translated but unmarked was consistent with the spatiopolitical realities that he was documenting, in which language usage, as much as architecture and history, becomes multilayered and inseparable from the issues of proximity, memory, and loss that his film essays.[17]

Aljafari further dramatizes the continual Israeli expropriation of Palestinian property in a short but evocative sequence that is set in the same living room of the house we saw in *The Roof*. There, the camera arrives to take measure of a bulldozer's assault on a Palestinian home whose entire front wall has been ripped off. Its owner vows on film to have it rebuilt, and in *Port of Memory*, Aljfari returns to that home. Now, the front of the building has been rebuilt, although one can trace the vertical line in the plaster where the repaired wall is grafted onto the original structure. We first see a small group of people moving furniture and taking down paintings from the wall, including one of Jesus's "last supper." In a room to the side, a woman and her elderly mother sit on the bed watching. Then, the small film crew sets up a shot in which an Israeli man stands under an ornate door lintel and proclaims proudly, in Hebrew, that he built the decorative stained glass windows above him with his own hands. The director orders multiple takes so that his actor might inflect the statement convincingly, and asks him to add a line about the ceiling, too, urging him to "say it like you really own it." While the scene is not explained, taken together with other such ambiguous vignettes, it generates the overwhelming sense that a Palestinian architectural history is being erased and rewritten through multiple means, including the cinematic. Later, as we shall see, *Port of Memory* uses extant Hollywood and Israeli features to further expose the remapping of Palestinian space within fictional diegeses, but here the viewer of *The Roof* is privileged for having seen this house once "exposed" by dint of its partial destruction by a bulldozer, and now "reexposed" and threatened once again through a fictionalized cinematic encounter (of the kind that has occurred throughout Jaffa's history and that continues still).

For while this film-within-a-film scene rings uncannily "false" as documentary (we sense its performative staging), it is nevertheless firmly embedded within the actual politics of Jaffa's Arab neighborhoods. In a final chapter committed to theorizing a space of conviviality between Palestinian and Jewish Israeli residents, LeVine (2005: 215–248) takes up the contemporary politics of the "New-Old Jaffa." He emphasizes the way that Jaffa exists within Tel Aviv's dualistic imaginary – as simultaneously a dilapidated, violent, dangerous streetscape ready for transformation and renewal, and an "ancient," "romantic," "exotic," and "historically Jewish space, one that was 'liberated from Arab hands'" to become available for development "as a cultural and historical center" (2005: 220). Crucially, LeVine points out that such an ideological construction of Jaffa derives in part from moving-image cultures of television and film which are not incidental to the forces of dispossession that have grown around Jaffa, having in fact been complicit with the very destruction of neighborhoods that "urban renewal" later officially codified. LeVine, quoting Andre Mazawi, notes that Jaffa, and especially the neighborhood of Ajami, in which *Port of Memory* takes place, "is the site of many crime and war movies and television shows since the 1960s because 'it resembles Beirut after the bombardments – dilapidated streets, fallen houses, dirty and neglected streets, smashed cars'" (2005: 220).[18]

Among the many unnamed films that LeVine and Mazawi allude to, two in particular are relevant here: *Kazablan* (1974) and *The Delta Force*, both directed by the Zionist Israeli director Menachem Golan. *Kazablan*, a musical, was part of the genre of *"bourekas"* films, dominant in Israeli cinema between 1967 and 1977 (Shohat, 2010: 113), which projected fantasies of reconciliation between the deeply divided and socially stratified communities of Ashkenazim (Central and Eastern European Jews) and Mizrahim (Jewish Arabs) within Israel, often through exaggerated stereotyping. Kazablan (sometimes spelled Casablan, after Casablanca), played by Yehoram Gaon, is a Moroccan Jew who falls in love with a young Ashkenazi woman. Her family eventually accepts him, but not before he has spent most of the film socially ostracized by his Ashkenazi neighbors, who refer to him and his Arab friends with racialized insults like *vilde khaye* ("wild animal").[19] *Kazablan's* setting is the same Jaffa neighborhood as in Aljafari's film, but in Golan's film it is populated only by Jews, both those of Mizrahi and Ashkenazi origin. The government wants to tear down their dilapidated homes, but the residents band together to restore the buildings for themselves. In a sentimental musical sequence in the film, Kazablan wanders the seafront streets of Jaffa, singing nostalgically in Hebrew of his homeland in Morocco, a place that he remembers as paradise before the displacement and loss that he experiences in Israel. No less important for its role in Jaffa's cinematic history is Golan's later film, *The Delta Force*. Here Chuck Norris appears as a US commando, fighting Palestinian "terrorists" in the midst of civil-war-torn Beirut.[20] The production team of *The Delta Force* not only took over Jaffa in order to cast it as Beirut but created its own urban mayhem in the process. As part of what Aljafari (2008) has termed a "cinematic occupation," the producers arranged for their fictional conflicts to include actual explosions that destroyed real buildings, thus provoking real consequences for Jaffa's residents and its ever-more-threatened built environment.[21] Elsewhere, Aljafari has spoken about being a child in Jaffa during this period, watching the explosions as the city was transformed around him.

> The road around my grandmother's house had been covered with posters of Ayatollah Khomeini and Hezbollah flags. I was standing next to a group of other children and I waited for the [film] shooting to commence. Suddenly a car appeared with the name of my school, "Saint Joseph," on its door. Two blond men were standing in the car and were firing in all directions … I remember that the children told me that one of the men in the car was the American actor, Chuck Norris. (2010)

These two films, then, have production narratives that are thoroughly embedded in the layered histories of spatial exploitation and transformation that have built and unbuilt Jaffa. *Kazablan* depicts – and both films figure in – a politics of social relations and urban practices that writers like Monterescu (2007) and others (Tamari, 2009; LeVine, 2005) have documented and analyzed. *Port of Memory* forces a reflection on the uncanny (literally, in Freud's terms, the *unheimlich* or unhomely) effects of watching and experiencing such filmic narratives from a subject position inside that urban space of home.[22] For a Palestinian in Jaffa, we might say, now internally displaced and denied a genuine homeland, this kind of cinema contributes even further to the erasure of that space.

With such erasures in mind, Aljafari's decision to integrate sequences from both films within the diegesis of his own, unmarked and unannounced except for a reference in the end credits, constitutes a radical gesture that further intervenes in the spatial politics and critiques that others have advanced around the site of Jaffa. In *The Roof*, as we have seen, Aljafari's uncle takes a walk around his neighborhood and leads the viewer in a tour of demolition and urban gentrification. In the newer film, Salim sets out on another walk in the same neighborhood, but this time he becomes a kind of ghost, haunting the mise-en-scène of Golan's film, *Kazablan*. Aljfari inserts an entire sequence constructed from pieces of *Kazablan*: as a shot is held of Salim looking out over the ocean, music from the earlier film comes up in the mix, and we cut to a shot of the Jaffa waterfront where children play as the camera pulls back and pans right to reveal Kazablan beginning to walk into frame. He sings in Hebrew, subtitled as: "There is a place beyond the sea where the sand is white and home is warm," and the camera tracks and follows him as he continues a walk from the oceanfront into the streets of Jaffa, all the while singing nostalgically of the "home beyond the sea," the neighborhoods he left behind, the women and children playing while the sabbath bread bakes in the oven. In this original sequence, Kazablan continues his walk through the derelict streets of Jaffa, further establishing for the viewer the harsh conditions for Mizrahi Jews who found themselves caught between the Zionist vision of a Jewish homeland and the realities of prejudice in the (usually ghettoized) neighborhoods or camps that they were placed in upon arrival.[23] *Kazablan*'s neighborhood is portrayed as somewhat mixed, but only between Mizrahim and Ashkenazim, in keeping with the film's endeavor to project a multicultural space of Jewish nationhood, one that excludes Palestinians entirely.

Indeed, in *Kazablan*, while the neighborhood is subjected to the same threat of evictions and gentrification depicted in *Port of Memory*, the former removes Palestinians entirely from the diegesis. Consequently, as Kazablan's promenade proceeds in Aljafari's film, we begin to see a ghostly reclamation of the original material. As Kazablan rounds a corner and walks down an alley, Salim enters the frame from behind a building, catching a quick glance at the newcomer before retreating behind a wall (Figure 9.3). In the next shot, Kazablan continues his walk toward the camera as Salim again materializes within the frame and quickly overtakes him as he leads the way through the empty lane. From this shot on, the mise-en-scène of *Kazablan* continues, but its protagonist is replaced by the figure of Salim, who "ghosts" each shot as he continues the walk around Jaffa's streets in a scene that also incorporates material from two later sequences in Golan's film (a walking sequence after Kazablan is released from prison, and a scene in which his lover, Rachel, visits him at his house; there Salim replaces Rachel (Figure 9.4)). The effect of the collapsing diegeses is extremely disorienting since the bleached-out color of *Kazablan*'s diegetic world here contrasts slightly with Alajfari's own footage in the preceding and subsequent shots;[24] even a viewer who has not seen *Kazablan* will likely notice that something is awry in

Home beyond the sea...

Figure 9.3   Salim reinhabits Jaffa, in *Port of Memory* (dir. Kamal Aljafari, prod. Novel Media).

Figure 9.4   Ghosting *Kazablan*, in *Port of Memory* (dir. Kamal Aljafari, prod. Novel Media).

the sequence. Aljafari also removes the sound from the original footage, now constructing a walking sequence with only the sound of Salim's footsteps reverberating loudly, and the noise of the wind continuing through each subsequent shot.

The merging of diegetic spaces that Aljafari effects is critical for the film's intervention into the spatial politics of Jaffa and for the question of cultural memory that is alluded to in the film's title. The sequence effectively remaps Golan's Jaffa – ethnically-cinematically cleansed of Palestinians – with the ghostly body of a Palestinian resident present throughout yet absent to the diegetic world of a Zionist cinema like Golan's. Aljafari renders visible the "repressed Palestine" (Shohat, 2010: 282) that Golan's film strives to cover over and, in so doing, creates a sequence that relies on a productive haunting of nationalist space by that which it represses. In her book *Ghostly Matters*, Avery Gordon (2008: 63–64) repositions the ghost as a "social figure" who "imports a charged strangeness into the place or sphere it is haunting." Producing a sense of the uncanny in those who perceive it, the ghost operates as "a symptom of what is missing" but also "represents a future possibility, a hope" and, finally, demands that we "offer it a hospitable memory *out of a concern for justice*" (emphasis in original). Aljafari's ghostly uncle here recaptures the space from which he was excluded, evoking the Palestinians missing from *Kazablan* as well as those alluded to in the posters, seen earlier, which line the streets of Jaffa, thus demanding justice in the present. Yet the sequence does so through an articulation of cultural memory that, like the space of Jaffa itself, is itself layered with competing languages and allegiances.

The sequence in fact complicates an ethnically oppositional reading of Palestinian–Jewish conflict by relying heavily on the evocative music and lyrics of the Hebrew song that Kazablan sings. This song is one of exile, but its evocative construction of Morocco is here retooled for another's exilic yearning. On the one hand, the sequence functions to reinhabit and reclaim a disappearing Jaffa on behalf of those displaced in the past and those threatened with displacement in the present (the very next shot is a slow vertical pan across a broken terrain that includes the detritus of buildings already destroyed). But it is also the song of the exilic and transnational filmmaker. Aljafari (2009) has referred to the *Kazablan* number as his song, too: "feeling displaced and missing home, that's my narrative!" In representing that narrative for himself, however, Aljafari nevertheless retains the Hebrew song and music from the original film, which are not mixed out until late in the sequence. Part of his intervention, then, is to allow the Hebrew language to serve as the narration for a Palestinian experience, in much the same way as Shammas, cited in the introduction to this chapter, did with his groundbreaking novel *Arabesques* (1988), written in Hebrew. Aljafari does so in full knowledge of the potentially controversial implications of that choice from the standpoint of Palestinians who regard Hebrew as the language of the occupier; yet, as he (2009) has said, "it's just a language; you can feel with that language," and his implicit recognition of the polyglot nature of Palestinians within Israel was confirmed for him at the film's première in Abu Dhabi where, he recounts, many Arab audience members commented on how emotional they felt at hearing the song and seeing the sequence. In this respect, it is significant, too, that the two women whose house is taken over for the film shoot are Christian. In one scene, we see the younger woman praying before a makeshift domestic shrine of candles and religious icons; in a second, disarmingly funny, sequence, we observe her and her mother watching a televised scene of Christ's baptism by John the Baptist, as their cat sprawls out on top of the VCR and TV, twitching when a dove appears as the Holy Spirit. *Port of Memory*, then, depicts Jaffa as a multiconfessional space whose conflicts are generated by historical and contemporary acts of colonization and not by the identifications of religion, ethnicity, or language.

If Aljafari's use of *Kazablan* perhaps offers the ghostly promise of a reclamation of fictional history toward recognition of actual Palestinian presence,[25] *Port of Memory*'s incorporation of a clip from *The Delta Force*, which introduces the film's final scenes, reminds us that Israel's cinematic and real occupation of Jaffa continues into the present. As we have seen, Salim's carefully shot and structured walks in Jaffa in this film and *The Roof* serve to remap the city as a site of continuous Palestinian habitation and history, recording built spaces that are at risk of destruction as well as those that have been transformed by years of use and reuse as the town is reinscribed with other histories and policies. As the *Kazablan* walk concludes and we return to its establishing shot of Salim looking out to sea, we cut to a long-shot of a hillside that has been razed and refigured as a kind of memorial park of picnic tables, a lookout, and flagpoles, its slopes punctuated by lonely streetlamps and empty roads. Following this bleak panorama, one that is tellingly reminiscent of the suspended space and "empty" shots at the end of Michelangelo Antonioni's *The Eclipse* (1962), we see Salim descending a flight of steps. We have seen the same street earlier in the film but this time, as Salim passes out of frame, there is a cut to a tighter framing of a street scene in which we recognize an almost completely identical architecture. Suddenly, a Volkswagen van careens down the steps with a jeep speeding after it, as if chasing Salim, as the sounds of automatic weapon fire and an offscreen helicopter accompany the screech of engines: *The Delta Force* has invaded Jaffa. Chuck Norris leans out of the van, firing back at his pursuers, and a gun battle continues in successive shots as the van speeds through the Jaffa streets. Aljafari's insertion has removed the implied diegetic location of Beirut from the mise-en-scène, placing the American film and its imagined street fight between US soldiers and "Arab terrorists" back into the Jaffa neighborhoods in which the production actually took place. The scene is brief, ending with a shot of a minaret that we have seen in the *Kazablan* sequence as well as earlier in *Port of Memory*, but the effect is to further stress the operation of a "force" of colonial image-making upon Jaffa. The full effects of such force are shown to the viewer shortly after, in one of the film's concluding and most disturbing images. In an extreme long-shot, the unnamed motor-scooter rider returns to the memorial park. As the camera cuts in closer, it isolates him at the top of the hill, sitting on his machine, laughing maniacally as the crab-like arm of a digger appears just over the crest of the hill; his face, the film suggests, is the face of an Israeli-colonized Jaffa (Figure 9.5).

Figure 9.5 The face of colonized Jaffa, in *Port of Memory* (dir. Kamal Aljafari, prod. Novel Media).

Conclusion

In this series of three films, Aljafari establishes himself as a Palestinian artist whose work is produced interstitially and financed transnationally through a wide variety of sources.[26] While his work, like that of many German filmmakers, has relied upon a mix of European funds, his own geographical mobility and the emergence of new Gulf film production funds have oriented him toward other sources, too. Aljafari's focus on predominantly Palestinian locations and narratives and his deployment of an aesthetic honed within a European art and film context situates him within a small stable of other Palestinian filmmakers working on "Palestine-in-Israel" from a position of exile (Shohat, 2010: 276; Alexander, 2005: 154). While one can historically situate Aljafari's emergence as a filmmaker within such a context, or even within the domain of interstitial accented filmmakers more generally, this chapter has argued that Aljafari's work is distinctive in its consistent focus on a spatial politics of home in Palestine/Israel, rendered in a style in which long-shots, minimal action, and an obsession with physical surfaces builds a highly political and poetic discourse even, or especially, in the absence of a declarative political rhetoric from the film's ambiguous characters. In so doing, if Aljafari approaches the goal signified by his own quotation of Adorno – in which cinema becomes a homeland for a people that has none – then it has been by reestablishing a Palestinian presence within the contingencies of colonial space as it is wrought by the Israeli state. His cinematic homeland is one which never carries the force of an easy or utopian nationalism and yet, in exploring the layers of the past, his films still offer the material for a possible future out of the rubble of the present. If one might risk a hopeful note in closing, it could be this: While the production history of Aljafari's *The Roof* shows the need for the filmmaker's vigilant resistance to the Eurocentric vision of Palestinians that his German producers wished to present, the recent success of *Port of Memory* in European festivals[27] might be one sign that his work is finding an audience that wants to see Palestine differently.

Notes

1   The author wishes to thank the filmmaker for his cooperation in the research for this chapter and the editors of the volume for their helpful comments.

2   Here I must register my own role in drawing the filmmaker into such networks: in 2008 I organized a panel on Palestinian cinema at the Society for Cinema Studies and Media Studies in Philadelphia, United States, and invited Aljafari as a panelist. Thanks in part to the work of one of this volume's editors, his work was also screened at the conference, generating considerable interest and library sales of his work. Aljafari received a Radcliffe Visiting Artists Fellowship at Harvard University for 2009–2010 and, at the time of writing, holds a position as a faculty member at the New School in New York City. Such occurrences function to provide further creative possibilities for the artist, while simultaneously producing him as a desirable commodity within a global terrain of academic and critical work and festival programming.

3   The eccentricity of filming a space with no apparent function was immediately evident to some Genevans who, during the shoot, expressed surprise that the filmmaker was concentrating on such a dirty and run-down space amid the beauty of the Swiss city.

4   I deploy the term here after LeVine's (2005: 350) discussion of Jaffa: LeVine borrows it from Holston's (1989: 5) discussion of modernist planning in Brasilia which involved a similar dynamic.

5   For more on Israel as a settler state, see the foundational work by Maxime Rodinson, *Israel: A Colonial-Settler State?* (1973), which argues that Israel's creation was characterized by the same logic of European occupation and domination of an indigenous population as other settler-colonial environments like Australia and New Zealand. The concept informs much of the recent post-Zionist work on Israel, such as Pappe's (2006), as well as some studies of cinema in Palestine/Israel, notably Shohat's *Israeli Cinema* (2010). For more on settler-colonial practices as they are rendered cinematically in the United States, Australian, and New Zealand settings, see Limbrick (2010).

6   The caged bird is a motif that appears in other films from or about Palestine and that features prominently in the titles of the Palestinian film, *A Caged Bird's Song* (Sobhi al-Zobaidi, 2003), about schoolchildren in Gaza and the West Bank, and the Iranian film, *Canary* (Javad Ardakani, 2002). Thanks to the editors of this volume for bringing these to my attention.

7   These events, of course, were not particular to Aljafari's family but were part of the *Nakba*, the "catastrophe" experienced by Arabs across Palestine at the founding of Israel in 1948. There is a substantial literature on this topic; see e.g. Masalha, 1992; Sa'di and Abu-Lughod, 2007; Haim Bresheeth's essay on cinematic depictions of the *Nakba* in Sa'di

and Abu-Lughod; or Pappe, 2006. For more details on the ethnic cleansing operations in Ramle and on the conflict in Jaffa and surrounding areas, see Pappe, 2006; Benvenisti, 2000; LeVine, 2005. Of the events also described by Aljafari's family, LeVine writes: "Fighting in Jaffa began in December 1947 and continued until the city's surrender on May 13, 1948, which followed the flight of all but 3,500 of the city's prewar Palestinian Arab population of 70,000" (LeVine, 2005: 215). Pappe (2006: 103) adds: "people were literally pushed into the sea when the crowds tried to board the far-too-small fishing boats that would take them to Gaza, while Jewish troops shot over their heads to hasten their expulsion. With the fall of Jaffa, the occupying Jewish forces had emptied and depopulated all the major cities and towns of Palestine. The vast majority of their inhabitants [...] never saw their cities again."

8 Jaffa is, according to LeVine (2005: 2), one of the oldest port towns in the world, and its long history as a connecting site between Arab and Ottoman societies and other parts of the Mediterranean was crucial to its cosmopolitan modern status before 1948. On Jaffa's importance to the region, see also Tamari, 2009. Its depopulation and surrender to Israeli forces in 1948 was a major moment in the war. Post-1948, the city has been eclipsed by Tel Aviv and now functions as the holder of traditional architecture and "heritage" beauty; Palestinian families remaining in the "old city" are under considerable pressure to leave in favor of developers and Jewish Israeli families.

9 See e.g. Monk (2002); Weizman (2007).

10 See Khalidi (1992).

11 My dates here are taken from LeVine (2005: 29–36), who constructs a detailed history of Jaffa focused mostly on the "modern" period from Napoleon to the present.

12 It is precisely this proximity and fluidity of movement between Levantine Arabs that Israeli leader David Ben-Gurion objected to when he argued, "We are duty bound to fight against the spirit of the Levant, which corrupts individuals and societies, and preserve the authentic Jewish values as they crystallized in the Diaspora" (Shohat, 2010: 106). Here Ben-Gurion reveals not only his contempt for Arabs, whether Jewish or not, but also (ironically) highlights how Zionism, despite its rhetoric about the restoration of a preexisting Jewish Israel, relied upon the colonial imposition of diasporic and European Jewish values onto the existing local terrain.

13 See Shohat (2010), and particularly her postscript, for a succinct discussion of the pressure exerted on official Zionist narratives by recent work in Israeli history and culture. See also Whitelam (1996); Sand (2009).

14 On the historical shift between certain versions of nationalism in Palestinian cinema and the treatment of nation and nationalism in recent Palestinian films, see the postscript to Shohat (2010: esp. 277, 287, 294).

15 Such a tendency, perhaps intensified in the present case by the moral obligation Germany has traditionally felt toward the state of Israel, is discussed by Randall Halle in his essay on transnational European art films. Halle (2010: 314) identifies in many transnational European productions a "dynamic of Orientalism" that "supports the production of stories about other peoples and places that it, the funding source, wants to hear. Under the guise of authentic images, the films establish a textual screen that prevents apprehension of the complexly lived reality of people in not-too-distant parts of the world."

16   For example, in the first year of its existence as a development and postproduction fund, Sanad, under the wing of the Abu Dhabi Film Festival, has provided a total of $US 500 000 in grants to Arab filmmakers including Syrian directors Omar Amiralay and Mohammad Malas, Lebanese filmmakers Khalil Joreige and Joanna Hadjithomas, and Algerian filmmaker Tariq Teguia, among many others. See http://www.abudhabi-filmfestival.ae/en/sanad/projects (accessed October 16, 2010). The phenomenon of transnationally mobile festival directors and curators at such festivals has also led to cooperative programming arrangements across Arab and US venues.

17   This question of polyphony, here as much a question of documentary and fictional voices overlapping and intersecting as of actual spoken languages, is also stressed in Shohat's postscript to her *Israeli Cinema* (2010: 263), in which she notes that contemporary Israeli and Palestinian films tend to use polyglossia or multiple languages as an integral part of their cinematic realism, in a rejection of the monocultural and monolingual Hebrew representations favored by earlier Israeli productions. We will return to this point later with respect to Aljafari's use of the film *Kazablan* (1974).

18   Most recently, Ajami was the setting for the Israeli film *Ajami* (2009), which partly sold its bleak vision of life in the neighborhood as the product of a rare and "daring" collaboration of an Israeli Jew and a Palestinian.

19   In one key scene, as we are introduced to Kazablan and his gang, one of his friends exposes the racist logic of the girl's father, Feldman, suggesting sarcastically that as a *schwartzer* ("nigger"), Kazablan is clearly not good enough for the man's daughter. For more on the racialized dimensions of the *bourekas* genre, see Shohat (2010).

20   On the preponderance of movies involving Arab terrorist characters, see Shaheen (2009).

21   In this regard it is worth noting that the film had the full support of the Ministry of Defense and the personal blessing of Yitzhak Rabin and Ariel Sharon (Shohat, 2010: 220), who, before their political careers, were two of the most storied and aggressive Israeli military commanders. Director Menachem Golan (who adopted his surname following Israel's annexation of the Golan Heights from Syria) began his Israeli film production career with his cousin, Yoram Globus (who, like Golan, went into filmmaking after military service), forming Noah Films in 1963 and making softcore porn and exploitation features. The two went on to take over Cannon, an American production house, turning it into a multinational and vertically integrated company that, by the time it made *The Delta Force*, owned significant European and British theater chains and had major interests in other entertainment businesses around the world (Stanbrook, 1986).

22   Freud (1919). See also Royle (2003).

23   See Shohat (1988) and Swirski (1989) on the historical aspects of the migration of Mizrahim to Israel and their social conditions upon arrival. These authors argue that the Mizrahi Jews were not typically Zionists (Zionism having emerged as a European response to oppression of Ashkenazim) and that their relationship to the new state after 1948 was fundamentally different from that of Ashkenazi Jews, who saw themselves as superior to all Arabs, Jewish or not.

24   *Port of Memory* was shot on super-16 mm film and blown up to 35 mm for release. Aljafari manipulated the *Kazablan* footage, as well as that of *The Delta Force*, so as to distinguish them more from the surrounding material. The effect, Aljafari has suggested (personal communication), might be read as a symptom of memory.

25 On this point is worth noting that Aljafari's intentions were formed in response to a comment by Jean-Luc Godard in *Notre musique* (2004): "In 1948, the Israelis wade into the water towards the Promised Land, the Palestinians wade into the water towards their drowning; shot, reverse-shot. The Jewish people encounter fiction while the Palestinians encounter documentary" (Aljafari, 2010; my translation). Aljafari's response in this film was to reposition Palestinians through fiction, in the process juxtaposing two historical narratives that would usually never meet. It is this (non-)meeting of fiction and reality, he suggests, that is one of the main preoccupations of his film.

26 While based in Germany, Aljafari also completed an installation project named *Album*, commissioned for the 2008 Home Works IV forum in Beirut by Ashkal Alwan: the Lebanese Association for Plastic Arts. The installation involved a two-channel display of still images of balconies in Ramle and Jaffa, shot from the street with an accompanying soundtrack of early morning location sound – birds, cars, sea. Very reminiscent of both *The Roof* and *Port of Memory* in its look, *Album* again uses images of pre-1948 architecture to suggest a narrative of occupation in the doubled senses of the word, evoking both domestic habitation and the forced evacuation and annexation of Palestinian homes by Israelis during and after 1948.

27 In 2010 *Port of Memory* won the Louis Marcorelles Prize at the Cinéma du Réel festival, under the auspices of the French Ministry of Foreign Affairs.

References

Adorno, T. (2005) *Minima Moralia: Reflections on a Damaged Life*. 1951 (trans. E.F.N. Jephcott), Verso, London.

Alexander, L. (2005) Is there a Palestinian cinema? the national and transnational in Palestinian film production, in *Palestine, Israel, and the Politics of Popular Culture* (eds R.L. Stein and T. Swedenburg), Duke University Press, Durham, NC, pp. 150–172.

Aljafari, K. (2008) A cinematic occupation: reality and fiction in Jaffa. Paper presented at the Society for Cinema and Media Studies, Philadelphia.

Aljafari, K. (2009) Unpublished interview with the author, November 21.

Aljafari, K. (2010) Entretien avec Kamal Aljafari. *Journal du réel* 2, http://blog.cinemadureel.org/2010/03/19/journal-du-reel-n°2-entretien-avec-kamal-aljafari/ (accessed June 9, 2010).

Al-Qattan, O. (2006) The challenges of Palestinian filmmaking (1990–2003), in *Dreams of a Nation: On Palestinian Cinema* (ed. H. Dabashi), Verso, London, pp. 110–130.

El-Asmar, F. (1975) *To Be an Arab in Israel*, Frances Pinter, London.

El Avram Group (1995) *Israeli Popular Hits*, Monitor Records, Israel.

Benvenisti, M. (2000) *Sacred Landscape: The Buried History of the Holy Land Since 1948*, University of California Press, Berkeley.

Bresheeth, H. (2007) The continuity of trauma and struggle: recent cinematic representations of the Nakba, in *Nakba: Palestine, 1948, and the Claims of Memory* (eds A.H. Sa'di and L. Abu-Lughod), Columbia University Press, New York, pp. 161–187.

Davidson, J.E. (1999) *Deterritorializing the New German Cinema*, University of Minnesota Press, Minneapolis.

Freud, S. (1919) The Uncanny, in *The Standard Edition of the Complete Psychological Works of Sigmund Freud*, vol. 17. 1953–1974 (trans. and ed. J. Strachey), Hogarth Press, London, pp. 217–256.

Galt, R. (2006) *The New European Cinema: Redrawing the Map*, Columbia University Press, New York.

Gordon, A. (2008) *Ghostly Matters: Haunting and the Sociological Imagination*, rev. edn, University of Minnesota Press, Minneapolis.

Hake, S. (2008) *German National Cinema*, 2nd edn, Routledge, New York.

Halle, R. (2008) *German Film after Germany: Toward a Transnational Aesthetic*, University of Illinois Press, Urbana and Chicago.

Halle, R. (2010) Offering tales they want to hear: transnational European film funding as neo-orientalism, in *Global Art Cinema: New Theories and Histories* (eds R. Galt and K. Schoonover), Oxford University Press, Oxford, pp. 303–319.

Holston, J. (1989) *The Modernist City: An Anthropological Critique of Brasilia*, University of Chicago Press, Chicago.

Jiryis, S. (1976) *The Arabs in Israel* (trans. I. Bushnaq), Monthly Review Press, New York.

Khalidi, W. (ed.) (1992) *All That Remains: The Palestinian Villages Occupied and Depopulated by Israel in 1948*, Institute for Palestine Studies, Washington, DC.

LeVine, M. (2005) *Overthrowing Geography: Jaffa, Tel Aviv, and the Struggle for Palestine, 1880–1948*, University of California Press, Berkeley.

Limbrick, P. (2010) *Making Settler Cinemas: Film and Colonial Encounters in the United States, Australia, and New Zealand*. Palgrave, New York.

Limbrick, P. (2011) From the interior, in *The Cinema of Me: The Self and Subjectivity in First Person Documentary Film* (ed. A. Lebow), Wallflower Press, London.

Masalha, N. (1992) *Expulsion of the Palestinians: The Concept of 'Transfer' in Zionist Political Thought, 1882–1948*, Institute for Palestine Studies, Washington, DC.

Mazawi, A. (n.d.) Film production and Jaffa's predicament. Unpublished paper, quoted in M. LeVine (2005) *Overthrowing Geography: Jaffa, Tel Aviv, and the Struggle for Palestine, 1880–1948*, University of California Press, Berkeley.

Monk, D.B. (2002) *An Aesthetic Occupation: The Immediacy of Architecture and the Palestine Conflict*, Duke University Press, Durham, NC.

Monterescu, D. (2007) Heteronomy: the cultural logic of urban space and sociality in Jaffa, in *Mixed Towns, Trapped Communities: Historical Narratives, Spatial Dynamics, Gender Relations and Cultural Encounters in Palestinian-Israeli Towns* (eds D. Monterescu and D. Rabinowitz), Ashgate, Aldershot, pp. 157–178.

Naficy, H. (2001) *An Accented Cinema: Exilic and Diasporic Filmmaking*, Princeton University Press, Princeton, NJ.

Nichols, B. (2001) *Introduction to Documentary*, Indiana University Press, Bloomington.

Pappe, I. (2006) *The Ethnic Cleansing of Palestine*, Oneworld, Oxford.

Renov, M. (2004) The subject in history. *The Subject of Documentary*, University of Minnesota Press, Minneapolis.

Rodinson, M. (1973) *Israel: A Colonial-Settler State?* (trans. D. Thorstad), Pathfinder, New York.

Royle, N. (2003) *The Uncanny*, Manchester University Press, Manchester.

Sa'di, A.H. and Abu-Lughod, L. (eds) (2007) *Nakba: Palestine, 1948, and the Claims of Memory*, Columbia University Press, New York.

Sand, S. (2009) *The Invention of the Jewish People* (trans. Y. Lotan), Verso, London.

Schindler, S.K. and Koepnick, L. (eds) (2007) *The Cosmopolitan Screen: German Cinema and the Global Imaginary, 1945 to the Present*, University of Michigan Press, Ann Arbor.

Shammas, A. (1988) *Arabesques* (trans. V. Eden), Harper & Row, New York.

Shammas, A. (2002) Autocartography: the case of Palestine, Michigan. *Palestine-Israel Journal of Politics, Economics, and Culture*, 9 (2), 111–119.

Shaheen, J.G. (2009) *Reel Bad Arabs: How Hollywood Vilifies a People*, rev. edn, Interlink, Northampton, MA.

Shohat, E. (1988) Sephardim in Israel: Zionism from the standpoint of its Jewish victims. *Social Text*, 19–20, 1–35.

Shohat, E. (2010) *Israeli Cinema: East/West and the Politics of Representation*, 1987, rev. edn, University of California Press, Berkeley.

Stanbrook, A. (1986) The boys from Tiberias. *Sight and Sound*, 55 (4), 234–238.

Swirski, S. (1989) *Israel: The Oriental Majority*, Zed, London.

Tamari, S. (2009) *Mountain against the Sea: Essays on Palestinian Society and Culture*, University of California Press, Berkeley.

Weizman, E. (2007) *Hollow Land: Israel's Architecture of Occupation*, Verso, London.

Whitelam, K.W. (1996) *The Invention of Ancient Israel: The Silencing of Palestinian History*, Routledge, London and New York.

Filmography

Ajami (Scandar Copti and Yaron Shani, Germany/Israel, 2009).

Album (Kamal Aljafari, 2008) (installation with two-channel video and sound).

Caged Bird's Song, A (Sobhi al-Zobaidi, Palestine, 2003).

Canary [Ghanari] (Javad Ardakani, Iran, 2002).

Chronicle of a Disappearance [Sijil 'Ikhtifa'] (Elia Suleiman, Palestine/Israel/USA/Germany/France, 1996).

Delta Force, The (Menahem Golan, USA/Israel, 1986).

Divine Intervention [Yadon, Ilaheyya] (Elia Suleiman, France/Morocco/Germany/Palestine, 2002).

Eclipse, The [L'eclisse] (Michelangelo Antonioni, Italy/France, 1962).

Hole, The [Dong] (Tsai Ming-Liang, Taiwan/France, 1998)

House [Bayit] (Amos Gitai, Israel, 1980).

In Working Progress (Alexandre Goetschmann and Guy Davidi, Israel/Palestine/Switzerland, 2006).

Kazablan (Menahem Golan, Israel, 1974).

London (Patrick Keiller, UK, 1994).

Notre musique [Our Music] (Jean-Luc Godard, France/Switzerland, 2004).

Port of Memory (Kamal Aljafari, Germany/France/UAE/Palestine, 2009).

Roof, The (Kamal Aljafari, Germany, 2006).

Stranger than Paradise (Jim Jarmusch, USA/West Germany, 1984).

Time that Remains, The (Elia Suleiman, UK/Italy/Belgium/France, 2009).

Visit Iraq (Kamal Aljafari, Germany, 2003).

Wedding in Galilee (Michel Khleifi, Belgium/France/UK/Germany, 1987).

10

Fatih Akın's Homecomings

Savaş Arslan

"From this point on, it is none of your business." At the end of the film, before they close the bedroom door, this is what the protagonists say as they turn their heads and address the camera in Halit Refiğ's 1964 film *Evcilik Oyunu* (Playing House). As indicated by this typical trope of high Yeşilçam (Turkish studio) films of the 1960s and 1970s,[1] films can present adventures beyond everyday reality which may be opened and closed through direct spectatorial address. Such protocol often belonged to lighthearted Yeşilçam melodramas, romantic comedies, or comedies. When Yeşilçam became realistic, however, its films often left this playful and traditional performative practice and employed bold statements about the dire conditions of the people, following the blueprint of realist cinemas of the West and attempting thereby to separate fiction from reality. Yet during such attempts, Yeşilçam films fell short of reproducing a vocabulary of Western realism, which often presented a clear-cut separation between the fictional and the real. Even the films of Yılmaz Güney, who, in his late career, was internationally acclaimed for social realist works, present various departures from realism and references to everyday reality. For instance, during the filming of his *Duvar* (The Wall, 1983) in France, Güney created a minor scandal in that country because "he sought realism by slapping and verbally abusing [the child actors] on the set so that their tears would look real" (Arslan, 2011: 14). In his action film *Canlı Hedef* (Live Target, 1970), one of the characters is named after his real-life daughter, from whom Güney was living apart and sending messages through his films (Arslan, 2011: 180–187). In other words, coupled with their technical and filmic deficiencies and the mistakes often resulting from low-budget filmmaking, Yeşilçam films featured various nonillusionistic and nonrealistic visual and narrative threads. Such departures from realism in Yeşilçam were a result of employing both a non-Western form of realism, which had its precursors in the performance tradition of Turkey, and of chronic low-budget

A Companion to German Cinema, First Edition. Edited by Terri Ginsberg and Andrea Mensch.
© 2012 Blackwell Publishing Ltd. Published 2012 by Blackwell Publishing Ltd.

production conditions. This may be seen as Yeşilçam's modality, which laid out a structure and/or language of filmmaking having different manifestations across Yeşilçam's various films (see Arslan, 2011: 80–83).

The new cinema of Turkey, on the other hand, is not only visually and narratively different from Yeşilçam, but also caters to a new spectatorial practice which is closer to the reception of Hollywood and contemporary global cinemas. In this respect, contemporary Turkish spectators, following a break in film-going during the late 1980s and the early 1990s,[2] are widely exposed to the illusionism of Hollywood and, in part, demand this also from domestic films. This is also especially the case for the younger generation of contemporary Turkish filmmakers who consumed Yeşilçam mainly through television and thus became distanced from it, at times developing an ironic attitude directed against Yeşilçam's failures of film language (e.g. continuity mistakes, low-budget techniques, poor special effects, etc.). In addition, many popular Turkish films are nowadays marketed according to the high percentage of their budgets spent on elaborate visual values and special effects. Given this kind of scenario, while there is a rift between the Yeşilçam and post-Yeşilçam periods,[3] crosscurrents and continuities nonetheless exist between the two.

One such association is locatable between Yeşilçam's often male-driven, social realist direction and its contemporary counterparts in the art-house or festival circuits. Similar to Güney's opening of the filmic world to the real one, especially through inscription or projection of their personal experiences, some post-Yeşilçam directors have also articulated personal elements, especially their masculine identities, into their films. The films of Çağan Irmak, Zeki Demirkubuz, and Nuri Bilge Ceylan often carry overt or figurative references to their directors' personal histories, not least through stories revolving around a central male character who experiences an identity crisis as he tries to cope with the changing conditions of contemporary Turkey (see Arslan, 2009).[4] These masculine melodramas, which focus on the unheard cries of their central male characters while marginalizing their central female characters, reflect contemporary changes in Turkey, which over the past two decades has begun to experience a dismantling of the mainstream statist ideology associated with Kemalism, and to move toward a more liberal, decentralized understanding of the Republic.[5]

An extension of such male-centered realist narratives of the new cinema of Turkey may also be found in transnational or migrant Turkish films. This chapter will discuss some of the films of Turkish-German director Fatih Akın and explore their connections to the cinema of Turkey: their occasional treatment of Yeşilçam tropes of nonillusionism and of the drama of central male characters with respect to their identities and bonds to fathers and homes. In so doing, I shall position Akın's cinema as a part of the (new) cinema of Turkey, and thus as not necessarily Turkish nor clearly definable by a strict national cinematic category, since the new cinema of Turkey includes Kurdish and transnational films often made in, and funded at least in part by Germany, as well as Turkey. Although the arguments I make below may be extended to other Akın films, here I will focus only on three: the realistic dramas *Short, Sharp, Shock* (*Kurz und Schmerzlos*, 1998), *Head-On* (*Gegen die Wand*, 2004), and *The Edge of Heaven* (*Auf der anderen Seite*, 2007). Regarding these films, I will analyze three main themes – the use of sound and music, the central male characters' identity-crises, and the figuration of home – by application of Jean-Luc Nancy's thesis on listening (a tension of straining toward a sharing of meaning and sense) and of Slavoj Žižek's reading of the Lacanian triad (the Real, the Imaginary, and the Symbolic) as these may help explain the films' knotting of the male characters' identities to an idea of a home.

It is possible to add to this list the realistic dramas *In July* (*Im Juli*, 2000) and *Solino* (2002), although their central male characters are neither Turkish nor of Turkish background, which, to an extent, makes it difficult to assume an authorial connection to the central male character. While I will not discuss them, then, both films do nonetheless fall under the reach of my argument on home and identification with it. Two other Akın films not treated here are the documentary *Crossing the Bridge: The Sound of Istanbul* (2005) and the comedy *Soul Kitchen* (2009), even though both of them also reflect aspects of my argument about sound, particularly its treatment by Yeşilçam. Put another way, the three films discussed in this chapter present us with a different form of authorship than the one which is recognized and promoted commonly in Western cinemas. As introduced in French cinema circles, auteur cinema is often related to an artist's individuality, personal expression or style. However, as I shall indicate, in both Yeşilçam and these three films of Akın, the incursion of a director's personality into the cinematic text takes on a distinct form. As noted, these films do not attempt to maintain a separation between the real and the fictional but instead are identifiable by their dissolution of this precise separation. That dissolution is also marked by the introduction of a specific trope: the main character's – and by extension the director's – pursuit of a home.

Unlike the earlier auteur cinema or the work of contemporary global auteurs, what defines this pursuit is a *juxtaposition* of the main character's personality with that of the director and his wishes. Hence this chapter proposes to see Akın's films in relation to a different strand of filmmaking, since they depart from the prevailing discourse of global and transnational authorship by inviting a *metaphorical* return to the home. This sense of a return is marked by a series of differences and separations. Instead of building bridges (a concept often fostered by scholars of transnational cinemas and cultures),[6] this chapter invites a reading of Akın's films in terms of their relation to and separation from the (Turkish) home culture. However, this particular relation to the home culture will not be seen through the rubric of multiculturalism, which takes Akın's films as serving a greater European Unionist ideology propagating the assimilation of the EU's others.[7] Instead I shall illustrate how Akın's films are indebted to a specific, non-Western modality of realism that is closer to the Turkish home culture than to that of the German host.[8] This is why, I shall argue, Akın's films project a relationality in which the separation from and return to home, rather than the bridging and intermingling of home and host, are at stake.

Yeşilçam filmmakers, and partly their contemporary heirs, do not necessarily blur the line intentionally between the filmic and the real. The various effects of nonillusionism or nonrealism produced by their films indicate Yeşilçam's cinematic backdrop in the performative and visual traditions of Turkey. One may speak, for instance, of the nonexistence of a proscenium in the theater-in-the-round, which allows for interaction between actors and audience through direct address, or one may refer to the nonexistence of linear perspective, hence coupled with a narrative realism that attempts to present more than what is visible in a given pictorial frame in miniature paintings. In addition, the aural-centered nature of traditional story-telling, also inherited and employed by Yeşilçam, is likewise critical. Very often Yeşilçam films did speak: the action which could have been presented solely in visual terms is also coupled with the actors' voices telling the spectator what is going on or what is being done. More importantly, during the long history of Yeşilçam – from the late 1940s to the late 1980s – almost all films made in Turkey were postsynchronized: films were shot silently and then frequently dubbed by professional dubbing artists who gave voice to the actors onscreen. Alongside its narrative structure, visual storytelling conventions, and acting techniques, Yeşilçam was an aural cinema for which listening to a film was also possible: Yeşilçam had an audience, more so than it had spectators. That is why one Yeşilçam scriptwriter, Bülent Oran, was able to claim, "Turkish spectators watch films with their ears" (quoted in Arslan, 2011: 121).

"What does *to be* listening, *to be* all ears, as one would say 'to be in the world,' mean? What does it mean to exist according to listening, for it and through it, what part of experience and truth is put into play?" asks Jean-Luc Nancy in his book *Listening* (2007: 5). By separating hearing from the other senses and knotting it to understanding or to the making sense of something, instead of to a "perceiving sense," Nancy places listening as "straining toward a possible meaning" (Nancy, 2007: 6). This sense of listening – what we listen to when we watch a Yeşilçam film that speaks – is that of a *pursuit* of meaning. Nancy ties this sense to a "mutual referral" between meaning and sound, whereby, during the act of listening and by one's presence in a space of sensing, a "self" is positioned "in a relationship *to* self, or of a presence *to* self" (2007: 8). In the act of listening, in other words, unlike that of watching, what is at stake is the sensing of another self who acknowledges one's self, in itself or in another self. Thus listening involves a movement in which one relates to one's self, and this movement entails a "straining toward or in an approach to the self." The act of listening is about a search, a pursuit of the other and of one's self. "When one is listening, one is on the lookout for a subject, some-thing (itself) that identifies *itself* by resonating from self to self, in itself and for itself, hence outside of itself ..." (2007: 9).

Fatih Akın's *Head-On* is also a film that can be watched with ears. It thus places the spectator into a critical relationship to his sense of subjectivity. The film opens in Istanbul with an Ottoman court music band performing a folk song that is not tied in any way to the filmic narrative. This moment recalls Yeşilçam's singer melodramas as well as Indian and Egyptian musical melodramas, all of which include song sequences not directly related to or integrated within the narrative's spatiotemporal setting. Instead such song sequences are nonillusionistic, and in turn serve to partition the film into distinct chapters. The lyrics of such songs also bear little if any direct relation to the filmic narrative; they seem to be there by mere coincidence – but they compel the spectator to listen to them by making him strain toward a meaning. More than simply inside jokes or ironic references to the history of cinema in Turkey, these song scenes indeed are in fact composed of a contemporarily altered form of Ottoman court music known as *fasıl*. Normally a *fasıl* is composed of separate movements, including an opening, a song sequence, and improvisations. The song scenes used in *Head-On* are indeed drawn from a *fasıl* – like performance by the band. The film is not only partitioned by these song scenes, but the musical performances themselves are also partitioned, and in a way that rings similar to Yeşilçam's tendency of laying out a basic pattern or ground on which the different performances float at different altitudes (see Arslan, 2011: 80–83). As they thus reiterate Yeşilçam's modality, the nondiegetic song scenes in *Head-On* disrupt narrative continuity; the music either starts before we see the *fasıl* band or continues once the band has disappeared. In other words, one may think of the songs as a part of the film's soundtrack, but then, what is to be made of the images of the band!

The nonillusionistic coming together of the visual and the aural in *Head-On* likewise opens up a rift between these two registers. Visually, the song scenes are picturesque, featuring contiguous red carpets on which the band is situated; in effect, a foreground is formed that seems clearly separated from the silhouette of the Süleymaniye Mosque and the Beyazıt Tower in the background. The song scenes are also relatively motionless, perhaps in order to position the spectator into the act of listening and away from that of gazing. Unlike the gaze, where the referral is between subject and object, the act of listening refers the subject to itself: "the visual is tendentially mimetic, and the sonorous tendentially methexic (that is, having to do with participation, sharing, or contagion)" (Nancy, 2007: 10). Thus for Nancy, along with forging a relation to the self as subject vis-à-vis other selves, listening bears a *"relationship in self "* by its status as tension, as a straining toward, knowing that the self is not present, not given, while presenting it before or with "the resonance of a return" (2007: 12–13). This sense of return indicates two acts: the movement of the self between itself and another self, hence in the end returning back to itself; and the acknowledgement of the other in the course of this return. At the end of *Head-On*, Sibel (Sibel Kekilli), who falls in love with Cahit (Birol Ünel) in Germany but upon her return to Turkey marries someone else, decides not to join Cahit. Cahit is left alone and feels foreign to Istanbul, so he takes a bus to his father's hometown. While on the bus, Cahit deliberately addresses the camera by looking into it; and as the bus moves, we hear the music of the *fasıl* band greeting the spectator with a concluding performance. Here again, two returns converge: Cahit's return of the audience's gaze; and the return of Cahit and the audience to their respective homes – if they are still there to be found. Even more at stake than these two senses of return is the intermingling of the visual and the aural, which forms a relationship, a referral that foregrounds the character's tension, particularly with respect to his return.

Similarly, in the final sequence of Fatih Akın's *Short, Sharp, Shock*, after the death of Serbian Bobby (Alexander Jovanović) and Greek Costa (Adam Bousdoukos), the Turk Gabriel (Mehmet Kurtuluş), who had always wanted to return to Turkey to escape his migrant life in Germany, meets German Alice (Regula Grauwiller). When Alice asks Gabriel whether he will go to Turkey, he nods his head in the affirmative. Then she asks whether he will return, and he says he is not sure. After they hug, Gabriel goes to his parent's apartment, where he finds his father (Mustafa Enver Akın) praying. The father at prayer does not see but instead hears Gabriel placing a gun in a drawer, then turns his head toward his son and says: "My son, let's pray together. As you know, like the films end, this life will also come to an end." As Gabriel's father starts speaking, a Sezen Aksu song containing lyrics by poet Metin Altıok becomes audible: "My body is cold, my heart hurts / Ah poplars, poplars … / With rough scissors / Ah, they carved me from an old picture. / Half of my cheek left there / Complements itself in nowhere."[9] Gabriel then starts praying with his father, but at that point the camera moves away from them and zooms in on a photograph of three friends: Gabriel, Costa, and Bobby.

These concluding scenes from two of Akın's films bring together the nonillusionism of Yeşilçam realism and the methexic character of Yeşilçam's aurality within the context of transnational or migrant films that may thus be positioned on the margins of the contemporary cinema of Turkey. In *Short, Sharp, Shock*, the father openly refers to the end of the film with his analogy of life to film, as if to say, "From this point on, it is none of your business" – because the film ends here and life starts (or is it vice versa?). After Gabriel enters the room, his father feels his presence without seeing him, in effect addressing him through hearing and thus sensing his presence by hearing. In a way, the religiosity of the father's presence is clear. In speaking of Yeşilçam, Nezih Erdoğan (2002: 243) associates this phenomenon with the uniform voice of a shadow-play master who in fact represents a sacred voice, that of Logos dictating the narrative and morality of these films. It may seem difficult to generalize Erdoğan's claim to all Yeşilçam films, yet the sense of voice of the father in *Short, Sharp, Shock* is actually augmented by the actors who play Gabriel's family: the real-life parents of director Akın. Much like Nuri Bilge Ceylan, who also employs family members as actors in his films, this kind of personal connection between the filmic and the real remains in concert with Yeşilçam, where the real-life names of actors are often used in films (as with Sibel in *Head-On*). However, while it is possible to link this practice to the concept of a shadow-play master who controls the diegetic space and introduces extradiegetic elements which dislocate cinematic illusionism by punctuating the filmic narrative, this sense of a penetrating directorial voice only approximates the idea of vocal and/or aural presence in the act of listening or hearing. In other words, we are not speaking of a dominant, omniscient voice which prescribes a hierarchical relationship between characters or interpretive layers. Instead, following Nancy, what is at stake in this scene is the methexic quality of the sonorous: "in semi-Lacanian terms, the visual is on the side of an imaginary capture (which does not imply that it is reduced to that), while the sonorous is on the side of a symbolic referral/*renvoi* (which does not imply that it exhausts its amplitude)" (Nancy, 2007: 10). It is in this sonorous time and space that the father knows what his son has done, as the father hears the sound of the gun being placed in the drawer and tells his son to redeem himself – a statement to which his son listens. And as Gabriel listens to his father and joins him in prayer, he finds himself in tension, marked as a "resonance of a return."

There are two different aspects to this return. The first has to do with a returning back to himself, a referring to himself in a tension and as an impossibility. The second has to with a returning (back) home. When Alice asks Gabriel whether he will go or stay and then, later, whether he will return, she speaks of another sense of home, insofar as Gabriel wants to return to his father's homeland which, at film's end, is also signaled by his return to his father's home in Germany, to the Law, symbolized in Lacanian terms by the name of the father. Similarly, in the opening scene of *The Edge of Heaven*, university professor Nejat Aksu (Baki Davrak) visits his father Ali's (Tuncel Kurtiz) hometown, to which he has moved after being released from prison. As Nejat stops at a gas station along the way, he hears a contemporary version of a folk song from the Black Sea region and asks the cashier about it. The cashier tells him about the singer. In effect, Nejat's return to his father's home is signaled by his estrangement from it. Yet as a return, it also signals his acceptance of the father's law. His uncertain alignment with this law is supported by the Abraham and the child of sacrifice story he relates to Susanne (Hanna Schygulla), who has come to Istanbul upon word that her daughter, Lotte (Patrycia Ziolkowska), has been murdered accidentally, and who is shocked by the sacrifice of animals she witnesses during the Muslim holiday of Eid al-Adha (Festival of Sacrifice). Nejat tells Susanne that when he was a kid, he always feared his father would sacrifice him. The possibility that this story might signal a detour, by which the guilt Nejat feels for his actions which may lead to his sacrifice might, recalling Deleuze,[10] be transferred at least partly back onto the father, is quickly abandoned, however, and the Freudian Oedipal story is restored: Nejat tells Susanne how he later came to recognize that his father always cared for and protected him.

One might propose that what surfaces during this play of the symbolic economy (especially regarding the father and his metonymic equivalent, the return home) is the Real, which registers beyond the Symbolic, being sensed as both present and absent, as always already there. After noting the need to set aside "the naïve ideological opposition between 'hard reality' and the 'world of dreams,'" Žižek notes not only that the real of our desire emerges in dreams, but also that everyday reality is "an illusion resting on a specific 'repression': on ignorance of the real of our desire" (Žižek, 1999: 21). For Žižek, the relationship of enjoyment to the later Lacanian concept of the Real is exemplified by Michel Chion's notion of *rendu*, a sonorous means of cinematic realism "which is opposed both to the (imaginary) simulacrum and the (symbolic) code." With the development of sound technology, films can amplify sounds which may not be audible to the human ear, whereupon the soundtracks of such films become "the primary frame of reference that orientates us in the depicted diegetic reality," in effect taking up the function of an establishing shot (Žižek, 1999: 25–26). This sense of *rendu* is apparent in the final scenes of two of the Akın films. In *The Edge of Heaven*, Nejat is filmed from behind as he sits on the beach of his father's hometown waiting for him to return from sea. As he stares at the sea, viewed only from behind, the sound of waves overtakes the scene before the final credits roll. In *Short, Sharp, Shock*, the scene opens with a shot of the father praying in the foreground, while Gabriel opens the drawer in the background. Subsequently a close-up of Gabriel placing the gun in the drawer is coupled with a reinforced sound of the gun hitting the surface of the drawer, even though the weapon is meant to be wrapped in a piece of cloth. Following Žižek, these moments are perfect metaphors for psychosis, for which "the Real is a lack, a hole in the middle of the symbolic order … an 'aquarium' of the Real encircling isolated islands of the Symbolic" (Žižek, 1999: 26).

This sense of the Real exceeding enjoyment likewise registers the symbolic order in other, older films. In *Lady in the Lake* (Robert Montgomery, 1947), a Hollywood *film noir* shot from the point-of-view of protagonist Philip Marlowe (Robert Montgomery), the objective shot is denied, making the spectator feel as though s/he were "imprisoned in a psychotic universe without symbolic openness" (Žižek, 1999: 27). However, this sense of *rendu* is only approximate, because it entails "the prohibition of something" (in this case, an objective shot) but not, as in the Akın films, of "something *that is already in itself inaccessible*" (e.g. the incest prohibition that founds the symbolic order) and thus indicative of "a second lack, the lack of a lack itself" (Žižek, 1999: 28). In the first sense, *rendu* signifies in its etymological sense; it is about giving back or returning *something*, for instance an objective reverse-shot or the sound of a gun hitting the wooden surface of a drawer, which serves to restore the symbolic order. It is not also about *renvoi* – a return to, or a referral of a tension marking the impossibility of returning (back) home.

According to Žižek, the later Lacan engages the entire network of communication with four discursive fields – the Master, the University, Hysteria, and the Analyst, all of which inscribe this second sense of lack, the constitutive absence of symbolic communication, and thus "a certain space in which signifiers find themselves in a state of 'free floating'" (Žižek, 1999: 29). The later Lacan presents us with this sense of signification and its enjoyment through the notion of "*le sinthome*: the point which functions as the ultimate support of the subject's consistency" (Žižek, 1999: 30). It is this sense of "the ex-sistence of the Real, of the Thing embodying impossible enjoyment," which remains separate from the Imaginary (fantasy) and the Symbolic (meaning) and marks the fundamental moment of psychoanalysis: *"identification with the sinthome"* (Žižek, 1999: 30). The *sinthome* represents the outermost limit of the psychoanalytic process. In *Short, Sharp, Shock*, the *sinthome* is the home, the free-floating signifier, the One which does not signify anything but *sheer* enjoyment, that is, "the Thing embodying impossible enjoyment," the impossibility of the Real in the symbolic order of the father – because it is Gabriel's father, and everything he is positioned to represent, which figures the home(land). In the film, before (the Greek) Costa is killed, Gabriel goes to a travel agency to buy a one-way airplane ticket to Turkey. However, the agent gives him a return ticket, claiming it is cheaper. Additionally, when answering Alice's question, Gabriel tells her he is not sure about returning. At the end of *Head-On*, Cahit makes an unanticipated journey to his Southern Turkish hometown, without being able to communicate well in Turkish, and without his lover, Sibel, in pursuit of whom he has ostensibly returned to Turkey in the first place. At the end of *The Edge of Heaven*, Nejat arrives in his hometown as a stranger, staring blankly toward the sea and awaiting his father, who perhaps will never arrive.

Again according to Žižek (1999: 30), the home may be fantasmatic, "the imaginary scenario which, with its fascinating presence, screens the lack in the Other, the radical inconsistency of the symbolic order," or it may be symptomatic, "the coded message in which the subject receives from the Other its own message in reverse form, the truth of its desire." When it surfaces in the Akın films as a fantasy, the home is lived in Germany; and when it is experienced as a symptom, it is Istanbul (as site of enjoyment), to which all three male characters (Gabriel, Cahit, and Nejat) first return. However, the home signified by the *sinthome* is neither fantasy nor symptom but "the point marking the dimensions of 'what is in the subject more than itself' and what it therefore 'loves more than itself' " (Žižek, 1999: 30). This home for Akın is nowhere to be found: Gabriel's home is unidentified; Cahit's is not yet arrived at, because at film's end, we leave him on the bus, en route; and Nejat's is *auf der anderen Seite* – on the other side, at the edge of heaven. Instead of a ludic, ritualized "acting out" ("a symbolic act, an act addressed to the great Other"), this other home is a "passage to the act," an identification with "the *sinthome*, the pathological 'tic' structuring the real kernel of our enjoyment" (Žižek, 1999: 33). It is the identification with the *sinthome* as home which is at stake in Akın's films. It is the knot that makes identification possible, yet it exists only *auf der anderen Seite*.

Notes

1   Yeşilçam ("green pine") is the name of a street in downtown Istanbul where the majority of production companies were headquartered, and refers to the popular film industry of Turkey that existed roughly from 1950 to 1990.
2   For a variety of reasons (including but not limited to the Hollywood majors' control of the Turkish domestic film distribution market, the rise of television, a new sociocultural

climate that arose after the 1980 military intervention, and the inclusion of a new generation of filmmakers and filmgoers), a new cinematic culture has emerged in Turkey since the 1990s.

3 The history of cinema may be bracketed into three broad eras: *pre-Yeşilçam* until the late 1940s, *Yeşilçam* between 1950 and 1990, and *post-Yeşilçam* since 1990. By placing Yeşilçam at the center of film history in Turkey, this periodization attempts to pinpoint changes in film production, distribution, and exhibition in Turkey (see Arslan, 2011).

4 Among such films are Çağan Irmak's *My Father and My Son* (*Babam ve Oğlum*, 2005), Zeki Demirkubuz's *The Confession* (*İtiraf*, 2001), and Nuri Bilge Ceylan's *Climates* (*İklimler*, 2006).

5 Turkey's move away from a statist economy and its integration into the global capitalism started as early as the 1980s. This process was accelerated during the 1990s, in particular through the dissolution of the Eastern bloc, the implementation of reform programs in Turkey meant to complete the country's bid for EU membership, and the rise of neoliberal globalization. These developments changed the shape and nature of the Turkish establishment, by limiting the strength of its isolationist, statist, and autocratic ideology.

6 For instance, a recent collection of conference proceedings edited by Steven D. Martinson and Renate A. Schulz is entitled *Transcultural German Studies: Building Bridges* (2008).

7 The first European Parliament Lux Prize, awarded to films addressing the issues of European integration, went to Akın's *The Edge of Heaven* in 2007.

8 Another article that deals with the notion of Akın's homecomings is Berghahn (2007), which ties the trope of home in Akın's films to the *Heimatfilm* genre of German cinema. Perhaps Berghahn's article, from which I have borrowed the rendering of "homecoming," may be thought of as the "other side" of an impossible homecoming.

9 While Metin Altıok is a well-known poet in Turkey, Sezen Aksu is often accepted as the diva of Turkish pop music. The translation is mine and the original Turkish lyrics are: *"Bedenim üşür, yüreğim sızlar. / Ah kavaklar, kavaklar… / Beni hoyrat bir makasla / Eski bir fotoğraftan oydular. / Orda kaldı yanağımın yarısı, / Kendini boşlukla tamamlar."*

10 In *Anti-Oedipus: Capitalism and Schizophrenia*, Deleuze and Guattari indicate that, unlike the Oedipal myth in which guilt is attributed to the son, the Abraham and Isaac myth permits one to question the actions and intentions of the father. In contrast to the usual accounts of psychiatrists, Deleuze and Guattari therefore address delirium and, in turn, guilt in "a field that is social, economic, political, cultural, racial and racist, pedagogical, and religious" (Deleuze and Guattari, 2003: 274).

References

Arslan, S. (2009) Venus in furs, Turks in purse: masochism in the New Cinema of Turkey, in *Cinema and Politics: Turkish Cinema and the New Europe* (ed. D. Bayrakdar), Cambridge Scholars, Newcastle, pp. 258–267.

Arslan, S. (2011) *Cinema in Turkey: A New Critical History*, Oxford University Press, Oxford, New York.

Berghahn, D. (2007) No place like home? Or impossible homecomings in the films of Fatih Akın. *New Cinemas: Journal of Contemporary Film*, 4 (3), 141–157.

Deleuze, G. and Guattari, F. (2003) *Anti-Oedipus: Capitalism and Schizophrenia*, 11th edn (trans. R. Hurley, M. Seem, and H.R. Lane), University of Minnesota Press, Minneapolis.

Erdoğan, N. (2002) Mute bodies, disembodied voices: notes on sound in Turkish popular cinema. *Screen*, 43 (3), 233–249.

Martinson, S.D. and Schulz, R.A. (eds) (2008) *Transcultural German Studies: Building Bridges*. Peter Lang, Bern.

Nancy, J-L. (2007) *Listening* (trans. C. Mandell), Fordham University Press, New York.

Žižek, S. (1999) The undergrowth of enjoyment: how popular culture can serve as an introduction to Lacan, in *The Žižek Reader* (eds E. Wright and E. Wright), Blackwell, Oxford, Malden, MA, pp. 11–36.

Filmography

Canlı Hedef [Live Target] (Yılmaz Güney, Turkey, 1970).

Climates [*İklimler*] (Nuri Bilge Ceylan, Turkey/France, 2006).

Confession, The [*Itiraf*] (Zeki Demirkubuz, Turkey, 2001).

Crossing the Bridge: The Sound of Istanbul (Fatih Akın, Germany/Turkey, 2005).

Duvar [The Wall] (Yılmaz Güney, Turkey, 1983).

Edge of Heaven, The [*Auf der anderen Seite*] (Fatih Akın, Germany/Turkey/Italy, 2007).

Evcilik Oyunu [Playing House] (Halit Refiğ, Turkey, 1964).

Head-On [*Gegen die Wand*] (Fatih Akın, Germany/Turkey, 2004).

In July [*Im Juli*] (Fatih Akın, Germany, 2000).

Lady in the Lake (Robert Montgomery, USA, 1947).

My Father and My Son [*Babam ve Oğlum*] (Çağan Irmak, Turkey, 2005).

Short, Sharp, Shock [*Kurz und Schmerzlos*] (Fatih Akın, Germany, 1998).

Solino (Fatih Akın, Germany, 2002).

Soul Kitchen (Fatih Akın, Germany, 2009).

11

Lessons in Liberation

Fassbinder's Whity at the Crossroads of Hollywood Melodrama and Blaxploitation[1]

Priscilla Layne

Introduction

There is a black mother. Her son says, I don't want you to sing those songs.
What songs? Black songs! The son is of mixed blood. Whity!

(Rainer Werner Fassbinder, Kardish, 1997: 91)

These lines could stem from one of many American narratives about the precarious position of the mulatto in a society dependent on the binary of whiteness and blackness. *Whity* (1970) is indeed told as an American story by German director Rainer Werner Fassbinder. Fassbinder's engagement with this topic reminds us that not only American society, but also German society, has historically forced citizens into a black and white dichotomy.[2] Despite the erasure of the term race (*Rasse*) from the public discourse after World War Two (Tissberger, 2006: 92–93), racialization continued to have very real effects in Germany. Afro-German children born to black GIs and white German mothers in the postwar period were constantly confronted with the perceived boundary between black and white.[3] Among several proposals to deal with the "race problem" posed by so-called *"Mischlingskinder,"* some German child welfare offices sought potential African American adoptive parents for Afro-German children, several of whom ended up in orphanages (Fehrenbach, 2005). Popular opinion in the German public was that an Afro-German child was inherently African and could not thrive in a German environment. This message was famously packaged for a German audience in R.A. Stemmle's melodrama *Toxi* (1952). However, despite the national rhetoric, many mothers of Afro-Germans kept their children and in the 1960s and early 1970s, a generation of Afro-Germans came into adulthood.[4] When Fassbinder

A Companion to German Cinema, First Edition. Edited by Terri Ginsberg and Andrea Mensch.
© 2012 Blackwell Publishing Ltd. Published 2012 by Blackwell Publishing Ltd.

approached the topic of the mulatto of American slavery, he took an American story of racism and revealed it to be a German story.

Such efforts at drawing transatlantic connections between American and German culture in respect to the African Diaspora are ongoing. Recently, I attended the reading of a play still in revision by Jackie Sibblies.[5] Sibblies' play, *We are Proud to Present a Presentation about the Herero of Namibia, Formerly Known as South-West Africa, From the German Sudwestafrika, Between the Years 1884–1915*, is a metatheatrical piece: five American actors struggle to put together a performance based on letters written by a German soldier who participated in the genocide of the Herero. In a scene where two German soldiers round up Herero men and put them in concentration camps, the white actors' accents suddenly metamorphose into a Southern twang. Unexpectedly, the Herero man running from German soldiers becomes a black slave running from an American lynch mob. There is historical evidence for this transatlantic link. In her analysis of the German reception of Harriet Beecher Stowe's *Uncle Tom's Cabin* (1852), Heike Paul (2009: 141) argues that the idealization of this novel in nineteenth-century Germany can be read as a "projective justification of German colonial intentions." In fact, prior to the genocide of the Herero, German travelogues from America suggested an annihilation of Blacks as an answer to America's "African problem" (Paul, 2009: 141–142). What the characters in Sibblies' play approached as a single historical moment in distant Africa is revealed to be a common history shared on both sides of the Atlantic; the German story becomes an American story.

Both Sibblies' play and Paul's analysis of *Uncle Tom's Cabin* are examples of cultural mobility. In *Cultural Mobility: A Manifesto*, Stephen Greenblatt proposes that although cultures tend to hide the mobility that drives them, it is important to investigate specific moments of cultural exchange in order to understand what constitutes cultural identities, how these identities persist over long periods of time and what forces might disrupt them. Americans recognize their history of slavery, but associate genocide with Nazi Germany's crimes during the Holocaust. Germans acknowledge Nazi Germany's genocide, but view slavery as an alien institution that existed in America. And most average Germans are unaware of the reality of the country's colonial past. Sibblies' play disrupts these separate cultural identities and reveals transatlantic commonalities between the two countries – indicting both in the persecution and forced diaspora of African people.

Fassbinder's Least Successful Film

This chapter attempts to reveal the same significance of cultural mobility in Fassbinder's film *Whity*. *Whity* is often considered a mere exercise in melodrama. Fassbinder's most famous tribute to this genre was *The Marriage of Maria Braun* (*Die Ehe der Maria Braun*, 1979). *Maria Braun*, the first in his BRD-trilogy, fits comfortably within Fassbinder's oeuvre which mostly consists of films that are read as allegories for West German history. Many of his films are very domestic, set in the postwar era in German cities like Munich and Berlin. Bearing this in mind, *Whity* stands out as an anomaly, for it is set in the nineteenth century in the American Western frontier and its protagonists are not Germans, but American planters, cowboys and a mulatto servant. In order to simulate the American West, *Whity* was shot in Spain and was therefore the first film Fassbinder shot outside of Munich (Thomsen, 1997: 77). *Whity* was also Fassbinder's least successful film at the box office. Herbert Spaich describes *Whity* as

> commercially one of the most catastrophic infractions in Fassbinder's career [...] The film was booed at the Berlinale in 1971. No distributor could be found for Fassbinder's until then most expensive production (680 000 Mark). Even ARD and ZDF were not interested. Only in the early 1980s did the private television station Pro 7 broadcast the film. (1992: 138) [6]

A short synopsis of the film reads as follows:

> Somewhere in the American West in 1878 in a large house that is more like a mausoleum than a home, lives the Nicholson family. It includes Ben, the domineering patriarch; Katherine, his second wife, a nymphomaniac; and his sons by his first wife, Frank, a homosexual, and Davy, who is mentally retarded. Serving and being abused by the family is a young black man, Whity, Ben's illegitimate son who wants to belong. (*Rainer Werner Fassbinder Werkschau*, 1992: 18)

Although this description offers background to the story, the plot that drives the film is key to understanding any analysis. Ben distrusts his young wife Kate and arranges for Garcia to pass himself off as a doctor and tell Kate that Ben is dying. Suspicious of Kate's love for him, Ben is curious about her reaction to the news. After Garcia informs Ben that Kate was not only happy about the news but also slept with the "doctor," Ben shoots Garcia and claims that he was avenging Kate's "rape." Hanna, a prostitute and songstress at the saloon, corroborates Ben's statement for a bribe and he escapes any punishment. Even though the family is under the impression that Ben is dying, their greed for the inheritance leads to a string of murder plots. Frank asks Whity to kill Ben. Kate asks Whity to kill Frank. And the normally obedient Whity hesitates about killing anyone.

Because of its unusual time and setting, past critics have disassociated *Whity* from Fassbinder's other films. Thomas Elsaesser (1993: 273) states "nothing at first sight could be further from an allegory of the political events of the day than WHITY." Peter Jansen and Wolfram Schütte (1992: 135) share this viewpoint: "The past films all intended, or were interpreted as intending, to say something about the society of the Federal Republic [of Germany], even if it was in an estranged form. With WHITY, Fassbinder associates himself with Hollywood for the first time and with Hollywood's most despised genre, the melodrama."

Because the film ends with Whity shooting the entire Nicholson family and fleeing to the desert with Hanna where they die of thirst, Christian Braad Thomsen reads *Whity*'s rebellion and death as a critique of terrorism and therefore a predecessor to Fassbinder's later films on the subject, *Germany in Autumn* (*Deutschland im Herbst*, 1977) and *The Third Generation* (*Die dritte Generation*, 1979). Meanwhile, Elsaesser (1993: 323) reconciles *Whity* with Fassbinder's oeuvre by stressing the film's focus "on the group knit tightly by mutual hatred." Fassbinder himself described filming *Whity* as an experiment; an opportunity to allow his antitheater group to view itself from an outside perspective (Spaich, 1992: 138).

While I do not disagree with either Thomsen or Elsaesser's readings of the film, I would like to expand *Whity*'s relevance beyond Germany by investigating it as a moment of cultural mobility.[7] My guiding question in this chapter is to what extent the performance of race in *Whity* is informed by "black cultural traffic"[8] to Germany. For the purpose of this chapter, I consider black cultural traffic the movement of African Americans, the circulation of cultural products like music, films and literature by or about African Americans and the portrayal of African Americans in the media from Hollywood films to news reports.

When one considers its portrayals of race, *Whity* appears to be at the crossroads of two American trends in the film industry: the Hollywood melodrama and Blaxploitation. Fassbinder admits to the influence of Hollywood on *Whity* by citing Raoul Walsh's Civil War melodrama *Band of Angels* (1957). However *Whity* seems to diverge from this more classical portrayal of slavery. Around the same time that Fassbinder portrayed the oppression and liberation of an African American protagonist, African American directors were doing the same with Blaxploitation films. Black liberation had been of interest to the German student movement since the 1960s. Furthermore, the Black Power movement influenced the violence of the students' more radical wing, including the emerging left-wing terrorist group the Rote Armee Fraktion (Red Army Faction). I believe *Whity* can be considered an example of the Blaxploitation genre in Germany. In order to prove this point, I will first consider the film's historical context and then look at how *Whity*'s portrayals of race differ from Hollywood melodramas. Finally, I will explore the similarities between *Whity* and Melvin van Peebles's Blaxploitation "ghetto Western" *Sweet Sweetback's Badaasssss Song* (1970). I do not argue that Fassbinder's film contributes to the struggle of racial Others. Rather, I agree with Katrin Sieg (2009: 154), who reads leftist German artists' portrayals of the Other as "less about minority advocacy than it is about antifascist writers' search for a revolutionary subject at precisely those historical moments when that revolutionary subject, whether constituted as the working class or as women, seemed more divided and resistant to intellectuals' administrations than ever." My aim is to show how Black cultural traffic influences Fassbinder's portrayal of an African American revolutionary subject and to insist that discussions of Blaxploitation films are opened up to include transnational examples.

The Historical Moment

One first wonders why Fassbinder would film a Western set in the 1800s. Germans have been interested in the Western genre since the nineteenth century, as is most evident in Karl May's popular *Winnetou* novels. Much like these novels, early Western films functioned as an escape from modernity and a means to cushion the shock of modernity through dealing with the past (Verhoeff, 2006). In early German films, fears of modernity were often displaced to the American West (Göktürk, 1998). The Western taught viewers to accept "a beneficial sacrifice of unrestrained masculine individualism in the interests of civilisation, law and culture" (Mulvey, 1989: 40). Following World War Two, Westerns continued to be popular in West Germany, demonstrated by the successful Technicolor film adaptations of May's novels shot in Yugoslavia. In the 1960s alone, over ten Winnetou films were made. The Karl May adaptations were so popular that in order to appease the demands for these Western European co-productions, East Germany also created several Socialist Westerns.

Whity is by no means a classical Hollywood Western, rather it is a good example of Fassbinder's ability to, in Gerd Gemünden's (1994: 56) words, "combine or reconcile Hollywood's formulas of recognition and identification with distancing techniques in order to preserve a space for social critique."[9] One of the Brechtian techniques apparent in *Whity* is its unusual time and setting. The story's location in the American West sets up parallels between American slavery and contemporary West German discrimination against and exploitation of racial Others. At the same time, the foreign setting allows enough distance between the story and the audience for social critique. Secondly, despite the diegetic location in America, the characters all speak German which adds to the story's artificiality. Additionally, Hanna the prostitute's occasional camp performances of English songs interrupt the action and add a further layer of estrangement and artifice. Finally, the performances of race, especially Marpessa's blackface which I will explore later, point to the distinction between the actor and the role. All of these strategies of alienation make the audience aware that they are "watching a performed reality" (Gemünden, 1994: 63–64) and these techniques challenge the construction of race and the hierarchies of power established in the world of the film.

Wallace Steadman Watson (1996: 86) suggests Fassbinder plays with the Western genre and presents characters that are "caricatures of American Western types." Other critics liken *Whity* to an Italian "Spaghetti" Western, not only because it was shot on the set of Sergio Leone's *Once Upon a Time in the West* (1968), but also because of its "emotive music and exaggeratedly slow pace" (Thomsen, 1997: 77). In the 1960s and 1970s, with the Western losing popularity in the United States, European-made Westerns catered to the market. The most popular thereof were the Spaghetti Westerns which enjoyed much success in Germany. Spaghetti Westerns typically broke genre conventions: filmmakers could ignore the censorship laws of the United States, they introduced morally ambiguous heroes, intensified violence and occasionally featured explicit homoeroticism and masochism.

Interesting trends in both European and American Westerns of the 1960s and 1970s were a focus on race and criticism of hegemonic white culture. For example in the 1967 film *Hombre* directed by Martin Ritt, Paul Newman plays a white man who is raised by Apache Indians and is referred to by other whites as "Red Skin" because he has adopted the ways of Apache culture and rejected his own – a parallel to *Whity*. According to Georg Seeßlen and Claudius Weil, these political Westerns of the 1960s

> did not adhere to the optimism of integration, like the films of the 50s, rather they adhered to the optimism of change and solidarity with other racial minorities, whose idealism and humanity could break the brutality of the greedy Yankee hegemony ... the hero is the bi-racial one, the voluntary "Indian," the Mexican and the negro who recognizes possible allies in the fight for emancipation. (1979: 175)

An important influence on this trend in the Western was the global student movement of the 1960s. For young people critical of capitalism, imperialism and individualism, the loner hero of the Western was less appealing than collective heroes. And when there was an outcast, s/he could no longer believably be integrated into society which had been common for the classical Western. When one considers these new trends in the Western as well as Fassbinder's interest in genre and marginal characters, it is understandable that he would choose an African American protagonist for his first attempt at a Western. One must, however, consider what images of African Americans existed in Germany at the time that might have influenced Fassbinder's portrayal of an African American on the screen.

In the postwar era, Germans' ideas of African Americans were not only informed by Afro-Germans and black GIs, but also by knowledge of the Civil Rights Movement and the Black Panther Party. Black culture such as Soul music and the Afro-look were popular with students who sympathized with minorities' struggles around the world. These youth were commonly not only interested in black culture but a variety of foreign cultural products, including Spaghetti Westerns (Ege, 2007: 116–117). Some students even saw themselves as the "Negroes" of German society because they were discriminated against based on their countercultural appearance. A few students attempted to organize with black students and GIs in Germany. When the Sozialistischer Deutscher Studentenbund (Socialist German Student Union or SDS) fragmented, its more radical wing viewed the Black Panthers and the concept of the urban guerilla as a model to follow.

Afro-Germans and black GIs were not the only population that counted as "Others." Since the 1950s, guest workers, whose social standing led journalist Ernst Klee (1984) to characterize them as the "niggers of Europe," came from Portugal, Spain, Greece, Italy, Yugoslavia, and Turkey. Germans initially assumed guest workers would stay temporarily and animosity toward them grew as increasing numbers opted to remain in Germany with their families. Fassbinder addressed racism and discrimination toward guest workers in the film *Katzelmacher* (1969) where Fassbinder himself plays a Greek guest worker and in *Ali: Fear Eats the Soul* (*Angst essen Seele auf*, 1974) – a love story between an older German widow and a Moroccan guest worker.

Hollywood and Fassbinder's "Deep South Melodrama"

One of Fassbinder's inspirations for filming *Whity* was *Band of Angels* which he referred to as "one of the loveliest films I've ever seen" (Thomsen, 1979: 82). Ed Guerrero categorizes *Band of Angels* as belonging to the second phase of the Hollywood plantation melodrama – a subgenre of the melodrama which romantically portrayed the antebellum South as a utopian fantasy to which white Americans wished to return. In contrast to the first wave which consisted of films like *Birth of a Nation* (1915) and *Gone with the Wind* (1939), *Band of Angels* was shot when "Hollywood's plantation mythology underwent a period of significant revision that softened some of the genre's supremacist assumptions about slavery" (Guerrero, 1993: 10). At the time, Hollywood began paying more attention to black protest against negative stereotypes in films because Blacks needed to be convinced of their important role in America and their duty to fight overseas in World War Two.

The film's main protagonist is Amantha Starr, daughter of a plantation owner. When Amantha's father passes away, she discovers that her deceased mother was one of his black slaves and she is therefore not a legitimate heir to her father's inheritance, but one of his slaves. Amantha is forcefully brought to Louisiana to be sold. At a slave auction she is bought by Hamish Bond, played by Clark Gable. Although Amantha initially shuns Hamish, when he saves her from a deadly thunderstorm she falls in love with him. Like Amantha's deceased father, Hamish is kind to his slaves. Hamish's mulatto housekeeper Michelle insists that the bars on the estate's windows are there to keep the outside world out, and not her in. And Hamish's black servant Dollie refers to his plantation as a paradise retreat from the city – "the land of honey."[10]

Although *Band of Angels* belongs to the second wave of plantation melodrama, it is still guilty of reproducing racial stereotypes from older films. Rather than condemn slavery, the film seeks to redeem the good white man. This is evident in the romance between Hamish and Amantha, and in the story of Sidney Poitier's character Rau-Rau. In contrast to most of Hamish's adoring slaves, Rau-Rau despises Hamish because he recognizes that it is precisely Hamish's kindness that keeps the slaves in their bonds. After Rau-Rau joins the Union soldiers, he encounters Hamish on the run and intends to turn him in. However, when Hamish reveals the story of how he saved Rau-Rau from a brutal African king while he was a baby, Rau-Rau forgives his slave trading past. Rau-Rau eventually helps Hamish escape and be reunited with Amantha. Hamish proclaims about Rau-Rau's actions, "I guess he thought he couldn't be free until I was," thus reversing Hegel's master–slave dialectic; instead of the master having to acknowledge his slave's freedom in order to be free, the slave must ensure his master's freedom in order to be free.

When Fassbinder expresses his adoration for Walsh's film, in the same interview he describes his own films as stories about people who are oppressed and unhappy but do not have the courage to or know any better to live differently. In contrast, *Band of Angels* shows oppressed people who are happy and are incapable of living better. *Band of Angels* implies that inequality and segregation are not necessarily wrong as opposed to an extremist kind of racism; an argument which Germans learned over a century ago from Stowe's novel. Both Amantha's father and Hamish Bond are portrayed as the good white master. The film's underlying argument is that freedom will only make the slaves lazy, while under the paternal care of kind whites they had structure and a good life, even if they were denied subjectivity; like the female slaves who enjoy sexual relations, what historically was most often rape (Hartman, 1997), with their white masters.

Fassbinder's relocation of Walsh's plantation melodrama to the West is unusual but not inaccurate. There were small numbers of slaves, especially domestic servants, in the Western frontier (Savage, 1998). In fact, setting *Whity* in the West challenges Hollywood's misleading portrayal of racism as existing solely in the South (Guerrero, 1993: 18). Yet the film's time frame, 1878, is 13 years after slavery was abolished. Despite Fassbinder's historical inaccuracies, there *were* scenes in the script of other slaves working in fields on the Nicholson estate, which Fassbinder eventually chose not to film (Thomsen, 1997: 77). Thus Whity and his mother Marpessa are meant to be slaves and we can examine the differences between the portrayal of slavery in *Band of Angels* and *Whity*.

Although Fassbinder speaks fondly of *Band of Angels*, he turns much of Walsh's film on its head. First of all, Walsh's film opens with establishing shots that help the audience locate the film's setting in the South, in Kentucky's flourishing bluegrass fields. Such idyllic scenes of pastoral prosperity would not fit in a Western. In fact, one of the historical obstacles against the Western expansion of slavery was the environment – cotton crops could not survive in the conditions (Savage, 1998). *Whity* does not even begin with an establishing shot of the West, rather it begins with a green screen followed by the credits appearing over a medium close-up of Whity lying seemingly lifeless face-down in the dirt. In Brechtian fashion, this unusual opening eliminates all suspense; for Whity's disembodied voice is heard singing lyrics that foretell the film's violent ending. Here, music is used to break the connection between the devoted slave and the white master, in contrast to how slave spirituals are used in Hollywood plantation melodramas. This opening and *Whity*'s Western setting convey a pessimistic tone. The film's setting suggests that the protagonists' relationships and futures are as dead and dried out as the landscape – a dire message compared to the optimism reflected in the decadent plantation estates of Hollywood films.

What is also missing from *Whity* are panning shots of happily waving slaves or even slaves working in fields. Most of the action is limited to constraining, interior spaces like the Nicholson estate, Hanna's room and the saloon. Because Fassbinder forgoes establishing shots of the Nicholson plantation he goes against the classic Western's tradition of conveying freedom in its wide open spaces. Instead, Fassbinder stresses the feeling of being trapped, employing Brechtian distancing techniques by framing Whity within the frame using a window or a door as he longingly looks in on the other characters.

Despite its similar Technicolor and Cinemascope grandeur, compared to *Band of Angels*, *Whity* is shrouded in grotesque images. As Spaich (1992: 146) suggests, "Fassbinder takes the rituals [of the Western] and the sentiment implied in the genre and exaggerates them into the realm of the grotesque: the protagonists, caricatures of human existence, are made up like clowns. Günther Kaufmann is at times reminiscent of Al Jolson." Spaich's comparison of the film's characters to clowns refers to their makeup. The black cook Marpessa is played by actress Elaine Baker in blackface. The Nicholsons also wear makeup that is white with a green tint, making them appear undead, which recalls Fassbinder's comparison of their estate to a mausoleum. Due to their unusual complexion, the Nicholsons' whiteness seems just as constructed as Marpessa's blackness. Their green tint and unnaturally white eyebrows and eyelashes, which Fassbinder had bleached, challenge the belief that there is such a thing as a pure white complexion. Fassbinder's exaggeration of the racial difference between Marpessa and the Nicholsons is perhaps best read as what Sieg calls "ethnic drag." In Sieg's reading of *Katzelmacher*, she argues that Fassbinder's self-portrayal of the foreigner combines an adaptation of the critical *Volksstück* with elements of Brechtian theater. According to Sieg (2009: 155), by blatantly drawing attention to the racial Other through masquerade, Fassbinder stresses the "disjunction of social role and racial essence" and "denounce[s] the process of detecting and pronouncing racial difference in the body of the Other as a violent, collective process."

One of the black stereotypes in *Band of Angels* is the black mammy – a stock figure in plantation melodramas – a jovial, round woman with a grinning face who likens the iconic Aunt Jemima. In contrast, Marpessa does not convey the same warm feelings of maternal, domestic security. She typically has her eyes and mouth open wide, in a look of grotesque surprise. Her black makeup is much darker compared to Kaufmann's natural complexion (Figure 11.1). When we first encounter Marpessa, artificial light from behind and above causes her face to appear so dark, that when her head is down while working, the shadow of her large afro wig adds an additional layer of black completely erasing her facial features, further eliminating her subjectivity. She is not wearing the quintessential Mammy's headscarf, perhaps so that the abnormal nature of her afro wig is even more exaggerated. When Marpessa leans to the right, the large collar of her dress

Figure 11.1 Marpessa and Whity in the kitchen, in *Whity* (dir. R.W. Fassbinder, prod. Anti-teater-X-Film).

reveals a small spot on her body where the dark makeup was not applied evenly and one sees that her skin color is merely a disguise. Part of her makeup is also rubbed off during a struggle with Frank.

By blackening up Elaine Baker and pointing to the farce of her appearance, Fassbinder stresses Marpessa's difference. This disjunction between the actress and the role foregrounds the constructed nature of race and allows for multiple layers of performance. In *Toxi*, childhood actress Elfie Fiegert's biography of being an Afro-German orphan was subsumed with the role she was playing, suggesting something especially authentic about her performance (Fenner, 2009). In contrast, Elaine Baker's blackface performance not only severs the tie between actress and role, but allows for the possibility that Marpessa is also performing – and even undermining – a certain stereotype of blackness. Blackface might also be useful for the diegesis because it is important that Marpessa is darker than Whity in order to exaggerate his dilemma as a "tragic mulatto." In Douglas Sirk's melodrama about "passing," *Imitation of Life* (1959), the black mother Annie is shockingly darker than her mulatto daughter Sarah Jane, which makes it difficult for the other characters to believe the two are related, therefore increasing the melodramatic tension. Exaggerating Marpessa's blackness conforms to this tradition while simultaneously indicting a German audience for their essentialist ideas of black people as having a certain skin tone in order to be authentically black. Unlike her mulatto son, Marpessa is "really" black and must therefore have visibly darker skin. For this reason, Fassbinder could not darken Kaufmann's appearance and instead he stresses Whity's difference by exposing the actor's body in a voyeuristic manner.

In the film's opening scene, Marpessa is in the kitchen preparing food, cutting off the head of a fish. Traditionally the kitchen should be a space of domestic innocence, but Marpessa's appearance and her work are far from comforting.

The camera frames her from the waist to the neck, focusing on her hands and cutting off her head. This medium close-up of her hands has several functions; it focuses on her labor (something one rarely sees in *Band of Angels*) and devalues her individuality suggesting that for the family she is merely a pair of laboring hands. Furthermore, by cutting off her head equivalence is made between Marpessa and the fish she is butchering. This equivalence between the confined Marpessa and the animals she prepares for the family continues, when the camera pans left and tilts up to reveal a chicken hanging in a cage. With this visual language, Fassbinder addresses the inhumanity of racist living and working conditions. This comparison recalls a scene in Austro-Hungarian director Géza von Radványi's *Uncle Tom's Cabin* (*Onkel Toms Hütte*, 1965) when, during the slave revolt, the master's mulatto mistress burns down the house, but makes sure to free the caged birds first. By substituting the more common figure of the happily smiling mammy with a grotesque black cook who is clearly distressed by her situation, Fassbinder never tries to suggest that there was anything pleasant about slavery. The onscreen sound, what appears to be the buzzing of a fly, supports the scene's dark tone. The presence of flies in the kitchen helps negate any warm feeling of domesticity. The sound of flies also suggests that both the meat and the inhabitants of the house are decaying.

While working, Marpessa starts singing "Glory, Glory Hallelujah." Her singing references plantation melodramas which typically included slave spirituals. Performances of slave spirituals, especially by black actors, were meant to give the films more authenticity. These songs were portrayed as entertainment for whites and a way to make the slaves' labor more enjoyable. Although Marpessa begins singing "The Battle Hymn of the Republic," she ends with the song "When the Saints Go Marching In." It is possible that Fassbinder was not aware that these were two different songs. However, his use of blackface clearly invokes the tradition of minstrelsy that began in the nineteenth century in the United States and also became popular in Europe. Perhaps combining the two songs is an intentional attempt at inauthenticity; further revealing the constructed nature of race.

Spaich's comparison of Afro-German Günther Kaufmann's performance to that of Al Jolson in *The Jazz Singer* (1927) is a comment on Whity's exaggeratedly submissive behavior which appears more like a caricature of blackness than a realistic portrayal. This points to another difference from *Band of Angels*; in *Whity* there is no pleasant white master and yet, Whity thanks his master for the whippings all the same. This adds an element of masochism to the film and exaggerates Whity's role as the melodramatic hero whose suffering is a testament to his virtue. Whity's deadpan expressions of gratitude for his abuse seem absurd. While *Band of Angels* does not ask us to question the slaves' happiness, *Whity* does. Fassbinder has said of oppressive relationships, "to enjoy pain is always cleverer than simply to suffer it. That goes for all minorities" (Thomsen, 1979: 94). Whity has perhaps learned to accept his punishment as a means of survival.

Dissecting Whity's Character

Thomsen (1997: 76) describes Whity as "the ideal slave type to such a degree that he hardly sees himself as oppressed. He thinks his status is natural and just and makes it a point of honour to satisfy his masters." Traditionally, in American literature and film there were not many roles for Blacks to choose from. The roles available included obedient "toms," comedic "coons," "tragic mulattos" and violent "bucks" (Donald Bogle, quoted in Pieterse, 1992: 152). Whity's behavior resonates with the "Uncle Tom" – a term which stems from Stowe's novel. According to the Oxford English Dictionary, the term "Uncle Tom" is "used allusively for a Black man who is submissively loyal or servile to White men" (OED). As is apparent from this term, Stowe's novel had a dramatic effect on how African Americans were viewed in Europe. Prior to the book's publication, former slaves like Frederick Douglass had already been traveling through Europe and telling their life stories. After Stowe's novel was published, such ambassadors for the black American experience found it difficult to stress their reality compared to her portrayal of Blacks as "dependent, long-suffering, and in need of paternalism" (Elam and Jackson, 2008: 1–3).

Stowe's novel is a well-known cultural reference in Germany that replaced earlier accounts of modern free Blacks in the North with a simplified image of the obedient, child-like black slave. "The cultural mobility of Stowe's novel in the mid-nineteenth century thus – instead of adding complexity and flexibility to the German perception of African Americans – reduces the popular image of black people in America to a single, highly generalized and – above all – static stereotype" (Paul, 2009: 135). References to Stowe's novel can be found throughout German culture. At the beginning of the 1900s there was a beer garden in Berlin named *Onkel Toms Hütte* which would lend its name to the subway station built in 1929 along with an *Onkel Toms Strasse* (Paul, 2009: 138). I already mentioned the film adaptation by von Radványi. The term was also used in Germany by both black GIs and Germans (Ege, 2007: 108, 114). And finally, when Barack Obama won the election for US president in 2008, the left-wing German newspaper *Die Tageszeitung* printed a picture of the White House on the front page with the title "Onkel Baracks Hütte."

Whity demonstrates his submissive nature and devotion to his white masters during the opening scene, when he enters the kitchen to inform Marpessa that the Nicholsons are not happy with her food. The mother and son have the following exchange:

WHITY: They don't like it.
MARPESSA: There's a lot they don't like.
WHITY: I believe you've misunderstood me. I want them to like everything.[11]

After this brief exchange, Whity addresses his mother's singing with the reproach I quoted earlier from Fassbinder's notes, "You shouldn't always sing these songs ... black songs," to which Marpessa responds by spitting in his face and cursing him with "Whity" – his degrading nickname (his real name is Samuel). Fassbinder perhaps chose the nickname "Whity" after having encountered its use, most often spelled "whitey," in leftist student circles. For example, in a flyer written by the SDS in 1968 as an attempt to get black GIs to join their demonstration, German students expressed understanding if Blacks were reluctant to go to demonstrations organized by "whities." The word "whitey" had been suggested by William Van Deburg as a derogatory term black revolutionaries could use against Whites (Ege, 2007: 104, 123).

In the film, the nickname "Whity" refers to both the character's internalized racism and his innocence, represented in a light suit he wears whenever he leaves the estate. Whity's naiveté and internalized racism explain his initial lack of resistance to his situation. Whity is the typical melodramatic hero who does "not fully grasp the forces [he is] up against" (Mulvey, 1989: 41). When Hanna implores him to escape from his servitude and go East to Chicago with her, he adamantly declines and insists that he is content in his current state.

Aside from his similarity to an "Uncle Tom," Whity's character is also based on the "tragic mulatto." In American literature and film, the mulatto was described as "tragic" because s/he was seen as being trapped between two worlds – not entirely black nor white. According to the "one-drop rule," which has dominated American discussions about race since 1915, "a person is black if she has a black forebear, and that forebear was black if she had a black forebear, and so on" (Zack, 1993: 19). There are many fictional and nonfictional accounts of African Americans who attempted to "pass" as white. This was popular subject matter for Hollywood melodramas like *Band of Angels* and *Imitation of Life*. The resolution of this conflict of *Schein* vs. *Sein* can differ. In *Band of Angels*, Amantha and Hamish presumably leave the United States for a place where the former slave master and slave can be together irrespective of race. At the conclusion of *Imitation of Life*, the light-skinned Sarah Jane is finally accepted into the white community after her dark-skinned mother passes away. Just as in *Band of Angels*, the funeral is used as a setting for the mulatto's confrontation with his/her racial identity; as if either the black or white self were being buried.

Thus, the mulatto is considered tragic not only because s/he is "trapped" between two identities, but in order to successfully join the white community – a rare occurrence – s/he must kill the black identity. Unlike Amantha and Sarah Jane, however, Whity makes no attempt to pass as white. Amantha believes her claim to the Starr family name should secure her status and keep her from being treated like other Blacks. In contrast, Whity denies himself the name Nicholson. His rejection of the Nicholson name could be a further expression of internalized racism and an act of submission: regardless of who his father is, he is black. Read positively, Whity's refusal to perform whiteness further stresses the performance aspect of his blackness.

Whity's position as an American mulatto is what makes him so different from the other ethnic minorities in Fassbinder's films. The Othered characters in *Katzelmacher*,

Ali: Fear Eats the Soul and *The Marriage of Maria Braun* are Others-from-Without – a Greek and Moroccan guest worker and African American GIs respectively.[12] These Others are never *really* familiar to the Germans in the films nor are they accepted as belonging to the German community. Whity, however, is an Other-from-Within. He is the slave who, in Richard Middleton's words (2006: 31), is "within the social system, and even the blood … a native-born slave, the subject-other within the household itself." Whity's mulatto identity is at the center of his melodramatic state. His presence is a constant reminder of Ben's desire for the black body, a desire which contradicts white superiority. Whity's performances of blackness and servitude relieve this tension by supporting the ruse of white superiority.

Blaxploitation: A Bad Ass Come to Collect Some Dues

Whity may start out as obedient as Poitier's character Rau-Rau in *Band of Angels*, but Whity eventually carries out the rebellion Rau-Rau only considers. Fassbinder's resistance to Poitier's role as the submissive, harmless black man is the first link between *Whity* and the Blaxploitation genre. Guerrero (1993: 69) describes Blaxploitation films as a genre "which arises from the film industry's targeting the black audience with a specific product line of cheaply made, black-cast films shaped with the 'exploitation' strategies Hollywood routinely uses to make the majority of its films." Several factors contributed to the wave of Blaxploitation films created in the late 1960s and early 1970s: the growing political consciousness in the black community influenced by the Civil Rights Movement, Hollywood's near bankruptcy due to a declining and fragmented audience and its subsequent desire to capitalize on black audiences and the black community's backlash to the harmless, sexless black males portrayed by Poitier. Critics of Poitier felt his characters were "castrated" and "completely devoid of mature characterization or of any political or social reality" (Guerrero, 1993: 72).

Guerrero considers Van Peebles's *Sweet Sweetback* as part of Blaxploitation's peak – a film that helped provide the formula for the genre. Blaxploitation films allowed African Americans the fantasy that one could fight "the Man" and win. Burly, hypersexual and suave black heroes gave black men *and* women a feeling of confidence and power which Hollywood films prior to that could not have achieved. These films also allowed for many more African Americans to find work in the film industry, whether as directors and screenwriters or working on the set. That there was not such a movement in Germany likely has to do with the relatively smaller black community in Germany at the time; and the fact that the few Afro-Germans present would not be recognized as a community for at least another decade.[13] Despite the lack of a large Afro-German audience to push for changes in the portrayals of Blacks in German film, I believe *Whity* puts forth a more complex and less essentialist portrayal of Blacks on the German screen.

There are several interesting parallels between *Sweet Sweetback* and *Whity*. In both films, blackness and queer sexuality are closely intertwined – Sweetback performs in queer, interracial sex acts for a live audience; Whity has several intimate encounters with men and women. These queer black protagonists violently rebel against their white oppressors and must go on the run. And both Sweetback and Whity's journeys end in the desert. Yet, there are two significant differences to consider. Sweetback's single act of revolt happens near the beginning of the film and leads to a string of episodes: close escapes and negotiations with other characters to ensure his safety. He escapes in the end, which feeds black viewers' fantasies of successfully resisting oppression. In *Whity*, however, the rebellion is not the cause, but the result of all the other incidents and Whity does not survive his flight. Thus, just as in several of Brecht's works, it is not the act of violence, but the reasons leading up to it that are foregrounded.

Sweet Sweetback and *Whity* were shot within a very close timespan. Although the script for *Sweet Sweetback* was finished in March 1970, shooting did not take place until May and June of the same year. Fassbinder's *Whity*, on the other hand, was shot during April 1970, sandwiched in between the writing and shooting of *Sweet Sweetback*. It is entirely possible that Melvin van Peebles knew Fassbinder at the time or was at least familiar with his work. Van Peebles was married to the German actress Maria Marx prior to filming *Sweet Sweetback* and he had worked in Europe for a time. His film about racial discrimination in the US army, *The Story of a Three Day Pass* (1968), is considered one of the first Blaxploitation films and was shot in France. Van Peebles's familiarity with German *Sprachgesang* and his creation of a short film for German television suggest that he had experience working in Germany as a filmmaker as well (James, 1995: 1, 7). As far as Fassbinder's familiarity with Blaxploitation films, at least one early Blaxploitation film premiered in West Germany before *Whity* was filmed – Gordon Flemyng's *The Split* (1968) screened in March 1969.

A further link between *Whity* and *Sweet Sweetback* is the importance of sexuality. Sweetback a.k.a. Leroy is a sex worker in a brothel. The film opens with a troubling scene where young Sweetback, played by Van Peebles's son Mario, gets his nickname while being seduced/raped by a black female prostitute. After the opening credits, one sees a now adult Sweetback performing in an interracial, queer sex show at the same brothel. And when Sweetback is on the run from police, he often uses sex as a means for survival.

The purpose of Sweetback's hypersexualized nature is contended. Van Peebles admits attempting to cut production costs by marketing *Sweet Sweetback* as a pornographic film. This could partly explain the numerous sex scenes, which Van Peebles insists were not staged. However, critics have also suggested that Sweetback's sexuality was conceived to counter Poitier's "castrated" characters with a character for whom sex is power. Many young black men identified with Sweetback positively and it became fashionable to refer to men who were especially successful with women as "Sweetbacks" (Guerrero, 1993: 105).

Actually, the term "sweetback" had already existed in the black community prior to Van Peebles's film. Steven Knadler (2002: 900) describes the sweetback as "a much more ambiguously gendered and sexualized hustler, whom the 'younger generation' of Bohemian artists fashioned into their own 'subcultural epistemology.'" Knadler suggests that the sweetback character was used by some male writers of the Harlem Renaissance who linked sexual deviance with race consciousness and wished to "counter white supremacist theories of the black man's emasculation" not with hypersexualized characters but with a "queer black male body that is ... 'politically volatile' precisely because its desires are unpredictable and in excess of the normative discourses of race and heterosexuality" (2002: 900). By naming his protagonist Sweetback, Van Peebles might have also been drawing on this link between radical politics, race and queer sexuality in order to make his protagonist even more dynamic.

Like Sweetback, Whity also draws power from his sexuality. As opposed to the other Nicholsons who all appear sickly, Whity is quite vital. The fact that he wears a red suit while in the estate stresses this vitality and his potential for rebellion. As a slave, Whity's source of power is that the Nicholsons not only depend on his labor and his loyalty (confiding in him with their darkest secrets), but they are also unable to resist his sexual appeal; an appeal that can be attributed to his muscular physique, exoticness and submissive nature. Whity exemplifies the paradox of the black male slave who generates competing fantasies in the white imaginary of power (because he is enslaved) and submission (because he is the hypersexual Other). On separate occasions, Whity has intimate encounters with Kate and both of his brothers. In each of these encounters, the Nicholsons might come on to Whity, but he is always the one who determines how far these interactions go. He even walks out on Frank who corners him wearing ladies underwear.

By far the most suggestive sexual scene does not take place between Whity and his lover Hanna, toward whom he is surprisingly passive, but between Whity and his father Ben. In a scene I would like to examine more closely, Ben initially whips Davy for spying on his parents during sex. Whity interrupts the beating, offering himself up to be whipped in Davy's place. Ben agrees to Whity's request and tells him to get undressed, after which Whity takes off his shirt. This is one of several times Whity's naked torso is displayed. In a later scene in Hanna's room, he lies on her bed in an open shirt and holds out a handful of money, propositioning her for sex. Instead of focusing in on the money or the female at whom desire is typically directed, the camera pans 180 degrees revealing a medium close-up of Whity's face and naked torso. The fact that this is shot without cuts makes the pace of the scene especially slow and draws attention to the voyeur's desire to consume the black male. The cover of *Uncle Tom's Cabin* (Figure 11.2) also exemplifies this desire to see the naked abused body of the slave. It features the backside of a black man's nude muscular body as he stands with his hands chained behind his back. Depicted from behind, the black man becomes a faceless sexual object.

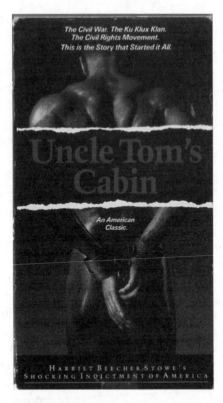

The Civil War. The Ku Klux Klan.
The Civil Rights Movement.
This is the Story that Started it All.

Uncle Tom's
Cabin

An American
Classic.

HARRIET BEECHER STOWE'S
SHOCKING INDICTMENT OF AMERICA

Figure 11.2 Cover of the VHS of *Uncle Tom's Cabin (Onkel Toms Hütte)*, from *Uncle Tom's Cabin* (dir. Géza von Radványi, prod. Avala Film).

As Whity gets undressed, Ben plays with the whip – a phallic symbol which is also carried by one of the cowboys, played by Fassbinder. During the whipping scene, the camera frames Ben and Whity from a low frontal angle (Figure 11.3). Because of this camera angle, Ben appears behind Whity and off to the left and only their torsos are visible. The fact that Whity is topless and one cannot see his lower body makes this appear to be a sexual act. When Ben whips Whity in Davy's place, the whipping stands in for the sexual intercourse that the impotent Ben is unable to perform in bed. While his wife fails to arouse him, Ben clearly gets pleasure from beating Whity. During the beating he yells, "Scream Whity, scream" and he only stops once Whity lets out one final scream suggestive of a climax. Ben concludes the act with a patronizing comment about his performance which likens pillow talk between two lovers: "That was pretty good huh, Whity."

Although Whity is beaten in this scene, he still exhibits a certain amount of strength. He chooses when and where he is beaten. He can take the blows without being tied down like Davy was. And just as in the scene with Hanna, Whity *allows* Ben, and Kate and Frank who are spying from the balcony, to receive pleasure from

Figure 11.3   Ben whips Whity, in *Whity* (dir. R.W. Fassbinder, prod. Anti-teater-X-Film).

this exhibition of his body. His control of his sexual allure is a large part of his power for it counters white supremacist ideology. During American slavery, sexual control was typically used to reproduce enslavement and racial subordination (Hartman, 1997: 84). As an erotic act, whipping Whity allows Ben to enact his sexual attraction to blackness, while also beating black male sexuality into submission and therefore stifling the castration threat.

If black male audiences derived a sense of empowerment and positive identification from Sweetback's many sex scenes, what kind of enjoyment would a white German audience derive from these scenes of submission and subjection? Because slaves in America were considered property, they were unable to consent to or resist (sexual) violence (Hartman, 1997: 81). Their lack of agency combined with the myth of the hypersexual Black meant that slaves were considered "always willing." According to Saidiya Hartman (1997: 8), the "simulation of agency and the enactment of willful submission" was a typical occurrence.

However, Whity does not just consent to the whipping, he requests it. Thus, this scene perhaps relieves white viewers of the guilt of objectifying the black body. More specifically, this scene could enact Fassbinder's own fantasy. In his autobiography, Kaufmann claims Fassbinder's motivation for shooting *Whity* was his attraction to the actor. According to Kaufmann, Fassbinder booked a hotel room for them to share and he had to get Fassbinder drunk each night so that he could avoid the director's advances (Kaufmann and Droste, 2004: 126). Having Whity consent to his own subjection might have entertained Fassbinder's hopes of winning Kaufmann's affections. After all, in their relationship Fassbinder was the one in power. He had the ability to promote or stifle Kaufmann's acting career.[14] In fact, Kaufmann's slighted teenage ambitions of becoming an entertainer likely made him more vulnerable to Fassbinder's promises of stardom.[15] Although Kaufmann denies there was ever a physical relationship between them, some scholars insist the two were lovers (Thomsen, 1997; Watson, 1996).[16]

Aside from the voyeuristic scenes discussed earlier, there are other instances when Whity's sexuality is emphasized in a way that reproduces negative stereotypes about black men. Whity's incestuous relationships with his father and brothers recall Freud's claims in *Totem und Tabu* that so-called "primitive" people are more prone to incest. And in two of the intimate encounters between Whity and his brothers occur in the horse stable. In both scenes, his brothers touch the horse in the mise-en-scène either as a substitute for or an initiation to touching Whity. Thus, his equivalence with the horse suggests something animalistic about Whity. I believe there is tension between Fassbinder's personal desire for Kaufmann and his attempt to portray sexuality during slavery in a way that critiques racism. It was radical of Fassbinder to diverge from portrayals of the willing black woman and the violent black male rapist in classical Hollywood films by foregoing heterosexual sex scenes and instead implying sex between the master and the *male* slave. Queering the white master undermines the power of the dominant patriarchal and heteronormative narrative. Yet, the voyeuristic scenes of Whity's half-naked body and his consent to his subjection seem to fulfill white fantasies about the "always willing" black other.

Oppressed Victim or Blaxploitation Antihero?

While Spaich compares Whity's obedient behavior to minstrelsy, I would argue that Fassbinder's portrayal of Whity is more sophisticated and resonates with Blaxploitation films. Hollywood films like *Band of Angels* offered the kind slave master as an explanation for the slaves' complacent behavior. Blaxploitation films, however, made it explicit that the black man allows himself to be used by whites because he has been conditioned to accept it and knows no other way. For example, Eithne Quinn (2010: 97) refers to a scene in *Superfly* (1972) to exemplify the same "self-conscious internalization of racial inequality" that we see in *Whity*: "'That honky's using me,' he [Eddie] says of their white drug wholesaler. 'So what? You know, I'm glad he's using me ... People been using me all my life.'"

In the aforementioned interview with Thomsen (1979: 93), Fassbinder states "relationships between people are always sado-masochistic as a direct result of their upbringing." Fassbinder portrays Whity as someone who has convinced himself that he deserves his oppression which allows him to take pleasure in it as a kind of survival tactic. Compared to *Band of Angels*, with *Whity* we progress from the black subject in Hollywood films who is happy *and* unaware of his/her oppression (Amantha) to a black subject who has taught him- or herself to accept the oppression (Whity). While *Whity* does reproduce common black stereotypes from American literature and film, such as the "Uncle Tom" and the "tragic mulatto," at some point the film departs from the tradition of *containing* blackness, to liberating it as in Blaxploitation films.

Sweetback's rebellion transpires one night, when the owner of the brothel lends him out to a pair of white LA police officers. The policemen intend to feign their attempts to counter black-on-black crime by bringing in Sweetback as a "captured perpetrator." On the way to the station, the police pick up a Black Panther, Mu-Mu, whom they beat up in an alley. While the policemen are beating Mu-Mu, Sweetback suddenly intervenes, saving Mu-Mu's life and beating the policemen.

Like Sweetback, Whity exhibits a similar sudden change in behavior – a spark of violent resistance. Prior to his execution of the Nicholsons, Whity is in Hanna's room, where she tries one last time to convince him to run away with her. She tells Whity about Ben's murder of Garcia and then gives him the bribe money as proof. During this scene, Whity stands timidly in the corner with his hands folded and his eyes cast down. Hanna then grabs him and kisses him forcefully, demanding that he "Kill them. Kill all of them. You have to free yourself from them. You're a human being, too." Her overdramatic plea is an example of the exaggerated moral registers found throughout the film. Immediately following this scene, Whity enters the saloon by descending the stairs from Hanna's room. Previously, Whity always entered her room from the outside, scaling the side of the building. Now Whity has the confidence to not only be open about his relationship with Hanna, but confront the cowboy played by Fassbinder who beat him up earlier.

When Whity descends from Hanna's room into the bar, it is as if the money and his knowledge about Ben's murder give him an additional source of strength and masculinity. When Whity first entered the saloon toward the beginning of the film, he was not only beaten up and thrown out of the bar, but he did not put up any resistance during the struggle and the scene ends with him lying face-down in front of the saloon in his light suit. In contrast to the weakness he exhibited during the beating, when Whity enters the saloon from Hanna's room, he stops on the stairs and defiantly returns the patrons' stares. He then walks to the bar and drinks half a bottle of whisky. Like the shot of Whity on Hanna's bed, this was also filmed without any cuts, exaggeratedly slowing down the action and embellishing his feat. As soon as Whity pulls out his money and demonstrates his masculinity by drinking the whiskey, he is accepted at once. With his money and newly exhibited strength, the white cowboys who denied him access to their group earlier are now happy to include Whity in their card game.

The acceptance Whity gets in the saloon is not, however, based on real change, but money and the performance of masculinity. Just because the cowboys invite Whity to join their game does not mean their racist views have changed. Whity's contentment with the group shows he is only concerned with his own integration and not a revolution – a parallel to Jorgos in *Katzelmacher* who is eventually accepted by the German group of friends only to leave town because he does not want to work with a Turk. According to Linda Williams (Williams, 2001: 35), the American melodrama "offers hope … that it may not be too late, that there may still be an original locus of virtue, and that this virtue and truth can be achieved in private individuals and individual acts." In such a traditional melodrama, Whity's violence and subsequent death in the desert could be read as Hegel's slave choosing death over servitude – making him a martyr. However, Fassbinder's message is that neither Whity's sole integration nor his rebellion and subsequent death can really change anything. Fassbinder has said of the film, "In reality, the whole film is directed against the Negro ... In the end, he may shoot the people who oppressed him, but afterwards he goes into the desert where he dies ... if he had really thought about his actions, he would have showed solidarity with other oppressed peoples" (Fischer, 2004: 223). Whity's killing of his family is a personal act of revenge rather than a challenge to racism in the larger society. This might explain why Whity only wears his red suit in the Nicholson estate – his potential for rebellion is confined to the domestic realm.

In his analysis of *Sweet Sweetback*, Robert Reid-Pharr (2007: 165) accuses Sweetback of this same individualism. Reid-Pharr refers to the scene when Sweetback saves Mu-Mu. Afterward Mu-Mu asks, "Where are we going?" to which Sweetback merely responds "Where you get that *we* shit?" Reid-Pharr argues that Sweetback not only runs from white violence:

> what Sweetback also runs from, what he also fears, is the equally real, equally palpable reality of the Black American's culpability, his lack of innocence. As this brief sketch of Van Peebles's own filmography is meant to suggest, the difficulty faced by the midcentury Black American intellectual was the recognition that, the power of the erotic being what it is, supposed black and white combatants might indeed have become so intimate by the early 1970s that it was difficult, if not impossible, to see where black innocence began and white guilt ended.

Sweetback's sudden act of resistance might have helped Mu-Mu at that moment, but it does not erase the fact that Sweetback had never had a problem with catering to the "Man" before. As the "Negro in revolt," Sweetback is not free from scrutiny. For example, by committing acts of violence against black women during his flight, he upholds the master narrative of patriarchy. As Reid-Pharr (2007: 151) suggests, rather than just the oppressed black man, he is revealed to be a culpable agent of oppression: "the hegemonic works in both directions, from top to bottom, bottom to top." Sweetback spends the rest of the film running from this truth, trying to reclaim his innocence.

A similar argument could be made for Whity. Prior to his rebellion Whity learns that Ben is guilty of an unjust murder. But it is not a sudden realization of Ben's false morality which leads to Whity's change in behavior. Rather, Whity's rebellion is motivated by the money Hanna gives him. This money enables him integration into the group of cowboys and like Sweetback, Whity is revealed to be not an innocent victim, but a willing participant in the very system that oppresses him. Whity's rebellion is as individualist as Sweetback's flight. Whity not only does not seek out other oppressed people, according to Thomsen (1997: 77), the scenes deleted from the script show Whity together with other slaves who are working in the fields. He despises their revolutionary songs when he rides over the fields with his white masters and uses his whip on members of his own race if they're not working fast enough. Over the oppressed, Whity can enjoy to the full the sweetness of power and experience his own worth.

The song Whity sings at the end of the film, while he dances with Hanna in the desert, demonstrates that he has not reached any profound conclusions about race, nor thought about countering racism on a larger scale. In English, he repeats a song Hanna sung earlier: "It doesn't go together. Your way of life and mine … Goodbye, my love, goodbye." Whity succumbs to the same separatist racist ideals he internalized throughout the film. Concluding that there is no place for him and Hanna to be together, he capitulates, settling for death with his loved one.

Conclusion

As this chapter has argued, a connection can be made between 1968 European filmmakers' critical engagement with Hollywood and the Blaxploitation genre. In their portrayals of race, Fassbinder and Van Peebles were both working with and against the same stereotypes from Hollywood melodrama: the Uncle Tom, the violent buck or "anti-Tom," the tragic mulatto and the mammy, among others. Both directors had the goal of liberating black characters from these confining, degrading images. In 1967, French filmmaker Jean-Luc Godard said filmmakers "should try to provoke two or three Vietnams in the bosom of the vast Hollywood-Cinecittà-Mosfilm-Pinewood etcetera empire, and, both economically and aesthetically, struggling on two fronts as it were, create cinemas which are national, free, brotherly, comradely and bonded in friendship" (Godard, quoted in Mulvey, 1989: 22–23). Fassbinder and Van Peebles's resistance to Hollywood's racial stereotypes accomplishes such cinema.

Both Hollywood plantation dramas and Blaxploitation films commonly used melodrama to evoke either sympathy for the white woman or the black slave to make a moral argument (Williams, 2001). *Sweet Sweetback* and *Whity* stand out as deviating from this practice. Van Peebles's antihero is morally questionable and Fassbinder uses melodrama ironically, evoking sympathy for none of his characters. What is also unique about the protagonists Sweetback and Whity is that although they are both thrust from innocence and must leave their home neither actually arrives anywhere. Sweetback presumably keeps running and Van Peebles's warning at the film's ending, "Watchout – a baad assss nigger is coming to collect some dues," suggests his rebellion will continue until he can find a new home. Thus, *Sweet Sweetback* points to an optimistic future and promotes the individual hero that triumphs in films like *Shaft* (1971) and *Coffy* (1973). Whity, however, is condemned to death because he does not unite with others.

Where *Whity* and *Sweetback* converge marks a time when African American experiences as articulated by the Civil Rights Movement and the Black Power Movement were prominent in worldwide debates about oppression. In the late 1960s and early 1970s, the German discourse about race and oppression was primarily led by white leftists concerned with racial oppression in the United States and in Third World countries. The integration of Afro-Germans had been deemed a success and Afro-Germans were therefore "rendered invisible" and lacked a strong public presence (Fehrenbach, 2005: 185). Guest workers lacked the capital (financial and cultural) for a strong voice in the mainstream. In the United States, the Civil Rights Movement, Black Power and Afrocentrism were eventually followed by black commercial culture, individualized style and "romanticized ghetto entrepreneurs" (Quinn, 2010: 104). In Germany, however, the 1980s were the pinnacle for Afro-Germans and guest workers' community building. Although *Sweet Sweetback* and *Whity*'s similarities reveal a link between African American and European critical responses to Hollywood, the triumph of individualism in *Sweetback* versus the importance of community in *Whity* may point to a forthcoming divergence between the black political movements in the United States and Germany.

Notes

1   I would like to thank Deniz Göktürk, Anne Nesbet and the Visual Cultures Working Group at the University of California in Berkeley and Heike Raphael-Hernandez at the University of Maryland University College Europe for reading earlier drafts of this chapter.
2   In past discourses, Jews were also racialized as dark (Gilman, 2005).
3   Biracial children constituted 2% of German births immediately following the war (Fehrenbach, 2005: 74).
4   "Neither segregation nor emigration could solve the social problem of postwar *Mischlingskinder* for a simple, if unanticipated, reason: only a small percentage (under 13 percent) of the children's birth mothers were willing to surrender their custodial rights and allow them to stand for adoption" (Fehrenbach, 2005: 160).
5   Sibblies is an MFA candidate in playwriting at Brown University.
6   All translations from German to English are by the author.
7   I use this term as it is defined by Stephen Greenblatt (2010: 250–252). Greenblatt gives five essentials for the study of cultural mobility: take mobility literally, "*shed light on hidden as well as conspicuous movements* of peoples, objects, images, texts and ideas," "*identify and analyze 'contact zones' where goods are exchanged*," "*account in new ways for the tension between individual agencies and structural constraint*," and "*analyze the sensation of rootedness*" (italics in original).
8   I take this term from Elam and Jackson (2008). In the book's introduction, Jackson defines black cultural traffic as "actual movements of black cultural material from place to place, rather than in a conceptual sense ... Between black performances and

the viewers looking in on those performances, there occurs trade in ideas, styles, impressions, body language, and gestures" (Elam and Jackson, 2008: 8).

9 Nevertheless, Fassbinder adamantly denied any Brechtian influence on his work. See his famous interview with Norbert Sparrow (2004).

10 All dialogue excerpts are based on the DVD release of the film.

11 All dialogue excerpts are based on the German-language dialogue as it is heard in the DVD release of the film (based on subtitles and the author's translation).

12 I am using the terms "Other-from-Within" and "Other-from-Without" as they are defined by Michelle M. Wright. An "Other-from-Within" is seen as different, but still belonging to the national community, while an "Other-from-Without" is completely foreign (Wright, 2003).

13 Audre Lorde was key in helping Afro-Germans gain a sense of community in the 1980s. In 1984, Lorde taught a course on African American female poets and led a poetry workshop in English at the *Freie Universität* (Free University) in Berlin, in which several Afro-German women participated. Lorde encouraged these women to document their experiences of living in Germany and this motivated several of the participants to publish the book *Farbe bekennen* (Showing Our Colors) in 1986. For personal accounts on the feeling of isolation many Afro-Germans experienced in the postwar era see Oguntoye, Opitz, and Schulz, 1992; Hügel-Marshall, 1998.

14 Kaufmann had been working as a salesman when he was first approached about acting in Volker Schlöndorff's play *Baal*. Kaufmann met Fassbinder on this set and immediately attracted the director's attention.

15 Kaufmann had wanted to become a trumpet player as a young man and his music teacher felt he had a promising future in music. His stepfather, however, did not agree that being a musician was a respectable occupation and insisted that Kaufmann become a printer's apprentice (Droste, 2004: 42–43).

16 Fassbinder also had a relationship with the Moroccan star of *Ali: Fear Eats the Soul*, El Hedi ben Salem.

References

Belting, H. (1999) Interview: February 5, 1999, in *Marcel Odenbach: Ach wie gut, daß niemand weiß* (ed. U. Kittelmann), Verlag der Buchhalter Walther König, Cologne, pp. 52–69.

Ege, M. (2007) *Schwarz werden: "Afroamerikanophilie" in den 1960er und 1970er Jahren*, Transcript Verlag, Bielefeld.

Elam, H.J. and Jackson, K. (eds) (2008) *Black Cultural Traffic*, University of Michigan Press, Ann Arbor.

Elsaesser, T. (1993) *Fassbinder's Germany: History, Identity, Subject*, Amsterdam University Press, Amsterdam.

Fehrenbach, H. (2005) *Race After Hitler: Black Occupation Children in Postwar Germany and America*, Princeton University Press, Princeton, NJ.

Fenner, A. (2009) Reterritorializing enjoyment in the Adenauer era: Robert A. Stemmle's *Toxi*, in *Framing the Fifties: Cinema in a Divided Germany* (eds J. Davidson and S. Hake), Berghahn Books, New York.

Fischer, R. (2004) *Fassbinder über Fassbinder: Die ungekürzten Interviews*, Verlag der Autoren, Frankfurt am Main.

Gemünden, G. (1994) Re-fusing Brecht: the cultural politics of Fassbinder's German Hollywood. *New German Critique*, 63, 54–75.

Gilman, S. (2005) Die jüdische Nase: Sind Juden/Jüdinnen *weiß?* Oder: die Geschichte der Nasenchirurgie, in *Mythen, Masken und Subjekte: Kritische Weißseinforschung in Deutschland* (eds M. Eggers, G. Kilomba, P. Piesche and S. Arndt), Unrast, Münster.

Göktürk, D. (1998) *Künstler, Cowboys, Ingenieure: kultur- und mediengeschichtliche Studien zu deutschen Amerika-Texten 1912–1920*, Wilhelm Fink, Munich.

Greenblatt, S. (ed.) (2010) *Cultural Mobility: a Manifesto*, Cambridge University Press, New York, Cambridge.

Guerrero, E. (1993) *Framing Blackness: The African American Image in Film*, Temple University Press, Philadelphia.

Hartman, S. (1997) *Scenes of Subjection: Terror, Slavery, and Self-making in Nineteenth-century America*, Oxford University Press, New York.

James, D. (1995) *That's Blaxploitation!: Roots of the Baadasssss 'tude (Rated X by an All-whyte Jury)*, St Martin's Griffin, New York.

Jansen, P.W. and Schütte, W. (1992) *Rainer Werner Fassbinder*, Fischer, Frankfurt am Main.

Kardish, L. (ed.) (1997) *Rainer Werner Fassbinder*, Museum of Modern Art, distrib. Abrams, New York.

Kaufmann, G. and G. Dröste (2004) *Der Weiße Neger Vom Hasenbergl*, Diana Verlag, Munich.

Knadler, S. (2002) Sweetback style: Wallace Thurman and a queer Harlem Renaissance. *MFS Modern Fiction Studies*, 48 (4), 899–936.

Middleton, R. (2006) *Voicing the Popular: On the Subjects of Popular Music*, Routledge, New York and London.

Mulvey, L. (1989) *Visual and Other Pleasures*, Indiana University Press, Bloomington.

Paul, H. (2009) Cultural mobility between Boston and Berlin: how Germans have read and reread narratives of American slavery, in *Cultural Mobility: a Manifesto* (ed. S. Greenblatt), Cambridge University Press, Cambridge and New York.

Pieterse, J.N. (1992) *White on Black: Images of Africa and Blacks in Western Popular Culture*, Yale University Press, New Haven and London.

Quinn, E. (2010) "Tryin to Get Over": *Superfly*, Black politics, and post-civil rights film enterprise. *Cinema Journal*, 49 (2), 86–105.

Rainer Werner Fassbinder Werkschau (1992) Exhibition catalog, May 28–July 17. Berlin/Potsdam, Germany.

Reid-Pharr, R. (2007) *Once You Go Black: Choice, Desire and the Black American Intellectual*, New York University Press, New York.

Savage, W.S. (1998) Slavery in the West, in *African Americans on the Western Frontier* (eds M.L. Billington and R.D.H. Niwot), University Press of Colorado, Boulder.

Seeßlen, G. and C. Weil (1979) *Western-Kino*, Rowohlt, Reinbeck bei Hamburg.

Sieg, K. (2009) *Ethnic Drag: Performance, Race, Nation, Sexuality in West Germany*, 2002, University of Michigan Press, Ann Arbor.

Spaich, H. (1992) *Rainer Werner Fassbinder: Leben und Werk*, Quadriga, Beltz; Weinheim.

Sparrow, N. (2004) "Ich lasse die Zuschauer fühlen und denken": Rainer Werner Fassbinder über Douglas Sirk, Jerry Lewis und Jean-Luc Godard, in *Fassbinder über Fassbinder. Die ungekürzten Interviews* (ed. R. Fischer), Verlag der Autoren, Frankfurt a.M.

Thomsen, C.B. (1979) Five interviews with Fassbinder, in *Fassbinder* (ed. T. Rayns), Carl Hanser Verlag, Munich, pp. 82–101.

Thomsen, C.B. (1997) *Fassbinder: The Life and Work of a Provocative Genius* (trans. M. Chalmers), Faber & Faber, London and Boston.

Tissberger, M. (2006) The project(ions) of "civilization" and the counter-transferences of whiteness: Freud, psychoanalysis, "gender" and "race" (in Germany), in *Weiß - Weißsein - Whiteness: Kritische Studien zu Gender und Rassismus* (eds M. Tissberger, G. Dietze, D. Hrzán, and J, Husmann-Kastein), Peter Lang, Frankfurt a.M.

Verhoeff, N. (2006) *The West in Early Cinema: After the Beginning*, Amsterdam University Press, Amsterdam.

Watson, W.S. (1996) *Understanding Rainer Werner Fassbinder: Film as Private and Public Art*, University of South Carolina Press, Columbia, SC.

Williams, L. (2001) *Playing the Race Card: Melodramas of Black and White from Uncle Tom to O.J. Simpson*, Princeton University Press, Princeton, NJ.

Wright, M. (2003) Others-from-Within from Without: Afro-German subject formation and the challenge of a counter-discourse. *Callaloo*, 26 (2), 296–305.

Zack, N. (1993) *Race and Mixed Race*, Temple University Press, Philadelphia.

Further Reading

Broeck, S. (2003) Travelling memory: the middle passage in German representation. *The Massachusetts Review*, 44 (1–2), 157–166.

Clark, W.B. (2006) Robert Penn Warren's *Band of Angels* at Fifty. *Southern Quarterly*, 43 (2), 176–185.

Eggers, M., Kilomba, G., Piesche, P. and Arndt, S. (eds) (2005) *Mythen, Masken und Subjekte: Kritische Weißseinforschung in Deutschland*, Unrast, Münster.

Frayling, C. (1981) *Spaghetti Westerns: Cowboys and Europeans from Karl May to Sergio Leone*. Routledge & Kegan Paul, London and Boston.

Freud, S. (1925) *Totem und Tabu: einige Übereinstimmungen im Seelenleben der Wilden und der Neurotiker*, Internationaler Psychoanalytischer, Leipzig.

Gilroy, P. (1993) *The Black Atlantic: Modernity and Double Consciousness*, Cambridge University Press, Cambridge.

Göktürk, D., Gramling, D. and Kaes, A. (2007) *Germany in Transit: Nation and Migration, 1955–2005*. University of California Press, Berkeley.

Graham, A. (2001) *Framing the South: Hollywood, Television and Race during the Civil Rights Struggle*, Johns Hopkins University Press, Baltimore.

Hügel-Marshall, I. (1998) *Daheim unterwegs: ein deutsches Leben*, Orlanda Verlag, Berlin.

Klee, P. (1984) *Die Nigger Europas. Zur Lage der Gastarbeiter*, Patmos Verlag GmbH, Mannheim.

Lott, E. (1995) *Love and Theft: Black Minstrelsy and the American Working Class*, Oxford University Press, New York.

Mazon, P. and Steingröver, R. (eds) (2005) *Not so Plain as Black and White*, Rochester University Press, Rochester, NY.

Mennel, B. (1995) Masochistic fantasy and racialized fetish in Rainer Werner Fassbinder's *Ali: Fear Eats the Soul*, in *One Hundred Years of Masochism* (eds M.C. Finke and C.N. Finkes), Rodopi, Amsterdam, pp. 191–207.

Nelson, G. (1994) *Blackface: Reflections on African Americans and the Movies*, HarperCollins, New York.

Oguntoye, K. (ed.) (1992) *Farbe bekennen: afro-deutsche Frauen auf den Spuren ihrer Geschichte*, Fischer, Frankfurt am Main.

Rogin, M. (1996) *Blackface, White Noise: Jewish Immigrants in the Hollywood Melting Pot*, University of California Press, Berkeley.

Silverman, K. (1992) *Male Subjectivity at the Margins*, Routledge, New York.

Talty, S. (2003) *Mulatto America: At the Crossroads of Black and White Culture: a Social History*, HarperCollins, New York.

Tissberger, M., Dietze, G., Hrzán, D. and Husmann-Kastein, J. (eds) (2006) *Weiß - Weißsein - Whiteness: Kritische Studien zu Gender und Rassismus*, Peter Lang, Frankfurt a.M.

Filmography

Ali: Fear Eats the Soul [Angst essen Seele auf](R.W. Fassbinder, West Germany, 1974).
Baadasssss Cinema (Isaac Julien,USA, 2002).
Badass (Mario Van Peebles, USA, 2003).
Band of Angels (Raoul Walsh, USA, 1957).
Beware of a Holy Whore [Warnung vor einer Heiligen Nutte] (R.W. Fassbinder, West Germany, 1971).
Birth of a Nation (D.W. Griffith, USA, 1915).
Fox and His Friends [Faustrecht der Freiheit] (R.W. Fassbinder, West Germany, 1975).
Germany in Autumn [Deutschland im Herbst] (R.W. Fassbinder *et al.*, West Germany, 1978).
Gone with the Wind (Victor Fleming, USA, 1939).
Hombre (Martin Ritt, USA, 1967).
Imitation of Life (Douglas Sirk, USA, 1959).
Jazz Singer, The (USA, Alan Crosland, 1927).
Katzelmacher (R.W. Fassbinder, West Germany, 1969).
Marriage of Maria Braun, The [Die Ehe der Maria Braun] (R.W. Fassbinder, West Germany, 1979).
Once Upon a Time in the West [C'era una volta il West] (Sergio Leone, Italy/USA 1968).
Spaghetti West, The (David Gregory, USA, 2005).
Split, The (Gordon Flemyng, USA, 1968).
Story of a Three Day Pass, The (Melvin Van Peebles, USA, 1968).
Sweet Sweetback's Baadasssss Song (Melvin Van Peebles, USA, 1971).
Third Generation, The [Die Dritte Generation] (R.W. Fassbinder, West Germany, 1979).
Toxi (Robert Stemmle, West Germany, 1952).
Uncle Tom's Cabin [Onkel Toms Hütte] (Géza von Radványi, West Germany, 1965).
Veronika Voss [Die Sehnsucht der Veronika Voss] (R.W. Fassbinder, West Germany, 1982).
Whity (R.W. Fassbinder, West Germany, 1971).

12

Sexploitation Film
from West Germany

Harald Steinwender and Alexander Zahlten

Standard histories of German film have almost uniformly ignored the section of film production, distribution, and exhibition that utilizes sexual themes as a generic feature. The exclusion of sexploitation film from "official" history takes place despite the fact that for a period of almost ten years from the late 1960s onward, this genre must nearly be equated with popular cinema in West Germany. By some counts sexploitation film at its peak in 1970 made up more than 50% of all German releases (Miersch, 2003: 108), and in 1971 the three most successful films in Germany were the first two installments in the *School girl Report* (*Schulmädchen-Report*) series and the first installment in the *Housewives Report* (*Hausfrauen-Report*) series. The next year, three of the five most successful films were again follow-ups of the *School girl Report* or *Housewives Report* films (Sigl, Schneider, and Tornow, 1986: 145–146).[1] Yet officially these films don't seem to have existed at all. More or less deliberate exclusion of sex film from the study of the history of German cinema simply follows the typical presupposition that sex-themed production is generally situated in a "discrete realm of representation, cut off and clearly distinct from other forms of cultural production" (Nead, 1997: 374). One aspect of creating such a hermetic generic space is the inevitability of a founding myth, in the case of German sexploitation films usually pinpointed in the immense success of *Helga* (*Helga–Vom Werden des menschlichen Lebens*) (1967, Erich F. Bender), a film the German film industry body SPIO (*Spitzenorganisation der Filmwirtschaft e.V.*) initially categorized as a documentary. Well aware that there are no such definite delineations of "birth" and "death" in genre, this chapter will follow such a chronology only tentatively and for the practical means of charting the continuities and reformulations that accompanied the immense rise in popularity of explicitly – and often performatively – sex-themed theatrical films from the late 1960s onward. This will include a wide array of films that utilized sexual themes as

A Companion to German Cinema, First Edition. Edited by Terri Ginsberg and Andrea Mensch.
© 2012 Blackwell Publishing Ltd. Published 2012 by Blackwell Publishing Ltd.

one of their main points for attracting audiences, while not relying or focusing on visually explicit "proof" of sexual activity.[2] It will map the reference points the genre relied on, reaching as far back as Weimar cinema, and trace the discourses of the national and international, of gender and generation. The main concern, however, must be to provide a first overview of the genre's trajectory, hopefully to stimulate and encourage future research.

Perspectives on Sexploitation

Analyses of West German sexploitation film are virtually nonexistent outside of Germany itself, possibly due to the heavy influence of German language departments on the study of film from West Germany. It is only recently that popular genres in West German film have received attention at all, notably from within film studies departments (for positive examples see Bergfelder, 2006; Moltke, 2005). Even within Germany, the academic publications have been few and far between, in the case of sex films mostly restricted to unpublished disserta- tions (Wente, 1992; Wardenbach, 1993), and rare examples of case studies (Miersch, 2003). While there are several fan-oriented publications (see e.g. Phelix and Thissen, 1986; Haufen, 1990a, 1990b, 1991), academically the genre has mostly been treated briefly in psychological (Ertel, 1990) or film-historical (Seeßlen and Weil, 1978; Seeßlen, 1994) approaches concerned with the wider topic of pornographic or "erotic" film. There are also occasional feminist approaches with an explicit self-understanding as interventions (Gramann *et al.*, 1981; Rückert, 2000). A glance at the standard histories of German film shows an almost complete reduction of the late 1960s to late 1970s to the films of New German Cinema (e.g. Prinzler, 1995; Elsaesser and Wedel, 1999; Hake, 2008; Jacobsen, Kaes, and Prinzler, 2004). This almost exclusive historiographic focus on New German Cinema problematically perpetuates an opposition of legitimate and illegitimate culture that erases the rich constellation of social and cinematic discourses sexploitation film was embedded in. At the same time it encourages the construction of essentialist models of German high culture linked to modernist ideas of auteurism and the avant-garde.

The marginalization of the study of sex film is also, however, connected to certain arguments made by New German Cinema itself. This generation of self-conscious filmmakers and their famous rallying cry at the Oberhausen festival of 1962 that "Daddy's cinema is dead" proclaimed a strong opposition to the domestic genre cinema often identified with the *Heimatfilm*. This dominant genre of the 1950s was now considered both an aesthetic continuation of the escapism of former National Socialist cinema and escapism from the issues of war responsibility in the 1950s. Scholars such as Tim Bergfelder (2006: 2) have pointed out that the antipathy of the New German Cinema "towards 'Daddy's cinema' [...] was a symbolic act of rejection of a politically compromised parental generation, projected wholesale, and without taking hostages, on to the films, filmmakers, and not least [...] the audiences of an indigenous popular cinema." Although the best-known exponents of New German Cinema such as Wim Wenders, Rainer Werner Fassbinder, and Werner Herzog were not completely opposed to genre cinema – with Wenders adapting the American road movie for German audiences, Fassbinder working in the context of melodrama, and Herzog directing a remake of F. W. Murnau's *Nosferatu* (1922) – the West German auteur filmmakers and many of their supporters generally adopted the opposition to German popular cinema (Garncarz and Elsaesser, 1995: 304–305). Ulrich Gregor (1983), for example, one of the founders of the Friends of the German Kinemathek in Berlin and former chief programmer for the Forum section of the Berlin International Film Festival, nearly completely ignores the genre cycles of the postwar era and explicitly rejects the *"Kommerzfilm"* ("commercial cinema") and its directors in his influential *Geschichte des Films*. Similarly normative evaluations of commercial cinema dominate the accounts of German film history to this day (for a more detailed account see Steinwender and Zahlten, 2009a).[3]

The rejection of sexploitation film followed the larger logic of this politico-generational discourse: Sexploitation film, on the one hand often viewed as a new phenomenon breaking with traditional views on sexuality and proper film production practice, was on the other hand guilty by association with the cinema of the past. The most active directors in sexploitation film were, biographically, positioned squarely in "Daddy's cinema": Franz Josef Gottlieb (known for several entries in the Edgar Wallace series), Franz Marischka, Adrian Hoven, or Hans Billian. The key producers involved in sexploitation, of which more will be said later, were mostly fairly young but also had all made their first steps in "Daddy's cinema" before endeavoring into sexual themes.

The young generation of directors, eager to mark a rupture with German cinema of the immediate postwar period – and by extension confirm their distance from UFA (Universum Film Aktiengesellschaft) cinema under National Socialism – were not partial to the possibilities a marginalized (as opposed to marginal) film genre offered both politically and aesthetically. This is one of the reasons why, despite exceptions,[4] sex film in Germany never broadly achieved a progressively subversive status for the student movement or engaged in antiauthoritarian politics in the way that the Pink Film sexploitation genre did in Japan from the mid-1960s on.[5] Discourses on continuity/discontinuity are thus key to both how sexploitation film in West Germany was regarded and which direction it took aesthetically and thematically. At the same time, the narrow focus on personalized continuity blurred the view on a different set of thematic and stylistic continuities running through sexploitation film, ranging from traditions as old as the 1910s, most prominently the *Sittenfilm* (vice film) of the Weimar Republic.

The *Sittenfilm* and its Influence on Sexploitation Cinema in West Germany

While often referred to, and usually quoted by its more lurid film titles such as *Der Weg, der zur Verdammnis führt, 2. Teil – Hyänen der Lust* (The Road to Damnation, Part 2: Hyenas of Lust) (1919, Otto Rippert), the *Sittenfilm* has in fact received fairly sparse academic attention, with few recent exceptions (see e.g. Hagener, 2000). As a genre, the *Sittenfilm* was defined by its often sensational use of stories that touched upon public morals, such as prostitution, abortion, or sexually transmitted diseases. Its exploitative image has in retrospect been joined with the myth of the *zensurlose Zeit* ("time without censorship"), situated in the two years between the abolishment of centralized censorship after the German Revolution of 1918 and the institution of the new film laws in the form of the *Reichslichtspielgesetz* of 1920.[6] Although the *Sittenfilm* was a common phenomenon until the early 1930s, the association with a temporally delimited (supposed) absence of censorship would again suggest a relegation of sex-themed film to the "discrete realm of representation." Ironically, Siegfried Kracauer (1966: 45–46) – usually quite eager to draw even implausible lines across history – saw them as neither connected to the sudden release of pressure brought about by the end of the war, nor to the "revolutionary erotic feelings" that "quivered in contemporary literature." Instead these were "just vulgar films selling sex to the public," apparently with no sociological or media-theoretical significance.

Recent research, however, has pointed out the connections of the *Sittenfilme* to various societal discourses and to other contemporaneous media such as the *Sittenroman* or theater. The immensely successful *Cyankali* (Cyanide) by Hans Tintner (1930) was based on Friedrich Wolf's theater piece, itself situated firmly within the proletarian movement. The film took a stance against the criminalization of abortion through the infamous paragraph 218 by portraying the miserable fate of the young unmarried couple Hete (Grete Mosheim) and Paul (Nico Turoff). Unable to afford a child, Hete fails in obtaining a legal abortion and finally dies when an abortion "medicine" she receives from an old lady turns out to be cyanide. The film was famously censored but achieved great popularity nonetheless (Dohrmann, 2000).

That a film such as *Cyankali* would be grouped into the category of the *Sittenfilm* points to another larger vector these films were a part of. There is actually a considerable overlap of what is referred to as *Sittenfilm* with the category of the *Aufklärungsfilm/Sexualaufklärungsfilm* ((sex) education film) that in turn is largely seen as part of the drive for classification and the development of techniques of social control associated with modernity. A great number of the latter were produced or sponsored by the state (Schmidt, 2000), and the *Sittenfilme* more or less consciously reference or even share their didactic thrust. Richard Oswald graphically divulged the dangers of syphilis in one of the first of the

Aufklärungsfilme, Es werde Licht! (Let There Be Light! 1917), sponsored by the German Society for Combating Venereal Disease. A pioneer and a kind of auteur of the *Sittenfilm*, Oswald was able to consistently combine social activism with commercially successful attention-grabbing topics, in 1918 also shooting the first gay rights film *Different from the Others* (*Anders als die Andern – Sozialhygienisches Filmwerk*, 1919) with the participation of social reformer and sexologist Magnus Hirschfeld. This model of the *Aufklärungsfilm*, utilizing experts for sometimes more and sometimes less sincere educational purposes as well as an appeal to social change, would also inform the greater part of sex films in the 1960s and 1970s, although with decisive differences. The extraordinary (international) success of *Helga* in 1967 initiated the sexploitation film boom while relying on the same didactic framework and official sponsorship.

In comparison to the straight-faced activism and sensationalism of the *Sittenfilme*, however, most of 1970s sexploitation is deliberately and openly farcical to a degree that *The School Girls* and the endless stream of *Report* films that followed often seem like elaborate in-jokes. In contrast, even evocative titles of the 1910s and 1920s such as *Madame Lu, die Frau für diskrete Beratung* (Madame Lu, the Woman for Discrete Consultation) (1929, Franz Hofer), another dramatization of the problems involved with abortion laws, or *Sex in Chains* (*Geschlecht in Fesseln – Sexualnot der Gefangenen*, 1928, Wilhelm Dieterle) were infused with earnest designs for educating the (urban) masses. The latter especially seems almost parodic for contemporary viewers, hyperbolically dwelling on the torturous plight of prisoners. Refused the right to sexual activity, they – and their spouses – commit themselves to hysteria, suicide or – an almost equally terrible fate in the context of the film – homosexuality. Nonetheless, *Geschlecht in Fesseln* is obviously serious about its own goals. This is not to say that the greater part of the *Sittenfilme* – although with so few left or even accessible for viewing today it is difficult to conclusively say – were not primarily made with commercial considerations in mind. This impression is inevitably enhanced by the considerable gap between the flamboyantly suggestive advertisements and the restrained visualizations – the "time without censorship" notwithstanding – and usually quite conservative conclusions. Malte Hagener goes as far as to position them as "paratextual attractions," as films based on spectacle that takes place largely outside of the filmic texts themselves, in sensationalist posters, booklets, and references to transgressive behavior (Hagener, 2000: 18).

The *Bürgerlichkeit* expressed in the *Sittenfilme* is committed to typically modern themes such as social control, "scientific" categorization and strict gender divisions. The former becomes explicit in the many references to a rhetoric of *Sozialhygiene* ("social hygiene") and the eugenic politics of films such as *Der Fluch der Vererbung* (The Curse of Heredity, 1927, Adolf Trotz). However it is not necessary, as Ulf Schmidt stresses, to position the vocabulary of social hygiene and *Volksgesundheit* ("national health") common in the *Sittenfilme* on a straight trajectory to the eugenics of the so-called Third Reich

(Schmidt, 2000). Such a reflex simply obscures the political diversity and often contradictory discourses running through and surrounding the *Sittenfilm*.

The question of gender elucidates this complexity. The string of films criticizing (and several propagating) abortion restrictions and the innumerous urban peril films such as *Die Minderjährige* (The Minor, 1921, Alfred Tostary) or *Der Weg, der zur Verdammnis führt, 1. Teil: Das Schicksal der Aenne Wolter* (The Road to Damnation, Part 1: The Fate of Aenne Wolter, 1919, Otto Rippert) use rape and violence against the female body as the main pedagogic instrument for dramatizing their arguments. Violence against women thus becomes the typical channel for broadcasting the modern human condition, a trope that would be continued in a large part of the sexploitation films 50 years on. The innumerous films reiterating the dangers of venereal diseases often use the figure of the prostitute as a kind of archetype, while the basic underlying fear being expressed through the trope of infection is that of urbanity and modern mass culture. It is perhaps no coincidence that Walter Ruttmann, best known for his experimental and modernist urban portrait *Berlin – Symphony of a Great City* (*Berlin – Die Symphonie der Großstadt*, 1927), also shot the film *Feind im Blut* (Enemy in Your Blood, 1931) on the dangers of syphilis.

While anxiety vis-à-vis the younger generation still plays a determinant role for the films of the 1960s and 1970s, the focus has become more diffuse and is not concerned with urbanity or modernity per se. The more or less didactic-minded *Sittenfilme* tended to address audiences across gender lines. Even as violence against the female body was standard, they were geared to address a general audience and thus wider societal concerns, a breadth of appeal that is mostly absent in West German sexploitation, at least from the moment the *Report* films set in. It is a sign of an increasing binarity between German productions targeted at male and those targeted at female audiences. This development is exemplified by the 1970s' division of box-office successes between sex films and films based on the bestselling humanist-melodrama books of Johannes Mario Simmel, nicely elaborated on in the documentary *Von Sex bis Simmel* (From Sex to Simmel, 2005, Hans Günther Pflaum and Peter H. Schröder). This also entails a shift in the neuralgic points the films address, but it is a shift that was only gradually fleshed out in the early years of the sexploitation boom.

West German Sexploitation Film – The Formulas of the 1960s and 1970s

Though the German sexploitation film of the 1960s and 1970s soon developed its own aesthetics and narratives and is thus sometimes referred to as an "independent genre" (Miersch, 2003: 37), it is important to point out that the sex film of this era is by no means an *aesthetically* coherent body of films. In fact, there has been a varying and surprisingly rich pool of subgenres or formulas, many of which appeared side by side but often merged into new generic cycles. Booming in the late 1960s and early 1970s and with a production apex in 1970, when 40 of 79 released films of West German origin could be subsumed to it (Miersch, 2003: 108), the bulk of the genre's output consists of very low-budget productions that belong to or reference a limited number of series.

Some scholars, Thomas Elsaesser (1989: 23) among them, have argued that these films – partially screened in the so-called *Bahnhofskinos*, the shabby cinemas located near railway stations in bigger cities, but in case of the most successful series also in average cinema houses – were mostly popular with the so-called *Gastarbeiter*, a claim that may have originated with sexploitation producer Alois Brummer's statements in Hans Jürgen Syberberg's documentary *Sex-Business – Made in Pasing* (1969). Between 1955 and 1973 over two million of these immigrant workers moved to Germany, many from Turkey, Italy and Spain, as part of a formal "guest worker" program to help build up the economically booming country. But by no means does a certain number of immigrant workers living in Germany at this time explain the average domestic sale of more than six million tickets for each of the first installments of the *Schoolgirl Report* cycle (Bergfelder, 2006: 230). There is virtually no empirical data on the audience of the sexploitation films, but it seems safe to presume that these films attained viewers from across the entire social spectrum, with male adults comprising the lion's share of the audience. Rather than being a niche product the sex film of the 1970s appears to have been a popular phenomenon, the result of a society in social, political and historical transition and at least partially an expression of a reevaluation of public discourses on sexuality.

Such a reevaluation was well under way in contemporary debates, with the writings of Wilhelm Reich and Sigmund Freud exerting considerable influence especially among the burgeoning student movement.[7] However, the defining development here may have been the popularization and commercialization of these discourses, a process also connected to new models of society. Herbert Marcuse (1962: ix–x) has written that "to the degree to which sexuality obtains a definitive sales value [...] it is itself transformed into an instrument of social cohesion." Indeed, the commodification of discourses on sexuality came to define a certain contemporary sense. Alfred Kinsey's studies on sexual behavior (1948/53) received enormous press coverage and inspired numerous successful imitators in the industrialized world, for example Günther Hunold's *Schuldmädchen-Report* (Schoolgirls Report, 1970) in Germany. Magazines began to provide their readers with series of articles on marriage counseling and "how-to sex" sections, "the pill" became broadly used and Beate Uhse's sex-shop chain mushroomed all over the country. This was paralleled by a trend in the tabloid press to cover the supposed "sexual revolution" of the late 1960s in often projective articles illustrated by exploitative pictures – in many ways the journalistic equivalent to some of the sex film formulas. The sales value and commercial success of sexuality gradually began to provide it with legitimacy as well. The era also saw the liberalization of parts of the penal code dealing with sexuality, and the boom of the sexploitation film in West Germany was also partially a result of an increasingly liberal approach taken by the *Freiwillige Selbstkontrolle der Filmwirtschaft* (FSK / Organization for the Voluntary Self-regulation / Film Classification Board of the German Film Industry), that still approves the release of nearly every film shown in German cinemas.

1950–1967: Postwar Predecessors of the Sex Film Boom

The retrospective homogenization of 1950s West German cinema into the exclusive domain of the *Heimatfilm* must be seen as a rhetorical and polemical maneuver with roots in the manifesto of Oberhausen. In fact there were quite a few attempts at serious engagement with social concerns and a sizeable amount of commercial projects that were well aware of the box-office value of sexual themes. One of the earliest postwar examples is Willi Forst's bleak melodrama *The Story of a Sinner* (*Die Sünderin*, 1951) that not only caused a public furor for its topic and some very brief nudity by Hildegard Knef, but also made the film extremely successful at the German box office. Other homegrown films like *Forbidden Paradise* (*Das verbotene Paradies*, 1958, Max Nosseck) and *Liane, Jungle Goddess* (*Liane, das Mädchen aus dem Urwald*, 1956, Eduard von Borsody), featuring scenes of female nudity, succeeded in using the sexual angle in a more systematic way. In the late 1950s producer Wolf C. Hartwig – later to strike gold with the *Schoolgirl Report* series – began to systematically exploit the interest in cinematic explicitness. His career began with a scandal when he distributed the Italian-French co-production *Lucrèce Borgia* (*Lucretia Borgia*, 1953, Christian-Jaque) which was temporarily banned in Germany as a result of an orgy sequence (Hartwig and Miersch, 2003: 10). Hartwig also established the "West German Jayne Mansfield" Barbara Valentin with a series of exploitation films in the late 1950s and early 1960s (for a detailed description see Bergfelder, 2006: 208–212). Even the notorious Veit Harlan, having previously directed National Socialist propaganda films such as *Jud Süß* (Jew Süss, 1940) and *Kolberg* (1945) as well as more trivial entertainment, shot *Bewildered Youth* (*Anders als du und ich*, 1957). The film drew on the *Sittenfilme* – the title referring to Oswald's 1919 *Anders als die Andern* – of the silent film era and oscillated between homophobic melodrama and exploitation film. 1964 saw the release of *Fanny Hill*, nominally directed by the "king of nudies" Russ Meyer, a rather tame German-American co-production with involvement by Artur Brauner's CCC studios. Alois Brummer – owner of a small theater chain and later a key figure in sexploitation production – began distributing films that were sometimes, as in the case of the crime drama *Jungfrau aus zweiter Hand* (Second-hand Virgin, 1967, Akos von Rathonyi), enhanced with "erotic" scenes. However, these precursors of the later sex films are possibly less important than the emergence of highly controversial art films from Scandinavian countries. Especially Ingmar Bergman's *The Silence* (*Tystnaden*, 1963), Vilgot Sjöman's *491* (1964) and his *I Am Curious – Yellow* (*Jag är nyfiken – Gul*, 1967), all from Sweden, proved extremely successful in Germany, with *The Silence* becoming by far the most successful film of the years 1964/65 (Garncarz, 1996: 385). Its release was accompanied by a public campaign of mostly Christian lobbyists against "dirty" movies that no doubt provided additional advertisement. The impact of these controversial art films on public opinion resulted in some of the later German semisex films and pseudodocumentaries using Scandinavian locations and/or stock footage from these countries to signal yet another *Schwedenfilm*, as the art films were known in the 1960s (examples are *Do You Believe in Swedish Sin?* (*Nach Stockholm der Liebe wegen*, 1969, Gunnar Höglund); *Pornography in Denmark* (*Pornographie in Dänemark – Zur Sache, Kätzchen*, 1970, Michael Miller)). Popular fantasies were also fueled by the legalization of pornography in Denmark in 1968 and the import of porn magazines from Scandinavian countries (Seeßlen, 1994: 170–174, 204–205).

1967–1972: Semirespectable "Marriage Manuals" and Sex Education Films

The success story of systematic sexploitation film production began with help from an unexpected side. While the sex-themed films of the 1970s were usually realized without government subsidies (*Filmförderung*) or the participation of television stations (Sanke, 1994: 47), the boom was in fact initially fueled by federal government money. The prototype of the so-called *Aufklärungsfilm*, the 1967 release *Helga*, was produced on the insistence of health minister Käte Strobel (of the Social Democratic Party in the newly minted coalition government, certainly a large factor in the government's involvement) and financially supported by the Federal Center of Health Education. Initially planned as two half-hour education films, distributor Hanns Eckelkamp and producer Martin Hellstern decided – influenced by successful screenings of exploitation flicks like Erle C. Kenton's *Bob and Sally* (1948, released in Germany under the title *Brautzeit und Ehe*) – to fabricate a feature film from the material (unpublished authors' interview with Hanns Eckelkamp, conducted September 17, 2009). The shoestring plot centers on the sexually inexperienced Helga (Ruth Gassmann) who wants to marry and thus visits a gynecologist who lectures her (and the audience in the cinema) on sexual intercourse and birth control. Soon Helga gets pregnant and seeks more information on the upcoming birth which is delivered by nurses and varying doctors. After a lengthy birth sequence which uses footage of an actual birth presented in detail – sexual intercourse on the other hand is never shown – the film closes to triumphant music with Helga being a happy young mother and her husband helping her in the kitchen. Despite the sometimes clumsy editing and extremely wooden acting, *Helga* unexpectedly became a huge success in Germany. It received the film industry award *Goldene Leinwand* for its exceptional box-office results and was successfully exported to European countries like Italy where it became one of the biggest box-office earners of 1968 (Seeßlen, 1994: 175). Nearly forgotten today, the film allegedly reached 40 million spectators worldwide in the first year of distribution (Thissen, 1995: 194) and together with the swiftly produced sequels *Helga and Michael* (*Helga und Michael*, 1968, Erich F. Bender) and *Helga und die Männer – Die Sexuelle Revolution* (Helga and the Men – The Sexual Revolution, 1969, Roland Cämmerer) earned 150 million DM (currently ca. 250 million Euros when adjusted to inflation) in two years (Bergfelder, 2006: 224).

At the time of its release controversially discussed by critics who doubted its value as an education film, *Helga* nevertheless established the sex education formula virtually overnight. The opening sequence provided a blueprint for the later *Schoolgirl Report* films, with a reporter conducting street interviews and asking average people questions on their sexual knowledge. As in many of the sex education films, the credits provide a list of academic advisors that legitimize the consumption of the following images and pose as evidence of its "scientific" value. There are also montage sequences intercutting images of foreign countries and impressions of idyllic nature and landscapes that establish, together with a voiceover commentary, a discourse that insists on the *trias* of love, sexuality and marriage as "natural," "good" and "healthy." A strategy followed throughout the film is the interlinking of images of sexuality and nature as well as commentaries on the importance of birth control in "the interest of the *Volksgesundheit.*" As in many of the later semi-education films, the explanations given by "experts" often directly address the audience in the cinema by speaking into the camera and thus attacking the fourth wall of narrative cinema.

Among the "marriage manual movies" and sex education films that followed, the most successful are inseparably conjoined with the persona of the 1928-born journalist and author of popular counseling books Oswalt Kolle. Between 1968 and 1972 Kolle produced eight semidocumentaries that earned him the title of unofficial "head of sexual education in Germany" and proved like the *Helga* films extremely successful, with the first film selling over 6 million tickets in Germany, and four of the following installments clocking in more than three million German cinemagoers each. Even though Kolle usually didn't direct the films, he wrote the screenplays, appeared on screen (as himself) and his name was often an integral part of the film's title. His first entry to the genre was *The Miracle of Love* (*Das Wunder der Liebe*, 1968, Franz Josef Gottlieb), a documentary with a pronouncedly serious tone and a liberal agenda. Kolle's documentaries not only supplied their audience with sexualized images but also followed the mission of the popular author to "free" the repressed sexuality of modern men and women. In *The Miracle of Love*, Kolle argued for women's liberation and – unusually for the genre – showed as much male as female nudity in a presentation that is far removed from the aggressive sexism of the later *Report* films. Kolle followed this liberal agenda throughout his career and in the succeeding films argued for social acceptance of homo- and bisexuality, the *Freikörperkultur* ("free body" or "nude culture") or partner exchange as well as the legalization of pornography. Other education films like *Du – Zwischenzeichen der Sexualität* (You – Subtle Signals in Sexuality, 1968, Gerhard Zenkel) and *Freedom to Love* (*Freiheit für die Liebe*, 1969, Phyllis and Eberhardt Kronhausen) clearly followed this trend, whereas the latter film was intended by its directors as a "socially critical," even "revolutionary" entry to the cycle (Schifferle, 2007: 15).

The first *Helga* film and the Kolle series took up the heritage of the silent era and seemed to incorporate a sincere social activism, to a certain degree distancing them from full-blown exploitation movies.[8] Like their predecessors in the silent era, the education films of the late 1960s initially avoided the onscreen depiction of sexual intercourse and thus "the education took place on the level of (voiced-over) words rather than that of images" (Schifferle, 2007: 15). *Helga* and the Kolle films lacked the strong melodramatic bent of the more serious *Sittenfilme*, and instead presented concerned but understanding couples (Kolle) or a near-catatonic main actress passively floating through stainless doctor's offices and lecture halls, always ready to submit to scientific authority (*Helga*). Structurally, they often used stock footage with a voiceover commentary, presented "experts" – scientists, physicians, journalists and judges, usually all male – and utilized staged round-table discussions on human sexuality, followed by short sequences where actors illustrated the sexual everyday problems of "normal" couples. The semirespectable construction and the overall cleanliness of these films, both in terms of the actual sets and the exposed actors' bodies and morals, allowed directors and producers to introduce thematically risky subjects and to stretch the limits of censorship. Soon more graphic films like *Liebestechnik für Fortgeschrittene* (Love Techniques for the Experienced, 1970, Kurt Palm) and *Abarten der körperlichen Liebe* (Perversions of Physical Love, 1970, Franz Marischka) followed, the latter a rare case in German sexploitation film in showing gay sex between men (although, as the title suggests, framed as "perversion"). Ernst Hofbauer's *Teenage Sex Report* (*Mädchen beim Frauenarzt*, 1971) presented an *en détail* gynecological examination of a young woman including the onscreen introduction of a speculum. *Teenage Sex Report* already has one foot in the *Report* films, which would lead sex-themed films along a much less socially ambitious though no less influential path. Despite the continuities with Weimarian cinema, the films were at the time presented as a sensational and eruptive development as well as a break with established discourses on sexuality. For the audience, it seems that the films that emphasized a more or less serious didactic approach could still attract the general audience. The soon to appear *Report* films, however, supported a gradual development toward audience fragmentation, and increasingly set their focus on an all-male target group.

The New Subgenre of the 1970s: The *Report-Film*

The *Report-Film* as the most important production cycle from the West German sexploitation genre evolved directly from the pioneering education films and enjoyed considerable success between 1970 and 1974. Approximately sixty of these semidocumentary films were released theatrically between 1967 and 1980. As a formula, the *Report-Film* typically claims to investigate the love life and sexual attitudes of a selected social group, profession or, less often, geographical region and predicates to deliver the unbiased, but somewhat shocking "truth" on its subject. Their truth-value was obviously in question, and in the case of *Nurses Report* (*Krankenschwestern-Report*, 1972, Walter Boos) the nurse's guild went to court and tried to suppress the release of the film. Though by no means difficult to recognize as complete fabrications, the overall design claims authenticity, and according to some readings the technical inadequacies of the films enhanced the sense of immediacy (Seeßlen, 1994: 180), although it does seem questionable whether the films were actually accorded any "authenticity" by the audience. Many of these very low-budget, episodically structured films borrow elements from journalistic reportage and documentary cinema. They thus offer a mixture of faked and in some of the earlier films actual street interviews, statements of real or so called "experts" on sexuality, and reenacted case-studies, but are much more sensationalist in tone than the education films that preceded them.

All of these films have a contemporary setting, and there have been some *Reports* on male subgroups like bath attendants, male pupils and husbands. But the main object of inquiry of the films is female: teenage pupils (the *Schoolgirls Report* series beginning with *The School Girls* (*Schulmädchen-Report: Was Eltern nicht für möglich halten*, 1970, Ernst Hofbauer)), stewardesses (*The Swingin' Stewardesses* (*Die Stewardessen*, 1971, Erwin C. Dietrich)), nurses (*Nurses Report*), and housewives (*Housewives Report* (*Hausfrauen-Report: Unglaublich, aber wahr*, 1971, Eberhard Schröder)). The best-known and most successful variants are the *Schulmädchen-Report* series of 13 films, produced between 1970 and 1980, and the *Hausfrauen-Report* cycle of six parts, released between 1971 and 1978. According to producer Wolf C. Hartwig, his *Schoolgirls Report* series found an audience of roughly 100 million worldwide. As the first installments of the cycle were shot in 17–19 days for approximately 220 000 DM each, these films were extremely profitable in comparison to films from other genres (or film industries) as well as in relation to their production costs (Hartwig and Miersch, 2003: 11, 26–28).

Stylistically, some *Report* films like *Abarten der körperlichen Liebe*, *Teenage Sex Report* or *Virgin Report* (*Jungfrauenreport*, 1972, Jess Franco) show a relation to the Italian "shockumentaries" of the *Mondo* cycle and films like *Women of the World* (*La donna nel mondo*, 1963, Paolo Cavara, Gualitiero Jacopetti and Franco Prosperi). As in the Italian pseudodocumentaries of the 1960s, the German version used statistics and facts rather freely and the voiceover commentary was highly misogynistic while feigning compassion and moral outrage. But contrary to the Italian counterparts and the few "true" *Mondo* films of German origin like Rolf Olsen's *Shocking Asia* (*Shocking Asia – Sünde, Sex und Sukiyaki*, 1976) these German "documentaries" are not interested in the exotic, the unusual or the alien, instead focusing exclusively on the ordinary and the everyday, if with a middle-class twist. The interiors of these films are usually (petit) bourgeois, very seldom located in the working class, and the actors are mostly nonprofessionals carefully chosen for their average looks.

Apart from the *Housewives* series, the bulk of the subgenre is interested in the sexuality of underaged girls. The exploitative dealings with the subject included sex scenes of supposedly 13–15-year-old girls (usually portrayed by grown-ups) with males between 40 and 60, which push these films, by today's standards, rather uncomfortably toward child erotica. Also common for the *Schoolgirls Report* series of directors Ernst Hofbauer and Walter Boos are sequences that reenact incest between brother and sister, father and daughter or grandfather and niece as well as rape scenes that are justified via voiceover or through narrative constructions such as court scenes. Because of these scenes, the original versions of most of these films are presently on the German *Index für jugendgefährdende Schriften* (Index for Youth-Endangering Media) and thus their advertising and sale are restricted. The rape myth of female culpability argued for here is also very much in line with the series' overall characterization of an aggressive female sexuality constantly demanding sexual acts, while young men in these films are usually inexperienced, frightened and/or unattractive. The films generally express fear of an active and mature female sexuality, and at the same time often punish the sexual interest of young women with either violence (rape) or social problems (e.g. bad grades in school). Their narrative strategies and tropes indicate that the *Report Film* was directed mainly at (male) representatives of older generations and thus indeed at the original audience of the despised "Daddy's cinema." This is supported by the fact that more than half of the films' titles feature subtitles addressing parents, such as *What Parents Don't Consider Possible* or *What Parents Should Really Know*. Viewed from this perspective, the series has been described as an example of "sexploitation films dealing with the West German generation gap" (Schifferle, 2007: 16). It also seems striking that, notwithstanding the contemporary political atmosphere, there are virtually no hippies or political protestors visible in these films, and as Bergfelder (2006: 231) has pointed out, they could be understood as part of an ideological project opposed to the sexual libertinage of the 68ers as they "circumvent and suppress the dangerous link between sex, politics, and history that the 68ers addressed, while taking on board some of their more superficial attractions." The films indeed construct a strictly male heterosexual petit-bourgeois perspective, and homosexuality – besides occasional lesbian scenes – was completely absent in Hartwig's *Report* cycle.

With the new *Report* formula, the genre thus underwent a major transformation. The target audience seems to shift from a general audience across gender and generational lines to male spectators, and although certainly a sizeable youth audience initially supported the films, at least the explicit addressees are of a somewhat older generation, one anxious about the generational shifts in values and lifestyles. The diversification within the genre accelerated as well; the sole reliance on sex as spectacle necessitated intensified product differentiation in increasingly fast production cycles.

Localized Sex Comedies and Other Formulas

With the *Report-Film*, the German sex education film abandoned most of its legitimizing strategies and now developed into a variety of formulas that on the contrary performatively emphasized their status as exploitation. These films were episodic and agglomerated, compared to the American *nudies,* a high number of simulated sex scenes. They also usually incorporated humorous episodes and comic side characters with an emphasis on low-brow humor that was to become an increasingly central aspect of the genre. These comedic flavorings were often tied to regional characterizations in a further attempt at producing variety with sexploitation.

The most successful variant of the regional twist in West German sexploitation is set in the distinctive rural locations of Bavaria and could be best described as *Heimat* sex comedies. From the 1968 *Pudelnackt in Oberbayern* (Stark Naked in Upper Bavaria, Hans Albin) to the 1983 *Sechs Schwedinnen auf der Alm* (Six Swedes in the Alps, Erwin C. Dietrich), more than 40 German sex films appeared that used Bavarian locations or stereotyped Bavarian themes, with a production apex in 1974 when approximately half of the released sex films could be added to the "Bavarian sex film" (Wardenbach, 1993: 27–34). As in the case of the *Report-Film* and its *Schoolgirl* variant, it was a central series that established the cycle at the box office; the *Liebesgrüße aus der Lederhose* series of directors Franz Marischka and Gunter Otto. Starting with *Liebesgrüße aus der Lederhose* (From the Lederhosen with Love, 1973, Franz Marischka) the series comprises six parts until 1982. Oscillating between simplistic slapstick comedy (often with roots in the *Bauerntheater*, the Bavarian stage comedies), scenes exposing the rural landscapes, and the mandatory softcore sex scenes, the series was significantly more revealing than its predecessors from the *Report* films though still missing the explicit "meat shots" of hardcore pornography.

Directors like Franz Antel, Hans Albin, Franz Marischka and Hans Billian had of course directed their share of *Heimat* films and comical musicals before turning to the sex film. Interestingly, and despite the association with "Daddy's cinema," these films can also be seen as an acerbic yet apolitical critique of the popular *Heimat* genre. Most of these films use local signifiers like *"Lederhosen,"* "yodeling" or *"Dirndl"* in their titles and some referred directly to *Heimat* films of the 1950s.

In this vein *Wo der Wildbach durch das Höschen rauscht* (Where the Mountain Torrent Rushes Through the Panties, 1974, Jürgen Enz) was a play on *Wo der Wildbach rauscht* (Where the Mountain Torrent Rushes, 1956, Heinz Paul). While the *Heimat* films delivered escapism and assurance that Germany, despite the crimes of Nazism and the atrocities of the war, was still essentially intact, the *Heimat* sex comedy ridicules the stock characters of the traditional genre as impotent or solely driven by sexual needs. Conflicts between modernity and rural life, an important *topos* of the *Heimat* film, were transformed into a parodic standoff between cinematic clichés.

Other formulas were strictly rooted in urban settings. Besides a small number of films set in Berlin like *Confessions of a Campus Virgin* (*Die Schulmädchen vom Treffpunkt Zoo*, 1979, Walter Boos), one noticeable example is the *Lass jucken, Kumpel!* series (1972–1981), a cycle set in the Ruhr area and directed by Franz Marischka. These bawdy sex comedies with an antiauthoritarian twist used worker's flats as "authentic" settings, a coarse language mixed with local dialect and a – fairly shallow – social critique. Like the Bavarian sex comedies, they were extremely low-budget productions while highly profitable. The prototype of the series, *Lass jucken, Kumpel!* (Scratch the Itch, Coal Miner, 1972), followed a folksy novel by former miner Hans Henning Clear; shot in four weeks with a budget of 350 000 DM, it supposedly made roughly 12 million Marks in return (Wardenbach, 1993: 23–26). Next to Marischka's five follow-ups until 1981, rip-offs by Sigi Götz (aka Siegfried Rothemund) (*Bohr weiter, Kumpel!* (Drill along, Coal Miner, 1974)) and Alois Brummer (*Kursaison für scharfe Kumpel* (Spa Season for Raunchy Coal Miners, 1981)), cashed in on the minor trend of working-class sex comedies.

Another regional variant that often fared well in export was set in Hamburg and used the red-light district St Pauli as its setting. Usually merging themes of the crime film and the sex film, these are the closest German approximation to the American *roughies*. Examples are *Erotic Center* (*Eros Center Hamburg*, 1969, Günter Hendel), *Hotel by the Hour* (*Das Stundenhotel von St. Pauli*, 1970, Rolf Olsen) and *St. Pauli Nachrichten – Thema Nr. 1* (St. Pauli News – Topic No. 1, 1971, Franz Marischka). The almost touristic perspective of this short-lived subgenre may be deduced from poster artwork like that of distributor Constantin for *Das Stundenhotel von St. Pauli* which promised "The new 'true' Hamburg movie."

One strain of films produced what parallels a standard of the hardcore pornographic film: the sexualized parody. Beginning with *Grimms' Fairy Tales for Adults* (*Grimms Märchen von lüsternen Pärchen*, 1969, Rolf Thiele), *The Naked Wytche* (*Lass uns knuspern, Mäuschen*, 1970, Franz Josef Gottlieb) and *Dornwittchen und Schneeröschen* (Sleeping-White and Snow-Beauty, 1970, Erwin Klein), sex films using the typology of the fairytale were popular in the early 1970s and exploited motifs from local folklore. There were numerous spoofs of popular novels or film genres like the sexploitation/swashbuckler mix *The Sex Adventures of the Three Musketeers* (*Die Sexabenteuer der drei Musketiere*, 1971, Erwin C. Dietrich) and the Nibelung parody *The Long Swift Sword of Siegfried* (*Siegfried und das sagenhafte*

Liebesleben der Nibelungen, 1971, Adrian Hoven) as well as an attempt at science fiction with *2069: A Sex Odyssey* (*Ach jodel mir noch einen – Stosstrupp Venus bläst zum Angriff*, 1974, Georg Tressler) or a comic fallback on the "white slavery" subgenre like *Der lüsterne Türke* (The Lecherous Turk, 1971, Michael Miller).

Compared to the bulk of the genre, however, these variants are comparatively few in number. Another more successful exception to the performative-realism tradition of German sexploitation is the escapist sex comedy borrowing motifs from the period film. Examples are the five *Frau Wirtin* films (1967–1973) of director Franz Antel, on the exploits of a female innkeeper / stage performer in the early nineteenth century, that began with *The Sweet Sins of Sexy Susan* (*Susanne, die Wirtin von der Lahn*, 1967), or the series that revolved around the "adventures" of the Viennese courtesan Josefine Mutzenbacher, directed by Kurt Nachmann: *Naughty Knickers* (*Josefine Mutzenbacher*, 1970); *Don't Get Your Knickers in a Twist* (*Mutzenbacher 2. Teil: Meine 365 Liebhaber*, 1971); and *Teach Me* (*Auch Fummeln will gelernt sein*, 1972). Especially the Sexy Susan (*Frau Wirtin*) series was, in comparison with the greater part of contemporaneous sexploitation, outfitted with a fairly structured script and relatively high production values, probably due to its status as an international co-production. The *Sexy Susan* films also seem highly exceptional in how they move their settings easily across European borders, making the rest of the genre and its focus on the West German microcosm look all the more parochial. However, for West German sexploitation the question of nation is more complex than it appears at first glance.

Production/Genre, Distribution/Nation

During the opening credits of *The Hostess Exceeds All Bounds* (*Frau Wirtin treibt es jetzt noch Toller*, 1970, Franz Antel), an upper-class Viennese bureaucrat – played by popular star Gunther Philipp – peeps through a keyhole into the dressing room of the eponymous *Frau Wirtin* Susan (Teri Tordai). The keyhole perspective shows her performing several time-consuming undressing procedures, while the keyhole perspective cuts off her head and the keyhole opening is positioned to the far right of the frame, leaving the greater part of the screen black. It is a perfect encapsulation of how the West German sexploitation film – especially in comparison with the *Sittenfilm* – on the one hand claimed to voyeuristically show more, but on the other proceeded to narrow down perspective, both in terms of the audiences and the social themes it addressed. In exchange it left a large unmarked space, a black projective field of anxiety that it partially produced and partially fed off.

The partitioning of the sexes that this scene enacts in terms of space and the gaze is one of the most significant arguments made by sexploitation cinema, and is complexly connected to discourses of nation. Tim Bergfelder (2006: 232) has written that the sex film boom of the late 1960s "ultimately led to a reorientation of the West German film industry towards a more nationally and less internationally minded mode of production." Such a phrasing, however, injects causality into chronology and is not strictly true. In fact, the level of international diffusion and co-production of West German sexploitation is quite astonishing, although it does show a distinct shift away from internationalism on the level of textual immanence. While films such as the unusually high-budgeted *Sexy Susan* series (in the context of sexploitation film) employed an international cast and featured locations in southern Germany, Austria or France, the greater part of sexploitation film was resolutely local in terms of (West German) themes and the semiotic reservoir it exploited.[9]

The local/national fixation that these films show on the textual level is especially striking when compared to the international casts and settings of the Edgar Wallace films, the Karl May Westerns or the Jerry Cotton series in the early 1960s.[10] The case of Wolf C. Hartwig is exemplary in this respect. Hartwig produced a spate of somewhat suggestive fantasy-exploitation films such as *Horrors of Spider Island* (*Ein Toter hing im Netz*, 1959, Fritz Böttger) in the early 1960s, then transitioned to only mildly raunchy thrillers set in Far East locations in the mid-1960s, and finally moved on to the sexual microcosm of West German *Bürgerlichkeit* in the *Report* films of the early 1970s. A film such as *Virgins of the Seven Seas* (*Karate, Küsse, Blonde Katzen*, Ernst Hofbauer and Chih-Hung Kuei), a white slavery-themed co-production with the Shaw Brothers of Hong Kong shot as late as 1974, was a distinct exception to this inward-bound sexploitation trajectory, although it of course reinforced essentialist ideas of gender, nation and race by juxtaposing them.

However, such a shift back – at least superficially – to a national framework led to an at best very uneven homogenization. Following the logic of product differentiation when the hook line – sex – was the same for all films meant that the erotic and cinematic benefits of mixing supposed opposites continued to inform West German sexploitation film. That the opposing of national or local contexts was a mainstay of these films shows how the category-fixation of sexploitation film seemed to be, on several levels, a step backwards in terms of the tentative but general development toward valorizing hybridity and transnationalism in early 1960s cinema in Western Europe. The hard work of confusing national delineations via Euro-Westerns, Euro-Spy films and the Euro-*Krimi* had to be reversed in order to create marketable, eroticizable tensions. An initially one-trick dog such as the sex-themed film saw itself in constant danger of exhausting itself in ever-shorter series and production cycles. Major film series of the 1960s had been based on well-known material such as the Karl May or Edgar Wallace books. But apart from the *Schoolgirl Report* series, based on the aforementioned book by Günther Hunold, producers in the new low-budget environment shied away from buying rights and instead relied on established genres, formulas, and easily marketable gimmicks. Sexploitation, for a maximum of efficiency, obsessively constructed friction between the most basic of binaries: man–woman, local–foreign, and between seemingly unconnected genres. That such a shift back into strict binaries was accompanied by a broad shift to the comedic, epitomized by the perplexingly popular Bavarian-set *Lederhosen* films, may show that it was at this point difficult to perform such cinematic backtracking with a straight face.

Producers

Keeping in mind the shift to West German interiority that sexploitation film performed on the textual level, the films were perhaps surprisingly successful exports. One important aspect is that some of the main players that emerged in the West German sexploitation business were very experienced in transnational production and distribution strategies, with several of them not originally based in Germany at all. The Austrian Karl Spiehs (with his company Lisa Film) participated in the boom from the start, and was quite active in utilizing "exotic" contrasts – both national and generic – to market his product, especially after the initial attraction of the sexploitation cycle had ended: *Ding Dong* (*Drei Bayern in Bangkok*, 1976, Sigi Rothemund) set the *Lederhosen*-subgenre into an exotic locale, *Dracula Blows his Cool* (*Graf Dracula beißt jetzt in Oberbayern*, 1979, Carl Schenkel) provided a combination of *Lederhosen* antics with comedy-horror, *Nympho Girls* (*Drei Schwedinnen auf der Reeperbahn*, 1980, Walter Boos) mixed the Hamburg-film with the *Schwedenfilm* subgenre, and a number of other films attempted to profit from the allure of popular travel destinations such as Greece or Ibiza.[11]

The restless Swiss producer/distributor/exhibitor Erwin C. Dietrich used his small battalion of German-based production and financing companies to churn out international co-productions from a wide array of subgenres, often employing exploitation expert Jess Franco: *Higher and Higher* (*Ich, ein Groupie*, 1970, Erwin C. Dietrich) made a star of Ingrid Steeger; *Barbed Wire Dolls* (*Frauengefängnis*, 1975, Jess Franco) perpetuated the women-in-prison theme; and *She-Devils of the SS* (*Eine Armee Gretchen*, 1973, Erwin C. Dietrich) made use of the international fad for sadiconazista (for more on sadiconazista see Stiglegger, 1999). Dietrich's films are the ones most diffuse on the level of national signifiers and were the most consistently successful in terms of international distribution. Although a large portion of his productions are listed as Swiss, these films were highly successful within the West German sexploitation boom and usually shot as international co-productions with participation by Dietrich's German-listed companies.

Among the group of producers that found their fortune in sexploitation film, Alois Brummer appears as somewhat of an exception. Now mostly remembered for being the main focus of Hans Jürgen Syberberg's documentary *Sex-Business – Made in Pasing*, the owner of a small theater chain produced some of the more outrageous sex comedies such as *Graf Porno und die liebesdurstigen Töchter* (Count Porno and his Love-Hungry Daughters, 1969, Günther Hendel). Going straight into sexploitation production to supply his own theaters, the films mostly retained a rural focus and stayed within national distribution channels. On the whole, however, Spiehs, Dietrich and Hartwig were very active in international distribution of their films. Claiming a nation-centered tunnel vision on the level of narrative and setting, the films in fact did not solely rely on the German market, but used a focus on German signifiers as a tool for distinguishing themselves in the international sexploitation market as well.

Veteran industry powers, such as producers Artur Brauner, Ludwig Waldleitner, and Horst Wendlandt, made some tentative steps into sex-themed production, but never fully adjusted to the shifting market, enhancing the impression of fundamental changes in the film industry. However, the changing of the guard that took place with the rise of sexploitation can paradoxically also be viewed as the last stand for genre production and international distribution of the West German film industry. Eventually of course the at the time probably quite rational reliance on sex as the main audience attractor eventually led – especially after the legalization of hardcore pornography – to a frenzied spiral of self-cannibalizing genre recombinations and ever more intricate product differentiation. The trail leads from the fusing of the successful "coal miners" sex series *Lass jucken, Kumpel!* and the *Liebesgrüße aus der Lederhosen* series in the efficiently double-titled *Zwei Kumpel auf der Alm: Liebesgrüße aus der Lederhose 2. Teil / Lass jucken, Kumpel! 4: Zwei Kumpel auf der Alm* (Two Coal Miners in the Mountains: From the Lederhosen with Love Part 2 / Scratch the Itch, Coal Miner 4: Two Coal Miners in the Mountains, 1974, Franz Marischka) and ending in films such as *Sechs Schwedinnen auf der Alm*, now made for an exceedingly small audience.

Sexploitation cinema was in a sense always in the wrong corner. While the proponents of the New German Cinema saw the sexploitation films as guilty by association with "Daddy's cinema," the main producers driving the genre were in turn seen as destructive forces by the established film industry. And while Hartwig, Dietrich and Spiehs indeed to some degree were attempting to perpetuate the model of a popular and genre-based cinema that was internationally distributable, they had to rely on the emphasis on discontinuity and the spectacle of the new. Trying to assemble the second largest audience group still viable at the time – the male half of the population – they became a driving force in partitioning a general movie audience into niche audiences, beginning with the fault line of gender.

The Legacy of Sexploitation

For the general public in Germany today, theatrically released sexploitation cinema is (for the former West Germans) not more than a memory occasionally refreshed on late-night television. For researchers, the films provide complex and sometimes perplexing documentation of a web of discourses running through society and film in the 1960s and 1970s. The film-industrial legacy of these films, however, is uncertain. They did not, as Pink Film did in Japan, provide a fertile training ground for young scriptwriting and directing talents that could help sustain the domestic mainstream film industry in years to come.[12] Only in exceptions did this low-budget genre enable "artistic" experimentation, but it provided an easy entry into the film industry or simply a place to work for directors such as Gustav Ehmck, Siegfried Rothemund (often under the name of Sigi, or Siggi, Götz), or Fassbinder-collaborator Ulli Lommel (although the genre did launch the careers of a surprisingly high number of popular German film and TV actors, among others Ingrid Steeger, Elisabeth Volkmann, Konstantin Wecker, Sascha Hehn, and Heiner Lauterbach).

The films are, however, interesting as examples of a mode of a popular European cinema that is far removed from the style of filmmaking described by Bordwell, Staiger, and Thompson (1985) as "classical Hollywood style." Most of the films belonging to the sex film cycle of the 1960s and 1970s are certainly not "good movies" from the traditional (Euro-American) perspective, that is, technically well-made films with credible actors and a five-act narrative based on psychologically motivated characters. Nearly all of them use a loosely connected episodic structure, blend different genres and present their attractions – the naked female body and titillating comical or slapstick sketches – in a mode that is more reminiscent of the early "cinema of attractions" (Gunning, 1990). But a great many of them also utilize nonlinear storytelling and extreme manipulation of time. The convoluted narrative levels in the first *Schoolgirl Report* films, for example, are quite complex, and Bergfelder (2006: 229) points out that these "incoherent, elliptical and muted [films], marked by strangely emotionless characters [...] frustrate rather than confirm visual pleasures and narrative expectations in a manner that, perversely, is closer to avant-garde cinema than to the conventions of popular genres."

It was not, however, a subcutaneous avant-gardism that brought on the genre's rapid decline in popularity. While market saturation and the rise of home video played a role, the main reason for the genre's gradual demise from the mid-1970s onwards was the partial liberalization of pornography with the revision of the sexual crime legislation on January 28, 1975. Some of the later genre entries, for example the films of Hans Billian (the only one of the former *Heimatfilm* directors to make the switch to hardcore sex films), were now shot in both hard- and softcore versions (Schifferle, 2007: 14–15), but soon hardcore pornography – which was not allowed to be exhibited in normal cinemas – pushed the semipornographic films aside.

From 1967 to 1980 all in all more than 300 of the 782 solely West German produced films could be counted as sex films and thus over a period of 13 years the genre provided an average of 40% of the West German production output (Miersch, 2003: 131). The genre then virtually disappeared, only to experience a revival in the early 1990s when the commercial TV stations RTL+ and Sat 1 broadcast nearly all of the German sex and *Report* films with great success (with RTL+ aided greatly by its excellent connections to Karl Spiehs). Again, the domestic variant had significantly higher audience ratings than comparable foreign films and became a staple of Friday and Saturday late-night programming. A typical Saturday like May 18, 1991, for example had RTL+ air, between 11 p.m. to 4 a.m., *Lass laufen, Kumpel!* (Let it Go With the Flow, Coal Miner! 1981, Franz Marischka), two broadcasts of *Gaudi in der Lederhose* (Fun in the Lederhose, 1977, Jürgen Enz), and *Monika und die Sechzehnjährigen* (Monika and the 16 Year Olds, 1975, Charly Steinberger) as well as the Italian "nunsploitation" film *The Lady of Monza* (*La Monaca di Monza*, 1969, Eriprando Visconti). The counterprogramming of Sat 1 at the very same time slot included, besides one hour of sports, two broadcasts of *Teenage Sex Report* and the sex film spoof *Drei Lederhosen in St. Tropez* (Three Lederhosen in St. Tropez, 1980, Franz Marischka). On this randomly chosen Saturday both TV stations broadcast nearly nine combined hours of German sex films. On account of the scurrilous effect of the highly dated (by this time) portrayals of sexuality and their focus on self-conscious spectacle, it is perhaps not surprising that some of these films attracted a cult following, especially in the case of the *Schoolgirl Report* series. In the wake of the new popularity the comparatively lavish scores of this most successful German cinema series up till today were re-released on LP and CD. Television and DVD remain the media where the conventions of sexploitation film still persist to a limited degree, especially in sexuality-focused "informational" programs such as *Liebe Sünde* (Beloved Sin, 1993–2000) or *Wa(h)re Liebe* (True (Commodified) Love, 1994–2004), which however primarily reference the early phase of the sex education films. Even Oswalt Kolle, who published articles on the topic up to his death in 2010, cooperated with the private-owned German TV station ProSieben in 2008 for the successful five-part documentary *Sexreport 2008 – So lieben die Deutschen* (Sex Report 2008 – How the Germans Love, 2008), the title of which deliberately references his successes of the 1960s. Thus film-industrially and aesthetically West German sexploitation film remains largely inconsequential for film production today, an idiosyncratic and at times puzzling phenomenon now – at best – locked in cult film reception practice.

Notes

1 It must be emphasized that any statements on box-office and audience numbers from this era have to be regarded as possessing only approximate value. There are very few actually reliable numbers on the film industry available from the 1960s and early 1970s, much less about sexploitation film specifically.

2 The criterion of "simulated sexual activity" as opposed to "actual sexual activity," apart from the problem of a purely physical definition of sexuality, is of little value when there were a fair amount of films released in both hardcore and softcore versions in the 1970s.

3   There are a few exceptions to this tendency. Next to Seeßlen's pioneering works on popular cinema, e.g. his book on erotic cinema (1978, with Weil), Garncarz's 1996 study on popular cinema aimed at provoking a reevaluation of German popular cinema. The above-mentioned more recent studies are Bergfelder (2006) and Moltke (2005), while the volume edited by Halle and McCarthy (2003) also deals with German popular cinema of various eras.

4   Although there are in Germany examples of directors such as Monika Treut that explore sexual themes with political implications, this was not a common feature of the sex film genre per se. Some of the few "progressive" exceptions during the genre's heyday are the Munich-based sex films of Marran Gosov, e.g. *Angel Baby (Engelchen – oder die Jungfrau von Bamberg*, 1968), Gustav Ehmck's realistic melodrama *Die Spalte* (The Slit, 1971), and Rosa von Praunheim's gay rights film *It Is Not the Homosexual Who Is Perverse, But the Society in Which He Lives (Nicht der Homosexuelle ist pervers, sondern die Situation, in der er lebt*, 1971).

5   Pink Film are roughly defined as independently produced one-hour-long films with a fixed number of sexual scenes, shot on 35 mm film and released as triple bills in specialized theaters (a definition which mainly refers to its form from the early 1970s onward). Achieving explosive popularity in the first half of the 1960s they are still being produced today, albeit in much smaller numbers. Pink Films were, especially in the late 1960s, sites of explicit and usually leftist politics; while producer/director Kôji Wakamatsu is the (today) best-known example, this was actually a general tendency in the genre. For more on Pink Film, see Zahlten (2007) or Sharp (2008).

6   Local censorship remained in place, however, so that essentially every local police station could shut down a film deemed inappropriate. As Hagener correctly points out, this is actually an even more problematic situation for the film industry than a predictable centralized censorship policy (Hagener, 2000: 15).

7   Particularly Reich's *Die Massenpsychologie des Faschismus* (1933) and *Die Sexualität im Kulturkampf* (1936), the latter re-released in a revised edition under the title *The Sexual Revolution (Die sexuelle Revolution)* in 1966, provided students with catchphrases (Reich, 1971, 1993).

8   Another indicator of the deliberate recourse to the silent era are the two Rialto productions *Ideal Marriage (Van de Velde: Die vollkommene Ehe*, 1968) and *Van de Velde: Das Leben zu zweit – Sexualität in der Ehe* (Van de Velde: Life in a Partnership – Sexuality in Marriage, 1969, both Franz Josef Gottlieb), which mirror two early Weimar era films based on the works of Dutch gynecologist Theodoor Hendrik van de Velde: *Marriage (Die Ehe)* and *Fruchtbarkeit* (Fertility, both 1929, Eberhard Frohwein).

9   It is important to point out that other European cinematographies experienced similar trends toward sexploitation at this time. In Italy the success of Pier Paolo Pasolini's *The Decameron (Il Decameron*, 1971) and *The Canterbury Tales (I Racconti di Canterbury*, 1972) launched a boom of literary adaptations heavily relying on a sex angle, that were followed from the mid-1970s on by the frivolous sex comedies of the *film sexy* that remained one of the last successful domestic genres in Italy until the early 1980s (Brunetta, 2009: 273–277). In France the *Nouvelle Vague* generation's new relationship to sexuality was soon followed up by more obviously commercial filmmakers and sex film cycles like the *Emmanuelle* series (1974–1993), launched by Just Jaeckin's *Emmanuelle* (1974).

10   These highly successful series of 1960s popular German cinema showed a shift away from the German/Austrian settings of the *Heimatfilm* toward (supposedly) foreign locations. The Jerry Cotton series was based on a German pulp-fiction novel series about an FBI agent in New York; the Edgar Wallace films were set in a fantasy Britain based on convoluted murder plots and stereotypes of the British upper class (and on the books by the author of the same name). The Westerns, based on the books of German novelist Karl May, virtually ruled the box office during the 1960s. According to Bergfelder's excellent book on 1960s German cinema, the Jerry Cotton series comprised eight films, the Karl May series 17 films, and the Edgar Wallace cycle a whopping 38 films (plus an additional 10 from the spin-off Brian Edgar Wallace series) (Bergfelder, 2006: 251–260).

11   A very late addition to the penchant for exotic locations is the *Eis am Stiel* series (*Eskimo Limon*, aka *Lemon Popsicle*), an interesting exception to the West German sexploitation pattern. Initially an Israeli youth film that was nominated for the Golden Globe, it turned into a series of sex comedies that was co-produced with a German company from the third installment onward. The series ran between 1978 and 1988 with a total of eight films, the first few of which were highly successful in West Germany.
     The switch from regional to international settings partly reflects a change in the vacation patterns of the German population, resulting in a shift in the distribution of fantasies tied to certain localities. This entails certain significance for discourse of nation, as Germany appears, in the films set in southern Europe, as a more homogenous entity that than in the regional emphasis of the *Lederhosen* or *Hamburg* films. The films focusing on regional settings played off of urban/rural dynamics (strongly connected to a long-established North–South dynamic), and thus implied certain aspects of the discourse on a "new" democratic, modern and affluent Germany. The films set in popular travel destinations already have this affluence and international embeddedness as a precondition, but also draw on traditional German tropes regarding "romantic" Southern Europe that already featured prominently as far back as Goethe.

12   The sex-themed cinema of late 1970s/early 1980s Turkey was similarly incapable of providing a bridge to the mainstream and to help sustain general production in the long run.

References

Bergfelder, T. (2003) Exotic thrills and bedroom manuals: West German B-film production in the 1960s, in *Light Motives. German Popular Film in Perspective* (eds R. Halle and M. McCarthy), Wayne State University Press, Detroit, pp. 197–219.

Bergfelder, T. (2006) *International Adventures. German Popular Cinema and European Co-Productions in the 1960s*, Berghahn Books, New York, Oxford.

Bordwell, D., Staiger, J. and Thompson, K. (1985) *The Classical Hollywood Cinema: Film Style and Mode of Production to 1960.* Columbia University Press, New York.

Brunetta, G.P. (2009) *The History of Italian Cinema: A Guide to Italian Film from Its Origins to the Twenty-First Century*, Princeton University Press, Princeton, Oxford.

Dohrmann, O. (2000) "Kämpfer für eine Reform des § 218," "Limonade" oder Gretchentragödie? *Cynakali* im sozialhistorischen und intermedialen Kontext, in

Geschlecht in Fesseln. Sexualität zwischen Aufklärung und Ausbeutung im Weimarer Kino 1918–1933 (ed. M. Hagener), edition text + kritik (ein CineGraph Buch), München, pp. 102–118.

Elsaesser, T. (1989) *New German Cinema. A History*, Rutgers University Press, London, Basingstoke.

Elsaesser, T. and Wedel, M. (eds) (1999) *The BFI Companion to German Cinema*, BFI, London.

Ertel, H. (1990) *Erotika und Pornographie. Repräsentative Befragung und psychophysiologische Langzeitstudie zu Konsum und Wirkung*, Psychologie-Verlags-Union, München.

Fay, J. (2004) The Schoolgirl Reports and the guilty pleasure of history, in *Alternative Europe: Eurotrash and Exploitation Cinema Since 1945* (eds E. Mathijs and X. Mendik), Wallflower Press, London, pp. 39–52.

Garncarz, J. (1996) *Populäres Kino in Deutschland. Internationalisierung einer Filmkultur 1925–1990*. Habilitationsschrift. University of Cologne, Köln.

Garncarz, J. and Elsaesser, T. (1995) New German Cinema, in *Encyclopedia of European Cinema* (ed. G. Vincendeau), Cassell/BFI, London and New York, pp. 304–305.

Gramann, K. *et al.* (eds) (1981) *Lust und Elend. Das erotische Kino*, Bucher, München, Luzern.

Gregor, U. (1983) *Geschichte des Films ab 1960. Band 3*, Rowohlt, Reinbek bei Hamburg.

Gunning, T. (1990) The cinema of attractions: early film, its spectator and the avant-garde, 1986, in *Early Cinema: Space, Frame, Narrative* (ed. T. Elsaesser), BFI, London, pp. 56–62.

Gutknecht, C. (2004) *Ich mach's dir mexikanisch. Lauter erotische Wortgeschichten*, C.H. Beck, München.

Hagener, M. (ed.) (2000) *Geschlecht in Fesseln. Sexualität zwischen Aufklärung und Ausbeutung im Weimarer Kino 1918–1933*, edition text + kritik (ein CineGraph Buch), München.

Hagener, M. and Hans, J. (2000) Von Wilhelm zu Weimar. Der Aufklärungs- und Sittenfilm zwischen Zensur und Markt, in *Geschlecht in Fesseln. Sexualität zwischen Aufklärung und Ausbeutung im Weimarer Kino 1918–1933* (ed. M. Hagener), edition text + kritik (ein CineGraph Buch), München, pp. 7–22.

Hake, S. (2008) *German National Cinema*, 2nd edn, Routledge, London.

Halle, R. and McCarthy, M. (eds) (2003) *Light Motives: German Popular Film in Perspective*, Wayne State University Press, Detroit.

Hartwig, W.C. and Miersch, A. (2003) Vorspiel: "Das war alles aus dem Leben gegriffen." Interview mit dem Produzenten der *Schulmädchen-Reporte*, in *Schulmädchen-Report. Der deutsche Sexfilm der 70er Jahre* (ed. A. Miersch), Betz, Berlin, pp. 7–36.

Haufen, G. (aka Karsten Rodemann) (1990a) Die Lust zu zweit. Sex-Aufklärung made in Germany. *Splatting Image*, 2 (4), 17–20.

Haufen, G. (1990b) Tatsachenbericht der jungen Liebe. Schulmädchen von Heute. *Splatting Image*, 2 (5), 17–20.

Haufen, G. (1991) Tatsachenbericht der jungen Liebe. Teil 2. Der deutsche Hausfrauen-Report. *Splatting Image*, 3 (6), 39–42.

Hunold, G. (1970) *Schuldmädchen-Report. Sexprotokolle*, Kindler, München.

Jacobsen, W., Kaes, A. and Prinzler, H.H. (eds) (2004) *Geschichte des Deutschen Films*, 2nd edn, Metzler, Stuttgart, Weimar.

Kracauer, S. (1966) *From Caligari to Hitler. A Psychological History of the German Film*, Princeton University Press, Princeton, NJ.

Kracauer, S. (1979) *Von Caligari zu Hitler (erste vollständige Ausgabe). Eine psychologische Geschichte des deutschen Films*, Suhrkamp, Frankfurt a.M.

Marcuse, H. (1962) *Eros and Civilization*, Vintage Books, New York.

Miersch, A. (2003) *Schulmädchen-Report. Der deutsche Sexfilm der 70er Jahre*, Betz, Berlin.

Moltke, J.V. (2005) *No Place Like Home. Locations of Heimat in German Cinema*, University of California Press, Berkeley, Los Angeles.

Nead, L. (1997) The female nude: pornography, art, and sexuality, in *Gender Violence. Interdisciplinary Perspectives* (eds L.I. O'Toole, J.R. Schiffman, J.R. and Edwards, M.L.K.), New York University Press, New York, London, 374–382.

Phelix, L. and Thissen, R. (1986) *Pioniere und Prominente des modernen Sexfilms* (ed. C. Bandmann), Goldmann, München.

Prinzler, H.H. (1995) *Chronik des deutschen Films 1895–1994*, J.B. Metzler, Stuttgart, Weimar.

Reich, W. (1971) *Die Massenpsychologie des Faschismus*, Kiepenheuer and Witsch, Köln.

Reich, W. (1993) *Die sexuelle Revolution*, Fischer, Frankfurt a.M. (1st edn, 1936: *Die Sexualität im Kulturkampf*).

Rückert, C. (2000) Gute Frauenerotik und schlechte Männerpornographie. *tv diskurs. Verantwortung in audiovisuellen Medien*, 4 (12), 28–34.

Sanke, P. (1994) Der bundesdeutsche Kinofilm der 80er Jahre. Unter besonderer Berücksichtigung seines thematischen, topographischen und chronikalischen Realitätsverhältnisses. Doctoral diss. Philipps-Universität Marburg, Marburg, http://archiv.ub.uni-marburg.de/diss/z1995/0493/pdf/dps.pdf (accessed February 11, 2011).

Schifferle, H. (2007) Sex-business made in Germany. Anmerkungen zum deutschen Erotikkino der 60er und 70er. *epd Film*, 24 (9), 14–16.

Schmidt, U. (2000) "Der Blick auf den Körper." Sozialhygienische Filme, Sexualaufklärung und Propaganda in der Weimarer Republik, in *Geschlecht in Fesseln. Sexualität zwischen Aufklärung und Ausbeutung im Weimarer Kino 1918–1933* (ed. M. Hagener), edition text + kritik (ein CineGraph Buch), München, pp. 23–46.

Seeßlen, G. (1994) *Der pornographische Film. Von den Anfängen bis zur Gegenwart*, 2nd edn, Ullstein, Berlin, Frankfurt a.M.

Seeßlen, G. and Weil, C. (1978) *Ästhetik des erotischen Kinos. Eine Einführung in die Mythologie, Geschichte und Theorie des erotischen Films*, Roloff und Seeßlen, München.

Sharp, J. (2008) *Behind the Pink Curtain. The Complete History of Japanese Sex Cinema*, FAB Press, Surrey.

Sigl, K., Schneider, W. and Tornow, I. (1986) *Jede Menge Kohle? Kunst und Kommerz auf dem deutschen Filmmarkt der Nachkriegszeit. Filmpreise und Kassenerfolge*, Filmland Presse, München.

Steinwender, H. and Zahlten, A. (2009a) Einige Überlegungen zum europäischen Populärfilm. *MEDIENwissenschaft. Rezensionen. Reviews*, 26 (4), 371–391.

Steinwender, H. and Zahlten, A. (2009b) Unpublished interview with Hanns Eckelkamp, September 17.

Stiglegger, M. (1999) *Sadiconazista. Faschismus und Sexualität im Film*, Gardez! St Augustin.

Thissen, R. (1995) *Sex verklärt. Der deutsche Aufklärungsfilm*, Heyne, München.

Wardenbach, G. (1993) *Bayern als Lokalität im deutschen Sexfilm*. Masters thesis, University of Cologne, Köln.

Wente, B. (1992) *Protagonisten und Ensemble im deutschen Sexfilm der 70er Jahre*. Unpublished MA thesis, University of Cologne, Köln.

Zahlten, A. (2009) *The Role of Genre in Film from Japan. Transformations 1960s–2000s*, UMI, Ann Arbor.

Further Reading

As mentioned in the introduction, academic literature on West German sexploitation film is few and very far between, and most of it is in German. The case study on the *Schulmädchen Report* series by Miersch (2003) provides valuable insight into the production boom of the early 1970s and close textual analysis. The volume on the *Sittenfilm* edited by Hagener (2000) is exemplary in both the breadth and depth of its articles. Garncarz's 1996 study of popular cinema in Germany was one of the earliest reevaluations of popular genres in Germany. It provides data on the box-office appeal of German films from 1925 to 1990 that corrects some methodically problematic aspects of the nevertheless useful overview delivered by Sigl, Schneider, and Tornow (1986). Seeßlen's books on erotic cinema (1978, with Weil) and pornographic films (1994) are not completely reliable in terms of facts, but were pioneering works in the German language and are full of often thought-provoking arguments. Phelix and Thissen (1986) and Thissen (1995) both deliver decidedly nonacademic but at least partially useful overviews of West German sexploitation. In English, Bergfelder (2006) supplies an invaluable account of the general production context of the 1960s including a chapter on the German B-film and the sexploitation cycles. Fay (2004) reviews the *Schulmädchen-Report* series as unconscious representations of repressed German history. Finally, Syberberg's film *Sex Business – Made in Pasing* (1969) is an interesting documentation of the extremely low-budget production environment German sexploitation existed in, and can be ordered directly from his website.

Filmography

Early *Sittenfilme*

Cyankali [Cyanide] (1930, Germany, Hans Tintner).
Different from the Others [*Anders als die Andern – Sozialhygienisches Filmwerk*] (1919, Germany, Richard Oswald).
Es werde Licht! [*Es werde Licht! 1. Teil*/Let There Be Light!] (1917, Germany, Richard Oswald).
Feind im Blut [Enemy in Your Blood] (1931, Germany, Walter Ruttmann).
Der Fluch der Vererbung [*Die nicht Mutter werden dürfen*/The Curse of Heredity] (1927, Germany, Adolf Trotz).
Fruchtbarkeit [*Fruchtbarkeit – Das Problem der Mutterschaft*/*Das Problem der Mutterschaft – Ein Van de Velde-Film*/Fertility] (1929, Germany, Eberhard Frohwein).
Madame Lu, die Frau für diskrete Beratung [Madame Lu, the Woman for Discrete Consultation] (1929, Germany, Franz Hofer).
Marriage [*Die Ehe*/*Die Ehe – Ein Film von Van de Velde*/*Die vollkommene Ehe*] (1929, Germany, Eberhard Frohwein).
Die Minderjährige [*Die Minderjährige – Zu jung fürs Leben*/The Minor] (1921, Germany, Alfred Tostary).

Sex in Chains [*Geschlecht in Fesseln (Sexualnot der Gefangenen)/Geschlecht in Fesseln – Die Sexualnot der Strafgefangenen*] (1928, Germany, Wilhelm Dieterle).

Der Weg, der zur Verdammnis führt, 1. Teil: Das Schicksal der Aenne Wolter [The Road to Damnation, Part 1: The Fate of Aenne Wolter] (1919, Germany, Otto Rippert).

Der Weg, der zur Verdammnis führt, 2. Teil – Hyänen der Lust [The Road to Damnation, Part 2: Hyenas of Lust] (1919, Germany, Otto Rippert).

The *Helga* films

Helga [*Helga – Vom Werden des menschlichen Lebens*] (1967, West Germany, Erich F. Bender).

Helga und die Männer – Die Sexuelle Revolution [Helga and the Men – The Sexual Revolution] (1969, West Germany, Roland Cämmerer).

Michael and Helga [*Helga und Michael*] (1968, West Germany, Erich F. Bender).

The *Kolle* series

Female Sexuality [*Oswalt Kolle: Deine Frau, das unbekannte Wesen*] (1969, West Germany, Alexis Neve).

Miracle of Love, The/The Wonder of Love [*Das Wunder der Liebe/Das Wunder der Liebe – Sexualität in der Ehe/Oswalt Kolle: Das Wunder der Liebe*] (1968, West Germany, Franz Josef Gottlieb).

Oswalt Kolle: Liebe als Gesellschaftsspiel [Oswalt Kolle: Love as a Party Game] (1972, West Germany, Werner M. Lenz).

Oswalt Kolle – Pay Example: Adultery [*Oswalt Kolle – Zum Beispiel: Ehebruch*] (1969, West Germany, Alexis Neve and Oswalt Kolle).

Oswalt Kolle: Was ist eigentlich Pornografie? [Oswalt Kolle: What, By the Way, is Pornography?] (1970, West Germany, Oswalt Kolle).

Sensual Male, The [*Oswalt Kolle: Dein Mann, das unbekannte Wesen*] (1970, West Germany, Werner M. Lenz).

Sexual Partnership [*Oswalt Kolle: Das Wunder der Liebe II – Sexuelle Partnerschaft/Das Wunder der Liebe II*] (1968, West Germany, Alexis Neve).

Your Child, That Unknown Creature [*Oswalt Kolle: Dein Kind, das unbekannte Wesen*] (1970, West Germany, Werner M. Lenz).

The *Schulmädchen Report* series

Blue Dreams/Confessions of a Naked Virgin/Secrets of a Naked Virgin [*Schuldmädchen-Report 11. Teil – Probieren geht über studieren*] (1977, West Germany, Ernst Hofbauer).

Campus Swingers/Schoolgirl Report Part 4: What Drivers Parents to Despair/Sex Education/Barely Innocent [*Schuldmädchen-Report 4. Teil – Was Eltern oft verzweifeln lässt*] (1972, West Germany, Ernst Hofbauer).

Carnal Campus/Blue Fantasies [*Schuldmädchen-Report 12. Teil – Wenn das die Mammi wüsste*] (1978, West Germany, Walter Boos).

Further Confessions of a Sixth Form Girl/Schoolgirls' Report – Why Parents Lose Their Sleep [*Der neue Schulmädchen-Report 2. Teil: Was Eltern den Schlaf raubt/Schulmädchen-Report 2. Teil: Was Eltern den Schlaf raubt/Der neue Schulmädchenreport*] (1970, West Germany, Ernst Hofbauer).

Naughty Coeds [*Schuldmädchen-Report 8. Teil – Was Eltern nie erfahren dürfen*] (1974, West Germany, Ernst Hofbauer).

Naughty Freshmen/Schoolgirl Report Part 5: What All Parents Should Know [*Schuldmädchen-Report 5. Teil – Was Eltern wirklich wissen sollten*] (1973, West Germany, Ernst Hofbauer and Walter Boos).

School Girls, The/Confessions of a Sixth Form Girl [*Schulmädchen-Report: Was Eltern nicht für möglich halten*] (1970, West Germany, Ernst Hofbauer).

Schoolgirls Growing Up/Schoolgirl Report Part 3 [*Schulmädchen-Report 3. Teil – Was Eltern nicht mal ahnen*] (1972, West Germany, Walter Boos and Ernst Hofbauer).

Smartie Pants [*Schuldmädchen-Report 10. Teil – Irgendwann fängt jede an*] (1976, West Germany, Walter Boos).

Sweet Young Trouble [*Vergiss beim Sex die Liebe nicht – Der neue Schuldmädchen-Report 13. Teil*] (1980, West Germany, Walter Boos).

Teenage Playmates/Lucifer's Angels [*Schuldmädchen-Report 7. Teil – Doch das Herz muss dabei sein*] (1974, West Germany, Ernst Hofbauer).

When Girls Make Love [*Schuldmädchen-Report 9. Teil – Reifeprüfung vor dem Abitur*] (1975, West Germany, Walter Boos).

The *Hausfrauen-Report* series

Give 'em an Inch [*Hausfrauen-Report 3. Teil/Hausfrauen-Report 3*] (1972, West Germany, Eberhard Schröder).

Hausfrauen-Report 6. Teil: Warum gehen Frauen fremd? [Housewives Report Part 6: Why Are Women Unfaithful?] (1978, West Germany, August Rieger).

Housewives on the Job [*Hausfrauen-Report International/Hausfrauen-Report 5. Teil: Hausfrauenreport international*] (1973, West Germany, Ernst Hofbauer).

Housewives Report/On the Side [*Hausfrauen-Report: Unglaublich, aber wahr*] (1971, West Germany, Eberhard Schröder).

Most Girls Will [*Der neue Hausfrauen-Report, 2. Teil/Hausfrauen-Report 2*] (1971, West Germany, Eberhard Schröder).

Sensuous Housewife, The/Wide Open Marriage [*Hausfrauen-Report 4. Teil*] (1973, West Germany, Eberhard Schröder).

Other German, Austrian or Swiss Sexploitation Films and Nudity- or Sex-themed Films

2069: A Sex Odyssey/Sex Odyssey [*Ach jodel mir noch einen – Stoßtrupp Venus bläst zum Angriff/Stoßtrupp Venus – 5 Mädchen blasen zum Angriff*] (1974, West Germany/Austria, Georg Tressler).

Abarten der körperlichen Liebe [Perversions of Physical Love] (1970, West Germany, Franz Marischka).

Angel Baby [*Engelchen – oder die Jungfrau von Bamberg*] (1968, West Germany, Marran Gosov).

Asia perversa/Shocking Asia [*Shocking Asia – Sünde, Sex und Sukiyaki*] (1976, West Germany/ Hong Kong, Rolf Olsen).

Barbed Wire Dolls/Caged Women [*Frauengefängnis*] (1975, Switzerland, Jess Franco aka Jesús Franco Manera).

Bewildered Youth [*Anders als du und ich/Das dritte Geschlecht/Anders als du und ich (§ 175)*] (1957, West Germany, Veit Harlan).

Bohr weiter, Kumpel! [*Glück auf – Der Steiger kommt!/Im Kohlenpott wackeln die Betten/*Drill along, Coal Miner] (1974, West Germany, Sigi Götz aka Siegfried Rothemund).

Confessions of a Campus Virgin/Train Station Pickups/Confessions of a Sixth Form Virgin [*Die Schulmädchen vom Treffpunkt Zoo*] (1979, West Germany, Walter Boos).

Ding Dong [*Drei Bayern in Bangkok/Was treibt die Maus im Badehaus?/Drei Oberbayern auf Dirndljagd*] (1976, West Germany, Sigi [Siegfried] Rothemund).

Do You Believe in Swedish Sin?/Swedish Sin [*Nach Stockholm der Liebe wegen*] (1969, West Germany/Sweden, Gunnar Höglund).

Don't Get Your Knickers in a Twist [*Mutzenbacher 2. Teil: Meine 365 Liebhaber/Josefine Mutzenbacher – Meine 365 Liebhaber*] (1971, West Germany, Kurt Nachmann).

Dornwittchen und Schneeröschen [*Dornwittchen und Schneeröschen (Mal mit, mal ohne Höschen)/* Sleeping-White and Snow-Beauty] (1970, West Germany, Erwin Klein).

Dracula Blows his Cool [*Graf Dracula beißt jetzt in Oberbayern*] (1979, West Germany/Italy, Carl Schenkel).

Drei Lederhosen in St. Tropez [Three Lederhosen in St. Tropez] (1980, West Germany, Franz Marischka).

Du – Zwischenzeichen der Sexualität [You – Subtle Signals in Sexuality] (1968, West Germany, Gerhard Zenkel).

Erotic Center [*Eros Center Hamburg*] (1969, West Germany, Günter Hendel).

Fanny Hill – Memoirs of a Woman of Pleasure [*Fanny Hill*] (1964, West Germany/USA, Russ Meyer and Albert Zugsmith).

Forbidden Paradise [*Das verbotene Paradies*] (1958, West Germany, Max Nosseck).

Freedom to Love/Freedom of Love [*Freiheit für die Liebe*] (1969, West Germany, Phyllis and Eberhardt Kronhausen).

Gaudi in der Lederhose [Fun in the Lederhose] (1977, West Germany, Jürgen Enz).

Graf Porno und die liebesdurstigen Töchter [*Ein Graf in Oberbayern/*Count Porno and his Love-Hungry Daughters] (1969, West Germany, Günther Hendel).

Grimm's Fairy Tales for Adults/The New Adventures of Snow White [*Grimms Märchen von lüsternen Pärchen/Schneewittchen … doch ein Flittchen*] (1969, West Germany, Rolf Thiele).

Higher and Higher/Me, a Groupie [*Ich, ein Groupie*] (1970, West Germany/Switzerland, Erwin C. Dietrich).

The Hostess Exceeds All Bounds [*Frau Wirtin treibt es jetzt noch Toller*] (1970, West Germany/ Austria, Franz Antel).

Hotel by the Hour [*Das Stundenhotel von St. Pauli*] (1970, West Germany, Rolf Olsen).

Ideal Marriage/Intimate Desires of Women [*Van de Velde: Die vollkommene Ehe*] (1968, West Germany, Franz Josef Gottlieb).

It Is Not the Homosexual Who Is Perverse, But the Society in Which He Lives [*Nicht der Homosexuelle ist pervers, sondern die Situation, in der er lebt*] (1971, West Germany, Rosa von Praunheim).

Jungfrau aus zweiter Hand [Second-hand Virgin] (1967, West Germany, Akos von Rathonyi).

Kursaison für scharfe Kumpel [*Kursaison im Dirndlhöschen/Dirndljagd in Oberbayern/ Lederhosenzauber*/Spa Season for Raunchy Coal Miners] (1981, West Germany, Alois Brummer).

Lass jucken, Kumpel! [Scratch the Itch, Coal Miner!] (1972, West Germany, Franz Marischka).

Lass laufen, Kumpel! [*Lass jucken, Kumpel! 6. Teil/Ran an die Möpse, Kumpel!*/Let It Go With the Flow, Coal Miner!] (1981, West Germany, Franz Marischka).

Liane, Jungle Goddess [*Liane, das Mädchen aus dem Urwald*] (1956, West Germany, Eduard von Borsody).

Liebesgrüße aus der Lederhose [From the Lederhosen with Love] (1973, West Germany, Franz Marischka).

Liebestechnik für Fortgeschrittene [Love Techniques for the Experienced] (1970, West Germany, Kurt Palm).

Long Swift Sword of Siegfried, The/The Erotic Adventures of Siegfried [*Siegfried und das sagenhafte Liebesleben der Nibelungen*] (1971, West Germany, Adrian Hoven).

Der lüsterne Türke [*Der lüsterne Türke – Seine Nächte mit Eliza, Suleika und Ranah … und wie es ihm erging/Die blonde Haremsdame/Die blonde Sex-Sklavin*/The Lecherous Turk] (1971, West Germany, Michael Miller).

Monika und die Sechzehnjährigen [Monika and the 16 Year Olds] (1975, West Germany, Charly Steinberger).

Naked Wytche, The [*Lass uns knuspern, Mäuschen/Hänsel und Gretel verliefen sich im Wald*] (1970, West Germany, Franz Josef Gottlieb).

Naughty Knickers [*Josefine Mutzenbacher*] (1970, West Germany, Kurt Nachmann).

Nurses Report [*Krankenschwestern-Report*] (1972, West Germany, Walter Boos).

Nympho Girls/Three Swedish Girls in Hamburg [*Drei Schwedinnen auf der Reeperbahn/Auf St. Pauli ist die Hölle los*] (1980, West Germany, Walter Boos).

Pornography in Denmark [*Pornographie in Dänemark – Zur Sache, Kätzchen/Beim Sex ist alles erlaubt (2. Teil)*] (1970, West Germany, Michael Miller).

Pudelnackt in Oberbayern [Stark Naked in Upper Bavaria] (1968, West Germany, Hans Albin).

Sechs Schwedinnen auf der Alm [Six Swedes in the Alps] (1983, West Germany, Erwin C. Dietrich).

Sex Adventures of the Three Musketeers, The/The Three Musketeers and Their Sexual Adventures [*Die Sexabenteuer der drei Musketiere*] (1971, West Germany, Erwin C. Dietrich).

She-Devils of the SS/Fräuleins in Uniforms [*Eine Armee Gretchen*] (1973, Switzerland, Erwin C. Dietrich).

Spalte, Die [The Slit] (1971, Gustav Ehmck).

St. Pauli Nachrichten – Thema Nr. 1 [St. Pauli News – Topic No. 1] (1971, West Germany, Franz Marischka).

Sweet Sins of Sexy Susan, The [*Susanne, die Wirtin von der Lahn/Frau Wirtin von der Lahn*] (1967, Austria/Italy/Hungary, Franz Antel).

Swingin' Stewardesses, The/Naked Stewardesses/Sweet Sensations/Stewardesses Report [*Die Stewardessen*] (1971, Switzerland, Erwin C. Dietrich).

Teach Me/The Games Schoolgirls Play [*Auch Fummeln will gelernt sein*] (1972, West Germany, Kurt Nachmann).

Teenage Sex Report [*Mädchen beim Frauenarzt*] (1971, West Germany, Ernst Hofbauer).

Van de Velde: Das Leben zu zweit – Sexualität in der Ehe [Van de Velde: Life in a Partnership – Sexuality in Marriage] (1969, West Germany, Franz Josef Gottlieb).

Virgin Report [Jungfrauenreport/Jungfrauen-Report] (1972, West Germany, Jess Franco aka Jesús Franco Manera).

Virgins of the Seven Seas/The Bod Squad/Enter the Seven Virgins [Karate, Küsse, Blonde Katzen/ Yang chi] (1974, West Germany/Hong Kong, Ernst Hofbauer and Chih-Hung Kuei).

Wo der Wildbach durch das Höschen rauscht [Witwen Report/Sexgrüße aus dem Lederhöschen/ Where the Mountain Torrent Rushes Through the Panties] (1974, West Germany, Jürgen Enz).

Zwei Kumpel auf der Alm: Liebesgrüße aus der Lederhose 2. Teil/Lass Jucken Kumpel 4: Zwei Kumpel auf der Alm [Lass jucken Kumpel 4/Two Coal Miners in the Mountains: From the Lederhosen with Love 2. Part/Scratch the Itch, Coal Miner 4: Two Coal Miners in the Mountains] (1974, West Germany, Franz Marischka).

Other Films and Documentaries

491 [491] (1964, Sweden, Vilgot Sjöman).

Berlin – Symphonie einer Großstadt/Berlin – Symphony of a Great City/Berlin: Symphony of a Metropolis [Berlin – Die Symphonie der Großstadt] (1927, Germany, Walter Ruttmann).

Bob and Sally [Tell Our Parents/The Story of Bob and Sally] (1948, USA, Erle C. Kenton).

Canterbury Tales, The [I racconti di Canterbury] (1972, Italy/France, Pier Paolo Pasolini).

Decameron, The [Il Decameron] (1971, Italy/France/West Germany, Pier Paolo Pasolini).

Emmanuelle (1974, France, Just Jaeckin).

Going all the Way/Lemon Popsicle [Eskimo Limon] (1978, Israel, Boaz Davidson).

Horrors of Spider Island/Body in the Web/It's Hot in Paradise/The Spider's Web/Girls of Spider Island [Ein Toter hing im Netz] (1959, West Germany/Yugoslavia, Fritz Böttger).

I Am Curious – Yellow [Jag är nyfiken – Gul] (1967, Sweden, Vilgot Sjöman).

Jud Süß [Jew Süss] (1940, Germany, Veit Harlan).

Kolberg [Kolberg] (1945, Germany, Veit Harlan).

Lady of Monza, The/The Nun of Monza [La Monaca di Monza] (1969, Italy, Eriprando Visconti).

Nosferatu [Nosferatu – Eine Symphonie des Grauens] (1922, Germany, F. W. Murnau).

Sex-Business – Made in Pasing [Sex-Business – Made in Pasing] (1969, West Germany, Hans Jürgen Syberberg) (TV).

Sexreport 2008 – So lieben die Deutschen [Sex Report 2008 – How the Germans Love] (2008, Germany) (TV).

Silence, The [Tystnaden] (1963, Sweden, Ingmar Bergman).

Sins of the Borgias [Lucrèce Borgia/Lucretia Borgia] (1953, Italy/France, Christian-Jaque).

Story of a Sinner, The [Die Sünderin] (1951, West Germany, Willi Forst).

Von Sex bis Simmel [Von Sex bis Simmel – Anmerkungen zum deutschen Film der 70er Jahre/From Sex to Simmel – Notes on German Film in the 1970s] (2005, Germany, Hans Günther Pflaum and Peter H. Schröder) (TV).

Wo der Wildbach rauscht [Where the Mountain Torrent Rushes] (1956, West Germany, Heinz Paul).

Women of the World [La donna nel mondo] (1963, Italy, Paolo Cavara, Gualitiero Jacopetti and Franco Prosperi).

13

A Documentarist at the Limits of Queer

The Films of Jochen Hick

Robert M. Gillett

The relationship between German cinema, queer cinema, and documentary cinema has rarely been the focus of critical interest. There are excellent studies on German queer cinema, on German documentary cinema, and on queer documentary cinema, but virtually nothing on German queer documentary. Alice Kuzniar (2000), for example, takes the aesthetics of the New Queer Cinema and the discourses of Queer theory and applies them to an array of German films ranging in date from 1919 to 1997. Along the way, she rightly points out that "although scholarly response to the global 1990s trend in queer filmmaking has been dynamic [...] it bypasses the conspicuous differences that characterize and comprise the tradition established in Germany" (Kuzniar, 2000: 4). But she also concedes that "the documentary format" is "underrepresented" in her own book (Kuzniar, 2000: 15). Nora M. Alter (2002: 2) sets out to investigate "a discrete 'nonfiction' unit that is close to, but not entirely part of, dominant [German] feature film production." Where Kuzniar notes a "dynamic" scholarly response to global queer filmmaking, Alter (2002: 4) is able to document "an explosion of studies on nonfiction and documentary film. But Alter, like Kuzniar, is left asking: "What, then, might explain the neglect of this genre by German film studies?" (Alter, 2002: 4). If Kuzniar's study has a "particular orientation," Alter's has a unifying theme, *Projecting History*. And the word "queer" is avoided with a sedulousness that feels programmatic.[1] By contrast, the 1997 collective volume edited by Chris Holmlund and Cynthia Fuchs foregrounds the term "queer," and applies it specifically to documentary. In their introduction, Holmlund and Fuchs (1997: 2), like Kuzniar and Alter, lament the unfocused treatment of their subject in a plethora of previous and contemporary publications. The self-evident focus of this American book, though, is on American film. Hence, in her "film and videography" *(sic)*, Lynda McAffee (1997: 242) restricts herself to films available in the United States, noting

A Companion to German Cinema, First Edition. Edited by Terri Ginsberg and Andrea Mensch.
© 2012 Blackwell Publishing Ltd. Published 2012 by Blackwell Publishing Ltd.

that "unfortunately this last criterion of distribution excludes [...] international documentaries." And indeed her list includes only one film that is attributed unambiguously to "Germany" (McAffee, 1997: 249).

That one film is *I Am My Own Woman* (*Ich bin meine eigene Frau*, 1992), by Rosa von Praunheim. The first two films of Praunheim's AIDS trilogy, *Silence = Death* (*Schweigen = Tod*, 1989) and *Positive* (*Positiv*, 1990), are also included, as German-American co-productions; so too is Monika Treut's *Female Misbehavior* (1992) (McAffee, 1997: 257, 255, 246–247). Two further films by Praunheim are featured in Thomas Waugh's essay from the same collection on "Lesbian and Gay Liberation Documentary of the Post-Stonewall Period 1969–84" (Waugh, 1997: 109, 113–116, 121). Alter for her part includes not only Praunheim, but also Elfi Mikesch, in a list of important German-speaking essay filmmakers (Alter, 2002: 84). Kuzniar invokes documentary in her discussion of films by Jürgen Brüning, Jörg Fockele, and Claudia Schillinger (Kuzniar, 2000: 189, 220). And the filmmaker she does not feel able to do justice to because of his use of the documentary format is Jochen Hick (Kuzniar, 2000: 15).

The sheer number and weight of these names, and the contexts in which they occur, suggest that something important has been marginalized. The mechanisms by which this occurs, of course, form part of the context of German queer documentary filmmaking. Most obviously, the unspoken, and often even unconscious, reluctance of the straight majority to accommodate queer has a direct impact on the funding possibilities for, and hence the aesthetic parameters of, the films concerned. The dominance of the United States in the fields both of queer and of the cinema has had a direct effect on the subject matter and form of German queer documentaries. It is not for nothing, after all, that both Treut and Praunheim figure in McAffee with German-American co-productions. And the fraught relationship between truth-telling and performance that is at the center of queer not only helps to determine the relationship between the feature film and the documentary, but also subtends the whole genre of the queer documentary itself, as the notion of "performative documentary" shows.[2]

The specifically German contribution to these debates is as prominent as it is distinctive. It is not just that canonical filmmakers associated with the New German Cinema have been massively concerned with documenting performances. Rainer Werner Fassbinder, after all, both came from, and frequently filmed in, the theater.[3] And Werner Herzog's documentary portrait, *My Best Fiend – Klaus Kinski* (*Mein liebster Feind – Klaus Kinski*, 1999), can be seen as a performative study of performance itself. The German context is also informed by a uniquely important body of writing about the nature and purpose of realism. Of central importance here, alongside Siegfried Kracauer, is Bertolt Brecht. Brecht's pervasive influence can be seen in the work of filmmakers as different as Straub/Huillet, Alexander Kluge, and Volker Schlöndorff.[4] And in the controversial trilogy by Hans Jürgen Syberberg, comprising *Ludwig* (1972), *Karl May* (1974) and *Hitler* (1977), Brecht enters into an unlikely alliance with Richard Wagner.[5]

This combination not only fantastically encapsulates the "dialectic of the Enlightenment" – it also neatly helps to mark out the parameters of German queer documentary.[6] It is of course a particularly German pairing, and in his trilogy Syberberg is very concerned to explore German history and the German imagination. The counterintuitive yoking together of analysis and myth, minimalism and excess, sober, even cynical observation and camp performance, as practised by Syberberg, also informs and helps to define queer aesthetics. Thus none of Syberberg's three films is straightforwardly heterosexual, and the diegetic perspective adopted is often predicated upon a nonstraight sexuality.[7] The subject matter moreover to which Syberberg applies his disparate techniques is neither invented nor fictionalized. Rather, it is so well known, and has so often been the subject of fictional, semifictional and nonfictional treatments that it can be said to have attained the status of discourse. And this wholesale and multifaceted interrogation of discourses is one of the chief aims and achievements of queer documentary.

All these considerations apply to Jochen Hick, who has come to be hailed (e.g. in the influential weekly *Der Spiegel* (see Anon, 2009)) as a leading exponent of the genre. Born and raised in Germany, Hick studied in Hamburg, inter alia with Helke Sander, and won his first prizes in Oberhausen, so his German credentials are impeccable. He is known to be gay, though he insists that he is not a gay filmmaker (see Hoo, 2009: 11). Throughout his career he has faced a constant struggle to find funds – a fact that has found its way both into his films themselves and into reviews of them.[8] The United States features prominently in his output. Indeed, several of his films were made in English, so globalization is written into his practice as well as being a theme. The fundamental gestures of his films are looking and listening, recording and presenting. That is to say: they spring from a realist impulse and are indebted to a realist aesthetic. Much of what is recorded and presented, though, has the status of self-conscious performance. This has the effect of attenuating both the intrusiveness of Hick's camera and the films' claims to veracity. It also offers an instructive parallel to the importance laid on performance in queer theory. Several of the performances depicted are generically pornographic, which makes acutely explicit the issue of viewing pleasure. At the same time, the disjunction between truth-effects and reality, between façade and fact, is gently insisted upon. This gentleness, and what could be called an undemonstrative sobriety of style, is a feature of Hick's work that is often praised. But concealed within it there are often contrasting moments of excess, shock, and naked emotion. One of these, indeed, is presented explicitly as operatic. And very often the effect is to call into question the safe assumptions of postmodern discourse as peddled in the West.

Historically, queer arose as a response to a very particular set of discourses and silences: those surrounding the emergence of AIDS. In his short *Welcome to the Cathedral* (*Willkommen im Dom*, 1991) Hick literally holds these discourses up to the camera. The film records a demonstration of people with AIDS against the Catholic synod, and the telling reactions of the faithful. As one reviewer put it: "Rabid rosarists punched gays on the nose and kicked them up the backside. Women called sporadically for gassing" (Riepe, 1992: 19; my translation).[9] It is noticeable however that, in an oeuvre mainly made up of documentaries, the two other films in which Hick foregrounds AIDS, namely *Via Appia* (1989) and *No One Sleeps* (1999), are both works of fiction. Critics, admittedly, have invoked documentary in their discussions of both. Thus Astrid-Elke Kurth (2002: 200 and passim) refers to *Via Appia* as "pseudodocumentary" and Stefanie Wilke (2000) describes the gaze in *No One Sleeps* as "dokumentarisch." Yet in both films Hick actually uses the generic possibilities of the feature film to call into question the truth effects of AIDS discourse. In *Via Appia* he uses the quest motive and the road movie to debunk the search for first causes. His protagonist Frank returns to Rio to revisit old haunts and reenact the scenario of his infection. The lynchpin of that scenario was a Brazilian called Mario. So when the film is constituted as a search for that Mario, it is tempting to read this a quest to discover the source of Frank's infection. (The fact that Mario is a resident of a Third World country, of course, complicates that temptation and, especially for North American critics, reinforces it.[10]) Ultimately, though, the quest turns out to be futile. Indeed, in one of the scenes in which the camera is characteristically hunting itself into a dead-end round the corners of a hotel corridor, Frank derisively cites the population statistics of the city of Rio, thus showing how insultingly simple-minded – and imperialist – this take on the film actually is.

In *No One Sleeps* Hick uses the trope of the detective story to offer fictional proof of a real theory about the virus in order to demonstrate both the bootlessness of such theorizing and the generic emotions invested in it. There the protagonist Stefan Hein is the son of an East German virologist who travels to San Francisco to present and find proof for his father's theory that the virus was deliberately cloned from sheep for use by the Pentagon in the Cold War.[11] By the end of the film, he has the proof that he needs, but is made aware by the policewoman who restores it to him of just how little he can do with it. The steps which lead to this discovery – including the frantic illegal rummaging through an office at night – are so obviously generic conventions that their fictionality is never in doubt. With the help of these conventions, though, Hick is able to invest with tension his concomitant discourse about the fate of information. And the gruesome murder of informants gives a new twist to the equation of silence with death.

The proximity of the protagonist to these murders, and the structuring of the film in a sequence of scenes that we realize with hindsight are a series of lucky escapes, enable Hick to explore and expose another ubiquitous saw of the AIDS debate: the yoking of sex and death.[12] Buying in neither to the moralistic claptrap which sees the syndrome as a punishment for sexual misdemeanors, nor to the perverse psychopathology of the Freudian *Todestrieb*, nor to the Romantic mystifications of the Wagnerian *Liebestod*, Hick allows his protagonist to be saved with the help of sex, not killed by it. Along the way, true to the conventions of his thriller genre, he takes the discourse of danger, omnipresent *ex negativo* in the discourse of "safe sex," and turns it inside out. The same can be said, *mutatis mutandis*, for *Via Appia*. We know we are on the eponymous street of Rio's red light district because Jose, our Brazilian guide, reminds us of the American who was murdered there. And the camera inches us warily into it, leaving us in no doubt as to the sort of place it is supposed to be. Indeed, the movement of the camera and lighting effects are used again and again in this movie to create the filmic equivalent of the sex/death/danger discourse. At one point, for example, we see infected blood gleaming unnaturally red in the half-light of a scene of mayhem. Yet the people who are in real and constant danger on the Via Appia are not the clients but the prostitutes, who are subject to periodic visits from the panda cars of the so-called "Salvation Army," and who cannot but regard the advancing camera as a comparable threat. By contrast, despite the expectations set up by the mise-en-scène, nothing serious happens to Frank and his friends at all. Even the mayhem in the hotel room is created not by some violent intruder, but by Frank himself – who had earlier insisted that elementary precautions would be sufficient for survival.

Whether Frank himself survives we do not know for certain, because Hick refuses closure. At the edge of the sea in someone else's dawn, the quest just stops. The film stock runs out. Hick's point is precisely that we must resist the temptation to aestheticize the syndrome. As he said in an interview accompanying the first television airing of the film: "Gays are exploited by being sent to die heroically" (Korf, 1990; my translation).[13] Any attempt to construe AIDS as a tragedy entails a failure to come to terms with the senselessness of the syndrome, and is ideologically suspect. Hence Hick's repudiation of what he calls the "bias" of "gay melodramas" (Korf, 1990). For him, AIDS is neither sexy nor sleazy, neither morally significant nor spiritually cathartic. It is not amenable to the logic either of praise and blame, or of cause and effect. It is the sort of shit that happens, and utterly banal.[14]

The filmic form that is most appropriate to the exploration of this banality is, precisely, pseudodocumentary. As documentary, this form eschews the dramatizations inherent in fictional genres; but because it is not genuine, it also refuses both the constitutive gesture of truth-telling and the danger of exploiting a real-life dying subject. And so it is that the style of Hick's film is at once self-conscious and realistic, playing games with notions of cinéma vérité, while at the same time constantly emphasizing the presence of the camera. *Via Appia* is among other things a film about how films get made, about the difficulties of finding suitable locations, about the need to negotiate access, about the cost involved. There is also a discourse in it about the marketability of narratives, especially AIDS narratives.[15] At the same time, the film-within-a-film makes this a film about film as a site of cultural intervention. Thus it is the camera crew that acts as bait for Jose, who is ambitious to use the medium to escape from the milieu of the Via Appia. At one point the director remarks: "Sie glauben sowieso wir wollen einen Porno drehen" ("Anyway, they think we're making a porn film"), which raises the questions both of sexual exploitation and of audience motivation. By the same token, one of the terrified hustlers on the Via Appia is literally hunted down by the camera. Another draws attention to the thoughtless cruelty of those who simply go to stare. And a third uses the word "programinha" to refer both to a small television program and to venal sex.

Via Appia has itself been described as a *kleines Fernsehspiel,* or "television minidrama."[16] A striking feature of the film, in this context especially, is the number of television screens that appear in it. Together these thread together an untranslated Portuguese soundtrack to the film, offering those who understand that language a whole series of resonant references to the economic situation in Brazil, to the tourism on which that country relies and to the children which are its blightable future. And the only time we actually get to see a sex act in the film is on one of these ubiquitous hotel-room televisions. A similar technique is used in *No One Sleeps,* which was also made with funding from German Television. There, however, the sex occurs in full view – though it does not in fact occupy the screen for very long. In other respects too this later film abandons the restraint of its predecessor and works instead with ironic overdeterminism and excess.[17] Thus there is a strong religious dimension to the film, present in the Christological implications of the splayed corpses, and picked up again in a huge tattooed cross and the violent removal of a crucifix before sex. But ultimately this merely fulfils the function of a red herring. The whole film can be read as homage to Susan Sontag, since the person here in charge of investigating HIV-related deaths bears an uncanny resemblance to the author of *AIDS and Its Metaphors* (1989). On the other hand, the language our detective Tolliver speaks is considerably closer to the gutter than the elegant prose of the celebrated cultural critic. Equally, an emotional climax is reached in the film when a mortally sick AIDS patient and a celebrated opera singer together belt out a duet version of the aria from Puccini's *Turandot* which gives the film its title. Yet at the level of the plot this moment is presented as a gratuitous, retardatory distraction.

More widely, the use Hick makes of what he himself calls the "gayest of all operas" in this film can be seen as an exemplary combination of the mythic and the analytical. Even the translation adopted for the title allows for slippage from the imperative of an imperial decree to an indicative description of the perturbation caused by a mass murderer or a pandemic. What is at stake in both is the complicity of the state and its henchmen in the indiscriminate murder of millions. Moreover, it is hard not to see in Hick's thoroughgoing use of an operatic leitmotiv a corrective reference to Jonathan Demme's AIDS melodrama *Philadelphia* (1993). In that film the gay protagonist Beckett clearly and unironically identifies with the doomed diva of Umberto Giordano's *Andrea Chenier,* wooing his bemused straight lawyer with a rather exalted paean linking love and death. Hick brings matters down to earth by having his aria hummed by a macho ex-convict, who is described by one critic as being "built like a lumberjack" (Fricke, 2000: 15). The association of such a figure with the legendary princess opens up a series of ironic disjunctions which draw attention among other things to issues of gender, power and socioeconomic dependency which are barely touched on in *Philadelphia*. Conversely, it is oddly appropriate to take as an intertext for a detective thriller an opera that turns on riddles, including a riddle of identity, and that uses the dramatic unities to set the clock ticking. It is even possible to see in the broken triad of Turandot's riddles, with their evocation of hope, blood, and a murderous mistress, an unsentimental alternative to *Love! Valor! Compassion!* (1997). In short, by suturing an archetypal tale from the *Thousand and One Days* onto a plausible story of scientific research in a modern gay metropolis just up the coast from Hollywood, Hick is able to bring off a multiple act of emotive *Verfremdung* (see Brecht, 1964) rendering "strange" both Puccini's opera and the (filmic) discourses of AIDS.

Elsewhere in Hick's oeuvre, AIDS appears as a self-evident fact alongside other salient features of the modern gay experience. *Menmaniacs* (1995) is dedicated to two of the protagonists who succumbed to the syndrome between the making of the film and its release. In *Talk Straight (Ich kenn' keinen – Allein unter Heteros*, 2003), it was the discovery of his positive status that finally drove one of the interlocutors to come out. In the two-part *Sex/Life in LA* (1998, 2005) the syndrome is implicated both in the bleakest failure and in the most heartening success. And one of the things that have changed by the second part is the introduction of barebacking. In *Rainbow's End* (2006) positive status is presented as a ground for discrimination and bureaucratic chicanery. And one of the many ironies of *The Good American* (2009) is that the goodness of the title is achieved not just in spite of HIV-positive and hence illegal alien status, but also, indirectly, because of it.

The protagonist of that film, Tom Weise, after hearing his diagnosis and experiencing German reactions to it, decides to leave and go to the United States – even though at the time it was illegal for anyone with HIV to enter that country. In doing so he is following a significant trend in German queer cinema, represented perhaps most famously by Monika Treut. Alice Kuzniar (2000: 157–173), indeed, devotes a whole chapter to what she calls "The Queer Nationhood of Treut *et al.*," using a term which was originally synonymous with the United States to refer to the ways in which queer as a global phenomenon undermines and reinforces notions of a national cinema. Once in the United States, Weise experiences the American dream in all its horror and glory, descending into homelessness and rising to a riverside apartment with a view of the Statue of Liberty. Having made it, he is ready to turn himself into a "good American," exercising commendable charity and offering help to those who need it. He is also inclined to follow the Euro-American dream of going back to his country of origin to show those who doubted him that he has actually made something of himself. And in the end he marries the love of his life, so his fairytale biography is complete.

As a documentarist, though, Jochen Hick does not tell tales. And one of the remarkable things about his film is the way in which it consistently refuses the teleology of these narratives. Because the Weise we meet has already made it, we never discover how he got into the States in the first place. We are party neither to his fall nor to his rise, except as disembodied narrative, and we have to take on trust what he says about his altruistic initiatives. Even when we do accompany him home, we are denied the expected showdown and presented instead with some very flat footage of a shut dry cleaner's. And the marriage that is concluded at the end is a contract between two sick people from two different cultures, whose complicated relationship definitely does not promise a glib "happily ever after."

Moreover the way in which the film is shot and edited engages ironically and disruptively with specifically American legends. For one thing, the film refuses to script an emotionally satisfying scenario. Instead it follows an aleatoric aesthetics which allows in the name of realism precisely those elements of ambiguity, uncertainty and facticity that Hollywood excludes (see Hoo, 2009: 9). It works with structures of repetition and contrast, which enable us vicariously to experience the downside of the American dream, visually to understand the profligate prudishness of sex without nudity, and dramatically to grasp the often unspoken association of the much-vaunted American freedom with hard cash. One of the specific techniques used for the purpose is Hick's trademark emphasis on mise-en-scène (see Lannert, 2009). The spaces in which people live and work, the backgrounds against which they allow themselves to be filmed, gradations of lighting and details such as food in a fridge, are all used explicitly not only to convey information about personality, history, and socioeconomic status, but also to mark out the emotional rhythm of the film and to indicate the contingency of what is said in it. Thus the cramped living spaces of the escorts, when compared to Weise's spacious apartment, speak volumes about the latter's good fortune and the exploitation on which it is based. The inevitable confusion of Weise's farewell event, emphasized by being literally shot from the sidelines, echoes the emotional complexity surrounding his decision to leave and the performative aspect of the brave face he puts on it. And the simple contrast between the modern penthouse in New York and the freshly renovated, but stylistically traditional, flat he moves into in Berlin neatly symbolizes everything that is different and difficult about his new venture.

One area in which these differences impinge especially on Weise's fortunes is that of the relationship between sex, particularly gay male sex, money, and freedom. That is to say: the perspective that is adopted in this film is specifically queer. Most obviously, the same-sex wedding ceremony, filmed at least partly from an oddly exalted perspective, entails a freedom not available in many US states and not always presented as desirable within queer discourse. Equally, the way in which Weise made his money – by establishing a website for rent-boys and organizing huge events at which a variety of gay sex-workers could display their wares – adds an unmistakably queer slant to his rags-to-riches trajectory. In both cases what is foregrounded is the postmodern, performative aspect of gay sexuality, allied, in the case of the "Hustlaballs," to a self-evident enactment of extreme practices. In this respect it is noticeable that, while the film does tell the story of the successful organization of such an event, with all the vicissitudes that need to be overcome along the way, it refuses to adopt the conventions of a standard "behind the scenes" documentary. Where the latter would posit the successful staging as its telos, Hick remains faithful to the messy details on the one hand and the naked flesh on the other. The way in which the two cancel each other out makes for a characteristic viewing position which is also indicatively queer. (The point is even underlined by the programmatic inclusion of a casual cum-shot.) The incidental thematization of sexually transmitted diseases in this film, including not only HIV but also hepatitis, takes us in a formal circle back to, but also beyond, the origins of queer. So too does the chilling vignette of the escort who received death threats after outing a highly placed cleric in a book. But above all it is the juxtaposition, without comment, of "pretend family values," complete with partner and dog, and a promiscuous indulgence in the illegal practices of prostitution and extreme pornography, which enables this film to straddle the gay/queer divide. And the ironic superimposition and fragmentation of familiar narratives – the love story, the self-made man story, the successful production story – offers a very striking example of the way in which documentary can undo discourse.

To some extent, *The Good American*, which is Hick's most recent full-length release, can be read as a palimpsest of his earlier work, especially of previous films set in the United States. Thus the "Hustlaballs," organized by our good American, recall the "Drummer Balls" of *Menmaniacs* – which in turn resonate with the drag balls of Jennie Livingston's *Paris Is Burning* (1990).[18] *Menmaniacs* is a study of the international fetish community represented by the International Man of Leather competition, the special interest *Drummer* magazine and the parallel competition organized under the latter name. A noticeable feature of the film is the fact that the simulated sex performances which are a necessary part of the Drummer competition are so very bad. This makes us think again not only about the criteria by which we judge such things, but also about performance itself and its relationship to identity. Again in *Menmaniacs* we meet a master–slave couple who have just renewed their contract. For the slave, this contract includes a particular dress code, confinement to the domestic sphere and the requirement to be submissively available when the master returns from work. For the master, it includes the necessity of opening doors for his deliberately incapacitated other half – as we witness in an extended sequence that is almost surreal in its ritual repetitions. It is thus not hard to see in this arrangement a knowing parody which, like drag, shows up the constraints of the standard marriage contract by consciously imitating them, without for all that necessarily disavowing an ethics of fidelity or discounting the possibility of a genuine emotional attachment. Equally, the rhetoric which makes of Mr Weise a "good American" has an unsettling equivalent in the touching parodic-seeming genuineness with which, in *Menmaniacs*, the HIV-positive Mr Leather for Portland, Oregon, lays out for us the details of the secondhand shop he runs for the benefit of his fellow positives. By contrast, the simple mention, in *Menmaniacs*, of the sums spent by those attending the leather convention, prefigures in its cynicism the comparable moment from *The Good American* when the greater paying power of the Hustlaballers leads to the quiet removal from a Las

Vegas hotel of other guests who had voiced their objections. Perhaps unsurprisingly, the earlier film places rather more emphasis on the necessity of "going out" from the closed community into the wider world. To that end it makes typically programmatic use of mise-en-scène, exploiting both the claustrophobic interiority of the hotel setting and the openness, both liberating and threatening, of the streets outside. By much the same token, the moments where the camera is allowed intimate access to, say, the disorder in a person's hotel room, are matched and counteracted by others where it is denied entry to, say, a lift full of people going out together. Moreover, where *Menmaniacs* briefly interrogates the composition of the community by including the testimony of a woman and invoking the discourse of political correctness, *The Good American*, though the only woman it includes is a neighbor of the protagonist's parents, self-evidently features an African-American and other non-Caucasians. And where *The Good American*, in its title, its plot, and the comments of its characters, thematizes nationality from a bicontinental global perspective, *Menmaniacs*, while insisting that the leather community is a global phenomenon, uses its dual US–German perspective to hold up to scrutiny the constituent discourses, and indeed performances, of Americanness. It is not for nothing that the opening voiceover of the film, constituting as it were the mental equivalent of establishing images of the Chicago skyline, concerns the American attitude toward sex. And the film constitutes itself as an opposite of this by including, for example, found footage of a German-made, Dutch-distributed S/M porn film which the Americans put on the index.

One aspect of the phenomenon of Americanness, which subtends *The Good American*, is absent from *Menmaniacs*: the so-called "American dream." Because the latter is exclusively concerned with the sexual personae performed by its protagonists, it is sublimely indifferent to their "real life" careers and aspirations. By contrast, the aspirations of a variety of interlocutors are of central concern to the pair of films collectively entitled *Sex/Life in LA*. In the first film, Hick offers insights into the work of nine men involved in the marketing of bodies in the city of Hollywood. In the sequel, he adds some eight more, at least one of whom subsequently has a cameo performance in *The Good American*. But he also follows the further careers of selected protagonists from his earlier film. And he chronicles changes to the business – notably those associated with the medium that made Tom Weise's fortune, the Internet. Together, then, the two films thematize time and turnover, and the human cost of both. Along the way we do get to witness the sort of parabolic career implicitly attributed to the "Good American." At the same time, the homelessness that was merely mentioned in that film is here actually presented in the form of a hustler without a driver's licence who lives in his car. The drama of homecoming which Weise denies us or displaces is here repeatedly played out. The US–German perspective is also emphasized, not least by the LA-born performance artist Ron Athey, who is more successful in Europe than in his native country and who has some correspondingly scathing things to say about American attitudes. Here too, as in *The Good American*, religion puts in a surprising stagy appearance, this time in the form of a profession of faith intoned by a homeless hustler who prays before working out. There is even a comparable book, which here however seems to be less in the business of unmasking hypocrisy than of endorsing the illusion of glamour. And the casual cum-shot, which in *The Good American* was a kind of housewarming present, is here attributed to a supermodel relieving stress – and later counterbalanced by the strenuous, and not wholly successful, efforts of a porn actor to achieve orgasm.

What is particularly striking about the masturbation scene from *Sex/Life in LA* is the manner in which it is shot. For one thing it is explicitly framed with a discourse of expectation and anticlimax. When Tony Ward looms up in silhouette against a candlelit background, the scene takes on obvious overtones of ritual or performance. The candles themselves have a clearly phallic dimension, underlined when the indistinctly clothed character portentously lights another one. The announcement, no less momentous in tone, that he is going to have a bath, conjures up associations with romantic indulgence. Immediately, though, there is a cut to Kevin Kramer, waiting for the phone to ring. And by the time we are actually allowed into the bathroom, the light in there is bright enough to allow explicit filming, reducing the candle to the status of a continuity citation. As he gets into the bath, Tony is talking to the cameraman, whom we briefly glimpse in a mirror on the wall that figures repeatedly in the subsequent scene. Only at the end, though, do we get to see the cameraman again, grinning this time at the joke of the stress relief. The effect is to make us uncomfortably aware of the process of filming. This is underlined by the fact that the first glimpse we get of Tony in the bath, talking about his hard-on, is a reflection in another, larger, mirror. It is only when Tony talks of letting himself go and gets down to it that the camera too is allowed to focus in unashamed alternation on his face and his prick. And once he has reached his orgasm we return, after the brief moment of literal self-reflection, to documentary business as usual, with Tony addressing his not especially profound remarks to a cameraman who has retreated back to invisibility, but not silence.

What is happening here is a very careful juggling of performance and authenticity, intimacy and exhibitionism, documentary and pornography, accompanied by an extreme focus on perspective and hence the gaze, and an ironic distrust of what is said and shown. That is to say, this film actively works to dismantle the simple category of truth, just as it carefully complicates our viewing pleasure. By mapping documentary onto pornography and vice versa this film involves the viewer in an exploration of the nature of both, and hence of the relationship between identity and performance, authenticity and illusion, perspective and desire (see Buss, 1998). It is not for nothing that the first intradiegetic remark we hear is deludedly concerned with correcting misapprehensions. Nor is it an accident that reviewers have invoked the category of voyeurism when describing their reaction to the film.[19] In what is often literally a hall of mirrors reflecting naked flesh back to an implied camera, the viewer is constantly called upon to consider and revise his response. Thus when a naturally worried hustler, feeling the camera on him, breaks into an involuntary but uncertain smile, the emotional desire to invest that smile with truth almost outweighs the objective certainty of its falsehood. When Tony Ward refers to the world in which Madonna moves as "the Kingdom" and his removal from it as both an "expulsion" and a return to the status of a peasant, the effect is not only to point up the archetypal applicability of the American dream and the power structures that feed it. It also helps us affectively to understand all those expulsions that litter literature from the Fall onwards. And when in a subsequent scene we find ourselves literally looking up at the star's distant hilltop castle in the company of a tourist "doing" celebrity homes, the collapsing of the aura into reality is at once salutary and uncomfortable. Similarly, when ex-addict John Garwood's past tense, "epic" account of his removal to hospital is impossibly acted out for us by a man with a limousine, complete with overdetermined filmic glances in the rear view mirror and a literally tinted retrospective of Santa Monica Boulevard, the self-conscious artifice of the device alerts us to the factitiousness of what we are watching and makes us reconsider our own perspective. Or when Patrick, the hustler with the car but no driver's licence, intones for us in profile a litany about how obsessed people are with sex, and then turns to us to insist that he is not exaggerating, we realize with a shock that with this implausible performance he has been not only talking about us, but also baring his soul to us.

By the time of the sequel, Patrick has disappeared and John Garwood is dead. Garwood's death gives Hick the opportunity to lament the senseless loss of young life, not to AIDS, but to addiction. The mode in which *Cycles of Porn* (2005) mourns him is almost classical, with a talking head tribute and found footage presumably including outtakes from the previous film. With this death, but perhaps also more generally, a clearer note of condemnation enters the later film. Thus the scene in which Kevin, apprised of John's death, is briefly stung but soon recovers his composure, exemplifies a callousness which is later explicitly excoriated. The naked exploitativeness of the industry becomes clear with the damning revelation that the inmates of the Big Brother-type *Live and Raw* house are thrown out just before they qualify for national insurance and unemployment benefits. Indeed, it is freely and drastically admitted in the analogy one producer draws with the slaughtering of a hog. The claim that working for the industry is better than working as a clerk in a retail store is visually contradicted when the person who makes it is seen carrying out exactly the sort of pre-lockup tasks that a store would have required. The solo simulated fisting session he coordinates is filmed so bluntly that we can both see the chemical disengagement of the actor concerned and feel the attendant boredom. Because this film covers a house wired with webcams and features footage of actual porn shoots, it is full of diegetic cameras and thus thematizes more explicitly than its predecessor its own relationship with voyeurism and pornography. There are even two DVDs of the film. The explicit version is literally plastered with flesh and proclaims its own success at the GAYVN awards ceremonies the film screens at. On the other cover, the flesh is confined to the actual title, and we are presented instead with a photograph we see being taken in the film and qualified as "beautiful." The person responsible can be seen as a benign equivalent of Rick Castro, who, in *Sex/Life*, seems to make good money out of snapping destitute hustlers. And the model, marvellously, proclaims: "I like to watch."

The rhythm this implies is central to *Cycles* and helps to define its self-conscious status as a sequel. Alongside the less understated style that reflects the changed conditions in the industry, there is a curious, countervalent sedateness. Full-face egotism and ambition is counterpointed with an insistence, in profile, on renunciation. Vicarious and throwback promiscuity is contrasted with a surprising stress on relationships, accompanied by an emphasis on genuinely domestic interiors, a use of photographs that is sentimental rather than pornographic, and pets. Geographically, the calm of Palm Springs is set against the freneticism of LA. And woven into the fabric of the film is a rhetoric, both accusatory and conciliatory, of before and after. For as long as he was still a resident in the *Live and Raw* hotel, Johnny Law appeared to keep up a positive attitude toward everything that went on there. After his expulsion we see him behind bars and abandoned, and learn that he had a massive problem with alcohol – though even that may just be a way of trying to reconcile his eviction with his self-esteem. Having previously construed his HIV-positive status as a death sentence, Rick briefly fulfils a dream by becoming the successful porn star Cole Tucker, and then returns to business as usual with a day job, a partner and a dog. Being of the same generation as Hick himself, he helps him to confront the otherwise ubiquitous "Peter Pan syndrome." There is even a moment when, accompanying youth to a party, we leave them to their own devices in order to catch up with an old friend. The most emotionally intriguing has-been of the film is ex-porn star Matt Bradshaw (Keith). A former hairdresser, Keith reminds us that jobs outside the porn industry are no more secure than those within it. As an actor, Matt was consummately professional and conspicuously at ease with Hick's camera (even if he did allow himself a distancing fit of the giggles). Filmed as he returns home to live with his sister, he becomes nervous and slightly camp. Through him, the film becomes a portrait not just of sex/life in LA, but also of life without sex in Baton Rouge, Louisiana. Not that we get to see any footage of the place Keith calls "Hickville." Instead we are literally confined to the house, almost, it sometimes feels, behind closed shutters. With its angles, the camera appears to measure out this interior like a pacing prisoner. Only once do we see Matt escape, in a van equipped with sex-toys and videos, on what is posited as a regular trip in search of culture and adventure in New Orleans. In these respects, Keith's experience prefigures that of the protagonists in Hick's most celebrated film. Originally planned as a German counterpart to *Sex/Life in LA*, *Talk Straight*, which won the Teddy for best documentary at the Berlin film festival in 2003, explores the living conditions of homosexuals in provincial Swabia, Southern Germany. The forester Stefan regards his small village as central because it is about as far from either Munich or Stuttgart as New Orleans is from Baton Rouge. The mise-en-scène and costumes are so extraordinarily apt, shot from such telling angles and so brilliantly intercut, that instant recognition is tinged with disbelief, often provoking laughter. At one point, for example, we are transported from a church hall with a prominent crucifix to a sex shop with dildos gleaming like church silver behind glass. And where Keith, testing depth with a dipstick, insists on the very heterosexual nature of Baton Rouge, Hick is able again and again to find characters who tell the camera, with complete seriousness, that they have never yet met a gay man or a lesbian.

Like *Via Appia*, *Talk Straight* can be seen as critically engaging with certain prevalent discourses of homosexuality. Most obviously, it questions the triumphalist trajectory of gay liberation by demonstrating how gay men in the provinces live literally on the edges of homophobic discourse. In the very first scene, we are presented with an archetypical German pub philosopher airing liberal prejudices against homosexuality and anal sex, before the camera pulls back to reveal a gay man who has been sitting next to him all the time. The limits of liberalism are revealed when we are repeatedly made party to the Nazi-inspired murderous impulses that certain parents claim to have felt when their children first came out to them. This National Socialist shadow, reinforced by the presence of two gay men who survived it and a perhaps excessive concentration on members of the older generation, here complicates the discourse of coming out. How emotionally fraught this can be is made clear not only by the heartrending scene in which two young men plan how to do it and imagine possible reactions, but also by the fact that the Christopher Street Day parade in Ravensburg actually reduces two people to tears. The ability of human beings to overlook the obvious is underlined when a series of pictures showing Stefan in what with hindsight are overdeterminedly gay poses is overlaid with a commentary from his mother explaining how she never suspected, or when an acquaintance of a man we know to be out still denies knowing any gay men. The hegemonic use of the category of the "normal" is underlined when the term is used, alongside the barely translatable "gesittet" ("discreet" or "decent") to describe the behavior of overweight German tourists paying off nubile Thai girls in full view in the hotel compound. The person who uses it, and the person to whom it applies, are part of an astonishing array of unlovely middle-aged heterosexuals who in this film are made to sit around, not infrequently in rows, and react with various degrees of embarrassment to the presence and views of their homosexual fellow-citizens. (That the women are often to be found in the background on these occasions is likewise no accident.) Very often, these people are shown as forming problematical communities, to which the film opposes a discreet discourse of foreignness. Thus Stefan's mother moved from the Rhineland to Swabia and is an outsider. Erika, the Catholic activist mother of two gay sons, is married to an Italian. And the assistants in both the sex shop and the souvenir shop in Berlin are also foreigners. Programmatically, though, the attitude of the film toward its small-town Germans is neither inimical nor hostile. Rather they are often shown up by their hesitations to be the victims of a discourse whose lack of logic they are unable to compensate. And nowhere is this

truer than in the case of the Catholic Church, whose representatives in this film
run the gamut from stubborn parroting, through oleaginous hypocrisy, to tell-tale
pauses.

Welcome to the Cathedral both recorded and was itself a protest against the
Church. *Hallelujah* (2006) comparably documents a noisy gay and lesbian caucus
protesting the Pope's visit to Cologne. In *Rainbow's End*, which Hick made together
with Christian Jentzsch, the complicity of the Roman Catholic Church in murderous violence against homosexuals is graphically illustrated in the events
surrounding Polish Gay Pride marches. In this sense, the title of the film is
significantly ambiguous. On the one hand it might sometimes seem that gay men
and lesbians in certain parts of Europe have in fact finally attained their elusive
prize of legal recognition. And in the light of this, there are those who would
conclude that the whole campaign, for which the rainbow was a symbol, is at an
end. Conversely, though, we all know that the rainbow, exemplum of the spectrum
and hence of diversity and sign of a new covenant after a murderous flood, is an
optical illusion. The law, whatever the intentions behind it, is necessarily normative,
and what it prohibits is very often a real and present danger. And what happens
when the campaign is abandoned is homophobic business as usual. In short, what
you find at the end of the rainbow is not a pot of gold, but a backlash.

Accordingly, in the film itself, there is disturbing footage of two men who, in the
so-called gay capital of Europe, are afraid to leave their apartment because of fear
of homophobic violence from young North African immigrant neighbors. And
one gay Dutch Muslim quietly explains that the reason he moved to Amsterdam is
that in his home town he was beaten up so badly that he had to spend three nights
in hospital. The tale is also told of the implicitly homophobic chicaneries meted
out to a would-be immigrant to the United Kingdom. The effect of the juxtapositions in the film is to underline the implication that the graphic depictions of the
aggression, condoned by the police and hence by implication coordinated by the
state, which was vented upon participants in the March for Equality in Krakow, is
not as exotic or exceptional as it might appear. By the same token, the point is
made repeatedly that the progress achieved in some countries should not blind
us to what goes on elsewhere. Even ostensibly humanist organizations such as the
United Nations are shown to be bureaucratically obstructive and diplomatically
divided.

Yet we are also presented in the film with a gay couple in the liberal German
capital of Berlin. Berlin has an openly gay mayor and a vibrant nightlife which
attracts visitors from all over Europe, including the new plutocrats of the former
Soviet Union. Far from taking advantage of these freedoms, though, our gay
couple remain glued to the computer screen. What they are looking for is vicarious
titillation; their computer stands for the anonymous commoditization of gay
sexuality in the postmodern age. What they find, however, are websites promul-
gating the death penalty for homosexuals. Their comfortable consumption is in
tension with the need for political action. By focalizing their film explicitly through

this perspective, Hick and Jentzsch make that tension ours. At the same time, they dramatize the issue of point-of-view and cultural understanding. And they show that beneath the shallow uniform satisfaction of globalized late capitalism, there lurk abysses where the rainbow has never been heard of.

A similar thesis and a comparable play of perspective inform the film *East West Sex and Politics* (2008). If in *Rainbow's End* we saw Polish Catholics braying for blood, in *East West* we are presented with the unsettling spectacle of Russian Orthodox believers who look and behave like Hell's Angels, and whose violence is actually consecrated by a priest. Yet this English-language German film begins with a sequence which emphasizes nonunderstanding and outsiderhood. And the film constantly brings us up short by disappointing our expectations or flouting our assumptions. Having learned from the experiences of demonstrations to align Russian Orthodoxy with homophobia, we are not a little surprised to learn that those we have been following in their fight against homophobia are also believers. When the homophobic slogans of the orthodox mob are replaced on the sound-track by gay-friendly ones from an earlier event in Geneva, it takes a while to register the change. The attendant disappointment not only helps to measure the distance between Russia and Switzerland, but also encourages critical reflection about the nature and purpose of Pride marches. And the irony of seeing exclusions practised by a man whose exclusion we had previously been encouraged to disapprove of amply underlines the political, sexual, and epistemological complexity of the problems explored in the film.

In many ways, indeed, this trademark complexity can be seen to undo discourse in exactly the same queer way as in Hick's other films. The title *East West*, for example, is no less double-edged than *Rainbow's End*, suggesting as it does a kind of posthistorical triumphalism which the film itself radically disavows. And the recurrent thematization of the media and the market for photographs, though perhaps more explicit in this film than elsewhere, clearly invites comparison with others of Hick's films. In particular, there is a striking parallel between Sergei Golovach in *East West* and Rick Castro in *Sex/Life*. And the effect is not only to underline a shared self-consciousness, but also to call into question the facile distinctions often drawn between the East and the West. Like the Berlin of *Talk Straight*, Moscow is here presented as a Mecca for gays and lesbians. As in Hick's Americans films, though, the freedoms they enjoy there depend on their socioeco-nomic status. Concretely, where in *Sex/Life* Kevin unthinkingly endorses a ban on cruising because he can afford an apartment, in *East West* the closure of a park is doubly painful because we have experienced visually both the freedom offered by such spaces and the cramped living conditions they help to alleviate. And at the end of the film, the lawyer who organized the Prides is building on his contacts to the European parliament, but the security guard who just joined in has lost her job. Outside the capital, in Eriwan, for example, queers are every bit as rare as in Swabia, and for the same reason. Hence most of the people we meet in Moscow are not Muscovites, but outsiders. One of them indeed is not sure whether the beating he received was because of his sexual orientation or the color of his skin. The xenophobia this implies, though extreme, is at least economically plausible when breezily asserted by a rickshaw rider; and it is not unrelated to the ostracism of a boy at a US boarding school for refusing to love America. And the violence involved, exacerbated by officially sanctioned hate speech, is not different in kind to that meted out for a year and a month to that same boy in the Land of the Free.

The problem of homophobic violence, of course, was one of the constitutive issues facing the queer movement. And it is massively thematized not only in *East West*, but also in many other films by Jochen Hick. Equally, the assimilation of sexual identity with performance, drag, camp etc., which is central to queer theory, not only dominates *Menmaniacs* and crucially informs both parts of *Sex/Life*; it is also to be found in *East West*, where a man kissing a woman declares that he is gay, but a man who revels photographically in male nudity and frequents men only nightclubs roundly declares that he is not. The absurd semiotics of gender, which queer is concerned to deconstruct, and which is touched on in the phallic performances of *Menmaniacs* and *Sex/Life* or the military fetishism of *Talk Straight*, here informs not only certain dialogues of drag artist Ahasver, but also the active/passive rhetoric of homophobic hate-speech. Queer's insistence on matters of socioeconomic, class, racial and postcolonial, as well as sexual disadvantage, is written into all of Hick's films, including *East West*. And the discursive intractability of the notion of a "queer nation," which subtends all of Hick's global filmmaking, are neatly summarized at the end of *East West*, when a small, swift and little publicized demonstration by anarchists declares there is no sex and no nation.

In the process they – and of course Hick with them – make telling use of visual props: banners, flags, costumes and masks, as well as choreographed movement. In *East West*, indeed, the latter is used in a classical manner to convey the violence of demonstrations. Here, as in all Hick's films, the masterly use of mise-en-scène, including animate extras, such as cats, and the contrast between interior and exterior scenes, draws properly queer attention to issues of socioeconomic freedom. The sometimes disjunctive use of space and the writing of the city is used here, as elsewhere in Hick, to underline the systemic constraints operating on individuals. The inclusion of staged performances and found footage (sometimes, indeed, of found footage of stage performances, as in Putin's speech) makes us aware, as throughout Hick's work, of the factitiousness of the artefact and the inauthenticity of its truths. By the same token, the characteristic quick cutting between informants seems to guarantee composite veracity, but might equally construct a shared ideology. The attendant need constantly to add to or subtract from what is said and shown forces the viewer into a position of analytical detachment which is anything but stable. And again and again in Hick's films we are brought up short with a heart-stopping realization, as when, in *East West*, Alexei quietly tells us of the violent death of his boyfriend.

The rhythm that keeps these truths in play without overdramatizing them, the trust that allows them to be said and the skepticism that sets them off, the camera that sometimes cannot bear to watch and sometimes cannot tear itself away, the editing which keeps us on the qui vive and juxtaposes for us any number of significant details, in short Hick's whole mastery of the art of documentary is evident in these moments. The effect is to shatter irrevocably the complacency of the viewer; to make painfully clear the constitutive relationship that links discourse, including the discourses of the Christian Church and other ambitious politicians, with murderous violence; to make achingly plausible the need to dismantle discourse and to fight its effects; to emphasize the complicated relationship between the private and the political, the particular and the universal; and so to force us to reassess everything we thought we knew about East and West, sex and politics. At the same time, Hick's films offer new insights into what it might mean to be German and queer, and how these positions might affect the watching and making of documentary films. And that, ultimately, is what makes Jochen Hick not just a documentarist at the limits of queer, but one of the exemplary practitioners of the German queer documentary.

Notes

1 For example, Ulrike Ottinger is introduced, inadequately and periphrastically, as "a maker of feminist films that problematize gender constructions" (Alter, 2002: 9).

2 On the "performative documentary," see Nichols (1994). A good number of the films discussed by Nichols are part of the canon of the New Queer Cinema. Naturally, Nichols mentions not a single German film; but his text is nonetheless available in German (see Nichols, 1995). For the central importance of performance and performativity in queer theory, see Jagose (1998: 83–93) and Sullivan (2003: 81–98).

3 Thus both *Katzelmacher* (1969) and *The Bitter Tears of Petra von Kant* (1972) exist both as films and as stage plays. And Fassbinder made film versions of plays by Ibsen (*Nora Helmer*, 1974), Marie-Louise Fleißer (*Pioneers in Ingolstadt*, 1971) and Claire Booth Luce (*Women in New York*, 1977), as well as *Theater in Trance* (1981), a study of theater itself.

4 On Straub/Huillet, see Walsh (1981); Brady (2008). On Kluge, see Lutze (1998). Schlöndorff, of course, famously filmed Fassbinder as Baal.

5 On Syberberg, Brecht, and Wagner, see Sandford (1992); Sharrett (1981/1982).

6 The reference, of course, is to Adorno and Horkheimer (2002), an enormously influential book about the disjunction between the alleged progress of reason and the horrors of National Socialism, whose thesis is perhaps best summed up in the apophthegm: "Myth is already enlightenment, and enlightenment reverts to mythology" (p. xviii).

7 For a recent treatment of Syberberg in a queer context, see Bolduc (2009).

8 See Gillett (2005) on *Via Appia*; and cf. Diehl (2000) on *No One Sleeps*.

9 "Rabiate Gebetsaufsager […] schlugen Schwulen auf die Nase und traten sie in den Hintern. Frauen forderten vereinzelt Vergasung."

10 For a discussion of critical reactions to *Via Appia*, see Gillett (2005). Rather than understanding the film as a critical engagement with discourses – such as that which seeks to blame AIDS on the "third world," critics often reproduce that discourse and assume that Hick was trying (unsuccessfully) to do the same.

11   For a succinct overview of such conspiracy theories, including that associated with
      Jakob and Lilli Segal, see http://www.copi.com/articles/guyatt/paids.html (accessed
      February 3, 2011).

12   Compare the resonant title of Leo Bersani's "Is the Rectum a Grave?" (1987).

13   "Da werden Schwule missbraucht, um heroisch in den Tod zu gehen."

14   At one point the syndrome is referred to explicitly as "Diese Scheiße" ("this shit").

15   Thus after the first section of the film has been completed, we are told that the next
      installments of the funding have been canceled in favor of a project about homeless
      gypsies.

16   Commissioned by German television, Hick's film was originally due to be aired in
      March 1989. However, it was pulled at the last minute and not actually shown until
      August 28, 1990 at 11:15 p.m.

17   As with *Via Appia*, the obtuseness of certain critics' responses can serve as a measure
      of the film's intelligence. Thus anyone who has paid any attention to the film would
      be able to offer clear and convincing answers to the barrage of rhetorical questions
      with which Harald Peters seeks to damn it. See Peters (2000).

18   For a comparison of *Menmaniacs* with *Paris Is Burning*, see Rahayel (1995: 19).

19   Curiously, both Kolja Mensing and the semi-anonymous review in the *Frankfurter
      Rundschau* attribute voyeuristic tendencies to the camera itself. See Mensing (1998);
      "ros" (1998).

References

On Jochen Hick

Anon. (2009) Der Berlinalist. *Kultur-Spiegel*, 2, 20–23.

Buss, C. (1998) Träume und Triebe: Porno als Erfüllung, Pornos als Verhängnis. Jochen
    Hicks Gay-Doku *Sex/Life in LA* hat in Hamburg Premiere. *taz Hamburg*, June 11, 134.

Diehl, A. (2000) Schwuler Film? Heute: *No One Sleeps* im Abaton. *taz Hamburg*,
    October 9, 23.

Fricke, H. (2000) Aids als Thriller: Jochen Hicks *No One Sleeps*. Lästern, zanken, ficken. *taz
    Hamburg*, October 6, 15.

Gillett, R. (2005) Disavowing a deleterious discourse: Jochen Hick's *Via Appia*. *KulturPoetik*,
    5 (2), 225–242.

Hoo, J. (2009) Talking straight. *The Ex-Berliner* (February suppl.), 8–11.

Koll, H-P. *et al.* (eds) (2002) *Lexikon des internationalen Films*, rev. edn, 4 vols,
    Zweitausendeins, Frankfurt a.M., pp. 2106, 2303, 2792, 3431.

Koll, H-P. *et al.* (eds) (2005) *Lexikon des internationalen Films, Filmjahr 2004*, Schüren,
    Marburg, p. 235.

Koll, H-P. *et al.* (eds) (2006) *Lexikon des internationalen Films, Filmjahr 2005*, Schüren,
    Marburg, pp. 80, 137.

Korf, C. (1990) Spurensuche in Rio. *Stern-TV*, October 28, 23.

Kriest, U. (2008) *East/West – Sex and Politics*. Film-dienst, 61, 25, 26.

Kurth, A-E. (2002) *Via Appia:* cruising the traumatized self, in *Words, Texts, Images. CUTG Proceedings*, Vol. 4 (eds K. Kohl and R. Robertson), Lang, Oxford, pp. 199–214.

Lannert, K. (2009) *The Good American. Zitty*, 18, 63.

Mensing, K. (1998) Sex, Träume und Video. Die Kamera geht mit zur Arbeit: Eine Dokumentation über die schwulen Bilderwelten von Los Angeles. *Berliner Zeitung*, August 27, 8.

Peters, H. (2000) Die schwulste aller Opern. *No One Sleeps*: ein Film über Schnauzbärte. *Berliner Zeitung*, September 29, 17.

Rahayel, O. (1995) *Menmaniacs – The Legacy of Leather. Film-dienst*, 48 (20), 19.

Riepe, M. (1992) Praktisch ausgelöscht. "Dienstag," 22.45, Hessen 3. *taz Hamburg*, March 26, 19.

"ros" (1998) Heute zum Film. *Sex Life in LA. Frankfurter Rundschau*, May 16, 22.

Sander, D. (2008) Freie Liebe unerwünscht. Homosexuelle Doku. *Spiegel Online*, November 27, http://www.spiegel.de/kultur/kino/0,1518592942,00.html (accessed January 14, 2010).

Wilke, S. (2000) *No One Sleeps. Cinema*, 10, 88.

Other

Adorno, T.W. and Horkheimer, M. (2002) *Dialectic of Enlightenment* (trans. E. Jephcott), Stanford University Press, Stanford, CA.

Alter, N.M. (2002) *Projecting History. German Nonfiction Cinema 1967–2000*, University of Michigan Press, Ann Arbor.

Bartone, R.C. (2005) Documentary film, in *The Queer Encyclopedia of Film and Television* (ed. C.J. Summers), Cleis Press, San Francisco, pp. 94–100.

Bersani, L. (1987) Is the rectum a grave? *October*, 43, 197–222.

Bolduc, M. (2009) Mourning and sexual difference in Hans-Jürgen Syberberg's *Parsifal*," in *Queer Movie Medievalisms* (eds T. Pugh and K.C. Kelly), Ashgate, Farnham.

Brady, M. (2008) Brecht in Brechtian cinema, in *Verwisch die Spuren! Bertolt Brecht's Work and Legacy: A Reassessment* (eds R. Gillett and G. Weiss-Sussex), Rodopi, Amsterdam, New York, pp. 295–308.

Brecht, B. (1964) *Brecht on Theatre: The Development of an Aesthetic* (trans. and ed. J. Willett), Methuen, London.

Chin, D. (2005) New Queer Cinema, in *The Queer Encyclopedia of Film and Television* (ed. C.J. Summers), Cleis Press, San Francisco, pp. 220–222.

Holmlund, C. and Fuchs, C. (1997) Introduction, in *Between the Sheets, In the Streets. Queer, Lesbian, Gay Documentary* (eds C. Holmlund and C. Fuchs), University of Minnesota Press, Minneapolis, London, pp. 1–12.

Jagose, A. (1998) *Queer Theory: An Introduction*, New York University Press, New York.

Kracauer, S. (1960) *Film Theory. The Redemption of Physical Reality*, Oxford University Press, New York.

Kuzniar, A.A. (2000) *The Queer German Cinema*, Stanford University Press, Stanford, CA.

Lutze, P.C. (1998) *Alexander Kluge: The Last Modernist*, Wayne State University Press, Detroit.

McAffee, L. (1997) Film and videography, in *Between the Sheets, In the Streets. Queer, Lesbian, Gay Documentary* (eds C. Holmlund and C. Fuchs), University of Minnesota Press, Minneapolis, London, pp. 241–263.

Murray, R. (1998) *Images in the Dark: An Encyclopedia of Gay and Lesbian Film and Video*, 3rd edn, Titan, London.

Nichols, B. (1994) Performing documentary, in *Blurred Boundaries. Questions of Meaning in Contemporary Culture*. Bloomington, Indiana University Press, pp. 92–105.

Nichols, B. (1995) Performativer Dokumentarfilm (trans. M. Hattendorf), in *Perspektiven des Dokumentarfilms* (ed. M. Hattendorf), Diskurs-Film-Verlag, Munich, pp. 149–166.

Nichols, B. (2001) *Introduction to Documentary*, Indiana University Press, Bloomington.

Rich, B.R. (1992) Homo pomo: the New Queer Cinema. *Sight and Sound*, 2 (5), 30–34.

Roth-Bettoni, D. (2007) *L'homosexualité au cinéma*, La Musardine, Paris.

Sandford, J. (1992) Hans Jürgen Syberberg: films from Germany, in *Syberberg. A Filmmaker from Germany* (ed. H. Stewart), Hill & Garwood, Watford, pp. 5–12.

Sharrett, C. (1981/82) Epiphany for Modernism: Anti-illusionism and theatrical tradition in Syberberg's *Our Hitler. Millennium Film Journal*, 10/11, 141–157.

Sontag, S. (1989) *AIDS and Its Metaphors*, Farrar, Strauss & Giroux, New York.

Stacey, J. and Street, S. (2007) Introduction: queering *Screen*, in *Queer Screen. A Screen Reader* (eds J. Stacey and S. Street), Routledge, Oxford and New York, pp. 1–18.

Sullivan, N. (2003) *A Critical Introduction to Queer Theory*, New York University Press, New York.

Walsh, M. (1981) *The Brechtian Aspect of Radical Cinema*, British Film Institute, London.

Waugh, T. (1997) Walking on tippy toes: lesbian and gay liberation documentary of the post-Stonewall period 1969–1984, in *Between the Sheets, In the Streets. Queer, Lesbian, Gay Documentary* (eds C. Holmlund and C. Fuchs), University of Minnesota Press, Minneapolis, London, pp. 107–124.

Further Reading

Jochen Hick's work has so far attracted very little scholarly attention. For German speakers, the *Lexikon des Internationalen Films* (Koll *et al.*) and its supplements supply basic information on all Hick's full length films up to and including *Rainbow's End*. (The 2009 supplement was not available for consultation at the time of writing.) For those with French, Didier Roth-Bettoni's *L'homosexualité au cinéma* includes Hick in a discussion of depictions of AIDS in German cinema, and in a note on the importance of documentary in New Queer German Cinema. Otherwise, Raymond Murray's *Images in the Dark* provides some careful information on each of Hick's first three films. Hick's own website, www.galeria-alaska.de, provides a large and motley collection of secondary material from newspapers and the net, including quite a lot of material in English and other languages. However, this is not always reliable, and is more useful as a bibliography than an actual source. There is also a fair amount of repetition. As far as I know there are only two academic articles on Hick. Astrid-Elke Kurth's discussion of *Via Appia*, "Cruising the Traumatized Self," is an offshoot of a broader dissertation about German artistic responses to AIDS. And my own, also on *Via Appia*, is about "Disavowing [the] Deleterious Discourse" of AIDS in that film. Alice Kuzniar discusses Hick only once, but her book is nonetheless indispensable as a mine of information and a model of how to write about *The Queer German Cinema*. Bill Nichols's

Introduction to Documentary is the best in a crowded field at marrying history, theory and basic information. And anyone wanting to understand "New Queer Cinema" should read the *Sight and Sound* article by B. Ruby Rich, in which the term was first coined, and Nikki Sullivan's *Critical Introduction to Queer Theory*.

Filmography

Films by Jochen Hick

Cycles of Porn (= Sex/Life in LA, Part 2) (Germany, 2005).
East West – Sex and Politics (Germany, 2008).
Good American, The (Germany, 2009).
Hallelujah (Germany, 2006).
Menmaniacs – The Legacy of Leather (Germany/USA, 1995).
Rainbow's End (w/Christian Jentzsch, Germany, 2006).
No One Sleeps (Germany, 1999).
Sex/Life in LA (Germany/USA, 1998).
Talk Straight [Ich kenn' keinen – Allein unter Heteros] (Germany, 2003).
Via Appia (West Germany, 1989).
Welcome to the Cathedral [Willkommen im Dom] (Germany, 1991).

Other films

Baal (Volker Schlöndorff, West Germany, 1969).
Bitter Tears of Petra von Kant, The [Die bitteren Tränen der Petra von Kant] (R.W. Fassbinder, West Germany, 1972).
Female Misbehavior (Monika Treut, Germany/USA, 1992).
Hitler, A Film from Germany [Our Hitler; Hitler – ein Film aus Deutschland] (Hans Jürgen Syberberg, West Germany, 1977).
I am my own Woman [Ich bin meine eigene Frau] (Rosa von Praunheim, Germany, 1992).
Jeffrey (Christopher Ashley, USA, 1995).
Karl May – In Search of Paradise Lost [Karl May – Auf der Suche nach dem verlorenen Paradies] (Hans Jürgen Syberberg, West Germany, 1974).
Katzelmacher (R.W. Fassbinder, West Germany, 1969).
Kuhle Wampe (Slátan Dudow, Germany, 1932).
Love! Valor! Compassion! (Joe Mantello, USA, 1997).
Ludwig – Requiem For a Virgin King [Ludwig – Requiem für einen jungfräulichen König] (Hans Jürgen Syberberg, West Germany, 1972).
My Best Fiend [Mein liebster Feind – Klaus Kinski] (Werner Herzog, UK/Germany/Finland/USA, 1999).
Nora Helmer (R.W. Fassbinder, West Germany, 1974).
Paris Is Burning (Jennie Livingston, USA, 1990).

Philadelphia (Jonathan Demme, USA, 1993).

Pioneers in Ingolstadt [*Pioniere in Ingolstadt*] (R.W. Fassbinder, West Germany, 1971).

Positive [*Positiv*] (Rosa von Praunheim, West Germany, 1990).

Silence = Death [*Schweigen = Tod*] (Rosa von Praunheim, West Germany, 1989).

Theater in Trance (R.W. Fassbinder, West Germany, 1981).

Women in New York [*Frauen in New York*] (R.W. Fassbinder, West Germany, 1977).

14

Models of Masculinity in Postwar Germany

The Sissi *Films and the West German* Wiederbewaffnungsdebatte

Nadja Krämer

Introduction

Rockets exploding in bright, white flashes tinged with blue and red flares shooting toward a dark night sky, accompanied by thunderous blasts and smoke – these are in the opening shot of the trailer promoting the first *Sissi* film, which debuted in Vienna on December 21, 1955 and on the following day in Munich. This fiery display may initially have reminded some audience members of the bombings of Austrian and German cities in the not too distant past, but viewers quickly realized that the images projected were those of fireworks, not explosions, as subsequent shots displayed a celebration of Austrian Emperor Franz Josef I's marital engagement to German Princess Elisabeth of Bavaria, called "Sissi," in 1853.

This exuberant expression and celebratory mood exhibited on screen may also point to the phenomenal success that the film, entitled simply *Sissi*, had garnered with German-speaking audiences in the year following its premiere. *Sissi* became the most successful German film of the 1950s, a blockbuster of its time.[1] Its success was planned, but the overwhelming audience response to it was not anticipated. "Sissi-fever" had broken out throughout Europe and beyond.[2] This incredible triumph at the box office prompted immediate plans to extend the *Sissi*-franchise – along with an unprecedented public relations campaign that not only printed film posters and advertisements, but also reproduced the cinematic image of Sissi along with Franz on postcards, matchboxes, dolls etc. (Lowry and Korte, 2000: 115; Jary, 1993: 149). In fact, the *Sissi* trilogy made the two main actors, Romy Schneider and Karlheinz Böhm, household names and created a new star cult.[3]

A Companion to German Cinema, First Edition. Edited by Terri Ginsberg and Andrea Mensch.
© 2012 Blackwell Publishing Ltd. Published 2012 by Blackwell Publishing Ltd.

Two more, equally successful films followed: *Sissi – The Young Empress* (*Sissi – Die junge Kaiserin*, 1956) and *Sissi – The Fateful Years of an Empress* (*Sissi – Schicksalsjahre einer Kaiserin*, 1957).[4] The production plans of a fourth film had to be abandoned, because Romy Schneider declined to be cast again, despite a salary offer of 1 million Deutschmark, a sensational amount at the time (Barthel, 1986: 244). Even the distributor of *Sissi 3*, the UFA Filmverleih (Lowry and Korte, 2000: 114), tried to explain the *Sissi*-phenomenon in its press release:

> In a world of nuclear reactors, satellites, supersonic speeds, psychoanalysis and theory of relativity, in a world of the Iron Curtain and economic battles [...], in short, in a world, which has become more and more abstract and efficient, there is almost no space in which the human soul can settle down with its dreams. [...] And still or exactly for that reason people are yearning for a beautiful unreality, for a far-away unknown, for a time in which everything was totally different, bigger than ever before.[5]

Clearly, the producers viewed the *Sissi* phenomenon against contemporary, mind-boggling technological advancements as well as in the context of the frightening fortification of the Cold War fronts, while also suggesting a yearning for escape to a simpler, splendid time that existed only in the imagination and would remove moviegoers from their bleak, postwar realities. *Sissi* films allowed a return to dreams, fairy tales and the glory of past times without appearing overtly nationalistic and chauvinistic, as was the case with *Münchhausen* (Josef von Baky, 1943). According to Eric Rentschler (1990: 21), that film, under the guise of recounting the legendary life and fantastic travels of the titular historical figure, Baron Münchhausen (1720–1797), employed spectacular costumes and elaborate set designs that revealed a "fascinating and fantasizing fascism."[6]

Even now, contemporary and international audiences respond well to the *Sissi* films, as they evoke the charming and fresh image of Sissi and her upright husband, Franz, and their romance. The films are aired frequently on television and have found a worldwide audience, perhaps because they touch upon a persistent cultural and psychological yearning for a romantic and harmonious world that celebrates the sentimental (Lowry and Korte, 2000: 118).

The affection that audiences share for these characters is also evidenced by the strong interest expressed in a television remake of *Sissi* that aired in December 2009.[7] The *Sissi* trilogy is part of the collective, cultural memory of German-speaking audiences and has even been referenced, parodied, and become iconic in gay subculture (Lowry and Korte, 2000: 116).[8]

While the *Sissi* films have been embraced by their audiences and become a beloved staple of so-called light entertainment, they received dismissive and negative critiques at the time of their original releases, when they were referred to as "folk-epics in which world history is reduced to a small-town level, and every criticism slides off its nifty design as from a well-oiled wrestler's body" (*Der Spiegel*, quoted in Bessen, 1989: 328).[9] Scholarly attention has generally been limited to plot descriptions in German and Austrian film historiographies (e.g. Bessen, 1989: 319–328; Barthel, 1986: 239–249; Jary, 1993: 143–152). A few scholars have expanded the investigation, among them Susanne Marshall (1997) and Gerhard Bliersbach (1985), who offer more comprehensive and insightful readings, pointing out that the films' settings within the Habsburg Empire during the 1850s can be seen to represent the 1950s, since their depictions of the imperial family examine complex family structures and dynamics which are much more germane to the social situation in postwar West Germany than to the Austro-Hungarian Empire. Current research on these immensely popular films is available almost exclusively in German. It has looked at the trilogy mostly in terms of its popular appeal and focused largely on the titular female protagonist. In these investigations, Sissi is usually seen as young, vulnerable, and humane, fighting the traditional power structures of the Vienna court through her spontaneity, innocence, and authenticity (Lowry and Korte, 2000: 117). Georg Seeßlen (1992a) points to the Sissi character and her 1950s significance in light of postwar destruction and Holocaust guilt. Sissi plays a "central role as a 'figure of salvation'"[10] who functions through her "innocence and energy to 'deliver' men from their guilt and at the same time give new glory to qualities necessary for reconstruction" (Seeßlen, 1992a: 12).[11] In other words, Sissi represents the "promise of regeneration," a concept suggested by Heide Fehrenbach (1995) in her leading study of popular German cinema of the 1950s (which nonetheless neglects the *Sissi* series completely). Even more recently published collections of German cinema of the 1950s, such as the anthology *Take Two: Fifties Cinema in a Divided Germany* (Davidson and Hake, 2007), barely mentions the *Sissi*-series. The only notable exception here is Erica Carter's chapter, "Sissi, the Terrible: Melodrama, Victimhood, and Imperial Nostalgia in the *Sissi* Trilogy" (2010), which looks at the *Sissi* series in the contemporary framework of the 1950s and focuses on the Sissi character. Carter conducts a formal analysis of the color palette, composition and camera movement in service of an aesthetic memory of the Austrian Empire and its imperial past through "representational models [...], nineteenth century Biedermeier and Third Reich film" (Carter, 2010: 93).

Sissi certainly elevates the men around her, namely her husband, Emperor Franz Josef I, as well as her personal assistant, Major Böckel (Josef Meinrad), both of whom this chapter will discuss. I argue, however, that the Sissi character plays only a supporting role with respect to her significance for social and political interpretations of 1950s discourses, despite her titular role in all three films. Instead I contend that she serves primarily to transform the male protagonists in her immediate surroundings. The films' representation of the main male characters suggests the emergence and privileging of alternative forms of masculinity in wartorn German society, where traditional models of manhood had been utterly compromised, and which therefore was perceived as suffering from a dirth of male role models.

Ironically, Sissi's transforming and validating influence on these men originates in another man: her father, Duke Maximilian Josef of Bavaria (Gustav Knuth).

Maximilian plays only a secondary role in the series; however, I read him as the characterological matrix, the ideal man who imparts the values of *Heimat*, a central cultural construct deployed during the postwar years in an attempt to redefine and reestablish German identity vis-à-vis the country's devastating Nazi legacy. This postwar attempt entailed problematic recuperation of ideas appropriated into Nazi mythology. According to Fehrenbach (1995), during the 1950s, "the concept of *Heimat* was used to facilitate the messy process of political and moral reconstruction" (Fehrenbach, 1995: 151) understood in terms of an essential, unchanging, German spiritual "rootedness in the earth" manifest in "nonrational, deep soulfulness" (Wilhelm Michel, quoted in Fehrenbach, 1995: 150) and emotional ties to a locale and its natural space that instilled a strong sense of identity (p. 150). Sissi is shaped by her father and possesses a deep sense of *Heimat* and belonging which she eventually articulates to her husband who is more determined by the demands of nation and *Realpolitik*. Franz internalizes the emotional concept of *Heimat* and carries it forward as the new national leader: a New Man who merges *Heimat* and state into a driving political force, the new citizen in uniform in a democracy ready once again to defend fatherland and nation in times of war. Hence the seemingly innovative and fresh image that the female Sissi appears to carry in the form of what I shall discuss is an egalitarian marital relationship and an approach to the future which breaks decisively with the parent generation, ultimately affirms a conservative, male-dominated hierarchy that reestablishes the German male into a patriarchal authoritarian leadership position, once more in uniform and heading the nation, albeit as a citizen of a democracy. Franz serves as a model for reforming, reconciling, and defending the West German state: when he becomes head of household, he proves himself not only a husband and father but a human being, in effect reconstructing the German family in a gentle, unforceful manner that reinstates conservative values regarding family organization without obviously evoking the male-centered fervor associated with Nazism (see Moeller, 1989: 157). As Ursula Bessen (1989: 326) states, "*Sissi* is a film in which – almost silently – men return to their rightful place."[12] The male characters in the *Sissi* trilogy thus reflect the conservatism of the Adenauer era, during which traditional family organization and citizenship were seen as necessary to the future of Germany.

At the same time, crucially, this discourse carried international significance with respect to the so-called *Wiederbewaffnungsdebatte* – debates over West German postwar rearmament. This debate, begun as early as 1949, revolved around the issue of reintroducing a West German military into the postwar European arena. It resulted in the founding of the *Bundeswehr* (Federal Defense Force) in 1955, which, through German accession to NATO, legitimized the West German state by repositioning it back onto to the international political stage. These developments created the "*Bürger in Uniform*," a citizen soldier who stood for the integration of the military into democratic government structures. This new model of a German soldier was supposed to be a citizen who acted within a democratic system, a militarily trained yet free human being who did not blindly follow orders as *Befehlsempfänger* ("mere recipient of orders" and, by extension, "unquestioning executioner of orders"), but executed them because of his conviction of their legality under the rule of law and in accordance with the new West German constitution. These monumental structural shifts within West Germany, and the conclusion of a heated debate over Germany's future military role coincided with the premiere of the first *Sissi* film in 1955.

The reintroduction of military forces into democratic postwar Germany necessitated a redefinition of German nationhood and identity that would uphold the constitution in accordance with Western ideological parameters. The reestablished military forces would need to negotiate the tainted German past and redefine themselves, both domestically and internationally, as a cooperative and committed partner in the Western alliance. Doing so, however, presented a problem for the reigning political philosophy of fundamental state sovereignty and self-determination. The classical definition of political sovereignty entails the power of a nation-state to make foreign policy decisions concerning war and peace as well as to declare a domestic state of emergency (Römer, 1988: 76). Hence the creation of a standing military was seen as an essential step toward regaining German sovereignty, even as it forced the issue insofar as that the creation of a West German army was contingent upon the country's joining a Western alliance led by a former enemy, the United States. Before even considering the reestablishment of its military, then, Germany was compelled to confront the fact that, as aggressors and instigators of two world wars, and perpetrators of the annihilation of European Jewry and numerous other wartime atrocities, its national standing was completely compromised. The *Wiederbewaffnungsdebatte* was therefore part of a much larger complex of questions, to which the *Sissi* films were poised to respond: How should models of masculinity be articulated in postwar Germany? How should they be negotiated to create national identity and a commitment to democracy? How could German men be reinstated as leaders, whether at home, in the military, or in governmental offices in the context of mounting Cold War tensions?

The *Sissi* Trilogy – A Set of "German" Films?

Before proceeding to answer these questions, we must first ask whether interpreting the *Sissi* trilogy, an Austrian production, is justified within the West German context. Without dismissing the series' Austrian provenance and the possibility of reading the films in terms of postwar Austrian subjectivity, I want to examine the postwar West German and Austrian film industries.[13] This will reveal a close and complex interconnection between them by which German distributors had significant influence on scripts, casting, and directing. At the heart of these developments lay parameters set by the Allied authorities after World War Two that organized media production and distribution networks and structured economic arrangements which fostered a symbiotic relationship between the two Germanophone industries.[14]

The postwar Austrian film industry was chronically underfunded, while film productions in West Germany during the early 1950s enjoyed national support and a proactive advancement system (*Deutsches Filmförderungsgesetz*) (Steiner, 1987: 75).[15] The West German economy experienced a recovery through the massive support of the Marshall Plan and was further stabilized through a currency reform that ended postwar inflation (Moeller, 1989: 140). In 1949, after the West German film industry agreed to voluntary self-regulation (*Freiwillige Selbstkontrolle*), the Western Allies in turn lifted legal restrictions on West German film production. These new regulations prevented government censorship as well as intervention by the Western occupational forces. The German film industry therefore achieved more independence and was able to recover more quickly than the Austrian, which lacked necessary funding and stability within a limited national market. Hence the Austrian film industry was compelled to look toward the West German market as a means of viable recovery. West German productions, on the other hand, sought audiences in Austria. These mutual if uneven interests resulted in an annual agreement regulating trade in West German and Austrian films. Between 1950 and 1953, an average of 14 Austrian films were promoted on the German market, and between 75 and 95 West German films were distributed in Austria (Steiner, 1987: 85). According to Walther Urbanek,

> At that time, they all saw the liberalization of film exchange with the Federal Republic of Germany as the ideal of their dreams, those producers in Vienna, but Bonn allowed only two-dozen films into the country. Hence the aforementioned footrace for each of these [...] [films]. (quoted in Fritz, 1984: 94)[16]

Along with intense competition for the Austrian film market came a specific form of financing. For Austria, film distribution was an important means of obtaining foreign currency. Therefore, credits for film production were guaranteed through the Austrian government in order to advance the export of Austrian films. Financing was conducted through Austrian banks, but these would only provide credit upon receipt of proof that the proposed film had already been approved for import by Germany. Having one's film selected by the Austrian trade contingency was highly coveted and only granted once the production's economic success had been virtually assured. Hence the focus on the German market was at once a stabilizing factor for the Austrian film industry and a factor in its dependence on German distribution within a complex system of governmental and financial institutions as well as Austrian production companies, the most prominent of which was Wien-Film GmbH, the producer of the *Sissi* series.[17]

German distributors, however, were the deciding factor in this process. They had absolute power, initiated production, and shaped the film market and industry: "Productions were often materializing only through the direct order of the distributors" (Steiner, 1987: 86).[18] Film production was thus rigged. German distributors would agree to distribute an Austrian film only if the plot, actors, and script were agreeable to their interests, which were informed by projected box-office success and a sense of the film's ideological appropriateness for a West German audience.[19] As one critic commented rather cynically in 1952,

> Today, banks only give credits for film productions if the deal is dead certain. "Dead certain" clearly means the participation of proven film stars and a plot so stupid that the "people" can process it without complication. The distributor decided on the film's appearance, and the bank on its creation. (quoted in Fritz, 1984: 82)[20]

Once a German distributor was located and financing guaranteed, an Austrian production company could submit the film for consideration under the Austrian trade agreement:

> Consequently, the paradox emerged that all parties were dependent on German distribution, including the [Austrian] Department of Commerce, which permitted a film's export only after its distribution had been confirmed. (Steiner, 1987: 87)[21]

As such, the *Sissi* films are indeed Austrian productions, but the German distributors' influence on script development, casting, and directing was immense. Sometimes German distributors applying for worldwide distribution rights would even "forget" to list Austria as the film's country of origin (Fritz, 1984: 94), which caused a trade dispute in 1957 over this practice to market Austrian titles as German (Carter, 2010: 81).[22] Austrian actors such as Paul Hörbinger, who featured alongside Romy Schneider in *A March for the Emperor* (*Die Deutschmeister*, 1955), made adjustments to his acting to please West German audiences:

> Based on my rich experience […], I have adopted a Viennese dialect that also can be understood in Berlin and Hamburg. Since Austrian cinema can never pay off in Austria, we must stage our films according to the wishes of the entire German-speaking audience. (Fritz, 1984: 111)[23]

The Austrian producer of all three Sissi films was Wien-Film, but the worldwide distribution for the first two *Sissi* films was undertaken by the West German company, Herzog, located in Munich, and the third film was distributed by the West German UFA.[24] Since their worldwide distributors were German, the *Sissi* films attempted to appeal to West German audiences, not least by shedding a favorable and conciliatory light on Germany. For this reason, a focus on the trilogy's West German social and political context is both warranted and legitimate.

Production Background and the Plot of the *Sissi* Trilogy

In order to assure the first *Sissi* film's surefire success, the experienced and successful director, producer and screenwriter, Ernst Marischka (1893–1963), strove to fulfill the requirements of the Austrian and West German film exchange:

> Ernst Marischka produced what he considered edifying culture for the so-called little man, and of course, he had to produce what the German distributor dictated, without which an Austrian film could not be released. (Fritz, 1984: 73)[25]

In fact, the biggest popular and financial Austrian film successes during the 1950s were produced under his guidance. Marischka began working as a screenwriter as early as 1913 and continued during the 1930s and 1940s on operetta-like films, among them also a *Sissi* musical in 1932 with Paula Wessely (Carter, 2010: 82). These films were usually set in Vienna and part of the *"historische Wiener Filme"* (historical Viennese films) (Fritz, 1984: 74). These formed an entertaining genre of period pieces featuring traditional music, glamorous costumes, and colorful uniforms, often structured through comedy of error and always accompanied by a love story and happy ending – but never any wars.[26]

The trailer for the first *Sissi* film references Marischka's previous successes, with *A March for the Emperor* and *Victoria in Dover* (*Mädchenjahre einer Königin*, 1954), which starred a 16-year-old newcomer Romy Schneider, whom Marischka was systematically preparing for future stardom, in the character of a "sweet, innocent girl" (Steiner, 1987: 209).[27] *Victoria in Dover* served as model for the first *Sissi* film, in which a young Queen Victoria falls in love with Prince Albert, whom she is slated to marry (Steiner, 1987: 209).[28] In both preceding projects, Marischka worked with Herzog Film, with which he would continue collaborating through *Sissi 2*.[29] Marischka paired Romy Schneider with her mother, Magda Schneider, an audience favorite in West Germany since their dual appearance in Hans Deppe's *When the White Lilac Blooms Again* (*Wenn der weiße Flieder wieder blüht*, 1953). Such steps were taken to ensure the success of the first *Sissi* film, whose basic plot Marischka had already staged as an operetta in 1932 based on the story by Marie Blank Eismann (Steiner, 1987: 208; Jenny, 1998: 124).

Whereas the *Sissi* films are based on historical figures and events, their fictionalized portrayals are highly selective, and the events are presented out of chronological order (Westermann, 1990: 119). The first film tells the story of the 16-year-old, delightful and refreshing Sissi, who lives a sheltered and uninhibited life free from courtly formalities with her father, Duke Maximilian Josef, her mother, Ludovika (Magda Schneider), and her seven siblings at Lake Starnberg in Possenhofen, Bavaria. Sissi unexpectedly meets Austrian Emperor Franz Josef, whose domineering mother, Ludovika's sister Archduchess Sophie (Vilma Degischer), has arranged for him to marry Sissi's older sister, Nene (Uta Franz).

After spending only a few minutes with Sissi, however, Franz decides instead that he wants to marry her. The film proceeds with their courtship, portraying a relationship based on love, and concludes with a glorious wedding ceremony. The second film depicts the ongoing adjustments Sissi must make to the strict etiquette of the Viennese court, dramatizing the conflicts which arise between Sissi's personal desires and the political demands made of her. Tensions peak when Sophie removes Sissi's new-born daughter from her care, ostensibly to enable Sissi to focus strictly on affairs of the court. Initially Franz approves of Sophie's actions, which leads to a first, apparently irreconcilable disagreement between the couple. The film ends, however, with their reconciliation: Sissi's demand that she raise their child herself is met as, in the realm of political affairs, the couple is crowned King and Queen of Hungary, which serves to reunite the Austro-Hungarian Empire. The final film of the trilogy portrays a series of extended separations between Sissi and Franz. First Sissi takes refuge from the formalities and regulations in Vienna by retreating to the less restrictive Hungarian countryside. She leaves to return to Franz, only to fall ill with a serious lung disease, for which she is sent to Portugal and Greece for rehabilitation. Finally recovered, Sissi accompanies Franz on a diplomatic tour of Milan and Venice, where the royal couple is given an initially cold reception that becomes a respectful and popular celebration capped off with a blessing from the Catholic clergy.

Locality, *Heimat* and the Model of Masculinity: Duke Maximilian Josef in Bavaria

After World War Two, the German film industry struggled to reinvent itself after having been co-opted by the Nazi regime. Many actors from the 1930s and 1940s continued to be cast following the war; very few new faces appeared on postwar screens (Koetzle *et al.*, 1998: 92). A large number of people who had worked in the Nazi film industry proceeded to run the postwar industry, employing the same personnel and utilizing the same studios and equipment. The film industry of the Third Reich had mined heroic male figures, especially from the Seven Years War, the Napoleonic Wars of German Liberation, and World War One, such as the aforementioned Baron Münchhausen as well as Frederick the Great and the "Hohenzollern," the latter of which had been elevated by the Nazis into a "cult of Prussia" for celebrating war-related themes and heroic sacrifice vis-à-vis a multitude of enemies (Rother, 1998: 68). The postwar film industries faced the problem of reintroducing masculine role models and historical periods exemplary for their assertions of German nationalism, which was particularly troubling during a period in which such images were especially difficult to sustain, let alone justify. The *Sissi* films were evidence that this dilemma could be solved through nostalgic and mystified representations of historical and political events and figures (Rother,

1998: 75), even and especially those which served to salvage and promote ideals sacrificed in the name of dynasty or Empire, as has been pointed out on numerous occasions.

The *Heimatfilm* was crucial to this process. A popular genre during the 1950s, it provided an opportunity for reviving local traditions and imagining provincial settings comprised of pristine landscapes and unspoiled, pastoral backgrounds. The *Heimatfilm* portrayed nature through an unambiguous moral lens based on an ideology of family and love uncontaminated by modernity. Plot conflicts were localized, classically melodramatic, apolitical and sentimental, and resolved peacefully (see von Moltke, 2002). Recognizable, iconic landscapes – mountains, forests, and the flora and fauna of the heath – situate the realm of nature outside history, far away from the wartorn urban spaces in which most of the genre's audiences lived. The *Heimatfilm's* male characters defend their villages or regional identities and cultures against foreign invasion and nontraditional ways, that is, city dwellers and modern notions. In the case of the *Sissi* films, the plots and settings of 1850s Bavaria and Austria provide integrative references to a shared past and shared meaning, and therefore encourage and attempt to justify the nation (see Fehrenbach, 1995: 150). This recognition and celebration of the local and the mundane, this sense of belonging to a birthplace, landscape, and dialect provided a nonthreatening mode of identification for Germans and *Ostflüchtlinge* (refugees from the East) that would in turn project a nonaggressive "Germanness" to the country's European neighbors. The *Heimatfilm* is thus ideal for presenting ideological solutions to emotional and political quandaries. As Thomas Elsaesser (quoted in King, 2003: 131) contends, "Its perennial usefulness – for filmmakers and audiences – would be then that it [the *Heimfilm*] articulates, albeit in clichés and stereotypical formulas, the crisis of authority and legitimation so crucial to German history and Germany as a nation."

The appealing authenticity and humanity of the *Sissi* trilogy's aristocratic characters overcoming personal as well as political hardship was certainly reassuring to German audiences of the 1950s. Lighthearted, "folksy" segments from the ostensibly more harmonious 1850s, the films provided nostalgic escapes into the presumably more secure, imperial past. Viewers were transported to familiar destinations: *Sissi 1* supplied wide panoramic shots of Alpine forests, the mountains of the Upper Austrian *Salzkammergut*, and a scenic boat cruise along the Danube. All of these locations encouraged national pride and identification with the beautiful landscapes of the German *Heimat*, even if visiting them was only possible cinematically. Only 18% of West Germans dared travel to foreign countries in 1954 for fear of resentment from former wartime enemies (Bliersbach, 1985: 74). The sequels take audiences to more exotic places – Hungary, Madeira, Corfu, and Venice – thus expanding the idea of travel and middle-class lifestyles, and offering a sense of normalcy and economic restoration.

The *Heimatfilm* is rooted in the concept of *Heimat*, which Celia Applegate has explored in her groundbreaking *A Nation of Provincials: The German Idea of Heimat*

(1990: 240): "Heimat was attractive for representing something truer than the Nazis' 'community of blood,' but something essentially peaceful, noneventful. The notion of Heimat also expressed the immortality of the community to which one belonged ..." Therefore, the construct of *Heimat* enabled the possibility of "embody[ing] the political and social community that could be salvaged from the Nazi ruins" (Applegate, 1990: 242); its "integrity of the locality within a national state" (p. 243) could serve as the new German foundation. The ideological concept of *Heimat* would resuscitate a distinctly German tradition of patriotic sentiment untainted by grandiose Nazi concepts of community based on blood rather than locality. *Heimat*, and by extension the *Heimatfilm*, could become a "cathartic space" for the collective experience of community while also appealing to a larger, national audience (Bechthold-Comforty, 1989: 28):

> If democracy could not be rooted in Germany as a whole, it could be rooted in the German locality, the Heimat: from such small beginnings would grow national traditions. (Applegate, 1990: 243)

The essence of *Heimat*, and therefore the foundation of the new state in the *Sissi* films, is Sissi's father. He instills the Bavarian rootedness in Sissi, while she herself transcends this specific locality into the national (German) or transnational (Austrian) tradition. While Sissi learns to negotiate her identity as it changes from that of local Bavarian princess to Empress of Austria-Hungary, she rearticulates her father's sense of belonging to that of her husband, the Emperor of Austria, who represents a new *Heimat* for her and in turn is secured into his *Heimat*, thus becoming elevated to the status of "new *Mensch*" (human being, a masculine noun in German) and, ultimately, citizen of a new, purportedly democratic state.

Maximilian represents a patient, gentle father amused by his rambunctious children. He does not lecture or try to control them, but instead supports them unconditionally and insists on the uninhibited unfolding of their lives as "God's will." This atypically accepting and close, caring relationship with children contrasts the traditional German image of the strict, authoritarian paternal figure. Especially loving and close is Maximilian's relationship with Sissi, whose relationship with her mother is far more contentious. Yet his special disposition is first conveyed in *Sissi 1*'s opening shot, where he is introduced as a man of nature seeking to escape orderly court protocol by fishing and, when greeted formally by local fishermen, responding informally, overlooking caste distinctions. In fact, hierarchies based on birth are meaningless to Maximilian, as his informal interactions are measured solely by character, not social status. Maximilian is the only man of noble birth in the trilogy consistently dressed in civilian clothes – mostly traditional Bavarian outfits – rather than a military uniform. He is the civilian *Bürger* who dons a uniform only when the situation – here, stately ceremonial occasions – calls for it, as if to emphasize that the uniform is only a contingent aspect of Maximiliam's otherwise civilian life,

Figure 14.1   Sissi and her father, Maximilian, in *Sissi 1*.

the film shows him checking the size of his hat and military outfit to see if they still fit, and his sons play with the hat as if it had lost its acrimonious meaning in the Possenhofen household.

Maximilian's atypical disposition is set up from the film's onset, as is the affinity between him and Franz. Maximilian's unconventional, bourgeois behavior is criticized by the Archduchess Sophie and labeled as *"dunkler Punkt,"* or "dark spot" of the family, while her son, the Emperor, finds him most remarkable – the only Bavarian family member he has remembered, and remembered best. The very idea of "remembrance" or *Erinnerung* is introduced through association with Maximilian. Further illustrating this point is an immediate cut to the next scene, in which Sissi and Maximilian are shown hiking through the Bavarian forest near their home. Their outing represents a foundational performance of German identity, and it becomes the paradigm of their relationship throughout the *Sissi* trilogy (Figure 14.1).[30] The scene is echoed by a later one in the first film in which Sissi, walking alongside future husband Franz in the hills of Bad Ischl, Austria, offers a philosophical quote from her father, whereupon the Emperor then falls in love with her and decides he must marry her (Figure 14.2).

Sissi explicitly identifies with her father as she listens to his paternal advice during their walk through the forest: "Do you know that I am so very happy to have a father like you?"[31] Her identification becomes explicit and extraordinary in the later scene, in which she repeats the conversation to Franz: "I believe I will be just like him one day."[32] The conversation thus doubles in a way that reflects a self-assured, bourgeois sense of redemption, salvation, and strength through nature. As Sissi quotes her father verbatim:

Figure 14.2   Sissi and her future husband, Franz Josef I, in *Sissi 1*.

If you are ever upset or worried, go through the forest with open eyes. And in every tree, in every shrub, in every flower and in every creature, the Almighty God will reveal Himself to you and give you solace and strength.[33]

The visual constellation represented by these two scenes also foreshadows Franz's replacement of Maximilian. The forest not only suggests a deeply nationalistic locale; it is a space onto which is projected a number of prominent Germanic images: it is nature, not civilization, it is uninhibited, wild, and free, it is the place of mythic Germanic origin as "'initia gentis' [where the race first arose]" (Schama, 1996: 84); since the Napoleonic Wars of German Liberation (1813–1815), the forest has been declared by nationalists a genuine German landscape that functions as a symbol of national identity (75–134). The forest is recognized as untainted and pure, an embodiment of regenerative powers (Applegate, 1990: 234). Both Maximilian and Franz carry rifles when in the forest on a hunt, but they do so with their rifles secured and load only when preparing to shoot. Needless to say, neither one is actually shown ever firing a shot, let alone killing any animals; Sissi's calculated sneezing or waving of her hat at opportune moments prevents that. Clearly, the *Sissi* films depict the forest as a pacific space of (postwar) German nationhood.

Maximilian's formative advice to Sissi entails walking through the forest while reminding her to recognize the divine presence in the beautiful surroundings, which ground her life. He not only reaffirms a traditional and conservative faith, but revives a pantheism rooted in German Romanticism, by which the Alpine context becomes a space of grandeur and transcendence through beauty and the sublime. This realm of nature offers a refuge from the social woes associated with modernity, as well as an anchor for home and belonging in a universal, sacral and harmonious landscape (Schulz, 1996: 101). Purpose and meaning are therefore locatable to a *Lebensphilosophie* (philosophy of life) that predates Nazism – German idealism, for which the alienating spoils of modern mass culture can be circumvented. Not coincidentally, this philosophy was also eventually co-opted by Nazism.

When Sissi quotes her father to Franz, he is impressed but only later realizes that she and Maximilian actually do live their deeply felt connection to *Heimat*, by finding spiritual comfort in nature. Duke Maximilian Josef of Bavaria is the male role model who thus serves as an ostensibly uncompromised basis of German identity, assuring national continuity along with untainted renewal within the emerging postwar German democracy. The film establishes him as a beacon of democratic ideals, which achieve credibility insofar as he and his family belong to a branch of the house of Wittelsbach involved neither in Bavarian power politics nor the sorts of incriminating history associated with the Hohenzollern. In a heated exchange with her future mother-in-law Sophie, Sissi defends her father in the spirit of freedom and truth: "I want to live free without pressure and constraints. [...] [I speak] the language my father has taught me, who holds freedom and truth above all else."[34] In this way mediated through Sissi, Maximilian will teach Franz a new model of masculinity appropriate to postwar Germany. As Bessen (1989: 326) describes it: "Riches and power are now put in the hands of simple people. The command is not with the women any longer, but with the men. Or it is with such women, who love their fathers more than their mothers."[35]

The Nation, the *Wiederbewaffnungsdebatte,* and the Making of the New Man in Uniform

During the waning months of World War Two, the division of Germany into four Allied sectors, and the complete dismantlement of the German *Wehrmacht* had already been decided (Mahlmann, 1985: 95). The Yalta conference in February 1945 and subsequent meetings in Potsdam the following summer set into motion two of the most contentious issues in German postwar politics: the division of Germany, and the rearmament debate. The latter led to the forgone conclusion that West German remilitarization would only come at the cost of reunification with East Germany and the possibility of a new military conflict in which Germans on both sides would end up fighting one another (Mahlmann, 1985: 96).

Discussions about West German militarization were initiated in 1949 by West Germany's first chancellor, Konrad Adenauer (1876–1967), a devout Catholic and committed anti-Communist who headed the conservative Christian Democratic Union (CDU). Because 85% of West Germans rejected any form of military service, Adenauer secretly extended an offer to the Western allies assuring them of

West German military support in the event that a European army was formed to help secure the Western zones against a potentially rearmed Soviet-occupied Eastern zone (Mahlmann, 1985: 96). Cold War tensions quickly heightened when East Germans started "voting with their feet," that is, leaving the GDR for permanent residence in the West (Mahlmann 1985: 98). It was the outbreak of the Korean War in 1950, however, and a concomitant increase in anti-Communist sentiment and anxiety fostered by the "domino theory" that finally legitimized West German rearmament in the eyes of its domestic and international proponents. Equating the Korean situation with the division of Germany, advocates of West German remilitarization found growing public support, whereupon the conservative Adenauer government pursued a "politics of strength," seeking to regain military standing and achieve political rehabilitation through a reestablishment of a German military (Large, 1996: 7).

Adenauer's plans of military reorganization were rebuffed in heated domestic debates by strong oppositional forces that established an unrelentingly "Ohne mich" ("Without me"), pacifist stance. But there were also voices from the Left who claimed to be more nationalistic by rejecting remilitarization, since they advocated the reunification of the divided Germany and saw rearmament as shutting the door on that possibility (Doering-Manteuffel, 1981: 1).

Vying international interests fueled these discussions. Western occupational forces sought to contain West German military ambitions by integrating them into larger, anti-Soviet defense organizations such as the European Defense Community and later NATO. In return, the Adenauer government had to prove that the West German military had undergone a fundamental structural shift that entailed commitment to a democratic, constitutional state worthy of Allied trust. For one, the new *Bundeswehr* had to be integrated into the civilian government under the auspices of the Ministry of Defense; it could not exist as a separate entity within the state. The task of this new military would be to defend the democratic constitution of the FRG (Federal Republic of Germany), and in that sense it was to constitute a purely defensive army, serving to protect its citizens and their legal rights as well as defend West German territory along with potential NATO allies.[36] Each individual soldier had to swear to uphold the constitution rather than pledge allegiance to a political leader. He would in turn retain his civilian rights, whereupon he was permitted the right to disobey orders that were found to violate human dignity or international law. These provisions rendered the new German soldier a *Bürger in Uniform* (a citizen in uniform).[37] On May 5, 1955, amid continued opposition but with the approval of the Western Allies, the *Bundeswehr* was founded, and a rearmed West Germany joined NATO four days later. The *Bundeswehr* solved the problem of a compromised *Wehrmacht* tradition by aligning itself with the resistance movement associated with Claus von Stauffenberg, whose officer corps had attempted to assassinate Hitler on April 20, 1944 on the belief that true obedience and fulfillment of duty means resisting the injustice even of one's own compatriots.[38]

The *Sissi* films project an awareness of past German military traditions, in that they evidence support for the creation of new military forces alongside a new, democratic *Bürger*. The promise of a viable West German future is posited in the *Sissi* films, which in turn reassures the community of nations (as well as Germans themselves) that the new FRG would promote stability, humanism, and peace. The film series addressed a range of issues pertinent to the rearmament debate. The idea of a changed military tradition, the assertion of German nonaggression, and the mission to protect as part of an imperative to refuse unlawful orders, all addressed the contemporary discourse, itself guided by a strong anti-Communism apparent from the very onset of the Cold War. The conservative notions of reunification, reconciliation, and forgiveness are expressed additionally throughout the trilogy.

The *Heimatfilm* genre and its deployment by the *Sissi* trilogy served to reestablish national-political identity by projecting a renewed sense of German strength, honor, and sovereignty onto images of men in uniform. Combining these issues helped appease concerns about German aggression: "Heimat was something that one fought for, but never something that participated in battle" (Alon Contino, quoted in Fehrenbach, 1995: 150). Insofar as *Sissi 1* was released in December 1955, a mere month after the first volunteers were accepted into the *Bundeswehr*, while its production took place amid intense debate about West German rearmament, its release is interpretable as a cultural means for containing the very serious questions raised by and within that debate.

Whereas calls for military service, duty, and patriotic responsibility carried a dubious ring during the 1950s, they are recurrent and critically unremarked in the *Sissi* films. The Emperor and Major Böckel are consistently dressed in uniform and represented as servants of their country, a fact of which Franz speaks on several occasions. Only during his most private moments (his first date with Sissi, and their later honeymoon), when he appears in Alpine surroundings rather than at court, does Franz wear civilian clothing. Böckel's changes in appearance and dress only become apparent in *Sissi 3*, where he wears civilian clothing while pursuing his previously unexplored interests in foreign languages and cultures as well as romance. While Franz remains the leader of the state and the "maker of history," Böckel represents the *Bürger in Uniform*. As such, both characters embody issues that emerge during the rearmament debate.

When Franz is seen in uniform, he is wearing white gloves and a saber, which he takes off whenever entering a room or acting in stately affairs or with family members. Weapons are not used aggressively, but symbolically. Power is not defined politically through weapons, organization, money, or technology; the weapons are solely used in terms of the authority they signal for this young, dynamic and noble leader (Seeßlen, 1992b: 72). Franz's leadership fits the ideal of a well-mannered, disciplined, hard-working man whose patriotism is devoid of dubious associations with the Hohenzollern or Prussia.

Franz represents the desired new model of a German citizen and of the new political leader in his role as both soldier and civil servant committed to legal

Figure 14.3   The Emperor at his desk in the Vienna Hofburg, in *Sissi 1*.

justice. When he is presented with execution orders for eight young men accused of "rebellion, sedition and lèse-majesty,"[39] Franz makes inquiries into the proportionality of their crime vis-à-vis the proposed punishment, and finally refuses to approve the sentence, despite the urging of a court officer backed by the highest military tribunal as well Sophie herself. By relying upon his own judgment and rejecting the ruling of the court martial, a military institution, as well as his own mother's wishes, in favor of real evidence and a civil court proceeding, Franz embodies the dual role of soldier and civil servant. And by rejecting the idea that expressing an unfavorable opinion should warrant the death penalty, he affirms the fundamental right to free expression that would later be considered integral to West German democracy.

Another pertinent aspect plays out in this scene when Franz rejects the judgment of his mother. Here the camera angle shifts to a low-angle position that is reinforced by the actor's upright stance: in effect, he is portrayed as having become more powerful after having negated his mother's authoritarian and often bigoted attitude toward popular social reform – an attitude exemplified by the prominent placement of a gigantic portrait of Empress Maria Theresia (1717–1780) behind Franz's figure in the frame (Figure 14.3).

This constellation suggests that Franz stands literally in the shadow of his country's past while also representing its new beginning. The past may be rejected in part, but Franz does not reject it entirely. There were perceived positive aspects of Maria Theresia's rule: she unified Eastern Europe under the Habsburg dynasty and increased Austria's international standing by promoting commerce and agriculture and reorganizing the military (Beller, 2006: 85). Franz thus stands in a tradition within which he can selectively choose past accomplishments while initiating his own reforms – a direct analogue to the postwar rearmament debate. As the scene ensues, the idea of civil law is reinforced and, furthermore, distinguished from the lip-service of the Nazi judicial system. Franz may work at a desk, but he is not a *Schreibtischtäter* ("desk perpetrator") who routinely signs off execution orders. This new judicial structure must be accepted as the deep bow that Franz Joseph's court officer signifies. The Emperor is the uniformed ruler: his composed, formal demeanor and elevated status make him an ideal model of both military leadership and bourgeois citizenship.[40]

Much more problematic is the behavior of Major Böckel. Initially, he does not appear suspect, since Josef Meinrad's performance overplays the character's physical clumsiness as it riddles his interactions with faux pas and slapstick. However, Böckel's behavior veils virtues of the sort that were highly compromised under Hitler; they are subject to transformative redemption in the course of the *Sissi* trilogy. In the beginning, Böckel is keenly aware of the hierarchy of authority: obedience and submission are his dominant disposition. In *Sissi 1*, Böckle receives direct orders from Sophie to protect the Emperor from assassination. He is eager to please despite his lack of experience, as he claims. "Theoretically, I know every trick a bodyguard needs to know."[41] The term "Überwacher" in the original German literally means "guardian"; however, it also connotes "minder," which is clearly consonant with Sophie's habit of private intrusion and secret surveillance of family members. The film does not, however, critically address the possibility that her order as well as Böckel's own claim to "theoretical knowledge" might signify something much more malevolent: the Nazi recruitment of citizen spies. Following Sophie's orders, Böckel proceeds to instruct his subordinates to control strictly all persons in the Emperor's vicinity. Like Franz (Figure 14.3), he is situated behind a desk, ordering his three attentive subordinates to arrest anyone who appears "suspicious or refractory":[42] "Better to arrest one too many rebels than to let an innocent man get away" (Figure 14.4).[43]

This rather confused yet serious order is softened through the physical comedy of two of the soldiers bumping into each other while receiving it, distracting from the order's extremism. Böckel's behavior echoes their overzealousness to obey orders, even to the extent of detaining persons who may appear out of place or awkward and preventing their release despite their innocence. His attitude is presented in *Sissi 1* as a leftover from the tainted past, softened through comedy and very much in contrast to the assertive, critical, and idealized demeanor Franz exhibits when he refuses to sign the execution orders.

Nevertheless, Böckel remains a sympathetic character, mostly because of the comic relief through which he renders harmless his authoritarian actions and their

Figure 14.4   Oberst Böckel at his desk in Bad Ischl, in *Sissi 1*.

consequences, through his undignified and dull-witted subordinates. "The film never criticized the system, but only its excesses, and those were only held up to ridicule" (Barthel, 1986: 256).[44]

Yet the audience is shown that Böckel's actions originate from his sense of loyalty and patriotic duty and are thereby salvaged, even affirmed, when he is promoted in *Sissi 2* to personal attaché. Despite his social awkwardness, he has proven his loyalty, and Sissi, while amused by his behavior, believes he is kind-hearted and trusts his service (Marshall, 1997: 381). This is noteworthy with respect to the rearmament debate. By 1951, the commander-in-chief of NATO, Dwight D. Eisenhower, assured Adenauer the honorable conscription of *Wehrmacht* soldiers, thus indicating trust in a West German military partnership. This suggested a certain national redemption, which in turn cleared the path for the reintegration of officers into the newly founded *Bundeswehr* who could not otherwise have been supplied by the military leadership due to a lack of trained and experienced professionals (Doering-Manteuffel, 1981: 124). Böckel's role in *Sissi 1* suggests something similar: he is committed to serving his country and the royal family; however, his "extreme" understanding of obedience is merely misguided. In the course of the trilogy, and largely with Sissi's inspiration, he proves adaptable and capable of learning how to think for himself, pursue his better judgment, and discover his individuality. His developmental progress is evidenced by his refusal to follow an explicit order, apropos of the new *Bundeswehr* code and in line with Franz's prior example.

In *Sissi 2*, Sissi surreptitiously leaves the palace in Vienna with a small entourage after a falling-out with Franz and Sophie. Böckel secretly telegraphs the court that Sissi is returning to her family in Bavaria. While concordant with Sophie's wont to monitor her family at court, and redolent once again of Nazi-instilled paranoia, Böckel's intervention ensures a conciliatory reunion between Sissi and Franz, who follows her to Possenhofen. By the same token, it affirms the foundations of the new German military with respect to questioning and disobeying orders. Böckel's initiative appears to be disloyal in that it directly contradicts the wishes of Sissi, who had taken care not to reveal her destination upon leaving Vienna. Countering superior orders and initiating contact with the court on his own accord represents a tremendous change in Böckel's behavior.

This change is in fact so remarkable that it becomes a topic of discussion during a scene directly subsequent to that of the royal couple's reconciliation. Duke Maximilian inquires whether Böckel ever indeed sent the telegram, and Böckel affirms, bowing his head and averting his eyes guiltily. Whereas the orders Böckel disobeyed were benign, Maximilian, the model of the "new citizen," refers to Böckel's actions as "almost a historical act" for their having facilitated the royal couple's reunification and ensured their leadership over Austria's own reunification with Hungary.[45]

Böckel's remarkable transformation continues. Initially, he had to undergo schooling in court etiquette and language in Vienna in *Sissi 2*. In the course of *Sissi 3*, as part of Sissi's entourage, he travels to Hungary, Portugal, and Greece, where he begins to expand his knowledge of history and learns, with considerable success, new languages and cultures. He discovers his humanity and experiences both personal and professional success, which thrives despite his predisposition toward clumsiness and social awkwardness. Böckel may be insecure about his new position and role, but his show of effort endears him to the audience, providing them with a font of hope regarding their own, contemporary struggles.

Böckel's transition becomes most apparent when he shifts to wearing his uniform to wearing civilian clothes – a suit – while romantically pursuing a Greek woman (Figure 14.5). Sadness is brought about by his break-up with a Hungarian woman, another love interest while stationed in Hungary, itself necessitated by his duty to accompany Sissi in her ongoing travels. Meinrad's over-the-top performance allows for a man in uniform to cry (Figure 14.6), yet despite his open display of emotion, he is always the dominant and determining party in this and his other romantic relationships, hence ultimately maintaining traditional gender hierarchies that are nonetheless tempered by the patriotic call to duty.

Böckel in effect changes from a manic and clumsy security guard whose intentions are to defend the monarchy, to a cultured, liberal citizen. He may wear a uniform in fulfillment of duty, yet he also discovers a new, civilian world to which

Figure 14.5 and 14.6 Böckel's expression of emotion and transformation to the new *Bürger* discovering his humanity, in *Sissi 3*.

he happily adjusts. Thus *Sissi*'s German audience is provided with a means by which to identify with a nonmilitaristic national revival, as Böckel becomes the model for an "ethics of demilitarization" (Marshall, 1997: 380).

While Major Böckel represents the reformation and demilitarization of German society, Franz represents the leader and representative of a government that permits rearmament. For this purpose, the model invoked is that of the medieval knight, a masculine ideal detached from the bloody and self-sacrificing Nordic hero of Nazi propaganda, and especially evident during the coronation scene in *Sissi 2*, when Franz, wearing uniform, cloak, and crown, enters riding a white

Figure 14.7 Franz Josef I during his oath as King of Hungary, in *Sissi 2*.

horse and carrying a sword with which to take the oath of King of Hungary following an elaborate church ceremony (Figure 14.7).

This representational choice suggests the image of the knight horseman as expression of noble rank and deed. It points very subtly to reforms undertaken during the tenth century, under Catholic Church auspices, which transformed the pillaging, "barbaric" warrior into a stately Christian soldier whose actions and behavior were ostensibly charitable and virtuous. The knight thus became an ideological phenomenon for legitimating the use of weapons on moral grounds (Bumke, 1992: 68). In *Sissi 2*, the image of the virtuous knight places this very model into question with specific regard to the fact that such romantic ideals were also used to rationalize and justify violent and irrational behavior during the anti-Muslim Crusades and anti-Jewish pogroms – and, later, the Holocaust.

Throughout the *Sissi* trilogy, Franz is portrayed as mild-mannered, respectful, and kind. He presents an alternative model of masculinity based on traditional values of steadfastness, inner strength, and determination coupled with "softer" qualities of empathy, sentimentality, and romantic love (Lowry and Korte, 2000: 116). The coronation underscores his ascription to these values, his knightly performance allegorizing the new, postheroic identity of the *Bundeswehr* and of the Adenauer administration. Franz's raised sword is not an aggressive gesture but instead reinforces his oath to unify and protect the Hungarian people. It also recalls the medieval *"Schwertleite,"* the bestowal of the knightly sword and belt upon entry into honorable military service, which bound their newly endowed carrier to the weapon's strictly good and pious use – apropos of the argument for rearmament (Bumke, 1992: 69).

Whenever Franz appears in public for major state functions, members of the Catholic Church are present, approving his actions and leading the ceremony. In *Sissi 2*, the coronation ceremony in the church preceding his public oath-taking is presented in great detail. Throughout the trilogy, representatives of the Catholic Church are prominently featured in the climactic finale scenes. In *Sissi 1*, it is Sissi and Franz's wedding ceremony; in *Sissi 2*, it is the coronation; and in *Sissi 3*, the clergy becomes the proponent of forgiveness and reconciliation. The prominence of the Catholic Church in these films recapitulates the strong stance it took in favor of rearmament. During the postwar years, "the Catholic church served as [...] a sounding board for conservative attitudes" and for government officials who in turn translated Church concerns into legislation (Fehrenbach, 1995: 93). Conservative Catholic policy-makers were untainted by the Prussian-Protestant military tradition and thus able to help legitimate Adenauer's attempts to integrate the new West German military into civilian government structures (Doering-Manteuffel, 1981: 6).

The Church sought to promote faith as a basis for individual conduct and as a bulwark against the atheism of communist Eastern Europe (Mahlmann, 1985: 100). In his 1948 Christmas message, Pope Pius XII called for a united front against communism. Adenauer, a devout Catholic, aligned his politics with this position, which included strong condemnation of the 1956 Soviet invasion of Hungary (Doering-Manteuffel, 1981: 4). The invasion itself, lamented by a papal encyclical, coincided with the release of *Sissi 2*.[46] The revival of the teachings of Thomas of Aquinas (1225–1274) after World War One facilitated this alignment by making it seem possible to reconcile rearmament with Christian moral values. By arguing that each state has a duty to protect its citizens from "unjust" incursions, these teachings actually rationalized military necessity in the name of self-defense (Doering-Manteuffel, 1981: 5). On this perspective, only defensive wars were justifiable (Doering-Manteuffel, 1981: 10). As the papal encyclical implied, Soviet intervention into an Eastern European country perceived as Christian necessitated a military response. It was on this basis in addition to the threat of war in Korea that the Catholic Church in West Germany became such a staunch supporter of Adenauer's rearmament plans.

In *Sissi 2*, Franz's oath is the climax of the new leadership's public display. The preceding scenes, however, add further legitimacy to Franz's status as benign ruler by depicting a quasi-religious ritual. The idea of the reunification of the Hungarian people is presented when each region in Hungary contributes soil to build an elevation on which Franz takes his oath – in effect reuniting all regions under the Austro-Hungarian Empire. This gesture also suggests the possibility of building and unifying the German nation in contemporary political conditions of the 1950s, and it furthermore suggests the West's supportive stand for Hungary, which was invaded by Soviet troops on October 23, 1956, only two months before the release of *Sissi 2* in December 1956. The man on the white horse becomes the defender of *Heimat*, the builder of a nation that is not, presumably, an aggressive conqueror.

Affirmation of Traditional Family Structures and Nation-Building

"Since 1942, the nights of bombardment turned all possessions into ashes. After that, during the flights and displacements, all form and substance of middle-class life disintegrated" (Michael Stürmer, quoted in Bliersbach, 1985: 68).[47] Besides material devastation, there was a sense of social degradation after the lost war (Bliersbach, 1985: 67). The postwar years saw the destruction of a host of familiar bourgeois, middle-class structures. A large number of Germans saw their families disrupted by the loss of their male members during the war. Men who eventually did return, as well as their families, confronted enormous destruction, hardships, and material scarcity. A good number "were often physically and psychological scarred, unwilling and unable to work" (Moeller, 1989: 140).[48] Along with this reality came the need to adjust to a dramatically changed family organization in which women had taken on traditional male roles to ensure their families' wartime survival. Women had become indispensable, and their "authority within families was greatly enhanced" (Moeller, 1989: 147). The Adenauer administration actively sought to redefine family along conservative lines in order to reintegrate returning men as smoothly as possible into familiar structures. It promoted the reinstatement of men as traditional breadwinners and encouraged women to limit their activities to housekeeping and childrearing (Moeller, 1989: 144). Gainful male employment was considered essential to national renewal, on the patriarchal belief that "men, not women 'founded families'" (Moeller, 1989: 144; Trimborn, 1998: 121). To this end, the "individual as the agent of work," and the family as a "fundamental social unit" came to constitute the core structural values upon which the new West German state would define itself and undertake nation-building efforts (Moeller, 1989: 142). Applegate puts it succinctly:

> Democracy and "healthy" attitudes would have to begin in the family, the home, the locality, and grow from those "roots" into a new nation and a new national identity. (1990: 229)

The *Sissi* trilogy addresses several issues raised by the West German social policies ensuing from these efforts. First and foremost, it dismantles and exposes as harmful the dominant role of the women in the parent generation. Family relations in the *Sissi* trilogy prove deceptive, since they only appear loving and conciliatory. Franz's parents are portrayed in ways that disqualify them as proper postwar role models. Franz's father, Franz Karl, has abdicated his claim to the throne for lack of interest and fear of responsibility. His weak, disinterested status is overcompensated by Sophie, who assumes the role of head-of-family as a ruthless, calculating tactician who rules the Empire *de facto*. With Sophie's heartless, controlling depiction as "the only man at court in the Hofburg,"[49] the film certainly calls into question the reversal of traditional gender roles; despite her shrewdness, Sophie is ultimately domesticated, as she relinquishes her position and defers leadership to Franz. She may be head-of-family, but she cannot be head-of-state.

On the other hand, Sissi's family in Possenhofen is represented as bourgeois: Traditional, civilian clothing is worn by all, the furniture is old and solid and appears to be family heirlooms, the actors (attempt to) speak a Bavarian dialect and undertake private, domestic activities such as housekeeping, fishing, hiking, hunting, and consuming hearty food and drink. Ludovika is positioned at the family's center, from which she attempts to instill decorum and etiquette by managing the daily routine. In several scenes, her domestic abilities and responsibilities are overtly emphasized: she instructs her daughters how to keep house and change diapers, and she takes charge of the kitchen on special occasions. The way in which she raises her daughters is perfectly in line with the traditional family model being promoted by the Adenauer administration. This seemingly ideal bourgeois household is overturned, however, when it becomes clear that Ludovika's ambitions have entailed deception and subterfuge, especially toward her husband. Under the guise of a harmless outing to Bad Ischl, she excludes Maximilian from major decisions that affect the entire family, as she secretly intends the trip to serve as an occasion for announcing Nene's engagement to Franz. Sissi is present on the outing solely in order to distract Maximilian from any suspicions he may have about these plans.

Hence Duke Maximilian Josef of Bavaria is frequently interpreted as a weak, peripheral bourgeois interested only in his private pursuits: fishing, hunting, and indulging in beer and brats in the company of nonaristocratic friends, distanced from political activity and familial insight.[50] But unlike Franz Karl, Maximilian, as I have argued, represents *Heimat*: he is a man who can in fact become a role model. He represents the foundation on which the new generation might rebuild and expand national identity into the idea of a "kinder, gentler" Germany. This new idea is meant to further the ideals that Maximilian represents, reorganizing and reinstating traditional family structures not through revolt and chaos in a wartorn country, but through a quiet change that promises redemption and salvation (Lowry and Korte, 2000: 117).

Positioning Sissi and Franz as central protagonists, the *Sissi* films present a relationship that appears equal and in which Sissi even seems to lead, for instance, by dissolving political tensions between Franz and some Hungarian nobles whom Sophie has effectively insulted. Yet Sissi accomplishes this task with charm rather

Figure 14.8   Sissi and her husband Franz Josef I in her parents' home, in *Sissi 2*.

than political wit, which she explicitly disavows. It is Franz who makes the major decisions in their relationship: he announces their engagement publicly notwithstanding Sissi's reservations; he initially sides with his mother concerning the removal of their child from Sissi's care; and he and his mother attempt to hide Sissi's life-threatening illness from her.

Although Franz is often reminded of his wife's wishes, they conform to the traditional family and gender values propagated by the Adenauer administration. Sissi calls on Franz to make more time for her, but through this request she merely affirms Franz's work ethic, itself reinforced by frequent shots of him working at his desk and in conference with ministers and diplomats – all for the good of the country. He and Sissi are shown arguing only once, in *Sissi 2*, over the matter of their child. While Sissi's parents side with Franz concerning the imperative that she support his duty to nation, Ludovika sees Sissi's retreat to Possenhofen as completely justified: a mother must care for her child. Hence the film asserts the return of women to house and home but veils that call with the strongest romanticism, which is underscored by violin music and a contrived reconciliation. When Sissi is finally reinstated in her role as mother, Franz is presented as a man interested in the details of childrearing. When Franz assures Sissi that, from now on, "everything will be done as you want it,"[51] Sissi has the final word: "No! As you want it."[52] This false parity is visually reinforced during an ensuing scene in which Franz, seated in a chair, pulls Sissi toward him so that she is veritably kneeling at his feet. Franz tells her that getting to know her new country will cure her of her homesickness, as if her retreat to Bavaria was nothing more than her desire to return home (Figure 14.8).

Franz, who will soon show her the Austrian mountains, thus takes a leadership role in defining the new *Heimat* for Sissi, merging the familiar with the new, assuring his wife not only of her new life in a new country, but also of his leadership within the family, to which she consents. Sissi displays her readiness for sacrifice and subordination through this particularly submissive constellation, the setting of which is still the Possenhoffen house, with its bourgeois core starkly contrasting the imposing and outdated royal palace. Hence whereas Maximilian, the model of the New Man, appears in this setting as weak and only peripheral to his apparently domineering wife, Franz is visually reinstated, by virtue of his repositioning within the setting, as the bourgeois head-of-household, even as the uniform he – unlike Maximilian – continues to wear signifies the success with which he, and by extension the state, have managed to shape and facilitate a personal relationship with Sissi.

Conclusion

The final sequence in *Sissi 3* represents a culmination of an intact family structure under male leadership and, by extension, an effective and courageous political leadership drawing upon facing its country's past for salvation. After Sissi's convalescence, Franz meets up with her to undertake a joint diplomatic tour through the Italian provinces of Lombardy and Veneto, which are hostile to the crown and have threatened to secede from the Empire. While their reception in Milan has comic undertones, the final sequence in Venice, which concludes the trilogy, is downright threatening. When Franz and Sissi ride in a gondola along the Grand Canal toward Piazza San Marco, the entire sequence is an interplay of silence, short exchanges between Franz and Sissi, fragments of the freedom choir in Giuseppe Verdi's opera *Nabucco* (1842) and of the melody from the Haydn composition that became the German national anthem, *Das Lied der Deutschen* ("The Song of the Germans") (1797) – but which was sung with different lyrics during the nineteenth century in the form of an Emperor's Hymn entitled *Gott erhalte Franz den Kaiser* ("God Save the Emperor Franz").[53] This hymn, simultaneously exalting Franz, the Emperor while also functioning as the national West German anthem, had been audible previously throughout the *Sissi* films, although only in short fragments. This final sequence eventually manages by its end to present the entire second movement of the Haydn quartet, effectively celebrating Franz, the new West German man and leader, while affirming West Germany's nationhood. Ironically, the Chorus of the Hebrew Slaves' *Va, pensiero, sull'ali dorate* ("Fly, thought, on wings of gold") from the third act of *Nabucco* has been considered a traditional Italian freedom song and remembers the biblical narrative of Jewish exile after the first destruction of the Temple in Jerusalem by the Babylonians. Of course, this account takes on a completely different meaning during the 1950s, vis-à-vis Germany's recent horrific history, especially the Holocaust (literally "burnt sacrifice"), against which context the rest of the scene plays out. There the German anthem carries additional meaning, since it was adopted by the Nazis who sang only the first stanza with the infamous opening line, *Deutschland über alles* ("Germany above all").

Naively, Franz does not expect a hostile reception from the Venetians, who shut their windows and turn their backs on the royal couple. However, Sissi points out that he should not have expected otherwise, since the people know him only as the signator of death warrants (issued in reality by his predecessors and local authorities).[54] He agrees, replying vaguely that "Too many mistakes have been made,"[55] and Sissi responds that she would like to have spared him this humiliation; but, in compliance with his assessment, Sissi assumes the role of supportive wife who faces adversity with dignity and courage alongside her husband. The mechanical protocol they fulfill by walking along the red carpet on the Piazza San Marco is abruptly lent a decidedly human face when, suddenly, Sissi spots her daughter, accompanied by Ludovika, and breaks her even stride to run toward and embrace her young child, whom she had not expected, when ill, ever to see again. At this moment, a connection is made with the Italian spectators. Here Sissi appears not as the oppressor or foreign invader but as a mother. Of course, Franz had planned this surprise all along for Sissi, a fact that makes him the author of the scene, which he in turn exploits as an Italian man exclaims, "Viva la mamma!" The acknowledgement of the basic humanity of Franz and Sissi as parents and human beings shows a family that can transcend any divisions that the past may have created. The explicit affirmation comes via absolution from church representatives, bishops who sanctify the intact, loving relationship between mother and child over protocol, which of course also insinuates that the church transcends nationality and is thus positioned to offer forgiveness and absolution to the Germans as a whole. And finally, when the Italians show respect by removing their hats to greet their enemies, they make a political gesture that is stunningly reinforced by the triumphant complete rendition, albeit without the lyrics, of the Austrian/German anthem. When the melody reaches the German anthem's line *Blüh' im Glanze dieses Glückes* ("Bloom in the splendor of this happiness") a frontal shot is provided of the Basilica di San Marco. More men remove their hats, and a large number of Venetian pigeons, now ostensibly doves of peace, take flight, propagating the political message of a peaceful West Germany and the possibility of forgiveness and reconciliation. The concept of a hopeful, nonaggressive German nationhood has come full circle. With the repetition of *"Blüh' im Glanze dieses Glückes,"* an intercut occurs that represents that "happiness," as Franz holds his daughter and salutes, and Sissi smiles at her husband and child, surrounded by clergy and flanked in the background by grandmother Ludovika (Figure 14.9).

Figure 14.9   The final shot of the trilogy: the royal family in Venice, in *Sissi 3*.

This final shot of the *Sissi* trilogy is a representative image that shows the convergence of discourses of gender and global politics that were deployed to rehabilitate highly conservative social structures in Germany and Europe, while also seeking to legitimize Germany's return to the world political stage. The image displays the notion of German redemption and salvation in an international context as sanctioned and displayed prominently by the Catholic Church, while also representing the reinstatement of traditional, conservative and bourgeois family structures under male leadership.

The image depicts the New Man at center stage, framed by adoring women who are now reduced to their role as mothers. Women have apparently willingly accepted their traditional roles in support of their husbands, and the consequent return to an ostensibly ethical society leads to redemption, which in turn provides a catharsis for the films' audience. Franz is reintroduced as an agent of his destiny and a maker of history. It is remarkable who is not shown: Franz's parents, who are disqualified from this future by their general conduct, as well as Max, the original model of masculinity, whom Franz has replaced because he is now the new model: a man who has been transformed into husband, father, political and military leader, and human being, now holding the child whom Max had proudly pronounced as Sissi's very likeness, merging past and present into a double-edged hope for a better German future.

Notes

1   There are no exact attendance records for the screening of the *Sissi* trilogy in movie theaters, since those were not officially kept, but it is estimated that between 20 and 25 million tickets were sold. See http://www.sissi.de/aktuell/filme_trilogie.php (accessed May 26, 2011).

2   See, for instance, Embacher (2004) for analysis of *Sissi*'s reception in Israel.

3   Both actors tried for years to escape the typecasting and overwhelming audience attention which their roles had garnered for them. Karlheinz Böhm played the title role of a psychopath in Michael Powell's *Peeping Tom* (1960), which shocked his audience and led to a rupture in his career. He was eventually rehabilitated during the 1970s by his work on a number of projects with Rainer Werner Fassbinder. Romy Schneider also sought a radical departure from her role as Sissi and "escaped" to France to work with Claude Chabrol, Luchino Visconti, and Orson Welles on fundamentally different projects, each of which alienated her German-speaking audience, who were not ready to relinquish her wholesome image as Sissi. Under the direction of Visconti in *Ludwig* (1972), Schneider returned to her role as the Empress of Austria, this time with a completely different portrayal of Elisabeth as a complex and difficult modern woman. In "Romy Schneider, *La Passante du Sans-Souci*: discourses of *Vergangenheitsbewältigung*, Feminism and Myth" (2005), Nina Zimnik gives an in-depth reading of Jacques Rouffio's *The Passerby* (*Die Spaziergängerin von Sans-Souci*, 1982), addressing Schneider's projects in France and the issue of the lingering threat of fascism against which Schneider took an adamant stance. Zimnik looks closely at the discourses of Schneider's personal transformation in terms of liberal political agendas and feminist representations in light of the problematic German past and Schneider's reception in Germany. In addition, she also points to Schneider's contentious relationship with her parents: Magda Schneider, who plays alongside her daughter in the *Sissi* trilogy and five other films between the years 1953–1961, and Wolf Albach-Retty. Both actors were stars of the Third Reich cinema "who entertained close relations with high politicians and the *Führer* himself (Zimnik, 2005: 263). Daniela Sannwald was the curator of an exhibit entitled *Romy Schneider. Wien – Berlin – Paris* (December 5, 2009–August 29, 2010) in Berlin's *Deutsche Kinemathek*, which traced the differing roles and images of Romy Schneider's career through images and installations, especially from the previously neglected and important 1960s, and documented her mythologization and appropriation by fans. For a visual impression and a short interview with Daniela Sannwald in German or French translation, see also http://videos.arte.tv/de/videos/ausstellung_romy_schneider_neu_entdeckt_-3137782.html (accessed May 26, 2011).

4   In the following pages, I will refer to the respective films in the trilogy as *Sissi 1*, *Sissi 2*, and *Sissi 3*.

5   In the following pages, all translations of quotes appearing in the main text are my own. The original German quote is: "In einer Welt der Atomreaktoren, Erdsatelliten, Überschallgeschwindigkeiten, der Psychoanalyse und der Relativitätstheorie, in einer Welt mit Eisernem Vorhang und Wirtschaftskämpfen […], kurzum in einer Welt, die immer abstrakter und rationeller wird, ist kaum noch ein Platz, an dem die menschliche Seele sich mit ihren Träumen ansiedeln kann. […] Und dennoch oder gerade deshalb

ist die Sehnsucht der Menschen nach der schönen Unwirklichkeit, nach dem fernen Unbekannten, nach einer Zeit, in der alles ganz anders war, größer denn je."

6 "Fascinating fascism" is a term coined by Susan Sontag (1974) in her seminal essay of the same name. Rentschler (1990: 21) reads *Münchhausen* as a "male fantasy of control."

7 The co-production of Austrian ORF, German ZDF and Italian RAI was filmed for television in two parts and aired December 16 and 20, 2009 under the title *Sisi* [sic]. The television series was directed by Xaver Schwarzenberger, with David Rott and Cristiana Capotondi in the main roles, and was filmed on location in Austria (see http://programm.org.at/?story=3815, accessed May 17, 2010). The film shows a much more contentious political atmosphere within the Austrian Empire and between the two protagonists. It is now available on DVD by Universum Film, thus far only in German without English subtitles.

8 Tom Tykwer named his main character "Sissi" and references the original in his film *The Princess and the Warrior* (*Der Krieger und die Kaiserin*, 2000). Michael "Bully" Herbig produced an animated parody, *Lissi und der wilde Kaiser* (Lissi and the Wild Emperor, 2007). The popularity of the *Sissi* films in queer iconography has been identified by the campy appeal of their storylines, sets, and costuming. Andrea B. Braidt (2008: 269) quotes William Spurlin's investigation about Lady Di, applying his concept to Sissi, whom she sees as "a kind of bourgeois woman in aristocratic 'drag'" playing "princess." Furthermore, the term "sissy" carries in English a derogatory connotation for a gay male. As will become clear in the course of the discussion in this chapter, the character Sissi defers her subjectivity in the film series onto the male characters by transferring "kinder, gentler" attributes and qualities to them. In effect, the German postwar masculinity is "sissy-fied" – at the expense of course, of actual gay men (who at the time were still criminalized in Germany under the infamous paragraph 175) and of women and feminism, for the films served the ideological purpose of rearmament which both gay and feminist liberation politics would likely have opposed. In addition, Heidi Schlipphacke (2010) points to the fact that both main actors portrayed homosexual characters in later works: Romy Schneider as Manuela von Meinhardis in the 1958 remake of *Girls in Uniform* (*Mädchen in Uniform*), directed by Géza von Radványi; and Karlheinz Böhm as Max in Rainer Werner Fassbinder's *Fox and his Friends* (*Faustrecht der Freiheit*, 1974) (Schlipphacke, 2010: 235).

9 "Volks-Epen, bei denen sich die Weltgeschichte aufs Kleingärtnerniveau begibt und an deren raffinierter Machtart jede Kritik wie an einem gut geölten Catcherkörper abgleitet."

10 "zentrale Rolle als 'Erlösungsgestalt'."

11 "Unschuld und Tatkraft [...] die Männer von ihrer Schuld [zu] 'erlösen' und zugleich für den Wiederaufbau nötigen Qualitäten neuen Glanz [zu] geben."

12 "Sissi ist ein Film, in dem – fast lautlos – die Männer wieder in ihre Rechte eintreten."

13 Mary Wauchope (2002) has explored the *Sissi* trilogy in the specific Austrian context of the treaty of 1955 and the postwar restoration of identity, pointing to the foundations of the Austrian state and of the Second Republic of Austria. She explores Austrian national identity through cultural promotions of Austrian nationhood as they are represented in the *Sissi* films. However, Wauchope also contends that the

historical grandeur and timeless natural beauty of the Austrian landscapes do not reflect specific political Austrian perspectives and circumstances. Instead she suggests that the series subscribes to basic ideals of Western democracy: freedom, truth, tolerance, and equality (Wauchope, 2002: 173). Wauchope also links the films to the renewed and intensified interest in the historical Elisabeth of Bavaria during the late 1990s, in the wake of the 1986 Waldheim Affair, which jeopardized positive postwar images of Austria by exposing the downplayed former Nazi involvements of Austria's then-president-elect, Kurt Waldheim.

14   In addition, Sabine Hake (2001: 153) has pointed out the continuities of this symbiotic relationship of "German Austrian film relations and Austria's total dependence on Germany for film imports and exports" that reach back to the film industry during the Third Reich. Erica Carter (2010: 95) discusses the aesthetic of the *Sissi* films that are also grounded in the Third Reich and points to the cinematography of Bruno Mondi, who collaborated, among other films, with Veit Harlan on *Jud Süss* (*Jew Süss*, 1940).

15   For a concise English-language description of the Austrian film studios and financial structures, see Gertraud Steiner (1995).

16   "Zu jener Zeit sahen sie alle in der Liberalisierung des Filmverkehrs mit der Bundesrepublik Deutschland das Ideal ihrer Träume, die Herren Produzenten in Wien, aber Bonn ließ nur zwei Dutzend Streifen ins Land. Daher besagter Wettlauf um jeden dieser [...] [Filme]."

17   Sabine Hake (2001) discusses the accommodations that the Austrian Wien-Film AG conducted after its foundation in October 1938 to adhere to the artistic and ideological imperatives of the Reich Cultural Chamber (*Reichkulturkammer*) in Berlin and under the leadership of UFA film studios, the monopoly parent company of the Nazi film industry.

18   "Produktionen kamen meist nur durch den direkten Auftrag der Verleihe zustande."

19   In the case of *Sissi 1*, Walter Fritz (1984: 118) contends that scenes at Sissi's Bavarian home were included specifically to please German audiences.

20   "Die Banken geben heute nur Filmkredite, wenn das Geschäft totsicher ist. Unter 'totsicher' versteht man die Mitwirkung bewährter Filmstars und eine so dumme Handlung, dass sie das 'Volk' ohne Komplikationen verdauen kann. Der Verleih bestimmte das Gesicht des Films und die Bank seine Zeugung."

21   "Somit trat also der paradoxe Fall ein, dass alle Beteiligten vom deutschen Verleiher abhängig waren – auch das Handelsministerium [Österreichs], das erst bei einer Verleihzusage die Ausfuhr genehmigte."

22   The trade dispute was actually triggered by the marketing of the *Sissi* trilogy. The Austrian daily "Tiroler Tageszeitung" reported about the co-optation of Austrian productions on January 9, 1957 under the headline "Sissi as 'German' film!" (Carter, 2010: 81).

23   "Aufgrund meiner reichen Erfahrungen [...] habe ich mir einen Wiener Dialekt zugelegt, der auch in Berlin und Hamburg verständlich ist. Da sich der österreichische Film in Österreich nie amortisieren kann, müssen wir unsere Filme nach den Wünschen des gesamten deutschsprachigen Publikums inszenieren."

24   For the turbulent and taxing history of Wien-Film during the 1938 Annexation, its subsequent integration into the German film industry during World War Two, and its continuation and eventual decline during the 1970s and 1980s see Bernhard Frankfurter (1988).

25 "Ernst Marischka produzierte, was er für erbauliche Kultur für den sogenannten kleinen Mann hielt, und er musste natürlich auch produzieren, was der deutsche Verleih, ohne den der österreichische Film nicht auskommen konnte, diktierte."

26 Sabine Hake (2001: 156) conducts an insightful discussion of the traditional genre of "Vienna" films in the Third Reich and concludes that it resulted in a "German view point of Vienna as a variation on, if not alternative to, true Germanness."

27 "süßes, unschuldiges Mädel."

28 This film is also part of the Koch Lorber *Sissi* film collection; see Further Reading.

29 Marischka worked very efficiently when collaborating with distributor Herzog, reflecting the close connection of *Mädchenjahre einer Königin* to *Sissi 1* and *2* by even using the same illustrations for the all films' opening credits.

30 According to Internet Movie Database (IMDb), the shooting of Sissi's Bavarian home and surroundings actually took place in Fuschl, Austria not far from Salzburg.

31 "Weisst du, dass ich sehr glücklich bin, dass ich einen solchen Vater hab'."

32 "Ich glaube, ich werde auch einmal so werden wie er."

33 "Wenn du einmal im Leben Kummer oder Sorgen haben solltest, dann geh' wie jetzt mit offenen Augen durch den Wald. Und in jedem Baum, in jedem Strauch, in jeder Blume und in jedem Tier wird dir die Allmacht Gottes zu Bewusstsein kommen und dir Trost und Halt geben."

34 "Ich will frei leben ohne Zwang. [...] [Ich spreche] die Sprache, die mich mein Vater gelehrt hat, dem die Freiheit und die Wahrheitsliebe über alles geht."

35 "Reichtum und Macht kommen nun in die Hände einfacher Menschen. Das Sagen haben nicht mehr die Frauen, sondern die Männer. Oder solche Frauen, die ihre Väter mehr lieben als ihre Mütter."

36 See paragraphs 6, 7, and 8 of the Legal Status of Soldiers (*Gesetz über die Rechtsstellung des Soldaten – Soldatengesetz Deutsche Bundeswehr*), http://rk19-bielefeld-mitte.de/info/Recht/Soldatengesetz/inhalt.htm (accessed May 26, 2011).

37 See paragraph 22.1 of the Military Penal Law (*Wehrstrafgesetz*), http://www.gesetze-im-internet.de/wstrg/__22.html (accessed May 26, 2011).

38 See the *Bundeswehr* statement on its history by following the link, "Streitkräfte," to "Tradition," at http://www.bundeswehr.de/portal/a/bwde (accessed May 26, 2011).

39 "Rebellion, Aufwiegelung und Majestätsbeleidigung."

40 In contrast to this benign depiction, Erica Carter (2010: 83), drawing from Robin Orkey (2001: 160–161), asserts, "Following the 1848 liberal revolutions, the Austrian Empire returned to absolutist rule under Kaiser Franz Joseph [...]. 1848 had left its mark on the empire in reforms that included the introduction of jury trial, improved rights of association, provisions for communal self-government, and mother-tongue education among a multilingual populace. By the time Franz Joseph married [...] [Elisabeth of Bavaria in 1854], the young Kaiser had, by contrast, overseen a process that reasserted monarchical authority by dismantling the jury system, replacing the new system of ministerial government with absolutist governance, and tightening the state's grip on public opinion and behavior through newly stringent press laws, a revised criminal procedure, and an 'omnipresent' role for a newly created gendarmerie."

41 "Theoretisch kenne ich jeden Winkelzug eines Überwachers."

42 "verdächtig oder renitent."

43 "Besser einen Rebellen mehr verhaften, als einen Unschuldigen laufen lassen."

44   "Der Film kritisierte nie das System, sondern nur dessen Auswüchse und die wurden lediglich der Lächerlichkeit preisgegeben."

45   "fast eine historische Tat."

46   "Our paternal heart is deeply moved by the sorrowful events, which have befallen the people of eastern Europe and especially of Our beloved Hungary, which is now being soaked in blood by a shocking massacre. And not only is Our heart moved, but so too are the hearts of all men who cherish the rights of civil society, the dignity of man, and the liberty which is due to individuals and to nations." For the complete speech, see "Encyclical of Pope Pius XII urging Public Prayers for Peace and Freedom for the People of Hungary, October 28, 1956," at *Papal Encyclicals Online*; see Websites.

47   "In den Bombennächten seit 1942 wurde Besitz zu Asche. In den Fluchten und Vertreibungen danach zerfielen Form und Substanz bürgerlichen Lebens."

48   For an in-depth account of postwar German social policy that focuses on the reconstruction of family and nation-building, see Moeller, 1989.

49   "der einzige Mann in der Hofburg."

50   Ursula Bessen states that the existence of fathers in the *Sissi* trilogy is acknowledged, but that they are represented as weak; while Bärbel Westermann suggests that the men / fathers only appear to wield authority.

51   "alles geschieht so, wie du es willst."

52   "Nein! Wie du es willst."

53   Franz Joseph Haydn (1732–1809) had composed the melody in 1797 for the "Emperor's Hymn." Lorenz Leopold Haschka (1749–1827) wrote the lyrics in honor of Franz II (1768–1835), Emperor of the Holy Roman Empire and later of Austria, to express Austria's patriotic sentiment against the threatening stance of France. The lyrics for the German national anthem were written much later, in 1841, by Heinrich Hoffmann von Fallersleben (1798–1874) as a call for a unified Germany in the *Vormärz* era marked by the German Revolution of 1848.

54   This notion expressed by Franz is in line with postwar German apologeticism, when a majority of Germans rejected guilt and responsibility for genocide by arguing that they themselves were neither present in the Nazi camps nor approved or took part in the killings.

55   "Zu viele Fehler wurden gemacht."

References

Applegate, C. (1990) *A Nation of Provincials: The German Idea of Heimat*, University of California Press, Berkeley, Los Angeles and Oxford.

Barthel, M. (1986) *So war es wirklich. Der deutsche Nachkriegsfilm*, Herbig, Munich and Berlin.

Bechthold-Comforty, B. (1989) *Der deutsche Heimatfilm: Bildwelten und Weltbilder: Bilder, Texte, Analysen zu 70 Jahren deutscher Filmgeschichte*, Tübinger Vereinigung für Volkskunde, Tübingen.

Beller, S. (2006) *A Concise History of Austria*, Cambridge University Press, Cambridge and New York.

Bessen, U. (1989) *Trümmer und Träume. Nachkriegszeit und fünfziger Jahre auf Zelluloid. Deutsche Spielfilme als Zeugnisse ihrer Zeit. Eine Dokumentation*, Studienverlag Brockmeyer, Bochum.

Bliersbach, G. (1985) *So grün war die Heide. Der deutsche Nachkriegsfilm in neuer Sicht*, Beltz, Weinheim, Basel.

Braidt, A.B. (2008) "What a Sissy!" Romy Schneider als Schwulenikone, in *Romy Schneider. Film. Rolle. Leben* (ed. K. Moser), Filmarchiv Austria, Wien, pp. 259–276.

Bumke, J. (1992) *Höfische Kultur. Literatur und Gesellschaft im hohen Mittelalter. Band 1*, dtv, München.

Carter, E. (2010) Sissi, the terrible: melodrama, victimhood, and imperial nostalgia in the *Sissi* Trilogy, in *Screening War: Perspectives on German Suffering* (eds P. Cooke and M. Silberman), Camden House, Rochester, NY, pp. 81–101.

Davidson, J. and Hake, S. (eds) (2007) *Take Two. Fifties Cinema in a Divided Germany*, Berghahn Books, New York and Oxford.

Doering-Manteuffel, A. (1981) *Katholizismus und Wiederbewaffnung*, Matthias Grünewald, Mainz.

Embacher, H. (2004) *Sissi* als Kassenschlager in Israel. Die k.u.k Monarchie in israelischen Erinnerungen, in *Populäre Konstruktionen von Erinnerung im deutschen Judentum und nach der Emigration* (eds Y. Hotam and J. Jacob), Vandenhoeck and Ruprecht, Göttingen, pp. 225–241.

Fehrenbach, H. (1995) *Cinema in Democratizing Germany*, University of North Carolina Press, Chapel Hill and London.

Frankfurter, B. (1988) Die Wien Film. Ein Beitrag zur Dreieinigkeit von Staat, Film und politischer Kultur in Österreich, in *Medienkultur in Österreich. Film, Fotografie, Fernsehen und Video in der Zweiten Republik* (eds H.H. Fabris and K. Luger), Böhlau, Wien, pp. 103–116.

Fritz, W. (1984) *Kino in Österreich 1945–1983. Film zwischen Kommerz und Avantgarde*. Österreichischer Bundesverlag, Wien.

Hake, S. (2001) The annexation of an imaginary city: the topos "Vienna" and the Wien-Film AG. *Popular Cinema of the Third Reich*, University of Texas Press, Austin, pp. 149–171.

Jary, M. (1993) *Sissi. Traumfabriken made in Germany. Die Geschichte des deutschen Nachkriegsfilms 1945–1960*, edition q, Berlin, pp. 143–152.

Jenny, H.A. (1998) *Sissi: Liebe, Tragik und Legenden: zum 100. Todestag der Kaiserin Elisabeth*, F. Reinhardt, Basel.

King, A. (2003) Placing *Green Is the Heath* (1951): spatial politics and emergent West German identity, in *Light Motives. German Popular Film in Perspective* (eds R. Halle and M. MacCarthy), Wayne State University Press, Detroit, pp. 130–147.

Koetzle, M., Sembach, K.J. and Schölzel, K. (1998) *Die Fünfziger Jahre. Heimat, Glaube, Glanz. Der Stil eines Jahrzehnts*, Callwey, München.

Kreimeier, K. (1985) Der westdeutsche Film in den fünfziger Jahren, in *Die fünfziger Jahre. Beiträge zu Politik und Kultur* (ed. D. Bänsch), Gunter Narr, Tübingen, pp. 283–305.

Large, D.C. (1996) *Germans to the Front: West German Rearmament in the Adenauer Era*, University of North Carolina Press, Chapel Hill and London.

Lowry, S. and Korte, H. (2000) Romy Schneider – vom süßen Mädel zur problematischen Frau. *Der Filmstar. Brigitte Bardot, James Dean, Götz George, Heinz Rühmann, Romy Schneider, Hanna Schygulla und neuere Stars*, Metzler, Stuttgart, pp. 109–143.

Mahlmann, T. (1985) Kirche und Wiederbewaffnung, in *Die fünfziger Jahre. Beiträge zur Politik und Kultur* (ed. D. Bänsch), Gunter Narr, Tübingen, pp. 90–107.

Marshall, S. (1997) Sissis Wandel unter den Deutschen, in *Idole des deutschen Films* (ed. T. Koebner), edition text + kritik, München, pp. 372–383.

Moeller, R.G. (1989) Reconstructing the family in reconstruction Germany: women and social policy in the Federal Republic, 1949–1955. *Feminist Studies*, 15 (1), 137–169.

Moltke, J.v. (2002) Evergreens: the *Heimat* genre, in *The German Cinema Book* (eds T. Bergfelder, E. Carter, and D. Göktürk), British Film Institute, London, pp. 18–28.

Moltke, J.v. (2005) *No Place like Home. Locations of Heimat in German Cinema*. University of California Press, Berkeley.

Orkey, R. (2001) *The Habsburg Monarchy, c. 1765–1918: From Enlightenment to Eclipse*, Palgrave Macmillan, Basingstroke.

Rentschler, E. (1990) The triumph of the male will: *Münchhausen* (1943). *Film Quarterly*, 43 (3), 14–23.

Römer, P. (1985) Die Verfassungsentwicklung in den fünfziger Jahren, in *Die fünfziger Jahre. Beitrag zu Politik und Kultur* (ed. D. Bänsch), Gunter Narr, Tübingen, pp. 71–89.

Rother, R. (1998) Vom Kaiserreich bis in die 50er Jahre. Der deutsche Film, in *Mythen der Nationen: Völker im Film* (ed. R. Rother), Koehler & Amelang, München, Berlin, pp. 63–81.

Schama, S. (1996) *Landscape and Memory*, Vintage, New York.

Schlipphacke, H. (2010) Melancholy empress: queering empire in Ernst Marischka's *Sissi* films. *Screen*, 51 (3), 232–254.

Schulz, G. (1996) *Romantik. Geschichte und Begriff*, Beck, München.

Seeßlen, G. (1992a) Eine Geschichte vom Mädchen, das Frau werden sollte. Zum 10. Todestag von Romy Schneider am 29. Mai. *epd Film*, 52, 10–14.

Seeßlen, G. (1992b) Sissi – Ein deutsches Orgasmusdrama. Hans-Arthur Marsiske, *Zeitmaschine Kino. Darstellungen von Geschichte im Film*, Hitzeroth, Marburg, pp. 64–79.

Seidl, C. (1987) *Der deutsche Film der fünziger Jahre*. Heyne, München.

Steiner, G. (1987) *Die Heimat-Macher. Kino in Österreich 1946–66*, Verlag für Gesellschaftskritik, Wien.

Steiner, G. (1995) *Film Book Austria*, Federal Press Service, Vienna.

Trimborn, J. (1998) *Der deutsche Heimatfilm der fünfziger Jahre. Motive, Symbole und Handlungsmuster*, Leppin, Köln.

Wauchope, M. (2002) Sissi revisited, in *Literature Film and the Culture Industry in Contemporary Austria* (ed. M. Lamb-Faffelberger), Peter Lang, New York, Frankfurt, pp. 170–183.

Westermann, B. (1990) Sissi. *Nationale Identität im Spielfilm der fünfziger Jahre*, Lang, Frankfurt, pp. 116–129.

Zimnik, N. (2005) Romy Schneider, *La Passante du Sans-Souci*: discourses of *Vergangenheitsbewältigung*, feminism, and myth, in *Rhine Crossings. France and Germany in Love and War* (eds A.M. Brueggermann and P. Schulman), SUNY Press, Albany, pp. 251–271.

Websites

Bundeswehr. Official site of the Federal Armed Forces of the Federal Republic of Germany. http://www.bundeswehr.de/portal/a/bwde (accessed August 15, 2010).

Gesetz über die Rechtsstellung des Soldaten – Soldatengesetz Deutsche Bundeswehr. Military Law governing the Bundeswehr (Federal Armed Forces). http://rk19-bielefeld-mitte.de/info/Recht/Soldatengesetz/inhalt.htm (accessed August 15, 2010).

Papal Encyclicals Online. Encyclical of Pope Pius XII Urging Public Prayers for Peace and Freedom for the People of Hungary October 28, 1956. http://www.papalencyclicals.net/Pius12/P12LUCTU.HTM (accessed August 29, 2010).

Romy Schneider – neu entdeckt? Report on Romy Schneider exhibit in Berlin's *Deutsche Kinemathek.* http://videos.arte.tv/de/videos/ausstellung_romy_schneider_neu_entdeckt_-3137782.html (accessed October 5, 2010).

"Sisi" – Der grosse Zweiteiler von Xaver Schwarzenberger als ORF-Event. Report on the contemporary Austrian TV production of the *Sissi* story. http://programm.orf.at/?story=3815 (accessed May 17, 2010).

Sissi Trilogy. Comprehensive overview of the *Sissi* films. http://www.sissi.de/aktuell/filme_trilogie.php (accessed March 9, 2010).

Wehrstrafgesetz. Military Law governing the *Bundeswehr* (Federal Armed Forces). http://www.gesetze-im-internet.de/wstrg/__22.html (accessed August 15, 2010).

Further Reading

Scholarship in the *Sissi*-trilogy is almost exclusively written in German. Especially helpful here are Susanne Marshall's "Sissis Wandel unter den Deutschen," in *Idole des deutschen Films* (1997), and Gerhard Blierbach's "Ein westdeutsches Aschenputtel: Sissi erster Teil (1955)," in his *So grün war die Heide. Der deutsche Nachkriegsfilm in neuer Sicht* (1985). Both texts perform close readings against cultural and political discourses of the 1950s. Very few sources regarding the *Sissi* films are accessible in English. Among them are Erica Carter's "Sissi, the Terrible: Melodrama, Victimhood, and Imperial Nostalgia in the *Sissi* Trilogy," in *Screening War: Perspectives on German Suffering* (2010). The essay looks at the reception history of the *Sissi* series and conducts a thoughtful reading and in-depth formal analysis of the films set against the German and Austrian postwar struggles. Mary Wauchope's "Sissi Revisited," in *Literature, Film, and the Culture Industry in Contemporary Austria* (2002), compares the reception of the *Sissi* films in Austria during the 1950s and 1990s and explores Austria's identity formation after World War Two. Heide Fehrenbach gives a comprehensive overview of the West German postwar cinema in "Popular Cinema, Spectatorship, and Identity in the Early 1950s," in her *Cinema in Democratizing Germany* (1995). She presents the use of the concepts of *Heimat* in a number of films (yet does not address the *Sissi* films directly), and traces the attempts to rehabilitate the role of the German man in order to establish the identity of the newly founded state.

All three *Sissi* films are available on DVD on NTSC format (region 1/North America) in German with English subtitles through Koch Lorber Films (http://www.kochlorberfilms.com). The collected Koch Lorber edition of the *Sissi* films contains the trailer for the first film in part 1 – *Sissi.* Part 2 *Sissi – the Young Empress* has the featurette "The Making of Sissi" and part 3 *Sissi – Fateful Years of an Empress* contains the trailer for the third film. It also holds a version dubbed in English entitled *Sissi – Forever My Love,* which Kinowelt Entertainment had released together with Paramount Pictures in 1960. It is a compilation of all three original films (139 mins in length) and includes the "Making of *Sissi*" featurette as well as the trailers in German for all three films that have English subtitles. This version has different opening credits and significant omissions and is not suitable for a close reading of the films. The Koch Lorber collection contains the film that also served as the model for the *Sissi* character who is also played by Romy Schneider – *Victoria in Dover* (1954).

The original PAL version (region 2/Europe) of the DVD collection was released by Kinowelt Home Entertainment, Germany and has some additional features that the English subtitled version from Koch Lorber does not contain. In addition to the film's trailer, *Sissi* also has a critical featurette entitled "Legende Romy Schneider," which contextualizes the life and career of Romy Schneider in light of her overidentification with her title role by the German-speaking public. *Sissi – Die junge Kaiserin* also includes a feature regarding the making of the film, and *Sissi – Schicksalsjahre einer Kaiserin* includes additional biographical information for Romy Schneider as well as the Empress Elisabeth of Austria.

Filmography

Fox and his Friends [*Faustrecht der Freiheit*] (R.W. Fassbinder, West Germany, 1974).

Girls in Uniform [*Mädchen in Uniform*] (Géza von Radványi, West Germany/France, 1958).

Jud Süss [*Jew Süss*] (Veit Harlan, Germany, 1940).

Lissi und der wilde Kaiser [*Lissi and the Wild Emperor*] (Michael "Bully" Herbig, Germany, 2007).

Ludwig [*Ludwig: The Mad King of Bavaria*] (Luchino Visconti, Italy/France/West Germany, 1972).

March for the Emperor, A [*Die Deutschmeister*] (Ernst Marischka, Austria, 1955).

Münchhausen [*The Adventures of Baron Munchhausen*] (Josef von Baky, Germany, 1943).

Passerby, The [*Die Spaziergängerin von Sans-Souci*] (Jacques Rouffio, France/West Germany, 1982).

Princess and the Warrior, The [*Der Krieger und die Kaiserin*] (Tom Tykwer, Germany, 2000).

Sisi (Xaver Schwarzenberger, Italy/Germany/Austria, 2009).

Sissi (Ernst Marischka, Austria, 1955).

Sissi – the Young Empress [*Sissi – Die junge Kaiserin*] (Ernst Marischka, Austria, 1956).

Sissi – Fateful Years of an Empress [*Sissi – Schicksalsjahre einer Kaiserin*] (Ernst Marischka, Austria, 1957).

Victoria in Dover [*Mädchenjahre einer Königin*] (Ernst Marischka, Austria, 1954).

When the White Lilac Blooms Again [*Wenn der weiße Flieder wieder blüht*] (Hans Deppe, West Germany, 1953).

15

Crossdressing, Remakes, and National Stereotypes

The Germany–Hollywood Connection

Silke Arnold-de Simine

The performance aspects of crossdressing afford a spectacle well suited to film and, before that, popular theater. Crossdressing is only one aspect of a broader comedy concept based on disguise, role reversal, and mistaken identity in which all social variables used to define individuals – gender and sexual orientation, race, ethnicity, nationality, class, age – can be switched. For example, by changing into *Mrs. Doubtfire* (USA, 1993), the unemployed actor Daniel Hillard not only pretends to be female, but assumes a different nationality (Scottish), a different age (elderly), a different social class (working class), and therefore also a completely different personality. The comedy stems from the accumulated and exaggerated discrepancies between appearance and behavior, on the one hand, and the allegedly authentic identity, on the other hand. In comedies, this perceived clash not only results in absurd situations but also goes unpunished and might even be rewarded.

Stories centering around disguise and mistaken identity can be seen as playfully countering anxieties concerning the successful fulfilment of social roles and mobile identities. They can equally be geared to subvert or to provide symbolic reassurance, questioning or confirming the boundaries of social conformity (Garber, 1992: 12, 28). According to Alexander Doty (2000: 80), comedy as a genre is fundamentally queer because it "encourages rule-breaking, risk-taking, inversions and perversions in the face of straight patriarchal norms" only contained by traditional narrative closure. In that sense, the subgenre of the "crossdressing comedy" seems to be something of a tautology, an intensified form of comedy in which both elements raise each other to a higher power. In its survey (http://www.afi.com/100years/laughs.aspx) of the one hundred best screen comedies, the American Film Institute ranked two crossdressing films at the top: Billy Wilder's *Some Like It Hot* (USA, 1959) at number one, followed by Sydney Pollack's *Tootsie* (USA, 1982).[1] Some recent releases such as *Connie and Carla* (USA, 2004) are based on those classics; in this case, the script

A Companion to German Cinema, First Edition. Edited by Terri Ginsberg and Andrea Mensch.
© 2012 Blackwell Publishing Ltd. Published 2012 by Blackwell Publishing Ltd.

is a mixture of *Some Like It Hot* and *Victor/Victoria* (USA/UK, 1982). But some of these Hollywood classics are themselves remakes of earlier films and scripts from Weimar cinema.

Up until the 1920s, the German film industry was an important economic competitor and cultural rival of Hollywood. Its successful filmmakers and actors were very much drawn to the American film industry, and close ties and networks of contacts were established which fostered a lively exchange not just of personnel but also of stories, scripts, and films. Transnationalism in film is not a recent phenomenon: circulation across borders and the employment of international personnel were typical of the cinema from its inception, and with national barriers only really employed upon arrival of the talkie and (recorded) speech. These crossdressing comedies did not become transnational commodities simply upon being remade in Hollywood; they superseded national boundaries right from the start, in that they were filmed in different languages and with international casts or in different countries altogether, a fact that serves to reflect "the dissolution of any stable connection between a film's place of production and/or setting and the nationality of its makers and performers" (Ezra and Rowden, 2006: 1).

German(-speaking) directors, scriptwriters, and actors who emigrated from Germany to America exported a Weimar modernity defined by the increasing visibility and agency of women and a heretofore unknown mobility of classes, races, and genders. This notion of "impermanence," however, fostered not only experiments with (sexual) identity, but also created social anxiety. Weimar cinema was one of the most prolific cultural sites for the expression of those experimentations and anxieties. According to Richard Dyer, between 1918 and 1933 the majority of films representing queerness hailed from Germany (Dyer, 1990: 5). Therefore Weimar cinema could provide Hollywood with scripts and talents well versed in gender-bending.

Whereas during the second half of the twentieth century, most crossdressing films featured men dressed as women, films from the century's first decades just as often showcased female crossdressers, for example in Ernst Lubitsch's *I Don't Want to Be a Man!* (*Ich möchte kein Mann sein!* Germany, 1918). This phenomenon was linked to a long-established stage tradition in which the female-to-male britches role was the "transvestite norm" (Marjorie Garber, quoted in Kuzniar, 2000: 31). Several major female stars of the Weimar cinema had appeared in "Hosenrollen" (britches roles), for example Asta Nielsen (*Jugend und Tollheit* (Youth and Madness, 1912/13); *Das Liebes ABC* (The ABCs of Love, 1916)), and Elisabeth Bergner (*The Violinist from Florence* (*Der Geiger von Florenz*, 1925/26); *Doña Juana*, 1927) (Dyer, 1990: 45). Their films were often screened uncensored throughout Germany – in contrast to many of the male-to-female crossdressing films and comedies which, insofar as female impersonation was becoming closely affiliated with a socially marginalized and illicit gay culture, were considered much more problematic (e.g. for public morale and underage audiences). This problematicity was echoed in the United States, where Mae West's Broadway play, *The Pleasure Man*, created a major scandal by showing the actors not just performing crossdressing but doing so back-stage, where they behaved as campily as they did onstage. On October 3, 1928, police stormed the Biltmore Theater in New York City, and the play was banned (Hamilton, 1993: 107). In effect, increasingly "it was not sexual activity that labelled a man homosexual but his choice and use of particular signifying gestures of social gender role enactment" (Meyer, 1992: 77).

While male-to-female crossdressing was associated with homosexuality, female-to-male crossdressing accrued a certain quotidian banality and thereby lost much of its sex appeal and/or comical potential. During both world wars, especially the second, a marked increase in female participation in the labor force saw women taking up jobs formerly deemed suitable only for men. Women readily embraced these real-life "britches roles," and although considered only a temporary arrangement, these jobs gave women a sense of newfound confidence and independence that was difficult to reverse after the wars. "The traditional order and the individual's fixed sense of identity became de-stabilized, unleashing a new fluidity that inspired both fear and desire – fear of the new and uncertain, and desire for liberation from traditional norms" (McCormick, 2001: 21). Women in men's roles and clothing became threatening to men returning from war who feared both the competition for jobs and the loss of their traditional roles as providers and heads of family.[2] This was especially true in Germany where the self-esteem of returning soldiers had already taken a major blow from defeat; some returned from years as prisoners-of-war only to find wives and families who had learned well to do without them. But the problem was also apparent in 1950s America, where the Cold War climate of paranoia and fear (that would quickly spread to Germany) fostered a conservative idealization of the bourgeois nuclear family and women's traditionally perceived roles therein as wives and mothers, in defense against these insecurities. Women were encouraged or even forced into domestic work, whether in their own homes or, as in the case of black women, other people's homes, while men retook higher paying jobs in pursuit of the breadwinner role.

Hollywood played a major, if not unambiguous role in disseminating and naturalizing these dominant ideologies. While a decrease occurred in overall US film production during the 1950s, the period saw an increase in remakes of crossdressing films. This may indicate more generally the perceived importance of such films during times of cultural crisis, insofar as they signify a return to conservative notions of gender as well as address changes in gender identity. After all, even the most mainstream formula films are never ideologically monolithic: filmmakers may try to inscribe "preferred readings," but the exigencies of commercialized "passing" entail their negotiating controversy with enjoyable spectacle, a strategy which may open up performative spaces that carry unpredictable and often uncontrollable aesthetic effects and potentially critical counterreadings. The disruptive power of women's changing roles also meant, that male-to-female crossdressing comedies (and their remakes) faced an increasingly difficult task. The paradigm in which men can fail at performance must be based on a very narrow, stereotypified concept of femininity, which of course had been irrevocably challenged. Hence modern crossdressing comedies choose settings in which such stereotypes persist, for example beauty pageants, middle-class suburbs, and conventional drag culture itself.

Transnational and transcultural remakes offer a prime opportunity to observe the cultural and historical gender-role transformations across such films. With Judith Butler (1999: 146), we can interpret a remake as a performative repetition that also constitutes the process of "doing gender." According to Butler, gender is constituted by performative repetition. Performative repetition is exactly what happens in remakes. Remakes which repeat performances of gender are therefore performative repetitions of performative repetitions. In films which focus on the performance and spectacle of gender, on sexual tensions and their incongruities, the question of how such performative (but also normative) repetitions vary becomes crucial. Remakes can either stick to an original plot, thus exposing its datedness, or alter the original story line to accommodate perceived shifts in audience attitudes or differing cultural norms. Remakes of crossdressing comedies by necessity also problematize the notion of authenticity, in that they reveal the constructedness of the "original": "By virtue of this reiteration … gaps and fissures are opened up as the constitutive instabilities in such constructions, as that which escapes or exceeds the norm, as that which cannot be wholly defined or fixed by the repetitive labor of that norm" (Butler, 1993: 10).

The term *remake* usually indicates that a film has taken over the story, dramaturgy, and characters from a source film, usually changing time and place to adapt the story to a different period and culture. Apart from new technological achievements such as the "talkie" and the color film, this supplies one of the central justifications for producing remakes, especially in Hollywood. The American film market rejects dubbed or subtitled (foreign) films and favors its own stars, value system, and cultural standards. Recycled material also helps minimize production costs. Remakes and their originals operate within the transnational network and crosscultural tradition of the global film industry. Weimar films and scripts were remade in 1950s Germany as well as in Hollywood, where remakes provided a niche for émigré directors as well as a fertile source of stories that had already proven commercially successful across national boundaries. In a climate in which Hollywood was under threat from television, dwindling audiences, and McCarthyist blacklisting, cinematic response was sought that would play both cards: conservatism and innovation. Indeed remakes of prewar films became popular not only because they were financially viable, but also because their gender performances carried updated social relevance: they were, in effect, the perfect commodities.

Comparing such remakes with their originals and one another can be illuminating on several levels. First, romantic comedies themselves are marked by codified genre conventions which are constituted by and at the same time prescribe specific gender conventions. Romantic comedies, which feature crossdressing as their major narrative device, show how gender identities are the effect of repeated (and more or less successful) performances and strategies of attribution. Transcultural and transnational remakes of crossdressing comedies must negotiate historically changing, culturally variant gender constructs and sexual norms. By comparing German and Hollywood remakes of Weimar crossdressing comedies, this chapter aims to investigate how gender codes are negotiated in a cinematic genre, the focus of which is the potential failure of gender performances based in specific cultural contexts where they acquire a defining and stabilizing function in gendered discourses of (national) identity.

The films which will serve as prominent examples are *Viktor and Viktoria* (*Viktor und Viktoria*, Reinhold Schünzel, Germany, 1933), its German remake, *Viktor and Viktoria* (*Viktor und Viktoria*, Karl Anton, Germany, 1957), and its Hollywood remake, *Victor/Victoria* (Blake Edwards, USA/UK 1982), as well as *Fanfaren der Liebe* (Fanfares of Love, Kurt Hoffmann, Germany, 1951), the original of the legendary crossdressing comedy, *Some Like It Hot* (Billy Wilder, USA, 1959), both based on the 1930s script by Michael Logan and Robert Thoeren, and its sequel *Fanfares der Ehe* (Fanfares of Marriage, Hans Grimm, Germany, 1953). Each remake acknowledges the fact that it is indebted to an earlier version, by including a reference to the original in the opening or end credits (Verevis, 2006: 9). Only the 1957 German remake of *Viktor and Viktoria* (1933), however, reached an audience that might also have seen the earlier version(s). By contrast, the Hollywood remakes did not have to take into account that their audiences might have compared them with earlier versions, for it was highly unlikely that these audiences had ever seen or even heard about the originals.

Viktor and Viktoria (Germany, 1933, 1957) and *Victor/Victoria* (USA/UK, 1982)

The introduction of sound at the end of the 1920s brought with it a rise in German entertainment genres, "particularly comedies, operetta films and musicals drawing on Hollywood models and German theatrical traditions." (Thompson, 2002: n.p.). *Viktor and Viktoria* (1933) is a mixture of all those genres, but more importantly it is the last in a long line of crossdressing comedies to exploit the comic potential in the "sexual crisis" which characterized the Weimar Republic. The film was highly successful – *the* German box-office success of 1933. It was released after the National Socialists had come to power and, over the following years, had transformed the film industry from a private oligopoly to a state-run monopoly. Nonetheless, surprisingly little of the film was censored, which is noteworthy given that it alludes openly to female homosexuality and covertly to male homosexuality, the latter criminalized at the time under Germany's section 175 (Grau, 1995: 18f). These homosexual undertones are obvious despite the fact that the narrative closes with two romantic heterosexual couples. Director Reinhold Schünzel had long been associated with Berlin's homosexual subculture. He had starred in *Different from the Others* (*Anders als die Anderen*, 1919), a polemic against paragraph 175, which was not revised until 1969 and finally revoked until 1994. He had also produced and written the screenplay for the crossdressing comedy, *Heaven on Earth* (*Der Himmel auf Erden*, 1926/27). Considered a "Half-Jew" by the Nazis, he needed a special working permit. His situation in the German film industry was precarious, and in 1937 he left for the United States on an offer by Metro-Goldwyn-Mayer.

Weimar culture was characterized by battles over changing gender perceptions and relations. Anxieties about the loss of national power and standing sparked a crisis of male subjectivity, especially among conservative and far-right constituencies who felt emasculated by Germany's defeat in World War One and humiliated by the ensuing Treaty of Versailles, which diminished Germany's economic and military power. A sense of betrayal was circulated by the old aristocracy and bourgeoisie about a perceived unpatriotic homefront ("*Dolchstosslegende*");[3] the old elites resented the new social democracy and the granting of suffrage and equal rights to all German citizens – including women. From 1908, women had been welcomed into the universities, and while they were grossly underpaid, their move into low-level, "pink collar" jobs was nevertheless unprecedented. For this kind of work, traditional gender roles lost their relevance, and the widely publicized image of the so-called "New Woman" came to carry a distinctly androgynous look: with a short haircut ("*Bubikopf*"), men's accessories ("*garçonne*"), and slim, athletic body ("*girl*"), she was the embodiment of female emancipation, inadvertently provoking reaction to women's potential economic and sexual autonomy. The French and American terms chosen to describe these new female positionalities evidenced widespread perceptions of them as ungermanic and of foreign influence. The Far Right described them as a "new race" "bred" in the United States: "For the National Socialists, it was clear that this dystopia of reversed gender roles could only lead to racial decline and had to be avoided" (Graf, 2009: 671). At the same time, a rhetoric of a German feminization took hold, based on the fact that, since two million male citizens had died in the war, women now made up the majority of the adult German population.

These social and cultural changes in gender roles and perceptions were thematized overtly in the cinema. Crossdressing takes literally the alleged assimilation of the sexes in fashion and behavior, but in the film comedies, crossdressing is never motivated by variant sexual orientation, ambiguous sexual identity, or mere playful gender-bending. Instead, it is a necessary last resort, or at least an instrumental means, for someone in relatively dire straits. A joyful element of masquerade and of the subversion of clear-cut gender identity nevertheless often results from crossdressing, even as they must be suppressed in conformity with conventional gender roles and the compulsory heterosexual couple(s) who mark the narrative closure.

The original 1933 version of *Viktor and Viktoria* not only features both female-to-male and male-to-female crossdressing but complicates matters even further by introducing a case of double crossdressing: a woman pretending to be a man pretending to be a woman. The removal of Viktoria's wig at the end of her performances does not reveal her "authentic" sex; on the contrary, that act signals the start of an actual crossdressing. The unsuccessful actor, Viktor Hempel (Hermann Thimig), who earns his living as a female impersonator, meets Susanne Lohr (Renate Müller), who wants to succeed in show business. Her motivation is less extreme than Blake Edwards's unemployed singer in the 1982 US/UK remake, who cannot afford even a meal and faints of hunger. When Viktor catches cold and is unable to perform, she allows him to persuade her to fill in for his role as "Mr Viktoria." During her performance, Viktor insists on guiding her, from the audience, through the lyrics of "Lady from Seville," and her efforts to mimic him lead to a comical performance. An impresario sees the act and signs Mr Viktoria. Although Susanne has her doubts, she is shunted off to London, where she performs before high society. Audience members Sir Douglas Sheffield (Fritz Odemar), Ellinor (Hilde Hildebrand), and Robert (Adolf Wohlbrück) fall for the act, but that same night, Robert overhears a conversation between Viktor and Susanne in which her true sex is revealed. Keeping her secret, he offers to show Mr Viktoria around London, in turn subjecting him/her to a tour-de-force of activities in which she must prove his/her masculinity: drinking, smoking, flirting with prostitutes, fighting in rough bars, and getting a shave at the barber shop. Having already fallen in love with Robert, Susanne goes along with Ellinor's attempts to seduce her, because she fears that Robert is going to marry Ellinor. At the same time, a rumor is spreading that Mr Viktoria is in fact a woman, which brings the police onto the scene. As a result, Susanne desists from her masquerade and rejoins Robert, as Viktor, who has been pursuing one of the chorus girls (Friedel Pisetta), reclaims his act and, making high comedy of his mishaps, likewise becomes a big success, both onstage and off.

On the surface, Susanne's masquerade as a man purports to aim for convincing illusion, but the film itself insists on highlighting its discrepancies by tailoring Susanne's suit to her feminine waist and hips. Although most of the diegetic characters fall for the illusion, the cinematic audience is encouraged to see the woman through the costume. She is a woman coded nonetheless as masculine and bearing male attributes: short hair, pantsuits (with flat cap or tuxedo), and deep voice; and she is forced to smoke, drink whiskey, fight with men, and flirt with women. Women of all ages and social standing, whether in the elegant Savoy Hotel or working-class East End pubs, find themselves attracted to the very feminine Mr Viktoria. Although set in London, here the film evokes 1920s Berlin's vibrant lesbian subculture, which offered a variety of lesbian clubs and bars that could even be found in tourist guides advertising the city's nightlife (Dyer, 1990: 8). It is just as Viktor promised the aspiring singer: "As a man everybody will be crazy about you."[4] Yet the attraction Mr Viktoria holds, and the desire s/he evokes in both men and women, both onstage and off, lie in the ambiguous gender codes she displays. In effect, Mr Viktoria represents the proverbial "third sex," an intermediate gender position famously propagated by Ernst von Wolzogen's novel, *Das dritte Geschlecht* (1899), and by the German sexologist Magnus Hirschfeld (see Lauritsen and Thorstad, 1974: 73–76), who argued that male and female attributes are present in random distribution in all human beings and that homosexuality is only one of various possible libidinal orientations within a broad range of nonnormative and fluid expressions of sexuality to which we now commonly refer as "queer."

Viktor and Viktoria was not only a German phenomenon. A simultaneously released Francophone version, *Georges et Georgette* (George and Georgette, Reinhold Schünzel and Roger Le Bon, Germany, 1933), was shot and released, and an Anglophone version was planned but for unknown reasons never completed. A subsequent British film, *First a Girl* (Victor Saville, UK, 1935), was an imitative remake – in parts virtually a literal adaptation[5] – but it placed more emphasis than its predecessors on class rather than gender transgression. Yet this version and the later Hollywood remake diverge most notably from the earlier films with respect to setting. Whereas the 1933 German and French version locate Mr Viktoria's celebrity in London – a site of "otherness" for both German and French audiences – the British and Hollywood versions are set in Nice and Paris, respectively. Gender transgression and sexual deviance are commonly associated with the national or ethnic "other." In Weimar cinema, androgynously coded actresses such as Asta Nielsen (Danish) or Greta Garbo (Swedish) were usually non-German, and Marlene Dietrich's sexual ambiguity was only cemented after her emigration to the United States.[6] In the 1933 *Viktor and Viktoria*, as well as in the US/UK remake from 1982, female impersonation acts center around an exotic Spanish señora.

The 1957 remake of *Viktor and Viktoria* was written by Curt J. Braun "after an original idea by Reinhold Schünzel," although the credits also state that it is a "new cinematic creation,"[7] thus masking the fact that the majority of the film is a literal – if sanitized – imitation of the 1933 original. Many Weimar musicals and comedies were remade in Germany during the 1950s; their apparent apoliticality gave underemployed Nazi-era filmmakers a means by which to ally themselves publicly with Germany's brief interwar democracy. Perhaps not coincidentally, it was often the misogynist and paranoid elements of Weimar film that reappeared in those postwar comedies, the pervasive fear that a humiliated "male" Germany needed to keep "others" – women, foreigners, homosexuals – in check in order to regain power (McCormick, 2001: 25). Hence both the original and the 1957 remake tried to reorder the social and civil relationships – between the sexes, between family and state – which had been disrupted by war.

Whereas the plethora of Hollywood musicals had no significant box-office impact in Germany during the 1950s and 1960s, the musical films produced in West Germany were immensely popular there. Their generic hybridity, for example their combination of the *Heimatfilm* genre (Elsaesser, 1989) with the musical forms of the traditional German folksong, or "Schlager," was tailored to the ideological climate and cultural framework of the postwar West German market (Bergfelder, 2000: 80).

For the remake, Braun changed both time (from the 1930s to the 1950s) and place (Paris instead of London). Unlike London, Paris had been successfully conquered by the German army and was therefore associated with German military prowess. The significance of Paris as a realm of sensuality linked this military strength to sexual power. Apart from a short backstage scene in which Viktor (Georg Thomalla) is seen in drag, the emphasis is exclusively on the suffering that Erika (Johanna von Koczian) undergoes in that her female-to-male crossdressing keeps her from her "natural" feminine state. Her insecurity and discomfort in her male role enables Jean Perrot (Johannes Heesters) to indulge in some erotically charged and rather patronizing witnessing of her failure to make it as a man. The polyvalent potential of the gender constellations is very much repressed in this version.

Blake Edwards and Hans Hoemburg may for this reason have ignored Braun's version when conceiving *Victor/Victoria* and instead revisited the 1933 original. In contrast to the tame 1957 version, here the subtle interrogation of gender roles in the 1933 version was not only made explicit but transposed into a definitively queer arena. Edwards, like Schünzel before him, was known for a playful attitude towards sexual codes (Brandlmeier, 1989: 28) and for "overtly explor[ing] and critique[ing] normative sexuality" (Luhr and Lehman, 1989: 2). Both not only directed but wrote the scripts for, and even produced their own films. During the deregulated 1980s, Hollywood film production nearly doubled, and a high demand existed for screenplays. This led to an increase in remakes, especially of films not regularly shown on television or not yet available on video. These remakes were often used as mainstream star vehicles (Oltmann, 2008: 73). In Edwards's case, the star was Julie Andrews, famous for her double image as "prim and proper" (e.g. *Mary Poppins*, 1964) and rather improbable "queer" gay and lesbian icon (e.g. *The Sound of Music*, 1965) (Farmer, 2007: 134).

Julie Andrews had enjoyed a successful Hollywood career in which she did not hide but rather capitalized upon her British origins, and her portrayal of a sophisticated queerness is clearly associated with that background. The "Gay Paris" of Edwards's film was recreated in England's Pinewood Studios, whereby it was easily recognizable as an artificial filmset in which even snow and cold can be made to project the warm light and bright colors of an androgynous utopia: "The androgynous vision [...] indicates an age-old search for a place where the sexes complement and complete each other and where the self can experience an expansion of its gender and sexual identities."[8] (Benedek and Binder, 1996: 13). In contrast to the film's depiction of a masculinized, homophobic, violent and uncouth Chicago, hometown of leading man King Marchand (James Garner), its Paris evokes that city's reputation as the city of love and sexual liberation, which is in Edwards's film also associated with a European demimonde. Berlin, on the other hand, does not appear as a location in any of the films,[9] although its 1920s nightlife and gay scene were renowned for travesty cabarets that predominantly featured female-to-male crossdressing closely connected with a thriving lesbian subculture (Lehnert, 1997: 156).

In Schünzel's 1933 version, Viktor's female impersonation act is disassociated from homosexuality – Viktor's possible bisexuality is hinted at only subtly at points throughout – but firmly located in the music hall and vaudeville traditions.[10] In Edwards's version, by contrast, Carole "Toddy" Todd (Robert Preston), the counterpart to Schünzel's Viktor, who is indubitable gay, likewise compares Victoria's masquerade to a magician's trick, thereby placing it in the respectable Victorian (pun intended) institution of vaudeville and high camp. The camera encircles Victoria onstage in a single take, as if to emphasize the fact of the deceit for the cinematic audience. In Schünzel's version, a similar if less discreet perspective is conveyed when the camera peeps under Mr Victoria's flying skirts as s/he whirls about the stage.[11] The camera in both instances grants the allied cinematic audience a privileged insight that is nonetheless redundant given the lack of dramatic irony, whereupon they are positioned as complicit with the masquerade. When Toddy retakes his act at the film's end, he does not aim to deceive the gullible diegetic audience, but rather stresses the comical discrepancy between Toddy's beefy, cloddish body and his feminine attire and role: his makeup is deliberately crude, his dress does not fit properly, and he appears much more plump than he did previously in a tuxedo. His performance belongs to the tradition of the English *Pantomime Dame* (Senelick, 1993), apropos of which it stands as a diegetic, campy "remake" or parody of Victor/Victoria's act. For here Toddy openly fills in for Victoria, not the other way round, as in Schünzel's version; he is not simply any longer parodying a woman, but a woman pretending to be a man pretending to be a woman. The ensuing applause suggests that the diegetic audience enjoys this performance even more than the previous masquerade, because it does not evoke in them a "perverse" desire, a yearning for an unsettling or even taboo experience.

The nightclubs in Edwards's remake clearly cater to the Parisian sexual demimonde, where crossdressing is openly though not exclusively associated with homosexuality. Toddy pretends that "Victor" is his lover in an effort to make Viktor's female impersonation act more convincing; when we see Toddy perform, he does so in a tuxedo, and it is the diegetic audience, many of whom are transvestites in drag, which provides the visual spectacle. In both films, by extension, the playful imitation of gender stereotypes is not restricted to the stage. But whereas in *Victor/Victoria*, characters who mistake appearance for essence, and who thus theoretically negate the fluidity of gender and sexual desire, are ridiculed or lampooned – particularly King Marchand's lunkish bodyguard, "Squash" Bernstein (Alex Karras), and his birdbrained moll, Norma Cassady (Leslie Ann Warren) – in *Viktor and Viktoria* it is the failure to perform both genders convincingly and successfully which is the main source of comedy in the film. In contrast to *Victor/Victoria*, *Viktor and Viktoria* does not spend screen time focusing on Susanne's transformation into a man but rather concentrates primarily on her training in performance and her transformation into Mr Viktoria, which takes place in a backstage dressing room she must share with other male performers who are also shown transforming themselves into gender stereotypes, for example musclemen created with fake moustaches, makeup, and wigs.

Because of her limited acting experience, moreover, Susanne is more worried about her stage performance than about her masquerade as a man. When she takes to the stage as Mr Viktoria for the first time, she follows Viktor's lead as he directs her from the orchestra pit, religiously imitating his clumsiness. It is this which makes her stage performance unconvincing and comical. Although she manages to stay in character when Robert feigns to test her manhood, she also clearly feels more uncomfortable in the male role than Andrews's Victoria Grant, who with only a modicum of comic difficulty adopts the exotic persona of a gay Polish aristocrat, Victor Grazhinski, and does not attempt to imitate mainstream masculinity in order to enjoy her newfound freedom and confidence: "I am my own man." Victoria has been convinced by Toddy's claim that there are "all sorts of men who act in all sorts of ways" and simply declares herself "one sort of man" and the doubting Marchand "another." Susanne, on the other hand, continues to imitate Viktor and reiterates again and again that she hates performing as a man: "How I suffer by playing the ridiculous role of a man."[12]

The film itself, however, clearly indulges in the playfulness of crossdressing (Lehnert, 1997: 106). Robert tests not only Susanne's but also Viktor's masculinity: he pretends that Viktor has been asked to a duel, where Viktor's unsuccessful attempt to perform ideal male dauntlessness exposes him as a fraud and laughing stock. By thus failing to conform to the competent and self-assured masculinity portrayed by Robert, Viktor, like Susanne, comes to serve as comic relief in both his onstage ("real woman") and offstage ("real man") roles. Whereas in 1933, it is the woman, Susanne, and the "unmanly" man Viktor, who must perform the rites of masculinity, in 1982 it is the leading man, King Marchand, who is unsettled by the crossdressing and chooses to boost his macho image with boxing matches and heavy drinking. But even these proofs fail when Marchand's macho bodyguard, "Squash" Bernstein, reveals that his whole life as a footballer and rough guy has been a performance designed to cover up his homosexuality. By casting a well-known former professional football star in this part, Edwards "challenges common assumptions about the relationship between body type, [behavior] and sexuality" (Luhr and Lehman, 1989: 49). Bernstein's confession that he is also a pretender compels Marchand to face the fact that he himself has been performing the persona of a "hard man" by consorting with gangsters and blond bombshells. A demonstrative masculine habitus does not stabilize his male identity, which seems to elude conventional representation. In the commentary to the DVD release of the film (Warner Home Video, 2002), Julie Andrews describes how she modeled her male habitus by restraining her gestures and facial expressions and using only very little variation: "I took refuge in stillness." The significance of these tactics is supported by recent research: "Maleness is more invisible in its artificiality. Sociological studies have demonstrated that maleness is assumed, unless proven otherwise. Shown photographs of people with characteristics of both sexes, participants in such studies tend to see a man if there is any male signifier" (Solomon, 1993: 145).

Femininity, on the other hand, is always already associated with spectacle, masquerade, and illusion. Even though Norma refers to the sexual act when she tells Marchand, "We [women] are lucky – we can fake it," this also refers to her hyperfemininity which comes closest to a drag act. Her exaggerated and overstated performance is a caricature of the misogynistic stereotype of the highly eroticized peroxide-blonde epitomized by Marilyn Monroe (whose given name was in fact Norma). Norma insists that she was able to identify Victoria as Victor in his/her performance because, she argues, "real women" can always spot another "real woman." The audience, who is in on the joke of her error, must nonetheless face the destabilization of the concept "real woman," it implies. Norma thus represents "norma"-tive sexuality and desire, for instance when she tries to persuade Toddy that the "right woman" could reform him, but her own lover, Marchand, shows no sign of being attracted to her and fails to perform in bed with her. Eventually both Victoria and Marchand literally "come out of the closet." When Victoria's clothes are ruined in a rainshower, she dresses in Toddy's erstwhile lover Richard's (Malcom Jamieson) suit and, when he arrives unexpectedly, hides in the closet only to jump out and knock him down when he insults Toddy. Marchand hides himself in Victor/Victoria's hotel bathroom closet in order to peek at her naked body. The film does not show what he sees, although we are led to assume by his lewd facial expression that he has just reassured himself of her femaleness. Here Victoria is the object of the male gaze, but the audience does not participate in or share Marchand's point-of-view; instead it plays the voyeur to his voyeurism. Once he leaves the closet, he can allow himself to pursue his sexual attraction to Victoria, and when he kisses her, still in male attire, he says, "I don't care if you *are* a man." When the two are later shown in postcoital repose, Victoria is still wearing her button-down shirt, and her short hair is slicked back to give her a boyish appearance. Marchand is apparently prepared to keep up the pretense of being in a homosexual relationship because it serves his own interests. Only when the mob threatens to ruin him does Victoria revert to her female attire and identity.

The fact that *Victor/Victoria*'s plot ultimately revolves around Victoria's need to decide between the man she loves and her singing career is symptomatic of the rise in antifeminist discourse during the 1980s. Both the 1950s and the 1980s were characterized by a repressive conservative Right and the ascendancy of corporate business interests. In this context, the film industry's economic imperative of international expansion and circulation meant that the transcultural quality of these crossdressing comedies would render them more viable as global commodities: just as the comedies unsettle gender identity, they also reassert stereotypical national identities, which have great purchase in international markets and are readily consumed by multinational audiences.

Recalling Mae West's scandalized Broadway play, the carnivalistic goings-on in the Victor/Victora comedies are brought to an end by the police, who force their way into the theater to expose once and for all the true and unambiguous sex of Mr Viktoria and Victor/Victoria – when, crucially, they are performed by Viktor and Toddy, respectively. Where female gender codes are successfully imitated by men, the State resorts forcibly to the body as the source of an unequivocal determination of originary maleness (though not necessarily its sexual orientation). However, when the masquerade is performed by a female, the State authorities do not intervene (and in fact, lesbianism was never even mentioned in section 175); instead it is the task of the leading man to discover her "true" sex. In good comic tradition, the happy ending is affirmed by two romantic heterosexual couples, traditionally a serious, aristocratic couple mirrored by a comic servants couple; in the 1980s Hollywood remake, this is turned into a scenario in which the class differences are downplayed and the ostensible promotion of liberal tolerance of homosexuality is undermined: the heterosexual couple is mirrored by a comic homosexual couple, as Bernstein and Toddy pair up.

The fact that the plots of both versions are set in the world of the theater and vaudeville introduces the device of the play-within-the-play: the diegesis is split into stage and real world, performance and authentic identity. This device is used often in comedy, for it motivates the playful acquisition of another identity. As musicals, these films forego the pretence of realism, but *Viktor and Viktoria* takes things a step further by its structural convention around the rhythms of speech and music. When the actors are not singing, they use a form of *"Sprechgesang"* (blank verses and rhymes), their movements choreographed insofar as they are synchronized with the dialogue and accompanying music. In Edwards's version, the musical numbers are carefully integrated into the filmic narrative and, unlike the German version, always motivated by onstage performances, but even here theatricality, spectacle, and performance are by no means confined to the stage. In this carnivalistic, topsy-turvy world, crossdressing performance starts with the end of the stage show and the removal of the wig. All characters aim to be rewarded for their performances of those culturally and historically shaped images of femininity and masculinity into which they have been enculturated. Not the theater but everyday life is the stage on which gender is performed – and misled. Edwards's Reagan-era remake does not insist or hinge upon the unequivocal truth and authenticity of the body. The relevant question for it is not whether Victor/Victoria is a gender imposter, but rather who controls her (gender) performance, who gains and who loses power through that performance, and who is aware of it as performance, that is, who is qualified to "see," and who is not.

Fanfaren der Liebe (Germany, 1951)/*Some Like It Hot* (USA, 1959)

Together with the crossdressing comedy *Charley's Aunt* (*Charleys Tante*, Germany, 1934; remakes: Germany, 1955, 1963, 1996), *Fanfaren der Liebe* was the most popular German comedy of the 1950s. Its director, Kurt Hoffmann, had learned his trade by working, among other things, as assistant director for Reinhold Schünzel on *Viktor and Viktoria* (1933). Today *Fanfaren der Liebe* would be all but forgotten had Billy Wilder not based his immensely popular *Some Like It Hot* (USA, 1959) on that production and its screenplay. Laurence Maslon (2009: 26) may be exaggerating when he claims that "the source material for Wilder and Diamond's screenplay for *Some Like It Hot* remains one of the most elusive and most misattributed urtexts in cinema history," but Wilder's attempt to downplay the influence of the earlier version has certainly contributed to its having been widely overlooked in the discussion of his classic remake. The film's opening credits do clearly state that it was based on a script originally written by two German screenwriters, Michael Logan and Robert Thoeren, the latter of whom Wilder had allegedly already met as a fellow screenwriter in Berlin (Gmünden, 2008: 123). His years of work in Weimar cinema had a lifelong influence on Wilder, and one of the directors he continued to admire most was Ernst Lubitsch.

In 1933, Thoeren emigrated to France, where he sold a script entitled *Fanfaren der Liebe* to Solar Films. Richard Pottier, an Austro-Hungarian exile in Paris who had changed his name from Richard Deutsch, based the French film *Fanfare of Love* (*Fanfare d'amour*, 1935) on this script. When Thoeren emigrated to the United States in 1957, he persuaded Wilder to screen the 1951 German film.[13] Although Wilder described it as "a very low budget, very third-class German picture [...] absolutely terrible. Deliriously bad" (Crowe, 1999: 160), he nevertheless purchased a ten-year option for the rights to the screenplay. The remaking of German pictures for the North American market was a common feature in the careers of German(-speaking) émigré film workers, and to sell an already successful script/film was perceived as an entry ticket to Hollywood (Elsaesser, 1999: 109). *Some Like It Hot* was not only the third highest grossing film of 1959 (Maslon, 2009: 141) but went on to become a classic.

Wilder must have been intrigued by the story, not least because masquerade and play with appearances is a recurrent theme in his films and something in which he would clearly remain interested (Zolotow, 1987: 107). His American directorial debut was *The Major and the Minor* (USA, 1942), in which a young woman lacking the money for a regular train ticket from New York City to her hometown pretends to be an 11-year old girl named Sue-Sue in order to travel half-price. In his later *Irma La Douce* (USA, 1963), the upright policeman Nester Patour (Jack Lemmon) becomes the pimp of prostitute Irma (Shirley MacLaine), only to disguise himself as the rich and eccentric British "Lord X." The characters in these films are changed by their experiences of masquerade, and some even lose their sense of self. They are all forced to realize that behind all those impersonations lies no stable identity: if one mask goes, another will appear; masks can acquire lives of their own, and costumes are simply catalysts for metamorphosis. The identity politics in these films reflect the vulnerability of the immigrant who must work on the basis of a malleable transcultural identity. As successful immigrants to the United States, Wilder and his co-writer I.A.L. Diamond knew that social and cultural identities could and had to be adapted and reshaped in order to ensure one's survival. Cultural mimicry was literally a survival strategy. Europeans who wanted to make it in the American film industry were expected either to assimilate and integrate themselves seamlessly or to fashion themselves according to the cultural clichés and national stereotypes which were prevalent at the time, and which provided a market demanding satisfaction. The persona they created for themselves and the films they made needed to function as financially viable trademarks in order to ensure their economic survival in Hollywood. "If the dream factory was thus partly 'made in Europe,' the worlds of make-believe, disavowal, deception, and self-deception have their own share of historical reality, fashioned from the contradictory triangulations of migration, national or ethnic stereotyping and exile" (Elsaesser, 1999: 121).

Wilder not only directed but also wrote the script for *Some Like It Hot*. He always claimed that all he took from Hoffmann's film was the basic storyline and one scene in which the camera tracks the crossdressing musicians, Jerry / Daphne (Jack Lemmon) and Joe / Josephine (Tony Curtis), as they move through the train while being introduced to the members of the all-female band they have just joined. But even if *Some Like It Hot* is one of those rare examples of a remake that acquires the status of an "original," there are enough similarities in its storyline to categorize the film as in fact a remake. Wilder did alter the original setting by relocating the action to (again masculine-coded) Chicago and (feminine-coded) Miami during Prohibition, the rise of organized crime, and the onset of the Great Depression (1929), thereby distancing the audience historically from the diegetic present. However, he did not jump at the chance to shoot in color, a technological innovation then used to justify the production of remakes, but instead chose black-and-white. At a time when nearly every Hollywood film was being shot in color, this was undoubtedly a conscious decision at least partly meant to make the crossdressing appear less "garish" and "grotesque."[14] It also evoked the milieu of the 1930s gangster film, thus positioning the film as a period piece in which not only the crossdressers wore costumes.

Thus a comparison of *Some Like It Hot* to *Fanfaren der Liebe* and *Fanfare of Love* shows that "it is not [...] just the 'content' of comedy that is significant but also its 'conspiratorial' relationship with the viewer" (Horton, 1991: 9). Here, as in *Viktor and Viktoria*, gender and national stereotypes are combined, and the cultural differences they project usually become objects of the voyeuristic gaze. In Pottier's 1935 French version, the two desperate musicians, Jean (Fernand Gravey) and Pierre (Julien Carette), dress up in Bavarian Dirndl in order to play in an all-female band called the Dutch Tulips. This curious mix of national customs and symbols ties the gendered "other" to the national "other." In *Fanfaren der Liebe*, national and ethnic impersonations (as African Americans and gypsies) precede the drag performance, suggesting an escalation of masquerades. The resulting consolidation and compounding of "otherness" in turn serves to establish and underscore a difference between "authentic" subjects and those who cannot be incorporated into predetermined stable identity formations.

By employing this strategy in *Some Like It Hot*, Wilder opens up an array of subincongruities based upon genre, sex/gender, social class, and ethnicity/nationality which subvert rather than reinforce one another for comic effect. Wilder reworks and highlights familiar generic formulas through techniques of citation, hybridity, and parody. The film's opening sequences suggest a gangster movie or film noir; a group of mafiosi embody Italian machismo and pose a deadly threat to the two witnesses, Joe and Jerry, of the St Valentine's Day Massacre. But as the story progresses, the predominant theme of Prohibition becomes less and less associated with the strict alcohol laws that actually facilitated organized crime, and increasingly with a sex-gender fluidity which enables the law's gentler, more peaceful transgression. While the latter effort is counteracted by an ensuing romance plot based on the stabilizing norm of the heterosexual couple, the romance plot is in turn undermined by Joe's masquerade as "Junior," the Cary Grant-like heir to the Shell Oil fortune, and by Marilyn Monroe's auto-impersonation, a performance so campy that it can only be read as parodic (see Lieberfeld and Sanders, 1998: 132). Indeed the majority of the film's actors are deliberately typecast. In this way, the notorious St Valentine's Day Massacre becomes the image against which two foundational but conflicting American social myths collide: the holiday celebrating love vows features the killings between rival gangs and kicks off a crossdressing narrative that clashes with both the gangster film and the conventional romance genre.

This clash is heightened by jazz music, which drives *Some Like It Hot*'s narrative, making it much more fast-paced than *Fanfaren der Liebe*'s waltz-timed Schlager. Unlike Hoffmann, Wilder utilizes the device of ellipsis to dramatize the propulsion of incongruities toward more and more capers. In contrast to *Fanfaren der Liebe*'s detailed and extended focus on the protagonists' gender transformation, which includes shaving their (male) bodies, adjusting (female) wigs, and learning to walk and behave like "women," Joe and Jerry simply appear as men in one shot and reappear as women in the next. Both masquerades are diegetically convincing, but in the German version, the romance plot is foregrounded, and the motivation for the crossdressing quickly changes from the financial need that persists as an issue in the Hollywood version to libidinal desire for its own sake. In both films, the original male couple ("buddy-team") is already gender-coded; one partner is more masculine than the other. In *Some Like It Hot*, this is played out as Joe gets the girl while Jerry slips into another male–male relationship. By contrast, the romance plot in the German version ends in the conventional way, with two heterosexual couples integrating into the traditional partriarchal social via the aesthetic norm of the happy ending; and Hans Grimm's sequel shows all four of them living together in one room, indicating their ongoing financial problems but also the fact that the two male buddies remain bonded notwithstanding their marriages (a fact highlighted when their working wives leave them behind to cope with household and children), thus reestablishing the heteronormative homosocial.

Fanfaren der Liebe features two desperate musicians, Hans Martens (Dieter Borsche) and Peter Schmitt (Georg Thomalla), who try to find jobs in an orchestra by dressing up as gypsies, in a jazz band by donning black-face, and as girls ("Hansi" and "Petra") – just as the fashion dictates. In 1951, when the film was made, Germany was still feeling the aftermath of the lost war but was indulging in amnesia regarding the Holocaust and the war crimes committed under National Socialism. Predating the Economic Miracle phase, former soldiers returning from the war or wartime captivity faced obstacles to regaining their authority in families which had learned to live without them. Many jobs and a good deal of the reconstruction work had been undertaken by *Trümmerfrauen* ("rubble women"), whereupon the returning men often felt not only defeated and dishonored but expendable. In this historical context, Hans and Peter search for a way to regain their place in a postwar German society that seems to have no need for white, German, male musicians. When they inquire about work at a booking agency, they are told that gypsies, "Negroes," and women are all the rage. In effect, they find themselves in a world turned upside down – at least in terms of the Nazi ideology still canonical only six years prior, according to which ethnic and racial minorities were considered *Untermenschen* ("subhumans") and women were supposed to marry and bear children rather than work outside the home. That is exactly what two musicians from the all-female orchestra decide to do and why the agency is desperately seeking their replacements. The message is clear and actively expressed by the two musicians, a fact that plays no role whatsoever in Wilder's version. In the United States, a mass postwar displacement of women from their wartime jobs had also occurred, but by 1955, more women had (re)joined the workforce than during the war (Oltmann, 2008: 198).

Hans Grimm's sequel makes light of a commonly related German issue of the period: the fathering by black US soldiers of illegitimate German children, which upset the racial pride and posed an additional blow to the egos of the defeated (white) German men. In Grimm's sequel, the babies of the now married couples get mixed up, and instead of his daughter Peter discovers a black baby in the pram, which causes him to faint. Hence both crossdressing and the gender trouble it produces serve to expose and disavow traumatic holes in the social fabric of postwar Germany.

Fanfaren der Liebe's setting is also thus revealing. The story begins in a Munich that shows all signs of having been destroyed by Allied bombings, and therefore also of German defeat. There, threatened with masculine aggressiveness, Hans and Peter back down, their behavior only changing once the orchestra reaches its destination, a spa in the Alps. It is in this idyllic, rural location ostensibly untouched by modernity and characterized as eternal and unchanging, a setting evocative of another highly successful escapist German genre, the *Heimatfilm* ("Homeland film"), that the two men are able to reconnect with a familiar and traditional cultural heritage and thereby reassert their manhood.

Therefore it is no surprise that Wilder considered *Fanfaren der Liebe* too "Germanic" for American tastes. Wilder claimed that American male audiences required a stronger motivation for crossdressing than the unemployment which had motivated the German characters. He saw the American male world as predatory and violent, in relation to which crossdressing would become a matter of life and death. As witnesses to the St Valentine's Day Massacre, Joe and Jerry are stalked by the killers and flee to safety by joining Sweet Sue (Joan Shawlee) and her Society Syncopaters – an all-female jazz band headed for a gig in Florida. In this respect, the Hollywood version is more conservative than the German in its insistence upon providing an enforced reason for the crossdressing. But whereas Jerry/Daphne is finally delighted by the prospect of marrying million-aire Osgood Fielding III (Joe E. Brown), who will free him/her from existential and financial worries, Hans and Peter never worry about the fact that by risking the disclosure of their true identities through their incessant and seemingly natural pursuit of women, they may once again end up out of a job. The men simply use their masquerade to get near women, touch them, befriend them, while never for a minute losing sight of their sexual orientation and interests. They do not lose themselves in their female roles. Hans starts approaching the women in the orchestra as his male self almost immediately upon meeting these new female colleagues on the train. He is not afraid of blowing his and Peter's cover. Interested in Gaby (Inge Egger), he loses no time in preparing her (while in female masquerade) for the revelation of his male self, by reading her palm and feigning to predict that she will meet a composer the next day. In line with Dieter Borsche's star intertext as one of the most prominent leading men in 1950s German cinema (Hake, 2004: 193), in the end, Hans is not only romantically but also professionally successful, as the Schlager he composes is performed by the all-female band and becomes a hit.[15]

In the Wilder version, on the other hand, Joe, a saxophonist, does not try to seduce Sugar Kane (Monroe) by reverting to his male self, nor does he attempt to talk her into dreaming of a guy just like himself. On the contrary, he must first learn that Sugar had been disappointed by saxophonists in the past, who had all proven unreliable and exploitative. She insists that she does not dream of the proverbial American embodiment of powerful wealth (John D. Rockefeller) or of potent manhood (Johnny Weissmuller) but of bespectacled, unthreatening gentlemen who are "sweet, helpless" – and nonetheless rich. Joe/Josephine, trying to model him/herself accordingly, slips into the role of Junior, thus performing a double crossdressing: Joe as Josephine as Junior, who is just as phoney as his female impersonation. As would *Victor/Victoria* 33 years later, he in turn acts out a different social class and nationality, in this case performing his take on a British heir to the Shell Oil Company. In this role, he delivers a parody – in both speech and demeanor – of *the* male movie idol of the time, by imitating Cary Grant. Grant, who hailed from Britain, had tried to acquire an American accent for his movie roles, in the process developing a peculiar accent which Curtis/Junior imitates in his performance of Junior (as Jerry comments, "Where did you get that phoney accent from? Nobody talks like that!").[16] Junior's Britishness is likewise stereotyped through costuming – formal attire, even at the beach – and the performance of cultivated, asexual and cool behavior. In the postwar period a formerly powerful British imperialism had become impotent: this along with Junior's references to Shell's postwar expansion into Venezuela suggests a positioning of Wilder's film into a postwar political context in which, by 1959, US triumphalism had trumped an impotent, fallen and US-appropriated British colonial-imperialism.

There is of course also another way to interpret Junior's assertions that "girls just sort of leave [him] cold," "When I'm with a girl, it does absolutely nothing for me," and "now and then mother nature throws somebody a dirty curve and something goes wrong inside": these comments evoke stereotypical notions of homosexuality, known not coincidentally in France as the *vice anglais* ("English vice"). (Accordingly, English gentlemen were reputed to be effeminate and not infrequently homosexual.) Moreover, when Joe/Josephine kisses Sugar onstage near the film's end – their first sincere kiss, which reveals that s/he is actually in love with her – it undermines clear-cut distinctions between homosexual and heterosexual desire, fostering an ideological overlap between the two orientations and, in turn, a broad spectator identification with "kinder, gentler" conquest. This plays out more emphatically as the film finally ends with one fused heterosexual couple, Joe and Sugar, and one potentially homosexual couple, Jerry and Osgood, who, upon Jerry/Daphne's disclosure that he is a man, replies famously, "Nobody's perfect," implying a future for their romance. In effect, the sexual desire between the stereotypical heteronormative couple, Junior and Sugar, plays out not only on the basis of pretence and lies but in terms of performative and generic conventions. Recalling while transcending the film's enforced narrative impetus, it is not a return to authenticity that resolves the entanglements of the comic romance and ensures a happy ending, but the acceptance of complex structures of desire which do not necessarily conform to heteronormativity, even as the underlying conventions of nation and class are not essentially displaced by the narratological openness.

Indeed and in turn, Marilyn Monroe's star persona was not simply that of a pin-up girl but stood for all-American values. The Americaness Marilyn/Sugar embodies is epitomized by her childlike innocence coupled with a strikingly overt sexuality of which she is seemingly unaware, a trait that renders her at once endearing and unthreatening. The incongruity of Monroe's obvious status as sex symbol and Sugar's sincere belief in her (initially) unsuccessful attempt to arouse Junior are not only sources of comedy but metaphors for a nonawareness of her (sexual) appeal. Her potentially excessive female sexuality is easy to contain and readily instrumentalized for patriotic purposes – a strategy that was essential to Monroe's popularity. As Sugar, she sells kisses for the national Milk Fund, a long-established US children's charity, while offscreen she could be seen supporting US troops in Southeast Asia. At the same time, her vulnerability signals her need for male protection. Hence while *Some Like It Hot* transcends national as well as gender and class boundaries seen as autonomous cultural particularities, it still respects nationhood as a powerful and expansive symbolic force (Ezra and Rowden, 2006: 2).

In contrast to *Some Like It Hot*, *Fanfaren der Liebe* has no open ending, but its success nevertheless prompted a sequel: in *Fanfaren der Ehe*, Hans and Peter (played by the same actors) have married the two female musicians but are not able to provide for their wives. The world seems topsy-turvy, as the two wives find jobs on a luxury cruiseship and must leave their husbands and babies behind because the ship's captain will only employ single women. When Social Services dispatches a children's nurse to see that the babies are well looked after, Hans and Peter must again dress up as women. This gives them the idea to travel to Genoa with the babies, where they plan to meet up with the cruise liner and rejoin their wives. To accomplish this, they take on the identities, respectively, of an American millionaire, Mrs Yell, and her companion, Sister Rebecca. In this guise, however, they are unable to intervene when they find that their wives have attracted very persistent male admirers. Thankfully Hans closes a successful business deal for Mrs Yell, who generously shares the profit – knells of the approaching, US-contrived Economic Miracle. In the end, the two couples are reunited, and traditional German values of marriage and family are restored.

So while both films reflect a perceived need to reconstruct national and gender identities following the major upheavals of war and exile, in terms of identity politics the two versions could not be more different. Whereas *Fanfaren der Liebe* tries to negotiate political, economic, and sexual crises by reasserting the primacy of a traditionally patriarchal German masculinity vis-à-vis its veritable conquest by an ethnically and sexually coded "other," instrumentalizing masquerade to (re)instate men as lovers, husbands, fathers, and providers, *Some Like It Hot* embraces and celebrates the fluidity and performativity of identities in the context of US postwar ascendence and the comcomitant assimilation of new immigrant populations.

Résumé

Postwar US and German remakes were not necessarily competing as to who were the rightful heirs of Weimar film and its legacy, post-1945 Germany, or the emigrants who had left Nazi Germany and were now working in Hollywood. Even so, it is obvious that the US productions share with the Weimar scripts/films the highlighting of artifice and performativity, whereas the 1950s German remakes strive to authenticate sex, gender, and heteronormativity. According to Garber, crossdressing always points toward a social "category crisis" or irresolvable conflict which destabilizes comfortable binaries and limits and "displaces the resulting discomfort onto a figure that already inhabits, indeed incarnates, the margin" (Garber, 1992: 17). They mark displacements from the axis of ethnicity and nationality to the axis of gender. In the stifling climate of Adenauer's 1950s, the German remakes try to contain the gender fluidity and sexual ambiguity that was more or less present in the Weimar originals. While both German remakes discussed in this chapter update the Weimar comedies by resituating them into a contemporary, modern Germany – for example through the use of Agfa color stock, rock 'n' roll music, and fresh young actresses like Johanna Koczian in *Viktor and Viktoria* (1957) – they also curtail much subversive potential offered by the original scripts.

By contrast, the US remakes, whether from 1959 or 1982, unconventionally return the Weimar plots to their original milieus: 1929 (*Some Like It Hot*) and 1934 (*Victor/Victoria*). In further contrast to the German films, the US versions do not end with conventional heterosexual coupling, but add homosexual coupling. One could even argue that they transgress these clear-cut sexual binaries and allow for an even more radical viewing. Even so, the gender troubles which characterize the respective decades leave a mark on these films. As the comedies delight in playing with gender codes, they cannot help but exhibit the strategies and techniques by which gender is constructed and delimited. Their humor is based on the incongruities which arise from the rigid regulation of gender and sexuality and from the playful abandonment of those rules. But the crossdressing they depict is nevertheless almost always temporary and restricted to certain settings in which the pleasure principle can, for a short moment, be reconciled with the socially dominant symbolic order, not least as it contains the national and ethnic "other." By the same token, even if most of the crossdressing comedies discussed here aim for conventional narrative closure through the return to identifiable and stable identities and recognizable binary scenarios (heterosexual vs. homosexual), their couples are nevertheless attracted to one another on the basis of their ambiguous and oscillating gender identities and sexual desires. Gender is performed not only on- but also offstage – and in our ongoing negotiations of gender codes and conventions, transnational cinema and the film industries' imperative of economic expansion, competition, and cooperation have a major role to play.

Notes

1 *Mrs. Doubtfire* was ranked 67, and *Victor/Victoria* (discussed below) was ranked 76.
2 More recent films have exploited the perceived notion that emancipated women might have trouble performing the stereotypically fashionable and beautiful woman. E.g. in *Miss Congeniality* (USA, 2000), Sandra Bullock plays an FBI agent who goes undercover as a contestant in the Miss USA pageant. The film plays upon the patriarchal idea that

    successful, professional women in jobs previously reserved for men have lost their femininity; it deploys some of the same sight-gags (e.g. stumbling in high heels) found in male-to-female performances and films.

3   This "Stab-in-the-Back Myth" was deployed by patriotic right-wing and conservative political forces who wished to blame Imperial Germany's loss of World War One on war-sabotage by socialists, communists ("Bolsheviks"), and Jews, rather than admit to the Reichsheer's (National Army) military failure.

4   "Als Mann wird man sich um sie reißen." Even the worldly Ellinor attempts to seduce Mr Viktoria: "What an adorable boy this Viktoria is. And so well built" ("Ein reizender Junge, der Viktoria. Und so gut gewachsen"). And when the jealous Douglas tries to relativize: "He has a good tailor" ("Er hat einen guten Schneider"), she responds: "Why don't you, too, go to a good tailor?" ("Warum gehen Sie nicht auch mal zu einem guten Schneider?"). It is the clothes that make the man.

5   In *First a Girl*, the change of gender is most noticeably associated with a change in social status. In the context of the British class structure, the transformation of a poor delivery girl, Elizabeth (Jessie Matthews), into a high-society star who performs as "Bill" on the French Riviera was an obvious issue. Here, Robert (Griffith Jones) administers no masculinity tests once he discovers Bill's true sex; he is merely concerned about her living with Victor (Sonnie Hale). Once Victor assures him that he has been "father, mother, sister and brother to this girl," a fairytale ending ensues in which Victor couples with a wealthy princess (Anna Lee), and Bill/Elizabeth rejoins Robert, who happens to be the princess' ex-fiancé. The final misalliances involve not so much conventional gender but rather class transgressions. What is important to the princess is not that her husband performs in drag, but that he is successful. Victor in fact links his acting to high culture by constantly alluding frequently to Shakespeare (which is lampooned in the 1933 German version) and promising the princess, who pictures him as Hamlet, "Wait for my Cleopatra!". With this declaration he associates his crossdressing with the respectable tradition of Renaissance drama, in which (young) male actors were cast in the female roles.

6   Not coincidentally in *Victor/Victoria* (1982), a photograph of Marlene Dietrich dressed in male attire sits atop Toddy's (Robert Preston) nightstand. I shall discuss this film and character below.

7   "freie filmische Neuschöpfung."

8   "Die androgyne Vision […] verweist auf die seit Menschengedenken existierende Fahndung nach dem Ort der Geschlechter, der Forschung nach der Komplettierung des Selbst und der Expansion der geschlechtlichen und sexuellen Identitäten."

9   With one exception: when the couple in *First a Girl* goes on tour, a collage occurs of the various international cities (Rome, New York) where they perform, including Berlin, evoked by the Reichstag.

10   Hence in Edwards's film, both the male and female names comprising "Victor/Victoria" are derived from the female character's actual name; in Schünzel's film, they are derived instead from the male character's name, and Susanne is professionally and privately referred to simply as "Mr Victoria."

11   Later in the film, a similar cinematic perspective on the female body is conveyed through the use of overhead shots on a dance sequence in which the individual bodies of the showgirls appear to dissolve into a veritable mass ornament (Kracauer, 1995) of

complex geometrical and kaleidoscopic patterns after a technique made famous by Hollywood director Busby Berkeley.

12 "Wie ich leide, die lächerliche Rolle eines Mannes zu spielen."

13 In interviews, Wilder referred regularly to a German original from 1932, although such a film never existed.

14 Although Curtis and Lemmon were schooled in effeminacy not by a woman but by the legendary drag artiste Barbette (Vander Clyde) (Maslon, 2009: 67), Wilder wanted their gender transformation to appear as convincing as possible.

15 Slightly stern, Borsche was well known for playing doctors who embodied male authority in private and public life.

16 Not coincidentally, the breathy voice of Marilyn Monroe adopted for her film persona was described in a 1953 *New York Times* article as "a cross between a British accent and baby-talk" (Jamison 1953: 5).

References

Benedek, S. and Binder, A. (1996) *Von tanzenden Kleidern und sprechenden Leibern. Crossdressing als Auflösung der Geschlechterpolarität?* Edition Ebersbach, Dortmund.

Bergfelder, T. (2000) Between nostalgia and amnesia: musical genres in 1950s German cinema, in *Musicals: Hollywood and Beyond* (eds B. Marshall and R. Stilwell), Cromwell Press, Exeter, pp. 80–88.

Brandlmeier, T. (1989) Der Regisseur, in *Reinhold Schünzel, Schauspieler und Regisseur* (ed. J. Schöning), edition text + kritik, München, pp. 25–35.

Butler, J. (1993) *Bodies that Matter: On the Discoursive Limits of "Sex,"* Routledge, New York and London.

Butler, J. (1999) *Gender Trouble: Feminism and the Subversion of Identity*, Routledge, New York.

Crowe, C. (1999) *Conversations with Wilder*, Faber & Faber, New York.

Doty, A. (2000) *Flaming Classics. Queering the Film Canon*, Routledge, New York and London.

Dyer, R. (1990) Less and more than women and men: lesbian and gay cinema in Weimar Germany. *New German Critique*, 51, 5–60.

Elsaesser, T. (1989) The Heimatfilm, in *Deutscher Heimatfilm*, (ed. T. Elsaesser), Goethe Institute, London, pp. 1–14.

Elsaesser, T. (1999) Ethnicity, authenticity, and exile: a counterfeit trade? German film-makers and Hollywood, in *Home, Exile, Homeland: Film, Media, and the Politics of Place* (ed. H. Naficy), Routledge, London and New York, pp. 97–123.

Ezra, E. and Rowden, T. (2006) General introduction: what is transnational cinema? in *Transnational Cinema: The Film Reader* (eds E. Ezra and T. Rowden), Routledge, Abingdon and New York, pp. 1–12.

Farmer, B. (2007) Julie Andrews made me gay. *Camera Obscura*, 22 (2), 134–143.

Garber, M. (1992) *Vested Interests. Cross-Dressing and Cultural Anxiety*, Routledge, New York and London.

Gmünden, G. (2008) *A Foreign Affair: Billy Wilder's American Films*, Berghahn, New York and Oxford.

Graf, R. (2009) Anticipating the future in the present: "New Women" and other beings of the future in Weimar Germany. *Central European History*, 42 (4), 647–673.

Grau, G (ed.) (1995) *Hidden Holocaust: Gay and Lesbian Persecution in Germany 1933–45*, Cassell, Chicago.

Hake, S. (2004) *Film in Deutschland. Geschichte und Geschichten seit 1895*, Rowohlt, Reinbek bei Hamburg.

Hamilton, M. (1993) "I'm the queen of the bitches": female impersonation and Mae West's *Pleasure Man*, in *Crossing the Stage: Controversies on Cross-dressing* (ed. L. Ferris), Routledge, London and New York, pp. 107–119.

Horton, A. (1991) Introduction, in *Comedy/Cinema/Theory* (ed. A. Horton), University of California Press, Berkeley.

Jamison, B.B. (1953) Body and soul: a portrait of Marilyn Monroe showing why gentlemen prefer blondes. *The New York Times*, July 12, 5.

Kracauer, S. (1995) The mass ornament, in *The Mass Ornament: Weimar Essays*, Harvard University Press, London and Cambridge, MA, pp. 75–86.

Kuzniar, A.A. (2000) *The Queer German Cinema*, Stanford University Press, Stanford, CA.

Lauritsen, J. and Thorstad, D. (1974) *The Early Homosexual Rights Movement (1864–1935)*, Times Change Press, New York.

Lehnert, G. (1997) *Wenn Frauen Männerkleider tragen. Geschlecht und Maskerade in Literatur und Geschichte*, dtv, München.

Lieberfeld, D. and Sanders, J. (1998) Keeping the characters straight: comedy and identity in *Some Like It Hot*. *Journal of Popular Film and Television*, 26 (3), 128–135.

Luhr, W. and Lehman, P. (1989) *Returning to the Scene: Blake Edwards*, Vol. 2, Ohio University Press, Athens.

McCormick, R.W. (2001) *Gender and Sexuality in Weimar Modernity: Film, Literature, and "New Objectivity,"* Palgrave, Houndmills, Basingstoke, Hampshire.

Maslon, L. (2009) *Some Like It Hot: The Official 50ᵗʰ Anniversary Companion*, Pavilion, London.

Meyer, M. (1992) Unveiling the word: science and narrative in transsexual striptease, in *Remake, Premake: Hollywoods romantische Komödien und ihre Gender-Diskurse, 1930–1960* (ed. K. Oltmann), Transcript. Bielefeld.

Oltmann, K. (ed.) (2008) *Remake, Premake: Hollywoods romantische Komödien und ihre Gender-Diskurse, 1930–1960*, Transcript. Bielefeld.

Senelick, L. (ed.) (1992) *Gender in Performance: The Presentation of Difference in the Performing Arts*, University Press of New England, Hanover, NH and London, pp. 68–85.

Senelick, L. (1993) Boys and girls together: subcultural origins of glamour drag and male impersonation on the nineteenth century stage, in *Crossing the Stage* (ed. L. Ferris), Routledge, London and New York, pp. 80–95.

Sieg, K. (2009) *Ethnic Drag. Performing Race, Nation, Sexuality in West Germany*, University of Michigan Press, Milwaukee.

Solomon, A. (1993) It's never too late to switch, in *Crossing the Stage: Controversies on Cross-dressing* (ed. L. Ferris), Routledge, London and New York, pp. 144–154.

Thompson, R. (2002) He and she: Weimar screwballwerk. *Senses of Cinema*, 22, http://archive.sensesofcinema.com/contents/cteq/02/22/viktor.html (accessed February 14, 2011).

Verevis, C. (2006) *Film Remakes*, Edinburgh University Press, Edinburgh.

Zolotow, M. (1987) *Billy Wilder in Hollywood*, W.H. Allen, London.

Further Reading

In *Gender Trouble: Feminism and the Subversion of Identity* (1999) and *Bodies that Matter: On the Discursive Limits of "Sex"* (1993), Judith Butler argues that gender and sex are instituted by a stylized repetition of acts that create the appearance of substance and that crossdressing can be a strategy to expose this performance of a stable and essential gender identity. Marjoire Garber's *Vested Interests: Cross-Dressing and Cultural Anxiety* (1992) is a good start for further reading on crossdressing. Alice Kuzniar's *The Queer German Cinema* is the only monograph which looks exclusively at crossdressing in German film but it focuses mainly on avant-garde films from Weimar cinema to the end of the twentieth century. Whereas Gerd Gmünden (*A Foreign Affair: Billy Wilder's American Films*, 2008) and William Luhr/Peter Lehman (*Returning to the Scene: Blake Edwards*, 1989) compare the discussed source films and remakes thereby highlighting the subversive potential of *Some Like It Hot* and *Victor/Victoria*, Chris Straayer in her article "Redressing the 'Natural': The Temporary Tansvestite Film" (in C.S. *Deviant Eyes, Deviant Bodies: Sexual Re-orientation in Film and Video*, 1996: 42–78) emphasizes that the temporary transvestite films follow a heterosexual imperative. Richard W. McCormick's *Gender and Sexuality in Weimar Modernity: Film, Literature, and "New Objectivity"* (2001) provides useful insights into gender discourses in Weimar modernity. Constantine Verevis's *Film Remakes* (2006) is a useful introduction into the theory and practice of remakes.

Filmography

Different from the Others [*Anders als die Anderen*] (Richard Oswald, Germany, 1919).

Charley's Aunt [*Charleys Tante*] (Robert Stemmle, Germany, 1934; remakes: Germany 1955, 1963, 1996).

Das Liebes ABC [The ABCs of Love] (Magnus Stifter, Germany, 1916).

Doña Juana (Paul Czinner, Germany, 1927).

Fanfaren der Ehe [Fanfare of Marriage] (Hans Grimm, West Germany, 1953).

Fanfaren der Liebe [Fanfares of Love] (Kurt Hoffmann, West Germany, 1951).

Fanfare of Love [*Fanfare d'amour*] (Richard Pottier, France, 1935).

First a Girl (Victor Saville, UK, 1935).

Georges et Georgette [George and Georgette] (Reinhold Schünzel and Roger Le Bon, Germany, 1933).

Heaven on Earth [*Der Himmel auf Erden*] (Reinhold Schünzel, Germany, 1926/27).

I Don't Want to Be a Man! [*Ich möchte kein Mann sein!*] (Ernst Lubitsch, Germany, 1918).

Irma La Douce (Billy Wilder, USA, 1963).

Jugend und Tollheit [Youth and Madness] (Urban Gad, Germany/Denmark, 1912/13).

Mrs. Doubtfire (Chris Columbus, USA, 1993).

Some Like It Hot (Billy Wilder, USA, 1959).

Major and the Minor, The (Billy Wilder, USA, 1942).

Tootsie (Sydney Pollack, USA, 1982).

Victor/Victoria (Blake Edwards, USA/UK 1982).

Viktor and Viktoria [*Viktor und Viktoria*] (Reinhold Schünzel, Germany, 1933).

Viktor and Viktoria [*Viktor und Viktoria*] (Karl Anton, West Germany, 1957).

Violinist of Florence, The [*Der Geiger von Florenz*] (Paul Czinner, Germany, 1925/26).

Third Movement:
Disidentification

Once transnational cinematic tendencies and proclivities have been destabilized and dislocated, from what ground can German film scholarship speak? The present volume's third movement comprises chapters that understand the cinematic reinforcement of traditional identity-formations – whether sociocultural, ethnonational, or political-ideological – as an impediment to answering that question constructively. These chapters engage ongoing public debates and media controversies which have erupted since the *Wende* over aesthetic and intellectual challenges to prevailing understandings of tradition, its historical rendering and capacity to be transformed. The role and function of the cinematic apparatus – including television and digital media – in prompting and mediating social discourse, both historically and for the future, is an extenuating, pervasive concern of this third movement, as its constituent chapters attempt in the course of pushing the ideological envelope to envision a less violent, more genuinely balanced German cinema and social culture.

16

The Aesthetics of Ethnic Cleansing

A Historiographic and Filmic Analysis of Andres Veiel's Balagan

Domenica Vilhotti

"I'm sorry, but you're comparing our Holocaust to your filth. That's just too much."
(Madi/Zelma to Khaled Abu-Ali in Andres Veiel's *Balagan*)

To assail the fundamental righteousness of the Jewish state of Israel was an implicit obscenity in my home. When notions of the "birth of Israel" were questioned, my mother, who narrowly escaped Vienna in 1938 with her parents, would invariably conjure what became tantamount to an impenetrable and, in its retelling, sacred tableau: the silhouette of my grandfather listening to the radio and counting the number of votes necessary to establish Israel as a singular, Jewish nation-state in historic Palestine. Upon hearing that the requisite number of votes had been cast, his normally stoic nature was overcome with emotional release: at last he, and those who had come after him, would be safe. This emotional display from so stoic a man made a deep impression upon my mother and, indirectly, upon me, whereupon it was taken for granted that Israel was born, and henceforth would remain, a country founded in righteousness. My localized family assessment of the Jewish state can easily be recast as representing the overall associative logic within the US Jewish community and the larger, globalizing society of which it is a part that Israel was and continues to be an unassailable actor on the world political stage, its every act, however questionable, justified as necessary, in the long run, to mitigating antisemitism and preventing a second Holocaust.

German director Andres Veiel's *Balagan* (1994), a documentary covering the experimental Israeli station play, *Arbeit Macht Frei M' Toitland Europa* (Dudi Mayan, 1992–1993), shattered for me what Israeli historian Ze'ev Sternhell (1998) has famously called the "founding myth of Israel," as it directly challenges the notion,

A Companion to German Cinema, First Edition. Edited by Terri Ginsberg and Andrea Mensch.
© 2012 Blackwell Publishing Ltd. Published 2012 by Blackwell Publishing Ltd.

shared with US Jews by a significant number of Germans, that Israel was conceived immaculately, as it were, without "original sin" (see Beit-Hallahmi, 1993). Veiel, who was trained originally in psychology, is known for making critical and experimental documentaries examining the return of repressed and disavowed attitudes and ideological dispositions, especially as they may entail fascism and racism, across multiple generations in German society, German political culture, and the postwar German diaspora. *Balagan* serves up for judgment Israeli policy and priorities, which since – and even before – the country's inception, have received significant political and economic support from a Germany interested in encouraging Jewish habitation beyond German borders as well as maintaining European hegemony in the postcolonial Middle East. Veiel's film boldly questions rhetorically the *raison d'être* given for such support: Israel as a necessary sanctuary for oppressed Jews, to be maintained and preserved at all costs and regardless of historical circumstances. As expressed in this chapter's epigraph, one of *Arbeit Macht Frei*'s most cogent points is that the Israeli occupation of Palestine is comparable to Nazi policy under the Third Reich. In one performance piece, Ashkenazi-Israeli actress, Smadar "Madi" Ma'ayan, tropes Holocaust survivorship to Fellini-esque distortion, as her character, a middle-aged Holocaust survivor, screams hysterically at a Palestinian character, portrayed sympathetically by Palestinian-Israeli actor Khaled Abu-Ali, as he knocks on the window of her home, pleading desperately to engage in dialogue. Madi's character describes the Palestinian's implicit comparison of the Holocaust to the *Nakba*, the Zionist dispossession and displacement of Palestinians from their lands and homes during 1947–1949 (see Ginsberg and Lippard, 2010: 292–293), which she refers to as "your filth," as "just too much," and in turn refuses to engage, much less welcome him into her illegitimately acquired home. The woman's Holocaust-survivor husband, played by Jewish-Iraqi actor, Moni Yosef, intervenes, echoing symbolically the strategy of traditional Zionist historians by demanding vociferously that his Palestinian neighbor, and the entire line of critical questioning of Jewish statehood, "go away."

Terri Ginsberg's "Holocaust 'Identity' and the Israeli/Palestinian *Balagan*" analyzes how Veiel's documentary critiques the perceived "obscenity" of referring to modern Israel as originally tainted or morally flawed. Her use of the term *obscenity* derives from Ancient Greek theatrical tradition, in which the "obscene," a "species of the ugly," is permitted onstage only as a reconstitution of the "beautiful" (Ginsberg, 2007: 181). Apropos of this controlled aesthetic paradigm, the "ugly" that *Arbeit Macht Frei* forces its audience to experience is, in Madi's words during one of *Balagan*'s several offstage interviews, the comparison of the Holocaust to "our life as Israelis here and now." The play parodies the core of Jewish nationalism, which obscures Israel's "original sins" to the extent that the country may claim a veritable free pass to legitimacy, precisely by distorting Holocaust survivorship in the extreme, emphasizing its social stereotypicality in the confrontational, improvisational tradition of Polish stage director, Jerzy Grotowski (Ginsberg, 2007: 183–184). Madi's performances satirize the idea that, again in her words, Israel is "a nation that was raised upon the ashes," a common explanation that calls on and celebrates the ideological notion of Israel as literally the survivor of a "great, sacrificial conflagration" – the definition itself of *holocaust* – whose very existence justifies not only the *Nakba* but subsequent violent acts, including the post-1967 Occupation, the more recent Gaza invasion, and numerous other intervening atrocities (see Ginsberg and Lippard, 2010: 191–192, 215–216). Madi's post-theatrical continuation of the satire additionally underscores what Israeli "New Historians" and other scholars of Zionist history argue effectively is the pervasiveness of Israel's "founding myths" (see Morris, 1987; Segev, 1993; Shlaim, 2000; Pappe, 2001).

According to scholars as diverse as Benjamin Beit-Hallahmi (1993), and Idith Zertal (2005), this myth positions Israeli statehood within a christological framework for which Jews murdered by the Nazis are perceived to have suffered and died for the country's founding and ongoing "sins." The fruits of purported Jewish sacrifice, the ensuing salvation Israel supposedly offers as compensation for that holocaustal loss, are analogizable, in this framework, to a gift of eternal life: perpetual existence for a Jewish nation-state, and a promise of permanent habitation in historic Palestine forever free of the vulnerability and victimization which previously had marred Jewish-European life, and which Zionist ideology extends to all of world history. This new earthly paradise, this Father's Kingdom or "New Jerusalem," evokes a shared sense among Jewish Israelis of sacred inevitability. Before "resurrection" can take place, that is, death must have occurred; hence the martyrial significance of Holocaust survivorship: mass death made palpable – redeemed – by the promise of new life. Indeed such christological rationale feeds and reinforces itself: because I rise again, I must be righteous, and because I am righteous, I will always rise again.

But what of the possibility that, to follow this logic, Israel, too, shall be judged? If the cloak of unassailability were lifted, what conclusions might be drawn? Through its deployment of grotesque parody and performative irony, *Arbeit Macht Frei* and, in turn, *Balagan*, implicitly compare the crimes of the Third Reich, "our Holocaust," with those of Israel's establishment and subsequent occupation of Palestine, "your filth." The question remains of whether such a comparison can be substantiated beyond, much less within, the theatrical/cinematic setting, and if so, under what conditions and critical rubrics?

One could certainly examine, as have Nur Masalha (1992) and Ilan Pappe, Israel's maltreatment of Palestinians during the *Nakba*. Pappe's *The Ethnic Cleansing of Palestine* (2006) makes the controversial comparison by applying Drazen Petrovic's (1994) six-pronged definition of *ethnic cleansing*, which I shall outline below, to both the genocide in the former Yugoslavia and the 1948 *Nakba*. If one accepts Pappe's first claim that the conflict in the former Yugoslavia was a clear-cut case of ethnic cleansing, might one not also designate the Nazi treatment of German Jews under the Nuremburg Laws and similar legislation similarly? And if one likewise accepts Pappe's subsequent claim that the *Nakba* was also a case of ethnic cleansing, why have historians chosen not to pursue that claim's logical extension? That is to say, if the ethnic cleansing in Yugoslavia is likened to the *Nakba*, and if the Nazi racial laws are also known to have enabled an ethnic cleansing, then is not the German ethnic cleansing of European Jews comparable in large respect to the Zionist ethnic cleansing of Palestine? Thus far, such comparisons have only been worked out in the horrific dreamscape, the "obscene" theatrical arena, which *Arbeit Macht Frei/Balagan* present.

The purpose of this chapter is twofold. First I shall conduct an historical investigation of Pappe's use of "ethnic cleansing" to describe both the *Nakba* and the effort by the Nazi regime to render Germany and its imperial territories *Judenfrei* ("free of Jews") (Epstein and Rosen, 1997: 148). From there, I reference the concept's 1993 definition by the United Nations Council for Human Rights in order to hypothesize why the comparison has been considered so "obscene" within the academic literature, including that of many New Historians, where, until very recently, it has been alluded to with euphemisms such as "the Palestinian Question" or "the master plan." My conclusions shall lead us to three central issues documented and critiqued by *Arbeit Macht Frei/Balagan* concerning the contemporary Jewish reluctance to relinquish sole "ownership" of collective suffering and its legacy: (1) the fear that the perceived preeminence of the Judeocide will be undermined if *genocide* is "opened" to the ethnic cleansing of Palestine; (2) the ensuing fear, propagated within Israeli public discourse, of a resulting "domino effect," a prediction that the comparison of Nazi anti-semitism with Israeli anti-Palestinian policy will backfire against Palestinians and others seeking their liberation, insofar as the comparison threatens to divulge Palestinian victimhood as comprising, in part, Jewish Israel's uncanny "other"; and (3) the resulting perceived need to solidify the myth of Israeli foundational propriety and the country's ensuing sense of entitlement to an internationally sanctioned *carte blanche* with respect to its policy vis-à-vis the Arab and Muslim worlds, in terms of righteous Jewish sacrificialism.

Definitions of Ethnic Cleansing

In order to establish a transhistorical application of "ethnic cleansing" to the three mentioned instances – Yugoslavia, Palestine, Nazi Germany – the term itself must be defined carefully. Pappe reviews popular, encyclopedic, scholarly, and governmental definitions spanning sources from *Wikipedia* to *The Hutchinson Encyclopedia* to Petrovic to the US Department of State to the United Nations. For my purposes, it is appropriate to employ an academic definition, because it offers the most extensive grounds for contextualization.

Drazen Petrovic (1994) is cited frequently as having authored one of the most comprehensive and authoritative works, "Ethnic Cleansing: An Attempt at Methodology," defining and delineating the dimensions of ethnic cleansing. In it, he summarizes the issue:

It is the present writer's view that ethnic cleansing is a well-defined policy of a particular group of persons to systematically eliminate another group from a given territory on the basis of religious, ethnic or national origin. Such a policy involves violence and is very often connected with military operations. It is to be achieved by all possible means, from discrimination to extermination, and entails violations of human rights and international humanitarian law [...] Most ethnic cleansing methods are grave breaches of the 1949 Geneva Conventions and 1977 Additional Protocols. (Petrovic, 1994: 3)

Petrovic proposes six main tenets of ethnic cleansing: (1) its systematic character; (2) its official support by authorities through "either [their] participation or instigation, or at least by [their] refraining from taking action to restrain those responsible"; (3) its status as a victimology defined by the "ethnic, national, religious, or other" characteristics of a social grouping comprised predominantly by civilian noncombatants who are members of a larger population; (4) its definition of the target population "by its origin, and not by its activity"; (5) the refusal of its perpetrators to respect international humanitarian law despite their formal obligation to do so; and (6) the employment by its perpetrators of a range of forms and methods, depending upon the "global character" of their aims, ranging from "simple administrative and economic discrimination" to the extermination of the target group (Petrovic, 1994: 3).

Judenfrei: Anti-Jewish Legislation in Prewar Nazi Germany as Ethnic Cleansing

Petrovic's six main tenets of ethnic cleansing are applicable to Nazi Germany's actions against Jews, both before and during World War Two. Beginning as early as 1933, official acts of the German Parliament served to define and discriminate against the class of citizens designated racially "Jewish." The Law for the Restoration of the Professional Civil Service (Chronology, 2007: 7), for instance, promulgated in 1933, excluded Jews and the regime's political opponents from university and government positions. This and similar laws barring Jews from holding positions as lawyers, physicians, and teachers satisfy criteria of Petrovic's first, third, fourth, and sixth tenets. Passage of the Nuremberg Laws in 1935, which denaturalized German-born Jewish citizens and residents and prohibited Jews from acquiring German citizenship satisfies Petrovic's second tenet. These actions denying opportunities to Jews quickly escalated to actions designed to isolate and confine them geographically. The "transfer" of Jews to ghettos began in 1940 with the establishment of the Łódź Ghetto, the Nazis created a succession of additional ghettoes throughout Germany and its newly acquired Eastern European territories, including the Warsaw Ghetto, where "more than 350,000 Jews – about 30 percent of the city's population – [were confined] in about 2.4 percent of the city's total area" (Chronology, 2007: 36).

All of these actions are well documented and beyond dispute. The applicability of Petrovic's fifth component, however, is more difficult to establish, in that Nazi policies predated pertinent international efforts to promulgate prohibitions and criminalize human rights violations such as those committed so defiantly by the Nazis.

The Palestinian *Nakba* as a Clear-cut Case of Ethnic Cleansing

In his book's prologue, Pappe laments that the 1948 Zionist dispossession and displacement of Palestine, which he regards as an indisputable case of ethnic cleansing, has been erased almost completely from world history. Pappe has just cause to lament: once the Haganah (the central underground Zionist militia) decided to proceed with the codenamed "Plan D" (Plan *Dalet* in Hebrew), it took only six months for it to accomplish its mission. At that point, over 50% of the indigenous Palestinian population, or nearly 800 000 people, had been uprooted and disenfranchised. Eleven urban neighborhoods were cleared, and 531 villages were razed. This mission, in particular the fundamentally systematic nature of its implementation, indeed represents ethnic cleansing, and for that reason it is categorizable within contemporary international law as a crime against humanity (Pappe, 2006: xiii). The specifics of Plan D fit five of Petrovic's six tenets: (1) it was systematic in character; (2) it had official support; (3) its victims were defined by their ethnic, national, and religious character and (4) by their origins rather than their activity; and (6) its perpetrators employed a variety of methods, in this case forced removal from house and home. Again, Petrovic's fifth tenet, the refusal to respect international humanitarian law, is harder to argue; yet Pappe (2006: xiii) counters that, while Zionist policy was based originally upon an alleged imperative to retaliate against Palestinian reprisals enacted during 1947 against Zionist incursions vis-à-vis the imminent end of British Mandate Palestine, it was later transformed into an unwarranted imperialist drive to "ethnically cleanse the country as a whole in March 1948." In this respect, Israel may not have been violating international law explicitly, because no such law would be written until after 1948, after the promulgation of the 1949 Geneva Conventions. Nonetheless, as letters written by Israel's first prime minister, David Ben-Gurion, along with excerpts from Plan D prove, Israel was already willfully contravening agreements outlined in the 1947 United Nations Partition Resolution when it initiated the *Nakba* (Pappe, 2006: 40).

In fact, as illustrated by the following, dramatic passage from Pappe's preface, five of Petrovic's six tenets were satisfied by the mere inception of Plan D:

> In this building, on a cold Wednesday afternoon, 10 March 1948, a group of eleven men, veteran Zionist leaders together with young military Jewish officers, put the final touches to a plan for the ethnic cleansing of Palestine. That same evening, military orders were dispatched to the units on the ground to prepare for the systematic expulsion of the Palestinians from vast areas of the country. The orders came with a detailed description of the methods to be employed to forcibly evict the people: large-scale intimidation; laying siege to and bombarding villages and population centers; setting fire to homes, properties and goods; expulsion; demolition; and finally, planting mines among the rubble to prevent any of the villages and neighborhoods as the targets of this master plan. Codenamed Plan D [...] this was the fourth and final version of less substantial plans that outlined the fate the Zionists had in store for Palestine and consequently for its native population. (Pappe, 2006: xi)

The fact that a detailed military plan was drafted and methodically carried out speaks to Plan D's systematic character. Although Plan D was a covert initiative conducted by an underground militia, that group in fact became Israel's official army, the Israel Defense Forces, during the course of the *Nakba*, and was headed all along by Ben-Gurion (Pappe, 2006: 40). As early as a decade prior to the adoption of Plan D, Ben-Gurion had expressed unquestionable support for ethnic cleansing. In his June 1938 letter to the Jewish Agency Executive, he wrote: "I am for compulsory transfer; I do not see anything immoral in it" (quoted in Pappe, 2006: xi). Thus Petrovic's second tenet, official support from authorities, is satisfied.

Cultural historian Joseph Massad's discussion of the Zionist search for Jewish "genetic" markers is most helpful for ascertaining the applicability of Petrovic's fourth tenet. Massad (2005: 5) elucidates the historical irony that, as early as the 1930s, Zionists understood that, for the sake of justifying Jewish statehood, they, too, had to adopt the very racialist pseudoscience that had been used against Jews by the Nazis. Plan D called for the expulsion of Palestinians on false grounds that they comprised a distinct racial and religious grouping. Here it should be noted that the motivation for Palestinian dispossession and displacement was to create an irrefutable 80% Jewish demographic majority in historic Palestine – in racial, ethnic, and religious terms recently deconstructed by Israeli historian Shlomo Sand (2009) – in order to secure a permanent and estimable Jewish political bloc in the region. Without Plan D, that goal would have been difficult if impossible to meet, not least given the size of the Palestinian Arab population at the time – approximately 1.2–1.3 million (Morris, 1987: 8) – and the likelihood that the Jewish birth rate would not have been able to eclipse that of Palestinians. Ben-Gurion was well aware that no realistic amount of Jewish immigration would be sufficient to amass the necessary 80%, whereupon he declared forced expulsion, or ethnic cleansing, which included several documented massacres, both necessary and mandatory (Morris, 1990: 11).

Whereas the applicability of Petrovic's fifth tenet is, as mentioned, more difficult to prove, one can reasonably argue that Israel willfully sought to sidestep and break extant international law "despite formal obligation" (Petrovic, 1994: 3). Here I refer to Pappe's argument that, by engaging in Palestinian dispossession during March 1948, the Zionists were in fact violating the UN Partition Resolution, which Ben-Gurion had signed less than a year before, in November 1947 (Pappe, 2006: 40). As Israeli historian Benny Morris shows in his discussion of the Partition Resolution and Zionist military aims, moreover,

> The acceptance of partition, in the mid-1930s as in 1947, was tactical, not a change in the Zionist dream [...] Ben-Gurion told the Jewish Agency Executive that he supported partition "on the basis of the assumption that after we constitute a large force following the establishment of the State – we will cancel the partition of the country and we will expand throughout the Land of Israel." (1990: 9)

In other words, Ben-Gurion expressed clearly that he never had any intention of respecting international law, despite being formally obligated to do so. His implicit rejection of the Partition Resolution, to which he had signed his name, exemplifies Israeli perpetration of Petrovic's fifth tenet, notwithstanding Ben-Gurion's logical inability to have broken postwar humanitiarian law before the fact. Indeed his actions signaled a preparedness and willingness to break any such law once promulgated.

Petrovic's sixth tenet states simply that perpetrators may employ a range of forms and methods, depending on the "global character" of their aims. Israel's Plan D indubitably satisfies this final aspect of "ethnic cleansing." Plan D entailed a variety of methods for forcibly removing the Palestinian population. It began with mass intimidation, which, as Morris (1990: 14) delineates, compelled the emigration of professionals and intellectuals, or those with the necessary means, most of whom expected their exiles to be temporary. Widespread unemployment and food shortages followed, which served to weaken permanently the remaining population. After intimidation came overt offense, including the bombardment of urban and rural areas, the burning and destruction of homes and places of business, several massacres, overall mass expulsion, and the decimation of whole neighborhoods and villages in order to discourage the return of refugees.

The "Obscenity" of the Comparison of the Third Reich to the Founding of Israel

Using Petrovic's authoritative six-pronged definition of ethnic cleansing, the three cases of ethnic cleansing discussed in this chapter are clearly under-standable under that rubric. Apropos of Pappe, the *Nakba* may be likened to the ethnic cleansing in the former Yugoslavia. As outlined herein and throughout the academic literature and reference works, Nazi Germany engaged in an ethnic cleansing of Jews which resulted in genocide and which thus may also be likened to the Yugoslavian case. And as the current chapter is attempting to demonstrate, if events in both Israel and Nazi Germany are comparable to those in Yugoslavia, in that each country engaged in ethnic cleansing, then the actions of Israel in perpetrating the *Nakba* are directly analogous to those of Nazi Germany with respect to both countries having engaged in ethnic cleansing.

It is therefore troubling that mainline academic literature has refrained from making, much less exploring, this comparison. Instead most scholars have elided it, cautiously avoiding any references to Israeli massacres of Palestinians, and this despite the fact that the Israeli massacre of the Palestinian population of Deir Yassin, one of the Zionist militia's bloodiest incursions, was indisputably part of Plan D and its aim to deplete Palestine of its indigenous, non-Jewish Arab population. Such references and linkage might thus be described as *verboten* ("forbidden" in German), or as "obscene" in the sense outlined by Ginsberg.

Several New Historians and sympathetic US and UK scholars, however, allude frequently to the *Nakba* and its relationship to Nazi politics, but only via coded euphemisms and imagery, whereby the comparison is underplayed. And while use of "the Palestinian Question," for example, helps Maxime Rodinson (1983), Yosef Gorney (1985), and even Massad link the policies of Israel in albeit differing ways to those of the Third Reich, their work is largely theoretical and focuses primarily on Israeli and Jewish national identity – as does Ginsberg, whose critique of *Balagan* is concerned primarily with its ideological aesthetics. No historical analyses make the comparison on an explicit, policy-by-policy basis. Similarly, Pappe draws a myriad of implicit correlations between Israeli and Nazi policy, but he never makes an outright connection on the basis of his book's titular concept. His book's table of contents contains chapter headings and subheadings which evoke the notion of *Judenfrei*, such as "Finalizing a Master Plan" and "Final Cleansing of the South and East" (Pappe, 2006: v–vi); and in his initial discussion of ethnic cleansing in the former Yugoslavia, Pappe (2006: 1) makes an even bolder assertion: "The particular way some of the Serbian generals and politicians were using the term 'ethnic cleansing' reminded scholars they had heard it before. It was used in the second world war by the Nazis and their allies." The first image featured in the book is a photograph of Irgun (far right-wing underground) troops marching through Tel Aviv in a "show of strength" on the eve of Israel's declaration (Figure 16.1); the image undoubtedly evokes comparison with German SS troops marching in formation, as becomes clear when viewed alongside a shot from *Balagan* taken at a display in the Warsaw Ghetto Fighters Museum, Akko (Figure 16.2).

Figure 16.1 Irgun troops march through the streets of Tel-Aviv in a show of strength on the eve of the declaration of the State of Israel. *Source*: Pappe (2006).

Figure 16.2 Madi/Zelma at the Warsaw Ghetto Fighters' Museum, Akko, in *Balagan* (dir. Andres Veiel, prod. Journal Filmproduktion).

Why Is the German/Jewish–Israeli/Palestinian Analogy "Obscene"?

Interestingly enough, the comparison of Germans/Jews with Israelis/Palestinians is far from *verboten* when forwarded by groups diametrically opposed to the New Historians. A 2007 pamphlet published by the David Horowitz Freedom Center, a neoconservative thinktank, features on its cover a swastika encircled by a crescent moon, and is entitled *The Nazi Roots of Palestinian Nationalism and Islamic Jihad*. Apropos of the sloganeering typical of political pamphlets, the Horowitz publication's rhetoric is inflated, as it seeks to close off discussion in a perfunctory and premature manner distinct from academic protocol. Comparing the Muslim Brotherhood with the Nazis, both circa 1938, coauthor David Meir-Levi writes,

> It was during this time that the Muslim Brotherhood found a soul mate in Nazi Germany [...] Both movements sought world conquest and domination. Both were triumphalist and supremacist: in Nazism the Aryan must rule, while in al-Banna's Islam, the Muslim religion must hold dominion [...] Both worshipped the unifying totalitarian figure of the Caliph or Fuhrer. And both rabidly hated the Jews and sought their destruction. (2007: 7)

Why are such comparisons between Nazism and Arab and Islamic nationalism, however specious or distorted (see Becker, 2006), tolerated, while legitimate scholarly comparisons between Nazism and Zionism remain *verboten*? In order to answer this question, I must turn to the mentioned "ownership" of Jewish suffering and its legacy.

One reason why comparing the founding of Israel with any aspect of German fascism has been considered "obscene" is that, while both instances involved ethnic cleansing, including massacres and other atrocities, only the latter led – at least within the present perspective – to one of the most horrific genocides in modern history. Those who reject the comparison are often threatened specifically by the projected loss it may entail of the cultural and political privilege attained by Israel's claim to perpetual victim status vis-à-vis its nonetheless oppressed Palestinian inhabitants and weakened Arab neighbors as justification for its violent establishment and continuing acts of aggression and war against them. Mainline scholars as well as many progressives, for example, fear that *genocide* has become trivialized by alleged overuse within governmental and academic circles and in the popular vernacular, and that this trivialization will affect global policy toward Israel, especially by its European and North American allies. Alain Destexhe, for instance, the former Secretary General of Doctors without Borders, a progressive humanitarian organization, asserts that there have only been three examples of genocide in the twentieth century: the Armenian genocide, the Holocaust, and the Rwandan genocide. Destexhe excludes Yugoslavia, Palestine, and other instances of ethnic cleansing, such as those effected by India's partition, because he fears that the so-called ubiquitous use of the term will dilute its presumed specification of a hierarchy of heinous crimes distinguishable by the "single-minded intent behind the barbaric actions" (Becker, 2006: 7). Destexhe's criticisms implicitly decry New Historical revisionism, which seeks to expose the latent fallacies which belie Israel's founding myths, for its "too common usage of genocide" (Becker, 2006: 7). Citing the arguably exaggerated influence of Holocaust deniers, mainliners and progressives who strive to protect a veritably sacral conception of "genocide" and, by extension, the Holocaust insist that the overapplication of the term aids Holocaust denial by "bolster[ing] their horrible propaganda that the Nazi extermination camps and the 'final solution' were not really such a uniquely horrible period in history" (Becker, 2006: 7).

Of course, the retentive urge echoed across university campuses, media outlets, and nongovernmental organizations to keep "genocide" and, more specifically, the Holocaust narrowly defined itself carries larger policy implications. Is the resistance to extending transhistorically the definition of genocide a latent part of the reason why no serious global initiative has been implemented to stop the near-genocidal conditions in the Israeli-occupied Gaza Strip? Obviously, the global conditions of 1942 and the present are different; the United States could rationalize its entry into World War Two on grounds that it was fighting to prevent a fascist takeover of Europe, while its contemporary efforts on behalf of Palestinians would run counter to current Western hegemonic tendencies (cf. Rubenberg, 1986; Bennis, 2007). Could it be, then, that the comparative use of "genocide" is so controversial because the market has already been cornered, by Zionism, on holocaustal suffering? Does this mean that the West will remain complacent regarding Israeli crimes against Palestinian humanity?

Joseph Massad (2005) delineates reasons why the Palestinian–Israeli conflict has not yet been resolved. He describes Zionism as a logical outcome of the historical progression of reflexive antisemitism, settler-colonialism, racism, and nationalism which leads to the construction of Palestinians as, collectively, the Jewish-Israeli "other." Massad (2005: 13) references Michael Selzer's landmark book, *The Aryanization of the Jewish State* (1967), and extends its argument in order to claim that Nazi antisemitism "started a domino effect that began in Germany and ended in Palestine." Selzer had noted originally a Jewish-German tendency to project onto their generally less fortunate Eastern European co-religionists, known in German as *Ostjuden*, a stereotypical image historically deployed by antisemites, for which Jews are seen as "dirty and cunning, medieval, and effeminate" (Selzer, 1967: 86). Massad (2005: 13) understands Zionism as a logical extension of this tendency to establish a prideful national identity by creating an out-group, and he concludes that Palestinians have become the ultimate object of this displacement among Jews: "the Jewish population, regardless of ethnic origins, has internalized this antisemitic epistemology in describing the Palestinians." He argues that this tendency is not exceptional to Zionist thought, but rather its rule:

> This is not simply a superstructural neurosis [...] [but] the epistemological foundation on which [Zionism] rests. If Zionism proceeded from a rejection of all things Jewish in favor of European culture ... its pedagogical mission was to transform all Jews into that model. To justify its colonization efforts in Palestine to [...] [Europe], Zionism would present Jews as carriers of ... civilization to a land burdened by a barbaric ... population who ... transformed it into a desert. Much of what anti-Semitism projected onto European Jews would ... be displaced onto Palestinian Arabs, who were seen to embody ... attributes that both Zionism and anti-Semitism insisted had been ... embodied by diaspora Jewry. (Massad, 2005: 13)

I argue, further, that the mainline and Zionist rejection of comparisons between Nazi policy and the ethnic cleansing of Palestine is the effect of a complex "othering" of Palestinians which effects an uncanny disgust, indeed a return of repressed, internalized Jewish self-hatred vis-à-vis the very real suffering of Palestinians. *Arbeit Macht Frei/Balagan* expertly captures this uncanny sensibility, this liminal recognition of the comparison's "obscenity," in its carnivalesque parody of Israeli Holocaust survivors who insist that comparing their purported martyrial suffering under Hitler with Palestinian suffering at the hands of Zionism is "parasitical" and "just too much."

Balagan and the Aesthetics of Ethnic Cleansing

If the "obscene" comparison of Nazi ethnic cleansing with the *Nakba* is so threatening that it is only explored inversely within artistic provocations such as *Arbeit Macht Frei* and *Balagan*, then such occasions rightly deserve investigation. What, we could ask, might be an *aesthetics of ethnic cleansing*? In what ways does *Balagan* make comparisons between the widely acknowledged results of Nazi policy and the largely unacknowledged *Nakba*? I propose that *Balagan* inscribes an aesthetics of ethnic cleansing that entails a threefold rhetorical structure involving (1) perspective, a recontextualization of what one might call an economy of pain; (2) parallelism, an exposure of the similarities between Nazi and Zionist policy; and (3) desacralization, a demystification of the perceived sacrality of the Holocaust, what Madi calls "the new national religion" of Israel. These three strategies are underscored in the film by aesthetic practices of montage and abject imaging. What follows is an analysis of *Balagan*'s juxtaposition of expository footage, mainly of low-key scenes from *Arbeit Macht Frei* but also of the play's actors expressing their political views offstage, with scenes from the play that are exceptionally abject. I shall argue that this cinematic appropriation of the abject produces ironic or critically emphatic meaning intended to provoke *Balagan*'s spectator as well as *Arbeit Macht Frei*'s live, participatory audience. Sometimes projecting its provocations directly, these performative vehicles compel an acknowledgement of suppressed truths and of the discomfort they wreak on Israeli/Palestinian society.

Perspective: Recontextualizing the Economy of Pain

Playing Zelma, a museum docent at the Warsaw Ghetto Fighters Museum, Madi conveys, in her words, not a stereotypical, 70-year-old Holocaust survivor, but the archetypal "1000-year-old" Wandering Jew (see Ginsberg, 2007: 143–144). "Dead-alive," she is the ghost who asks uncomfortable questions. In one of her more disturbing provocations, Zelma proposes that the number of Judeocide victims must be seen in perspective relative to the much larger number of World War Two casualties, and that numbers signify differently across cultures. In so doing, she effectively deconstructs the mythic and often christological preeminence which many Israelis assign to "the six million." She confides in an offhand remark, without visible substantiation, to her increasingly uncomfortable audience that Gypsies collapse numbers higher than ten into an infinite "many," rendering the life of an 11th individual "no person, no potential, no world." The film then intercuts portions of an offstage interview with Madi, in which she describes the absence of grandparents on her father's side as a "wound, a well, a *schwarze loch* ['black hole']" that was "in the air" but nonetheless unspeakable and untouchable. The juxtaposition suggests that the loss of even one individual, by albeit prejudicial contrast, apparently means a great deal in the Israeli context; while Madi's illumination of the contested significance of the zero functions as a node of critical comparison of the Nazi ethnic cleansing that resulted in so much loss of Jewish life with the *Nakba* that resulted in a smaller but nonetheless significant loss of Palestinian Arab life. To repeat, within six months of Plan D's inception, "more than half of Palestine's native population, close to 800,000 people, had been uprooted, 531 villages had been destroyed, and eleven urban neighborhoods emptied of their inhabitants" (Pappe, 2006: xiii).

As the film cuts back to the museum scene, Zelma offers an answer to her questions regarding the significance of numbers, making one of the film's more cogent points:

> That's how statistics are. But talking about statistics, six million of a total loss of fifty-five million [is] roughly how much percent? Roughly? Eleven or twelve, right? Well, we may be tough, but in our hearts this raises a question, right? A most natural question. God, you're only ten percent! The whole word cried "woe is me! Why do you of all people make such a noise? Do Jews always have to be so special?"

Veiel aims his camera at the confused and offended audience, then cuts to one of *Arbeit Macht Frei*'s more abject performances, in which Madi/Zelma flails about histrionically onstage, then demands that we look closely at the number engraved on her arm, crying in triumphal desperation, "I went through the selection … I went through *the selection!*" Veiel responds with a close-up of her arm, while Khaled, carnivalizing the Palestinian "other," begins trying to scrub off the number. The taboo-breaking nature of these actions, along with the conflation within the scene of actor and role, serve to mitigate audience empathy with the historical Jewish suffering Madi/Zelma represents and instead to contend with her displaced positioning of Khaled, the Palestinian, as Israel's archetypal suffering servant. The point is clarified by the juxtaposed claim of one audience member, a self-identified Holocaust survivor, who points to her arm insistently and says, "I also have one [a tattoo]": it is no longer only the Holocaust generation's cries of woe, but also the silenced cries of Khaled's generation and people that are relevant. Moreover, in the post-Holocaust state of Israel, Palestinians, not Jews, are the current and primary victims of oppression. The question lingers: does Khaled not deserve to be "special"? Do "we"?

Parallelism: Exposing the Similarities between German and Israeli Nationalism

During the museum scene, Zelma initially sets about exploring the concept of German nationalism in an effort to expose its logical fallacy. Pointing to prewar Nazi propaganda depictions of the stereotypical "ugly Jew" who eats the blood of Christian children for self-purification, she segues into a discussion of Nazi racialism, which she appropriates into an ironic expression of the Zionist view that Palestinians are to Israelis as Germans are to Jews: "It is of all people the Arabs, our cousins, who are a pure race. The National Socialist theory of the pure race states that the Arabs are *reinrassig* ['racially pure']. Why? ... They did not mingle with others. The Arab's blood is ... very pure." She continues her ironical strategy with a twist, by asserting even more self-consciously, with prejudice drawn again from Nazi pseudoscience, that, by extension, unlike Arabs, Jews are necessarily a mixed people, "like the Gypsies. Animals, that's what we are." In effect, Zelma draws a most disconcerting, if implicit inference: Israelis have adopted lines of thought all too similar to those of Nazi racialists, "othering" the region's Palestinian inhabitants by projecting an internalized antisemitism onto them and in turn reacting fearfully to it, thus manifesting a vicious cycle of Jewish self-hatred played out against the persistently colonized Palestinian population. Nitzan S. Ben-Shaul (1997) has referred to this phenomenon as "siege mentality." As if to underscore the point, Zelma concludes her presentation by reminding her audience that to create a second-class population on the basis of their perceived "impurity" is to repeat a tragic history: "That's a license to destroy a big people."

In art and performance, the standard of proof is different from that of academic writing. Madi echoes the sentiments of Massad and of Selzer aesthetically, through associative suggestion rather than rational analysis, although reasoned conclusions may be drawn therefrom. Madi's comparisons of Zionist and Nazi thought, underscored by Veiel's editorial juxtapositions, render shockingly manifest cinematically what is only cautiously approached in academia. Massad (2005: 13) does argue methodically that modern Israeli policy and ideology emulate German nationalism: "Much of what anti-Semitism projected onto European Jews would now be displaced onto Palestinian Arabs, who were seen to embody the attributes that both Zionism and anti-Semitism insisted had been previously embodied by diaspora Jewry."

Desacralization of the Holocaust

A defining characteristic of religion is faith, or belief without reason. Part of *Arbeit Macht Frei*'s argument entails an aesthetic critique of the unimpeachable sense of entitlement – the "free pass" to exceptional behavior – which the experience of holocaustal suffering has presumably permitted Jewish Israelis. In that irrational framework, "Holocaust" becomes an ideological concept, a matrix of blind faith. As Madi observes in interview clips which bookend *Balagan*, "The Holocaust is the new religion … It is the opium of the masses in Israel." *Arbeit Macht Frei/Balagan* regards the sacralization of the Holocaust as a fundamental obstacle to political progress and critical thought, which it seeks to expose provocatively, through the event's uncanny profanation, its rendering historically comparable with other crimes against humanity, in particular the *Nakba*. Shocking visual ironies, abject and grotesque imagery, and disturbing metaphors all serve to mirror "obscenely" audience and spectator disgust at this comparison and thereby to prompt critical reckoning with repressed knowledge of its truthfulness.

During the scene in which characters played by Madi and Moni rebuke Khaled's character for making the comparison, and position him as an unwelcome "other," *Arbeit Macht Frei*'s theatrical troupe literally performs "obscenity." Before making us aware that Moni's character is an owner of (expropriated Palestinian) property, the play encourages us to misrecognize him as homeless and wandering, and his abode as an extension of the concentrationary universe. Drenched in sweat and blindfolded by a necktie, he stomps beggarlike amid the audience, here seated within an enclosed, makeshift concentration camp barracks. While banging together two Sierra cups as if to symbolize an encroaching Israeli army, and referring to the Jordan River dividing the Israeli-occupied West Bank from Jordan, he shouts at the Palestinian character, "This side – our side; that side … is ours too!" Literally blinded by the necktie, he grotesquely metaphorizes the relationship of bourgeois class interests both to the tragic history of the Eastern European Jews and their settler-colonization of Palestine, at once evoking and parodying audience/spectator revulsion at these "obscene" comparisons.

In another scene, *Balagan* presents a recurring image of Madi playing a skeletal concentration camp prisoner, naked save a cloth diaper. Her figure is often portrayed inversely crucified, hanging by her feet with torso flailing wildly. At other moments, she is shown climbing a silhouetted barbed-wire fence, a visual mainstay of Holocaust representation, only to form the shape of another crucifixion, here framed in alignment with an Israeli flag that waves in the background. Madi clarifies the connection in partial voiceover: "This survivor of the camp that is so skinny, for the Israelis, he is like a Jesus Christ. Someone who has this number, he has a ticket to paradise." The use of Christian symbolism in these scenes in provocative, in that it sets up for parody another "obscene" comparison – between the death of Jesus and the Judeocide. Appropriately, this "dead-alive" prisoner appears ghostlike, literalizing the uncanny, the return of the repressed. Her inverse crucifixion and histrionic flailing comprise carnivalesque performances which work to foreground and demystify the ideological ascription of martyrdom to Israeli Jews, especially those who are not actually Holocaust survivors but instead perpetrators of the *Nakba* and ensuing Occupation (see Beit-Hallahmi, 1993; Zertal, 1998; Sha'ban, 2005).

Aesthetics of Ethnic Cleansing: Juxtaposition and the Abject

As I have already demonstrated, *Balagan*'s aesthetic strategies include ironic juxtapositions of traditional expository footage with abject theatrical performances from *Arbeit Macht Frei*. In what follows, Madi's critique of Holocaust sacralization will continue to serve as an ideal entry point for exploring this strategy further. During one such performance, over which Madi's explanatory narration is once again heard, Veiel cuts to an offstage interview with her, as she continues: "Someone who has this number [engraved on his arm], he has a ticket to paradise. And to say, No, I don't care about it, I will take your identity and I will do it on my hand ...; it's terrible, it's a blasphemy, and it's forbidden ... and this is one of the reasons I did it." Here Madi directly expresses her rejection of Holocaust sacralization, capping it off with, "I don't give a fucking shit about the Holocaust." Next, however, Veiel juxtaposes her criticisms with their abject manifestation: Zelma, framed anamorphically, casts a seductive, demoniacal stare directly into the camera, challenging the speaker to watch her unravel a bandage wrapped around her arm to reveal the tattooed number. As Madi makes clear in later footage, Zelma and Madi are here performing a double-blasphemy: tattooed flesh is a Jewish sacrilege, but in Madi's Israeli culture, it is not only sacrilegious; its flagrant manipulation of Jewish historical fear and vulnerability makes it socially treasonous.

Balagan's strategy here is also visceral in its content and effects. Zelma, who should be dead but isn't, slowly collects her saliva and lets it dribble onto her arm, whereupon she attempts desperately to rub off the number before falling, face down, in exhausted defeat. According to Julia Kristeva (1982) writing famously on abjection, being confronted with excremental elements such as blood, urine, feces, semen, or saliva evokes a feeling of uncanny disgust, in that one is compelled thereby to recognize and contend with what was once part of the Self but subsequently separated from it – and discarded as waste or filth. By extension, abjection may be defined as the feeling of letting go what one would still like to keep – and for various reasons cannot. *Balagan* plays creatively with this extended notion, positioning Israel as desperately wishing to retain Jewish victim status as an unimpeachable cloak of exceptionalism, by presenting characters who expropriate and trample upon that sacral cloak to the point that it fails to impress – and undermines Israeli eminence in the process. Zelma, the eternal, ghostly wanderer, is Israel's uncanny mirror, projecting back onto it the persisting, chronic dis-ease and unsettled reality of illegitimate statehood.

At several points in *Balagan*, the progressive arrangement of excerpts from *Arbeit Macht Frei* mimes a phenomenological passage from superficial sentiment to unconscious, visceral reaction. The figure of Madi initiates one such progression by her explanation, given in voiceover, of some of the more disturbing images from the play, namely those of barely clad actors dancing and singing ritualistically within a staged concentration camp. Explicating the cacophony, she states: "This is not a scene, it is a screaming, and it comes from a tremendous amount of fear and aggression." The film then cuts to her seated in her apartment, her face underexposed to create a silhouette, as she observes, "Something is very wrong, but we are trying to hold on ... to our culture ... that was created here within the last forty years. We are trying to hold on to something that is collapsing. It's not working." With this assertion, Madi expresses verbally the sense of Israeli abjection which the play presents performatively, her shadowed, almost ominous figure serving to literalize that repressed feeling. Her shadowed visage in turn figures the anonymity of the Holocaust dead signified earlier during the museum scene, now evoked "obscenely" by her metaphorical facelessness.

Balagan's next scene depicts a raucous and jubilant Passover *seder* at Madi's family home. Her voiceover now offers a somewhat more amiable description of Zionist repression: the making of monsters. Observing her family's festive behavior, she rehearses the cultural commonplace that Israelis are loud because, following years of hiding out in silence during World War Two, they now rejoice excessively at the founding of the Jewish state, overcompensating with "the sound of a roaring monster." Madi hints at this monster's dysfunctionality, noting ironically that, "If we sing and we are together, it will be okay, we will pass the time." A shot of Madi singing and laughing at the *seder* table is then juxtaposed, however, with a montage of overt abjection from *Arbeit Macht Frei*: a naked woman in a barrel regurgitating and ingesting slop; another woman flailing in what appears her death throes while trapped within an airtight glass cage filled with shredded paper; and one more naked woman spinning in a large bowl while slapping her own buttocks. These extreme images serve to ironize visually Madi's verbal commentary; singing and being together will *not* make everything okay. An additional shot from the play portrays a silhouetted Madi hanging from the rafters until she falls into a dark abyss. The image reads as fecal: performing the abject, the moment reinscribes Madi's offstage insistence that, "We [Israelis] are trying to hold onto something that is collapsing."

In this very context, Madi's performance of abjection is shown in its relation to the maternal. Kristeva theorizes that we abject the maternal, that which creates us, in order to form independent identities. Madi illustrates this theory first by describing having been sexually stimulated by the skeletal images of dead concentration camp victims depicted in Holocaust documentaries, acknowledging her pornographic fascination with the paradigmatic footage. She links this fascination to her later anorexia and hiding of food in her vagina. These depictions are echoed visually by one of the film's most "obscene" images: Madi as emaciated prisoner "birthing" what appears to be a banana. To cavernous gallows music – screeching and gonging – she slowly raises the viscous phallus toward her mouth before Veiel cuts away. Recalling her earlier assertion that Israel is a nation "borne out of the ashes of the Holocaust," we can read Madi's birthing act as national allegory. The "child" is Israel, borne of a genocidal act symbolized by Madi's dead-alive, ethnically cleansed body. Because, as I have shown, to recycle and consume Nazism-cum-Zionism is to fundamentally offend the Jewish-Israeli symbolic order, the "obscene" connection between the two nationalist ideologies must be performed, via an aesthetics of abjection-cum-ethnic-cleansing.

Arbeit Macht Frei/Balagan does not perform Israeli/Palestinian abjection for its own sake, however; its "obscenity" is not, as Ginsberg (2007: 181) notes, merely a mere *épater le bourgeois* ("shock to the bourgeoisie"). Instead it positions the field of abjection as a space for healing. *Balagan* ends with a reconfigured christological tableau. Madi and Khaled, performing onstage their naked, dead-alive characters – stubborn remnants of the holocaustal imagination – embrace in what forms an undeniably christic image: Madi as Mother Mary holding Khaled as Baby Jesus, allowing him succor like a Madonna with Child. This classic image of predestined alienation and suffering, performed *in extremis* by a Jew and a Muslim, respectively, suggests that a genuinely repentant Israeli will cease abjecting the maternal and, allegorically, the stolen foundations of Jewish statehood: Palestine. Passive guilt will simply enable the problem to persist. Jewish creation must be altruistic rather than self-serving, by offering compassion rather than defensiveness in the face of the shameful past.

References

Becker, K. (2006) Genocide and ethnic cleansing, in *Model United Nations of the Far West: Addressing the Needs of the Vulnerable* (ed. R. Barrons), http://www.munfw.org/archive/50th/4th1.htm (accessed December 10, 2007).

Beit-Hallahmi, B. (1993) *Original Sins: Reflections on the History of Zionism and Israel*, Olive Branch Press, New York.

Bennis, P. (2007) *Understanding the Palestinian–Israeli Conflict: A Primer*, Oliver Branch Press, Northampton, MA.

Ben-Shaul, N.S. (1997) *Mythical Expressions of Siege in Israeli Cinema*, Edwin Mellen Press, New York.

Chronology of the Holocaust. United States Holocaust Memorial Museum, Washington, DC, http://www.ushmm.org/education/foreducators/resource/chronology.pdf (accessed December 11, 2007).

Epstein, E.J. and Rosen, P. (1997) *Dictionary of the Holocaust: Biography, Geography, and Terminology*, Greenwood Press, Westport, CT.

Ginsberg, T. (2007) Holocaust identity and the Israeli/Palestinian *Balagan*, in *Holocaust Film: The Political Aesthetics of Ideology*, Cambridge Scholars, Newcastle, pp. 176–202.

Ginsberg, T. and Lippard, C. (2010) *Historical Dictionary of Middle Eastern Cinema*, Scarecrow Press, Lanham, MD.

Gorny, Y. (1985) *The Arab Question and the Jewish Problem*, Am Oved, Tel Aviv.

Kristeva, J. (1982) *Powers of Horror: An Essay on Abjection* (trans L.S. Roudiez), Columbia University Press, New York.

Masalha, N. (1992) *Expulsion of the Palestinians: The Concept of "Transfer" in Zionist Political Thought, 1882–1948*, Institute for Palestine Studies, Beirut.

Massad, J.A. (2005) The persistence of the Palestinian question. *Cultural Critique*, 59, 1–23.

Meir-Levi, D. (2007) *The Nazi Roots of Palestinian Nationalism and Islamic Jihad*, David Horowitz Freedom Center, Los Angeles.

Morris, B. (1987) *The Birth of the Palestinian Refugee Problem, 1947–1949*, Cambridge University Press, Cambridge.

Morris, B. (1990) *1948 and After: Israel and the Palestinians*, Clarendon Press, Oxford.

Pappe, I. (2001) *The Making of the Arab–Israeli Conflict, 1947–1951*, I.B. Tauris, London.

Pappe, I. (2006) *The Ethnic Cleansing of Palestine*, Oneworld, Oxford.

Petrovic, D. (1994) Ethnic cleansing: an attempt at methodology. *European Journal of International Law*, 5 (3), 342–360, http://www.ejil.org/journal/Vol5/No3/art3.html (hypertext pages 1–5) (accessed December 1, 2007).

Rodinson, M. (1983) *Cult, Ghetto, and State: The Persistence of the Jewish Question*, Al Saqi Books, London.

Rubenberg, C.A. (1986) *Israel and the American National Interest: A Critical Examination*, University of Illinois Press, Urbana and Chicago.

Sand, S. (2009) *The Invention of the Jewish People* (trans. Y. Lotan), Verso, London.

Segev, T. (1993) *The Seventh Million: The Israelis and the Holocaust* (trans. H. Watzman), Hill & Wang, New York.

Selzer, M. (1967) *The Aryanization of the Jewish State*, Black Star, New York.

Sha'ban, F. (2005) *For Zion's Sake: The Judeo-Christian Tradition in American Culture*, Pluto Press, London.

Shlaim, A. (2000) *The Iron Wall: Israel and the Arab World*, W.W. Norton, New York.

Sternhell, Z. (1998) *The Founding Myths of Israel*, Princeton University Press, Princeton, NJ.

Zertal, I. (1998) *From Catastrophe to Power: Holocaust Survivors and the Emergence of Israel*, University of California Press, Berkeley.

Zertal, I. (2005) *Israel's Holocaust and the Politics of Nationhood*, Cambridge University Press, Cambridge.

Further Reading

Finkelstein, N.G. (1995) *Image and Reality of the Israeli–Palestinian Conflict*, Verso, London.

Rodinson, M. (1973) *Israel: A Colonial-Settler State?*, Pathfinder, New York.

Stein, S. (ed.) (2001) *Nuremberg Law for the Protection of German Blood and German Honor*, University of West England, Bristol, http://www.ess.uwe.ac.uk/documents/gerblood.htm (accessed December 13, 2007).

17

Margarethe von Trotta's
Rosenstrasse
"Feminist Re-Visions" of a Historical Controversy

Sally Winkle

Since its German release in the fall of 2003, Margarethe von Trotta's *Rosenstrasse* has unleashed a torrent of criticism and intense debate among German and American historians and film critics. German historian Wolfgang Benz called the film "historical kitsch" in his September 2003 polemic in the *Süddeutsche Zeitung*. Von Trotta in a subsequent radio interview ("Regisseurin von Trotta," 2003) accused Benz of indulging in a "male fantasy" for his interpretation of a controversial scene in the film. Meanwhile critics and historians joined in the fray, attacking and defending the film and its director in various media venues in Germany and the United States. Indeed, a *Süddeutsche Zeitung* headline labeled the furor a *Rosenstrassenkrieg* ("*Rosenstrasse* war") in one of their numerous articles on the film in 2003, and the H-Net list on German history hosted a lively online forum on *Rosenstrasse* in 2004 that lasted three months.[1]

The film tells the fictional stories of a woman and little girl whose lives were forever changed by the Berlin factory arrests of Jewish Germans in "mixed marriages" and by the demonstration of their family members, mainly women, on Rosenstrasse in Berlin from February 27 to March 6, 1943. Von Trotta's approach, featuring a complex temporal narrative structure, focuses on memory and supports a feminist perspective that emphasizes connections among women in the past and across generations. Similar to von Trotta's earlier films, *Rosenstrasse* links the personal with the political. As in her films of the 1970s and 1980s, such as *The Second Awakening of Christa Klages* (1978), *Marianne and Juliane* (1981), and *Sheer Madness* (1982–1983), *Rosenstrasse* highlights female subjectivity, relationships between women, and the importance of solidarity and female agency, providing a "feminist re-vision" of the present and past.

A Companion to German Cinema, First Edition. Edited by Terri Ginsberg and Andrea Mensch.
© 2012 Blackwell Publishing Ltd. Published 2012 by Blackwell Publishing Ltd.

The controversy and conflicting readings evoked by von Trotta's subjective re-vision of historical events in *Rosenstrasse* through fictionalized stories of individuals in the context of the German past, however, were already anticipated in the critical reception of several of her previous films. Although *Marianne and Juliane*, for example, received critical acclaim following its release, it was castigated by some critics and scholars for its subjective approach to politics in personalizing West German terrorism through the characterization of Marianne, the fictional stand-in for Gudrin Ensslin of the Baader-Meinhof Group (Byg, 1993: 265–266). The film was also criticized for conflating female sexuality and political militancy in its refusal to offer any plausible political explanation for Marianne's decision to join the Red Army Faction (RAF) and in its implication that Marianne's turn to terrorism might have been due to an extramarital sexual relationship rather than an autonomous choice based on political convictions (DiCaprio, 1996). In addition, in a critique of *Marianne and Juliane* that prefigures critical responses to *Rosenstrasse* many years later, Barton Byg objects to "von Trotta's manipulation of history in the service of her narrative" (Byg, 1993: 264).

In this chapter I analyze *Rosenstrasse* as a "feminist" film and simultaneously as a German heritage melodrama, caught in a contradiction resulting from a taboo felt by many German artists regarding works representing the Holocaust on the one hand, and the commercial demands of the entertainment film industry on the other. This study will focus on how von Trotta negotiated this contradiction in her film, the ensuing problems, and the reasons it provoked such controversy.

Rosenstrasse in the Context of Historical Controversy

Rosenstrasse presents a fictionalized narrative of an event in 1943 Berlin that was largely ignored until the 1990s. Beginning in 1993 it was commemorated in the German media, studied by historians, and subsequently became the subject of strident historical debate. While a few articles on the Rosenstrasse protest appeared in German magazines in the immediate postwar period, the event was largely omitted from the general narrative of German history, most likely due to the repression of the Nazi past in the 1950s as well as the lingering aversion of some conservative West Germans toward recognition of any acts of popular anti-Nazi resistance during the war, which could be interpreted as a rebuke to their own failure to actively oppose the Nazi regime. Although this attitude changed in the 1960s, it was not until after the fall of the Berlin Wall that the Rosenstrasse protest received more than cursory attention in the press or in history books in either German state (Gruner, 2003: 183). The renewed media interest in the Rosenstrasse protest can be attributed to the 50th anniversary celebration of 1993 as well as a perceived need in Germany following reunification (and the *Historikerstreit* of the 1980s) to reclaim and recount stories that cast German history during World War

Two in an at least marginally more "positive" light. The popular postwar account of the Rosenstrasse demonstration as a unique example of successful nonviolent protest by German women against the persecution of German Jews served this purpose (Gruner, 2003: 180–183; Gruner, 2005b: 14).

On Saturday, February 27, 1943, thousands of Jewish Germans, mostly forced laborers, were arrested in surprise raids on factories throughout Germany, with the largest raids concentrated in Berlin. Unlike previous roundups, intermarried Jewish Germans (that is, Jews married to "Aryan" Germans) and "Mischlinge" (part-Jewish Germans) were arrested as well. They were separated from the others, and in Berlin they were interned in the former Jewish administrative building on Rosenstrasse (Stoltzfus, 1996: 210–218; Gruner, 2005b: 61–69). In subsequent days almost 11 000 German Jews without "Aryan" relatives were transported to Auschwitz, including 7000 from Berlin (Gruner, 2005b: 75).

By the afternoon of February 27, family members of the interned intermarried German Jews began to gather on Rosenstrasse, having heard through word of mouth (the so-called *Mundfunk*) that their relatives might be held there. Details about the weeklong protest vary widely, with reports ranging from a modest gathering of 150–200 relatives to a huge, provocative demonstration of 1000 or more.[2] In the first 12 days of March 1943, Nazi officials released the intermarried Jewish German internees held in Berlin, with most set free from March 6 through March 8 (Gruner, 2005b: 111–116, 126–127).

Von Trotta's film inadvertently ignited a fierce debate concerning competing historical narratives on the effectiveness of public protest in persuading the Nazis not to deport the German Jewish husbands interned at Rosenstrasse in 1943.[3] In his research on Rosenstrasse, American historian Nathan Stoltzfus relied primarily on eyewitness interviews he conducted in the mid-1980s, supplemented by National Socialist government documents, Goebbels's diaries, postwar court reports, and other historical sources. Stoltzfus's book, *Resistance of the Heart* (1996: 223–231) highlighted the growing size of the demonstration, the courage and loyalty of the wives and mothers of the internees, and the feelings of solidarity they gained after days of watching, waiting, and defying the police, who threatened them and ordered them to leave. Stoltzfus reported one witness's description of the sixth day of the protest, in which she remembered seeing a thousand people on the street and hearing protestors screaming "You murderers" in addition to "Give us our husbands" (Stoltzfus, 1996: 243).

To Stoltzfus and the survivors he quoted, the protest on Rosenstrasse was clearly responsible for saving the German Jewish detainees in mixed marriages from deportation to Auschwitz. Stoltzfus (1996: 220–252) maintained that Goebbels ordered the release of the intermarried Jews and "Mischlinge" from Rosenstrasse on March 6, 1943 because he feared public protest and social unrest in the wake of the Nazis' devastating defeat at Stalingrad, thus disrupting official preparations for "total war." Stoltzfus argued that the support of German women on the home front was crucial for the stability of the Third Reich and that the women had a great deal of influence as a social group, especially in the waning years of the Nazi regime (Stoltzfus, 1996: 199–200).

German historian Wolf Gruner (2005b: 50–55), on the other hand, cited National Socialist documents indicating to him that the Nazi leadership had planned to release the intermarried German Jews held at Rosenstrasse all along. He argued that the protest, while laudable, played no role in the release of the detainees and that Goebbels had very little power over deportation decisions (Gruner, 2005b: 156–166). Gruner utilized predated release certificates received by some of the internees as evidence that the regime planned to set the victims free a few days after their arrest (Gruner, 2005b: 112–113). Gruner maintained that although 2000 intermarried Jewish Germans and "Mischlinge" were interned at Rosenstrasse, there were actually 8000 intermarried German Jews in Berlin in February 1943. Thus he read the arrest of a fraction of that number as an indication that the regime did not intend a radical action to rid the capital of all Jews at that time, despite the intentions Goebbels had proclaimed in his diary (Gruner, 2005b: 47–49, 107).

Gruner (2005b: 118–123) established two reasons for the brief internment of the German Jews with "Aryan" relatives: (1) to verify their "racial status" as Jews from "mixed marriages" and (2) to recruit intermarried Jewish Germans and "Mischlinge" with the necessary skills to replace the staff of the Berlin Jewish organizations who were to be deported with the other "full" Jewish Germans to Auschwitz or Theresienstadt. Gruner's historical method privileged documentary evidence over interviews with survivors; he dismissed individual memories as notoriously unreliable, especially eyewitness accounts of events that had transpired more than 40 years earlier (2005b: 140). Indeed, Gruner maintained that the legend of the Rosenstrasse protest as successfully saving the intermarried German Jews from deportation and death has become a part of Germans' collective memory, dating to the earliest reports in 1945 and eventually influencing the individual accounts of some witnesses years later (2005b: 201–202).

In the end the complex question of the reliability of survivors' memories as historical sources meant that contradictions in the witnesses' recollections provided evidence for both sides of the historical debate. Ultimately, the Rosenstrasse controversy was not about the occurrence of the event itself, which no one disputed, but about its historical role in prompting the release of the detainees. Resolution of this question had enormous implications for explaining the response or lack of response of the German populace to Nazi atrocities and for the feasibility of public protest to significantly change Nazi policies. Stoltzfus believed the courageous protest of the intermarried German women on Rosenstrasse showed that popular demonstrations and active opposition were possible and could have made a difference. Gruner, on the other hand, denied the efficacy of popular protest in a totalitarian system, particularly in the early 1940s, and doubted the power of such demonstrations to affect official decisions. Gruner's most vehement objections are directed at the conclusion that researchers and the public often draw from what they view as the successful protest on Rosenstrasse:

if more Germans had protested, the persecution and annihilation of the Jews could have been mitigated or even halted (Gruner, 2003: 184).

Utilizing a flashback frame, von Trotta's film joined the historical debate by privileging memory as the foundation of her narrative, thus clearly supporting Stoltzfus's point of view. As von Trotta explained to the press, it was not her intent to show definitively why the internees at Rosenstrasse were released in March 1943 but rather to "bring to life the individual experiences of the women who were eyewitnesses."[4] While von Trotta also read historical studies and memoirs on Nazi Germany and the Holocaust, in the end she relied heavily on survivors' stories and interviews in developing the film narrative. Indeed, the director's claim in a 2004 interview that "people are more important than documents" is a direct refutation of Gruner's approach (Sklar, 2004: 12).[5] Although von Trotta's preference for witness testimony corresponds to her laudable desire to highlight survivors' experiences, particularly women's voices, her demotion of historical documents tends to justify a problematic irrationalism, consisting of a predilection for the personal over the political, which can have conservative implications, for which she had been criticized in earlier films such as *Marianne and Juliane*, as noted above. This may be in part a result of the tension between the artistic and commercial requirements of her films, for which *Rosenstrasse* offers a cogent example.

Rosenstrasse and the Tension between the Artistic and Commercial Aspects of Film

A review of the history of *Rosenstrasse*'s production offers considerable insight into the tension within contemporary cinema as simultaneously an art form and a business. The road to production was long and arduous; the director created three versions of the script over a seven-year period before finally receiving financing in 2000–2001 as a German-Dutch co-production from Studio Hamburg Letterbox Filmproduktion, Tele München, and Get Reel Productions as well as support from a variety of German and Dutch film funds (Wydra, 2003: 110; Wiebel, 2003: 3). Von Trotta's efforts to produce *Rosenstrasse* demonstrate her struggle between accommodating her own ambitious objectives for the film with the demands of a film industry intent upon keeping costs low and attracting a popular audience accustomed to movie stars, high production values, and a comprehensible, entertaining plot.

The first draft, written in 1994, comprised a chronological narrative of the experiences of numerous characters during the factory arrests and demonstration on Rosenstrasse from February 27 to March 6, 1943. That script was considered too costly, and von Trotta created a second version concentrating on a few individuals caught up in the historical event. This narrative centered on her fictional rendition of a true story from the 1994 documentary by Michael Muschner of a girl who was able to visit her mother in 1943 in the collection center on Rosenstrasse before the mother was transported to the East (Wydra, 2003: 13). The second version includes many of the protagonists in the final draft with more details of their back-stories and more historically accurate information. Although it is framed by a few brief scenes of a middle-aged American woman in contemporary Berlin shown reading historical files, almost the entire narrative is set in the past. At the conclusion the story returns to the present, revealing that the American woman is the child whose mother was sent to Auschwitz from Rosenstrasse.[6]

The second draft was rejected as well and eventually shelved, which von Trotta attributed to the political climate in Germany and preference in the industry from the mid-1980s to mid-1990s for escapist comedies rather than historical films centering on the Nazi past (Wydra, 2003: 14, 174–177). Eric Rentschler (2000: 264–272) describes the changing trends in German cinema of the 1980s–1990s as a shift away from the innovative, socially critical, often political, unsettling films of New German Cinema and toward films that are unequivocally entertaining, with familiar stars and accessible scripts revolving around relationships, trendy, glamorous settings, lifestyle choices, and the personal problems of upwardly mobile characters, a trend that he calls the "German cinema of consensus." Certainly the conservative political landscape in the Federal Republic, beginning with the victory of the Helmut Kohl (Christian Democratic Union) government in 1982, contributed to the demise of the New German Cinema and the subsequent promotion of commercial viability and domestic success of German films in the following decade. With the new conservative government now in charge of distributing federal film subsidies and film prizes, Interior Minister Friedrich Zimmermann favored utilizing federal funds for popular, entertaining films that average Germans would find appealing (Rentschler, 2000: 265–266). Simultaneously, film financing became more centralized, television executives expanded their influence on film boards, and collaborations between television and film production companies became the norm, resulting in the increasing emphasis on commercial potential over artistic concerns (Rentschler, 2000: 267).

Margarethe von Trotta and her producer, Martin Wiebel, interpreted the changing political environment in the Federal Republic in the late 1990s, that is, the electoral victory of Social Democrats under Gerhard Schroeder and the formation of the Social Democrat/Green coalition in 1998, as facilitating a transformation in political attitudes and policies toward confronting the Nazi past and making the production of her film more feasible (Wydra, 2003: 14, 174–177). A convergence of political, economic, and cultural trends contributed to a proliferation of German feature films about the Holocaust and Nazi past from 1997 to 2000, as explained by Lutz Koepnick in his article, "Reframing the Past." These trends include: (1) the increasing commercialization of German filmmaking and recognition of its market value, (2) a new interest in Jewish culture in the Federal Republic since reunification paired with a growing culture of commemoration in Germany, and (3) the perceived need to preserve the memory of the

Holocaust because so many of the survivors were dying (Koepnick, 2002: 56–57). Margarethe von Trotta thus benefitted from what Koepnick described as a "culture of mass-mediated memory that has proliferated in Germany and elsewhere throughout the 1990s" (Koepnick, 2002: 49).

Von Trotta acknowledged the significance of television production funding for *Rosenstrasse*, an avenue made possible partly through her foray into TV work in the 1990s; in other words she pragmatically embraced the increasing commercialization of German cinema, which is noticeable in the casting and structure of her film. Indeed, von Trotta selected two of the biggest stars of German comedies of the 1980s and 1990s, Katja Riemann and Maria Schrader, to fill the major roles in her film. Von Trotta can therefore be seen as caught in a dilemma, committed to creating a popular, marketable, entertaining film set during the Holocaust, while being keenly aware of her responsibility as a German director to sensitively depict the traumatic experiences of Jewish Germans in Nazi Germany. By trying to please everyone, she ended up creating a controversial film full of noble intentions and internal contradictions, which marks the film as simultaneously fascinating and flawed.

Debates on the problematics of Holocaust representation have proliferated since Adorno's oft-cited and widely misunderstood statement describing the writing of poetry after Auschwitz as "barbaric." As Terri Ginsberg explains in her book, *Holocaust Film: the Political Aesthetics of Ideology*, "the Adornian taboo, as it is commonly interpreted, presupposes the Holocaust as a socially enabled occasioning of death so horrible, unprecedented, and historically paradigmatic that its representative artistic rendering is conceivable only as a mimesis of Nazi ideology itself" (Ginsberg, 2007: 4). Ginsberg argues that Adorno's commentary on the problematics of post-Holocaust culture is more complex, political, and theoretical than is evident from the ways it is usually understood. The misreading of Adorno's injunction has led scholars to emphasize the incomprehensibility of the Holocaust and the impossibility of achieving its cultural representation in artistic or cinematic form (Ginsberg, 2007: 5). Contrary to Adorno's socially critical emphasis, much film criticism tends to interpret the Holocaust in christological or Judeo-Christian terms as an example of Jewish (self-)sacrifice, as Ginsberg explains:

> Indeed, what for Adorno is etched indelibly at the barbaric core of Western civilization – of global capitalism and its ideological ethos – as an occurrence incomprehensible without sustained consideration of its social-institutional and especially political-economic determinants, becomes instead for Holocaust film criticism an index of human fallibility. (2007: 7)

To Ginsberg this critical shift in Holocaust film scholarship away from political interrogation in favor of moral lessons results in a refusal to address the issue of other victims of the Holocaust or of other earlier or later genocides and the economic, political, and social causes for all of these events (Ginsberg, 2007: 8).

Interestingly, Adorno's original injunction against *poetry* post-Auschwitz has served in the past three decades to particularly impugn commercial mass cultural cinematic and television productions representing the Holocaust (Bathrick, 2008: 12). In *Trauma and Media*, Allen Meek (2010: 135) argues that some scholars have used Adorno's critique to privilege witness testimony as an authoritative form of representation in contrast to Hollywood-style films relying on melodramatic conventions and narrative realism. According to Meek, this was particularly true among American intellectuals. "Adorno's concern was with the failure of German society to confront the significance of the Nazi era, whereas American psychotherapists and literary critics moved to make the victim/survivor a figure of collective identification and an embodiment of historical truth" (Meek, 2010: 136).[7] However, as Meek points out, "The impulse to protect the historical experience of the Holocaust from inadequate or appropriative media representations has lent support to a deconstructive critique of representation in which historical truth can only be made accessible through the absences, aporias and disruptions of narrative flow" (Meek, 2010: 158). This emphasis on language as insufficient in articulating trauma is ultimately unsupportable, since it effectively disallows communication of any lived experience; yet experience can only be related to others through some sort of linguistic communication, be it through witness testimony, documentation, oral history, or media (Meek, 2010: 158–160). To Meek, Adorno is actually highlighting the problematics of *all* cultural representations, not just representations of the Holocaust, "because representations are produced within an economy of exchange and calculation that itself informed the violence of the Nazi state at a fundamental level" (2010: 166).

A problematic aspect of much Holocaust representation and mass media transmissions that convey public trauma, such as those following 9/11, lies in the risks associated with their use to reinforce collective identification of certain groups of victims rather than other groups, thereby ignoring other acts of injustice or genocide. Such (mis)use of representations of public trauma can even serve to justify acts of violence in the name of democracy and in defense of national sovereignty. Meek (2010: 195) argues that while trauma can be and often is employed to shock members of a community for the purpose of advocating specific political or military goals, a critical understanding of historical trauma can serve to stimulate "critical reflection on the structures of sovereign power and political violence."

In contrast to such critical reflections on power, Margarethe von Trotta's film is aimed at inducing empathy and reflection on the repercussions of Nazi atrocities on survivors, which she attempts to achieve in a commercially viable cinematic form. At the end of the 1990s von Trotta had become aware of psychological studies showing that many Holocaust survivors who had repressed their experiences were later confronted with traumatic memories. In her third version of *Rosenstrasse*, written in 2000–2001, von Trotta created a film narrative focused on the importance of remembering for survivors and their families and on the consequences of their trauma, thus promoting the significance of witness testimony and Jewish survivors' experiences (Wydra, 2003: 15, 174–177; Wiebel, 2003: 9). The film achieved popular success, although it received mixed reviews, with numerous critics objecting particularly to the flashback frame of the narrative.[8]

In the 2003 film, von Trotta's fictional account of the historical events is couched in a complex narrative structure that spans over 60 years and two continents. *Rosenstrasse* begins in contemporary New York in the apartment of Ruth Weinstein, a Jewish woman whose mourning for the unexpected death of her husband leads to sudden traumatic flashbacks of her childhood in Nazi Germany. The first few flashbacks preceded by Ruth's blank stares reveal her disturbing memories of the day her mother was arrested during the Berlin factory raids in February 1943. Ruth's troubling confrontation with her traumatic past as a Holocaust survivor, along with her new-found interest in Orthodox Judaism, result in her abrupt rejection of her daughter Hannah's upcoming marriage to the non-Jewish Nicaraguan Luis.

Ruth's daughter Hannah learns that her mother had been cared for as a child by an "Aryan" woman in Berlin following the arrest of Ruth's mother Miriam in the factory raids, memories that Ruth had repressed and concealed from her children. The following week Hannah travels to Berlin to search for the elderly Lena Fischer, the woman who had saved her mother Ruth from deportation and death. Over the seven days that Hannah interviews the 90-year-old Lena in Berlin, Lena tells of her German Jewish husband Fabian's arrest in the factory raids and of her efforts to gain his release. Flashbacks to 1932 recount the back story of the lovers Lena von Eschenbach and Fabian Fischer, while flashbacks set in 1943 show Lena spontane-ously taking responsibility for the eight-year-old Ruth, whose mother Miriam is held with the others at the Rosenstrasse site. Miriam had been married to a German who divorced her, and she was deported to Auschwitz a few days after her arrest. Scenes portraying the solidarity, determination, and courage of the women protesting on Rosenstrasse and culminating in the release of their family members on March 6, 1943 form the center of the flashback narrative. The film concludes in present-day New York with a conventional happy ending culminating in reconciliation, love, and marriage.

Rosenstrasse as "Heritage" Film

In many ways *Rosenstrasse* can be considered a German "heritage" film, with carefully constructed, historically accurate mise-en-scène and costumes, well-known German actors, high production values, a fairly traditional classical narrative, and closure. Against the background of the Holocaust, German heritage films of the 1990s, such as *The Harmonists* (1997), *Aimée and Jaguar* (1999), and *Gloomy Sunday* (1999), tend to offer a celebratory rather than an investigative depiction of the past.[9] Whereas British heritage films of the 1980s were often criticized for their conservative ideology and nostalgic views of class-based, colonial, imperialist British society, German heritage films of the late 1990s provoke a different controversy among critics and scholars, since this mode of filmmaking, known for creating nostalgia for a lost past, is focused here on German-Jewish history, the Holocaust, and Nazi Germany. Thus German heritage films must "navigate a historical minefield," as Lutz Koepnick (2002: 51) put it. In *Rosenstrasse* von Trotta needed to reconcile contradictory imperatives as she attempted to both entertain her audience and authentically depict a controversial episode in the Nazi past.

Lutz Koepnick (2002: 52–57, 72) and Stephan Schindler (2007: 194–198) critiqued 1990s German heritage films for creating images of multicultural consensus in which Jewish and non-Jewish Germans share a harmonious common past; the film narratives tend to elide the distinct experiences of these groups during pre-Nazi and Nazi Germany, obscuring the fact that Jews and non-Jews suffered very different traumas, losses, and memories. On one level at least, *Rosenstrasse* can be interpreted as reinforcing the theme of Jewish–German harmony with its emphasis on German women in 1943 protesting out of love and loyalty for the release of their German Jewish husbands. Indeed, in his article on philo-Semitism in recent German film, Stuart Taberner (2005: 356–366) maintains that *Rosenstrasse* attempts to invoke a nineteenth-century ideal of assimilation in creating what he calls a "German-Jewish symbiosis" in the film's narrative and characters.

Nonetheless, I would argue that von Trotta's flashback structure suggests an alternative reading, one that adds another dimension to the genre by emphasizing two different levels of suffering experienced by Jewish and non-Jewish Germans in the Nazi era. Von Trotta attempts through flashbacks to depict two distinct experiences of memory for survivors of the Third Reich.[10] The first is lived by the Jewish victims, represented by the survivor Ruth, and expressed in her repression of her painful past as well as in sporadic flashbacks of her memories of those traumatic days in 1943. The second kind of memory is articulated by Lena and represents the recollection of non-Jewish Germans who lived through the war; this is revealed in flashbacks from Lena's point of view and in her account of her story to Ruth's daughter Hannah 60 years later.

Memory, Trauma, and the Melodramatic in *Rosenstrasse*

Some critics disregarded the film's potential for revealing distinct experiences of suffering and trauma among Jewish and non-Jewish Germans during the Holocaust; they simply derided the contemporary story as contrived, melodramatic, and superfluous (see Heine, 2003; Tilmann, 2003; Zander, 2003a; Stäheli, 2003; Kaufmann, 2004). Indeed, several film critics have labeled *Rosenstrasse* either pejoratively or positively as melodrama, a popular film style that most critics have disapproved of since the beginnings of cinema (see Göttler, 2003; Heine, 2003; Dargis, 2004). *Rosenstrasse* is not the first film in which von Trotta integrates melodramatic conventions in the constructions of her political, psychological dramas. In *Marianne and Julianne*, for instance, as Marc Silberman (1995: 202) explains, "von Trotta combines conventional melodramatic coding with radical political issues, translating ideological dilemmas into private predicaments." Von Trotta could be seen as following a tradition set by Fassbinder of utilizing Hollywood-style melodrama in such films as *The Bitter Tears of Petra von Kant* (1972) and *Ali: Fear Eats the Soul* (1974), a tendency motivated by Fassbinder's admiration of Hollywood director Douglas Sirk and by his desire to develop a popular yet critical cinema that would attract state funding as rules shifted to favor films with box-office draw over artistic innovation and social criticism.[11]

Melodrama is a complex and confusing term because although it has a long tradition in popular culture, it has accrued a wide variety of connotations over the years, mostly negative (Mayne, 1990: 358). Traditional melodramatic codes from nineteenth-century theater include sentimentality, spectacle, moral polarities, suffering victims, evil villains, music for dramatic effect, and a happy or satisfying end (see Rahill, 1967: xiv; Gledhill, 1987: 6–36; Mayne, 1990: 358–359). Linda Williams's evocative study on race and melodrama offers a useful point of departure for this analysis. Williams defines melodrama as a mode of "moving pictures" (2001: 12) that encompasses a variety of media across centuries in an attempt to address contemporary moral questions. Instead of condemning melodrama as hopelessly regressive and overly sentimental, Williams hails it as "a perpetually modernizing form that can neither be clearly opposed to the norms of the 'classical' nor to the norms of realism" (2001: 12). Williams argues that while one cannot claim that melodrama prevails in all popular films, one can say "that the mode of melodrama drives the production of a great variety of familiar film genres" (2001: 23). Williams's (2001: 24–26) description of melodrama, with its various combinations of pathos and action as well as its emphasis on recognizing virtue and on the innocent suffering victim or victim-hero, can easily be applied to many modern Holocaust films.[12] Certainly a large number of recent American and European films about the Holocaust can be classified as melodramas, including most of the German heritage films of the past fifteen years.

Von Trotta's use of melodramatic conventions in *Rosenstrasse*, including family drama, suffering victims, pathos, active victim-protagonists, and strong heroines, supports her emphasis on the significance of memory and the different levels of trauma suffered by Jewish and non-Jewish Germans in Nazi Germany, an emphasis that is in turn integrally related to the narrative structure of the film. While some critics complained of the overwrought emotions expressed in the contemporary frame narrative, an element commonly associated with melodrama, others skewered the film for omitting the story of the Jewish German internees in the last two years of the Nazi regime following their release in 1943 (see Heine, 2003; Stäheli,

2003; Tilmann, 2003; Zander, 2003a). The narrative structure of the film focuses almost exclusively on two time periods: the week-long protest from February 27 to March 6, 1943 and the weeks following Ruth's husband's death in 2001. The ellipsis between the shots of Ruth's impassive, expressionless face in her New York apartment as a widow and the flashbacks to her mother's internment at Rosenstrasse, for example, excludes almost all information of Ruth's life in those intervening 60 years, with the exception of brief verbal references to her journey to live with her aunt in America in 1946 and her marriage to a Jewish American professor, who, as she put it, "saved" her. Viewers know from the current story only that Ruth has two children and that she is mourning her recently deceased husband. The flashbacks are triggered by the trauma of her husband's death, thus establishing a narrative and emotional connection between the repressed traumatic memory of her mother's death in the Holocaust and her contemporary grief.

Ruth's memories are broken, disruptive, painful, and visual rather than verbal; her flashbacks picture scenes of her last meeting with her mother at the center on Rosenstrasse, of fleeing and hiding from the Nazis during the roundup of German Jews, and of watching as Lena discovers the body of Klara, one of the women of the Rosenstrasse protest, who committed suicide after her Jewish husband was deported. Ruth's flashbacks focus on her traumatic memories of fear, death, and the agonizing loss of her mother, her home, and familial stability, memories of a past she has suppressed and refuses to share with her children. Tellingly, the narrative structure does not depict Ruth recounting her story to her daughter; instead Hannah actively seeks out the German woman who can tell her mother's story. Hannah serves as surrogate in excavating the memories of her mother's experiences and in coming to terms with Jewish survivors' experiences in Nazi Germany during the Holocaust.

Whereas Ruth rejects any opportunity to verbally articulate her past, Lena willingly expresses her memories in interviews with Ruth's daughter Hannah, who preserves Lena's voice on a tape recorder, thereby signifying a validation of witness testimony to fill in the gaps left by her mother's silence. Lena's remembered actions, offered in dialogue and voiceovers as well as flashbacks, encompass her entire experience, pain and triumph, pride, determination, and desperation. Her recollections include the happier times of 1932 with Fabian and the solidarity she shared with the women protesting on Rosenstrasse as well as her relationship with little Ruth. She speaks openly about the past and at the end of her story she focuses on the victory and joy of her husband Fabian's release (Wydra, 2003: 18). Lena's memories are those of a non-Jewish German woman who, despite her hardships during the Third Reich and her marriage to a Jewish man, did not directly experience the overwhelming fear and loss that Ruth felt following the arrest and deportation of her mother.

Although von Trotta's melodramatic structure is effective in evoking viewer empathy as well as fostering a sense of the differing types of experiences and memories of Jewish and non-Jewish German survivors and the ramifications for their lives, it simultaneously exposes a disconcerting aspect of Holocaust heritage melodramas. In an article on "The Victim's Voice and Melodramatic Aesthetics in History," Amos Goldberg discusses historian Charles Maier's (2000) theory of two competing moral narratives of the twentieth century, one focusing on the Holocaust and/or Communist massacres and the other highlighting the devastating effects of colonialism and its legacy (see Maier, 2000: 826–831; Goldberg, 2009). Goldberg (2009: 234) argues that these narratives were interconnected in the 1950s and 1960s, but they have now split into two distinct approaches, in which the postcolonial account remains critical of Western democratic societies for continuing to support a racist politics of global hegemony, violence, and cultural domination, whereas the Holocaust has acquired the features of "a reassuring narrative." In this view, the Holocaust narrative is characterized by moral polarities and the image of the Nazis as the "bad guys" who destroyed everything, as opposed to the capitalist industrialized countries of the West representing the "good guys" who are committed to defending freedom and democracy.

The problematic of a melodramatic approach to the Holocaust for Goldberg is the kind of identification it tends to foster and the ensuing messages. "It is so easy to identify with the Jewish victim when the Jews – collectively and many times individually – are no longer the victims of history but rather powerful historical agents, and to silence any empathy toward currently suffering victims – an empathy that demands moral and political strength and a far more courageous and complex engagement" (Goldberg, 2009: 234). Despite von Trotta's careful attempts at creating a more complex picture of remembering and repressing the Nazi past, *Rosenstrasse*, with its melodramatic stereotyping of Nazi characters and its depiction of emotional intensity evoked by Ruth's repressed memories and past trauma, ultimately constructs a narrative that can be read as reassuring in its often Manichean juxtaposition of evil Nazis with the "good" Germans and Jews who were victims of the National Socialist regime. The empathy evoked is directed specifically at historical suffering of Jewish victims, and tends to prevent any interrogation of historical and political conditions that helped pave the way for the fascist regime and ensuing genocide.

Von Trotta as Feminist Filmmaker?

Like most of von Trotta's films, *Rosenstrasse* is a film told mainly from a female perspective, with a feminist focus on strong women struggling against injustice and adversity. In von Trotta's earlier films, as Marc Silberman (1995: 201) points out, a "network of doublings, parallels, and mirrorings among the women characters became a dominant structural pattern ..." *Rosenstrasse*, by contrast, presents a network of couplings, juxtapositions, and intergenerational pairings among women in familial or pseudofamilial relationships, enhanced by the complexity of the narrative structure and the emphasis on remembering. Connections among women are key in this film; the flashbacks (the past of the film) highlight relationships between the young Ruth and Lena and bonds among the protestors on Rosenstrasse through images of determined women standing together, comforting each other, sharing tea, and linking arms in resistance to Nazi threats. The contemporary story of the rapport between the elderly Lena and Ruth's daughter Hannah stresses female understanding across generations, while Lena's recollections stimulate compassion in Hannah for her mother's suffering as a child, thereby strengthening the mother–daughter relationship. Von Trotta's focus on memory and the flashback frame function to produce intergenerational solidarity among the female protagonists, contributing to a "feminist re-vision" of present and past.

After four decades, feminist film scholars have yet to agree on what establishes a film as "feminist." In a 1988 article on von Trotta's *Marianne and Juliane*, E. Ann Kaplan distinguished between film narratives that concentrate on women, their relationships, and their political struggles on the one hand, and films that question female representation as such, that is, the patriarchal construction of the "feminine," on the other. She referred to the former type of feminist film as "realist" and "essentialist" in its approach and to the latter as "antirealist" (Kaplan, 1988: 260–262). Although Kaplan defined von Trotta as a realist feminist film-maker, she argued that in *Marianne and Juliane* von Trotta exceeded the limitations of realist narrative structures by utilizing unsettling cinematic techniques, such as complicated flashbacks, that attempt to create distance in order to question "the construction of the family, the feminine, and terrorism" (1988: 262).

In her inquiries into the relationship between feminism and cinema, Annette Kuhn (1993: 5–8) discusses the concept of a feminist film or text in *Women's Pictures* as a feminist "intervention in culture." She asks, "Is the feminism of a piece of work there because of attributes of its author (cultural interventions by women), because of certain attributes of the work itself (feminist cultural interventions), or because of the way it is 'read'?" (p. 8). Kuhn's analysis emphasizes the significance of the film's spectators; she argues that the feminism of a text cannot be determined simply through its characteristics or through the author's intentions alone, but also through the readings and reception of the text (p. 16).

Kuhn's focus on the importance of reception is particularly relevant to von Trotta's films, since feminist critics have differed on interpretations of her work for decades. Susan Linville (1998: 92), for instance, unequivocally described *Marianne and Juliane* as "formally and thematically feminist and deconstructive." As noted, E. Ann Kaplan (1988) described the film as realist with feminist tendencies, while Charlotte Delorme (1981) attacked it and von Trotta as nonfeminist in her polemic review for *Frauen und Film*.

Von Trotta herself denied affiliation with *Frauenfilm* ("women's film") or feminist cinema early on, presumably in order to gain acceptance from a mainstream audience upon the release of her first solo feature film, *The Second*

Awakening of Christa Klages (Ward, 1995: 53). Von Trotta's efforts to distance herself from feminist filmmakers, including an unfortunate reference to women's cinema as a "thought ghetto" in a 1978 interview, might have contributed to the mixed reception of her later films by feminist critics, according to Jenifer Ward (1995: 53–54). Barbara Quart in her book on women directors hesitated to label von Trotta's films in what she considered inflexible feminist terms. "Still one is reluctant to call hers either a women's or a feminist cinema: she does far more than merely center on women characters, and yet, while she raises issues that are feminist, one hesitates to sum up her cinema with a word that suggests something ideological, programmatic (however appealing the ideology and the program)" (Quart, 1988: 93–94). Quart described von Trotta's films as "a women's cinema, *and* a feminist cinema, and more than these" (1988: 94). Susan Linville (1998: 161n9) commented that Quart's appreciative critique of the director nonetheless projects a limited understanding of feminism as ideologically rigid, a public perception that had undoubtedly exerted pressure on von Trotta to choose between feminist cinema and a mainstream audience at the beginning of her filmmaking career.

Despite her earlier reservations, in the past twenty years von Trotta has publicly acknowledged the female perspective of her films. While explaining in 2003 how her fascination with the actions of the women of Rosenstrasse led her to add yet another film centering on female protagonists to her repertoire, von Trotta rather ironically calls her almost exclusive cinematic focus on women her "prison": "And the fact that it was *women* who protested is connected once again to a personal point of view: my films are really mostly about women, that is *my* prison."[13] Certainly the strong feminist underpinnings of von Trotta's films are noted in numerous studies of her work.[14] Due to their interrogations of female subjectivity and identity construction within the patriarchal structures of German society, I would categorize von Trotta's earlier films (*The Second Awakening of Christa Klages*; *Sisters, or the Balance of Happiness* (1979); *Marianne and Juliane*; *Sheer Madness*) as feminist realist narratives.[15] However, the feminist aspects of *Rosenstrasse* seem more superficial and less integral to the structure of the film and the questions it explores. Indeed, *Rosenstrasse*, with its emphasis on active female protagonists, women's memories as witnesses and survivors, female solidarity, and intergenerational relationships among women, might be better described as a "woman-centered" film with feminist tendencies, in this case a rather problematical hybrid, an historically questionable, melodramatically structured "feminist re-vision," as will be discussed below.

In contrast to the disorienting flashback structure in *Marianne and Juliane*, which disrupts the linear development of the narrative, thus "opening up for her audience an ambiguous, intersubjective space of mourning," as Susan Linville (1998: 92) puts it, von Trotta created the flashback frame in *Rosenstrasse* to be much more comprehensible to the viewer, with clearer demarcations of time and location achieved through muted colors and softer lenses in the shots of the past, thus adhering more closely to classic narrative conventions of German heritage melodrama. As in her earlier film, however, von Trotta interrupts the flow of the story to reconstruct personal history in contentious political times through the frequent intercutting of scenes from the past and present, here mostly through Lena's point of view, and occasionally through Ruth's perspective. Von Trotta's flashback frame in *Rosenstrasse* is still complex and demanding, and *potentially* creates a space within which the characters and the film's spectators can reflect on connections between present and past, on the significance of memory, and on the importance of women's courage and solidarity in resisting injustice.

Trotta's "Feminist Re-visions" and Use of Melodrama in *Rosenstrasse*

In one of the flashback sequences at the end of Lena's story of the protest, von Trotta heightens the pathos of the experience by telescoping the releases of the internees to one day on March 6. The scene in question shows the women in the crowd on Rosenstrasse as individuals in sequential medium shots and close-ups being reunited with their husbands or children. Near the end of the scene the flashback juxtaposes a tender close-up of Lena and Fabian's joyful reunion as he is released with a high-angle long-shot of the eight-year-old Ruth and Lena's brother Arthur waiting all alone in vain outside the door on Rosenstrasse long after the others have left. The high-angle shot of the two looking at the blank windows accentuates Ruth's vulnerability, isolation, and hopelessness and then cuts to a medium profile shot as she asks Arthur "And my mommy? When is my mommy coming?"[16] The camera then pans through the upper story window to a view of an empty room of the detention center, throwing into relief the absence of Ruth's mother. The following shot is bridged by the elderly Lena's voice describing the release of the internees to Hannah as a victory, albeit "a small ray of light in the darkness." The scene cuts to a close-up of Hannah's stricken face as she wonders aloud what Ruth must have felt when her mother failed to appear. Ruth's daughter Hannah reacts to Lena's memories from the Jewish German survivor's perspective; she identifies with her mother and responds with horror and pain to the story of her mother's loss. Lena looked upon that period with pride and satisfaction, whereas to Ruth it was a time of overwhelming sadness, fear, and grief, which she needed to repress in order to survive.

Von Trotta's "feminist re-vision" of the Rosenstrasse protest shows the triumph of the intermarried German women from Lena's perspective while simultaneously using melodramatic codes of suffering and emotional intensity in Hannah's reaction to Lena's story, thus highlighting differences between Jewish and non-Jewish women's experiences in Nazi Germany. However, some have argued that von Trotta is rewriting history with regard to the women's influence in gaining the release of their family members, as Gruner (2005a) and Meyer (2004: 35) point out; the film narrative seems to be supporting Stoltzfus's interpretation that the solidarity of these women was responsible for forcing Goebbels's hand and changing Nazi policy in this instance. In any case, von Trotta's feminist focus on female agency tends to emphasize a rather romanticized notion of the non-Jewish German women characters' courage, strength, and determination in standing up to the Nazis and thereby saving their Jewish family members from deportation and death.

As a German director consciously constructing a commercially viable Holocaust melodrama that would sensitively depict Jewish experiences in Nazi Germany and the subsequent genocide, von Trotta fictionalized details of survivors' accounts in her film, privileging stories that added drama and pathos to the narrative. Historians such as Beate Meyer (2004: 26–36) and Wolfgang Benz (2003) condemned *Rosenstrasse*'s historical liberties as misleading falsehoods. Yet arguably most alterations were included to visually remind viewers that the majority of Jewish Germans arrested in the factory raids were sent to their deaths, even though the narrative centers on the intermarried German Jews and "Mischlinge" who were released. As a divorced intermarried Jewish German, it is not certain that Ruth's mother would have been transported to Auschwitz.[17] In addition, while the scene depicting her transfer to the deportation center at Levetzowstrasse all alone in a truck at night is historically improbable, it emphasizes the hopelessness of her situation, symbolizing the tragic fate of so many Jewish Germans who were transported to collection centers and then loaded onto trains to their deaths. The scene heightens the melodramatic pathos of her plight by focusing on her isolation and innocent suffering, in contrast to the heartless Nazis who ordered her deportation.

Similarly, the film depicts a group of intermarried Jewish German men who were sent from Rosenstrasse to Auschwitz in an emotionally intense scene showing the German wives swarming the truck as it pulls away. While the incident did actually occur, those intermarried Rosenstrasse internees were sent back to Germany two weeks later and spent the rest of the war in a work camp (Stoltzfus, 1996: 252–254; Gruner, 2005b: 166–172). Their return to Germany was not mentioned in the final version of the film, to the chagrin of historians such as Gruner, Benz, and Meyer; instead von Trotta wrote into the narrative the suicide of Klara, the wife of one of the deported men, thus emphasizing the despair of the victims and their families and increasing the melodramatic tone of the narrative. The unproduced second version of the script was more historically accurate in several instances, including a scene in which Klara receives notification that her husband Hans is being sent back from Auschwitz to a camp in Germany. The scene in this draft retains its emotional intensity and pathos, however, since the letter arrives too late, after Klara has already taken her own life (*Rosenstrasse*, 1995: 91). Von Trotta cut part of that scene in the final version, presumably sacrificing historical accuracy in favor of a contemporary narrative that stressed Jewish suffering and the significance of memory for Jewish survivors of the Holocaust. Scenes portraying representative experiences of Jewish Germans following the factory raids, such as a soldier threatening Fabian with a gun and the suicides of two young Jewish German women as they were being sorted at the main collection center, could be read as melodramatic clichés, and yet they illustrate the much higher level of distress, mortal danger, and fear that Jews experienced than their "Aryan" German relatives waiting outside.

Von Trotta also included a historically controversial scene near the end of the film in which Nazi officers set up machine guns aimed at the protesters, exaggerating the danger encountered by the non-Jewish German women on Rosenstrasse and contributing to the internal contradictions in the narrative text.[18] Obviously a part of her "feminist re-vision" and intended as a dramatic device to highlight the civic courage of the female protestors, a long slow pan shot of the women linking arms and of their expressive, determined faces emphasizes their bonds with each other in the face of deadly force. The scene establishes a connection between pathos and action, which Linda Williams (2001) terms a key aspect of melodrama. In this case action is defined by the defiance and resolve in the women's expressions and their stubborn presence on Rosenstrasse, accentuating female agency. In this scene the women on Rosenstrasse fulfill simultaneously the roles of what Williams calls the "virtuous sufferer and active hero" (Williams, 2001: 24). Indeed, scenes stressing the peril experienced by these women evoked the criticism that this is another typical rescue film celebrating noble gentile Germans saving helpless German Jews from the Nazis (Dargis, 2004).

Although *Rosenstrasse* includes a few of the seemingly obligatory Holocaust film shots of nameless masses in the deportation centers, the film introduces, albeit briefly, a nuanced depiction of several Jewish German internees as individuals rather than as anonymous victims. With few exceptions, most of those internees are portrayed as dignified and determined rather than weak and helpless. Von Trotta thus avoids the stereotype of Jewish protagonists as helpless victims, unlike her flat characterization of Nazi officers and guards (Seidel, 2003).

Ruth's mother Miriam, for example, appears in just a few scenes, and yet she is shown as primarily responsible for her daughter's survival. Miriam taught her child to hide from the Nazis, and when Ruth sneaks in to visit her mother at the Rosenstrasse center, Miriam gives the girl her ring for strength, telling her to find one of the women outside to take care of her. When the Gestapo discovers she is divorced, Miriam tells them she has a child, hoping it will lead to her release, but once she learns they intend to capture and deport her daughter as well, she lies about the child's whereabouts to protect her. Miriam's actions to save her child can be interpreted as another example of the melodramatic pairing of pathos and action in the same character, since Miriam is simultaneously innocent suffering victim and also active female protagonist within her very circumscribed situation as internee. Miriam also exemplifies Wolf Gruner's (1995b: 81–82) assertion in his book on Rosenstrasse to the effect that the many Jewish Germans who resisted Nazi persecution by fleeing, or in this case by helping a child to escape, belie the conventional image of Jews in Nazi Germany as passive victims.

Masculine Identity in *Rosenstrasse*

Von Trotta's efforts to reconcile her complex approach to memory and narrative structure with the need to create an accessible, popular film complete with happy end resulted in an internally contradictory text marked by rhetorical ambiguity and historical license, sparking critical controversy. For example, Lena's claim in *Rosenstrasse* that German Jewish men were gentle prompted conflicting readings of the film. Several Holocaust film scholars such as Esther Fuchs (2003: 84), Judith Doneson (1997: 144–147), and Sara Horowitz (1997: 126–127, 131) have remarked on the trend in many Holocaust feature films of depicting Jewish German males as passive, weak, and effeminate in comparison to their non-Jewish counterparts. In *Rosenstrasse*, however, I would argue that German Jewish men appear as humane and nonaggressive, but not weak; they are determined to survive, but as dignified human beings. Indeed the depiction of kind German Jewish men in von Trotta's text can be read as a feminist attempt to negotiate a new type of masculine identity in opposition to the images of aggressive, violent masculinity valorized by the Nazis, in effect another facet of her "feminist re-vision" of the historical conditions in the film.

While Lena's husband Fabian is not a dominant character, his appearances in the film focus on his musical talent and love for Lena in the 1932 scenes and on his dignity, compassion, and helpfulness following his arrest and internment in 1943. Fabian responds to threatened violence with perseverance and assists a young girl at the sorting center before they are both transferred with the others to Rosenstrasse. Fabian is portrayed as tender and sensitive but not as weak or effeminate. Another German Jewish character turns himself in at the center on Rosenstrasse to look after his daughter, thus revealing both courage and the desire to protect his child. A glaring exception to this pattern is the scene of Fabian's parents at the deportation center on Levetzowstrasse, where Fabian's coughing, physically fragile father says that he will never make it, while Fabian's mother asserts bravely, "I can work for both of us." This episode contradicts images of Jews in earlier scenes and, along with Lena's description of Jewish males as "gentle," led to charges that the film stereotyped German Jewish men as weak in contrast to strong Jewish and non-Jewish women (see *Film und Kritik*, 2003; Dargis, 2004; Meyer, 2004: 36).

Von Trotta's depiction of sensitive, courageous, nonviolent males also includes the one positively portrayed, prominent non-Jewish German male protagonist in the film, Lena's brother Arthur von Eschenbach, who was wounded in Stalingrad. Arthur represents the "other" kind of German typical of many German Holocaust films. Despite his status as a German officer returning from the front and often shown in uniform, he is a nonthreatening male. Arthur is caring, nonviolent, and supportive of his sister's marriage to the Jewish Fabian; he is aware and highly critical of Nazi atrocities. Through the Jewish German male protagonists and Lena's brother Arthur, von Trotta's "feminist re-vision" favors an antiviolent, nonaggressive, and sensitive depiction of masculinity in contrast to the National Socialist ideology of gender dichotomies.

The Nazis in *Rosenstrasse* are flat, stereotyped characters, typical of Holocaust melodramas. In addition they are almost exclusively male; they are mean, contemptuous, and aggressive. Patriarchy, masculinity, violence, and antisemitism are presented in the film as the foundations of National Socialism; there are no female guards or Nazi women in uniform and the few scenes showing callous antisemitic female neighbors in the second draft of the script were omitted in the final version of the film. In contrast, Lena's father, Baron von Eschenbach, appears as an ardent Nazi supporter and antisemite who has disowned his daughter for marrying a Jewish German. The few ambivalent non-Jewish German men are minor characters, such as the sympathetic policeman guarding the door at Rosenstrasse and the boss of Klara, one of the intermarried German women.

Rosenstrasse graphically dramatizes the incredible pressure that intermarried non-Jewish German women experienced in Nazi Germany, and yet the only instance in the film of a divorced intermarried German Jew is Ruth's mother, Miriam, who was sent to Auschwitz. As Lena tells Ruth's daughter Hannah of her grandmother's deportation, she counters Hannah's horror and condemnation with a defense of Miriam's husband, saying "Maybe he wasn't so awful, Hannah. Maybe he was just weak. Many men couldn't take the pressure. After all they would have had to give up their careers." In her article "Geschichte im Film," Beate Meyer argues that von Trotta's depiction of Ruth's mother, Miriam, an inter-married Jew who was divorced by her "Aryan" husband, is historically misleading. According to Meyer's research in Hamburg, more women than men divorced their Jewish German spouses. Meyer (2004: 27, 35–36) maintained that von Trotta thus projects the weakness of the German women who succumbed to pressure to end their marriages onto the intermarried German men in the film. While von Trotta's depiction of the loyal women of Rosenstrasse underscores the significance of female agency and solidarity in fighting injustice, Lena's statements about Miriam's ex-husband also exalt the strong, brave non-Jewish German women in mixed marriages in contrast with weaker, cowardly non-Jewish German men. This contributed to the controversy surrounding the film, and was construed by some as an example of essentialism and tendentiousness, typical critiques of cultural products with overt feminist messages (see *Film und Kritik*, 2003; Meyer 2004). Indeed, film critic Manohla Dargis (2004) accuses von Trotta of "twisting history into ideology" and resorting to "unhappy stereotypes" while adding to the number of rescue films showing Gentiles saving Jews from the Holocaust. Arguably, the film could be criticized for an allegoricality that is particularly problematic within the current context of our post-9/11 world, in which conservatives misappropriated and misused mainstream feminist arguments to defend an attack on Afghanistan as a way to "rescue" Afghan women from the Taliban, thereby implicitly labeling all Islam as inherently patriarchal and oppressive, and advancing a disingenuous pretext for war (see Ayotte and Husain, 2005).

Female Agency within the Patriarchy in *Rosenstrasse*

Undeniably, strong, determined women who resist the Nazis dominate the narrative. The proud, confident, aristocratic Lena is the major protagonist and active heroine; yet Nathan's wife Frau Goldberg emerges as the most resourceful and courageous of the protestors. She is the first to speak to Lena, advising her to approach the only sympathetic policeman present to find out whether Fabian is inside the building, and it is she who voices her discontent and begins the chant "I want my husband back." The other women follow her lead, showing perseverance, determination, and loyalty.

Meyer (2004: 35–36) accuses von Trotta of superimposing feminist notions from the 1970s women's movement onto the film's fictional storyline. Meyer argues that von Trotta created a feminist utopian myth through her emphasis on female solidarity, resistance, courage, and loyalty. She maintains that the women on Rosenstrasse are shown successfully confronting "a National Socialist regime marked by masculine brutality," thus saving their spouses, in contrast to weak German men who supposedly abandoned their Jewish wives in droves (p. 35).[19]

Contrary to Meyer's contention, however, von Trotta's film does not merely *project* modern feminist concepts of female independence, empowerment, and solidarity upon the historical narrative. Instead von Trotta's depiction of the women of Rosenstrasse places them firmly *within* the existing patriarchal structure in Nazi Germany of the 1940s, which stressed the importance of family and personal loyalty over women's participation in politics or public policy-making. In von Trotta's narrative, the women stood together on Rosenstrasse to protect their own families; their sole purpose in public protest was to preserve the sanctity and wholeness of their private, domestic sphere. In order to achieve this goal, they needed to make a public statement, to bear witness and confront policemen and Nazi officers in a public place. The film thus echoes interviews with eyewitnesses recalling the Rosenstrasse events, who asserted that they acted merely to support their husbands and children (Stoltzfus, 1996: 230). These women were not shown as acting on political principle, that is, they were not fighting the Nazis out of political conviction or to combat antisemitism in general, but simply to protect their husbands and families.

Female agency is a significant element in the film, and yet almost all the female protagonists are married and their efforts are centered on caring for their families; their actions are determined and circumscribed by their domestic circumstances. In other words, von Trotta emerges here as a realist filmmaker in her representation of women's place within the patriarchy of 1940s Germany. Von Trotta's "feminist re-vision" of the events valorizes antiviolent masculinity and extols the personal and political power of women's connections. In addition, as von Trotta explains, she was fascinated by the contradiction between the many female National Socialist supporters on the one hand, and the intermarried German women who defied the Nazis in defense of their Jewish husbands on the other (Wydra, 2003: 17; Wiebel, 2003: 12). The film thus exalts the protesters' subversive expression of loyalty, typically a Nazi feminine virtue, as the women fight for their husbands' release.

The Controversy of the Goebbels Scene

Undoubtedly the most controversial and hotly debated element of the narrative is the totally fictional scene in which a desperate Lena tries to flirt with Goebbels at a film premiere party. Goebbels lecherously looks on as Lena plays the piano; meanwhile her brother's attempt to talk to the propaganda minister about the protest on Rosenstrasse is rebuffed. The camera focuses on Lena's discomfort under Goebbels's penetrating gaze and then cuts to a shot of Lena, fully clothed, sitting on the side of the bed where she had changed into her evening gown, with a tear coursing down her cheek. Numerous critics interpreted the scene as indicating that Lena had sexual intercourse with Goebbels in order to save her husband, condemning it as outrageous historical kitsch (see Benz, 2003; Olbert, 2003; Hornaday, 2004; Kaufmann, 2004).[20] The American version of the DVD promotes this interpretation in its chapter titles by labeling the Goebbels scene "Lena's sacrifice." I believe, however, that a closer look at the costuming and mise-en-scène reveals that Lena did not sleep with Goebbels, since she is wearing a tightly fitted floor-length gown that buttons down the back, which her brother Arthur has to help her unfasten. This interpretation is confirmed by interviews with von Trotta in which she explains the protagonist's tears as signifying Lena's humiliation and lack of success in freeing her husband.[21]

In the Goebbels scene *Rosenstrasse* offers a fascinating example of disconnect between the author's intentions and the public reception of a text. Thus to some (e.g. Benz, 2003; Kaspar, 2003), von Trotta seems to undermine her own feminist focus on female agency through this ambiguously structured episode, thereby contributing to the controversy surrounding the film. However the contradictions and alternative readings lead to interesting questions. Is it crucial that the women's protest led to the release of the Rosenstrasse internees? Or would the courage, solidarity, and defiance of these women achieve their dramatic effect whether their relatives' freedom was the result of their efforts or not, as Gruner maintains in his book?[22] If the focal point of the film is the protest itself, as a brave public action against injustice and genocide, it would not matter whether the ambiguous Goebbels scene were interpreted as a sacrifice resulting in the release of the Jewish Germans. The significant point would be the strength, loyalty, and solidarity of these women and the dignity of their family members. Regardless of how the Goebbels scene is interpreted, however, it detracts from the focus on female solidarity and civic courage in the film by concentrating on Lena's individual actions rather than on the women's collective protest. Indeed, the scene can be read as undermining the film's alleged commitment to socopolitical protest through its muddled messages, thus adding to its internal contradictions and ambiguities.

Closure in *Rosenstrasse* – The Problematic Happy End

Von Trotta's narrative compromises to appeal to a mass audience are most evident in her embrace of a typical melodramatic convention, a convenient happy end, which was condemned by many critics (see e.g. Seidel, 2003; Stäheli, 2003; Tilmann, 2003). The film concludes shortly after Hannah's return to New York where in one brief scene she is shown reconciling with her mother followed by the final shots of Hannah and Luis's Jewish wedding. This emphasis on closure undermines the director's aim to inspire viewers to reflect on different kinds of memory for Jewish and non-Jewish German survivors as well as the devastating impact of repressing memories. Ultimately Ruth's voice is overshadowed in the text, first by the dominance of Lena's voice and recollections throughout the film and secondly by the rushed ending which tends to obscure the difficult task of mourning and of resolving ruptured relationships. Indeed, Ruth's role as Jewish survivor/witness actively recalling her memories to reconstruct and come to terms with her past is usurped by Lena and by Hannah, who serves as a surrogate for her mother in working through and mourning her traumatic past. Von Trotta intended to explore memory and recovery of experiences for Jewish and non-Jewish Germans during the Third Reich, but the conclusion of her film renounced an ending that could evoke interrogation and discomfort rather than reconciliation and closure.

The ending rings hollow with many critics, because, unlike von Trotta's earlier films, such as *Marianne and Juliane*, the flashback narrative structure does not adequately depict the reconstruction or working through of the past by the protagonist who is depicted as most damaged by her grief, pain, and loss, that is, Ruth. Ruth as an adult remains an enigma, signified by her impassive expressions throughout most of the film. When Hannah returns from Berlin with the ring that Ruth's mother had given the child in Rosenstrasse and that the little girl had thrown at Lena's feet when she was forced to leave for America to live with her aunt, Ruth's process of working through her grief and trauma as well as her ability to overcome her objections to her daughter's marriage to the non-Jewish Luis are elided into one gesture of taking her mother's ring from her daughter and immediately returning it to Hannah with a smile to signify that the ring will once again "make her dreams come true." The scene then cuts abruptly to Hannah and Luis's wedding in Ruth's apartment.

One could argue that the ending was intended as a resourceful effort to resist commodification of the Holocaust through an emphasis on closure and resolution rather than openness and ambiguity. As Ginsberg (2007: 25) points out, Holocaust discourse devoted to critical ambivalence and open debate can inadvertently "condone efforts to keep the issue a lucrative one," thereby contributing to its cultural commodification. Ultimately, this attempt at resolution was unsuccessful because of the internal contradictions and ambiguous narrative structure that suppressed the adult Ruth's voice and character in the film.

Conclusion

Von Trotta faced the challenge of creating an entertaining film from a terribly tragic subject, a task made more difficult by her focus on events already steeped in historical controversy and most clearly articulated in the Gruner–Stoltzfus debate. *Rosenstrasse* is a film caught between art and commerce, but largely devoid of social criticism. Von Trotta's film is determined by the difficulty of her situation; she is keenly aware of her responsibility as a German director to depict experiences of German Jews in the Holocaust and its effects on survivors authentically and fairly. As a consequence she attempted to achieve through a flashback structure and melodramatic form what most German heritage films have been accused as lacking: a moving depiction and simultaneously a critical interrogation of the different levels of suffering, experiences, and distinct memories of Jewish and non-Jewish Germans of the Holocaust and the Nazi German past. Simultaneously her efforts to sensitively portray Jewish persecution and annihilation during World War Two result in stressing the particularity of the Holocaust as a uniquely Jewish tragedy with traumatic ramifications for Jews in the present, which precludes giving sufficient attention to experiences of any other victims of the Nazis.

Von Trotta's emphasis on the particularity of Jewish suffering during the Holocaust is at least potentially susceptible to political misuse in the present. While her intentions may be laudable, the function and consequences of the director's revisionist approach are problematic. As Terri Ginsberg argues in *Holocaust Film*, the horrendous fate of so many Jews in the Holocaust has been misused to defend Israeli foreign policy in the Middle East and to justify denial of Israel's brutal treatment of the Palestinans. Through its relentless message of Jewish suffering and the traumatic impact of repressed memory on survivors, *Rosenstrasse* may be inadvertently giving validity to this kind of dissimulated denial.

Von Trotta's "feminist re-visions," designed to draw attention to an historical act of women's civic courage in the Nazi era, resulted in an ambitious, emotionally intense, complex film that is nonetheless marred by internal contradictions, rhetorical ambiguities, and confusing messages. Von Trotta's film certainly reached a mass audience and stimulated discussion, but whether it achieved its full potential as an effective, moving, reflective heritage film about the Holocaust will be a matter of continuing debate.

I wish to thank Ann Le Bar, Roderick Stackelberg, Terri Ginsberg, and Andrea Mensch for their valuable support and helpful suggestions for this chapter.

Notes

1   Of the numerous reviews and media articles on the film and its reception, see especially Benz, 2003; Kaspar, 2003; Kellerhoff, 2003; Nord, 2003; "Regisseurin von Trotta," 2003; Schlosser, 2003; Seidel, 2003; Stoltzfus, 2003; Tilmann, 2003; Dargis, 2004; *Rosenstrasse-Forum*, 2004; O'Sullivan, 2004; Thomas, 2004.

2   Gruner (2005b: 142–156) argues for a rather modest, quiet demonstration of 150–200 family members, whereas Stoltzfus (1996: 223–243) describes growing numbers throughout the week and cites a witness who recalls 1000 shouting protestors.

3   Stoltzfus's research is presented in his dissertation as well as in several articles and in his 1996 book, *Resistance of the Heart,* while Wolf Gruner first proposed his thesis on the reasons for the release of the intermarried German Jews in his dissertation and in articles in the 1990s and developed it later in a 2002 essay and in his 2005 book, *Widerstand in der Rosenstrasse.* A number of historians joined the discussion and interpretation of the Rosenstrasse protest in 2003–2004, but since Gruner and Stoltzfus represent the two major standpoints of the debate, I will focus on their views as articulated in their books and articles. See also Jochheim, 2002; Meyer, 2004; Leugers, 2005; Prause, 2005; Schröder, 2003.

4   The translation of *Die Welt's* paraphrase of von Trotta's interview is mine. The whole passage reads: "'Zu sagen, das war so und so, war gar nicht meine Absicht.' Unabhängig davon, weshalb die Gefangenen in der Rosenstrasse letztlich freigelassen wurden, gehe es darum, die einzelnen Erfahrungen der Zeitzeuginnen lebendig werden zu lassen" ("Regisseurin von Trotta," 2003).

5   The literature on debates among Holocaust historians concerning the merits of documentation versus witness testimony is extensive and daunting. As James E. Young (1997: 23–24) points out, witness testimonies have traditionally been discounted by historians as unreliable and limited due to their subjectivity. Certainly the validity accorded documents is evident in much of the current historical research on the 1943 Rosenstrasse protest. Nonetheless, in recent years witness testimonies have been recognized by some scholars, historians, and the public as legitimately adding victim's voices to a historical narrative long dependent on documents that represent mainly the perpetrators' perspectives. The scales often seem tipped in favor of the eyewitness and individual experience in twenty-first-century popular culture, a trend that is seen in recent Holocaust narratives as well (see Goldberg, 2009: 222–229). In addition discussions in Holocaust historiography on memory and documentation have been influenced by debates related to postmodern questions concerning historical objectivity, history as narrative and representation, and the relativity of truth. Examples of a few texts on these various historiographical debates include: Friedländer, 1992, 2000; Braun, 1994; Kansteiner, 1994; Lang, 1995; Young, 1997; Moeller, 2002; Rothberg and Stark, 2003; Goldberg, 2009.

  With regard to historical research of the Rosenstrasse events, Gruner (2005a) and Meyer (2004: 22–34) affirm the priority of documentation, whereas Nathan Stoltzfus

(2005) tends to approach National Socialist documents with skepticism. He perceives eyewitness accounts as offering more plausible insights into real-life experiences of the Holocaust. Such a perspective seems questionable to historians such as Meyer, who sees survivor testimony as one of the most complex types of historical sources. In addition to works by historians, two German monographs from the 1990s devoted to witness reports and testimony on the Rosenstrasse events have been influential in contributing to the collective memory in the Federal Republic of the 1943 protest; see Jochheim, 2002; and Schröder, 2003.

Of course the most significant and divisive historiographical debate in Germany on interpretations of National Socialism and the Holocaust was the so-called *Historikerstreit* of the mid-1980s. On the *Historikerstreit*, see Evans, 1989; Baldwin, 1990; Knowlton and Cates, 1993; Maier, 1998.

6 *Rosenstrasse* (1995). I wish to thank Nathan Stoltzfus for generously making a copy of this script available to me.

7 See Meek (2010: 135–137) for an explanation of this point, in which he refers in particular to Shoshana Felman's discussion of Claude Lanzmann's *Shoah*. Meek's analysis of empathy in mass media representations is also relevant here. As he points out, Adorno's reflections were often mistakenly viewed as related to theories of the Mitscherlichs, German postwar psychologists who maintained that Germans needed to develop empathy as an antidote for their refusal to face their own responsibility for and identification with Nazi racialist ideology of the past. Meek, however, argues "that this emphasis on empathy too easily colludes with an appropriation of the position of victim, a shift that was evident in later responses to television and film dramatizations of the Holocaust. Empathy can itself serve as a means of evading guilt and responsibility" (Meek, 2010: 135). Thus to some, the 1979 screening of the American television miniseries *Holocaust* in Germany, which became a huge media sensation, succeeded in helping West Germans to openly confront Nazi atrocities through their empathetic response, and yet the resulting collective identification with the victims could obscure responsibility of individual Germans for the Nazi past (Meek, 2010: 150–152).

8 These critics include: Heine, 2003; Kaspar, 2003; Seidel, 2003; Stäheli, 2003; Tilmann, 2003; Zander, 2003a; Kaufmann, 2004; O'Sullivan, 2004.

9 In her introduction to *Film/Literature/Heritage*, Ginette Vincendeau (2001: xviii) identifies celebration rather than investigation of the past as typical of British heritage films; this description applies to many German heritage films as well. British and French heritage films of the 1980s and 1990s are concerned mainly with literary adaptations or historical figures; examples include: *Chariots of Fire* (1991); *Jean de Florette* (1986); *A Room with a View* (1985); *Howards End* (1992); *Elizabeth* (1998); *Shakespeare in Love* (1998); and *Sense and Sensibility* (1995). For more on British and French heritage films, see Vincendeau 2001: xvii–xxi. For a detailed definition of German heritage film, see Koepnick, 2002: 49–52, 55–59. Koepnick maintains that rather than merely using history to provide a colorful background for melodramatic plots or adventure stories, heritage films "present the texture of the past as a source of visual attractions and aural pleasures." He argues that these films "transform the past into an object of consumption" (2002: 50).

10 For von Trotta's explanation of her concept of two kinds of memory, see Wydra, 2003: 18.

11 For information on Fassbinder and melodrama see Kuhn, 1984; Mayne, 1990; Corrigan, 1993.

12 "Westerns, war films, and Holocaust films, no less than women's films, family melodramas, and biopics thus participate, along with any drama whose outcome is the recognition of virtue, in the long-playing tradition of American melodrama" (Williams, 2001: 26).

13 The original quote reads: "Und dass es *Frauen* waren, die protestierten, fällt nun wiederum zusammen mit einem persönlichen Aspekt: Meine Filme handeln nun einmal meistens von Frauen, das ist *mein* Gefängnis" (Wydra, 2003: 16; my translation).

14 Ulrike Sieglohr (2002: 199) also places von Trotta among prominent German feminist filmmakers of the New German Cinema.

15 For feminist analyses that examine these questions in von Trotta's early films, see Kaplan, 1988; Quart, 1988; Möhrmann, 1993; Ward, 1995; Linville, 1998; Ooi, 2003; Hehr, 2000.

16 "Und meine Mutti? Wann kommt meine Mutti?" (*Rosenstrasse*, 2003; my translation).

17 According to Gruner (2005b: 135), most divorced Jewish Germans in "mixed marriages" were deported to Theresienstadt if at all. Other historians, such as Stoltzfus (1996) and Meyer (2004: 27) refer to divorce as a probable death sentence.

18 Very few witnesses of the many who were interviewed later about the Rosenstrasse events even mentioned the presence of machine guns during the protest; Stoltzfus (1996: 238–239, 243) cites two in his book who are recounting the events many years later. See also Schröder (2003: 32). For an analysis and critique of the conflicting descriptions of the demonstration and degree of threats to the protestors, see Gruner (2005b: 139–156, esp. 155–156).

19 See Meyer (2004: 35) for the entire quote: "So sind es die Frauen, die dem von männlicher Brutalität gekennzeichneten NS-Regime einen Sieg abtrotzen" (Thus it is the women who manage to wrest victory from a National Socialist regime marked by masculine brutality) (my translation).

20 Olbert (2003) erroneously describes Lena as dressed in a low-cut gown in that scene.

21 A few critics, such as O'Sullivan (2004) and Noack (2004), interpret the scene as von Trotta does; Noack also argues as I do that the costuming implies Lena did not have intercourse with Goebbels. Noack mentions as well that Goebbels was not interested in blonde women.

22 Gruner (2005b: 11–12, 202–203) argues that his conclusions concerning the events on Rosenstrasse in no way detract from the courage of the protestors. Von Trotta also discusses the courage of the demonstrators despite the reasons for the internees' release in the book on the film; see Wydra (2003: 18–20).

References

Ayotte, K.J. and Husain, M.E. (2005) Securing Afghan women: neocolonialism, epistemic violence, and the rhetoric of the veil. *NWSA Journal*, 17 (3), 112–133.

Baldwin, P. (ed.) (1990) *Reworking the Past: Hitler, the Holocaust, and the Historians' Debates*, Beacon Press, Boston.

Bathrick, D. (2008) Seeing against the grain? Re-visualizing the Holocaust. Intro. to *Visualizing the Holocaust: Documents, Aesthetics, Memory* (eds D. Bathrick, B. Praeger, and M.D. Richardson), Camden House, Rochester, NY, pp. 1–18.

Benz, W. (2003) Kitsch as kitsch can. *Süddeutsche Zeitung*, September 18, http://www.sueddeutsche.de/kultur/kritik-an-der-rosenstrasse-kitsch-as-kitsch-can-1.428859 (accessed April 28, 2009).

Braun, R. (1994) The Holocaust and problems of historical representation. *History and Theory*, 33 (2), 172–197.

Byg, B. (1993) German history and cinematic convention harmonized in Margarethe von Trotta's *Marianne and Juliane*, in *Gender and German Cinema* (eds S. Frieden, R.W. McCormick, V.R. Petersen, and L.M. Vogelsang), vol. 2. Berg, Providence, Oxford, pp. 259–271.

Corrigan, T. (1993) *New German Film: The Displaced Image*, University of Texas Press, Austin, pp. 43–69.

Dargis, M. (2004) Revisiting a Berlin protest that changed Nazi plans. Rev. of *Rosenstrasse*. *New York Times*, August 20, http://www.nytimes.com/2004/08/20/movies/film-review-revisiting-a-berlin-protest-that-changed-nazi-plans.html?scp=1&sq=Rosenstrasse+Dargis&st=nyt (accessed February 2, 2009).

Delorme, C. (1981) Zum Film, *Die bleierne Zeit* von Margarethe von Trotta. *Frauen und Film*, 31, 52–55.

DiCaprio, Lisa (1996) *Marianne and Juliane/The German Sisters*: Baader-Meinhof fictionalized, 1984, in *Perspectives on German Cinema* (eds T. Ginsberg and K.M. Thompson), G.K. Hall/Macmillan, New York and London, pp. 391–402.

Doane, M.A. (1987a) *The Desire to Desire: The Woman's Film of the 1940s*, Indiana University Press, Bloomington, Indianapolis.

Doane, M.A. (1987b) The woman's film, in *Home Is Where the Heart Is: Studies in Melodrama and the Women's Film* (ed. C. Gledhill), British Film Institute, London, pp. 283–298.

Doneson, J.E. (1997) The image lingers: The feminization of the Jew in *Schindler's List*, in *Spielberg's Holocaust: Critical Perspectives on Schindler's List* (ed. Y. Loshitzky), Indiana University Press, Bloomington, Indianapolis, pp. 140–152.

Evans, R.J. (1989) *In Hitler's Shadow: West German Historians and the Attempt to Escape from the Nazi Past*, Pantheon Books, New York.

Film und Kritik (2003) Rev. of *Rosenstrasse*. October 16, http://antville.medien.uni-weimar.de/filmkritik/topics/Rosenstrasse/(accessed May 18, 2009).

Friedländer, S. (ed.) (1992) *Probing the Limits of Representation: Nazism and the "Final Solution,"* Harvard University Press, Cambridge, MA.

Friedländer, S. (2000) History, memory, and the historian: dilemmas and responsibilities. *New German Critique*, 80, 3–15.

Fuchs, E. (2003) Gender and Holocaust docudramas: gentile heroines in rescue films. *Shofar*, 22 (1), 80–94.

Ginsberg, T. (2007) *Holocaust Film: The Political Aesthetics of Ideology*, Cambridge Scholars, Newcastle.

Gledhill, C. (1987) The melodramatic field: an investigation, in *Home Is Where the Heart Is: Studies in Melodrama and the Women's Film* (ed. C. Gledhill), British Film Institute, London, pp. 5–39.

Goldberg, A. (2009) Forum: On Saul Friedländer's *The Years of Extermination*: the victim's voice and melodramatic aesthetics in history. *History and Theory*, 48 (3), 220–237.

Göttler, F. (2003) Mädels im Märchenwald. Rev. of *Rosenstrasse. Süddeutsche Zeitung*, September 18, http://www.sueddeutsche.de/kultur/von-trottas-rosenstrasse-maedels-im-maerchenwald-1.431381 (accessed May 7, 2009).

Gruner, W. (2003) The factory action and the events at the Rosenstrasse in Berlin: facts and fictions about 27 February 1943 – sixty years later. *Central European History*, 36 (2), 179–208.

Gruner, W. (2005a) A Historikerstreit? A reply to Nathan Stoltzfus's response. *Central European History*, 38 (3), 460–464.

Gruner, W. (2005b) *Widerstand in der Rosenstrasse: die Fabrikaktion und die Verfolgung der "Mischehen" 1943*, Fischer Taschenbuch Verlag, Frankfurt a.M.

Hehr, R. (2000) *Margarethe von Trotta: Filmmaking as Liberation*, Axel Menges, Stuttgart, London.

Heine, M. (2003) Die Frauen und die Nazis. Rev. of *Rosenstrasse. Die Welt*, September 18, http://www.welt.de/print-welt/article260323/Die_Frauen_und_die_Nazis.html (accessed April 29, 2009).

Hornaday, A. (2004) "Rosenstrasse": truth was powerful enough. *Washington Post*, August 20, http://www.washingtonpost.com/wp-dyn/articles/A17318-2004Aug19.html (accessed July 30, 2009).

Horowitz, S. (1997) But is it good for the Jews? Spielberg's Schindler and the aesthetics of atrocity, in *Spielberg's Holocaust: Critical Perspectives on Schindler's List* (ed Y. Loshitzky), Indiana UP, Bloomington, Indianapolis, pp. 119–139.

Jochheim, G. (2002) *Frauenprotest in der Rosenstraße Berlin 1943: Berichte, Dokumente, Hintergründe*, Hentrich & Hentrich, Berlin.

Kansteiner, W. (1994) From exception to exemplum: the new approach to Nazism and the "Final Solution." *History and Theory*, 33 (2), 145–171.

Kaplan, E.A. (1988) Discourses of terrorism, feminism, and the family in von Trotta's *Marianne and Juliane*, in *Women and Film* (ed. J. Todd), Holmes & Meier, New York, pp. 258–270.

Kaspar, F. (2003) "Rosenstrasse": Haltung annehmen! Rev. of *Rosenstrasse. Kölner Stadt-Anzeiger*, September 17, http://www.ksta.de/servlet/ContentServer?pagename=ksta/page&atype=ksArtikel&aid=1063638249896 (accessed May 19, 2009).

Kaufmann, S. (2004) Stanley Kauffmann on films: Jewish fates. Rev. of *Rosenstraße. New Republic*, 231 (10), http://www.tnr.com/article/jewish-fates (accessed February 3, 2009).

Kellerhoff, S.F. (2003) Tagesstand der Geschichtsschreibung. Rev. of *Rosenstrasse. Die Welt*, September 24, http://www.welt.de/print-welt/article261720/Tagesstand_der_Geschichtsschreibung.html (accessed May 15, 2009).

Knowlton, J. and Cates, T. (trans. and ed.) (1993) *Forever in the Shadow of Hitler?: Original Documents of the "Historikerstreit," the Controversy Concerning the Singularity of the Holocaust*, Humanities Press, Atlantic Highlands, NJ.

Koepnick, L. (2002) Reframing the past: heritage cinema and the Holocaust in the 1990s. *New German Critique*, 87, 47–82.

Kuhn, A.K. (1984) Rainer Werner Fassbinder: the alienated vision, in *New German Filmmakers: From Oberhausen through the 1970s* (ed. K. Phillips), Ungar, New York, pp. 76–104.

Kuhn, A.K. (1993) *Women's Pictures*, Verso, London.

Lang, B. (1995) Is it possible to misrepresent the Holocaust? *History and Theory*, 34 (1), 84–89.

Leugers, A. (ed.) (2005) *Berlin, Rosenstrasse 1–4: Protest in der NS-Diktatur: neue Forschungen zum Frauenprotest in der Rosenstrasse 1943*, Plöger Medien, Annweiler.

Linville, S.E. (1998) *Feminism, Film, Fascism. Women's Autobiographical Films in Postwar Germany*, University of Texas Press, Austin.

Maier, C.S. (1998) *The Unmasterable Past: History, Holocaust, and German National Identity*, Harvard University Press, Cambridge, MA.

Maier, C.S. (2000) Consigning the twentieth century to history: alternative narratives for the modern era. *The American Historical Review*, 105 (3), 807–831.

Mayne, J. (1990) Fassbinder's *Ali: Fear Eats the Soul* and spectatorship, in *Close Viewings* (ed. P. Lehman), Florida State University Press, Tallahassee, pp. 353–369.

Meek, A. (2010) *Trauma and Media: Theories, Histories, and Images*, Routledge, New York and London.

Meyer, B. (2004) Geschichte im film: Judenverfolgung, Mischehen und der Protest in der Rosenstraße 1943. *Zeitschrift für Geschichtswissenschaft*, 52 (1), 23–36.

Moeller, R.G. (2002) What has "Coming to terms with the Past" meant in post-World War II Germany? From history to memory to the "history of memory." *Central European History*, 35 (2), 223–256.

Möhrmann, R. (1993) *Second awakening of Christa Klages*, in *Gender and German Cinema* (eds S. Frieden, R.W. McCormick, V.R. Petersen, and L.M. Vogelsang), vol. 1. Berg, Providence, RI, Oxford, pp. 73–83.

Noack, F. (2004) "Rosenstrasse": Margarethe von Trotta's homage to anti-fascism. Rev. of *Rosenstrasse*. H-Net Multimedia Review. H-German, July 26, http://h-net.msu.edu/cgi-bin/logbrowse.pl?trx=vx&list=h-review&month=0410&week=b&msg=Jke0xs%2bc4XAAfna%2b5lBijg&user=&pw= (accessed July 2, 2009).

Nord, C. (2003) Allgemeinmenschliches, allzu gemein Menschliches: Diskussionen um Margarethe von Trottas Film "Rosenstrasse." Rev. of *Rosenstrasse. taz*, September 24, http://www.taz.de/digitaz/.archiv/suche?mode=kompakt&tid=.%2F2003%2F09%2F24%2Fa0153.red&start=2&ListView=0&rev=1&name=askxZAzEO&tx=Rosenstra%DFe&ti=Diskussionen+Rosenstra%DFe&au=Nord%2C+Christine&sdd=22&smm=09&syy=2003&edd=25&emm=09&eyy=2003 (accessed May 7, 2009).

Olbert, F. (2003) Von der Wahrheit der Fiktionen.Rev. of *Rosenstrasse. Kölner Stadt-Anzeiger*, September 23, http://www.ksta.de/servlet/ContentServer?pagename=ksta/page&atype=ksArtikel&aid=1064245870107 (accessed May 19, 2009).

Ooi, S.J. (2003) Changing identity: Margarethe von Trotta's *The Second Awakening of Christa Klages*, in *Women Filmmakers: Refocusing* (eds J. Levitin, J. Plessis, and V. Raoul), Routledge, New York, pp. 84–96.

O'Sullivan, M. (2004) Rosenstrasse, simply heroic. Rev. of *Rosenstrasse. Washington Post*, August 20, http://www.washingtonpost.com/wp-dyn/articles/A15406-2004Aug19.html (accessed February 2, 2009).

Prause, P. (2005) Juden in "Mischehen" und "jüdische Mischling" als Opfer der "Fabrik-Aktion" – zur Notwendigkeit einer Re-Interpretation der Ereignisgeschichte. In *Berlin, Rosenstrasse 1–4: Protest in der NS-Diktatur: neue Forschungen zum Frauenprotest in der Rosenstrasse 1943* (ed. A. Leugers), Plöger Medien, Annweiler, pp. 19–46.

Quart, B.K. (1988) *Women Directors: The Emergence of a New Cinema*, Praeger, New York.

Rahill, F. (1967) *The World of Melodrama*, Pennsylvania State University Press, University Park, London.

"Regisseurin von Trotta weist Historiker-Kritik an "Rosenstrasse" zurück (2003) *Die Welt*, September 23, http://www.welt.de/print-welt/article261468/Regisseurin_von_Trotta_weist_Historiker_Kritik_an_Rosenstrasse_zurueck.htm (accessed April 29, 2009).

Rentschler, E. (2000) From New German Cinema to the post-wall cinema of consensus, in *Cinema and Nation* (eds M. Hjort and S. Mackenzie), Routledge, New York, London, pp. 260–277.

Rosenstrasse (1995) Drehbuch. Margarethe von Trotta. II. Fassung, December.

Rosenstrasse-Forum (2004) H-Net, H-German, July–August, http://www.h-net.org/~german/discuss/forums_index.htm (accessed July 2, 2009).

Rosenstrassenkrieg: Benz verteidigt sich gegen Trotta (2003) *Süddeutsche Zeitung*, September 20, http://archiv.sueddeutsche.apa.at/sueddz/index.php (accessed May 7, 2009).

Rothberg, M. and Stark, J. (2003) After the witness. *History and Memory*, 15 (1), 85–96.

Schindler, S.K. (2007) Displaced images: the Holocaust in German film, in *The Cosmopolitan Screen: German Cinema and the Global Imaginary, 1945 to the Present* (eds S.K. Schindler and L. Koepnick), University of Michigan Press, Ann Arbor, pp. 192–205.

Schlosser, E.M. (2003) Ein kleiner Funken Hoffnung. Rev. of *Rosenstrasse*. *Stuttgarter Nachrichten*, September 18, http://www.stuttgarter-nachrichten.de/stn/page/detail.php/506848 (accessed May 19, 2009).

Schröder, N. (2003) *Die Frauen der Rosenstrasse: Hitlers unbeugsame Gegnerinnen*, Heyne, Munich.

Seidel, H-D. (2003) Margarethe von Trottas "Rosenstrasse" provoziert Widerspruch – und pariert ihn zugleich. Rev. of *Rosenstrasse*. *Frankfurter Allgemeine Zeitung*, September 20, 33, http://m.faz.net/Rub117C535CDF414415BB243B181B8B60AE/Doc~EB80BD0659 7414549BF2CF82D8D6BEE1E~ATpl~Epartner~Ssevenval~Scontent.xml (accessed May 18, 2009).

Sieglohr, U. (2002) Women film-makers, the avante-garde and the case of Ulrike Ottinger, in *The German Cinema Book* (eds T. Bergfelder, E. Carter, and D. Göktürk), British Film Institute, London, pp. 192–201.

Silberman, M. (1995) The subject of identity: Margarethe von Trotta's *Marianne and Juliane*, in *German Cinema: Texts in Context* (ed. M. Silberman), Wayne State University Press, Detroit, MI, pp. 198–213.

Sklar, R. (2004) Invaded by memories of a Germany past: an interview with Margarethe von Trotta. *Cineaste*, 29 (2), 10–12.

Stäheli, A. (2003) Ein Triumph im Wasserglas "Rosenstrasse" – ein Film von Margarethe von Trotta. Rev. of *Rosenstrasse*. *Neue Zürcher Zeitung*, September 22, http://nzz.gbi.de/webcgi?WID=71882-4460321-90662_4 (accessed April 29, 2009).

Stoltzfus, N. (1996) *Resistance of the Heart: Intermarriage and the Rosenstrasse Protest in Nazi Germany*, Rutgers University Press, Rutgers, NJ.

Stoltzfus, N. (2003) Die Wahrheit jenseits der Akten. *Die Zeit*, September 30, http://www.zeit.de/2003/45/Rosenstra_a7e (accessed May 18, 2009).

Stoltzfus, N. (2005) Historical evidence and plausible history: interpreting the Berlin Gestapo's attempted "Final Roundup" of Jews (also known as the "Factory Action"). *Central European History*, 38 (3), 450–459.

Taberner, S. (2005) Philo-semitism in recent German film: *Aimée und Jaguar*, *Rosenstrasse* and *Das Wunder von Bern*. *German Life and Letters*, 58 (3), 357–372.

Thomas, K. (2004) "Rosenstrasse": wartime grief and women's heroism in this drama. Rev. of *Rosenstrasse*. *Los Angeles Times* August 20, http://pqasb.pqarchiver.com/latimes/access/680787921.html?FMT=ABS&FMTS=ABS:FT&date=Aug+20%2C+2004&author=Kevin+Thomas&pub=Los+Angeles+Times&edition=&startpage=E.12&desc=Movies%3B+MOVIE+REVIEW%3B+Wartime+grief%2C+women%27s+heroism+in+%27Rosenstrasse%27 (accessed May 18, 2009).

Tilmann, C. (2003) Aufstand der Frauen. Rev. of *Rosenstrasse*. *Der Tagespiegel*, September 17, http://www.tagesspiegel.de/kultur/art772,2105900 (accessed May 18, 2009).

Vincendeau, G. (2001) *Film/Literature/Heritage*, British Film Institute, London.

Ward, J. (1995) Enacting the different voice: *Christa Klages* and feminist history, in *Women and German Yearbook* (eds S. Friedrichsmeyer and P. Herminghouse), 11, 49–65.

Wiebel, M. (2003) *Rosenstrasse*. Film-Heft. Bundeszentrale für politische Bildung, Berlin, http://www.bpb.de/publikationen/T01VM5,0,Rosenstra%DFe.html (accessed August 27, 2009).

Williams, L. (2001) *Playing the Race Card. Melodramas of Black and White from Uncle Tom to O.J. Simpson*, Princeton University Press, Princeton, NJ.

Wydra, T. (2003) *Rosenstrasse: Ein Film von Margarethe von Trotta*, Nicolai, Berlin.

Young, J.E. (1997) Toward a received history of the Holocaust. *History and Theory*, 36, 21–43.

Zander, P. (2003a) Gartenzwerge und Zivilcourage. *Die Welt*, August 30, http://www.welt.de/print-welt/article256442/Gartenzwerge_und_Zivilcourage.html (accessed April 29, 2009).

Zander, P. (2003b) Vor acht Jahren wäre der Film anders geworden. Regisseurin Margarethe von Trotta im Gespräch. Interview with Peter Zander. *Die Welt*, September 18, http://www.welt.de/print-welt/article260322/Vor_acht_Jahren_waere_der_Film_anders_geworden.html (accessed April 29, 2009).

Further Reading

Kaplan, E.A. (ed.) (2000) *Feminism and Film*, Oxford University Press, New York.

Pribram. E.D. (ed.) (1988) *Female Spectators: Looking at Film and Television*, Verso, London.

Sjöholm, C. (2008) Margarethe von Trotta: Leviathan in Germany, in *Cinematic Thinking* (ed. J. Phillips), Stanford University Press, Stanford, CA, pp. 109–127.

Filmography

Ali: Fear Eats the Soul [Angst essen Seele auf] (R.W. Fassbinder, West Germany, 1974).

Aimée and Jaguar (Max Färberböck, Germany, 1999).

Andere Frau, Die [The Other Woman] (Margarethe von Trotta, Germany, 2004).

Bitter Tears of Petra von Kant, The [Die bittere Tränen der Petra von Kant] (R.W. Fassbinder, West Germany, 1972).

Chariots of Fire (Hugh Hudson, UK, 1991).

Elizabeth: The Virgin Queen (Shekhar Kapur, UK, 1998).

Harmonists, The [*Comedian Harmonists*] (Joseph Vilsmaier, Germany/Austria, 1997).

Holocaust: The Story of the Family Weiss (Marvin J. Chomsky, USA, 1978).

Howard's End (James Ivory, UK/Japan, 1992).

Ich bin die Andere [I Am the Other Woman] (Margarethe von Trotta, Germany, 2005–2006).

Jean de Florette (Claude Berri, France/Switzerland/Italy, 1986).

Marianne and Juliane [*Die Bleierne Zeit; The German Sisters*] (Margarethe von Trotta, West Germany, 1981).

Room with a View, A (James Ivory, UK, 1985).

Rosenstrasse (Margarethe von Trotta, Germany/Netherlands, 2003).

Second Awakening of Christa Klages, The [*Das zweite Erwachen der Christa Klages*] (Margarethe von Trotta, West Germany, 1978).

Sense and Sensibility (Ang Lee, USA/UK, 1995).

Shakespeare in Love (John Madden, USA/UK, 1998).

Sheer Madness [*Heller Wahn*] (Margarethe von Trotta, West Germany, 1982–1983).

Sisters, or the Balance of Happiness [*Schwestern oder die Balance des Glücks*] (Margarethe von Trotta, West Germany, 1979).

18

The Baader Oedipus Complex

Vojin Saša Vukadinović

The Eye-Terror Principle: "Illustrated History"

At the time of its release on September 25, 2008, *The Baader Meinhof Complex* (*Der Baader Meinhof Komplex*) was the most expensive production in German film history. Directed by Uli Edel and produced by Bernd Eichinger, both of whom have been associated with major commercial movie productions for decades, the film was based on the eponymous book by Stefan Aust (2008), which to this day has had a formative effect not only on the journalistic, but also on the academic reception of the *linksterroristische Organization* ("leftist terrorist organization"), the *Rote Armee Fraktion* (Red Army Faction (RAF)). *The Baader Meinhof Complex* makes an implied promise to depict the RAF *wie es eigentlich gewesen war* ("as it really was"), or rather, "*wie es gewesen sein könnte*" ("as it could have been"), as noted in *Der Spiegel* (The Mirror), Germany's premier liberal-centrist news magazine. The magazine echoed nineteenth-century historian Leopold von Ranke, who declared the historian's task to describe events thus, with the aim of evoking their ostensible experiential essence. This historicist imperative has to be criticized for disregarding epistemological differences across time, and for ignoring changing conceptions of reality as well as, more recently, the advent and unresolved challenges which deconstruction continues to pose for a historiography whose agenda still centers around standardized recountings of the past. By lauding *The Baader Meinhof Complex*'s adoption of this historicist credo, the review in *Der Spiegel* revealed its adherence to a simplistic concept of historical immediacy for which the task of a film is primarily descriptive. The magazine had always followed the evolution of the RAF closely, contributing greatly to its popular ascription as "the greatest drama in the history of the old Federal Republic" (Bönisch and

A Companion to German Cinema, First Edition. Edited by Terri Ginsberg and Andrea Mensch.
© 2012 Blackwell Publishing Ltd. Published 2012 by Blackwell Publishing Ltd.

Wiegreife, 2008: 53).[1] Subsequently dedicating a cover story to *The Baader Meinhof Complex*, it continued this sensationalism, sporting actors Martina Gedeck, Moritz Bleibtreu, and Johanna Wokalek as, respectively, Ulrike Meinhof, Andreas Baader, and Gudrun Ensslin – the co-founders of the RAF – on the cover, and a caption attributed to Brigitte Mohnhaupt, another RAF member (here played by Nadja Uhl), from the last line of the film: "Stop seeing them as they were not"; and underneath that: "A film destroys the myth of the RAF."

"Myth" in *Der Spiegel*'s usage does not refer, as it does for Roland Barthes (1964), to a semiological expression that names a linguistic or visual sign and the power relations structuring it. Instead it suggests quite literally a presumed misapprehension by the German Left of the RAF's political violence, according to which the myth of murder disguised as suicide in Stammheim and Stadelheim of 1976 and 1977 came quickly to be viewed as a right-conspiratorial lie among the group's sympathizers. The reference to the "myth of the RAF" and its ensuing analysis firmly established itself in German journalistic as well as academic circles, whereas it became romanticized within German pop culture (see Galli and Preusser, 2006). Significantly, however, it was members of the theoretically oriented radical Left itself who ultimately suspended the RAF myth by the mid-1990s, in the context of Germany's post-Wall reality (see Barth, 1996). It is still possible, then, to understand RAF history in Barthes' sense, as a German quotidian myth which has come to serve a commodity function. Indeed the RAF may be said, following Gilles Deleuze and Félix Guattari (1977), to resemble a modern zombie myth, in that its former membership has come to comprise a spectral presence, "living dead" who are unable to rest on account of having been granted an autonomous value that keeps them "alive," not only in the political marketplace but for a particular construction of "Germanness" that has sought fit to scapegoat the RAF, positioning it as the enemy outsider to a Germany bent on disavowing the group's integral, dialectical relationship – both real and imaginary – to the nation-state. This zombie characterization functions resolutely to contain any future rebellion, by positioning the RAF as an initially welcome development destined nonetheless to erupt in deadly terror, suggesting a teleological relationship between the "good" and "bad" aspects of its organizational program. By the same token, this zombie myth extends a political warning into the present. As Deleuze and Guattari maintain, "The only modern mythos is that of the zombie who, once returned to reason, will be good for work" (1977: 433).

Whenever the mythical aura of German *Linksterrorismus* has been conjured up, it is most often Antigone who delimits the horizon of RAF representation (Elsaesser, 2007). However, there is yet another myth invoked by the RAF drama and the politics of memory surrounding it. The pervasive concern in these representations with libidinal entanglements and fatal flaws – the stuff of *abjection* – along with a palpable apocalypticism, a projected belief in the imminent confrontation of humanity with some final and complete, existential "truth," are reminiscent of a Christianized Oedipus. One might therefore locate the impetus for the continuing obsession with RAF representation in Germany as emerging from a politically constructed need to misrecognize the organization as a nodal point of German subjectivity, a matrix that can serve to unify and stabilize a particular "Germanness" by supplying opportunities for its repeated identification with a conflictual family drama that is resolved through deadly violence. The resolute abjection particular to the cult of memory surrounding the RAF positions the group as if it had not originated in West Germany but instead had invaded it from the "outside," a practice which may in fact stem from the Federal Republic of Germany's (FRG) collective desire to bail out of this political tragedy.

This tendency is undoubtedly associated with another collective German trauma, from which the country has tried to extricate itself through countless distancing techniques, one of the more persistent of which has entailed transforming the official history of state confrontation with the RAF into a psychodrama meant to dissimulate knowledge about the prior Nazi era. Public discussion about the first organized political violence to have occurred in West Germany since the Second World War – accompanied by a concomitant neglect to thematize its origins and radicalization, not to mention its postwar plausibility within West Germany – became a transferential means of disavowing German guilt and externalizing the twentieth century's violent core. Since reunification, renewed debates about the RAF have continued to elide serious analysis of German violence by deflecting attention onto a sensationalized countercultural era, away from either the Nazi past or the post-Wall present, thus mythologizing the FRG as an innocent victim of a sudden, unprecedented, and unwarranted *un-German* attack.

The Red Army Faction, founded formally in May 1970, was certainly the most conspicuous, but neither the first nor the sole underground leftist organization in West Germany. It was preceded by the Tupamaros West-Berlin in the late 1960s (Kraushaar, 2005) and followed by the more anarchistic Bewegung 2. Juni (June 2nd Movement) and the social revolutionary Revolutionäre Zellen and Rote Zora during the 1970s, yet none of them accrued the same degree of public hysteria or came close to etching themselves as deeply into the German collective consciousness as did the RAF. Originally an offshoot of the 1968 student movement, the RAF saw itself as a Marxist-Leninist extension in Western Europe of Third World liberation struggles. The organization invested the energy accumulated during 1968, the year of protest, into devising a program of confrontational armed militancy, which it hoped would bring about a communist revolution in West Germany through rearmament of the German masses now mobilized and activated by the RAF as their vanguard. Deploying a theoretical eclecticism consisting of Maoism, Third World liberation rhetoric, ideological tracts by Che Guevara on the one hand and Herbert Marcuse on the other, as well as traditional Communist Party anticapitalism directed against what it considered to be the wealth-producing, self-enriching classes, the RAF projected itself as an integral part of a universally envisioned revolutionary plan. The "Fraktion" in its German name was meant to contextualize the organization's particular actions within the larger struggle for world communist revolution. The main target of its particular struggle, however, was never Germany itself, which the RAF considered a "colonized" victim of foreign power and influence, but the United States, the perceived center of global capitalist imperialism. In order to lend its rhetoric historical weight and legitimize its actions, the RAF employed an inflammatory vocabulary regarding the persistence of "fascism" that evidenced a fundamentally Manichean worldview into an axiomatic condemnation of the West (epitomized by the United States and Israel) and an unquestioned valorization of the Global South (especially countries in which leftist or left-nationalist liberation movements were active). The rhetoric of imminent "fascism," coupled with the evocation of a "new fascism," thus served an ahistorical programmatic, according to which logic the overthrow of the current political constellation required a collective response that itself was dependent upon a revolutionary cadre (the RAF) leading the West German masses. Revolutionary violence was in turn posited as an indispensable condition for genuine political change. Members of West Germany's underground leftist organizations conceived capitalism not as an anonymous, de/centralizing economic system of perpetually shifting coordinates, which is how Deleuze and Guattari described it at the time in a post-Marxist vein, but as a political formation owned and operated by an elite few. It was that very elite which the RAF denounced as "guilty," vis-à-vis whom it propagated its early underground credo: "Und natürlich darf geschossen werden" ("And of course one may shoot") (Meinhof, 1970: 74). An end to the RAF's war against world capitalism was not declared until 1998; it cost several dozen lives on the part of the German State, the RAF itself, as well as the citizenry – individuals whom the police assumed to be RAF members, or bystanders whom the RAF shot collaterally, for example during a 1979 bank robbery in Zürich. Having failed to construct or bring about communism in any form, the RAF finally disappeared from the political landscape during the 1990s, while continuing to haunt it intermittently, as specter of cultural, ideological, and historical conflict.

The Baader Meinhof Complex's plot rushes through the RAF's ten formative years from 1967 to 1977, beginning with a student uprising in West Berlin protesting a state visit by the Shah of Persia, which resulted in the police shooting of an unarmed student, Benno Ohnesorg, on June 2, 1967. The plot follows the political radicaliza-tion of journalist Ulrike Meinhof, student Gudrun Ensslin and her boyfriend Andreas Baader, and others, who would eventually, in 1970, declare war against the Federal Republic in the form of an urban guerilla outfit. The group robs banks and receives military training in the Middle East before bombing US Army installations, West German police stations, and other institutions in May 1972. Upon the almost immediate arrest of nearly the entire group, the "guerillas" continue their struggle in prison. While RAF cadre Holger Meins starves himself to death in the group's first major hunger strike, outside the prison a new "generation" of mostly young West Germans aims to continue the "Baader-Meinhof Group's" armed political militancy. After their unsuccessful attempt to liberate the imprisoned RAF leaders through a violent occupation of the West German embassy in Stockholm, a rescue strategy is developed by cadres from within the prison. After the highly publicized suicide of group founder Ulrike Meinhof, the authorities expand the number of RAF inmates in the Stuttgart-Stammheim prison in order to stave off allegations from group sympathizers about "isolation torture." Baader and Ensslin in turn instruct fellow RAF prisoner Brigitte Mohnhaupt, who is soon to be released, to reorganize the group into a new, functional combat unit. Immediately upon her release, Mohnhaupt goes underground again, and the remodeled RAF begins its "77 Offensive," beginning with the execution of Federal General Prosecutor Siegfried Buback, followed by that of the head of Dresdner Bank Jürgen Ponto, and ending with the kidnapping German Employer's Association president and former NSDAP member and SS officer Hanns-Martin Schleyer in September 1977. When it becomes apparent that the Bonn government is not willing to exchange Schleyer for 11 imprisoned RAF members, a Popular Front for the Liberation of Palestine (PFLP) commando hijacks the Lufthansa plane *Landshut* in an attempt to increase pressure on the West German government. At the Mogadishu airport in Somalia, the plane is raided by the German antiterror special unit GSG9, which frees all of the hostages. Devastated by the news, the RAF cadres in Stammheim, already serving a lifetime sentence, see no future for themselves or their cause. The next morning, Andreas Baader and Gudrun Ensslin are found dead, Jan-Carl Raspe dying, and Irmgard Möller severely wounded, all in their respective cells. The next day, October 19, 1977, the RAF executes Hanns-Martin Schleyer.

This plot, encompassing ten years, is identical with the one delineated by Stefan Aust. It is not the definitive history of the RAF, but it lends the group's history an appearance of closure, in the sense of exhausting it, and thus functions as a boilerplate for numerous ensuing accounts, including RAF recountings by Butz Peters (2004), Willi Winkler (2007), and Michael Sontheimer (2010). The plot furthermore functions as a condensation: a rapid succession of chronologically ordered events is connected through select focus on a few highly visible RAF personages whose various, often anonymous members disappear as quickly as they emerge. This narrative structure, in which individual perspectives dominate while the political nature of the drama is given far less attention, manifests the dominant historiography of *Linksterrorismus* in Germany. Rather than supplying the sort of genuinely new perspective claimed by *Der Spiegel*, such representation comprises an archetype of RAF depictions. This standardized recounting is traceable to official documents and chronologies, print media editorials, and textbooks, which treat the RAF largely as the private enterprise of a few key personalities rather than a postfascist phenomenon (Kowalski, 2010). *The Baader Meinhof Complex* projects a certain "realistic" quality, although its posthumous depiction of the RAF is more extensive in Stefan Aust's book, of which *The Baader Meinhof Complex*'s spectator is relentlessly reminded. The film's process of recapitulating and displacing information fragments circulated historically by the media about the RAF exemplifies Jacques Derrida's (1997) notion of an archive that generates rather than records events. Anyone even mildly familiar with popular RAF history can recite the book's – and the film's – plot by heart. Even though much official documentation about the RAF is still publicly inaccessible, Aust's treatise has been accepted as definitive with respect to the RAF's founding, early membership, the motivation for Ulrike Meinhof's suicide, and the appointed successor of Baader and Ensslin. *The Baader Meinhof Complex* retells the story repeatedly, which, because of its very predictability, comes to resemble an "antievent" (Derrida, 2003: 35). Indeed insofar as the film narrates RAF history in this way, its narrative is actually the least "complex" cinematic treatment of the topic to date (Nicodemus, 2009: 58).

All of this is important to emphasize, because the film's historical distance from the represented events has not resulted in much studied reflection but instead has produced rather limited understandings. Films about the RAF have historically been interested in examining the social realities of the FRG; the "RAF film genre" is definable less by films which focus specifically on the RAF itself than by those which depict and analyze the media, political, and social hysteria over *Linksterrorismus* within the West German public sphere.[2] Among them are Volker Schlöndorff and Margarethe von Trotta's *The Lost Honor of Katharina Blum* (*Die verlorene Ehre der Katharina Blum*, 1975), the omnibus film, *Germany in Autumn* (*Deutschland im Herbst*, 1978), and Rainer Werner Fassbinder's *The Third Generation* (*Die dritte Generation*, 1978) – all products of the independent and self-reflexive directors' cinema (*Autorenkino*) known internationally as New German Cinema. By contrast, the gesture of merely recording protocol, which *The Baader Meinhof Complex* projects, and which enables it to evade critical scrutiny, is indicative of a representational practice that has little in common with the original RAF film genre and more to do with the entertainment-oriented aspects of Eichinger's unofficial Germany Saga. This trilogy on the German twentieth century includes three cinematic productions: *Downfall* (*Der Untergang*, Oliver Hirschbiegel, 2004), *The Baader Meinhof Complex* (2008), and *Zeiten ändern Dich* (Time Changes You, Uli Edel, 2010), all especially noteworthy for their implicit historical revisionism regarding the Holocaust and Nazi era and its ghostly afterlife. *Downfall* represents the final days of National Socialism in the *Führerbunker*, giving the Nazi elites a human face while marginalizing the Holocaust; *Zeiten ändern Dich* restylizes a violent, illiterate rapper into a contemporary, anti-intellectual youth icon in times of growing acceptance of antisemitism; and *The Baader Meinhof Complex* detaches its RAF representation from the problematics of Post-Nazism in Germany, as if the group's political analysis simply devolved automatically into violent actionism during the 1970s – rather than, as this chapter shall argue, was an effect of unacknowledged and undertheorized German postfascist tendencies dissimulated for ideologicopolitical purposes as feminine-sexual perversity.

The focus of *The Baader Meinhof Complex*'s group biography, however, is not the psychological development of its protagonists but the chronological rehearsal of a series of events, the sensational depiction of which is meant primarily to promote historical voyeurism. *The Baader Meinhof Complex* operates by forcing a gaze that subjects the spectator to a visual assault in order to effect the sort of political catharsis that demands a classic Oedipal witnessing previously absent from the genre. The film constructs a phantasmatic desire for complete closure to the dramatic conflict, both through location shooting (e.g. in Stammheim's prison courtroom), which suggests authenticity, and an insistence on chronological faithfulness. Such closure is finally achieved, however, through a repetitive reduction symptomatic of the contemporary German memory cult: a rapid linkage of the events of 1967–1977 performed over and over like a narrative Moebius strip. With the exception of Ulrike Meinhof, who is positioned as a paradigmatic group victim in the sense of both failure and martyrdom, this performance is marked by a developmental stagnation that predetermines the figures' actions within a self-contained libidinal economy, making psychological ambivalence difficult if not impossible and minimizing space for critical reflection. Their characters are templates of the German memory cult, overdetermined by individualistic traits presumed constitutive of the RAF's mindset. As Dirk Kurbjuweit (2008: 45) stated in *Der Spiegel*, once again echoing Ranke, the generic transformation represented by *The Baader Meinhof Complex* "wants to show the people as they probably were in reality and simply strings the events together. It creates a work of history rather than a work of art. *Illustrated history*."[3]

Instead of braving an attempt to create a specific visual language with which to express the origins and radicalization of West German *Linksterrorismus*, and in turn offering a historiographical critique of the phenomenon, *The Baader Meinhof Complex* provides a complacent illustration of events. It does not deliver the definitive film about the RAF, but instead one about variegated yet persistent, mythologized images which for decades have been etched indelibly into the FRG collective consciousness, starting with the rally against the Shah and the police murder of student Benno Ohnesorg in West Berlin on June 2, 1967 and ending with the corpse of Hanns-Martin Schleyer during the so-called German Autumn of 1977 – the weeks of Schleyer's kidnapping, the hijacking of the *Landshut*, the Stammheim suicides, and Schleyer's assassination. It cements leftist militancy, especially during the film's first half, with the downright "eye-terror"[4] that rushes as quickly as possible through the years of the student movement and the formation of the RAF, and preempts a contemplative historical approach through a ceaseless, linear linking of events – as if trying to beat the organization with its own weapons. Whereas direct, experiential rendering of underground activities, killings, conditions of arrest and imprisonment were avoided by prior RAF films, the spectator is now privy to one violent act after another. In the haptic eye-terror of *The Baader Meinhof Complex*, the spectator is sutured into believing that, while *Linksterrorismus* did indeed emerge within West German society and was grounded in organized political protest and countercultural movements of the late 1960s, the deadly consequences of its later politics were inevitable. The film ostensibly wants to disallow an objectively distanced perspective toward both the West German state and the RAF, as well as to elide an historical verdict regarding the group – but it nevertheless transmits them through its relentlessness. The succession of images races along, the progression and ending a well-known matter of course.

"Illustrated history" in this respect suggests a disingenuously neutral discourse, an objectivation of a purely illustrative chronology that approximates "truth" *eventually*. In *Eine gewisse unmögliche Möglichkeit, vom Ereignis zu sprechen* (A Certain Impossible Possibility of Speaking about the Event) (2003: 21), Jacques Derrida theorizes that objectivized speech about events themselves is always subordinate to language, which thus acquires the status of mere afterthought and has always been connected to interpretation: one of the characteristics of the event is not only its unpredictability, and therefore the fact that it interrupts the usual progression of history, but also its absolute singularity. And so one can say that, speaking of the event, the imparting of knowledge *about* the event in a certain way misses *a priori* the always already singularity of the event – because of the simple fact that the utterance always comes too late and loses singularity to generality. In this light, there is a palmary moment of gender-related, political singularity which both *The Baader Meinhof Complex* and the public debate around it boastfully ignore, an unnamed omission which falls short of one of the RAF's earliest and perhaps most central historical peculiarities: that is, the abandonment of any recourse to the extensive debates which took place between 1970 and 1982 over the potential social origins – *Ursachenforschung* – of *Linksterrorismus* and its purported relationship to social movements, especially feminism.

From the Allegation of Feminism to *Femininism*: Sheer Killing is (Once Again) a Woman

In the public discourse about the RAF during the 1970s and early 1980s, a certain antifeminism was articulated that must be recalled if one is to understand the persistence of gendered discourse around the organization. This debate remains an unnamed conflict in *The Baader Meinhof Complex*. The film focuses on the RAF's confrontational attacks and its subsequent persecution by the State. The image of the RAF thus produced by the film comprises only a few, reductive aspects: group members themselves, their (re)actions, and their governmental opponents. Notwithstanding the deeper connotations of the "Wanted" signs posted at points throughout the mise-en-scène, as well as depictions of the various sites of attack, Stammheim Prison, and the kidnapping of Hanns-Martin Schleyer, which tap into the German collective memory, the film dissimulates the visually less accessible but nevertheless influential, interdisciplinary and transinstitutional debate, which at its core focused on feminism's political legitimacy. In *The Baader Meinhof Complex*, the debate experiences a spectral return that is dehystericized only upon first glance.

As the military clashes between the RAF and the FRG increased, self-declared experts on feminism from the government, academia, clergy, and media began to propagate the thesis that feminism was the actual thrust behind militant Marxism-Leninism in West Germany. They based this assertion not on a substantive engagement with the politics of anti-imperialism, but on the presumed high percentage of women in groups like the RAF. This "high" participation of women appeared as such only through abstract comparison, for example, when contrasted with the composition of the Bonn government, where at the time men held absolute majority. If compared with other Left groupings, especially the 1968 student movement from which it emerged, a less distorted, potentially less controversial image of the RAF becomes available, since there the participation of women and men was equally "high." The attribution of a falsely presumed female dominance within German *Linksterrorismus* can therefore be understood as a masculinist ideologem that served to position the RAF as a target of a socially and politically rooted antifeminism and its concomitant, discernible politics of *ressentiment*. This positioning was facilitated by common criminological images of the violent woman but went excessively beyond that. Denunciatory references to renowned French feminist Simone de Beauvoir in treatises on the RAF at the time rather indicate a dual discrediting of the RAF and feminism, the latter of which had become increasingly influential in West Germany during the 1970s. The fact that the RAF is now commonly remembered as women's history gone mad, and that few contemporary journalistic or academic texts fail to underscore the group's female membership, bespeaks the overdetermined effectiveness of this early debate.

The visual perspective of *The Baader Meinhof Complex* projects this discourse through a fetishization of female figures on the verge of a politicized nervous breakdown. Günter Nollau, then working in the Federal Ministry of the Interior, explained to *Der Spiegel* in 1971, barely one year after the RAF was founded, what in his estimation motivated the underground organization's actionism: "Even the Bonn security boss, Nollau, who was struck by the fact that 'so many girls are part of this,' sees 'something irrational in this whole thing.' He ponders: 'Perhaps what is now becoming clear is that this is an excess of woman's emancipation'" (*Der Spiegel*, 1971: 27).⁵ In 1972, Nollau became the president of the Federal Office for the Protection of the Constitution (Bundesamt für Verfassungsschutz). His notion of "women's liberation run to an excess" became the debate's influential and formative catchphrase, which in ensuing years would inspire a huge corpus of written works attempting to explain the genesis of the RAF and other underground leftist groups in terms of their purported connection to feminism. Nollau's colleague, Hans Josef Horchem, who was in charge of the Hamburg Office for the Protection of the Constitution, added further,

> The misinterpretation of reality, the total idea which developed from calculated, practical action, the undertaking of brisk and improvisational actions while renting apartments under false names or through middlemen, the sedulity of

reconnaissance – all of these things have characteristics that can only be explained by the decisive participation of women [...] 12 of the activists of the RAF's core group are women. Of the additional 20 activists who joined subsequently, eight are women. Their ideas and activities are also the result of the explosive emancipation of participating female activists. (1975: 26)[6]

The ensuing public debate contained all of the antifeminist buzzwords and included questions about abortion and the education of women under a rubric which attributed these issues to a presumed *Linksterrorismus–Feminismus* causal nexus. Thus in 1977, on the question of the RAF's roots, the German Bischofskonferenz (German Bishops Conference) (Sekretariat der Deutschen Bischofskonferenz, 1978: 21) declared: "Marriage and family, the rights of the unborn, and other ethical norms were attacked from different directions and on different levels. Did this not undermine the foundations without which our society loses its stability?"[7] Similarly the Christian "Psychagogist" Christa Meves stated in a psychiatrically oriented anthology concerning leftist militancy that education needs gender-differentiated programs based on the notion of two distinct sexes if female delinquency is to be prevented – itself considered a political activity in the broadest sense:

The neuroticization of young girls during their early years carries an additional, criminalizing effect if they are forced, contrary to their natural aptitudes, into unilaterally masculinized educational paths and sexualized lifestyles. This one-sided, masculinized "self-actualization" of women leads potentially to dissatisfaction, because it represents an additional denial of existing needs. For the first time in history, this condition has caused several, mainly young, intellectualized women to become terrorists. (Schwind, 1978: 78)[8]

Finally, *Der Spiegel* (1977: 22) likewise articulated an apocalyptic gender horizon for West German male citizens, which would now be visited upon them as "death in the shape of a young girl." As journalist Susanne von Paczensky (1978: 11) remarked at the time, the fight against terrorism increasingly became a symbolic fight against feminism.

This sampling of quotations from a debate that echoed across hundreds of publications points toward the fact that the political scandal embodied by the RAF was misrecognized as rooted not simply in the group's programmatic outline or of *Linksterrorismus* per se, but in an allegedly affiliated feminist politics. Although the antifeminist component of this debate is no longer directly addressed within the context of publicly remembering the German Autumn – whether in 1997 or 2007 – the purported relationship of the RAF to feminism has not been suspended entirely within these memory cycles. Instead its articulation has undergone a transformation, whereupon the guilt and responsibility associated with leftist militancy has been detached from the register of feminism and – more carefully and yet in some way just as unscrupulously – imputed to the femi*nine*: in effect, *Femininism*. As Kurbjuweit (2008: 47) put it: "With Nadja Uhl [as Brigitte Mohnhaupt,VSV], sheer killing invades, a blood rush unhinged from reason."[9] One of *The Baader Meinhof Complex*'s more conspicuous features is the sexualization of its female characters and of Andreas Baader, who is marked as a masculinist pervert. This strategic move elides a less conspicuously presented anti-imperialism, which might be termed a kind of aestheticized, desublimated Protestantism. The "astounding visual resemblance" of the actors to their historical counterparts, remarked in German reviews at the time of the film's release (see Kniebe and Kreye, 2008), attests to the effectiveness of visual style in conveying this updated antifeminism. Even the scenes of incarceration and hunger strikes are presented as hipster "coolness," as though nostalgia for past glamour could explain why the RAF's reputation radiated far beyond West German borders. An erotic fascination of attraction and repulsion is unmistakably constructed vis-à-vis this "radical chic" RAF, and is not surprisingly enacted across the actions and bodies of female characters.

This tendency toward a sexist rationale for the RAF is not new; *The Baader Meinhof Complex*'s cinematic precursors also seem inspired by 1970s debates over the alleged implications of the RAF's possible feminism-inspired politics. In 1997, for instance, the ARD television network broadcast Heinrich Breloers's docudrama, *Todesspiel* (*Death Game*), on the twentieth anniversary of the Schleyer murder, the "Landshut" hijacking, and the Stammheim deaths. This two-part telefilm comprises documentary coverage of public pronouncements made by the Mogadishu hostages which preceded the Stammheim suicides, as well as by government officials of the time, along with fictionalized representation of the hijacking and of the Schleyer kidnapping. The telefilm's binary gendering of the RAF members involved in these events is staged as a family melodrama encoded to allegorize the conflict between the RAF and the West German state. Schleyer, who symbolizes a German national father-figure, has been taken prisoner by his own wayward children. No longer dressed in an expensive suit but in a plain undershirt, he must endure disempowerment even with respect to his clothing – a phenomenon signaling a vulnerability that is usually found in the exposure of the women's bodies. Despite this humiliation, the war hero Schleyer remains composed and intellectually more adept than his captors. While the wayward sons merely act stupidly, moreover, the daughters behave in an especially viperish and trigger-happy fashion, interrogating and humiliating their prisoner. Such outrageous female behavior is particularly excessive during the prior abduction scene, when the female member of the commando turns her weapon on Schleyer's dead companions, their bodies riddled with bullets, and fires once again into the undamaged back window of a car, although there is no one left to kill at the crime scene. The image evokes Lombroso's criminological depiction of immoderate and irrational woman; or, as formulated by Horchem (1975), these women articulate a "decisive participation." Indeed in *The Baader Meinhof Complex*, it is the female member of the kidnapping commando who first raises her hand affirmatively during an RAF vote on the issue of whether the attack on Schleyer should be executed "hard," that is, through a direct assassination of Schleyer's bodyguards and driver during the abduction. In the following abduction scene, it is she who eventually shoots first.

The reified image of the gun-toting woman is by now, of course, a visual commonplace. Although possibly disturbing to a 1970s milieu not yet exposed to second-wave feminism, such imagery has now become *de rigueur*. In *The Baader Meinhof Complex*, however, this iconic image is resuscitated and redeployed retroactively in the name of rationalizing a past conflict. The credibility – and political uncanniness – of such an image is ensured as long as the history of German leftism remains mystified victimologically. Directing an ostensible desiring gaze toward this form of armed femininity mitigates the frightening potential of the underground's uncanniness. In short, the RAF is misconstrued as a women's political project in order that its program be explained away perfunctorily – "as it really was."

The Baader Meinhof Complex thus positions the RAF as a synecdoche for feminism. Just as feminism has been misunderstood as an irrational attack against men in order to dismiss it, rather than an analytical enterprise centering on issues of gender equality, social dehierarchization, redistribution of resources, and so forth, *The Baader Meinhof Complex* articulates a fear of women's emancipation that discredits its necessity and surrenders it to the historical dustbin. This is evident in the film's treatment of the abjection of women, especially those in leadership positions. While not explicitly critical of feminism, for instance, the relationship between Gudrun Ensslin and Ulrike Meinhof is presented as competitive rather than as one of solidarity between cadres. A drama of women's leadership ensues in which room is left for only one female boss – a conflict that inevitably ends in the death of both contenders anyway. In contrast to Ensslin, who supposedly underwent a quasi-religious self-actualization by becoming a militant Leninist, Meinhof comes off as a Jane-come-lately, a tainted idealist worthy of forgiveness for having recognized the error of her ways and, by her suicide, offered reconciliation to the FRG. Ensslin, on the other hand, functions as whip and exalted group alter-ego, who refuses to surrender the project until the very end, keeping it inflated with radical energy even when so-called "objective motives" behind the RAF, which Horst Herold, head of the Federal Criminal Police Office (Bundeskriminalamt), still wonders about – in *The Baader Meinhof Complex*, little more than perverse libidinal energies – have supposedly waned. Andreas Baader is a black hole of masculinity in comparison to whom any other male RAF member appears pale and secondary, and who displays excessively masculinist behavior.[10] Next to Ensslin, however, he comes across simply as a loyal follower, sublimely controlled by his girlfriend, someone who can only maintain his position in the group hierarchy by fits of screaming anger – a practiced form of political sadomasochism.[11]

It is therefore not surprising that the alleged successor to the group throne was not another man but instead another woman: "Brigitte Mohnhaupt" is perceived less as a proper name than as a phallic narrative principle within RAF lore, installing a matrilineal legacy that runs contrary to the usual cadre structure of far-left organizations. No RAF representation is complete without a rehearsal of Mohnhaupt's release from prison in early 1977.[12] In *The Baader Meinhof Complex*, the pertinent sequence is equipped with a particularly male-heterosexual fantasy of female sexual availability: "Five years in prison. That's how long I haven't fucked a man," says Mohnhaupt to a new RAF member, Peter-Jürgen Boock, immediately before returning to the underground. She emerges from prison looking surprisingly young, attractive, and energetic. The difference between her and Meinhof, who has just committed suicide in the film, couldn't appear greater. A libidinal suture then occurs between the old and new RAF guards. In the *Baader Meinhof Complex*'s only fornication scene (if one discounts Meinhof catching her husband *in flagranti* at the beginning), one witnesses the marriage of the RAF's so-called "first" (Mohnhaupt) and "second" (Boock) "generations." As a wedding gift, the bride offers the groom the group's most well-preserved secret: in a moment of (rare) postcoital relaxation, Mohnhaupt informs Boock that the Stammheim prisoners wish to decide their own fates and will do so at an opportune moment. In the face of imminent collective suicide, the sexual act becomes a pact which reinforces the primacy of female leadership, after which the Stammheim murder myth will be disseminated at an appropriate time for the ideological purpose of group preservation and recruiting new members. Through superimposition, a nude Mohnhaupt is then seen in the shower while Federal Prosecutor General Siegfried Buback, along with his driver and a bodyguard, are shot dead by the RAF's "Commando Ulrike Meinhof." Simultaneously Mohnhaupt's voice is heard reading the RAF's corresponding declaration. "Death in the shape of a young girl" has once again invaded the cultural memory.

Volker Schlöndorff's *The Legend of Rita* (*Die Stille nach dem Schuss*, 2000) provides a comparably voyeuristic, if somewhat sentimentalizing, heterosexual glance at the life story of a female underground leftist based loosely on the autobiography of former Bewegung 2. Juni and RAF member Inge Viett (1997). This film depicts the process by which a female member of an underground leftist group disassociates from it and goes into exile in the GDR, in turn romanticizing both her anti-imperialist militancy and the West German perspective she brings to her new life in the stolid, petit-bourgeois Communist State. Even a lesbian moment is used here in a decorative fashion, to dissimulate the more serious question of whether anti-imperialist and gay liberation or feminist politics have been related historically in West Germany. In a film of the early 1980s by Margarethe von Trotta, *Marianne and Juliane* (*Die bleierne Zeit*, 1981), *Frauenbewegung* (women's lib) is counterposed with leftist terrorism. These political modalities are embodied respectively by the disparate life-paths of two sisters, one of whom, resembling Christiane Ensslin, has opted for feminism, and the other, a Gudrun Ensslin prototype, has opted for *Linksterrorismus*, both in response to what they learned about the Nazi era during their strict Protestant childhoods. The film positions the two women in critical relation to public hysteria over the RAF, which was less interested in further investigating the organization's driving ideological constraints than in seeing it in melodramatic black-and-white (see DiCaprio, 1996). Andres Veiel's *Black Box BRD* (2001) draws a careful double portrait of the late RAF member, Wolfgang Grams, and Deutsche Bank CEO, Alfred Herrhausen, the latter of whom was murdered by the RAF in 1989. According to Rachel Palfreyman's (2006) analysis, Veiel's comparative biography, persuasive by its subtlety, goes beyond most contemporary academic and journalistic assumptions about why people join groups like the RAF, by revealing such choices as a matter of individual proclivity. Veiel's perspective on Grams is nevertheless political, since it does not privatize his decision, biographical conventions notwithstanding. At the same time, an image is projected of banker Herrhausen that starkly contrasts the one projected by the RAF in the assassination's declaration. Here, the ostensible capitalist monster metamorphizes into a representative of a vigilant attitude, which pleads for the release of Third World debt. What follows is an implicit comparison of the two protagonists that in some respects depicts them as alter-egos. Veiel's superimposition of the two biographies evokes an image of an era in which leftist radicals acted out their conflicts with more decisiveness than they presumably do today, and the director's dialectical subtlety becomes all the more convincing in that it abstains, unlike *The Baader Meinhof Complex*, from rehearsing every shot and every explosion and thus from forcing the spectator to witness the banal spectacle of a series of assassinations.

With respect to these assassinations, it is worth noting that *The Baader Meinhof Complex* does not present all victims of the RAF killings with equally respectful tribute. Murders committed by the group only count as sheer, unadulterated violence – and thus as excessive – when the victims are German. The dead of 1975 and 1977 – the victims of Stockholm, then Buback, Ponto, and Schleyer as well as their drivers and seven accompanying policemen – are positioned as the only "real" victims of the RAF, and thus as the only ones worth mourning, to the exclusion, for instance, of the US soldiers who were killed during the organization's series of bombings in May 1972. Likewise, references in the film to victims of other, very differently situated and theorized military struggles of the time – Vietnamese against US soldiers in Southeast Asia, Palestinian Arabs against Jewish Israelis in Israel/Palestine – position them as mere spectacle. The 1972 killings of 11 Israeli Olympic athletes by a PFLP commando falls outside the framework of complex, serious mourning-work as well. In fact, the then almost completely imprisoned RAF issued a blatantly antisemitic tract justifying the "Black September" attack, which is symptomatically never mentioned in the film (ID-Verlag, 1997: 151–177). Above all, *The Baader Meinhof Complex*, ostensibly concerned with historical accuracy, omits crucial details of RAF history which would have helped problematize the dominant narrative regarding this group of well-situated and allegedly well-intentioned West German bourgeois young adults who engaged in acts of terrorism against persons deemed representative of a persisting, post-Nazi-era "fascism." Among such uncomfortable details is the fact of residual antisemitism within RAF politics, which has not been addressed sufficiently in the German scholarly literature (see Colvin, 2009 for a notable, non-German exception) even as it has received serious criticism in reevaluations of the group from the Left (see Tolmein, 1992; Gerber, 2001; Tolmein, 2002; Bruhn and Gerber, 2007; Krug, 2007; Kowalski, 2010). In order to avoid this issue, the film's plot fixates upon the most illustrious of the RAF leaders, those – Baader, Ensslin, Meinhof, and Raspe – tried in Stuttgart in 1975, while Horst Mahler, an RAF founder and initially one of its high-ranking members, who today is serving another prison sentence for neo-Nazi involvements, disappears from the narrative at the moment of his 1970 arrest. Hence *The Baader Meinhof Complex* ignores the seemingly contradictory affinities between the RAF's anti-imperialist politics and their right-wing and Islamic variations (Tolmein, 2002).

What *The Baader Meinhof Complex* promotes, then, is an antipolitical polemic, the protagonists of which are not only uncannily sexy but one-dimensionally dogmatic. This spectacular fetishization of radicalism, its reduction and projection onto "others," bears remarkable affinity to the German self-same, symptomatizing a deep-structural simplification of power relations and political differences, which also suggests a longing for equally simplified structures of sexuality and gender. Despite the emancipatory fantasies the film evokes, gender and sexuality – not to mention race – remain underexamined not only with the filmic diegesis but within actual RAF texts on social inequality. The organization's writings focused so narrowly on anticapitalist violence that a systematic analysis of other social axes and their distinct, if not unrelated struggles was neglected. The RAF became increasingly alienated from the radical Left, its program devolving into self-referentiality. By and by, the group's references to victimization underwent further abstraction and devolved into the widest possible distance from the West German masses, as they came to focus vaguely on "people in the Third World" and in turn to fully unspecified "oppressed people" anywhere. The feminist, gay, lesbian, and migrant struggles (for the last see Bojadžijev, 2008) emerging in the FRG during the same period as the RAF were never touched upon by the group. These struggles often practiced particularized forms of emancipation which rejected transcendent, quasi-religious referents (*the* anti-imperialist struggle inciting *the* revolution) and concomitant idealism. The RAF's aim, by contrast, was an absolutist revolutionary "beyond," the sociopolitical prognosis of which remained an untheorized and abstract site of automatic social rectification, and thus came easily to serve as a commodificatory lure into violent fatalism.

Lizzie Borden's *Born in Flames* (1983), an American independent feature, supplies an instructive feminist counternarrative to these (and to *The Baader Meinhof Complex*'s) underexamined problematics. Situated in New York City ten years after a hypothetical socialist revolution, nonwhites and nonheterosexuals come to realize that white male privilege and class exploitation have not ended. Finally a disparate grouping of women and lesbians, the organizing core of which is black and working class, begin engaging in acts of militancy grounded in the wisdom of the Saharawi resistance movement in Morocco and aimed toward a mass base that eventually includes white, middle-class women and some men – after a fashion somewhat redolent of the Weather Underground.[13] In the early part of the film, the nascent group chases away potential rapists with whistles, while later, in a more radicalized effort to turn the public sphere into a dehierarchized zone, a more organized, militant formation engages in an action against a mainstream news station that leads to the destruction of its large, vertical antenna. These direct actions serve to demonstrate that militancy does not have to develop into physical violence and murder: the right combination of serious analysis and self-reflexive humor may enable a revolutionary group to produce a political praxis that is ethical and, above all, driven by a nonpaternalistic relationship to the other.

In this regard, Bruce LaBruce's *The Raspberry Reich* (2004) may be understood not simply as RAF porn but as a dual commentary about two opposing discursive positions regarding *Linksterrorismus*. On the one hand, the sexualization of female RAF members is subjected to a campy turn – from girls with guns to gays with guns who masturbate with their weapons and subordinate themselves to a female leader named "Gudrun." On the other hand, *The Raspberry Reich* may be seen as a reaction to the antisensualism of German anti-imperialist rhetoric, the aesthetics of which have tended to convene around tragedy and contempt (see ID-Verlag, 1997). As Klaus Theweleit (1998: 34) has remarked, RAF language has itself always been a radical rhetorical constriction of what was set forth as potentially liberating within the political and semiotic context of 1968. It is this formulaic sloganeering, however, that becomes fetishized in *The Raspberry Reich*, and which invests the organization's political demands with a hopelessly pre-Foucauldian concept: sexual liberation. Instead of engaging in a process of demystification, the film projects onto the political underground the serialized images of perversion commonly circulated about the RAF in the post-1968 discourse.

By the same token, *The Raspberry Reich* offers nothing to counter the RAF murder narrative which *The Baader Meinhof Complex* works obsessively to eliminate through its ironically ongoing mythologization. In fact the latter rehearses the persisting view that, one decade following the formal dissolution of the RAF, the time for historical reckoning has arrived – whereas such an ostensibly RAF-authorized reckoning has already been rendered obsolete. Irmgard Möller, the only survivor of the Stammheim "death night," has for years been denying the suicide narrative (see also Tolmein, 2003; Ohrt, Müller-Lobeck, and Fanizadeh, 1996; and Brunow and Skywalker, 2004), claiming that she and the others were assaulted by a secret service operation (of an unspecified country) that made the murders look like collective suicide. Resembling the practice of Christian confession, affiliation with the anti-imperialist milieu had for decades been organized around this conspiratorial murder myth – with those not subscribing to it becoming automatically positioned on the side of the enemy. More recently, however, similarly nondissident former RAF members who still have not renounced their political positions have either directly contradicted Möller or professed uncertainty about the matter – something which in those circles would have been unthinkable even as late as the 1990s (see Dellwo, 2007; Rollnik and Dubbe, 2004).[14] Indeed insofar as *The Baader Meinhof Complex* considers itself to be the work of popular cinematic demystification, the question remains of who still subscribes to the murder narrative – as dissident and excommunicated RAF member Peter-Jürgen Boock along with several former group members who had never previously distanced themselves from their militant pasts nowadays unequivocably declare that the Stammheim death night as well as the prior death of Ulrike Meinhof was a suicide. To complicate matters further, in 2009 it became public knowledge that the police officer, Karl-Heinz Kurras, who shot but was never convicted for killing Benno Ohnesorg, had been an agent of the Staatssicherheit ("Stasi"), East Germany's secret service; it was, in effect, a murder committed by a closeted communist that contributed to the radicalization of an entire movement which, ironically, had imagined the crime to have been perpetrated by a right-wing "fascist."

In any event, the film's nationalist victimology does reveal that the conflict between the RAF and the West German state was one of internecine rivalry, as both sides were obsessed with the country's longing for an alleged innocence before the Allied occupation after World War Two. Unable to relinquish this topos, the RAF's reactionary analysis of Germany evidenced a familiar authoritarian, paternalistic, and self-centered take on the First World, in anti-fascist guise. Thus analytically, this particular leftist formation did not launch its critique against the German nation per se but against a West German state perceived and experienced essentially as a cruel father figure. But "Daddy" loved Germany, and he has survived his rebellious child. Now he can exploit this victory by imagining himself the better part of a triangulated relationship, the one who acted correctly in that he abided by both official and Oedipal laws. He has chosen survival, while the rebellious child has surrendered to death – a mantra invoked repeatedly in German memorial culture, whenever Germany validates itself by declaring the RAF an ugly byproduct of broader protest movements, disavowing it as an integral part of its own history. Indeed, one revelation of *The Baader Meinhof Complex* is that the RAF must never die.

– Translated by Andrea Mensch

Notes

1 Hanno Balz (2008) has investigated the crucial role played by both sensationalistic and serious press coverage of 1970s *Linksterrorismus* for the phenomenon's political reception in its first decade.

2 For a general survey of cinematic adaptations of West German *Linksterrorismus* and its after-effects, see Kreimeier (2006); also Uka (2006).

3 "Eichinger will die Personen zeigen, wie sie wahrscheinlich waren, und reiht die Ereignisse schlicht aneinander. Er schafft weniger ein Kunst- als ein Geschichtswerk. *Illustrierte Geschichte*" (my emphasis).

4 I am indebted to Maja Figge for this concept.

5 " 'Irgendwas Irrationales in dieser ganzen Sache' sieht selbst der Bonner Sicherheitschef Nollau, dem auffiel, daβ da so viele Mädchen dabei sind.' Er sinniert: 'Vielleicht ist das ein Exzess der Befreiung der Frau, was hier deutlich wird.' " Sarah Colvin (2009: 195) discusses this matter in her book on Ulrike Meinhof.

6 "Die Fehleinschätzung der Realität, das hieraus entwickelte groteske Gesamtkonzept, die kalkulierte praktische Einzelaktion, das forsche und praktisch improvisatorische Handeln bei der Anmietung von Wohnungen unter falschen Namen oder durch Mittelspersonen, die Geschäftigkeit in der Erkundung und Aufklärung, alle diese Dinge tragen Züge, die nur durch eine entscheidende Mitwirkung von Frauen zu erklären sind [...] Von den Aktivisten der Kerngruppe der RAF sind 12 Frauen. Von den 20 zur RAF gestossenen Aktivisten sind acht Frauen. Konzept und Aktivität sind auch Ergebnis einer explosiven Emanzipation der beteiligten weiblichen Aktivisten."

7 "Aus verschiedenen Richtungen und auf verschiedenen Ebenen wurden Ehe und Familie, das Lebensrecht des Ungeborenen und andere ethische Normen angegriffen. Wurden so nicht Fundamente unterhöhlt, ohne die unsere Gesellschaft ihre Stabilität verliert?"

8 "Die Neurotisierung in den ersten Lebensjahren wirkt sich auf junge Mädchen in jenen Fällen zusätzlich kriminalisierend aus, in denen sie gegen ihre eigentliche Begabung in einseitig vermännlichende Bildungsgänge und sexualisierte Lebensweisen hinein-genötigt werden. Die einseitig vermännlichende 'Selbstverwirklichung' der Frau muss Unzufriedenheit potenzieren, weil sie für viele eine zusätzliche Abdressur vorgege-bener Bedürfnisse darstellt. Diese Gegebenheit bewirkt erstmalig in der Geschichte, dass vornehmlich einige junge, intellektualisierte Frauen zu Terroristinnen werden."

9 "Mit Nadja Uhl [als Brigitte Mohnhaupt, VSV] hält das schiere Töten Einzug, der Blutrausch, von Begründungen entkoppelt."

10 One might contrast Christopher Roth's *Baader* (2002), an affirmative and politicized variation of *Bonnie and Clyde* (Arthur Penn, 1967), in which many freely available "Bonnies" become taken with/by an apolitical "Clyde." Here, Andreas Baader is a rebel surrounded by energetic coolness, who dies an especially brutal death amid a hail of police bullets – a barely hidden but particularly clichéd and heroic variant of the Stammheim murder narrative.

11 In Fassbinder's *The Third Generation*, one of the most enlightening yet least discussed of the RAF films, the relationship between West German armed leftist militants and the FRG is imagined precisely as sadomasochism, yet without *The Baader Meinhof Complex*'s superficial reductivism. See Lode (1996).

12 Sontheimer (2010: 83ff) adds a few remarks to the description of Mohnhaupt's release from prison, referring to the RAF as "Feminat" and thus denigrating it in typical 1970s fashion, as women's liberation gone awry.

13 It should be emphasized that militant leftism since 1968 evidences little unified strategy or positionality. Thus the differences between West German and US anti-imperialist groupings are striking. The most serious of these entail the politics of murder: the Weather Underground, for example, in stark contrast to the RAF, concentrated on bomb attacks that would only destroy property, not people. The Weather Underground further distinguished its program by adopting a theoretical and practical openness which allowed the libidinal achievements of 1968, including feminism and the critique

of heterosexism to inflect its organizational structure. The RAF, on the other hand, reduced its analysis of capitalism to an absolutist rhetoric "against" but not beyond the State, and hence could only inevitably articulate a reactionary politics. For a historical comparison of the two groups, see Varon (2004).

14 Rollnik spent the last years of her 15-year sentence in Lübeck Prison, where Irmgard Möller was her fellow prisoner.

References

Aust, S. (2008) *Der Baader-Meinhof-Komplex*. Erweiterte und aktualisierte Neuausgabe, Hoffmann und Campe, Hamburg.

Balz, H. (2008) *Von Terroristen, Sympathisanten und dem starken Staat. Die öffentliche Debatte über die RAF in den 70er Jahren*, Campus, Frankfurt a.M.

Barth, V. (1996) Das Schweigen der Lämmer. Zur Historienschreibung um Ulrike Meinhof, *Die Beute. Politik & Verbrechen*, 1 (96), 28–33.

Barthes, R. (1964) *Mythen des Alltags*, Suhrkamp, Frankfurt a.M.

Bojadžijev, M. (2008) *Die windige Internationale. Rassismus und Kämpfe der Migration*, Westfälisches Dampfboot, Münster.

Bönisch, G. and Wiegreife, K. (2008) Massive Gegendrohung. *Der Spiegel*, September 8, 48–53.

Bruhn, J. and Gerber, J. (eds) (2007) *Rote Armee Fiktion*, ça ira, Freiburg.

Brunow, D. and Skywalker, L. (2004) "Zur Mythenbildung nicht geeignet": Im Gespräch mit Irmgard Möller. *testcard*, 12, 60–65.

Colvin, S. (2009) *Ulrike Meinhof and West German Terrorism. Language, Violence, and Identity*, Camden House, Rochester.

Deleuze, G. and Guattari, F. (1977) *Anti-Ödipus. Kapitalismus und Schizophrenie I*, Suhrkamp Verlag, Frankfurt a.M.

Dellwo, K-H. (2007) *Das Projektil sind wir. Der Aufbruch einer Generation, die RAF und die Kritik der Waffen*, Nautilus, Hamburg.

Derrida, J. (1997) *Dem Archiv verschrieben. Eine Freudsche Impression*, Brinkmann & Bose, Berlin.

Derrida, J. (2003) *Eine gewisse unmögliche Möglichkeit, vom Ereignis zu sprechen*, Merve, Berlin.

DiCaprio, L. (1996) *Marianne and Juliane/The German Sisters*, in *Perspectives on German Cinema* (eds T. Ginsberg and K.M. Thompson), G.K. Hall/Macmillan, New York and London, pp. 391–402.

Elsaesser, T. (2007) *Terror und Trauma. Zur Gewalt des Vergangenen in der BRD*, Kadmos, Berlin.

Galli, M. and Preusser, H-P. (ed.) (2006) *Mythos Terrorismus. Vom Deutschen Herbst zum 11. September*. Universitätsverlag Winter, Heidelberg.

Gerber, J. (2001) Auf der Suche nach Normalität. Der Antizionismus der westdeutschen Stadtguerilla. *Hallesche Beiträge zur Zeitgeschichte*, 10, 5–42.

Ginsberg, T. and Thompson, K.M. (eds) (1996) *Perspectives on German Cinema*, G.K. Hall/Macmillan, New York, London.

Horchem, H.J. (1975) *Extremisten in einer selbstbewußten Demokratie. Rote-Armee-Fraktion. Rechtsextremismus. Der lange Marsch durch die Institutionen*, Herder, Freiburg.

ID-Verlag (ed.) (1997) *Rote Armee Fraktion. Texte und Materialien zur Geschichte der RAF.* Edition ID-Archiv, Berlin.

Kniebe, T. and Kreye, A. (2008) Die Gesichter des Baader Meinhof Komplexes. *Süddeutsche Zeitung*, February 2–3, p. 13.

Kowalski, M. (2010) *"Aber ich will doch etwas getan haben dagegen!" Die RAF als postfaschistisches Phänomen.* Vergangenheitsverlag, Berlin.

Kraushaar, W. (2005) *Die Bombe im jüdischen Gemeindehaus*, Hamburger Edition, Hamburg.

Kreimeier, K. (2006) Die RAF und der deutsche Film, in *Die RAF und der linke Terrorismus* (ed. W. Kraushaar), Band 2. Hamburger Edition, Hamburg, pp. 1150–1170.

Krug, U. (2007) *Wie die-Werwölfe. Jungle World*, 43, 25.

Kurbjuweit, D. (2008) Bilder der Barbarei. *Der Spiegel*, September 8, 42–48.

Kurbjuweit, D., Röbel, S., Sontheimer, M., and Wensierski, P. (2009) "Verrat vor dem Schuss." *Der Spiegel*, May 25, 42–51.

Lode, I. (1996) Terrorism, sadomasochism, and utopia in Fassbinder's *The Third Generation*, in *Perspectives on German Cinema* (eds T. Ginsberg and K.M. Thompson), G.K. Hall/Macmillan, New York, London, pp. 415–434.

Meinhof, U. (1970) "Natürlich darf geschossen werden." Ulrike Meinhof über die Baader-Aktion. *Der Spiegel*, June 15, 74f.

Nicodemus, K. (2009) Death wish: German cinemas enduring fascination with the Red Army Faction. Film Comment, 55, 55–59.

Ohrt, R., Müller-Lohbeck, C., and Fanizadeh, A. (1996) "Wir meinten es ernst." Gespräch mit Irmgard Möller über Entstehung, Bedeutung und Fehler der RAF. *Die Beute*, 9 (1), 8–27.

Paczensky, S.v. (ed.) (1978) *Frauen und Terror. Versuche, die Beteiligung von Frauen an Gewalttaten zu erklären.* Rowohlt, Reinbek.

Palfreyman, R. (2006) "The fourth generation: legacies of violence as quest for identity in post-unification terrorism films," in *German Cinema since Unification* (ed. D. Clarke), Continuum, London, pp. 11–42.

Peters, B. (2004) *Tödlicher Irrtum. Die Geschichte der RAF*, Argon, Berlin.

Rollnik, G. and Dubbe, D. (2004) *Keine Angst vor niemand. Über die Siebziger, die Bewegung 2. Juni und die RAF*, Nautilus, Hamburg.

Schwind, H-D. (ed) (1978) *Ursachen des Terrorismus in der Bundesrepublik Deutschland*, Walter de Gruyter, Berlin.

Sekretariat der Deutschen Bischofskonferenz (ed.) (1978) "Erklärung der Vollversammlung der Deutschen Bischofskonferenz zum Terrorismus vom 21. September 1977," in *Ursachen des Terrorismus und Voraussetzungen seiner Überwindung*, Bonn.

Sontheimer, M. (2010) *"Natürlich kann geschossen warden." Eine kurze Geschichte der Roten Armee Fraktion*, DVA, München.

Der Spiegel (1971) "Löwe los," February 22, 26–34.

Der Spiegel (1977) "Frauen im Untergrund: 'Etwas Irrationales,'" August 8, 22–33.

Theweleit, K. (1998) *Ghosts. Drei leicht inkorrekte Vorträge*, Stroemfeld, Frankfurt a.M., Basel.

Tolmein, O. (1992) *Stammheim vergessen. Deutschlands Aufbruch und die RAF*, Konkret Literatur Verlag, Hamburg.

Tolmein, O. (2002) *Vom Deutschen Herbst zum 11. September. Die RAF, der Terrorismus und der Staat*, Konkret Literatur Verlag, Hamburg.

Tolmein, O. (2003) *"RAF – das war für uns Befreiung." Ein Gespräch mit Irmgard Möller über bewaffneten Kampf, Knast und die Linke.* Revised and updated 3rd edn, Konkret Literatur Verlag, Hamburg.

Uka, W. (2006) Terrorismus im Film der 70er Jahre: Über die Schwierigkeiten deutscher Filmemacher beim Umgang mit der realen Gegenwart, in *Terrorismus in der Bundesrepublik. Medien, Staat und Subkulturen in den 1970er Jahren* (eds K. Weinhauer, J. Requate, and H-G. Haupt), Campus, Frankfurt, New York, pp. 382–398.

Varon, J. (2004) *Bringing the War Home. The Weather Underground, the Red Army Faction, and Revolutionary Violence in the Sixties and Seventies*, University of California Press, Berkeley.

Viett, I. (1997) *Nie war ich furchtloser*, Nautilus, Hamburg.

Winkler, W. (2007) *Die Geschichte der RAF*, Rowohlt, Berlin.

Filmography

Baader (Christopher Roth, Germany, 2002).

Baader Meinhof Complex, The [*Der Baader Meinhof Komplex*] (Uli Edel, Germany, 2008).

Black Box BRD (Andreas Veiel, Germany, 2001).

Bonnie and Clyde (Arthur Penn, USA, 1967).

Born in Flames (Lizzie Borden, USA, 1983).

Downfall [*Der Untergang*] (Oliver Hirschbiegel, Germany, 2004).

Germany in Autumn [*Deutschland im Herbst*] (R.W. Fassbinder, Alexander Kluge, Volker Schlöndorff, *et al.*, West Germany, 1978).

Legend of Rita, The [*Die Stille nach dem Schuss*] (Volker Schlöndorff, Germany, 2000).

Lost Honor of Katharina Blum, The [*Die verlorene Ehre der Katharina Blum*] (Volker Schlöndorff and Margarethe von Trotta, West Germany, 1975).

Marianne and Julianne [*Die bleierne Zeit*] (Margarethe von Trotta, West Germany, 1981).

Third Generation, The [*Die dritte Generation*] (R.W. Fassbinder, West Germany, 1978).

Raspberry Reich, The (Bruce LaBruce, USA, 2004).

Todesspiel [Death Game] (Heinrich Breloer, Germany, 1997).

19

Dislocations

Videograms of a Revolution
and the Search for Images

Frances Guerin

Over 40 years, Harun Farocki has produced a body of work – films, new media installations and writings – that probes every level of the status, production, distribution, redistribution, storing, and perception of images. On every level, and from every perspective, the images that comprise Farocki's oeuvre interrogate the multifarious meanings, the realities and ambiguities, uses and misuses of images in the public sphere. He is particularly committed to the exposure of images that are used by the mass media, governments, and institutions set up in their name, science and industry, to perpetuate political, economic, and institutional power. Invariably, he approaches these discourses on the image via exposure, analysis, and usually a critique of its deployment to fuel the machinery of industry, consumer culture, and war. And always, the third party in the destruction that goes hand in hand with the production of such images is the camera of Harun Farocki, the imagemaker. Ultimately, the task of Farocki's films is didactic: his films are conceived and produced for an audience open to learning how to see and understand images. They are, so to speak, a form of training the viewer's eye and mind in the lifecycles of images.

The reach of Farocki's work is extensive: he creates, re-presents, dissects, and reflects on myriad images, no matter their form, that clog the visual environment. In over 90 films, Farocki turns the attention of his camera to subjects as apparently diverse as, for example, seventeenth-century Flemish painting (*Stilleben (Still Life)*, 1997), images generated in institutions such as prisons (*Gefängnisbilder (Prison Images)*, 2000),[1] the phenomenon of the shopping mall (*Die Schöpfer der Einkaufswelten (The Creators of the Shopping Worlds)*, 2001), and, perhaps most disturbingly, the role of the image in military strategies designed to map and destroy "enemy targets," the image as a weapon of wars that bleed uncontrollably into the spaces and events of everyday life (*Erkennen und Verfolgen (War at a Distance)*, 2003). Thus,

A Companion to German Cinema, First Edition. Edited by Terri Ginsberg and Andrea Mensch.
© 2012 Blackwell Publishing Ltd. Published 2012 by Blackwell Publishing Ltd.

in *Prison Images* Farocki's camera sees from the perspective of the all-seeing eye of the panopticon, and in *The Creators of the Shopping Worlds* the camera follows the way that our behavior in the mall is researched, planned in advance, and ultimately controlled through surveillance videos, body scans, computer generated projections. In films such as *Bilder der Welt und Inschrift des Krieges (Images of the World and the Inscription of War)* (1988) and *War at a Distance* – perhaps Farocki's best known films – he exposes, for example, how the development of image technologies in wartime such as the video head of a smart bomb in 1953 accelerates the development of televisual technologies in everyday life. The two spheres are thus intimately connected. Whether his camera is interrogating the inextricability of industry, the machinery of war and the television image (*Zwischen zwei Kriegen (Between Two Wars)*, 1978), between the production of Napalm B, the exploitation of human labor, and documentary filmmaking (*Nicht Löschbares Feuer (Inextinguishable Fire)*, 1969),[2] or between the "opinion industry" – porn magazines, advertising, and so on – and fiction filmmaking, it leaves no doubt of its own complicity in the corrosion of human freedom and democracy in the age of industrial capitalism. Despite the diversity of topics and the media in which they are represented, Farocki's films are, at heart, always about training the viewer in how images are produced, appropriated, mobilized by those in power to perpetuate their ideological and political agendas.

Simultaneously, alongside an overwhelming analysis of the contemporary use of images, Farocki's images embrace a belief in, and an interrogation of the revolutionary potential of images. Even as the image – of surveillance for example – entraps and debilitates, it sets the conditions of escape and possibility, it points to that which is outside its frame. Similarly, the image as instrument of measurement, calculation and automation embraces the possibility of indeterminacy, the tendency toward deviation and the potential to function as the ground of political and ideological protestation and contestation. And, while Farocki has made very clear, particularly through drawing attention to their industrial status and their function as visual mediation, even if his own films are complicit in the violence of twentieth-century industry and culture, he holds onto the last shred of belief that they still have the power to educate and effect change. In an obvious example, a film such as *Inextinguishable Fire* evidences the incineration of napalm on its innocent, unsuspecting victims, and traces the chemical back to the factories and workers responsible for its production, Dow Chemical in Michigan. With our eyes open to the film image as pivot in the process of witnessing such violence, Farocki leaves the viewer in no doubt of his teaching: "When napalm is burning, it is too late to extinguish it. You have to fight napalm where it is produced: in the factories."[3]

In the film's exposition sequence, Farocki reads the testimony of a Vietnamese victim of napalm burns. Because "you" (the viewer) will "close your eyes" if the film shows the burns of the young man, Farocki demonstrates the violence of napalm through an ersatz violence. He extinguishes a burning cigarette on his bare arm, announcing that a cigarette burns at 400 degrees while napalm burns at 3000 degrees. In this moment, Farocki in the frame, reading, is the image he made, performing an act of self-immolation to evoke (as opposed to representing) the destruction of napalm. This *mise-en-abîme* simultaneously educates the viewer in the destruction of napalm, and self-reflexively destroys Farocki's authority in an act of self-maiming. This oft-cited example is also the moment of *Inextinguishable Fire*'s regard for the potential change enabled through images. As we watch it, we recognize the relevance and effect of napalm in our lives, removed in time and place from the Vietnam War as we may be. When we cringe at Farocki's self-harm, so napalm is metonymically brought into our living rooms.

This moment of tension between the image as it is created in words of the burning of Vietnam villages and their people and the literal image of Farocki burning his arm is held together in what Elsaesser (2004a: 30) refers to as the dialectical nature of this filmmaking process. Public historical and private images are placed side by side, editorially manipulated, and as viewers we are able to "see" the consequences. Often in Farocki's films these juxtapositions, the so-called dialectic, comprise images from two different time-spaces: Vietnam in wartime, and the West at a supposedly peaceful historical juncture. Although he rarely uses the word, Elsaesser (2004a: 30) theorizes Farocki's practice as a dialectical process of image production that "brings to the fore a third definition of the two-image idea." If we accept this as Farocki's primary technique of editing, then it is in the conceptual spaces between the ersatz or juxtaposed images that the potential for revolution in images and inspired by images is located. To iterate, Farocki's is not a dialectic in the sense that it was conceived by the Soviet post-Revolutionary filmmakers. It is a dialectic of juxtaposition marked by a substitution that enables the contemporary Western viewer's recognition of how documentary images from an apparently distant time-space indeed contain urgent relevance to contemporary existence.

In the 1992 film *Videogramme einer Revolution (Videograms of a Revolution)*, a film that documents the fall of the Ceauçescu regime in Bucharest in 1989, this powerful double-entendre of image production and reception is at its most salient. Together with Andrej Ujica, Farocki makes a film that interrogates the use and misuse of images: images that both *enable* the momentous events in Romania and *distract* from the authenticity of their representation. That is, the various images in Farocki and Ujica's film stage an event like any other that defines the revolution, and simultaneously, they are a representation of the same revolution. Moreover, *Videograms of a Revolution* is made entirely of archival footage: footage filmed by the Romanian state television and the many amateur imagemakers who saw events from their own unique perspective, from rooftops, street level, around corners, from car windows, and so on. Together with Ujica, Farocki the filmmaker is here an editor of images; thus he creates meaning through assemblage rather than producing images, just as he did in his earlier films such as *Inextinguishable Fire*. Even when the images are filmed by Farocki, it is nevertheless in the editing of these and other images that the viewer becomes educated (and agitated) in reading images. Through compilation, various layers of images – the production and airing of television images, the recording of the revolution, the unearthing of these images from the archive, and their re-presentation in 1992 – come together in *Videograms of a Revolution* to create a trajectory that witnesses the repression, production, and destruction of political democracy, and social liberation. In Farocki's film, all of these phases of the revolution are in some way created by images. In this way, *Videograms of a Revolution* represents the realization of the radical aspiration of the image sought by documentary filmmakers throughout the twentieth century. The film finds images that are able to provide a framework for the possibility of social revolution. Only, it finds these images where we least expect them – in the real world outside of the frame of the moving image, that is, in this case, in the various modes of distribution, exhibition, and appropriation of images. Once again, it is not the single image itself that is bound to effect political and ideological change, but power resides in the way the image is deployed, manipulated, and received. And these aspects of the image are enabled through the juxtaposition of different perspectives, different kinds of images, and then, in the life lived by the image. To be sure, Farocki's process of image production is innovative, and it always gives over to the radicality of an image that educates and elucidates.

These discourses that point to the moment outside the production of the single image come closest to what Nora Alter (Elsaesser, 2004a) has called the "Im/perceptible" of Farocki's *Images of the World and the Inscription of War*. Alter is interested in Farocki's instantiation of a moment of "im/perceptibility" through the use of images that simultaneously reveal and conceal their political critique. In *Videograms of a Revolution*, however, I am more interested in the agitational and educative potential of what is beyond the moving images that we watch, both the film itself and the fragments Farocki brings together into the film as a whole. The outside, or the moment of dislocation/revolution that I identify in *Videograms of a Revolution* is not found or linked to the image aesthetic, even what the image represents. Rather, it is in that image which is not shown, in that phase of the image's life that we do not physically perceive. And, if Farocki's aspirations seem idealist, even Romantic in their determination to revolutionize, we must remember that the said Romanticism is always negated or compromised by Farocki's critique of his own intervention as a filmmaker from the West.

There is one more level of Farocki's filmmaking for which *Videograms of a Revolution* must be held up as an example. Farocki is devoted to rescuing, preserving, and archiving images as a way of articulating and understanding phenomena such as identity, culture, and the dissemination of knowledge. According to Farocki (2004: 264), film, as a modern techne, is one of the most effective forms of archiving and preserving images. In addition, the narrative is an aesthetic site at which to locate or situate the image. To this end, again and again, he prefers to reuse archival and found images, weaving them into film narratives that, as a result, become more than image repositories. Thus, for example, in a film such as *Der Ausdrück der Hände* (*The Expression of Hands*) (1997), Farocki redeploys fragments of classical film narratives in which the hand in close-up communicates through expression.

Farocki's film not only reflects on filmic representations of the hand and their history, but it segues into an exploration of the proliferation of uses of the hand in the economy of Western capitalism: as a conduit, a tool, a visual abbreviation. Once again, it is not at the literal level of representation that Farocki's films create meaning. While *Videograms of a Revolution* may seem distant from *The Expression of Hands*, the films are partners in their use of found footage to decipher and interpret both individual film fragments as well as the role of the fragment in larger narratives, here, the Romanian revolution and its retelling. In addition, this insistence on meaning as it is found in the space between, around and outside of the image remains consistent across these otherwise distant films. In both instances, this is achieved through Farocki's preferred method of linking by juxtaposing and substituting one image for another.[4]

Of course, Farocki's method of editing, his film aesthetic which has been characterized in a number of different ways, also reflects his relationship to the filmmaking practices that come before his, and those that were conceived in his environs. Most significantly, within the New German Cinema, the work of Alexander Kluge can be seen as ancestor to Farocki. Like Kluge, Farocki no longer believes in the cause and effect relationship of the image to the revolution. However, while Kluge politicized his audience by critiquing the image that persuades and "interpolates," thus making viewers reflect on how their opinions are formed in the first place, Farocki's film witnesses images that overthrow a government. Similarly, for Kluge, for those filmmakers and theorists in his midst, as well as for those who precede him, the political radicality of filmmaking lies in the production of a radical aesthetic. Farocki, however, locates, or dislocates, the radicality to a time-space outside of the image, but still within its force-field.

Videograms of a Revolution further demonstrates the multilayers of Farocki's work. In this film, he openly juxtaposes the formal concern of recycling with the theoretical impetus to politicize the image: every gesture of preservation is simultaneously a gesture of mediation and, subsequently, questioning the status of what is pictured. Another extremely articulate example of this complex form of image preservation and subsequent creativity can be found in *Images of the World and the Inscription of War*, particularly with reference to the wartime aerial reconnaissance image and the Nazis' visual documentation of their appalling crimes. The victim is pictured, thus documented, objectified thus trapped by the gaze of the camera and its operator, and ultimately, marked for destruction. The now familiar image of a beautiful young Jewish woman confronting the camera as she motions toward it on the platform at Auschwitz is exemplary of this conundrum of the image as it is archived, made into sense data, and seen through the viewfinder of destruction. Farocki himself discusses *Images of the World* on the voiceover and explains the woman's look as like that she would assume on a boulevard. While the woman's look puts her on a "platform," "the camp, run by the SS, is meant to destroy her and the photographer who captures her beauty for posterity is part of that same SS" (Elsaesser, 2004a: 199). Thus, the photograph, the photographer who takes it, and Farocki who reuses it, together work to memorialize (her image is forever recorded), incarcerate and destroy the woman at Auschwitz. And this complex process of documentation all the way through asking the viewer to rethink the relevance of Nazi manipulation and violence via the image is enabled through the juxtaposition of different perspectives, different discourses that create meaning outside of this image.

Thus, to reiterate, I am arguing that meaning is dislocated to the world outside of the image, enabled through Farocki's particular forms of montage, a dislocation that is the focus of the construction of the image. To achieve its multiple ends in *Videograms of a Revolution,* Farocki and Ujica reuse the wide range of images that documented (or tried to document) the revolution: official and unofficial State television, amateur film, home video, in short, whatever was available. Farocki has always worked in a number of media, a choice and decision that in interview he says has often been motivated by material conditions (Farocki, 2004). He insists that his choices of film, video, television, and more recently, digital images have been determined by conditions beyond the aesthetic: availability, the demands of a given commission, the specificity of the audience and the context that awaits his work. This said, as is so often the case with Farocki's words and images, there is a caveat to this deflection of focus away from the media specificity of a moving image. As Hal Foster (2004: 193) observes, and as so much of Farocki's work attests, however variant the "instruments of seeing and imaging … he is all but obsessed with the role, indeed the fate of cinema." It must be acknowledged this "obsession" was more prevalent in Farocki's work of the twentieth- than the twenty-first century, and, for its time, *Videograms of a Revolution* is both typical of and a departure from this obsession. It is, on the one hand, a film that is first and foremost about the capacity of the cinema, or moving images in their many forms, to bring life to a revolution. It is no accident that Farocki makes a film in a historical moment when reality is starting to be realized – sometimes literally – through digital production and reproduction of moving images. And yet, the imbrication of images and history in Romania is still firmly grounded in indexical inscriptions of the analog image. This paradoxical, perhaps anachronistic moment in the history of images provides the perfect opportunity for Farocki to "obsess" on the trajectory of cinematic images. On the other hand, the film is also, by necessity, about the life of the image beyond its aesthetic. Perhaps because of the prevalence of historical determining factors in Romania 1989, in keeping with the contingency of the image form and aesthetic, *Videograms of a Revolution* stumbles upon the realization that, while the aesthetic is important to the political efficacy of a radical image, it is the way that images are used and the contexts in which they are put that determine their place in history.[5]

Videograms of a Revolution quickly moves beyond the immediacy of its surface representations. The film's focus on the Romanian revolution and its representation provides access to bigger concerns. For example, it negotiates how images function and are mobilized to "deceive" or "distract" us from the truth, how historical events are represented usually in the popular press or through mass media. In a familiar Farocki strategy, the film also reflects on the way that history is written and visualized in the spaces that open up through the repetition and duplication of images. In *Videograms of a Revolution* and other of Farocki's films, this concern with repetition and the creative possibilities of proliferation is enabled through the recycling of images, through the revisualizations from another time and in another place. And to reiterate, it is at times through a process of juxtaposition and substitution that the viewer recognizes what the film does not show: her responsibility for what the image does show. For *Videograms of a Revolution*, these issues are secreted in the gaps created by the cut and subsequent montage of recycled film fragments. The gap, or missing link, what lies between film fragments, for Farocki, the successive recyclings, then and now, here and there, creates the spaces in which we the viewers are left to know and to see for ourselves. In this sense Farocki's films are an extension of the concerns of New German Cinema and particularly the work of Kluge: it is our vision or, our relationship to, and our reception of the image that is always at stake in this and other of Farocki's works.

The processes of recycling and revisualization are marshaled as a potent instance of Farocki's dependence on and simultaneous critique of the mass media. While it is standard practice for political documentary to re-present media images as the basis on which to vilify them, *Videograms of a Revolution* adds another layer of complexity.[6] The film itself embraces these strategies for its formal definition: it is put together through infinite reproduction and instantaneous communication of moving image mimesis, the *sine qua non* of global television. Subsequently, as I illustrate, the film deftly reorients these strategies to effect a searing critique of the particular strategies of ideological persuasion endemic to the mass media in both the socialist and capitalist worlds. *Videograms of a Revolution* not only goes a step further than Farocki's other films, it also expands the vocabulary of the political documentary when it replicates the very formal concerns of the media it confronts. Ultimately, all this is in the name of questioning and reorganizing the way we are conditioned to "see" – to perceive, to understand, to know the world through images – and in turn, this confrontation and reorientation of our vision forms the basis of a new political relationship to the world.

The Struggle of Images, The Struggle for Images

In a sequence close to the beginning of *Videograms of a Revolution,* we are taken to Victory Square for the live telecast of Nicolae Ceauçescu. He delivers his final speech to his people in what the voiceover tells us is an attempt to assert his endangered power at what would become the end of his 25 years of dictatorship. Very quickly, the centered, three-quarter shot of Ceauçescu on the balcony of the

Central Committee Headquarters begins to shake, the image is interrupted by the loss of tracking, and the television goes off the air. Elisabeth Neiman's voiceover in English (the English translation of the original male German voiceover) assures us that recording of the events continues in the station's mobile recording van. Her voice appears to belong to Farocki's film rather than to the culled footage. We believe the discrepancy she points up between what is being recorded and what is being televised. Her voiceover is given a certain authority when visual evidence accompanies it: red to represent the blank Televiziunea Romana image is inserted in the bottom left-hand corner of the image of the film we watch. The grand façade of the Central Committee fills the remainder of the screen. And when this background too loses clarity and becomes filled with the sky, the female narrator explains that the cameraman had received instructions to pan to the sky if anything unexpected occurred. And so we discover that the supposedly uninterrupted image of the events is itself a fabrication no more authentic than the balanced, three-quarter shots of the official broadcast. However immediate these shaky frames may appear, we are still seeing a highly constructed image. Similarly, at this early stage in the *Videograms of a Revolution* we still believe in the omniscience of its images.

When the television image is restored, the inset in the bottom left-hand corner replicates the full-sized image that fills the remainder of the screen. Gone is the red of the blank insert. Nevertheless, the confusion continues because Nicolae and Elena Ceauçescu appear not to realize that they are once again on air. The dictator's incessant cries for calm, and his tapping on the microphone continue as though in an appeal for the technology to be restored. At one moment, he even tells his wife to shut up. Despite these chattering pleas for quiet, the voiceover tells us that the sound is still off the air. What then are we hearing? Are these sounds that were nevertheless not broadcast to viewers in Romania at the time? Or has the sound in fact been restored? Perhaps the voiceover is confused? Or it might even be that the sounds are pre-recorded and belong only to the diegesis of Farocki and Ujica's film. The authority of the film begins to erode. Before *Videograms of a Revolution* answers these questions, sound and image are restored, we hear Ceauçescu and simultaneously see him in long-shot on the balcony as he vocally reinforces the independence and strength of the Romanian people.

However, the scene does not end there, because *Videograms of a Revolution* then sets out to discover the beginning of the disturbance. The same footage is replayed, and with the guidance of the woman's voiceover we watch carefully to see if we can detect the cause of the interruption. Our faith in her knowledge is thus restored when we watch the film appear to distance itself from the images it re-presents through a series of replayed fragments. However, nothing reveals itself. Undeterred, *Videograms of a Revolution* looks for yet another perspective: images from the weekly newsreel were able to record the disruption from a different perspective, so the female voiceover tells us. We see the rally from high above the sky, we look down at acute angles at crowds of people, like the vibrant palette of an impressionist painter, the mass of people take on the effect of a swarm of heads that color the length of the archival footage. We are given a bird's-eye view of the balcony on which Ceauçescu speaks. But still, these images cannot find what caused the disturbance. These are images without insight. *Videograms of a Revolution* leaves the footage running to reveal that the events we have just seen are in fact taking place on a television screen in a living room belonging to what the voiceover tells us is the apartment of an amateur cameraman. Not to be defeated, and still at a loss for an explanation of the unusual events, the amateur camera finds its way to the window and looks down at the street below to continue the search. Again, it sees crowds in long-shot, an image that represents the overwhelming commitment to revolution. Still, neither the amateur cameraman nor *Videograms of a Revolution* can find images to explain the interruption to events at Victory Square or their representation. We are left frustrated by the capacity of the image to objectively and coherently document the revolution.

This early sequence from *Videograms of a Revolution* conveniently lays out the film's four central concerns, concerns which act as a filter through which the broader discourses about the image and its imbrication in history unfold. First, we are introduced to the Romanian revolution as a revolution played out as a struggle for images: the dictatorship begins to topple as its image is interrupted, its performance rendered vulnerable. Later in the film, we will see the Romanian revolutionaries triumph when they occupy the national television station and "own" its broadcasts. By seizing control of the production and exhibition of the television image in Bucharest, the revolutionaries assume the power to govern. However, at this early stage in the film, there is no question that Ceauçescu's position on the balcony of the Central Committee is directly dependent on his control and manipulation of the image that represents him. Even its failures are orchestrated.

Second, here we learn that *Videograms of a Revolution* finds a new way for images to see this revolution, thus to gain new insight into its unfolding. Farocki's and Ujica's film, which is often indistinguishable from those of the "revolutionaries," bystanders, and other imagemakers who have filmed the footage in the first place, sees the different layers of social unrest through the uncertainty of a slowly unfolding, repetitive, sometimes confusing narration that ultimately reveals the same qualities in the events themselves – confusion and repetition. Thus, the films' uneven visual aesthetic is inseparable from those that comprise it: raw, out of focus, handheld, grainy, often interrupted by technical glitches, unable to locate the truth. The multiplicity of perspectives, the harshness of the image, the uncertainty of what it sees and hears are qualities we have come to associate with the truth available to a documentary camera. These are the techniques of the 1960s and 1970s, of direct cinema and cinema verité, techniques that propose to guarantee the authenticity of the image (Winston, 1988: 517–529). Like these documentary traditions before it, *Videograms of a Revolution* displays a belief in the power and agency of apparently authentic images – film, television, video as rehearsal for the digital, amateur, professional, official and unofficial. Irrespective, or more likely because of the ambiguity of what the cameras see, the immediacy of the images, apparently shot in real time, guarantees an authentic representation and simultaneous realization of the revolution. This aesthetic is typical of Farocki's oeuvre: even though the footage is shot by others, its reuse reinforces Farocki's didactic demonstration of the limitations and possibilities of the image. The truth, so to speak, of these images as they are recycled in *Videograms of a Revolution* is their representation of the revolution from different, often conflicting, sometimes blind perspectives.

However, the film's *mise-en-abîme* of images also challenges how images are made, the way they are interpreted, how they are used, who uses them, who owns them, who gives them meaning. Thus, *Videograms of a Revolution* illustrates its third concern: the film questions and critiques the valency of images, and in particular, it questions the images that are used in the support of the authoritarian regime. Ultimately, in the fourth important task of the film, *Videograms of a Revolution* moves beyond the events in Bucharest and Timisoara and their representation to embrace the paradox at the heart of twentieth-century iconoclasm. Namely, the film realizes the aspiration for a moving image that will help mobilize the masses to revolution, an aspiration sought by leftist, and particularly, Marxist intellectuals and image makers throughout the twentieth century.[7] At the same time, by extension, *Videograms of a Revolution* critiques the problematic role of media images in the official representation of public protest and civil unrest. Thus the film both documents the realized potential for the radical image in the twentieth century and vilifies the irresponsibility of its use by institutions working in the interests of those in power into the twenty-first. As I go on to demonstrate, through this fourth task, *Videograms* steps outside of itself to connect with and depart from its avant-garde documentary predecessors. This it achieves when it opens up to the possibility of visualizations of the present that ultimately lay the groundwork for the potential use of the image in political protest in the future. These four central concerns are achieved in *Videograms of a Revolution* through its "aesthetic of dislocation."

An Aesthetics of Dislocation

In the series of images described above, we see dislocation in abundance. First we see the dislocation of Ceauçescu's power: as it is, as it dissolves and as it and might have become. Second, there is a dislocation between what the people see and what the cameras see, between historical events and their representation. Third, and perhaps the most unexpectedly, there is a discrepancy between what Farocki and Ujica's film shows us and what we actually see. As a non-Romanian speaker, I, for example, am reliant on the narrator to locate the image, to tell me the time, the place and to whom the image belongs. Too often, I see one thing, for example, a camera looking for an image as it pans to the sky, and then the voiceover tells me I am seeing something different: here, the premeditated distractions of a socialist dictatorship. In other moments of the film, I rely on the narrator to clarify what the image documents. And when the information does not appear on the sound-track, this layering, or dislocation, results when the narrator claims the absence of sound at a moment when we clearly hear the goings on at the Central Committee. These inconsistencies in the image, the sound and the material dynamics at play in the relationship between them leave the film's audience dislocated by the conun-drum of the revolution and its inadequate representation.

Fourth, the televisual image is always dislocated. In this sequence we see the live broadcast interrupted by technical glitches that remind of the mediation involved. As Benjamin Young (2004) points out in one of the few articles in English on the film, the televisual image is always also a temporal dislocation. There is always a lag between the past of the events and the viewer's present, even as they are broadcast "simultaneously." Moreover, as we watch the film now 15 years later, we are further dislocated in time and space from the revolution and its representation. The intervention of Farocki and Ujica's film creates still more dislocations: for example, the dislocation of reality that is forged in the gap between the different perspectives – the official broadcast, the film camera from the weekly newsreel, an amateur cameraman filming from his apartment, Farocki and Ujica's film. As we have seen in this sequence, *Videograms of a Revolution* repeats events from different angles, through the perspectives of different cameras, sometimes with a different soundtrack, the one commenting on and establishing a dialogue with the others. As the film and its collaborative images keep searching we are led to acknowledge that there is no absolute image of this revolution, no such thing as an authentic perspective. This, in turn, eventually prompts us to recognize the dislocation of Farocki and Ujica as author-filmmakers.

We are never certain of whose or what images bear witness to the Revolution. The film we watch in the movie theater has the same status as the images of the amateur filmmaker, the demonstrator with a camera, which are, in turn, at times, on equal footing with the Televiziunea Romana footage and news broadcasts. As if we were not adequately dislocated by all these uncertainties, equally unclear in this footage is the medium we are watching: is it television, film, video? Because *Videograms of a Revolution* deflects authority through these various strategies, so in turn, Farocki and Ujica concede their authority as imagemakers, giving way to an image that reproduces the unscripted and democratic negotiation aspired to by revolutionary discourse in Bucharest and Timisoara. Their authority as film authors is dislocated in a gesture that reinforces the history and narrative of *Videograms of a Revolution*.

All of these dislocations amount to the film's conversation with what W.J.T. Mitchell (1986) calls "the iconic turn," a moment predicted, but yet to arrive. At the end of the line of generations who have denigrated the image in Western philosophy, art history, and visual studies, Farocki and Ujica's film might be understood to take up the call for the search for a way of conceiving the world visually, not through language. For *Videograms of a Revolution*, the details of the image's production is not important, its recognizeability and veracity are beside the point. What matters is the search for images to put in an archive of visual concepts. What matters is that the archive of images – in this case a film – will enable us to "understand," or at least remember, the historical moment of the Romanian Revolution.[8] As it turns out, the knowledge that we acquire from the film as image repository emphasizes that knowledge of the tumultuous events of the Romanian revolution is always subject to the positionality, or positionalities, of the representation. The experience is always necessarily a mediation, a mediation which in turn, according to *Videograms of a Revolution*, is in itself a form of historical knowledge.

The spaces or dislocations between camera perspectives, between images and history, between images and viewers are echoed everywhere throughout the film, both as comments on the problems of making images and of orchestrating this particular revolution. Perhaps most significantly, even the spaces and places at which the revolution is played out, Victory Square, the television station, the Central Committee, are represented as being dislocated from each other due to the camerawork that results from the urgency and simultaneous difficulty of getting close to, and ultimately, recording the events.

Appropriately, the struggle for images through an aesthetics of dislocation uses two symbolic sites of power in Bucharest as its stage: the television station and the Central Committee headquarters. We watch as the revolution unfolds and the revolutionaries take over these two sites as they physically dislodge Ceauçescu and the institutions that support him from their balconies and platforms. The revolutionaries command authority of and from these spaces, there struggling to define their own brand of national unity. However, these two symbolic foci are never stable markers – if only because as viewers of *Videograms of a Revolution* we are unsure of where they are in relation to each other. Often the most important moments and decisions in the process of revolution happen unexpectedly, not in or outside the television station, not on the balcony of the Central Committee or the square in front of it, but as the camera travels in trucks and cars along unremarkable streets somewhere between the two. The action is always spreading out beyond the confines of the film frame. The points of view of the many cameras are never fully adequate to capturing all of the action. In the moments of transition between sites, the films record events from ground level and the dislocation of events is mirrored in images seen through a jerky, handheld camera. Usually, these cameras are not sure of what they are watching or hovering around, sometimes it appears that they are expecting something momentous to take place. All the time we hear the firing of arms on the soundtrack as though the real action is taking place just out of eyesight. We are only ever allowed to assume this action thanks to the soundtrack because the camera does not present it to us. Even though the image is unsteady and can reveal a discrepancy with the soundtrack, these dislocations are the alert that in the times and spaces of transition, the cameras in Bucharest have ceased to be surveillance apparatuses, they become participatory in democratic negotiations and street-level rebellions.

When the image is grounded, thus located, in the television station, on the balcony of the Central Committee or watching over one of the two locations, the chaos of demonstration and revolution emerges. This chaos is communicated by the loss of the image and the confusion around the status of the image as in the example detailed above. The disorientation of the image, in turn, reflects the unpredictability of the revolution as it unfolds, and also the multiplicity of revolutionary actions. Alternatively, if the camera, the image and sound–image relations are coherent and comprehensible, there is nothing to see. Thus, when we see the demonstrators in their thousands as they motion along the street beneath an amateur cameraman's apartment, or when we become privy to the gatherings of spokespeople at Televiziunea Romana as they determine the ongoing process of revolution, nothing happens. At these moments, what we see and what we hear reflects another kind of transitory time-space or dislocation. And so, frustrated with its inability to document the key events, the film returns to footage shot from roof terraces a few streets away, watching the demonstrations from high above ground level, behind venetian blinds, at times in the blackness of night. A "better view" can be found that does not return to the surveillance strategies for which such perspectives were conventionally used in pre-1989 Romania. The bird's-eye view is now another option for noting the transformation of the image in support of the revolution. When the footage taken by amateurs and professionals manages to record the events it wants to see, or that must be televised to be realized – for example, when the Ceauçescus flee in their helicopter, or when Nicu Ceauçescu (the son) is captured – these visions are interrupted. Thus, a head comes to obscure the image, the camera is distracted by another event, or it just loses sight of what it was watching. Alternatively, Farocki and Ujica interrupt their film with a freeze-frame or, as we saw in the earlier described fragment, footage will show a camera pull back to depict a television in someone's living room, thereby revealing that we are in fact watching a televised version of events. And then a cut to black, or a broadcast interrupted by technical difficulties, the image degraded because it is a re-presentation of a low-quality transmission. It is impossible to find a location, a position from which to film and see the truth of these events. This impossibility comes despite the film's persistent effort to locate through subtitles and intertitles the time, the date and the place of the action. According to *Videograms of a Revolution*, the image is always a particular perspective, dislocated from other images, as well from the events, all attempting to represent the revolution as it takes place on the streets, and in the struggle to use the image to ensure the forward motion of that revolution, to inform, to expose, to mobilize people to take action themselves.

Liberation through Television?

The film continues. It persists with the dual motivation to document the Romanian revolution and interrogate its representation. Consequently, the film follows the revolutionaries in their successful seizure of Televiziunea Romana. But even as the people led by writers and artists assume the position of producers and controllers of the image, this new image is no less reliable, still dislocated through the wont of the producers to exploit it. Like the State functionaries before them, the artists, writers, and dramatists now at the helm of the Romanian television image refuse to allow the camera to record events until they have set the stage, rehearsed their lines, prepared the lighting and other aspects of the technical performance. The revolutionaries' control of the image sees them become wedded to and manipulate the power of its constructions. Their investment in the image produces, to use Farocki's (2004) words, the revolutionaries' "abstraction" from their "basic human condition," where abstraction refers to the process of reification that seduces them once they are in control of the image. The situation reminds us of Godard's insistence (especially in *Tout va Bien* (1972) and other of his *Dziga Vertov*-era films) that manipulation of the image to fulfill an ideological agenda will always alienate one's efforts in the interests of commodification. Thus we see *Videograms of a Revolution* engaged in similar struggles that have characterized the experiments of its politically motivated predecessors. And similar to Godard's pictured "revolutions," Ceauçescu and his regime are successfully toppled via the arrest of the images which enabled him. And, as we saw Godard warn of in *Tout va Bien*, *Videograms of a Revolution* demonstrates that once the image has been arrested, it is necessarily given over to another form of ideological system, in which equally biased decisions set new processes of representation in motion.

And so, Farocki and Ujica pry open the revolutionaries' hold over the image, and proceed to divorce the camera from those in power. Once again, this interrogation of the image as ideological battleground takes place in consciously inserted caesurae between images, between spaces, between events in the revolution. Thus, for example, the camera sits in an elevator filming the numbers of the floors as they pass by, or outside a closed door, vizualizing its inability to access events, its blindness to the goings on. The images of *Videograms of a Revolution* are always removed from the "real action." On the soundtrack in these moments we hear the revolutionaries, debating the images on which the forward motion of the revolution will hinge, insisting on a coherent and convincing message for the television viewers. Like Godard, Brecht, Straub–Huillet, and Kluge before them, the filmmakers simultaneously expose and question the use of the cinema through the cinematic manipulations of their own film.[9] The impotence of the camera, the resultant visual interruptions to the rhythms and patterns of revolutionary developments, thus the images of revolution, are everywhere mimicked by those of *Videograms of a Revolution*. And in another layer of reflexive critique, when the film finally enters the television studio, we watch the journalists watching television, as if they are watching and censoring their own images.

Toward the end of *Videograms of a Revolution*, the dust apparently begins to settle as Christmas greetings are broadcast on Televiziunea Romana. The revolution shifts to another symbolic location, apparently in the heart of Bucharest. The "enemy" (Ceauçescu loyalists) fire on the people from the empty buildings that surround at Victory Square. The unseen snipers hide in or between unfinished, unoccupied, nondescript high-rise buildings that Ceauçescu had built during his reign. The voiceover reflects on the equation between these characterless buildings, the faceless, intangible causes of fear that breed under a socialist dictatorship and the incompetence of global media in the face of these dynamics. In all three instances, the invisible enemy pervades the most visible, most symbolic of public spaces and the most "protected" of private spaces – the buildings on the Square, everyday life and the home.

When the center of the revolution shifts to Victory Square, the film remains at the scene of the action, thus, together with its revolutionary comrades, it is blind to the location and activities of the enemy.[10] The restless image depicts snippets of action: legs running down stairs, figures racing across the square to safety, the frenetic, almost desperate retaliation of the people's army, the cement eyesore buildings being the only constant in the background. Somewhere in the vicinity shots continue to be fired. The soundtrack thus alerts us to the presence of fighting, and consequently, we understand the people who run past the camera, often carrying shopping bags or a handbag as though out doing errands, are fleeing the gunfire. However, like those behind the cameras we are unable to determine who exactly they flee, their proximity or distance, the degree of their threat, the accuracy of the shooting. This sequence aptly illustrates the film's skillful representation that, "[a]s the Ceauçescus' fate becomes clear, more and more factions emerge whose relationship to Ceauçescu is increasingly unclear" (Privett, 1999: para. 10). The ambiguity of the enemy's location, the uncertainty of his next move, are accompanied at the level of the film by an absence of establishing shots, the disjunction between sound and image, the repeated loss of the image, and the self-reflexive unreliability of the narrator. Needless to say, all these factors add up to a dislocation of the viewer. Interspersed with these fragments of fighting, a British journalist is depicted to report on the same events we are watching. Technical difficulties in his broadcast abound; the sound doesn't work, the image is lost, the camera is in the wrong place at the wrong time.

In keeping with the pattern established by the film thus far, the same images are repeated again and again, as though in a continuous loop. We watch no less than four takes of the British news broadcast as the videocam and the reporter endeavor to make sense of the events, and struggle to overcome technical problems. Neiman's voiceover is also repeated with the visual reiterations, each time attempting to give a different perspective, but in fact, working as a commentator that demonstrates the manipulation of the media's version of events. Even in the hands of the revolutionaries and their Western sympathizers, the television image fails to locate the nerve center of the revolution. As we have already seen, these repetitive layers of flawed television images are woven into *Videograms of a Revolution* to witness the instability, and as Neiman's voiceover says, the impotence of the media which nevertheless, in its struggle with the revolutionaries for control of the image, enables the forward motion of the revolution.

Thus, together with this skepticism toward television images, *Videograms of a Revolution* witnesses the shift from images that create one kind of political reality and its accompanying version of history, through images that create another historical moment, a moment that is, via the use of the image, articulated as democratic. In one of the most powerful images of the film, we see the corpses of Elena and Nicolai Ceauçescu lay wasted in the gutter on Christmas Day, 1998. These images are also secondhand, thereby underlining the cheapness of the Ceauçescu lives within the narrative logic of revolution. The dead couple is shown at a distance, in a grainy image that would make identification without the voiceover impossible. The film then zooms outwards to reveal that the corpses are shown on a television screen, somewhere in the streets of Bucharest, three times removed from the reality of the viewer of *Videograms of a Revolution*. People are gathered around the television, they applaud, they celebrate while, and most importantly, their video cameras continue to record events in the midst. At this remove, Farocki and Ujica's film is uninvolved and thus, able to be more skeptical than the Romanian viewers of the diegesis, enabling the viewers of *Videograms of a Revolution* to wonder about the future of a unified Romania. Nevertheless, despite the distance and resultant ambiguity of the images of the Ceauçescu corpses, we are, at the very least, confident that radical change has been effected, the dictatorship has fallen. Somehow, somewhere in the gaps between what we have seen and what we now know took place, between the events and their representation, this uneven tapestry of found images has spawned a once unimaginable revolution.

Bigger Pictures

How to interpret this provocative trajectory? It is, on one level, the realization of the aspiration for a radical revolutionary image. Although in a very different guise, in response to a very different set of social and political parameters (communist dictatorship, as opposed to capitalist bureaucracy) *Videograms of a Revolution* finds what Eisenstein, Brecht, Godard, and Kluge among others were looking for. *Videograms of a Revolution* locates an image that inspires the masses to revolt against their oppression. Unlike the ancestors I am here attributing to the film, *Videograms of a Revolution* does not find an image that agitates through the force of its visual construction. While Farocki and Ujica's particular form of montage culls from the history of experimental filmmaking, those televisual, film and video images it discovers are not formally innovative. Together, the content of the re-presented images and their formal arrangement seize the necessity of realist legibility as the key to widespread accessibility. While *Videograms of a Revolution* is aesthetically innovative and at the vanguard of visual discourses of political possibility, it is reliant on images that claim to do no more than document what takes place before the camera. Through its distinction from the footage it appropriates *Videograms of a Revolution* demonstrates that the key to a revolutionary image lies in its production, distribution, exhibition contexts, and the audiences that await it. And, we could add, *Videograms of a Revolution* foregrounds what makes all of Farocki's images "revolutionary" or avant-garde. Namely, through his form of editing, of placing culled images together, Farocki's project is to school us to see and interpret images through revolutionary eyes. As W.J.T. Mitchell (2005) argues, it is not the image itself, but how it is used, the life that it leads which is at the heart of political mobilization. Thus, in their tapestry of second hand images, Farocki and Ujica find an image that not only creates and documents history, but more importantly, is an image that teaches us how to see and interpret that documentation or representation of history.

Is this why Farocki, the German filmmaker and theorist, whose intellectual formation took place in a post-Vietnam Berlin sieged by anger and radical possibility, is attracted to these events? Because here in Romania, he finds the ultimate imbrication of film and history, as the voiceover of *Videograms of a Revolution* observes, where the image is the condition of history and history is the condition of the image? I think for Farocki it is more than an opportunity to document this double-edged victory of the image, however cautious this documentation might be.

Romania 1989 is the perfect forum in which to confront the concerns of Germany and other European countries in 1992, concerns that also exceed national borders. Postunification Europe has continued to be preoccupied with questions such as how to negotiate political and economic inequality between member states, how to define national identity, belonging, relations between insiders and outsiders. Similarly, questions such as what is and should be the responsibility of one country to the histories of others? As in Romania, these questions have been asked in Germany especially against a background of attempts to reduce national sovereignty. And all the time, left-wing intellectuals have continued to influence and interrogate the parameters of the public sphere through images. Thus, the concerns of the newly unified Europe are also being worked out here in Socialist Romania. This is not to say that events and their aftermath in Romania are allegories of events in East Germany, but that they are relevant and share characteristics.

In his 1994 film *Die führende Rolle* (The Leading Role), Farocki gives us a glimpse of the imbrication of the image and history on the path toward confronting the conundrum created by the events of 1989 in Europe. The film uses all the familiar

Farocki strategies of culling and re-presenting images as it searches for an image that will describe, define, explain, and five years later, teach us how to see and interpret the widespread upheavals of the fall of the Berlin Wall in 1989. In keeping with Farocki's iconoclasm, there is no such ideal image, and yet, the search must nevertheless continue. In turn, the cinema and other moving images are the perfect way to represent and interrogate these questions, to continue the search. The cinema's mobility to transcend national borders – not only at the level of the aesthetic, but more recently in Europe, through its production, distribution and exhibition networks – is equal to the task of relocating the concerns of one country into those of another.[11] Today, with the advent of new technologies, and especially access to the World Wide Web, other forms of image production perhaps more easily access and generate socially and politically engaged street-level activism. However, in the 1990s, the cinema, video and television were still the available media to represent at all levels the mobility and international identities of a unified, if not coherent, Europe.

Bucharest and Timisoara, 1989 might thus be understood to present Farocki with the opportunity to continue the search for an image that was begun in Berlin 1989, and later, in *Die führende Rolle* in 1994. In Romania, Farocki and his co-image makers discover that the image of the revolution is elsewhere, dislocated from the still and moving images in which he had previously been looking. I have argued that *Videograms of a Revolution* finds this elsewhere in the way images are made, who makes them, who has access to their production, who consumes them, and how they are interpreted. The film's capacity to see this elsewhere is reflected in the spatiotemporal dislocations repeated at the level of the film's structure, dislocations that are, in turn, enabled by its choice to recycle and re-present the past and its images. As Young points out, the dead past and the possibility of a democratic future become visible in the lag between what happened and what is represented, what the image captures and the aleatory nature, thus the truth-status, of the events being documented. This is transposed to *Videograms of a Revolution* when the events retain the traces of authenticity because they always happen just offscreen, in the enforced pauses or structural spaces. To put it another way, the dislocation or disjuncture between Romania's communist past and democratic future is echoed in the empty spaces between film fragments to invoke by association a nostalgia for an image of the revolution that was never really found in other European countries, particularly in Germany. Images of revolution, and revolutionary images were perhaps harder to come by in Germany because of a number of structural factors relating to the unfolding of events that led to the eventual opening of the border between East and West. The quiet, peaceful secession of power was opposed to the relatively abrupt violent eruptions that resulted from the overthrow of Ceauçescu's Stalinist-like regime, a dictatorship that refused to loosen its grip on the media to the very end.

Lastly, in spite of my emphasis on *Videograms of a Revolution* as a film attributable to the oeuvre of Harun Farocki, Farocki the radical political documentarist, film author and essayist is simultaneously displaced, even dislocated, from the film. Indeed, this level of dislocation is both critical to the film's political edge and to its continuity with Farocki's other films. On the most obvious level, *Videograms of a Revolution* is a collaborative project written and produced with filmmaker Andrej Ujica.[12] Indeed, Ujica's preoccupation with the subject and form of *Videograms of a Revolution* preexists the film. His coedited collection might be considered a textual storyboard that extends from documentation to analysis to theorization of the "television revolution," just like *Videograms of a Revolution* (Amelunxen and Ujica, 1990). In addition, the writer-director-producer team diffuses its stability as a locus of meaning through the equal status given to their film, that of amateur film and video footage, and anonymous television images. Beyond these manifest diffusions of authorship, the film's belief that a revolutionary image is identifiable through appropriation of the contexts of production, dissemination and, most importantly, reception by us, is returned to the authorial distance from a definitive stylistic expression, narrative didacticism and identifiable conceptual maneuvers. Thus, as much as *Videograms of a Revolution* exemplifies the concerns of Farocki's other films, it also stands apart. The film's distinction is marked through its dislocation of the image it is looking for. And significant to the displacement of Farocki and Ujica as auteurs is the location of this image in a place where it was least expected – a television image produced by and for the people.

Farocki does not believe he can achieve what other image makers cannot. He may persist in the search for a revolutionary image, for images that revolutionize. However, *Videograms of a Revolution* also testifies to the impossibility of finding those images through the camera lens of the well-known filmmaker from the West. To be sure, his images are only a part of a process of continuing production and reproduction of images. Farocki's practice and politics are wedded to archives and repositories of used, discarded, forgotten images. This is perhaps why he has no problem with the reproduction of his own images.[13] The images which bring about the fall of the Ceauçescu regime have nothing to do with Harun Farocki's film. And neither are they stylistically vanguard, they do not break new aesthetic ground. On the contrary, the image that is used to challenge, and ultimately to set in motion the toppling of this dictatorship, the image of political agitation and revolution is produced by a realist, often handheld camera that portends a mimetic reflection of profilmic events. Quite simply, this revolution is enabled through the availability and accessibility of certain image making technologies. Television, home video, handheld 16 mm cameras are technologies that in 1989 Romania enabled the production and distribution of the image to be put in the hands of the people. It is this potential for the image to be appropriated by the people at every level, from production through spectatorship, which momentarily holds the promise of political agitation. For *Videograms of a Revolution* this promise is apparently only ever momentary because, in its anticipation of the Romanian revolution's eventual co-optation, as well as that of its images, the film takes on a nostalgia for that revolution that is always located outside the frame.

In conclusion, I want to suggest that *Videograms of a Revolution*'s belief in the power of images does not stop here, for it is visibly uncomfortable with, and distant from the results of the revolutionary action: the grotesque sight of the Ceauçescus lying dead by a wall as it was broadcast on television. The film thus goes one step further in a gesture that can be read as its stake to transgress national borders. The film implicitly critiques the instantaneity, superficiality, and sensationalism of global television reportage of this and similar events. On every level – aesthetic, production, distribution, and exhibition – this film is all that global television is not. *Videograms* compiles fragments of amateur and professional footage that invite us to witness the events unfold a day at a time over the course of ten days, sometimes an hour at a time, a minute at a time – always being careful to indicate the timing of the events through intertitles. The temporality of the slow-moving narrative, the accumulation of ideas and information enables a gradual revelation of the momentous nature of events. This monumentality is distinct from the spectacularization of historical events in the media. For the magnitude of the revolution is here depicted in all its complexity, with all of its contradictions and impossibilities exposed. It is of a different genre from the revolution shown on Western television in which the victory of democracy over dictatorship is an unqualified cause for celebration.

But, of course, *Videograms* also replicates the structure of cable television. As Farocki points out in a recent interview: cable television has several images on screen at once, "the stock information here and the weather information there, one correspondent in real time here and a tiny image with archival footage there … we're looking at several images, creating interrelations among images and texts. […] It's like having an editing table in front of us" (Griffin, 2004: 163). Farocki here connects the form of cable news and his use of multiple screens to create interrelations between frames, between images and texts, between fragments of used footage, within and between the three parts of his *Eye/Machine* trilogy (2001–2003). However, this conscious shift away from a linear, deductive narrative is already in place in *Videograms of a Revolution*. Similar to the viewer of cable television, or even of Farocki's multiscreen gallery installations, that of *Videograms* also finds history and its images in the gaps between different images, different locations, different cameras, between text and image. As in his later digital *Eye/Machine* works, the images that comprise *Videograms of a Revolution* are edited to create concepts, not as pieces of a larger story: Farocki leans on Benjamin's notion of the *Gedankenbild* here to articulate the innovation of his late twentieth century "idea-image."

Following the thread of the moebius strip, the gaps of *Videograms of a Revolution* are in stark contrast to the information sound bites of global television in its coverage of events as they happen, between commercials, in a format that prohibits both understanding and memory of the events." Because, as *Videograms of a Revolution* itself exposes, the mainstream media images may be multiple, complex, and fractured, but they are empty and amount to a singular perspective, a biased communication to a privileged Western audience. These commercial images feign to communicate truth, not the interface of history and representation. For *Videograms of a Revolution*, history emerges from the confusion and dislocation of the cameras, the back streets of Bucharest, on the road between locations, in all of those spaces where cameras, be they official, amateur, television, or film have difficulty going.

It must be conceded that, in spite of its relevance to a crosscultural, international audience, *Videograms of a Revolution* was released at select film festivals and is unlikely to be widely screened in the future. It has recently been released on DVD, but nevertheless, the film is unlikely to attract attention beyond a specialized audience of students and critics. And, unlike most of his other films, the film has never been reappropriated by Farocki for his gallery installations. Perhaps if it were to have a lot of attention, *Videograms of a Revolution* would lose its critical edge? For its success as an iconoclastic homage to the power of the image, its critique of the production, circulation, reception of what we might call the global television document, and by extension of its own aesthetic and function, is dependent on its distance from the aesthetic, exhibition, and reception of these images it appropriates with skepticism. While the film is international and reaches far beyond the specificity of that which it documents, it has to remain outside of the structures that enable it, in order for the critique of the same structures to carry credence.

Despite the differences between the work of Kluge, and other contemporaries such as Straub and Huillet, *Videograms of a Revolution* reintroduces the iconic possibilities of moving images into a politically and ideologically charged land-scape. And in this tumultuous arena, the film locates the potential revolutionary power for the image. However, this potency will not be discovered in the places and spaces where revolutionary filmmakers such as Vertov, Godard, Kluge carried out their explorations. According to *Videograms of a Revolution,* the search for a politically productive image has been dislocated from the radical aesthetic, in particular, the aesthetic of montage. It is, so Farocki and Ujica would have it, in the availability and accessibility of all stages of moving images – their production, distribution, exhibition and reception – to the people who make them, use them, comment on and believe them.

This research was supported by a Marie Curie Intra European Fellowship within the 7th European Community Framework Programme.

Notes

1 See also *Ich glaubte Gefangene zu sehen (I thought I was Seeing Convicts)* (2000). For a comprehensive filmography, see http://www.farocki-film.de (accessed February 14, 2011).
2 See Jill Godmilow's film, *What Farocki Taught* (1998).

3   This is taken from the film.

4   See Ernst and Farocki (2004). There is a growing literature on the found footage and compilation films, both of which can be thought of as antecedent to *Videograms of a Revolution*. Rather than reading Farocki's film within this context, I point the reader toward this literature. See, for example, Wees (1993); Bruzzi (2000).

5   This emphasis on the life of the image beyond the nevertheless experimental frame also places Farocki's work squarely within the tradition of radical political documentary. Filmmakers such as John Grierson and D.A. Pennebaker, Jean Rouch and Chris Marker become his predecessors. To follow Farocki's work along these lines, particularly as it relates to this tradition of filmmaking in Europe, see Guerin (2008).

6   Films such as Emile de Antonio's *In the Year of the Pig* (1968) and *Millhouse. A White Comedy* (1988) come to mind here as leading examples of this genre of found footage and compilation film.

7   Again, this is a conceptualization of film and mode of filmmaking that I discuss in "Radical Aspirations Historicized" (2008). It is perhaps most strongly associated with the work of Dziga Vertov and Sergei Eisenstein in the USSR, and Theodor Adorno and his student Alexander Kluge in Germany.

8   Farocki articulately explores this idea in his other films such as *Arbeiter verlassen die Fabrik (Workers Leaving the Factory)* (1995) and *Der Ausdruck der Hände (The Expression of Hands)* (1997). In both films, Farocki turns to the archives of film history in search of iconic images and gestures for a "visual archive of cinematic topoi" that might function like a dictionary of images for the future. See Ernst and Farocki (2004).

9   On the notion of Farocki as continuing Brecht's pursuit of film as a model for action and film as a didactic tool for the assumption of power and knowledge, see Elsaesser (2004b).

10 On this movement of the revolution between Timisoara and Bucharest, and again between different spaces and places that held immense symbolism, see Ujica (1990).

11 I am thinking here of the dramatic changes that have taken place in the structure of the European film industry. In particular, European Commission incentives at the level of funding, distribution, and exhibition policies have been developed to nurture a creative and economically successful industry. See, for example, Finney (1996).

12 Even though Ujica is Romanian born, during the conception of the film and its making he was living in Germany where he was a lecturer in literature and media at the University of Mannheim, 1985–1992.

13 Godmilow's *What Farocki Taught* (1998) is in fact a remake of Farocki's 1969 film, *Inextinguishable Fire*, which is about napalm B, the jellied gasoline manufactured by Dow Chemical and used during the Vietnam War.

References

Amelunxen, H.v. and Ujica, A. (eds) (1990) *Television/Revolution. Das Ultimatum des Bildes*, Jonas Verlag, Marburg.

Bruzzi, S. (2000) The event: archive and newsreel in *The New Documentary: A Critical Introduction*. Routledge, London, New York, pp. 11–39.

Elsaesser, T. (ed.) (2004a) *Harun Farocki: Working on the Sight-Lines*, Amsterdam University Press, Amsterdam.

Elsaesser, T. (2004b) Political filmmaking after Brecht: Harun Farocki, for example, in *Harun Farocki: Working on the Sight-Lines* (ed. T. Elsaesser), Amsterdam University Press, Amsterdam, pp. 133–153.

Ernst. W. and Farocki, H. (2004) Towards an archive for visual concepts, in *Harun Farocki: Working on the Sight-Lines* (ed. T. Elsaesser), Amsterdam University Press, Amsterdam, pp. 261–286.

Farocki, H. (2004) "Viewfinder": a conversation with Harun Farocki, *Artforum*, 43 (3), 162–163.

Finney, A. (1996) *The State of European Cinema. A New Dose of Reality*, Cassell, London.

Foster, H. (2004) Vision quest. *Artforum*, 43 (3), 156–161, 250.

Griffin, T. (2004) *Artforum*, 43 (3), 162–163.

Guerin, F. (2008) Radical aspirations historicized: the European commitment to political documentary, in *The Oxford Handbook of Film and Media Studie*s (ed. R. Kolker), Oxford University Press, New York.

Mitchell, W.J.T. (1986) *Iconology: Image, Text Ideology*, University of Chicago Press, Chicago.

Mitchell, W.J.T. (2005) *What Do Pictures Want? The Lives and Loves of Images*, University of Chicago Press, Chicago, London.

Privett, R. (1999) The revolution was televised. *Central European Review*, 1, 17, http://www. ce-review.org/99/17/kinoeye17_privett.html (accessed February 14, 2011).

Ujica, A. (1990) im Gespräch mit Livius Ciocârlie, Serban Foarta, Andrei Plesu and Mihai Sora, "Zeit und Bildplätze," in *Television/Revolution. Das Ultimatum des Bildes* (eds H.v. Amelunxen and A. Ujica), Jonas Verlag, Marburg, pp. 27–75.

Wees, W. (1993) *Recycled Images: The Art and Politics of Found Footage Films*, Anthology Film Archives, New York City.

Winston, B. (1988) Direct cinema: the third decade, in *New Challenges for Documentary* (ed. A. Rosenthal), University of California Press, Berkeley, Los Angeles, pp. 517–529.

Young, B. (2004) On media and democratic politics: videograms of a revolution, in *Harun Farocki: Working on the Sight-Lines* (ed. T. Elsaesser), Amsterdam University Press, Amsterdam, pp. 245–260.

Filmography

Between Two Wars [*Zwischen zwei Kriegen*] (Harun Farocki, West Germany, 1978).

Creators of the Shopping Worlds, The [*Die Schöpfer der Einkaufswelten*] (Harun Farocki, Germany, 2001).

Die führende Rolle [The Leading Role] (Harun Farocki, Germany 1994).

The Expression of Hands [*Der Ausdrück der Hände*] (Harun Farocki, Germany, 1997).

Images of the World and the Inscription of War [*Bilder der Welt und Inschrift des Krieges*] (Harun Farocki, West Germany, West Germany, 1988).

Inextinguishable Fire [*Nicht Löschbares Feuer*] (Harun Farocki, West Germany, 1969).

In the Year of the Pig (Emile de Antonio, USA, 1968).

I Thought I was Seeing Convicts [*Ich glaubte Gefangene zu sehen*] (Harun Farocki, Germany, 2000).

Millhouse: A White Comedy (Emile de Antonio, USA, 1988).

Prison Images [*Gefängnisbilder*] (Harun Farocki, Germany, 2000).

Still Life [*Stilleben*] (Harun Farocki, Germany, 1997).

Tout va Bien [Everything's All Right] (Jean-Luc Godard, France/Italy, 1972).

Videograms of a Revolution [*Videogramme einer Revolution*] (Harun Farocki/Andrej Ujica, Germany, 1992).

War at a Distance [*Erkennen und Verfolgen*] (Harun Farock, Germany, 2003).

What Farocki Taught (Jill Godmilow, USA, 1998).

Workers Leaving the Factory [*Arbeiter verlassen die Fabrik*] (Harun Farocki, Germany, 1995).

20

Germany Welcomes Back Its Jews
Go for Zucker! *and the Women*
in German Debate (aka Wiggie-leaks:
A Polemical Analysis)

Terri Ginsberg

LINDA [to "Janice"/Ghada]:	He took the wrong pill. Calm him down with a nice massage, some lavender …
"JANICE"/GHADA:	Shalom, Monsieur Zuckermann.
"SHMUEL"/SAMUEL ZUCKERMANN:	Shalom.
"JANICE"/GHADA:	Will you join me for a glass of tea?
JAECKIE ZUCKER [to Linda]:	Does she know what an Orthodox Jew is?
LINDA:	Sure, she's Palestinian.

(*Go for Zucker!* 2004)

This dialogue ensues as former East German sports announcer-turned-lawyer, Jaeckie Zucker (né Jakob Zuckermann) (Henry Hübchen), now a heavy drinker and poolhall gambler in debt to some unforgiving loan sharks, brings his estranged, ultra-orthodox Jewish brother, "Shmuel"/Samuel (Udo Samel), just returned from an exilic Frankfurt to Berlin for their mother's funeral, to a house of prostitution that Jaeckie owns, after Shmuel accidentally ingests the drug Ecstasy while visiting Jaeckie's lesbian, physical therapist daughter, Jana (Anja Frank). Jaeckie hopes that sex with a prostitute will soften up the strictly kosher Shmuel in accordance with their late mother's wish that her sons reconcile before inheriting her estate. This is especially important to Jaeckie, whose banker son Thomas (Steffen Groth) has called in one of Jaeckie's loans, and whose fed-up, goyische wife Marlene (Hannelore Elsner) has filed for divorce. Of course, such personal enjoyments as well as the exchange of money are forbidden during the *shiva* (week of mourning). As the intoxicated Shmuel nonetheless enters a private room with Palestinian prostitute "Janice"/Ghada (Ghada Hammoudah) at the behest of her madame, Linda (Renate Kröβner), Jaeckie sneaks out to compete at a pool tournament, where Jana cheers him on amid a raucus crowd. Parallel editing juxtaposes his

A Companion to German Cinema, First Edition. Edited by Terri Ginsberg and Andrea Mensch.
© 2012 Blackwell Publishing Ltd. Published 2012 by Blackwell Publishing Ltd.

successful plays with shots of Shmuel dancing and getting massaged by Janice, herself dressed in an ersatz belly-dancing costume combining elements of Turkish attire with a red-and-white Palestinian *keffiyeh*.[1] A similarly ersatz combination of Middle Eastern and klezmer music forms the soundtrack to this montage, which compares winning an illicit gamble to the (sexual) exploitation and corruption of Palestinians, in both instances by Jews, the former publicly, the latter privately – and both within the lumpenbourgeois, post-*Wende* (literally, post-[1989] shift) East Berlin setting of a film billed as "Germany's first post-1945 German-Jewish comedy" (Biehl, 2005).

Several months after *Go for Zucker: An Unorthodox Comedy!* (*Alles auf Zucker!* 2004) was released theatrically in Germany, a mildly contentious debate about it took place for a period of approximately one week over the Women in German ("WiG") listserv. WiG is an abbreviated name for the Coalition of Women in German, a scholarly forum in existence since 1974 that has published an annual scholarly yearbook since 1985 and has hosted an annual conference since 1995. The WiG mission statement describes the organization as, among other things,

> a democratic forum for all people interested in feminist approaches to German literature and culture or in the intersection of gender with other categories of analysis such as sexuality, class, race, and ethnicity [...] [and] dedicated to eradicating discrimination in the classroom and in the teaching profession at all levels."[2]

The debate over the WiG listserv initially concerned the function of humor in *Go for Zucker!* with respect to representations of Jewishness, but it eventually came to convene around the in/significance of Palestinian representation in the film and the ir/relevance of that to the publicity the film had received with respect to its post-reunification Jewish-German authorship. *Go for Zucker!* was directed by Dani Levy, a Germanophone Jewish Swiss, and produced by Germany's "'new' New German" X-Filme Creative Pool, a company co-founded by Levy, directors Tom Tykwer and Wolfgang Becker, and producer Stefan Arndt, and formed to create transnationally viable hybrids of pre-*Wende* German *Autorenkino* ("author's cinema") and commercial genre films including New Comedies (see Halle, 2008: 56–57).[3]

Approximately one year following the debate, in February 2006, listserv member Cary Nathenson, then an Assistant Dean of Graduate Programs at Northwestern University's School of Continuing Studies, published the first extant scholarly review of *Go for Zucker!* in H-German, a German studies listserv housed by H-Net: Humanities and Social Studies Online, entitled "A Polemical Review of Post-Wall Germany's First 'Jewish Movie.'" The review echoes and encapsulates the position Nathenson took during the WiG debate; namely, that "The movie has nothing to do with the Middle-East" (Nathenson, 2005c). Indeed Nathenson's first listserv post about the film, which kicked off the debate in response to an initial post from another list member who had inquired generally about the film, was meant to announce that his review of this film, which he strongly disliked, was already under consideration by H-German. Some months later, he followed up with an announcement of the review's imminent publication. Nathenson's first post presented his view that *Go for Zucker!*

> is an allegory of German reunification (that's also evident on a very superficial level – the East meets West plot line). But the part of the film that most interests (and disturbs) me is how unification is now in the hands of a Jewish family. The film, to me, presents a shifting of the burden of creating German normalcy onto the group whose victimization is the biggest obstacle to that normalcy. The fact that the director is of Jewish heritage is a red herring. Oh, and I didn't think it was terribly funny, either. (Nathenson, 2005a)

Nathenson's subsequent review in H-German expanded and elaborated this general criticism of the film for disingenuously using comedy to allegorize the tenuous secular–religious divisions within a post-*Wende* Jewish family onto the unhealed capitalist–communist, or Right–Left, divisions within post-reunification Germany. His review argues that this allegorization is presented in an antisemitic fashion replete with stereotypes of money-grubbing and sexually perverse Jews which harken to Nazi propaganda, and that its plea for unity and reconciliation comes at the expense of Jewish Holocaust victims and survivors in the form of an assimilationist discourse that also reinscribes the Nazi past. In this regard, Nathenson (2006: 3) is disturbed most apparently by a synagogue prayer sequence in which the film's "artifice of [Jewish-German] normality" is allegedly disrupted through usage of the circumscription, *Ha-shem* ("The Name"), rather than that of the actual name of the Jewish deity.

Whereas any number of films, German or otherwise, utilize the Jewish deity's circumscription when representing Jewish prayer and have not been called on it by critics of antisemitism, and insofar as Nathenson conveniently forgets that Judaism proscribes the name's actual usage within, among other places, secular representational contexts, one must infer that Nathenson's underlying concern is less that Judaic law, however misperceived, be respected and preserved in the cinema than that *Go for Zucker!*'s humor serves to dissimulate an invidious revisionist apologeticism regarding the Nazi past, which Nathenson believes, exaggeratedly, has entailed a significant increase in antisemitism since the *Wende* on account of Germany's perceived need to (re)establish itself "as a nation among nations, a normal country in a sense that has eluded both German states (and to a lesser degree Austria) since 1945" (Nathenson, 2006: 1). In fact, right-revisionist apologeticism, in the form of the renowned Holocaust historiography debate (*Historikerstreit*), began its surge at least a decade before the *Wende* (see Winkle, Chapter 17, in this volume) and, not unlike today's US Tea Party, was triggered by reaction to economic stagnation and crisis resulting at least in part from the evident role a nascent US-led neoliberalism was beginning to play in post(-Euro-)colonial world politics (see Meurer, 2000: 187–188) and their enabling conditions in the international oil trade, a crucial base of which was and remains the Middle East. By the time of the *Wende*, this revisionist reaction had already been "normalized" in the form of a conservative turn influenced on the one hand by Reaganism and prompted on the other hand by the rise of German *Linksterrorismus* (cf. Vukadinovic, Chapter 18, in this volume); it reinvoked the postwar Adenauer era, when popular German dissent regarding Cold War collaboration with US global interests – which itself continued similar Weimar- and Nazi-era collaborations (cf. Zachary, 2009) – was managed and contained (see Krämer, Chapter 14, in this volume).

Overlooking these crucial historiographic facts, Nathenson limits his gripe to a particularist contention that *Go for Zucker!*'s comedic call for Jewish-German normalization must be rejected because, in his view, it encourages Germans to forget the horrors of the Holocaust by projecting false images of "normal," "less 'foreign'" Jews rather than supposedly true images of them as different, as part of "a distinctly Jewish culture" (Nathenson, 2006: 3). According to his logic, only by upholding and asserting their difference, understood as a generalizable ethnicity, can Jews (and Germans) avoid another Holocaust. This promotion of Jewish "difference" is not only well-worn but coincides with Zionism, the ideology of Jewish nationalism, which purports to build on presumed empty desert a democratic nation-among-nations that is at once Jewish and secular by virtue of pragmatically promulgated racial laws (see Tekiner, 1989; Qumsiyeh, 2004: 87–88). Palestinian Arabs can live and work there, but only on highly circumscribed Jewish-Israeli terms enforced by a military-industrial apparatus funded largely by the United States and Europe and billed as the proven domain of a veritably reborn, tough and resilient Jew (see Beit-Hallahmi, 1992: 119–136; Boyarin, 1997). Indeed for early Zionist Max Nordau, "[The Zionist movement] has as its sole purpose the desire to normalize a [distinct, unassimilable] people" (Arthur Hertzberg, quoted in Taylor, 1974: 64). The fact that such ethnic categorization of Jews (not to mention Germans) has long been contested, not least by Jews (e.g. Sand, 2009), is implicitly misrecognized as antisemitic in Nathenson's view, on which the only postsacral alternative to a perceived self-destructive Jewish-German assimilationism, whether Eastern or Western, is identitarianism – an ironic position considering Nathenson's consistent, justifiable aversion to *German* identitarian tendencies.

In light of these historical elisions, it is telling that Nathenson omits the term "allegory" from his review, notwithstanding his use of it during the WiG debate, during which his proclivity to read *Go for Zucker!* as national allegory was critiqued as one-dimensional. Although the review persists in supplying an allegorical analysis, it – not unlike Nathenson's listserv posts – is concerned primarily to criticize the film's preponderant Jewish stereotyping while generalizing its perceived perniciousness to the film, and to post-*Wende* Germany as a whole, *sans* "allegory," as mere "play[s] for laughs, like everything else in this film" (Nathenson, 2006: 2). Listserv member Stefanie Knauβ, then at the (Catholic Theological) Karl-Franzens-Universät Graz, drew attention to this problem by averring that the film has a bit more depth than is obvious on first view, and that it deals with a lot of issues of Jewish life in Germany (both Germanies) in an interesting way. Of course, you can find all the stereotypes […] the jiddische Mamme, the Jewish seductress and JAP [Jewish American Princess] (just in German), the uncompromising Orthodox, the general preoccupation with inheritance […] but it might also be a question of whether you go looking for them […] The film has been criticized in comparison to *The Tango of the Rashevskis* (Sam Gabarski, 2003) as being a bit heavy-handed, typically German, and that might be true – most jokes are not very subtle –, but it had the courage to open the discussions on Jewish life in Germany today – with all its internal strives [sic] and in the context of Germany after the Wende. (2005a)

Knauβ clearly does not reject a national-allegorical analysis of the film, but her sense of its historicity adds dimension to Nathenson's more superficial, undertheorized reception. In fact Knauβ proceeded to argue that the film's ostensible antisemitic stereotypes are complemented and/or canceled out by the fact that its non-Jewish characters bear traits similar to those of its Jewish characters, thus underscoring the film's relevance to contemporary German reality. By the same token, Knauβ' commentary rejoins that of Nathenson, in her albeit welcoming, even apologetic emphasis on *Go for Zucker!*'s *German* allegoricality. Both critics are concerned more or less with the cinematic representation of Jewish identity in post-reunification Germany and the function comedy might serve there toward mitigating antisemitism and in turn propagating favorable images of Germany internationally. Their discourses therefore recall debates initiated during the 1990s over *Life Is Beautiful* (Roberto Benigni, 1997), an Italian comedy set literally in a Nazi concentration camp, and *Aimeé and Jaguar* (Max Färberböck, 1999), a German Holocaust film melodrama portraying a same-sex relationship in which a Jewish-German woman comes to stand as a romantic foil for her Christian-German lover and would-be rescuer (see e.g. Frost *et al.*, 2001; Sieg, 2002).[4] In effect, it is *Go for Zucker!*'s meaning and significance for the new Germany, especially as metonymized by "Jews" who (will) live there, that marks these "Wiggies'" (as some WiG listserv subscribers refer to themselves) primary concern.

It was amid this conflictual context that I – also a subscriber to the WiG listerv – decided to enter the discussion by calling attention to the film's *Jewish* allegoricality. While I agreed with Nathenson's estimation of the film "as a troubling allegory of German reunification that utilizes the 'Jew' – and, I would add, the 'queer' […] including the Jew AS queer […] as its figurative conduit" (Ginsberg, 2005a), I, in agreement with Knauβ, likewise did not see that as the film's essential problem or problematic. Instead, I wrote,

If Germans are able to feel more comfortable confronting their lingering (simmering?) racism in the context of humor, that's a sad statement. Moreover, such humor serves in "Alles auf Zucker" to mystify the social coordinates and functioning of German racism, insofar as *Jews are today NOT the primary victims of German/European racism, but rather Arabs, Turks, Greeks, Armenians, and so forth.* (Ginsberg, 2005a; emphasis added)

In the post-*Wende* era, as is commonly known, Germany's immigrant population from non-Western countries and regions has increased. Indeed as Jaeckie and Shmuel make their way to the brothel, they pass by a group of youths of immigrant and/or non-German background listening to "ethnic" music to which the drugged Shmuel begins to dance. By the same token, Germany's Jewish population has likewise increased, and investment by Jews and Jewish-owned companies in the German economy has been welcomed once again, at least by German elites (Hathaway, 2001; Siemon-Netto, 2003; Hall, 2005; Eggerz, 2006; "Chancellor Merkel," 2011; Runyan, 2011). A good deal of this activity, not all of it uncontroversial (Peck, 2005: 54–55; Schwartz, 2007), hails from the former Soviet bloc (Fisher, 1990; Bushinsky, 1991; Cohen, 2000) – but also, significantly, from Israel (e.g. Cronin 2009, 2010; Milk and Honey Tours, 2010), one of Germany's longstanding trading partners and aid recipients (see Deutschkron, 1970; Feldman, 1984; Kloke, 1994: Timm, 1997). Nathenson's review is thus correct when it questions *Go for Zucker!*'s central narrative motif, the retrieving and reinvesting of old Jewish money, but it loses credibility when it ignores the actual role some Jews as well as many Germans do in fact play as they try to foster German economic stabilization in the post-*Wende* era. Nathenson completely overlooks the historical question of the new Germany's global political economy – a continental configuration of neo-liberal transnational capitalism – by deploying the rhetorically more neutral term, "normalcy" (which he nonetheless knows carries post-Holocaust right-revisionist connotations), while suggesting in turn that *Go for Zucker!*'s failure to "portray authentic Jewish life in Germany" (Nathenson, 2006: 3) – as though such a thing exists, even according to Nathenson – is symptomatic of its "exploitation of Germany unity" in the name of "Jews [who] agree to overcome (overlook) the [Holocaustal] past and collaborate in [that] unity" (Nathenson, 2006: 3).

In my attempt to complexify Nathenson's dual allegation that *Go for Zucker!* is engaged in a sophisticated scapegoating of Jews for the failures of the *Wende*, about which he evinces a rather narrow scope, and that the ostensibly self-hating, opportunistic Jewish filmmaker Dani Levy is helping them do this, I first raised the issue of the sexual liberationism lampooned throughout the film in the form of excessive ludicity and incestuousness, connecting it to the film's global commodity function. *Go for Zucker!*'s narrative eventually reveals that Jana and her ultra-orthodox cousin, Shmuel's son Joshua (Sebastian Blomberg), once had an incestuous tryst that produced their daughter, Sarah (Antonia Adamik), whom Jana is now raising with her lesbian lover, Irene Bunge (Inge Busch). Likewise Jaeckie's sexually repressed banker son, Thomas, is seduced at film's end by his ultra-orthodox cousin, Shmuel's daughter Lilly (Elena Uhlig), a veritable nymphomaniac. I hypothesized that the "liberationism" exposed by these developments is largely contained by

the family values framework forwarded sentimentally by film's [happy, reconciled] end and condoned in essence by the film's orthodox Jewish characters in apparent contrast to its presentation of DDR "orthodoxy," which the film reduces and congeals for the sake of its neoliberal allegory/commodity, "Jewish Germany." (Ginsberg, 2005a)

Here I was aiming to confront the WiG debate's elision of political economic issues and their relationship to Israeli agency in and for the West, that is, its failure to address the possibility that the religious orthodoxy in the film is at least some kind of metaphor for the political orthodoxy associated with the former Eastern bloc, both of which ideological proclivities *Go for Zucker!* – uncannily apropos of Zionism – attempts to mitigate but not, finally, to eliminate through Jaeckie's "unorthodox" capers (to recall the film's Anglophone-release subtitle) and his daughter's "queer" orientation. Thus I also meant to challenge the limited readings the debate was thereby proffering of the film's Jewish and queer stereotyping, the latter of which would, like the Middle East and the ravages of neoliberalism, continue to be ignored or downplayed in Nathenson's published review and in ensuing scholarly treatment of the film (e.g. Allan, 2007; Benbow, 2009).

I subsequently returned to the question of Jewish victimhood by addressing Nathenson's concern that director Levy's Jewishness had become a foil for persisting German antisemitism and Levy's alleged collaborationism:

> About the director, I'm not sure his Jewishness is a red herring for anti-Semitism so much as a sad statement about the self-positioning by some Jews in line with the philosemitic mold ... I would be interested to know where the director stands on the Israeli–Palestinian conflict, especially the Separation Wall. If he is an apologist for Israeli "ethnic cleansing" (which is undeniably happening by way of that Wall), he may not be hard-pressed also to serve as an apologist for similar practices in Germany and beyond. (Ginsberg, 2005a)

I was referring, of course, to the scene between "Janice"/Ghada and "Shmuel"/Samuel. I wanted to know if anyone else on the WiG listserv had registered that scene and thought it meaningful. If, as Nathenson believes, *Go for Zucker!* is an apology for antisemitism where humor functions to reinforce post-*Wende* normalization at Jewish expense, what did it mean for the film also to include a scene in which an ultra-orthodox Jewish man high on a drug he received inadvertently from his lesbian niece whose daughter turns out to be his incestuously begotten grandchild, engages in sexual relations with a Palestinian prostitute at a house of gambling and ill repute owned by his assimilated, ex-communist, shyster, alcoholic brother with a price on his head? What might it mean, furthermore, if Shmuel – as stated in a program blurb in the November 2005 Museum of Modern Art (MoMA) Member Calendar announcing the film as part of its Kino! 2005: New Cinema from Germany series – was "now living in Israel"?[5] Although Marlene corrects Jaeckie about the family's place of residence when he states prior to the Frankfurt Zuckermanns' arrival that "My brother is an Israeli fanatic who throws rocks at cars on the Sabbath,"[6] the concomitant slippage, part of the scripted dialogue, is hardly accidental. What, in effect, is the figure of the Palestinian doing in this film?

Unfortunately I was not to receive an answer to my question. For as the debate escalated, the ensuing posts were at pains either to locate and confirm Levy's Swiss national origin (Mering, 2005; Vietor-Engländer, 2005), which I had initially mistaken as German (Ginsberg, 2005b) insofar as it is well-known that Levy, a child of Jewish-German Holocaust survivors (from Berlin), had at the time been living and working as a filmmaker in West Germany for 25 years (Benbow, 2009: 22); and to debunk the MoMA program blurb for having incorrectly placed the Frankfurt family residence in Israel (Pfitzner, 2005; Nathenson, 2005b,c; Eigen, 2005). Nathenson (2005b) proceeded to clarify his position by drawing attention to the way in which the film's humor purportedly exploits Jewish self-criticism and internecine division and reiterating her concern that the film renders "Jewish themes ... secondary to the story of a German family's coerced unification, a family with an Eastern and a Western branch *(not Israeli)*" (my emphasis) – a point blatantly contradicted by a press release (Lee, 2005) issued by First Run Features, the film's US distributor, which singularly highlights the fact that *Go for Zucker!* ran successfully in Israel for 15 weeks (Lee, 2005),[7] and also undercut by later mainstream print media reviews (Denby, 2006: para. 1; Alter, 2006: para. 4) comparing *Go for Zucker!* with a contemporary Israeli film, *Ushpizin* (Giddi Dar, 2004), that happens likewise, more directly to concern the Jewish religious–secular problematic. Only one post, from Sabine von Mering, then Executive Director of Brandeis University's Center for German and European Studies, seemed to reflect a good-faith engagement with my proposed reading and suggestion that the film's convoluted complexity be acknowledged and unpacked:

> I see [Levy] very much as part of a new generation intent on breaking new ground in approaching the topic of the Holocaust. Unfortunately, "Alles auf Zucker" was a big disappointment ... I found the sex scenes a lot more relevant and convincing in "Head on" [Fatih Akın, 2004] somehow than all those incestuous escapades in "Zucker" ... I wasn't convinced in the end that it was supposed to be a satire about German stereotypes. (2005)

Mering's intervention was very subtle, however, as though hinting in coded fashion that *Go for Zucker!* might be an allegory of a different order, one that acknowledges and laments the genocide of the European Jews while, as I had put it in a prior post, "allegorically 'hand-holding' their former (persisting?) German oppressors as if to say, 'We forgive you as long as you allow us to be the 'Jews' you've always wanted/needed us to be'" (Ginsberg, 2005a). Indeed in a critically well-remarked scene in which Marlene buys a book entitled *Wie Juden leben* ("How Jews Live")[8] as part of an ultimately unsuccessful attempt to placate the Frankfurt Zuckermanns by fooling them into believing that her own family is religiously observant, an adjacent placard in the mise-en-scène can be made out to read, "Sabra – The Spirit of Israel," among numerous other imported Israel goods lining the store shelves, many of which Marlene also buys and which, judging from the large amount of money (€436.49) she hands over to the cashier, are quite costly. Clearly, *Go for Zucker!* is not only concerned with Israel but overtly confuses Israeli with Jewish culture and identity – an erroneous tendency part and parcel of Zionist ideology as well as of German nationalism, both of which have positioned Jews as comprising an ethnonation in order to justify their colonial emigration to Israel or, for the latter during the Nazi era, their deportation and mass murder (see Selzer, 1967; Sand, 2009). Now, apparently, the same tendency is being used to rationalize their neocolonial return "home."

In response to Mering, I posted again, this time in an attempt to clarify the Israel/Palestine connection:

> While I appreciate Cary's qualification of her [sic] concept of the film's allegoricality, and agree with her reading of how Levy's Jewishness functions to deflect criticism (just as the moniker "antisemite" today functions to deflect legitimate criticism of Israeli policy) [...] I would argue that the "Jewish themes" in his film aren't secondary, they are part and parcel of the film's "German" meaning and significance, just as Jewishness is part and parcel of what it means to be German – although not necessarily in the way Levy proposes. That significance would include ... allegorization of Israeli/Palestinian non-normalcy ... and of the sordid standard of living of non-Jewish guest workers and immigrants in contemporary Germany (and maybe other places in the New Europe such as the current emblazoned France).
>
> Put bluntly, one simply can't talk about or portray contemporary Jews, especially in post-Wall Germany, without raising the spectre of the [Israeli] Occupation and of racisms much closer to home. THAT's the allegorical crux of this film which we must face up to, however taboo it may seem! In other words, it's not [just] Levy who's the "red herring" with respect to "Alles auf Zucker," it's Holocaust survival and the moral highground it has come to afford those who would interpret that horror's legacy in the wake of the Wende and its role in the heightening of neoliberalism and attendant global immiseration, whether such interpretation is expressed by victims OR perpetrators. (Ginsberg, 2005b)

In almost immediate reaction, a post finally appeared that not only took up these issues but did so by addressing me by name (for the first time since the debate had begun). Pascale Bos, a Professor of Germanic Studies at the University of Texas–Austin, took explicit issue with my reference to the fact that accusations of anti-Semitism have become a contemporary means of deflecting criticism of Israeli policy. She stated that, absent some delimitation on my part that would specify the makers and receivers of such accusations, my statement seemed like

> some kind of paranoid phantasy [sic] by some (right-wing?) Jews. Unfortunately, more often than I would like to admit, I have indeed seen forms of "modern" antisemitism disguised as "legitimate" anti-Zionism, in particular among German/ ist colleagues. There is furthermore such a long tradition of this on the German left (not to mention the right) that I don't want to see that reality so flippantly (parenthetically!) dismissed on this list. (Bos, 2005)

Bos forcefully, if indirectly insinuated that my reading of *Go for Zucker!* constituted antisemitism – at once left-wing and right-wing, Jewish and German – insofar as I did not direct my critical reference to the contemporary abuse of "antisemitism" specifically enough, to "some" critics of Israel, for example, or to an occasional articulation (Bos, 2005). Echoing sentiments critiqued explicitly by Edward Said at least a decade earlier,[9] Bos's position is noteworthy for its simultaneously commendable concern over antisemitism's contemporary persistence across the sociopolitical spectrum in Germany, and its failure to engage the real substance of my argument, which was that the mere expression of concern over Israeli brutality against Palestinian Arabs is consistently met with accusations of "antisemitism" and thus dismissed, regardless of that expression's origins or direction, within the contemporary public sphere. The implicit contradiction in Bos's position – it's okay to speak critically against antisemitism but not against anti-racism – served to belie her likewise implicit, rhetorical support for the coded and conceptually delimited readings which were in fact coming to comprise the debate's majority opinion that *Go for Zucker!* is, for better or worse, a film about post-*Wende* Jewish-German normalization devoid of significance for the Israeli–Palestinian conflict, and that to suggest otherwise is politically tendentious and ideological. As if that were not enough, ten minutes after Bos's post registered, Cary Nathenson upped the ante with the following astonishing message:

> While I don't have the film memorized (perish the thought!) there is, to the best of my recollection, no mention of Israel at all in the film. The family is from Berlin and Frankfurt. The movie has nothing to do with the Middle-East, and it's stretching it beyond credulity to try to make that connection even if there is any fly-by reference to the family's spending any time in Israel. (2005c)

With these responses, in which the word "Palestinian" is not once mentioned, Bos, Nathenson, and, by their accompanying reticence, the other Wiggies on the listserv presumed to determine, almost by default, without reasoned explanation, the permissible parameters of Jewish(-German) cinematic interpretability for German and German women's studies – a profoundly antisemitic act. Beyond that racialized horizon remained apparently unspeakable Palestinians, about whom former Israeli Prime Minister Golda Meir once famously quipped, "They did not exist" (Jansen, 1971: 152), but who in fact not only *do* exist but are represented, if marginally and reductively, as a metonymically congealed *allegory of both Jewish(-German) and German(-Israeli) collaborationism*, in *Go for Zucker!* These unspoken Palestinians are in reality not hidden or voiceless, even as *Go for Zucker!* and its critics on the WiG listserv would render them, via the typified Janice, as empty abstractions whose historical regrounding must necessarily signal "antisemitism" and marshal its purportedly justified defense, the expropriation and oppression of Palestinian Arabs in the disingenuous name of a co-opted Judaism (see Shahak and Mezvinsky, 1999; Vilhotti, Chapter 16, in this volume). In the specific instance of *Go for Zucker!* it is a Palestinian prostitute who comprises this reactive metonym, as if to propagate, in the absence of counterimages (contrasting the film's broad array of Jewish types), the orientalist view that all Arabs, understood reductively as minority third-worlders, are ready lackeys or collaborators with their European oppressors and therefore naturally incapable of self-determination (see Said, 1979). Here, in effect, the Palestinian becomes an "other" whose popular-real grounding in historic Palestine must be mystified and travestied in order to justify her continued domination and subjugation by the Jewish state of Israel.

The film's Israeli–Palestinian allegoricality was in fact picked up in a German review of *Go for Zucker!* (*CINEMA*) that appeared on the film's official website, itself selectively cited during the WiG debate (Nathenson, 2005c; Knauß, 2005b) in repetitive reference not to that review but to an interview posted there with Levy in which, according to Nathenson (2005c), he states that in an earlier draft of his screenplay he had the Frankfurt Zuckermanns living in the United States and returning to Germany for their mother's funeral, because he wanted to include issues relevant to German society (see Levy, n.d.). (This remark constituted perhaps Nathenson's only nod to US-led transnationalism either during the debate or his ensuing published review.) According to *CINEMA*,

> Jacob's Mamme, who had once fled to the West, has died. In her will, she stipulates that her two estranged sons, Jacob and Samuel, must reconcile – otherwise their inheritance is down the tubes. As the Berlin Zuckermanns and the orthodox relatives from Hesse meet for the first time, they naturally face each other more irreconcilably than *Israelis and Palestinians*.[10] (my translation; my emphasis)

The *CINEMA* review's tongue-in-cheek comparison of the diegetic conflict between Jaeckie and Shmuel to the Israeli–Palestinian conflict is stated in passing and thus warrants further analysis and critique – for that comparison, too, is relevant to German society, not to mention US-led transnationalism – as do the frequent, if passing references to Janice by several other reviews that were then posted to the film's official website or that have since appeared in print media and scholarly venues (e.g. Denby, 2006; Holden, 2006; Allan, 2007).[11] To date, however, Janice remains an open secret, not only for the WiG listserv, which has not revisited the issue substantively since Nathenson's review was published, but for *Go for Zucker!* (re)viewers; everyone sees her, many find humor in her scene with Shmuel, and while some critics acknowledge her existence, to explain its cinematic inscription and reception is clearly off-limits.

As proffered in my ensuing, final post to the debate (Ginsberg, 2005c), *Go for Zucker!*'s characterization of Janice is undeniably racist. The dialogue quoted verbatim at this chapter's outset, for instance, suggests that simply by virtue of her Palestinian heritage, this Palestinian woman would naturally know how to please a Jewish man. Although one might generously read the dialogue after a critical master–slave dialectic, whereupon Janice is lent a modicum of collaborative potential over her ostensible Jewish oppressor, that may be giving Levy too much credit, especially insofar as no mutually recognized organic relationship is diegetically evident between Janice and Shmuel: they are not related ethnically, religiously, nationally, filially, socially, professionally, or historically; hence, their implied power-play is at least gratuitous, at most ludic S/M. In effect, it is difficult if not impossible to interpret the sequence, much less its implications for the scene as a whole, the film's narrative thematic or its generic viability, as anything but baldly discriminatory toward Palestinians (and Turks and women) – as discriminatory, if not more so, than Nathenson finds the entire film is against Jews. Such a "laughable" characterization of a socially and economically privileged modern Jew being "victimized" by a Palestinian prostitute – in Germany – decontextualizes and reverses the German-European instrumentalization of Palestinians in the interests of Western hegemony, so that the centrality of Germany's historical instrumentalization of the European Jews remains the dominant, more important issue. For to offer an analysis and critique of minority and Third World collaborationism is one thing; there are countless examples of this in German film history (see e.g. Broe, Chapter 1; Layne, Chapter 11 (both in this volume)). It is another thing altogether to collapse the very idea of collaborationism into a broadly abstract homology, as has the US media regarding WikiLeaks' revelations of Palestinian Authority corruption, that whitewashes the coordinates of Western, European hegemony with an orientalist mise-en-abyme whose vanishing point is a sold-out, "prostituted" Palestine, whose horizon is a new, highly unstable Euro-dominant Germany, and whose sight-lines are a politically incorrect, irreverent, exceptional, "queer" Jewishness that facilitates and rationalizes collaborationism as both morally good and fun.

In fact the "Jewishness" in *Go for Zucker!* is anything but atypical. In its very juggling of secular and sacral modalities and practices, its concern for protocol and circumvention, and its interest in the body and physicality, it is – as Nathenson knows – undeniably stereotypical. The scene in which Marlene purchases *Wie Juden leben* is the most obvious case in point, but the later revelation that Shmuel is nearly bankrupt underscores the issue. Although these masquerades fail, as does Janice's before the inebriated Shmuel, who passes out and thus cannot perform sexually, their efforts all bear fruit: as the various plot lines untangle and resolve, the brothers reconcile, and so, when they proceed to learn from one Rabbi Ginsberg (former GDR star Rolf Hoppe), to whom their mother's will has been entrusted, that her estate is worthless, the stage is already set for these various and sundry characters to (re)build their Jewish-German lives and pursuits together in their new/ancestral home – Berlin.

In his scholarly analysis of *Go for Zucker!* Seán Allan (2007: 31n20) discusses Levy's stated intention "to revive a concept of Jewishness while at the same time rescuing Jewish identity from being type-cast in the role of the victim." Heather Benbow (2009) takes matters further by theorizing the humor that Allan (2007: 32) (whom she does not reference) also discusses as key to Levy's project, in the framework of Max Nordau: as a survival mechanism for Jews who "for the first time ... were permitted to believe that they weren't foreigners in the countries they lived in" (Nordau, quoted in Benbow, 2009: 23). Perhaps aware of the social contradictions implied by this ideological problematic, which entails upholding Jewish "difference" for both neo- and settler-colonial purposes (re: "settler colonialism" see Rodinson, 1973), the November 2005 MoMA Member Calendar may have intentionally, and in light of the film's frequent diegetic references to Israel, misrepresented the Frankfurt Zuckermanns as having previously resided there, thinking that the film's racist connotations might thereby be ameliorated, philosemitically and with a patronizing nod to Palestinian oppression, were its allegoricality redirected, apropos of the *CINEMA* review, toward the very internecine Jewish squabbling that ended up so disturbing Nathenson for its having reinvoked the ostensibly timeless, universal antisemitism which, although he does not acknowledge them, theorists and historians critical of Zionism (e.g. Selzer, 1967; Shahak, 1989; Beit-Hallahmi, 1992: 166–190; Massad, 2005) have argued is ironically necessary to justifying the strong and exceptional Jewish state.[12]

In *Go for Zucker!* as mentioned, this "humorous" positioning of the contemporary Jew as, paradoxically, a nonvictim with a victim mentality takes place on the backs of actually existing Palestinians – as well as, apropos of the WiG listserv debate, at the expense of those genuinely irreverent, politically incorrect, "queer" and exceptional Jews who are one way or another critical of such racism and its service to German nationalism and beyond.

In fact far from timeless, antisemitism is specific to Christian Europe, especially its Western components which today comprise the hegemonic center of the European Union, where X-Filme Creative Pool continues to co-produce new "popular art" films propagating a transnationalist cinematic aesthetics. In this context, one might legitimately surmise that the MoMA Members Calendar's "error" might also symptomatize an effort to support such an aesthetics in line with its institutional history of collaborating with the US government by co-opting cultural critiques of Western political economy (see Saunders, 2000). In any event, it is certainly questionable for a film, not least a post-*Wende* German production implicated structurally in the project of redeeming Germany's place on the world political stage, to position Jewishness conceived in this limited, Zionistic fashion as the mechanism of German, and by extension European, reunification. It is even more questionable for scholars discussing the film on the listserv of an academic, nominally feminist organization "dedicated to eradicating discrimination in the classroom and in the teaching profession at all levels" to ignore and deride attempts to raise the issue for intellectual analysis. While the bulk of contemporary interactive communication between scholars is now conducted over the Internet, its discursive status as public domain is too often forgotten, as computer equipment and interface technologies are mistaken as strictly private property, and email exchange is in turn misunderstood as personal or informal conversation lacking the permanence of public record. The WiG listserv – and the Coalition of Women in German of which it is a part – comprise one such public forum; however, its subscribers apparently overlooked that fact, and the protocols of authorial responsibility it entails, when the possibility surfaced that a film which a few of them were studying, and about which at least one of them was writing, might end up challenging their undertheorized assumptions and beliefs about the Israeli–Palestinian conflict within a specifically German context. This brief chapter has been a modest call to redress that regrettable oversight.

Notes

1 The *keffiyeh* is a traditional checkered headscarf worn by Arab and Kurdish men. In the contemporary period, it commonly signifies the Palestinian liberation struggle: a black-and-white pattern is usually associated with Fatah, the nationalist party founded by Yassir Arafat and currently the dominant power in the Israeli-occupied West Bank, and a red-and-white pattern is usually associated with the Palestinian Front for the Liberation of Palestine, a Marxist formation founded by George Habash that has rivaled Fatah historically.

2 The full WiG mission statement, which appears on the organization's website (http://www.womeningerman.org/), reads as follows: "The Coalition of Women in German provides a democratic forum for all people interested in feminist approaches to German literature and culture or in the intersection of gender with other categories of analysis such as sexuality, class, race, and ethnicity. Through its annual conference, panels at national professional meetings, and through the publication of the *Women in German Yearbook*, the organization promotes feminist scholarship of outstanding quality. Women in German is committed to making school and college curricula inclusive and seeks to create bridges, cross boundaries, nurture aspiration, and challenge assumptions while exercising critical self-awareness. Women in German is dedicated to eradicating discrimination in the classroom and in the teaching profession at all levels."

3 The company is responsible for celebrated festival/art-house fare, for instance *Run Lola Run* (Tom Tykwer, 1998), *Goodbye, Lenin!* (Wolfgang Becker, 2003), *My Führer* (Dani Levy, 2007), and *The White Ribbon* (Michael Haneke, 2009), which, like the New German Cinema before them, serve to promote provocative, self-critical images of Germany internationally.

4 Coincidentally, Dani Levy played a small acting role in *Aimée and Jaguar*.

5 The complete blurb reads: "This deftly scripted German-Jewish comedy won six Lolas, Germany's Oscar equivalent. Two estranged brothers – a gambler from former East Germany and a religious Frankfurt Jews now living in Israel – must reconcile to inherit their mother's estate" (MoMA Member Calendar, 2005: 10). (Among the awards *Go for Zucker!* ended up winning were best film, best director, best actor [Hübchen], and best screenplay (*Hollywood Reporter*, 2005: 77)).

6 The original German dialogue is: "Mein Bruder ist ein Fanatiker, so einer der in Israel mit Steinen auf Autos schmeißt, am Shabbat," which translates literally as "My brother is a fanatic, like those in Israel who throw stones at cars on the Sabbath" (my translation).

7 The press release's (Lee, 2005) exact wording is: "One of the most talked-about films in Europe this year, 'Go for Zucker' ('Alles auf Zucker!') premiered in Germany on January 6. It played 44 consecutive weeks in Germany and 15 in Israel; the film surpassed one million admissions in November, making it the highest-grossing German-ethnic film to date." The press release does not recount details of the film's run in countries other than Germany and Israel

8 The English subtitles, however, translate the book's title as "Living a Jewish Life." *Wie Juden leben* is in fact the main title of an actual book, *Wie Juden leben: Glaube – Alltag – Feste*, published in Germany in 1997.

9 "I am still firmly convinced that to defend Palestinian self-determination, and even to pronounce the word *Palestine* has been more difficult than any other political cause today. Despite our relatively modest actualities as a people, because of the understandable vehemence stirred up by a national community that has challenged Israel's behavior – Israel being seen as a state of survivors of the Holocaust – we have been cast as inheritors of the Hitlerian legacy. Israel and its supporters have not hesitated to exploit this" (Said, 1994: xix–xx).

10 "Jakobs Mamme, einst in den Westen geflüchtet, ist gestorben. In ihrem Testament hat sie verfügt, dass sich ihre entfremdeten Söhne Jakob und Samuel wieder vertragen müssen – sonst geht das Erbe flöten. Als sich die Berliner Zuckermanns und die orthodoxe Verwandtschaft aus Hessen erstmals begegnen, steht man sich freilich unversöhnlicher gegenüber als Israelis und Palästinenser."

11 Denby (2006: para. 3) refers to "Janice"/Ghada in passing as a "Palestinian party girl"; Holden (2006: para. 6) refers to her in passing as a "Palestinian beauty"; and Allan (2007: 36) refers to her, likewise in passing, as a "Palestinian hostess."

12 Zionist founder Theodor Herzl himself knew this and in fact, prior to "converting" to Zionism, expressed doubt that such an idea could actually unify an historically dispersed and diverse set of communities, many of which, beyond Christo-European borders or control, had not experienced or conceived of this sense of timeless persecution (Taylor, 1974: 63–71).

References

Allan, S. (2007) "Seit der Wende hat der Mann nur Pechgehabt. Jetzt soll er auch noch Jude sein": theatricality, memory and identity in Dani Levy's *Alles auf Zucker!* (2004). *Debatte* 15 (1), 25–42.

Alter, Ethan (2006) GO FOR ZUCKER. *Film Journal International*, 109 (20), 29–30, http://search.ebscohost.com/login.aspx?direct+true&db=f5h&AN=19680231&site+ehost-live (accessed October 26, 2010).

Beit-Hallahmi, B. (1992) *Original Sins: Reflections on the History of Zionism and Israel*, Olive Branch Press, New York.

Benbow, H. (2009) The gentleman and the rogue: Jewish protagonists in Lessing's *The Jews* and Dani Levy's *Go For Zucker! Australian Journal of Jewish Studies*, 23, 17–43.

Biehl, J.K. (2005) Germany breaks a taboo: Jewish comedy kosher as pork chops. *Spiegel Online*, January 1, http://www.spiegel.de/international/0,1518,338462,00.html (accessed October 15, 2010).

Bos, P.R. (2005) Alles auf zucker discussion. Email. Women in German women_in_ german@listlink.berkeley.edu, November 7, 09:09:27.

Boyarin, D. (1997) *Unheroic Conduct: The Rise of Heterosexuality and the Invention of the Jewish Man*, University of California Press, Berkeley, Los Angeles.

Broe, D. (2011) Have dialectic, will travel: the GDR *Indianerfilme* as critique and radical imaginary, Chapter 1, this volume.

Bushinsky, J. (1991) Germans welcome wave of Soviet Jews. *Chicago Sun-Times*, 1 May, http://www.highbeam.com/doc/1P2-4052043.html (accessed January 24, 2011).

Chancellor Merkel to travel to Israel for government consultations and bilateral talks (2011) Germany.info, January 26, http://www.germany.info/Vertretung/usa/en/__pr/P__Wash/2011/01/26__Merkel__Israel__PR.html?archive=1992696 (accessed February 5, 2011).

CINEMA (n.d.) *Alles auf Zucker!* – Überdiesen Film: Zweijüdische Familienliegenwunderbarmiteinanderim Clinch. *CINEMA*, http://www.cinema.de/kino/filmarchiv/film/alles-auf-zucker,1342061,ApplicationMovie.html (accessed January 24, 2011).

Coalition of Women in German. http://www.womeningerman.org/ (accessed January 24, 2011).

Cohen, R. (2000) Ex-Soviet Jews at home in Germany. *Charleston Gazette*, August 6, http://www.highbeam.com/doc/1P2-18568946.html (accessed January 24, 2011).

Cronin, D. (2009) EU remains cozy with Israel, despite the headlines. *Electronic Intifada*, December 21, http://electronicintifada.net/v2/article10956.shtml (accessed February 25, 2011).

Cronin, D. (2010) *Europe's Alliance with Israel: Aiding the Occupation*, Pluto Press, London.

Denby, D. (2006) Battle lines. *New Yorker*, January 23 (81, 45), 96–97, http://search.ebscohost.com/login.aspx?direct=true&db+f5h&AN=19481975&site+ehost-live (accessed October 26, 2010).

Deutschkron, I. (1970) *Bonn and Jerusalem: The Strange Coalition*, Chilton Book Co., Philadelphia and London.

Eggerz, S. (2006) In a post-Holocaust era: Germany welcomes Jews. *ACJ News*, Spring, http://www.acjna.org/acjna/articles_detail.aspx?id=406 (accessed January 24, 2011).

Eigen, S. (2005) alles auf zucker and Israel. Email. Women in German women_in_ german@listlink.berkeley.edu, November 9, 2005, 18:31:44.

Feldman, L.G. (1984) *The Special Relationship between West Germany and Israel*, Allen & Unwin, Boston.

Fisher, M. (1990) Migration of Soviet Jews to Germany stirs delicate debate. *Washington Post*, October 25, A25, http://pqasb.pqarchiver.com/washingtonpost/access/72626485.html?FMT=ABS&FMTS=ABS:FTanddate=Oct+25%2C+1990&author=Marc+Fisher&pub=The+Washington+Post+%28pre-1997+Fulltext%29&edition=&startpage=a.25&desc=Migration+of+Soviet+Jews+to+Germany+Stirs+Delicate+Debate (accessed January 24, 2011).

Frost, L., Hungerford, A., MacKay, J., and Wexler, L. (eds) (2001) Interpretation and the Holocaust. Special issue, *Yale Journal of Criticism*, 14 (1).

Ginsberg, T. (2005a) Re: Alles auf zucker. Email. Women in German women_in_ german@listlink.berkeley.edu, November 5, 11:32 am.

Ginsberg, T. (2005b) Re: Alles auf zucker. Email. Women in German women_in_german@ listlink.berkeley.edu, November 7, 01:12 am.

Ginsberg, T. (2005c) Re: Alles auf zucker. Email. Women in German women_in_german@ listlink.berkeley.edu, November 7, 11:31:08.

Hall, A. (2005) Jews flock to Germany. Totally Jewish, May 5, http://www.totallyjewish. com/news/special_reports/?content_id=383 (accessed January 24, 2011).

Halle, R. (2008) *German Film after Germany: Toward a Transnational Aesthetic*, University of Illinois Press, Urbana, Chicago.

Hathaway, W.T. (2001) A new beginning: Jews return to Germany. *Amarillo Bay*, 3 (2), http://www.amarillobay.org/contents/hathaway-william/new-beginning.htm (accessed January 24, 2011).

H-Net: Humanities and Social Sciences Online. http://www.h-net.org/ (accessed January 24, 2011).

Holden, S. (2006) Can't we all just get along? Yes, if there's money at stake. *New York Times*, January 29, E10.

Hollywood Reporter (2005) "Zucker" takes six Lolas: best actor win an upset. *Hollywood Reporter – International Edition*, July 12 (389, 49), 77, http://search.ebscohost.com/ login.aspx?direct=true&db=f5h&AN=17822408&site=ehost-live (accessed October 26, 2010).

Jansen, G.H. (1971) *Zionism, Israel and Asian Nationalism*, Institute for Palestine Studies, Beirut.

Kloke, M.W. (1994) *Israel und die deutsche linke: Zur Geschichte eines schwierigen Verhältnisses*, 2nd edn. Haag & Herchen, Frankfurt am Main.

Knauβ, S. (2005a) Re: Alles auf zucker. Email. Women in German women_in_german@ listlink.berkeley.edu, November 5, 09:37:23.

Knauβ, S. (2005b) Re: Alles auf zucker. Email. Women in German women_in_german@ listlink.berkeley.edu, November 7, 09:15:59.

Krämer, N. (2011) Models of masculinity in postwar Germany: the *Sissi* films and the West German *Wiederbewaffnungsdebatte*. Chapter 14, this volume.

Lau, I.M., Krupp, M., and Meislisch, S. (1997) *Wie Juden leben: Glaube – Alltag – Feste*, Gütersloher Verlagshaus, Gütersloh.

Layne, P. (2011) Lessons in liberation: Fassbinder's *Whity* at the crossroads of Hollywood melodrama and Blaxploitation. Chapter 11, this volume.

Lee, B. (2005) "Go for Zucker" opens in New York on January 20. *Go for Zucker. A Film by Dani Levy*. First Run Features, New York, 2.

Levy, D. (n.d.) Interview *Alles auf Zucker!* Official website, http://www.zucker-derfilm. de?interviewdanilevy.php (accessed November 7, 2005).

Massad, J.A. (2005) The persistence of the Palestinian question. *Cultural Critique*, 59, 1–23.

Mering, S.v. (2005) Alles auf Zucker. Email. Women in German women_in_german@ listlink.berkeley.edu, November 5, 2:00 pm.

Meurer, H-J. (2000) *Cinema and National Identity in a Divided Germany 1979–1989: The Split Screen*, Edwin Mellen Press, Lewiston, NY, Queenston, ON, Lampeter, UK.

Milk and Honey Tours (2010) Germany once again a homeland for Jews: Munich, Frankfurt and Berlin. UG Berlin, Open Group Programs, November suppl., http://jewish-vienna.at/ images/Germany%20Once%20Again%20a%20Homeland%20for%20Jews.pdf (accessed January 24, 2011).

MoMA Member Calendar (2005) *Alles auf Zucker!* Museum of Modern Art, New York, November.

Nathenson, C. (2005a) Alles auf zucker. Email. Women in German women_in_german@ listlink.berkeley.edu, November 4, 09:51:44.

Nathenson, C. (2005b) Re: Alles auf zucker. Email. Women in German women_in_ german@listlink.berkeley.edu, November 6, 08:54 PM.

Nathenson, C. (2005c) Alles auf zucker. E-mail. Women in German women_in_german@ listlink.berkeley.edu, 7 November, 09:19:19.

Nathenson, C. (2006) Review of *Alles auf Zucker*: a polemical review of post-Wall Germany's first "Jewish" movie. H-German, H-Net Reviews, http://www.h-net.org/reviews/show-rev.php?id=15462 (accessed January 24, 2011).

Peck, Jeffrey M. (2005) *Being Jewish in the New Germany*. Rutgers University Press, New Brunswick, NJ.

Pfitzner, I. (2005) Re: Alles auf zucker. Email. Women in German women_in_german@ listlink.berkeley.edu, November 6, 12:10:02.

Qumsiyeh, M.B. (2004) *Sharing the Land of Canaan: Human Rights and the Israeli–Palestinian Struggle*, Pluto Press, London.

Rodinson, M. (1973) *Israel: A Colonial-Settler State?* (trans. D. Thorstad), Pathfinder, New York.

Runyan, J. (2011) German state parliament welcomes first rabbinical delegation. Chabad-Lubavitch Media Center, January 13, http://www.chabad.org/news/article_cdo/aid/1411279/jewish/German-Legislature-Welcomes-Rabbis.htm (accessed January 24, 2011).

Said, E.W. (1979) *Orientalism*, Vintage Press, New York.

Said, E.W. (1994) *The Politics of Dispossession: The Struggle for Palestinian Self-Determination, 1969–1994*, Pantheon Books, New York.

Sand, S. (2009) *The Invention of the Jewish People* (trans. Y. Lotan), Verso, London.

Saunders, F.S. (2000) *The Cultural Cold War: The CIA and the World of Arts and Letters*, New Press, New York.

Schwartz, C. (2007) Inner rift among Germany's Jews: Eastern European Jews outnumber German Jews in Berlin: can the two groups reconcile? ABC News, May 14, http://abcnews.go.com/International/story?id=3173317&page=1 (accessed January 25, 2011).

Selzer, M. (1967) *The Aryanization of the Jewish State*, Black Star, New York.

Shahak, I. (1989) Zionism as a recidivist movement: origin of its separatist aims, in *Anti-Zionism: Analytical Reflections* (eds R. Tekiner, A. Abed-Rabbo, and Mezvinsky, N.), Amana Books, Brattleboro, VT, pp. 280–312.

Shahak, I. and Mezvinsky, N. (1999) *Jewish Fundamentalism in Israel*, Pluto Press, London.

Sieg, K. (2002) Sexual desire and social transformation in *Aimee and Jaguar*. *Signs: Journal of Women in Culture and Society*, 28 (1), 303–331.

Siemon-Netto, U. (2003) Jews flooding into Germany. UPI, June 5, http://www.upi.com/Odd_News/2003/06/05/Analysis-Jews-flooding-into-Germany/UPI-20971054848361/ (accessed January 24, 2011).

Taylor, A.R. (1974) *The Zionist Mind: The Origins and Development of Zionist Thought*, Institute for Palestine Studies, Beirut.

Tekiner, R. (1989) The "Who Is a Jew?" controversy in Israel: a product of political Zionism, in *Anti-Zionism: Analytical Reflections* (eds R. Tekiner, A. Abed-Rabbo, and Mezvinsky, N.), Amana Books, Brattleboro, VT, pp. 62–89.

Timm, A. (1997) The burdened relationship between the GDR and Israel. *Israel Studies*, 2 (1), 22–49.

Vietor-Engländer, D. (2005) Re: Alles auf zucker. Email. Women in German women_in_ german@listlink.berkeley.edu, November 6, 1:10 am.

Vilhotti, D. (2011) The aesthetics of ethnic cleansing: an historiographic and filmic analysis of Andres Veiel's *Balagan*. Chapter 16, this volume.

Vukadinović, V.S. (2011) The Baader-Oedipus-Complex, Chapter 18, this volume.

Winkle, S. (2011) Margarethe von Trotta's *Rosenstrasse*: feminist re-visions of a historical controversy. Chapter 17, this volume.

Zachary, G.P. (2007) *Endless Frontier: Vannevar Bush, Engineer of the American Century*, Free Press, New York.

Filmography

Aimée and Jaguar (Max Färberböck, Germany, 1999).

Go for Zucker!: An Unorthodox Comedy [*Alles auf Zucker!* (Bet It All on Zucker!)] (Dani Levy, Germany, 2004).

Goodbye, Lenin! [*Good Bye Lenin!*] (Wolfgang Becker, Germany, 2003).

Head-On [*Gegen die Wand*] (Fatih Akın, Germany / Turkey, 2004).

Life Is Beautiful [*La vita è bella*] (Roberto Benigni, Italy, 1997).

My Führer: The Truly Truest Truth about Adolf Hitler [*Mein Führer: Die wirklich wahrste Wahrheit über Adolf Hitler*] (Dani Levy, Germany, 2007).

Run Lola Run [*Lola rennt*] (Tom Tykwer, Germany, 1998).

Rashevski's Tango [*Le tango des Rashevski*] (Sam Gabarski, Belgium / Luxembourg / France, 2003).

Ushpizin [*Ha-Ushpizin*] (Giddi Dar, Israel, 2004).

White Ribbon, The [*Das weiße Band: Eine deutsche Kindergeschichte*] (Michael Haneke, Germany / Austria / France / Italy, 2009).

21

Screening the German Social Divide

Aelrun Goette's Die Kinder sind tot

David James Prickett

Introduction

Aelrun Goette has directed documentary and feature films that concern issues ranging from violent crimes committed by youth (*Ohne Bewährung – Psychogramm einer Mörderin* (Without Probation – A Psychological Profile of a Murderess, 1997–1998)) to the situation of women in the *Bundeswehr* (German standing army) (*Feldtagebuch – Allein unter Männern* (Field Diary – Alone among Men, 2001–2002)) to a case of maternal infanticide in Frankfurt (Oder) (*Die Kinder sind tot* (The Children Are Dead, 2002–2003)). "I began working with documentary film because I wanted to find topics which – how can I put this – are unsettling. Interestingly, it's never been difficult to find such topics" (Goette, quoted in Richter, 2005: para. 2).[1] Goette's films reflect her strong social conscience and her desire to effect change. Her films may be likened to collages: they present critically overlapping, intersecting glimpses into their subjects' lives, fears, and criminal activities, compelling audiences to connect the elements in order to make informed judgments about the figures in the films.

"Es ist Zeit, wieder zornig zu werden" ("It is time to get angry again") is the closing line of Goette's *Diplomarbeit* ("thesis") in directing, which she completed in 2000 at the Hochschule für Film und Fernsehen (College for Film and Television (HFF)) "Konrad Wolf" in Potsdam-Babelsberg. As reporter Dörte Richter notes, "Rage is a characteristic of her films" (Richter, 2005: para. 5).[2] When asked why she makes such films, Goette replied,

> The people whom I meet and about whom I make films – whether fiction or documentary – are all strong personalities. Perhaps that is the bind between them and me.[3] (quoted in Richter, 2005: para. 6)

A Companion to German Cinema, First Edition. Edited by Terri Ginsberg and Andrea Mensch.
© 2012 Blackwell Publishing Ltd. Published 2012 by Blackwell Publishing Ltd.

Goette has given numerous newspaper interviews and has appeared on German political talk shows, including *Im Palais* and *Anne Will*. In a 1997 interview published in *Die Welt*, Goette spoke at length about her documentary *Ohne Bewährung*. The film documents four years in the life of Jeannette, who was serving time in the *Justizvollzugsanstalt für Frauen* (Women's Prison) in Berlin-Plötzensee. Along with three friends, Jeannette tortured and killed 13-year-old Melanie in Schwedt, Brandenburg on March 11, 1992. Jeannette was 15 at the time of the incident.

Ohne Bewährung originated as Goette's 25-minute film, *Eine* (One, 1994). It was initially intended to serve as a cinematic letter to Jeannette's parents, from whom she had come to feel alienated (Wendt, 1997: para. 23). After agreeing to be Jeannette's guardian during her prison sentence, Goette began learning more about Jeannette's troubled family life. Both parents were alcoholics. When Jeannette was seven years old, she was sexually abused by her older brother – and no one believed her. "She was a ticking time bomb. Violence was the only means she had learned with which to settle conflict. And now she hit back" (Goette, quoted in Wendt, 1997: para. 13).[4] As in the majority of Goette's films, the protagonist is young, uneducated, and female. She is from the lower class and has little to no prospects. She lives in the shadow of domestic violence and has accepted violence as a means to solve conflicts. And she has been involved in a gruesome crime that alarms and alienates German society.

Despite the film's socially critical content, *Eine* was well received publicly. It supplies evidence that criminals like Jeannette, and the crimes they commit, resist simplistic categorization, thus prompting the viewer to consider the greater social factors involved in such cases. Goette remarked, "Back then I had already attempted to portray the ambivalence between 'good' and 'bad' and to show the victim behind the perpetrator" (quoted in Wendt, 1997: para. 23).[5] The film's theme, the protagonist's background, and Goette's struggle to capture the ambivalence between "good" and "bad," victim and perpetrator in cases of murder and abuse, are emblematic of her work. Thus, her focus is not only unique but also necessary for a post-Wall German society inured to a great extent by a collective *Wegschauen* ("turning a blind eye") to social issues such as child poverty and domestic violence. Due to their candid portrayal of these issues, Goette's films have begun to receive numerous awards and increased media attention. All the same, scholarly studies of Goette's oeuvre are lacking.

This chapter aims toward filling that gap in German cinema studies by providing a basis for scholarly attention to Aelrun Goette's films. It analyzes her documentary *Die Kinder sind tot* (2002–2003), investigating how it projects the post-Wall German divide onto former East German social conditions. The film shows the divide taking several forms – between men and women; between fathers, mothers, and children; between the "haves" and "have-nots" (the so-called *neue Unterschicht*).[6] It also indicates this divide's deepening effects on women's access to education, health care, and opportunities for a secure future in the former East Germany. It represents this divide both with respect to film production and by Goette's projection of a critical gaze.

In this respect, this chapter will indicate how Goette openly critiques and distances herself from Western feminism. I suggest, in effect, that materialist feminist thought shapes her cinematic work, which comprises a distanced, objective impulse for allowing a voice to female subjects, and a personal, subjective investment toward ensuring them an audience. Annette Kuhn has discussed this tension in terms of a distinction between "passionate detachment" and cinematic authorship – one that this chapter shall uphold in its analysis of *Die Kinder sind tot* and Goette's work in relation to it:

> Auteur theory may or may not embrace intentionalism. To the extent that it does, it will suggest that films mean only what their directors intended them to mean [...] If this notion of film authorship is accepted, we cannot necessarily take a film maker's [sic] word about her or his films – even if we have it – at face value. (1994: 10)

This chapter begins with an overview of Goette's biography and of German media perceptions of her as a woman filmmaker. Of particular interest is the strong attention lent Goette's status as a working mother; my interview with her provides insight into how she sees herself in these respects. The ensuing analysis of *Die Kinder sind tot* will illustrate the anthropological method employed by Goette with respect to her interview subjects and address how materialist feminism informed the making of the film.

Die Kinder sind tot focuses on the first of three major infanticide cases reported in the Eastern German city of Frankfurt (Oder): in June 1999, two young boys, Kevin and Tobias Jesse, were found dead from dehydration after their mother, Daniela, left them alone at home for 14 days. Goette's main concern is not Jesse's crime per se but rather the blatant *Wegschauen* displayed regarding it by the State, Daniela's neighbors, and her family. Daniela's children had experienced severe neglect at home and in their surroundings, where, following the collapse of the German Democratic Republic (GDR), many disenfranchised mothers and children now find themselves trapped in a downward spiral of unemployment and abuse. I will address these issues in the course of discussing how Goette's documentary understands them. Finally, I will investigate how the film's representation of the post-Wall German divide has been received critically in Germany as a whole.

Aelrun Goette: "Enduring the Balance"

In her interview with Dörte Richter, Aelrun Goette summarized her developmental years with a single, exaggerated zigzag gesture (Richter, 2005: para. 1) (Figure 21.1).

Figure 21.1 From the interview with Aelrun Goette ("Interview mit der Regisseurin Aelrun Goette") on DVD of *Die Kinder sind tot* (dir. Aelrun Goette, prod. zero film). Courtesy of zero film.

Born on July 6, 1966 in East Berlin, she was named after a Dutch captain, "Elrun," about whom Goette's mother had read in the newspaper (Junghänel, 2004: para. 11). When Goette was 14, her mother suffered a heart attack and died in her daughter's arms. Goette's father, a physicist, blamed her for her mother's death and sent her to a home for children, whereupon Goette was taken in by one of her mother's friends (Junghänel, 2004: para. 11). After completing the tenth grade, Goette was compelled to leave school, as she reportedly did not "demonstrate a mature Socialist personality" (quoted in Richter, 2005: para. 2).[7] She then began professional training as a nurse specializing in neurology and psychology. Goette enjoyed this training, because she liked working with the patients – and her schedule enabled her to forgo demonstrations of the Freie Deutsche Jugend (Free German Youth) (quoted in Richter, 2005: para. 2).[8]

It was also at this time that Goette began working in theater, which she described as a site of encounters, of political nay-saying, and a personal search (quoted in Richter, 2005: para. 2). She was a set and costume designer and a director up until the fall of the Berlin Wall. At that point, for Goette, the theater lost its political edge, or rather, its role as a site of political resistance, and she began focusing her energies elsewhere. After studying four semesters of philosophy at the

Humboldt-Universität zu Berlin, she found herself in front of the camera as a model and actress. Goette even appeared from 1993 to 1994 in the German soap opera *Gute Zeiten, Schlechte Zeiten* (Good Times, Bad Times) before moving on to study at the HFF "Konrad Wolf." Today, she occasionally offers seminars there: in 2010 she offered "Filmarbeit mit Profiregisseuren" (Filmmaking with Professional Directors) for theater students.

Practically every published interview and article makes a point of mentioning Goette's appearance:[9] "A Nice Figure – In Front of and Behind the Camera" opens with the following statement: "When this woman passes by, people turn their heads. Tall, blonde, a pretty face" (Lukaschewitsch, 1997: para. 1).[10] These articles do not reduce Goette to appearances, however; her remarked attractiveness is discussed in the context of professional modeling work.[11] Journalist Michael Lukaschewitsch stresses that Goette takes her work as a director quite seriously through her awareness of the cinema's manipulative potential: "Elias Canetti's *Crowds and Power* crosses her mind. She likes to talk about responsibility and privileges and wants to use both in order 'to work in an educational manner'" (para. 10).[12] Lukaschewitsch adds that Goette attended a seminar which renowned West German feminist film director, Margarethe von Trotta, offered at the HFF. However, he limits his commentary to a seminar photograph for which Goette had posed with von Trotta after having been selected again on account of Goette's perceived attractiveness. Were Goette a man, it is doubtful that her looks would have received such attention.

When she appeared on *Im Palais* on October 11, 2007, Goette participated on a panel about gender roles in Germany, entitled "When Frauen bezahlen [...]" ("When women pay [...]" Moderator Astrid Frohloff asked Goette to comment on how gender roles had been understood and passed on from generation to generation in the GDR. Goette responded,

> I can only relate my own experience – I grew up with a working mother. [...] That image is a crucial point for me: having a degree of financial independence and being able to make decisions with my partner.[13]

Frohloff also asked Goette to explain what it is like working in a profession largely dominated by men, and whether she has noticed a crisis of masculinity in the years following German reunification. Goette responded by shifting the focus back to the issue of parenting: "In my profession – as in many others – there are many women who have children and stop directing films. At some point, you are relatively alone."[14]

Although Goette herself does not stand alone, she certainly stands out as a female director. Her position is at odds with the Western German feminist perspective expressed by Frohloff, which ignores the public–private predicament of female labor, especially where child care services are underfunded or nonexistent, by turning women's economic concerns into a male psychological problem.[15] Yet the materialist gender analysis she had inculcated in the GDR does influence her thinking as well as her work as a director, instructor, and public figure:

> I've noticed that, in addition to what I communicate in my films, I function as an important role model for female students. [...] What is the image of the Eastern German woman – or of the young German woman, really? And how can we offer women today possibilities for identification, in which having children and a professional life can be fun?[16] (Prickett, 2009: para. 21)

When I asked Goette if she herself has any role models, she referred to colleagues who inspire and have accompanied her, such as the Austrian filmmaker, journalist, and writer Georg Stefan Troller. His statement, "Wir sind alle Menschenfresser" ("We are all cannibals"), both motivates and preoccupies her (Prickett, 2009: para. 48).[17] Commenting on film work he had done with cannibals on the New Hebrides, Troller draws a parallel between the cannibals, who ate their enemies in order to assume their strength, and documentary filmmakers, who "eat" their protagonists in order to take on and internalize the protagonists' solutions to the problems they face. By means of this "cannibalism," the documentary filmmaker is thought to learn "how one copes with sorrow and frustration; how one can utilize these feelings in order to become human again or also to be successful. You learn this from others" (Troller, quoted in Gallmeyer and Schwarz, 2006: para. 7).[18]

Troller's analogy of documentary filmmaking to cannibalism problematizes the relationship between a documentary filmmaker and his/her subjects in terms of film production, epistemology, and ontology. It also recalls Robert Stam's analysis of the trope of cannibalism in Brazilian Cinema Novo, in particular Joaquim Pedro de Andrade's 1969 adaptation of Mario de Andrade's *Macunaíma*.[19] In this context, the "cannibalist metaphor" has a "positive pole," "which idealize[s] the freedom of indigenous societies from restrictive Western social mores," and a "negative pole," "which ma[kes] cannibalism a critical instrument for exposing the exploitative social Darwinism of bourgeois society" (Stam, 1989: 145–146). In documentary filmmaking, however, directorial "cannibalism" figuratively consumes not only the filmic subject but also any claim to sheer objectivity on the director's part.

Goette is aware of these problematics. She has admitted that when filming *Die Kinder sind tot*, she was engaged in "cannibalism": "I wanted to give the monstrous events a human face" (Körte, 2004: para. 3).[20] She has stated that the responsibility of respecting her subjects is at times overwhelming. During the filming of *Die Kinder sind tot*, she often found it hard to strike a balance between protecting Daniela Jesse and not censoring herself. "This is a very difficult question because you are much more in control of the material than in a feature film" (Prickett, 2009: para. 50).[21] Goette compares her work as a documentary filmmaker to that of a "tightrope walker" who must maintain a fine balance between such "cannibalism" (i.e. a desire to know her subject intimately) and an immense responsibility to respect that subject as an autonomous, knowing person. If a director is only a "cannibal," s/he is a "pig," an all-consuming glutton who regurgitates the subject's narrative in the form of an ultimately self-serving cinematic project. But if the director is too cautious, s/he cannot gain the proper insight into a situation:

> You have to overstep boundaries in order to comprehend something, I think. Because in a safe space, you don't learn anything. And being able to endure this balance is a quality I've always sought in my colleagues. Troller is someone I have found who also deals with this – this is precisely what it's all about.[22] (Prickett, 2009: para. 48)

Goette's film projects consistently overstep boundaries of social mores, confronting the persistent German *Wegschauen* regarding those on the social margins.

Interrelated issues which frame *Die Kinder sind tot* – German *Wegschauen*, unemployed single mothers, child poverty, and the neglect and abuse of children – also comprise the core of *Keine Angst* (Don't Be Afraid, 2009), Goette's second narrative feature, set not in Eastern Germany but in the *Demonstrativbauvorhaben* ("model building project") in the Western German district of Porz in southeast Cologne. Since its screening at Kino Babylon in Berlin on September 3, 2009, *Keine Angst* has received numerous awards, including the *Deutscher Fernsehpreis* ("German Television Prize") for leading actresses Michelle Barthel (in the role of Becky) und Carolyn Genzkow (in the role of Becky's friend Melanie). However, reviews of the film have been mixed and have focused largely on two issues: the film's violence and its portrayal of the *neue Unterschicht* ("new lower class"). Barbara Gärtner writes that "a film like *Keine Angst* doesn't move you. It knocks you out" (Gärtner, 2010: para. 8).[23]

During the filming of *Keine Angst*, the actual residents of Cologne-Porz did not welcome Goette's cast and crew. A car was broken into, a crew member was attacked, and insults were slung. Perhaps due to her experience shooting *Die Kinder sind tot* on location in Frankfurt (Oder), Goette was able to sympathize with the residents' resistance. "'I felt we had the duty to prove that we did not want to film a dirty movie about a dirty world'" (Goette, quoted in Wick, 2010: para. 6)[24] (Figure 21.2).

Yet when considering the creative impetus of her work, it is in fact Goette's goal to challenge both her subjects and her audience. Ultimately, this impulse entails a deeply compassionate interest in personal tragedies of the sort experienced by Jeannette in *Ohne Bewährung*, Daniela in *Die Kinder sind tot*, and the female protagonists in *Keine Angst*. It is Goette's personal investment in analyzing and coming to understanding these women and the social conditions entrapping them that makes her films so compelling.

Figure 21.2   Aelrun Goette on the set of *Keine Angst* (dir. Aelrun Goette, prod. WDR/ Willi Weber). Courtesy of TAG/TRAUM.

Motherhood and the German Social Divide: *Die Kinder sind tot*

Introductory discussion

Die Kinder sind tot is Goette's most well-known documentary. While it is primarily a film about an overwhelmed single mother, *Die Kinder sind tot* is also an investigation of German motherhood gone awry. Every year, 100 children in Germany die from parental neglect and/or abuse ("Kinder als Opfer," 2007). Increased media coverage in Germany of filicide cases has not investigated the root causes of such crimes but only sparked a veritable panic about "unfit mothers." Goette has flatly denied any voyeuristic moments in her own films. However, she does believe that a "voyeuristic interest" lies at the heart of sensationalist reports on filicide, a phenomenon that has shaped the social imaginary "not just since Medea – it is a cause of great fear and thus naturally a fascinating topic" (Prickett, 2009: para. 17).[25]

During the Weimar period, the figure of the *Kindermörder* ("child-murderer") was the focus of much attention, as evidenced by the Düsseldorf child-murderer, Peter Kürten, and the figure of child-murderer Hans Beckert in Fritz Lang's *M* (*M: Eine Stadt sucht einen Mörder*, 1931). Scholar Maria Tatar explains,

> Although Lang harped repeatedly on *M* as a film with a social message about the importance of taking good care of children and as a film that stages a debate about

the death penalty, he made one particularly telling offhand observation about just what it was that fascinated him about the serial murders of the 1920s. In following various cases in the newspapers, Lang was struck by the way in which the unsolved murders seemed almost automatically to foster what he described as a psychosis of fear (*Angstpsychose*) – for him, a revolting mentality that mingled misanthropy with overzealousness to produce the kind of behavior that led to the denunciation of neighbors and other associates. (1995: 154)

The child-murderer – both real and fictional – served as a vehicle of panic-mongering in German society on several levels. First, the unassuming perpetrators could not be easily identified, consistently eluded the police, and thereby fed a "psychosis of fear" in society. Second, media reports fueled anxiety stemming from the police's failure to capture the perpetrator.[26]

Most germane to my analysis, however, is a third "level": the perceived role of the "unfit mother" in these child murders. Tatar observes that in Lang's *M*, the mothers, "who are anointed as the guardians charged with the protection of children from psychopaths, are themselves deeply implicated in the mental lives of the psychopaths who imperil children" (Tatar, 1995: 169). Accordingly, the children in *M* most likely would not have suffered such brutal deaths had their mothers kept better watch over them. In the world of *M*, notwithstanding Lang's self-proclaimed awareness of *Angstpsychose*, "unfit mothers" are deemed ultimately responsible for cases of child murder, regardless of whether the children die at the hands of others or at their mothers' hands.

Since the fall of the Berlin Wall, the German media has generally tended to locate such "unfit mothers" in the working class, especially in Eastern Germany. Even high-ranking politicians are not averse to issuing generalized, stigmatizing statements about the "Eastern German *Rabenmutter*" ("callous mother"). Responding to a case in Frankfurt (Oder) in 2005, General Jörg Schönbohm, former Secretary of the Interior in the State of Brandenburg, was of the opinion that the cause of filicide was "[…] rooted in the GDR regime, in the educational system of the East German state, in which the citizens were not taught values and lost their way" (quoted in Hein, 2005: para. 2).[27] When asked her opinion of Schönbohm's assertion, Goette cited Brandenburg's then-Minister of Education Horst Rupprecht, who "was almost as devastated by Schönbohm's statement as by the crime itself." She continued,

> In effect, [Rupprecht] puts a politician's statement on the same level as the death of nine children. That is obscene. Apparently, we are all currently resistant to human values. (quoted in Piepgras, 2005: para. 16)[28]

Schönbohm has not been the only politician to stigmatize and stereotype Eastern German mothers. Following the most recent case in Frankfurt (Oder) in February 2008, Prof. Dr Wolfgang Böhmer, Minister-President of the State of

Sachsen-Anhalt, remarked: "It seems to me as if cases of filicide – which of course have always occurred – have become a means of family planning" (quoted in Plewnia, 2008: para. 3).[29] Böhmer echoed a widespread misconception among Germans in the "old," or Western, Federal States that filicide is a phenomenon unique to the "new," or Eastern, Federal States.

In contrast to such blanket statements, by 2000 Goette had already begun seeking to identify the social factors which might lead to filicide. *Die Kinder sind tot* examines Daniela Jesse's life and crime in Frankfurt (Oder), unequivocally documenting the German social divide still prevalent in reunified Germany. By focusing on Daniela's double-bind as single mother and disenfranchised young, working-class woman, Goette's film resists stereotyping her conveniently as an "Eastern German *Rabenmutter*."

From Goette's perspective, Daniela's case reflects the ineffectiveness of post-reunification State agencies (e.g. the *Jugendamt* (Child Protective Services)) and the failure of neighbors and family to address and prevent such cases of child abuse and neglect. This problematic constellation was in fact the impetus for Goette making the film. After reading about Daniela in the newspapers, Goette became preoccupied with the case. She went to Frankfurt (Oder) – initially without a camera – to follow the trial. Sitting in the courtroom, Goette was unsettled as she observed others who had come to watch the proceedings, including many residents of Daniela's neighborhood, Neuberesinchen. Now largely home to the Frankfurt (Oder) working class, it was previously a prized district from its founding in 1977 until the fall of the Wall in 1989.[30] The atmosphere reminded Goette of both a rock concert and a public witch burning, whereupon it became immediately clear to her that she had to make a film about the case (Prickett, 2009: para. 35).

Despite Goette's resolve, she had trouble securing financing. Potential funders often denigrated the proposed topic, retorting, "Who cares about that?" (Prickett, 2009: para. 36). All the same, she began spending time with the residents of Neuberesinchen in order to learn more about them and their impressions of Daniela. Bit by bit, the concept of the film began to gel:

> It poses the question: how is something like this possible in Germany today? At the same time, the film deals concretely with the case and attempts to investigate this family tragedy. And not to judge. Viewers must decide for themselves how this all came to pass. That was my goal.[31] (Prickett, 2009: paras 35–36)

Goette defines the purpose of her film and reflects on her intention to provide her audience with questions rather than easy answers. Even the questions are meant to generate dialogue, debate, and, ultimately, ideas for social change, dislodging the audience's ideological resistances by triggering their emotional blocks: "For film is emotion. Always. Not reason. The discussions will come on their own" (Freitag, 2008: para. 9).[32]

The medium

Die Kinder sind tot evidences a cinema verité style. Alternating between very wide shots of desolate spaces and their inhabitants, and medium close-ups of selected individuals, Goette creates a cinematic frame meant to effect viewer empathy. A montage of unremarked images produces a tempo that is sometimes uncomfortably slow and at times overwhelming enough to tempt viewer participation. In this filmic context, the viewer is positioned to experience the unsettling silence and air of resignation that hangs over post-reunification Neuberesinchen.[33]

The story of Daniela, her children, and her mother – indeed of Neuebersinchen – is communicated largely via this visual narrative. Goette's reliance on editing and visual narrative is indicative of her adherence to cinema verité. Documentary theorist Bill Nichols (1991: 38) prefers to discuss documentary film in terms of the "*observational* and *interactive* modes of documentary representation*.*" The "observational mode" corresponds to cinema verité in that it "stresses the non-intervention of the filmmaker" and "cede[s] 'control' over the events that occur in front of the camera more than any other mode" (Nichols, 1991: 38).

Perhaps most importantly, the observational mode "gives a particular inflection to ethical considerations. Since the mode hinges on the ability of the filmmaker to be unobtrusive, the issue of intrusion surfaces over and over within the institutional discourse" (Nichols, 1991: 39). Therefore, like many followers of cinema verité, Goette has expressed aversion to the use of voiceover commentary, which she sees as manipulative. Goette also finds it tedious: "And that is the only thing that is really forbidden: to bore the audience" (Freitag, 2008: para. 13).[34] In her view, rarely do documentaries exhibit skilful use of voiceover, an exception being Mikhail Romm's 1965 *Triumph over Violence* (*Obyknovennyy fashizm*); most others use it as a contrived means of communicating what the camera does not (Freitag, 2008: para. 13). Goette finds it unnecessary and redundant simply to depict the life-story of a woman who abandoned her children (para. 13).

Die Kinder sind tot opens to the trial of Daniela Jesse, capturing vividly the voyeurism and media frenzy that so irritated Goette. A hand covers the camera lens, intermittently blocking the viewer's gaze. Both the viewer and the reporters depicted in the film wait anxiously for Daniela Jesse's arrival. Regaining focus, the camera turns on a police officer at the courtroom door. Positioned thus, and in light of his social role, he serves to represent State mediation: in this instance, between the media, the assembled spectators, and the accused; between the public and private spheres. His comportment – by proxy that of the State – is a mixture of boredom and nervous tension.

Finally, the door opens, and defense attorney Kerstin Boltz emerges to the cacophonous clicks and flashes of press cameras. She is followed by Daniela Jesse. Shrouded in a black veil, Daniela takes her place in the courtroom. The shot then freezes, and a violin is heard over the soundtrack playing a single, high-pitched note (Figure 21.3). As the image fades to black, an intertitle appears: "Daniela Jesse

Figure 21.3 Daniela Jesse in the courtroom, in *Die Kinder sind tot* (dir. Aelrun Goette, prod. zero film). Courtesy of zero film.

(23), sentenced to life in prison for the double murder of her children, Kevin (3) and Tobias (2)."[35] While the viewer thus registers the juxtaposition of Daniela's image with that of her captioned sentence, the preceding footage preempts a one-to-one equation of the woman with her crime. Other parties in this case, the technique implies, share in the guilt – on account of their own *inaction*. These include the police, the court, the media, and the inhabitants of Neuberesinchen.

An abrupt cut brings us to the Luckau Prison, in the State of Brandenburg, a year after the trial.[36] Goette is heard quietly asking Daniela, now framed in close-up, a brief series of questions. Her stolid tone indicates a conscious distance from Daniela and recalls the technique of documentarian Elizabeth T. Spira in its "empathic sternness" (Kuchenbuch, 2005: 279).[37] Goette has stressed her concerted effort to remain conscious of, and attempt to free herself from, any prejudices she might bring to her filmic subjects. For her, such prejudices only get in the way of filming (Prickett, 2009: para. 45). Nichols (1991: 195) likens such an effort to maintain objectivity to a "strategic ritual": "Rather than a sign of alienation or an anomic social order per se, objectivity has a functional value for the individual: it helps defend him or her against mistakes and criticism." However, Goette's objectivity was not only intended to protect herself but also the filmic subject Daniela in her prison setting. From the start, Goette spoke openly about her uncertainties with Daniela:

> I always said, "If we make this film, we will make it together. What is *your* reason for making this film?" Because that is what is so difficult in documentary film. It has its own dynamics. You arrive with a camera team, the person being filmed doesn't have

Figure 21.4   Title/sky, in *Die Kinder sind tot* (dir. Aelrun Goette, prod. zero film). Courtesy of zero film.

to go to work; instead, he or she is filmed – those kinds of things. So that person gets a special status. In order to avoid such a "star-status" in the prison framework, I think you always have to create a work situation and say, "OK, this is our work – what are we creating together, what do *you* want?" And that's what I've always done with documentary films. I always establish what my protagonist's main concern is. And then I incorporate it into the film.[38] (Prickett, 2009: para. 46)

Indeed, Daniela responds well to Goette, and Goette credits that to her openness with her subject, who speaks unhindered and seems relaxed, even happy – until Goette asks Daniela if she knows the day's date. Daniela nods trepidatiously, in anticipation of Goette's next question concerning what happened on that same date two years earlier. Daniela replies with pained expression: "I found my children dead."[39]

A second crossfade transfers our gaze to a blue sky onto which the film's title is transposed. From there, the camera pans slowly down to the sign at the tram stop for Neuberesinchen, where Daniela's family still lives. This visual pairing – montage – of the film's title and the station sign establishes an interrelation between Daniela's biography and crime, and the dysfunctional, disenfranchised social network in Neuberesinchen (Figures 21.4 and 21.5). The station sign also connotes a point of entry into this space, as it is followed by a longer, extreme wide-shot of the housing development in Neuberesinchen, which emits the sound of children singing, itself followed by a cut to the exterior of a school. Goette thus uses a series of establishing shots to shift the focus rapidly from Daniela, the "unfit mother," to the environs and conditions in which she lived when she committed

Figure 21.5 "Frankfurt (Oder) – Neuberesinchen," in *Die Kinder sind tot* (dir. Aelrun Goette, prod. zero film). Courtesy of zero film.

her crime. Although the tram stop is new, and the housing development is finally being renovated, both the development and the school date from the 1970s and are in great need of upkeep and repair. That Goette chooses to start her actual investigation of Neuberesinchen in a school is certainly no coincidence: her focus is on the neighborhood's children and their perceptions of the case, which one girl summarizes succinctly:

> Girl: "The mother, she went away, she went to visit a friend, and then she left the children alone. And she put a couple of milk cartons or something like that in the room and the children – they didn't share and when it was all gone, yeah – then they died of thirst."[40]

The girl's hesitation before mentioning the boys' death signifies what the film will reveal: a general hesitation among Daniela's former neighbors to talk openly about what happened.

A syntagm of bracketing shots of the housing development, its grey walls and empty courtyard set against a single violin note, serves as the next transition. While filming this scene, Goette noted in her diary, "the coldness creeps under your jacket here" (quoted in Piepgras, 2005: para. 8).[41] Appropriately, the film's working title was *Über die Abwesenheit von Liebe* (When Love Is Absent): Goette experienced Neuberesinchen as "a very, very cold world in which everyone longed for love but was unable to give it" (quoted in Press Book, 2003: 11).[42] Goette constructs syntagms such as this to underscore the stifling atmosphere and the taciturnity it seemed to produce in neighborhood residents. The ensuing shots further exemplify this technique, as the camera pans across the vacant courtyard of the *Plattenbau* (a typical Eastern German apartment block), then freezes upon reaching a wall. Moving from window to window, the camera fixates on some children looking out of one of them, while the same atonal violin music gradually increases in volume. The scene's final shot is of an open window, through which an arm suddenly reaches forward and pulls it shut. A woman then looks down through it toward the camera and walks out of the frame.

The elements of this syntagm are easily read as metaphorical. The children at the windows may remind the viewer of the entrapped and dehydrated Kevin and Tobias Jesse, who are known to have banged spoons against their window in a desperate attempt to gain their neighbors' attention. The windows – whether open or shut – suggest transparency and the ability to observe the goings-on within the various apartments from the outside. The woman at the window might stand in for the mother, Daniela, who felt compelled to abandon her children, or for the neighbors who closed their windows to block out Kevin and Tobias's quite audible cries. She might also represent one of many Neuberesinchen residents who were so preoccupied with her own problems that everything else seemed extraneous. On this metalevel, the syntagm allegorizes a larger social tendency, often considered redolent of German culture, to turn a blind eye to those in distress, and to believe that such distress has no bearing on one's personal life.[43]

During the scene's final shot, a man explains that Neuberesinchen was once a tree nursery, a true idyll. A cut follows to "Cindy's Beer Pub." In this scene, three things become apparent. First, no one wants to talk about the case. When Goette asks why, a man answers in dialect, "Because that doesn't concern me. I have my thoughts on the matter and – I'll keep them to myself."[44] Second, the majority of men in Neuberesinchen are not interested in founding a family or in proper child-rearing. Goette encountered many men in Neuberesinchen who bragged about the number of children they had conceived, but who maintained no contact with these children (Prickett, 2009: para. 13).[45] As the men in the pub speak, the film cuts to a window as a child presses his face against the glass, trying to observe the men in the bar, perhaps to gain their attention. Here again, the window metaphorizes the neighborhood's tendency toward poor communication, standing as a missed opportunity to communicate (visually), a stubborn desire to communicate (children with adults), a failure to communicate (the men's failure to notice the child), even a refusal to communicate (the neighbors who ignored Kevin and Tobias).

The refusal to communicate is the basis of the third point: the unwillingness and incapacity to communicate on the part of many Neuberesinchen residents (and, allegorically, residents of other Eastern German communities), which is undoubtedly linked to the disintegration of the social mix in such communities following the fall of the Wall. This translates into a general *Wegschauen*, a disinterest in the well-being of one's neighbors and children, or perhaps a fear or resistance to confront it. A man who had long kept silent speaks tersely: "I've got mine and then that's that – everything else is none of my business – that's how it is. That's none of my business. Every man for himself."[46]

The issue of responsibility – individual, collective, State – and of the many parties who turned a blind eye to Daniela and her children, is the interwoven narrative thread comprising *Die Kinder sind tot*'s thematic knot. With each syntagm and ensuing metaphor, the knot tightens. Goette speaks with a social worker who claims to have found evidence of neither abuse nor neglect, nor to have received telephone calls from neighbors. She also talks with neighbors who insist that they had called child services several times, displaying scrapbooks of newspaper clippings from the case in an attempt to prove their concern. Yet it slowly becomes clear that the film's primary thread is the dysfunctional relationship between Daniela and her mother, Rosemarie. A lack of communication, indeed, a refusal to communicate, has long divided mother and daughter – and this ultimately became the immediate cause of Kevin and Tobias Jesse's deaths. "Daniela's motivation to make the film was to figure out what kind of relationship she and her mother have had. A film like this can be helpful in such a process" (Prickett, 2009: para. 47).[47]

By constructing a montage of clips from interviews with Daniela and Rosemarie, Goette establishes a "dialogue" between the two women.[48] Each respectively describes, through an intercutting of interviews with them, the events of June 1999, to the point that their cinematically divided, sometimes conflicting narratives begin to merge. Although Rosemarie had often babysat the two boys, only Daniela's daughter, Katharina, actually was with Rosemarie during those fateful 14 days. Rosemarie claims certainty that the boys were with Daniela, whereas Daniela assumed that, like Katharina, the boys were with Rosemarie. This parallel syntagm, consisting of two interviews taking place at different times, brings to mind not only temporal but also spatial factors at play. Indeed, the events took place in a very limited space: witnesses report having seeing Rosemarie going into the apartment and one has to assume that she had seen the children. Thus in reconciling Daniela's and Rosemarie's conflicting narratives, the montage indicates that Rosemarie contributed to the circumstances which led to the boys' death. For Goette, this was not just another case in a series of cases of maternal filicide:

> That is certainly something really individual. You have to have become quite hardened not to reach a point and say, "I'm going to go there; I'm going to do something." And I can only explain this hardness based upon the personal relationship between these two.[49] (Prickett, 2009: para. 31)

Goette's careful attention to this strained relationship (in terms of the actual events and the filmic narrative) and her editorial strategy (in terms of the filmic montage) illustrates the emotional stand-off between Daniela and Rosemarie. In turn, the montage serves to shift attention away from *Rabenmutter* Daniela, thus lending the ostensible generational conflict, troubled communication, and

Figure 21.6   Daniela Jesse upon her arrival in Luckau prison, in *Die Kinder sind tot* (dir. Aelrun Goette, prod. zero film). Courtesy of zero film.

Wegschauen evident in both this family and their community a generalized, allegorical significance.

The result is the construction of compassion for Daniela in the skilfully composed segment, "'No Mercy': The Public Reaction to the Case."[50] Goette again transports the spectator away from public misconceptions about the case through close attention to its local conditions and effects. The opening alternates between footage of the March 2000 trial and Goette's interview with defense attorney, Kerstin Boltz. Over footage of people, mostly women, practically forcing their way into the courtroom, Boltz explains the case's contemporary popularity: "Women especially followed this trial with great interest."[51] The film qualifies this observation by cutting to unsympathetic reactions from the largely female attendees waiting outside the courtroom before the trial. A final comment in the series is exemplary: "Keine Gnade" ("No mercy").

An abrupt cut follows this comment, taking the viewer away from the courtroom setting to the Luckau Prison. Atonal music, heard earlier in the film, now expresses the desolation and resignation which accompanies Daniela from Neuberesinchen to her prison cell. What follows is perhaps the film's most uncomplicated and yet engaging scene. The viewer watches from outside Daniela's cell as a prison guard closes her cell door, and the scene cuts to the interior of the cell with an extreme close-up of Daniela lasting 22 seconds (Figure 21.6). She is portrayed in silence, staring into space, scratching her chin. Goette (Prickett, 2009: para. 40) explains,

> That is exactly how I experienced Daniela: trapped in herself and trapped by others. No prospects. […] That was an extremely authentic situation.[52]

Reception and broader impact

After *Die Kinder sind tot* was completed, it was rejected by the *Berlinale*: many questioned if it was appropriate to give a public platform to a woman who had killed her children. After the film won the Baden-Württemberg Documentary Film Prize and the *Prix Regards Neufs* at the 2003 *Visions du Réel* in Nyon, however, it received a theatrical release the following March (Körte, 2004: para. 4). The same year, *Die Kinder sind tot* won *Bester Dokumentarfilm* at the 54th German Film Prize Gala, where Fatih Akın's *Gegen die Wand* (*Head-On*, 2004) won the Filmpreis in Gold (Westphal, 2004: 29). Akın later remarked that Goette's film directly influenced his work. When conceiving his contribution, *Der Name Murat Kurnaz* (The Name Murat Kurnaz), to the film project *Germany '09: 13 Short Films about the State of the Nation* (*Deutschland 09: 13 Kurze Filme zur Lage der Nation*, 2009), Akın had been considering making a film about neglected children in Germany – until he saw *Die Kinder sind tot*. "No film can present this issue more accurately or powerfully than this film evinces" (quoted in Press Book, 2009: 6).[53]

Two reviews compare Goette's work to that of Romuald Karmakar, whom scholar Jay McRoy has identified as a director whose work challenges the commercially driven German "Cinema of Consensus" that emerged during the early 1990s. Karmakar's feature about Weimar-period serial murderer Fritz Haarmann (*Der Totmacher* (The Deathmaker, 1995)) evidences "intersections with documentary practices" and advances social critique via Haarmann as an element "'disruptive' to the functioning of a healthy social body" (McRoy, 2007: 93, 97). With regard to their respective works, journalist Martina Knoben writes that Goette and Karmakar "share an almost tender curiosity for encountering people whom others see as monsters" (Knoben, 2004: para. 2).[54] Goette is not only curious about such "monsters," she also strives to shift focus away from their scapegoated images to the social injustices overdetermining their criminal acts.

Nichols (1991: x) has written that "a good documentary stimulates discussion about its subject, not itself." To be sure, *Die Kinder sind tot* has served to enhance public awareness of maternal filicide in Germany, bearing witness to its social enabling conditions and helping deter prevailing social panic over the issue. Goette has remarked that, despite her East German background, she had experienced a largely negative reception in Frankfurt (Oder) during her research and filming. At its 2004 screening in Frankfurt (Oder), however, that mistrust had vanished (Prickett, 2009: para. 37). That the majority of the audience were women reflects the film's social contribution: the film's dissemination of Goette's materialist feminism helped raise the class consciousness of postunification women facing socioeconomic conditions similar to Daniela. One woman is quoted as asking, "Why did everyone look away? I still blame myself." Another admitted that she – along with her neighbors – had actually observed how dirty Daniela's children had become: "We live in a society that does not respect its children. Why would we expect that from a woman in extreme need?" (quoted in Junghänel, 2004: paras 5–6).[55]

One social worker in attendance stressed that neither Daniela's predicament nor the neighbors' disinterest prior to the boys' deaths were problems confined to Eastern Germany, reminding us that the number of filicide cases reported in the East nearly equals the number reported in the West (Junghänel, 2004: para. 5; Piepgras, 2005: para. 14).

A case in the district of Plön in the northwestern State of Schleswig-Holstein underscores this fact: in 2007, a mother had brutally killed her five boys. Following the incident, Goette appeared on Anne Will's political talk show to help elucidate the causes of maternal filicide.[56] The panel members debated the ineffectiveness of Child Services in preventing the boys' deaths. Will asked Goette whether, in the course of her work on *Die Kinder sind tot*, Goette had been able to determine why a mother would neglect or kill her children. Goette blamed a society that turns a blind eye to those in need, responding:

> It was a collective act. It didn't just have to do with the mother but also with a society that looked away. And the answer – or the attempt at an answer – that this film provides is namely that this can only happen when people do not respond collectively.[57] ("Kinder als Opfer," 2007)

Her response exemplifies the tightrope-walk she must perform as a documentary filmmaker in a reunified Germany where a privatizing State is exacerbating economic problems for working women. Clearly Goette's commitment to elucidating Daniela's Jesse story evidences her concomitant commitment to meeting the challenges that drove Daniela to abandon her children to such devastating ends.

Conclusion

In both her documentary and feature films, Aelrun Goette demonstrates the same quality that she seeks in her colleagues: the ability to "endure the balance" between cautious observer and "cannibal." This chapter has discussed Goette's "tightrope walk" as a documentary filmmaker in the context of *Die Kinder sind tot*, a film in which the ambivalence between "good" and "bad," perpetrator and victim, is especially acute. I have suggested that the "German social divide" represents a central concern of Goette's films. Her personal investment in the lives of her subjects – both real and fictional – and her resolve to express their "rage" places much-needed emphasis on the growing German social divide.

The analysis of this film has focused on three aspects of this divide – motherhood, child poverty, and the ghettoization of German cities – and the cinematic strategies and techniques which Goette employs to screen it. The case of Daniela Jesse not only underscores the image of the Eastern German *Rabenmutter* but caused actual outrage within Frankfurt (Oder). For many politicians and journalists, it seemed only natural that a case of maternal filicide would have occurred in Neuberesinchen, the "problem district" of Frankfurt (Oder), on the German–Polish border. Goette's work with Daniela Jesse provides the film's viewer with a unique opportunity to get to know the person behind the perpetrator: her troubled home life, her unfulfilled search for a stable partnership, her remorse and resignation. The viewer in turn comes to realize that, in effect, Daniela was not the only party responsible for her sons' deaths. Thus, the film raises serious questions about the deleterious roles played by Rosemarie Jesse, Child Services, and the neighbors.

As mentioned, one viewer at the local screening of *Die Kinder sind tot* admitted that Kevin and Tobias's dire situation was an open secret. *Die Kinder sind tot* examines the shame and fear, and resulting *Wegschauen*, associated with child poverty and its dangerous – indeed, deadly – consequences. Unemployed and/or underpaid parents find it difficult to provide for their children financially or emotionally. Neglected by family and neighbors, Kevin and Tobias died of dehydration. In Goette's subsequent *Keine Angst* as well, the fictional young teenage friends, Becky and Melanie, represent a class and generation of German girls who have no opportunities for self-development. In both films, disenfranchised women desperately seek a partner who will love and support them. Daniela Jesse and the fictional Becky and Melanie are victims of sexual abuse. Based on these films, it would even seem that stable family relationships within the German working class are simply not possible.

The German class divide translates into a German spatial divide in *Die Kinder sind tot* and *Keine Angst*, where Goette lends much attention to the ghettoization of Eastern German Frankfurt (Oder)-Neuberesinchen and Western German Cologne-Porz. Goette's cinematic focus on working-class apartment blocks transforms these buildings into sociospatial signifiers of entrapment and neglect. In *Die Kinder sind tot*, Goette's extreme long-shots of the buildings express the residents' overwhelmed sensibilities; her shots of graffiti-filled stairwells portray the residents' isolation. Although no one is present in such shots, loud children and adults arguing can be heard offscreen.

When considering Goette's work, the viewer appreciates Goette's efforts to allow her subjects to tell their stories, regardless of whether these have been documented or fictionalized. Goette has made a name for herself with these uncompromising portrayals of individuals that German society has apparently written off. By positioning their stories along the German social divide, she does a great service not only to German cinema but also to the human struggle she has enabled it to strengthen.

I would like to thank Aelrun Goette, the Deutsche Kinemathek–Berlin, Monika Moyrer, Nike Sommerwerk, TAG/TRAUM, zero film, and the editors of this volume for their valuable assistance and feedback.

Notes

1 "Ich habe angefangen, dokumentarisch zu arbeiten, weil ich Themen finden wollte, die – wie soll ich sagen – beunruhigen. Und interessanterweise ist es mir nie schwer gefallen, diese zu finden" (all English translations in this chapter are mine).

2 "Zorn ist ein Merkmal ihrer Filme."

3 "Die Menschen, denen ich begegne und über die ich Filme mache, egal ob fiktional oder dokumentarisch, sind alles starke Persönlichkeiten, keine reinen Opfer, und das ist vielleicht, was sich mit mir deckt."

4 "Sie sei damals eine tickende Zeitbombe gewesen. Sie hatte Gewalt als das einzige Mittel erfahren, Konflikte zu bewältigen – und nun schlug sie zurück."

5 "Ich hatte schon damals versucht, die Ambivalenz von 'Gut' und 'Böse' deutlich zu machen und auch das Opfer hinter der Täterin zu zeigen."

6 The controversial use of the term *neue Unterschicht* ("new lower class") reflects a fear of the social class divide that has been deepening since the introduction of *Hartz IV* (the fourth phase of the Hartz welfare reforms) in January 2005. In 2004, professor and cultural historian Paul Nolte sparked a debate with his *Generation Reform: Jenseits der blockierten Republik* (*Generation Reform: Beyond the Blocked Republic*), in which he refers to the idea of a *neu-alte Klassengesellschaft* ("new-old class society"). Nolte claims that, while wealth and education still divide German society along class lines, the "new lower class" has refused to adjust their "uncivilized" way of life to the bourgeois norms of the social majority, and that this presents the greatest threat to social order in the Federal Republic (quoted in Kessl, 2005: 2–3). Thus, the term expresses a value judgment about a person's (un)willingness to work and even carries racist undertones, as evidenced by former German Federal Bank Executive Board Member Thilo Sarrazin's *Deutschland schafft sich ab: Wie Wir unser Land aufs Spiel setzen* (*Germany Does Away with Itself: How We Are Gambling Away our Country*, 2010).

7 "[M]an [hatte] mir ziemlich deutlich zu verstehen gegeben, dass ich keine reife sozial-istische Persönlichkeit bin."

8 The Freie Deutsche Jugend was the only state-sponsored and recognized youth organ-ization in the GDR. Officially, membership (starting at age 14) was voluntary, but nonmembers faced hurdles in education and employment.

9 For example, "Aelrun Goette is a tall, attractive woman" ("Aelrun Goette ist eine grosse, attraktive Frau") (Richter 2005: para. 1); "Sie ist 1,80 Meter gross, blond, schlank" ("She is 1.8 meters tall, blond, slender") (Junghänel, 2004: para. 13).

10 "Eine gute Figur – vor und hinter der Kamera": "Nach dieser Frau dreht man sich um. Grossgewachsen, blond, ein ebenmäßiges Gesicht."

11 Goette sees her former modeling career as a burden: " 'Wenn ich fotografiert werde, lege ich immer dieses gestellte Gesicht auf,' sagt sie spöttisch" (" 'Whenever someone takes my picture, I make a staged expression,' she says sneeringly") (Lukaschewitsch, 1997: para. 2)

12 "Elias Cannettis 'Masse und Macht' fällt ihr ein. Sie spricht gerne über Verantwortung und Privilegien, will beides nutzen, um 'aufklärerisch zu arbeiten.' "

13 "Also, ich kann nur von mir ausgehen – ich bin mit einer berufstätigen Mutter gross geworden. […] Das ist so ein Bild, was für mich auch ein ganz entscheidender Punkt ist: Finanziell auch eine gewisse Unabhängigkeit zu haben und mitbestimmen zu dürfen."

14 "Es gibt natürlich in meinem Beruf – wie in vielen anderen auch – viele Frauen, die Kinder bekommen und aufhören, Regie zu führen. Irgendwann ist man an dieser Stelle relativ allein."

15 "Ich hatte mich nie so wirklich unter dem Mantel des Feminismus finden können" ("I was never able to find a place for myself under the mantle of feminism").

16 "Ich merke, dass auch bei Studentinnen, dass da neben dem, was ich so inhaltlich im Filmischen vermittle, ist, dass ich ganz stark als Modell fungiere. [...] Was ist eigentlich das Bild, der ostdeutschen Frau aber auch der jungen deutschen Frau, und wie kann man den Frauen heute Identifikationsmöglichkeiten anbieten, in denen es ihnen Spass macht, Kinder zu haben und zu arbeiten?"

17 In 2010, Troller was one of the first German directors to receive a star on the Boulevard der Stars at the Potsdamer Platz in Berlin. Others honored there include Vicco von Bülow, Doris Dörrie, Rainer Werner Fassbinder, Dominik Graf, Werner Herzog, Alexander Kluge, Fritz Lang, Max Ophüls, Wolfgang Petersen, Edgar Reitz, Margarethe von Trotta, Wim Wenders, Billy Wilder, and Konrad Wolf.

18 "Ich habe mal mit Menschenfressern auf den Neuen Hebriden gedreht. Sie verspeisen ihre Feinde, um sich ihre Stärke anzueignen. Der Fernseh-, Portraitfilmer verspeist die Leute, mit denen er dreht, um sich ihre Lösungen den Lebensproblemen gegenüber einzuverleiben. Er lernt wie man mit Trauer und Frust und so weiter fertig werden kann, was man damit anfangen kann, um sich wieder menschlich zu machen oder auch um Erfolg zu haben. Das lernst du von den anderen."

19 I would like to thank the Editors for this observation.

20 "Ich wollte den monströsen Geschehen ein menschliches Gesicht geben." Goette also cites Troller in her interview with Peter Körte: "We are all cannibals – even we documentary filmmakers" ("Wir sind alle Menschenfresser. Auch wir Dokumentarfilmer") (Körte, 2004: para. 3).

21 "Eine ganz schwierige Frage, weil man natürlich stärker als bei einem Spielfilm Herr und Meister des Materials ist."

22 "Und man muss Grenzen überschreiten, um etwas zu begreifen, glaube ich. Denn im geschützten Raum hat man keine Erkenntnisse. Und diese Balance immer auszuhalten, das ist das, wonach ich dann bei Kollegen immer gesucht habe. Und Troller ist jemand, den ich gefunden habe, der das auch thematisiert hat. Dass es genau darum geht."

23 "Ein Film wie *Keine Angst* berührt nicht. Er haut seine Zuschauer um."

24 "Ich habe uns in der Pflicht gesehen zu beweisen, dass wir keinen schmutzigen Film über eine schmutzige Welt drehen wollen."

25 "Dieses Thema 'Mutter, die ihre Kinder töten' [ist] ein ganz klassisches Thema [...]. Nicht erst seit Medea – es ist ein tiefstbeängstigendes aber damit natürlich auch faszinierendes Thema."

26 Author and journalist Gabriele Tergit found *M* tasteless and opportunistic, as the film premiered soon after Kürten's trial. However, she was equally shocked by the audience, who applauded when Beckert was apprehended by thugs: "Humans are thus constituted that they rush and want to find a victim quickly. If you scratch a bit, a Tartar will appear everywhere. There were many Tartars at the premiere in the Ufa-Theater at [Berlin]-'Zoo'" ("Der Mensch ist so beschaffen, dass er schnell rast und schnell ein Opfer will. Kratzt ein bisschen, und es kommt überall ein Tartar zum

Vorschein. Es waren viele Tartaren im Ufa-Theater am Zoo bei der Premiere") (Tergit, 1931: 845).

27 "[Schönbohm] meint, sie sei begründet in dem DDR-Regime, der Erziehung im ost-deutschen Staat, in dem den Bürgern keine Werte vermittelt wurden und sie verwah-rlosten."

28 "[E]r sei über Schönbohms Aussage fast so erschüttert wie über den Vorfall selbst. Er stellt also die Aussage eines Politikers auf eine Ebene mit dem Tod von neun Kindern. Das ist obszön. Offenbar sind wir alle derzeit gegen humane Werte resistent."

29 "Es kommt mir so vor, als ob Kindstötungen – die es allerdings immer schon gab – ein Mittel der Familienplanung seien."

30 Goette explains that since 1989–1990, the social structure in Neuberesinchen has radi-cally changed: "[T]here was a strong social mix: the doctor lived next to the refuse collection worker and next to the nurse. In this way, a completely different social fab-ric had emerged. This collapsed after the fall of the Wall" ("Die Menschen mischten sich untereinander. Also der Arzt hat neben dem Müllarbeiter, neben der Krankenschwester gewohnt, und dadurch war ein ganz anderes soziales Gefüge entstanden. Das ist nach dem Fall der Mauer weggebrochen") (quoted in Prickett, 2009: para. 7). For photos of Neuberesinchen taken in 1988–1989, see Bilder, 1988–1989; note the focus on happy children at play.

31 "Der stellt die Frage, wie kann so etwas sein, heute in Deutschland. Gleichzeitig bleibt der Film auch ganz konkret an diesem Fall und versucht, diese Familientragödie durchzuleuchten. Und nicht zu werten. Das muss der Zuschauer für sich selbst entsc-heiden, wie es dazu gekommen ist. Das war ja mein Ziel."

32 "Denn Film ist Gefühl. Immer. Nicht Verstand. Die Diskussionen kommen dann von ganz allein."

33 Compare to Hirokazu Kore-eda's *Nobody Knows* (*Dare mo shiranai*, 2004), "inspired by a real event known in Japan as 'the affair of the four abandoned children of Nishi-Sugamo'" (Scott, 2005: para. 1). Critic A.O. Scott (2005: para. 3) writes, "In observing the helplessness of the four children, you become acutely aware of your own inability to do anything for them. Mr Kore-eda's camera is so close to them – navigating the narrow, cramped spaces of their home, zooming in on their faces, hands and feet – that the sense of their aloneness becomes overwhelming. You are in on the secret of their existence and prevented from communicating it." I would like to thank Andrea Mensch for drawing my attention to this film.

34 "Und das ist das einzige, was wirklich verboten ist: Langweilen."

35 "Daniela Jesse (23), verurteilt zu einer lebenslangen Haftstrafe, wegen zweifachen Mordes an ihren Kindern Kevin (3) und Tobias (2)."

36 In 2006, the prison served as the setting for Chris Kraus's *Four Minutes* (*Vier Minuten*), which won several awards, including the Deutscher Filmpreis Bester Spielfilm in Gold (Press Book, 2006: 3, 10).

37 Filmmaker and theoretician Thomas Kuchenbuch describes Spira's method as being "not at all in the stance of a Samaritan; much rather with an empathetic sternness. Without any false empathy, she leaves the damaged soul its dignity" ("keineswegs in Samariterhaltung, sondern eher in der Haltung einer mitfühlenden Strenge. Sie lässt, ohne falsches Mitleid, dem beschädigten Leben seine Würde [...]")" (Kuchenbuch, 2005: 279). Spira is best known for her documentary series *Alltagsgeschichte* (Stories

of Everyday Life) on ORF (Austrian Broadcasting Corporation) and says of her interviewing technique: "For the most part, it is instinct. And you have to take your time. You can't simply approach someone and say, this is what I want, because you often get something quite different. I have a good sense for finding people who have an 'edge.' I see a face and say, I don't know what, but there's certainly something there. And I bore deeper if I encounter resistance or if the person works him- or herself into a rage" ("Zum Großteil aber ist das Instinkt. Und man muß sich Zeit lassen. Man darf nicht hingehen und sagen, das will ich von dem, denn dabei kommt oft was ganz anderes heraus. Ich bin sehr treffsicher beim Finden von Menschen, die etwas 'Eckiges' haben. Ich sehe ein Gesicht und sage, ich weiß nicht was, aber irgendwas kommt da heraus. Und ich stecke zu, wenn ich merke, ich stoße auf Widerstand, oder der Mensch redet sich in einen Wirbel" (quoted in Tscherkassy, 1993: 20)).

38 "Ich habe immer gesagt, 'wenn wir den Film machen, machen wir den gemeinsam – was ist dein Grund, diesen Film zu machen?' Weil das ist ja auch immer das Schwierige im dokumentarischen Arbeiten. Das hat ja eine Eigendynamik. Man kommt mit einem Kamerateam an, derjenige muss nicht zur Arbeit, sondern es wird gedreht und solche Sachen. Also er kriegt einen besonderen Status. Und um zu vermeiden, dass daraus ein 'Star'-Status innerhalb des Gefüges im Gefängnis wird, muss man meiner Ansicht nach eine Arbeitssituation herstellen und sagen, 'OK, das ist unsere Arbeit, was machen wir hier gemeinsam, was ist *dein* Anliegen?' Und das habe ich im Dokumentarfilm eigentlich immer gemacht, dass ich das Anliegen meines Gegenübers – danach gesucht habe. Und das dann auch mit in den Film hineinbringen."

39 "Da habe ich meine Kinder tot aufgefunden."

40 "Die Mutter, die ist weggegangen, die ist zu einer Freundin gegangen, und dann hat sie die Kinder alleine gelassen – und die hat ein paar Milchbeutel oder so was ins Zimmer gestellt und die Kinder – die haben das nicht geteilt und als nichts mehr da war, ja – dann sind sie verdurstet."

41 "Hier kriecht einem die Kälte unter die Jacke."

42 "Eine sehr, sehr kalte Welt, in der zwar alle eine grosse Sehnsucht nach Liebe haben, in der aber keiner in der Lage ist, Liebe zu geben."

43 Consider Siegfried Kracauer's (1998: 91) critique of the *Angestelltenkultur* ("salaried workers' culture") in Weimar Berlin: "'out of the business of work into the business of entertainment' is their unspoken motto."

44 "Weil das für mich kein Thema ist. Ich hab' meine Gedanken und – die behalte ich für mich."

45 "Die Männer, die ich dann getroffen habe, haben abends beim Stammtisch geprotzt, dass sie überall Kinder gezeugt hatten, und dabei kaum daran dachten, eine Familie zu gründen."

46 "Ich hab meins und dann ist gut – das andere geht mich nicht an – na so ist es. Mich geht das nicht an. Jeder ist sich selbst der Nächste."

47 "Und Danielas Anliegen war, sich darüber klar zu werden, was für eine Beziehung sie zu ihrer Mutter hat. Und dabei kann ein solcher Film hilfreich sein."

48 Ralf Schenk also refers to this montage as a "dialogue" in his critique of the film (2004: 21).

49 "Das ist natürlich dann was ganz Individuelles, weil man dazu ja eine ziemliche Härte entwickeln muss, dann irgendwann nicht zu sagen, 'ich gehe dahin und mache etwas.'

Und das kann ich nur mit dieser persönlichen Beziehung zwischen diesen beiden erklären."

50   " 'Keine Gnade': Der Fall in der Öffentlichkeit."

51   "Insbesondere Frauen haben dieses Verfahren sehr interessiert verfolgt."

52   "Das ist das, so wie ich eben Daniela erlebt habe [...] – wie sie in sich gefangen ist und dieses gefangen sein von außen – keinen Ausblick haben. [...] Das war eine ganz authentische Situation."

53   "Ich hatte noch ein anderes Projekt, da ging es um verwahrloste Kinder, aber während meiner Recherche habe ich diesen überwältigenden Dokumentarfilm *Die Kinder sind tot* gesehen – und richtiger oder eindringlicher, als dieser Film beweist, kann man das nicht verfilmen."

54   "Gemeinsam ist den beiden Filmemachern auch die fast zärtliche Neugier, mit der sie Menschen begegnen, die andere für Monster halten." Körte (2004: para. 11) makes the same comparison in his review.

55   "Warum haben alle weggesehen? [...] Ich mach mir heute noch Vorwürfe." "Wir leben in einer Gesellschaft, die an keiner Stelle Rücksicht auf Kinder nimmt. Wieso erwarten wir das von einer Frau, die so arg in Nöten ist?"

56   Anne Will's guests also included then: Federal Minister of Family Affairs, Senior Citizens, Women, and Youth, Dr Ursula von der Leyen (Christian Democrat); Ralf Stegner, Minister of the Interior of Schleswig-Holstein (Social Democrat); Gina Graichen, head of the special commission for *Delikte an Schutzbefohlenen* ("Crimes against State Wards") of the Berlin Office of Criminal Investigation; Georg Ehrmann, executive chairman of *Kinderhilfe Direkt e. V.*; Petra Ochel, head of Socio-Psychological Services of the Plön District; Anselm Brößkamp, head of Social Services of the Plön District; and Dr Ralf Kownatzki, pediatrician.

57   "Es war eine Kollektivtat. Es ging nicht nur um die Mutter, sondern auch um eine Gesellschaft, die weggeschaut hat. Und die Antwort – oder der Versuch einer Antwort, den dieser Film leistet, ist eben die, dass das nur geschehen kann, wenn kollektiv Leute nicht reagieren."

References

Bilder des Fotografen Herrn Thomas Klaber (1988–1989). *Chronik 1977/2007: 30 Jahre Neuberesinchen*, http://www.frankfurt-oder.org/pdf/buri/klaeber.pdf (accessed December 6, 2010).

Freitag, J. (2008) "Tatort"-Regisseurin Aelrun Goette: Mich fesselt vor allem das Abgründige. *Frankfurter Allgemeine Zeitung*, October 5, http://www.faz.net/-00mz7d (accessed September 7, 2010).

Gallmeyer, K. and Schwarz, F. (2006) "Ein Menschenfresser" in Paris: Georg Stefan Troller im Interview," *recontres.de: Das deutsch-französische Magzin/La revue franco-allemande*, September 1, http://www.rencontres.de/Film.80.0.html#6644 (accessed December 6, 2010).

Gärtner, B. (2010) Ein-Euro-Kinder. Deutsche Armut, fremde Welt: Ein Film von Aelrun Goette. *Süddeutsche Zeitung*, March 10, 15.

Hein, C. (2005) Vom unglücklichen Bewusstsein: Signifikant für unsere Gesellschaft ist nicht der mehrfache Kindermord in Brandenburg, sondern eher die Reaktion auf dieses entsetzliche Verbrechen. *der Freitag*, August 19, http://www.freitag. de/2005/33/05330301.php (accessed September 25, 2009).

Junghänel, F. (2004) Menschliches Versagen: Aelrun Goette stellte ihren Film "Die Kinder sind tot" in Frankfurt (Oder) zur Diskussion. *Berliner Zeitung*, March 13, http://www. berlinonline.de/berliner-zeitung/archiv/.bin/dump.fcgi/2004/0313/feuilleton/0024/ index.html (accessed April 29, 2009).

Kessl, F. (2005) Das wahre Elend? Zur Rede von der "neuen Unterschicht." *Widersprüche*, 25 (98), http://www.uni-bielefeld.de/paedagogik/agn/ag8/das_wahre_ elend.pdf (accessed February 4, 2011).

Kinder als Opfer: Wenn Eltern überfordert sind (2007). *Anne Will*. Will Media, ARD, Berlin, December 9.

Knoben, M. (2004) Mutter, Monster. Eine Frauensache: Aelrun Goettes Film "Die Kinder sind tot." *Süddeutsche Zeitung*, March 13, 14.

Körte, P. (2004) Der schmale Grat: Ein Mordfall, ein Roman und jetzt ein Film; Aelrun Goettes Dokumentation "Die Kinder sind tot." *Frankfurter Allgemeine Sonntagszeitung*, March 7, 34.

Kracauer, S. (1998) *The Salaried Masses: Duty and Distraction in Weimar Germany*, 1930 (trans. Q. Hoare), Verso, London and New York.

Kuchenbuch, T. (2005) *Filmanalyse: Theorien. Modelle. Kritik*, UTB Böhlau, Vienna, Cologne, Weimar.

Kuhn, A. (1994) *Women's Pictures: Feminism and Cinema*, 2nd edn, Verso, London and New York.

Lukaschewitsch, M. (1997) Eine gute Figur – vor und hinter der Kamera. Multitalent Aelrun Goette: Filmemacherin, Schauspielerin, Model und Moderatorin. *Berliner Morgenpost*, November 25, n.p.

McRoy, J. (2007) Joy-boys and docile bodies, in *Caligari's Heirs: The German Cinema of Fear after 1945* (ed. S. Hantke), Scarecrow, Lanham, MD, Toronto, Plymouth, UK, pp. 93–105.

Nichols, B. (1991) *Representing Reality: Issues and Concepts in Documentary*, Indiana University Press, Bloomington.

Nolte, P. (2004) *Generation Reform: Jenseits der blockierten Republik*, Beck, Munich.

Piepgras, I. (2005) "Hier kriecht einem die Kälte unter die Jacke": Gespräch mit Aelrun Goette, die einen Dokumentarfilm über einen Kindermord in Frankfurt/Oder gedreht hat. *Die Zeit*, August 11, 54.

Plewnia, U. (2008) Wolfgang Böhmer: "Ein Mittel der Familienplanung." *FOCUS Online*, February 24, http://www.focus.de/politik/deutschland/wolfgang-boehmer_ aid_262743.html (accessed October 20, 2009).

Press Book for *Deutschland 09: 13 Kurze Filme zur Lage der Nation* (2009). Piffl Medien, http:// deutschland09-der-film.de/files/D09_Pressemappe.pdf (accessed December 6, 2010).

Press Book for *Die Kinder sind tot* (2003) Ventura Film, http://www.hoehnepresse-media. de/kindertot/pdf/PH_DieKindersindtot.pdf (accessed October 24, 2008).

Press Book for *Vier Minuten* (2006) Piffl Medien, http://www.vierminuten.de/static/pdf/ vierminuten_presseheft.pdf (accessed December 6, 2010).

Prickett, D.J. (2009) Unpublished interview with Aelrun Goette, May 11, Berlin.

Richter, D. (2005) Aus der Ecke des Zimmers. Psychogramme: Die Berliner Regisseurin Aelrun Goette und ihre bemerkenswerte Dokumentation *"Die Kinder sind tot"* über eine

Mutter, die ihre Söhne verdursten ließ. *der Freitag*, April 1, http://www.freitag.de/datenbank/freitag/2005/13/psychogramme/ (accessed April 29, 2009).

Sarrazin, T. (2010) *Deutschland schafft sich ab: Wie Wir unser Land aufs Spiel setzen*, Deutsche Verlags-Anstalt, Munich.

Schenk, R. (2004) Rev. of *Die Kinder sind tot*, dir. Aelrun Goette. *film-dienst*, 57 (5), 21.

Scott, A.O. (2005) Abandoned children stow away at home. Rev. of *Nobody Knows* (*Dare mo shiranai*, 2004), dir. Hirokazu Kore-eda. *New York Times*, February 4, http://www.nytimes.com/2005/02/04/movies/04nobo.html (accessed December 8, 2010).

Stam, R. (1989) *Subversive Pleasures: Bakhtin, Cultural Criticism, and Film*, Johns Hopkins University Press, Baltimore, London.

Tatar, M. (1995) *Lustmord: Sexual Murder in Weimar Germany*, Princeton University Press, Princeton, NJ.

Tergit, G. (1931) Der Fritz Lang-Film: Der Film des Sadismus. *Die Weltbühne*, 27 (23), 844–845.

Tscherkassy, P. (1993) Das Angenehme ist, daß mir 99% der Österreicher sehr fremd sind: Ein Interview mit Elizabeth T. Spira. *Blimp: Film Magazine*, 26, 18–23.

Wendt, H-U. (1997) "Ich bereue, aber ich kann die Tat nicht rückgängig machen": Film über ein Mädchen, das mit 15 Jahren zur Mörderin wurde – Wie sieht die junge Frau sechs Jahre später ihre Tat und ihre Zukunft? – Die "Ambivalenz zwischen Gut und Böse." *Die Welt*, December 2, n.p.

Wenn Frauen bezahlen und Männer einkaufen gehen …: Wie verändern sich unsere Rollenbilder? (2007). *Im Palais*, rbb, rbb, October 11, Berlin.

Westphal, A. (2004) Lolas Grosskampfabend: Zur Vergabe des 54. Deutschen Filmpreises im Berliner Tempodrom. *Berliner Zeitung*, Feuilleton, June 19–20, 29.

Wick, K. (2010) Das Leben ist keine Insel: Herausragend: Alerun Goette und ihr sozialkritischer Milieufilm "Keine Angst." *Berliner Zeitung; Frankfurter Rundschau*, March 10, http://www.berlinonline.de/berliner-zeitung/archiv/.bin/dump.fcgi/2010/0310/medien/0006/index.html (accessed August 11, 2010).

Filmography

Deathmaker, The [*Der Totmacher*] (Romuald Karmakar, Germany, 1995).

Germany '09: 13 Short Films about the State of the Nation [*Deutschland 09: 13 Kurze Filme zur Lage der Nation*] (Fatih Akın et al., Germany, 2009).

Die Kinder sind tot [The Children Are Dead] (Aelrun Goette, Germany, 2002–2003).

Eine [One] (Aelrun Goette, Germany, 1994).

Feldtagebuch – Allein unter Männern [Field Diary – Alone among Men] (Aelrun Goette, Germany, 2001–2002).

Four Minutes [*Vier Minuten*] (Chris Kraus, Germany, 2006).

Head-On [*Gegen die Wand*] (Fatih Akın, Germany/Turkey, 2004).

Keine Angst [Don't Be Afraid] (Aelrun Goette, Germany, 2009).

Macunaíma (Joaquim Pedro de Andrade, Brazil, 1969).

M [*M: Eine Stadt sucht einen Mörder*] (Fritz Lang, Germany, 1931).

Nobody Knows [*Dare mo shiranai*] (Hirokazu Kore-eda, Japan, 2004).

Ohne Bewährung – Psychogramm einer Mörderin [Without Probation – A Psychological Profile of a Murderess] (Aelrun Goette, Germany, 1997–1998).

Triumph over Violence [*Obyknovennyy fashizm*] (Mikhail Romm, USSR, 1965).

22

A Negative Utopia
Michael Haneke's Fragmentary Cinema

Tara Forrest

The history of film contains a utopian strain – which is what accounts for the attraction of the cinema – but it is a utopia which, contrary to the Greek meaning of ou topos *=no place, is in existence everywhere and especially in the unsophisticated imagination. This unsophisticated imagination, however, is buried under a thick layer of cultural garbage. It has to be dug out. This project of excavation, not at all a utopian notion, can be realized only through our work.* (Kluge, 1981–1982: 210)[1]

In film reviews, Michael Haneke is often described as a pessimistic director whose work presents us with a bleak, dystopian outlook on the possibilities of the world in which we live.[2] In interviews, however, Haneke reacts vehemently to such claims, stating that his films are in fact utopian, albeit in a negative sense, because the grim scenarios they represent challenge the audience to conceive of the degree to which things could, in fact, be very different. "If," Haneke states, "there is a Utopia for me, that is worthy of its name, it can only be a negative one – a utopia that mobilises powers of resistance" (Assheur and Haneke, 2008: 133).[3]

Although this concept of negative utopianism could be productively explored in relation to Haneke's oeuvre more generally,[4] focusing on his 1994 film *71 Fragments of a Chronology of Chance*, the specific aim of this chapter is to examine how – and with what effects – its experimental form could be seen to "mobilise [… the audience's] powers of resistance" against the bleak image of society presented on screen. Drawing on the ideas of Alexander Kluge, Theodor Adorno, and Walter Benjamin, this chapter will argue that – far from being dystopian – *71 Fragments* encourages the audience to think critically and imaginatively about the degree to which the alienated image of life depicted on screen could, in reality, be transformed.

A Companion to German Cinema, First Edition. Edited by Terri Ginsberg and Andrea Mensch.
© 2012 Blackwell Publishing Ltd. Published 2012 by Blackwell Publishing Ltd.

Negative Utopianism

In an interview with Thomas Assheuer that took place in 2007, Haneke's interest in the productive effects of negative utopianism are revealed in a discussion about his early work in the theater. Reflecting on a production of Friedrich Hebbel's *Maria Magdalena* that he directed in Germany some thirty years ago, Haneke recalls a heated, postpremiere discussion that he had with a senior dramaturge, who was also a student of Adorno. As Haneke makes clear, what troubled the dramaturge about the production (which, for Haneke, was a great success) was the sense of "hopelessness" and "complete lack of utopia" characteristic of his staging of the play. *"What,"* Assheuer asks Haneke,

> *did you say in response to him?*
> That one has to fight against the production and the play and that Adorno himself surely would have understood that.
>
> *On account of the compelling aesthetic form?*
> On account of the form. What would the alternative be? Should art convey utopia, a message directly? Who is supposed to take that seriously? Only through the negation of utopia does the recipient have the opportunity to say no and to fight against it. (Assheuer and Haneke, 2008: 100)

As Haneke's comments both here – and elsewhere – suggest, this negative conception of utopia is, in part, indebted to Adorno's analysis of the role that art can play in challenging the limited, affirmative image of reality propagated by the culture industry. Utopia, Adorno states, can only be found "in the determined negation of that which merely is, and by concretizing itself as something false, it always points at the same time to what should be" (Bloch and Adorno, 1988: 12). In other words: utopia, in this sense, is manifested in the "determined negation" of that which is wrong, that which is morally reprehensible, and that which is rendered false because it threatens the potential for a world free from suffering and domination. According to Adorno, "determined negation" thus becomes the praxis through which the possibility of a different reality may be actualized.

Within this schema, it is therefore neither the role of the artist nor the filmmaker to represent "what should be" in a concrete way. While "there is," Adorno states, "nothing like a single, fixable utopian content" (Bloch and Adorno, 1998: 7), the role of the artist/filmmaker is to rejuvenate the viewer's capacity for imagination and to encourage him/her to reflect on the degree to which the world could be transformed into something very different. While the contours of this world are not, according to Adorno, something that can be predrawn,[5] it is clear that the utopia he invokes is both free from domination and organized, in part, around the minimization of suffering and the maximization of happiness, freedom and human potential.[6] However, as both Adorno and Haneke make clear, instead of presenting the viewer with a "message," or with a utopian image of the world as an ideal place, the primary aim of negative utopianism is to facilitate a desire for change. The "true thing," Adorno states,

> determines itself via the false thing, or via that which makes itself falsely known. And insofar as we are not allowed to cast the picture of utopia, insofar as we do not know what the correct thing would be, we know exactly, to be sure, what the false thing is. That is actually the only form in which utopia is given to us at all. (Bloch and Adorno, 1988: 12)

For Alexander Kluge (who was a close friend and associate of Adorno), film's ability to bring about change is intimately bound with its capacity to stimulate the imagination of the audience. What troubles Kluge about the mass media (he cites conventional narrative films and television news programs as examples) is the degree to which the image of reality they represent actively shapes our understanding of what is and isn't possible and impacts negatively on our capacity to conceive of the degree to which things could, in fact, be very different. As Kluge makes clear: The so-called "real" state of affairs "is not necessarily or certainly real." Alternative possibilities and the roads not taken "also belong to reality. The realistic result, the actual result, is only an abstraction that has murdered all other possibilities for the moment" (Dawson, 1977: 34). For Adorno, too, it is the standardized products of the culture industry (in the form of films, television programs, and popular music) that are "infecting everything with sameness" (Horkheimer and Adorno, 2002: 94). "The procedure," he writes, "follows the basic culture-industrial principle: affirmation of life as it is" (Adorno, 1989: 37).

If Haneke, too, is troubled by the standardized, affirmative character of the mainstream media, it is because of the negative impact it has on the audience's capacity to think critically and imaginatively about the ideas, values, and prejudices that actively shape the world in which we live. "People," Haneke states,

> can no longer bear ambivalences. Why? Because they have become so used to it from television and mainstream dramaturgy. They only know narrative forms that answer all their questions so that they are able to go home feeling pacified. That is what they pay for. [...] That is a type of commercialization of our understanding of reality that I don't want to accept. (Assheuer and Haneke, 2008: 130)

This reference to the mainstream media's "commercialization of our understanding of reality" can be read on at least two different – albeit interrelated – levels. In a very general sense, it refers to the role that the mass media (in the form of advertising, film, and television) play in the representation and idealization of a particular image of "reality" according to which the value and success of one's life are determined by one's capacity to purchase certain products. As Adorno outlines in his "Prologue to Television," by equating a happy, fulfilled life with the "fortunes of the department store," the commercially driven "utopia" presented by the mainstream media functions to "extirpate the idea of utopia from human beings altogether and to make them swear their allegiance all the more deeply to the established order" (Adorno, 1998: 57).

In relation to the specific concerns of this chapter, this commercialization process is also manifested in the passive, nonparticipatory mode of engagement fostered by the mainstream media and the "products" it produces. As Adorno writes in "The Schema of Mass Culture," it is "the pre-digested quality of the product [that] prevails" (Adorno, 2001: 67). By generating images, narratives, and ideas that reinforce audience expectations (expectations that have, in large part, been shaped by the culture industry itself), Adorno argues that mainstream media products cultivate a mode of engagement that does not require any effort on behalf of the spectator because "the message is invariably that of identification with the status quo" (Adorno, 2001a: 164). Put simply, the viewer becomes a consumer, in this context, because he/she is able to swallow the "premasticated" products whole (Adorno, 1989: 30).

Within this schema, Haneke's outline for an alternative filmmaking practice is driven by a desire to shake up the limited, commercial image of reality generated by the mainstream media and, in doing so, to undermine the passive, consumer-oriented mode of engagement that he associates with both mainstream television programs and Hollywood cinema. "My films," he states,

> should provide a countermodel to the typically American style of total production to be found in contemporary popular cinema, which, in its hermetically sealed illusion of an ultimately intact reality, deprives the spectator of any possibility of critical participation and condemns him from the outset to the role of a simple consumer. (Vogel, 1996: 75)

It is this emphasis on generating an active, participatory mode of engagement that is the driving force behind the production of *71 Fragments* and that aligns Haneke's delineation of the possibilities of the medium with Kluge's analysis of the "utopian strain" of cinema. As his comments in the epigraph make clear, for Kluge the utopian promise of film lies not in its capacity to present us with an ideal image of an alternate reality, but in its ability to disinter the spectator's capacity for imagination from the "thick layer of cultural garbage" under which it is buried. The audience, in this context, is thus not invited to passively immerse themselves in another world, but to reflect on the shortcomings of the reality on screen and, in the process, imagine how life could be transformed. Haneke describes this mode of engagement as a form of "resistance" because instead of consuming the film "whole," the audience is prompted by the experimental form of *71 Fragments* to reflect critically on the society in which the characters live – a society that is permeated by so much suffering, alienation, and despair. As Adriana S. Benzaquén has stated in her analysis of Adorno's work, it is "the reality of suffering [in this case, depicted on screen, that] testifies to the possibility *and* necessity of change" (Benzaquén, 1998: 152).

For both Haneke and Kluge, it is only by fragmenting the film's narrative and, in the process, undermining the passive mode of engagement that they associate with the "intact reality" generated by conventional narrative cinema that the audience is "jolt[ed] ... out of their attitude of consumerism" (Haneke, 2000: 174) and encouraged to actively participate in the meaning-making process. In a similar vein to Bertolt Brecht's analysis of the active, critical mode of engagement cultivated by the "radical *separation of the elements*" characteristic of Epic Theater (Brecht, 1998: 37), Kluge argues that film "is not produced by *auteurs* alone, but by the dialogue between spectators and authors" (Dawson, 1977: 37): a dialogue that is not manifested in the film itself, but in the thoughts and connections cultivated in "the spectator's head" by "the gaps [...] between the disparate elements of filmic expression" (Reitz, Kluge, and Reinke, 1988: 87).

As will be discussed in more detail in the following sections, it is the open, experimental form of *71 Fragments* – combined with Haneke's extensive use of long-shots and his predilection for truncating action and dialogue – that facilitates a genuinely cooperative, communicative relationship between the audience and the film. As will become clear, it is this active, participatory mode of engagement (and not the narrative content of *71 Fragments*) that constitutes the utopian promise of the film.

Communication that Doesn't Communicate

71 Fragments is the third work in a series of films that is often described as the "trilogy of glaciation" following Haneke's claim that the films are "reports on the progression of the emotional glaciation" of Austria (Haneke, 1992: 89). In keeping with the other films that constitute the trilogy,[7] *71 Fragments* is populated by lonely, alienated characters who are emotionally detached from the world in which they live. Among the key characters are: a young, homeless Romanian boy who has traveled to Vienna in the back of a truck because he has heard that Austrians "are nice to children"; a lonely, elderly man who spends most of his time in front of the television set and who has a difficult relationship with his bankteller daughter; a rogue member of the armed forces who steals – and trades in – military weapons; a couple who are seeking to adopt a young girl who rejects their attempts at familial communication; a university student named Maximilian who is also a table-tennis player; and a middle-aged security officer whose relationship to his wife is strained to the absolute limit. As the title suggests, the film itself is constructed out of 71 fragments that provide us with partial, interrupted access to

Figure 22.1 Anni in an uncomfortable moment at the zoo, in *71 Fragments of a Chronology of Chance* (dir. Michael Haneke, prod. Veit Heiduschka).

the day-to-day activities of this disconnected, largely nameless group of characters whose lives intersect by chance – and with disastrous consequences – at the end of the film.

Haneke has stated that the trilogy is "about the topic of communication that doesn't communicate" (Toubiana and Haneke, 2007), and it is clear that the characters who populate *71 Fragments* find it extremely difficult to connect and communicate with each other in a satisfactory and meaningful way. For example, in a scene that takes place at the zoo, we view the couple with Anni (the young girl whom they are seeking to adopt) as they watch the animated performance of the seals as they participate in their feeding-time ritual. While the couple and the girl appear to be enjoying the performance, the laughter of the former is somewhat forced and it is clear that these prospective parents are more interested in generating the appearance of familial fun, rather than relaxing and enjoying the experience for what it is. When the woman, however, puts her arm around Anni's shoulders, both the "fun" and the scene are abruptly brought to a halt by Anni's cold, angry expression and by her prompt rejection of the woman's hasty, somewhat stilted attempt at affection (Figure 22.1).

Haneke's emphasis on the difficult, forced nature of interpersonal relations is also made clearly apparent in scenes that revolve around the elderly man and his bankteller daughter. In an early scene at the bank, we view the daughter going through the motions of customer service, only to find out at the end of the transaction that the customer is in fact her father. "I don't," she states, "have any time now Father. Call in the evening and we can talk." When her father, however, follows her instructions, the call that ensues is frosty and awkward. In a

Figure 22.2   Television news footage, in *71 Fragments of a Chronology of Chance* (dir. Michael Haneke, prod. Veit Heiduschka).

scene that consists of one still, long-shot that lasts for more than eight minutes, we view the father on the phone in his flat, and imagine the daughter at the other end of the line participating begrudgingly in a conversation with a father whom she views – as the elderly man himself points out – as an irritating and tiresome burden.

This lack – but also suspicion – of familial warmth is, however, communicated most disturbingly in the film in a scene between the security guard and his wife who are eating dinner at the family table. When the security guard/husband interrupts the silence with an awkward, softly spoken "I love you," his wife is shocked and suspicious and immediately asks him if he is drunk. When the husband responds in the affirmative, she becomes angry and questions what he wants, noting that it isn't something that one says "out of the blue." Frustrated by his wife's comments and by his own unwillingness and/or inability to answer her questions, he slaps her violently in the face. After a moment's pause, however, the woman reaches out and touches his arm in a gesture of reconciliation, and they continue – albeit in an uncomfortable silence – eating their dinner at the table.

Although, as these examples make clear, the film is very much concerned with exploring what Haneke views as a breakdown in interpersonal communication, on another level, *71 Fragments* also interrogates the role that the mass media plays – on a much broader scale – in stunting, rather than facilitating, communication. Television screens and news broadcasts feature regularly in Haneke's films, but nowhere more than in *71 Fragments* which begins and ends with a montage of clips from a series of television news broadcasts (Figure 22.2). These clips (which also appear throughout the course of the film) provide us with access to footage from stories that were broadcast between October and December 1993, and that focus on events such as the Bosnian war; an Irish Republican Army bomb attack in Belfast; a strike by Air France workers; a Partiya Karkerên Kurdistan (Kurdistan Workers Party) attack in Eastern Anatolia; an address by Michael Jackson following allegations of child abuse; the United Nations war crimes tribunal for atrocities committed in former Yugoslavia; an Israeli military attack on southern Lebanon; and a shooting spree in a bank in Vienna undertaken by a university student. As will be explored in more detail in the following sections, the latter story is also reenacted in the film and serves both as the culmination point of Haneke's fictional account of events that led up to the shooting, and the site at which the lives of the various characters in the film intersect.

What troubles Haneke about television news programs is the degree to which their pace, organization, and narrative structure distance and – in the process – anaesthetize viewers from the issues and events depicted on screen and, in doing so, further contribute to what he describes as the "emotional glaciation" of the spectator. For Haneke, this glaciation process is very much a modern phenomenon. He argues that, prior to the development of the mass media, people's knowledge of the world was limited to "their immediate environment" and thus "nourished by their direct experience" (Assheuer and Haneke, 2008: 55). Today, he states, "we live in this environment where we think we know more things faster, when in fact we know nothing at all" (Sharrett, 2003: 31). Drawing on the cave allegory outlined in Plato's *The Republic* (Plato, 1987: 316–325), Haneke argues that our distant, heavily mediated relationship to the world around us is comparable to the experience of the prisoners described in Plato's story who mistake the shadows projected on the wall of the cave in which they are imprisoned for reality itself.[8] As Haneke makes clear,

> What we know of the world is little more than the mediated world, the image. We have no reality, but a derivative of reality, which is extremely dangerous, most certainly from a political standpoint but also in a larger sense to [sic] our ability to have a palpable sense of the truth of everyday experience. (Sharrett, 2003: 30)

This emphasis on the diminution in the capacity for communication and experience cultivated, in part, by the mass media resonates strongly with Walter Benjamin's analysis, in his 1936 essay, "The Storyteller: Reflections on the Work of Nikolai Leskov," of the modern decline in the "communicability of experience" that he associates with the rise of information culture (Benjamin, 1992: 86). Central to Benjamin's analysis of the growth of information as a means of communication is the decline in the art of storytelling and the communicability of experience with which he associates it. For Benjamin, what is significant about storytelling is the degree to which the storyteller is able to recount a tale in such a way that its meaning is not communicated to the listener directly. In a manner that anticipates Haneke's delineation of the task of a fragmentary film practice, Benjamin argues that "it is half the art of storytelling to keep a story free from explanation as one reproduces it" (p. 89). "The most extraordinary things, marvellous things," he writes, "are related with the greatest accuracy, but the psychological connection of the events is not forced on the reader" (p. 89).[9] Rather, the tale is recounted in a manner that prompts the listener to draw on his/her own experience and imagination in an attempt to fill out the contours of the story.

In stark contrast, Benjamin argues that the "prime requirement" of information "is that it appear understandable in itself" – a quality which, in "lay[ing] claim to prompt verifiability," is clearly at odds with "the spirit of storytelling" (Benjamin, 1992: 88). Taking the form and content of daily newspapers as his key example, Benjamin argues that the "replacement of the older narration by information [...] reflects the increasing atrophy of experience" (Benjamin, 1997: 113).[10] "Every morning," he writes,

> brings us the news of the globe, and yet we are poor in noteworthy stories. This is because no event any longer comes to us without already being shot through with explanation. In other words, by now almost nothing that happens benefits storytelling; almost everything benefits information. (Benjamin, 1992: 89)

In a similar vein to Benjamin, Kluge and Oskar Negt argue in their 1972 book *Public Sphere and Experience* that the emphasis on brevity and the cultivation of immediate comprehension characteristic of television news broadcasts impacts negatively, not only on the viewer's capacity to assimilate news items by way of his/her own experience, but on the viewer's ability to conceive of the meaning of a particular situation or event outside the terms within which it has been framed by the program. As Kluge and Negt make clear:

> A sensational news item (for instance about an air disaster) is broadcast; but it is not accompanied by programs that might meaningfully interpret this news in the light of social contradictions or develop it in relation to the viewer's own experience. It is only on such a broadened basis that grief, sympathy, incorporation into a historical context, or an autonomous reaction by the viewer become possible. [...] Insofar as experiences do manage to penetrate the items on the evening news, they are, in the commentaries, translated into an esoteric language that promotes the rapid consumption of events. (1993: 108)

For Haneke, too, it is the emphasis placed by the mass media (he cites television news programs and Hollywood cinema as examples) on presenting the viewer with rapidly edited, "pre-digested" bites of information that stunt our capacity to experience – but also to engage imaginatively with – the images on screen. "Contemporary film editing," Haneke notes, "is most commonly determined by practices of TV-timing, by the expectation of a rapid flow of information ... which can be quickly consumed and checked off" (Wheatley, 2009: 72). While information as a mode of communication can, in this sense, be easily registered, the mixed structure and rapid pace characteristic, for example, of television news programs stunts the audience's capacity to participate in the meaning-making process because the viewer is left with scant opportunity to reflect on the issues, ideas, and events at hand. "Television," Haneke states, "accelerates experience, but one needs time to understand what one sees, which the current media disallows" (Sharrett, 2003: 31).

As will be explored in more detail in the following section, if the spectatorial effects generated by the open, experimental form of *71 Fragments* differ from the mode of engagement fostered by the fragmentary structure, rapid pace, and information-driven content of television news programs, it is in part because the comparatively slow, meditative pace of Haneke's film provides the viewer with the opportunity to reflect on (rather than to simply register) the images and events on screen: to question the characters' motivations and the priorities of the society in which they live; and to think seriously and imaginatively about what would need to change for life to be transformed into something very different. Indeed, in a manner that resonates strongly with Benjamin's delineation of the storyteller's practice (within which the content and meaning of the tale are not communicated to the listener directly), Haneke argues that "[a] film's essential feature, its criterion of quality, should be its ability to become the productive centre of an interactive process" (Haneke, 2000: 171).

The Film in the Mind of the Spectator

It is not the office of art to spotlight alternatives, but to resist by its form alone the course of the world, which permanently puts a pistol to men's heads. (Adorno, 1990: 180)

71 Fragments opens with a black screen with white text that recounts in a clipped, journalistic style an event that took place in Vienna in 1993: "On 23.12.93 in the branch office of a Viennese bank, 19 year old student Maximilian B. shot three people and killed himself shortly afterwards with a shot in the head." This intertitle is immediately followed by a clip from a television news program that aired on October 12, 1993 and which contains three reports that focus on, among other issues, occurrences, and events: people fleeing war in Abkhazia; a US military attack in Somalia; and the tension generated by the presence of US warship *Harlan County* in Port-au-Prince. While the first and third news reports appear in truncated form, in a similar vein to the information contained in the intertitle, the style of the reports is very clipped, and the audience is provided with scant opportunity to understand or engage with the issues at hand.

In the first report about Abkhazia, for example, we are presented with images of weapons lighting up the night sky. This footage is quickly followed by images of people walking in a long line. The man at the front of the group is holding a piece of white cloth and the voiceover states (before shifting gear to a report about

Somalia): "With a handkerchief as a peace flag, the people walk through the firing lines. There are still more than one hundred thousand people fleeing the war." What is missing, however, from the report is the kind of context that would enable viewers to get a sense of the background and issues that led up to – or served as catalysts for – these events. Weapons (which, of course, have very real effects on their targets) are aestheticized as streaks of light in the sky, and while the people on screen are immediately recognizable as victims of war, the fast-paced, information-driven content of the report not only prohibits us from learning anything about their story, but provides us with little insight into what it would be like to experience such terror.

When, at the end of the film, Haneke reenacts the story about the shooting described in the opening intertitle, it is with the aim of undermining the detached, consumer-oriented mode of engagement cultivated by the information-driven focus of such reports, the structure and pace of which leave the viewer feeling "informed" but without any investment in – or sense of connection to – the issues and events in question. The reenactment scene is, in itself, quite brief: We view the security guard as he moves through the bank with an armored briefcase. As he walks toward the exit, we recognize the woman who was seeking to adopt Anni (but who has, in the meantime, chosen instead to take care of the young Romanian immigrant) as she participates in a conversation with a bankteller. We also notice the lonely, elderly man in the queue and we can see his bankteller daughter behind the counter. As the security guard prepares to exit the bank, Maximilian enters with his gun held high and immediately fires shots into the crowd. We hear the screams of the people in the bank, and then we view the student in an overhead shot that follows his movements as he crosses the road and enters his car, which is parked in a busy service station. The shot rests on the overhead image of his vehicle, a gunshot rings out, and the fragment cuts to black.

In contrast to the news report described above, these violent acts are certainly not aestheticized, and the camera follows the events as they unfold in a cool, distant, almost scientific manner that is characteristic of the style of the film as a whole.[11] Our relationship, however, to these random, horrific acts of violence is anything but distanced or detached. Unlike the people who feature in the news reports that intersperse the film, we are very familiar with the characters in (and their relatives outside) the bank whose lives will be disastrously impacted by the shooting. Although we view Maximilian firing into the crowd, Haneke refrains from providing us with any shorthand information about the consequences of his actions. The fragment thus generates what Benjamin describes as "an amplitude that information lacks" (Benjamin, 1992: 89) because the audience is encouraged to imagine how Maximilian's actions will change the lives of these characters whom we have followed throughout the film and who have already experienced so much unhappiness.

When, at the end of the film, we are presented with an actual news report about the shooting that was broadcast on Austrian television, we engage with the material on screen in a manner that differs from the distant, detached mode of engagement ordinarily facilitated by television news programs because, in this instance, we are able to fill in the human details that are occluded by the information-driven content of the report. While we learn, for example, that the attack took place in Billrothstrasse and that three people were killed as a result, when the voiceover states that the motive for the attack is "completely unclear," we beg to differ – not because the shooting is in any way justified, but because we are aware of the deep sense of human disconnectedness, alienation, and loneliness experienced not only by Maximilian, but also by the other characters who populate the film. As Haneke has stated in relation to the acts of violence committed in the trilogy:

> The real horror about them [...] is the suspicion that the supposedly irrational acts could have altogether rationally discoverable roots in our life style. This horror is dramaturgically productive. It makes it possible to have the spectators confront themselves, since they are forced to look for the answers which the film and its plot fail to give. (2000: 174)

This active, participatory mode of engagement is cultivated by the film on a number of different levels – all of which encourage spectators to become creative co-producers in the meaning-making process: to resist, rather than consume, the bleak image of society depicted on screen; and to imagine how life could – in reality – be transformed into something very different. Foremost among the devices employed by Haneke to this effect is the experimental form of the film itself which, as noted previously, consists of seventy-one fragments that are separated from each other by cuts to black and that are organized in a chronological, albeit open and ambiguous manner. Many of the fragments themselves also appear in truncated form with sentences, actions, and gestures cut off prematurely: a very effective device that works to open up, rather than close meaning down.

For example, in an early scene in the film, we view the security guard and his wife as they participate mechanically in their morning ritual. They get out of bed, attend to the baby, and heat the kettle on the stove. As the woman prepares to undress in the bathroom, we hear the sounds of her baby crying, and as her tired face reflected in the mirror begins to break into tears, the fragment abruptly cuts to black (Figure 22.3). This scene is immediately followed by a shot of the young Romanian boy who is eating food out of a bin located on the side of a busy road. As the passing cars draw to a halt, the boy looks over his shoulder, and we see a man and a woman in an expensive car staring at the boy in a dismissive way. Feeling uncomfortable, the boy walks away, the scene cuts to black and we are presented with another fragment, this one set in a university dorm where Maximilian and his roommate are participating in a conversation which we, however, enter midsentence. The discussion, we quickly

Figure 22.3   The security guard's wife breaks down, in *71 Fragments of a Chronology of Chance* (dir. Michael Haneke, prod. Veit Heiduschka).

learn, concerns a complicated puzzle that Maximilian is trying to crack and, as the roommate reveals the solution to his friend, the screen cuts to black, and to a new scene located in an orphanage.

Like the puzzle that features in the film, *71 Fragments* has an intriguing, puzzle-like structure, though it is not a puzzle that can be readily solved. Indeed, in keeping with the title of Haneke's 2000 film *Code Unknown* (a film which also deals with themes pertaining to war, migration, and strained relationships, and which is also highly fragmentary in its structure), the "code" for the 71 fragments that make up the film remains "unknown."[12] "[My] films," Haneke states, "pose certain questions, and it would be counterproductive if I were to answer these questions myself" (Sharrett, 2003: 29). Rather, in keeping with Kluge's delineation of the task of *Autorenkino* – within which the role of the viewer is not to "understand" the intentions of the director but to actively participate in the film's construction (Bitomsky, Farocki, and Henrichs, 1979: 510)[13] – what is crucial for Haneke is that the open, fragmentary form of the film facilitates the active, creative participation of the audience. "This," he notes,

> is my principle concern after all: the film should not come to an end on the screen, but engage the spectators and find its place in their cognitive and emotional framework. In short, film as such does not exist, it comes to exist only in the minds of the spectators. [...] The author of the film puts markers and signposts into place; the spectators' potential for fantasy and emotion then unfolds between these markers. (Haneke, 2000: 171)

It is clear from this statement that Kluge's ideas have had an important influence on the development of Haneke's work, an influence that is most clearly manifested in Haneke's reference to the film in "the minds of the spectators" – a phrase frequently employed by Kluge to describe the role that an experimental film practice can play in the establishment of an alternative public sphere within which viewers are encouraged to actively participate in the meaning-making process surrounding issues, policies, events, and ideas that impact on the world in which they live.[14] Haneke has certainly sought to achieve something similar through his portrayal of the shooting (and the events that preceded it) in 71 Fragments. Instead of presenting the viewer with an informative "reading" of these events – and instead of seeking to sway the audience's thinking in a particular direction – the open, unfinished character of the film encourages the audience to draw on their own experience in an attempt to fill in the gaps contained between the fragments and, in doing so, to engage imaginatively with the material on screen.

It is not, however, just the fragmentary structure of the film that cultivates this active, imaginative mode of engagement. Rather, as touched on previously in relation to the scene that focuses on a telephone conversation between the man and his daughter, Haneke frequently makes use of long-shots to stimulate the active, imaginative participation of the viewer. This emphasis on long-shots is extremely important, because it is by slowing down the pace that Haneke is able to cultivate a mode of engagement that differs significantly from the distant, "glacial" relationship fostered by television news programs, the latter of which (while also fragmentary in their structure) employ voiceover as a form of "glue" that both binds the fragments together[15] and irons out any ambiguities generated by the often eclectic collection of images on screen. Indeed, instead of packaging his stories in a manner that facilitates the rapid consumption of information, Haneke's extensive use of long-shots encourages the audience to really experience the image on screen; to inhabit the moment; and to feel the characters' pain, not through a process of identification, but by encouraging the audience to reflect on the kind of societal conditions that produce such alienation, loneliness, and despair.

For example, in an early scene in 71 Fragments, we view Maximilian standing at the end of a table-tennis table hitting balls that are being fired at him (at a rapid, relentless pace) by a machine that is partly visible at the bottom of the screen (Figure 22.4). The image is dominated by grey, and we watch the student's automated gestures, examine his distressed face, and listen to the sound of the balls bouncing on the table for an uninterrupted period of nearly three minutes. What is powerful about the scene is the way in which one's relationship to, and engagement with the image becomes more nuanced with both the repetition of his actions and the passing of time. Indeed, as Haneke himself has pointed out in relation to this scene, instead of presenting the shot in the form of "information" (Toubiana and Haneke, 2007) (a scenario in which we would only need to see the

Figure 22.4   Maximilian practicing his game, in *71 Fragments of a Chronology of Chance* (dir. Michael Haneke, prod. Veit Heiduschka).

shot briefly to register that Maximilian is practicing his game), the extended presentation of the shot prompts us to think in depth about what it is that we are actually viewing, to feel the mechanical rhythm of Maximilian's actions, and to reflect on the source of the anxiety written across his face. This highly reflective mode of engagement is also cultivated later on in the film when we are presented with a fragmentary image of a monitor featuring video footage of Maximilian participating in a competitive game of table-tennis. The shot remains on the monitor, but as we hear the voice of his coach analyzing the footage and aggressively chastising him for his mistakes, we feel the pressure and imagine the distressed, anxious look returning to Maximilian's face.

Growing Wings

Only by virtue of the absolute negativity of collapse does art enunciate the unspeakable: utopia. In this image of collapse all the stigmata of the repulsive and loathsome in modern art gather. Through the irreconcilable renunciation of the semblance of reconciliation, art holds fast to the promise of reconciliation in the midst of the unreconciled: This is the true consciousness of an age in which the real possibility of utopia – that given the level of productive forces the earth could here and now be paradise – converges with the possibility of total catastrophe ... as if art wanted to prevent the catastrophe by conjuring up its image. (Adorno, 1997: 41–42)

The picture of *71 Fragments* that has been sketched in this chapter is of a film that is disturbingly bleak. In addition to the acts of violence that take place at the end of the film, Haneke presents us with a series of characters whose lives are haunted by meaninglessness and whose relationships are marked, for the most part, by an absence of warmth, compassion, and human connection. In the news reports that intersperse the film, we learn that war, violence, terror, and despair are an every-day part of the world in which we live; a world that is presented in television news programs in a manner that renders viewers numb to the suffering on screen.

Haneke, however, has stated that his "films are the expression of a desire for a better world" (Toubiana and Haneke, 2007) and, although *71 Fragments* is very dark, the negative utopian approach that he has adopted renders the film far from nihilistic. "You should," Haneke states in a manner reminiscent of Adorno,

> always rebel against what's wrong. You can rebel against that in a film by showing it. But by showing it in a way that gives you a desire for an alternative, not in a way that makes it consumable. (Toubiana and Haneke, 2007)

As I hope to have made clear in this chapter, it is this emphasis on cultivating an active, imaginative mode of engagement which resists the image of reality depicted on screen that not only distinguishes *71 Fragments* from the "pre-digested" consumer products described by Adorno, but that aligns Haneke's delineation of the possibilities of film with Kluge's analysis of the utopian promise of cinema. Although, as Haneke himself has pointed out, the world isn't as bleak (or, at least, as uniformly bleak) as the world presented in the trilogy (Assheuer and Haneke, 2008: 52–53), in adopting a negative utopian approach, his aim has been to not only "mobilise [the audience's] powers of resistance" (2008: 133) against the alienated image of life presented on screen but, in doing so, to encourage the audience to imagine how – and with what effects – life could, in reality, be transformed into something very different. As Haneke notes in another context, the crucial point is to take the audience seriously and to "respect" their "capacity for perception and personal responsibility, that conceal in their gesture of refusal more utopia than all the bastions of representation and cheap consolation." It is only "[b]y leaving out the portrayal of happiness, [that] wishing," he writes, "grows wings" (Haneke, 1998: 558–559).

Notes

1 Emphases in the original.
2 Robin Wood (2006: 35ff), for example, has described Haneke as "perhaps the most pessimistic of all great filmmakers"; Monish Rajesh (2009) refers to the "trademark nihilism" characteristic of his work, and Claudia Puig (2010) states that Haneke has an "unrelentingly nihilistic world view."

3   All translations from German language sources are, unless otherwise noted, my own. See also Haneke's comments on this topic in Grissemann and Omasta (1991: 203).

4   This concept has not, to my knowledge, been explored in any detail in relation to Haneke's work. However, at the time of writing, an edited book entitled *The Cinema of Michael Haneke: Europe Utopia* (McCann and Sorfa, forthcoming) was still forthcoming. See also Kevin L. Stoehr's (2010, 489–491) very brief analysis of Haneke as an "antinihilist." Stoehr does not, however, discuss the idea of negative utopianism.

5   For an analysis of the degree to which Adorno's thinking in this regard has been influenced by the Judaic ban on graven images, see Benzaquén (1998).

6   See Adorno's comments in this regard in Bloch and Adorno (1998: 7).

7   The other films that make up the trilogy are *The Seventh Continent* (1989) and *Benny's Video* (1992).

8   See, for example, Haneke's comments in Assheuer and Haneke (2008: 55). Plato's cave allegory has also been extensively discussed by film theorists. See, for example, "Chapter 1: Plato's picture show – the theory of knowledge" (Falzon, 2002: 17–48).

9   "The value of information," Benjamin writes, "does not survive the moment in which it was new. It lives only at the moment; it has to surrender to it completely and explain itself to it without losing any time. A story is different. It does not expend itself. It preserves and concentrates its strength and is capable of releasing it even after a long time" (Benjamin, 1992: 89–90). See also Adorno's negative delineation of information as a mode of communication in Adorno (2001: 82, 85).

10 See also Benjamin's analysis of the information-driven focus of newspaper journalism in Benjamin (1999: 660).

11 In interviews, Haneke often expresses his aversion to films that aestheticize violence in order to render it palatable for the viewer. See, for example, Grabner (2005: 36–37).

12 For an analysis of *71 Fragments* and *Code Unknown* that explores, in part, the fragmentary structure of the films in relation to the ideas of Adorno and Jean-François Lyotard, see Grundmann (2010). Grundmann's analysis of the affinities between Haneke and Adorno does, however, differ from my own in the sense that he does not discuss the concept of negative utopianism explored in this chapter.

13 Drawing on the example of the child at play as the model of his conception of an active, imaginative spectator, Kluge claims that just as the imagination of children is more readily stimulated by building blocks than by electrical train sets, so too is the imagination of the spectator more effectively cultivated by films with the unfinished structure of a "construction site" or building in process (Lewandowski, 1980: 42). "I believe," Kluge states, "that it is … easier for the spectator to connect his experiences with a film that has breaks than with a perfect film. My editor always says: Weak films make strong viewers – strong films make weak viewers," to which Kluge adds: "a construction site is more advantageous than complete houses" (Bevers, Kreimeier, and Müller, 1980: 17).

14 See, for example, Reitz, Kluge, and Reinke (1988: 87).

15 This concept is taken from Siegfried Kracauer's analysis, in his 1926 essay, "Cult of Distraction: On Berlin's Picture Palaces," of the "glue" employed by "movie theaters" to transform films that are, in essence, fragmentary in their structure into "organic creations" (Kracauer, 1995: 328).

References

Adorno, T.W. (1989) *Introduction to the Sociology of Music* (trans. E.B. Ashton), Continuum, New York.

Adorno, T.W. (1990) Commitment, in *Aesthetics and Politics: The Key Texts of the Classic Debate within German Marxism* (ed. and trans. R. Taylor), Verso, London and New York, pp. 177–195.

Adorno, T.W. (1997) *Aesthetic Theory* (trans. R. Hullot-Kentor), Continuum, London and New York.

Adorno, T.W. (1998) Prologue to television, in *Critical Models: Interventions and Catchwords* (trans. H.W. Pickford), Columbia University Press, New York and Chichester, pp. 48–57.

Adorno, T.W. (2001a) How to Look at Television, in *The Culture Industry: Selected Essays on Mass Culture* (ed. J.M. Bernstein), Routledge, London and New York.

Adorno, T.W. (2001b) The Schema of Mass Culture, in *The Culture Industry: Selected Essays on Mass Culture* (ed. J.M. Bernstein), Routledge, London and New York, pp. 61–97.

Assheuer, T. and Haneke, M. (2008) *Nachaufnahme Michael Haneke. Gespräche mit Thomas Assheuer*, Alexander Verlag, Berlin.

Benjamin, W. (1992) The storyteller: reflections on the work of Nikolai Leskov (trans. H. Zohn), in *Illuminations* (ed. H. Arendt), Fontana Press, London, pp. 83–107.

Benjamin, W. (1997) Some motifs in Baudelaire, in *Charles Baudelaire: A Lyric Poet in the Era of High Capitalism* (trans. H. Zohn), Verso, London and New York.

Benjamin, W. (1999) The handkerchief, in *Selected Writings – Volume 2: 1927–1934* (eds M. Jennings, H. Eiland, and G. Smith; trans. R. Livingstone), MIT Press, Cambridge, MA and London.

Benzaquén, A.S. (1998) Thought and utopia in the writings of Adorno, Horkheimer, and Benjamin. *Utopian Studies*, 9 (2), 149–161.

Bevers, J., Kreimeier, K., and Müller, J. (1979) "Eine Baustelle ist vorteilhafter als ganze Häuser": Ein Gespräch mit Alexander Kluge. *Spuren*, 1, 16–19.

Bitomsky, H., Farocki, H., and Henrichs, K. (1979) Gespräch mit Alexander Kluge: Über *Die Patriotin*, Geschichte und Filmarbeit. *Filmkritik*, 275, 505–521.

Bloch, E. and Adorno, T.W. (1988) Something's missing: a discussion between Ernst Bloch and Theodor W. Adorno on the contradictions of utopian longing, in *The Utopian Function of Art and Literature: Selected Essays* (ed. E. Bloch; trans. J. Zipes and F. Mecklenburg). MIT Press, Cambridge, MA, London, pp. 1–17.

Brecht, B. (1998) The modern theater is the epic theater, in *Brecht on Theater: The Development of an Aesthetic* (ed. J. Willett), Hill & Wang, New York.

Dawson, J. (1977) But why are the questions so abstract?: an interview with Alexander Kluge, in *Alexander Kluge and The Occasional Work of a Female Slave*, Zoetrope, New York, pp. 26–42.

Falzon, C. (2002) *Philosophy Goes to the Movies: An Introduction to Philosophy*, Routledge, London.

Grabner, F. (2005) "Der Name der Erbsünde ist Verdrängung": Ein Gespräch mit Michael Haneke, in *Michael Haneke und seine Filme: Eine Pathologie der Konsumgesellschaft* (eds C. Wessely, G. Larcher, and F. Grabner), Schüren Verlag, Marburg, pp. 33–46.

Grissemann, S. and Omasta, M. (1991) Herr Haneke, wo bleibt das Positive?, in *Der Siebente Kontinent: Michael Haneke und seine Filme* (ed. A. Horwath), Europaverlag, Wien, Zürich, pp. 193–214.

Grundmann, R. (2010) Between Adorno and Lyotard: Michael Haneke's aesthetic of fragmentation, in *A Companion to Michael Haneke* (ed. R. Grundmann), Wiley-Blackwell, Malden, MA, Oxford, pp. 371–419.

Haneke, M. (1992) Film als Katharis, in *Austria (in)felix: zum österreichischen Film der 80er Jahre* (ed. F. Bono), Edition Blimp, Graz, p. 89.

Haneke, M. (1998) Terror and utopia of form. Addicted to truth. A film story about Robert Bresson's *Au hazard Balthazar*, in *Robert Bresson* (ed. J. Quandt), Toronto International Film Festival Group, Toronto, pp. 551–559.

Haneke, M. (2000) *71 Fragments of a Chronology of Chance:* Notes to the Film, in *After Postmodernism: Austrian Literature and Film in Transition* (ed. W. Riemer), Ariadne Press, Riverside, CA.

Horkheimer, M., and Adorno, T.W. (2002) *Dialectic of Enlightenment: Philosophical Fragments* (trans. E. Jephcott), Stanford, CA, Stanford University Press.

Kluge, A. (1981–1982) On film and the public sphere (trans. T.Y. Levin and M.B. Hansen), *New German Critique*, 24–25, 206–220.

Kracauer, S. (1995) Cult of distraction: on Berlin's picture palaces, in *The Mass Ornament: Weimar Essays* (ed. T.Y. Levin), Harvard University Press, Cambridge, MA, London, pp. 323–328.

Lewandowski, R. (1980) *Die Filme von Alexander Kluge*, Olms Press, Hildesheim, New York.

McCann, B. and Sorfa, D. (eds) (forthcoming) *The Cinema of Michael Haneke: Europe Utopia*, Wallflower Press, London.

Negt, O. and Kluge, A. (1993) *Public Sphere and Experience: Toward an Analysis of the Bourgeois and Proletarian Public Sphere* (trans. P. Labanyi, J.O. Daniel, and A. Oksiloff), University of Minnesota Press, Minneapolis, London.

Plato (1987). *The Republic* (trans. D. Lee), Penguin Books, London.

Puig, C. (2010) Elegant "White Ribbon" gets all tied up in monotonous gloom. *USA Today*, January 8, http://www.usatoday.com/life/movies/reviews/2010-01-07-whiteribbon08_ST_N.htm (accessed February 11, 2011).

Rajesh, M. (2009) Michael Haneke's Film Noir. *Time*, November 30, http://www.time.com/time/magazine/article/0,9171,1940236,00.html (accessed May 27, 2011).

Reitz, E., Kluge, A., and Reinke, W. (1988) Word and Film (trans. M. Hansen). *October*, 46, 83–95.

Sharrett, C. (2003) The world that is known: an interview with Michael Haneke. *Cineaste*, 28 (3), 28–31.

Stoehr, K. (2010) Haneke's secession: perspectivism and anti-nihilism in *Code Unknown* and *Caché*, in *A Companion to Michael Haneke* (ed. R. Grundmann), Wiley-Blackwell, Maldon, MA and London, pp. 477–494.

Toubiana, S. and Haneke, M. (2007) 71 Fragments d'une Chronologie du Hasard: Entretien avec Michael Haneke par Serge Toubiana. DVD extra on Haneke, M. *71 Fragments of a Chronology of Chance*, Madman Films, Collingwood, Victoria.

Vogel, A. (1996) Of nonexisting continents: the cinema of Michael Haneke. *Film Comment*, 32 (4), 73–75.

Wood, R. (2006) Hidden in plain sight: Robin Wood on Michael Haneke's Cache. *Artforum International*, 44 (5), 35–40.

Further Reading

A Companion to Michael Haneke (Grundmann, 2010) contains 32 chapters that provide the reader with a very comprehensive overview of Haneke's work. *Nachaufnahme Michael Haneke. Gespräche mit Thomas Assheur* (Assheur and Haneke, 2008) consists, in large part, of a long interview with Haneke that serves as a very good introduction to the concerns driving the production of his films. For further reading on Adorno's conception of negative utopianism, see Bloch and Adorno (1988) and Benzaquén (1998).

Filmography

Benny's Video (Michael Haneke, Austria/Switzerland, 1992).

Code Unknown: Incomplete Tales of Several Journeys (Michael Haneke, France/Germany/Romania, 2000).

71 Fragments of a Chronology of Chance [*71 Fragmente einer Chronologie des Zufalls*] (Michael Haneke, Austria/Germany, 1994).

Seventh Continent, The [*Der siebente Kontinent*] (Michael Haneke, Austria, 1989).

Index

A Companion to German Cinema, First Edition. Edited by Terri Ginsberg and Andrea Mensch.
© 2012 Blackwell Publishing Ltd. Published 2012 by Blackwell Publishing Ltd.